Introduction to Criminology

Nelson-Hall Series in Sociology

Consulting Editor: Jonathan H. Turner

University of California, Riverside

INTRODUCTION TO CRIMINOLOGY

Theories, Methods, and Criminal Behavior

Second Edition

Frank E. Hagan

Nelson-Hall
Chicago

Copy Editor: James L. Cambias
Interior Designer: Claudia von Hendricks
Photo Research: Judith Lucas and Tamara Deppen
Illustrator: Bill Nelson
Compositor: Fine Print, Ltd.
Manufacturer: R. R. Donnelley
Cover Painting: *The Arraignment*, Marcia Feldstein Danits, Oil

Library of Congress Cataloging-in-Publication Data

Hagan, Frank E.
    Introduction to criminology : theories, methods, and criminal
behavior / Frank E. Hagan. — 2nd ed.
      p.   cm.
    Includes bibliographical references.
    ISBN 0-8304-1221-2
    1. Criminology.   2. Crime—United States.   I. Title.
HV6025.H26 1990
364-dc20

89-29017
CIP

Manufactured in the United States of America

10 9 8 7 6 5 4 3 2

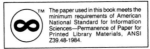
The paper used in this book meets the minimum requirements of American National Standard for Information Sciences—Permanence of Paper for Printed Library Materials, ANSI Z39.48-1984.

CONTENTS OVERVIEW

CONTENTS

4 CRIMINOLOGICAL THEORY I:
EARLY, CLASSICAL, AND
POSITIVISTIC THEORIES   119

5 CRIMINOLOGICAL THEORY II:
SOCIOLOGICAL THEORIES   163

PREFACE TO SECOND EDITION

This second edition maintains the original purpose of writing the text, and that is to serve the needs of instructors in criminology who wish to avoid the overly legal and crime-control orientation of many recent textbooks. While some familiarity with the legal and criminal justice systems is valuable, many introductory textbooks have so emphasized these elements that they have given short shrift to the vital core of criminological inquiry: theory, method, and criminal behavior. Such detailed analysis of social control agencies without adequate descriptions of criminal activity finds many works resembling an introduction to criminal justice systems rather than one dealing with basic criminology. More detailed descriptions and explanations of criminal behavior are a necessity for such agencies and social policies to be effective.

Although no social science inquiry can be entirely unbiased or value-free, the author has attempted to provide an eclectic theoretical view. If bias is to be acknowledged, the approach might best be described as liberal-conflict. In response to user and reviewer suggestions the order of chapters has been altered. It is my experience that instructors have their own chronology for chapter presentations and will organize their courses by their own preference for chapter order.

Chapter 1 begins with a general introduction to the study of criminology followed by an examination of research methods in Chapter 2. The latter involves an assessment of where the data on crime and criminals comes from. General patterns and variations in crime are then described in the third chapter. Throughout this second edition an attempt is made to use more international comparisons. Chapters 4 and 5 look at various theoretical explanations of crime and criminality, while Chapters 6-13 provide a detailed look at various forms of criminal behavior. These examinations are originally based on Marshall Clinard and Richard Quinney's criminal behavior systems typology, but considerably expand and modify both the model and examples.

Chapter 6 studies violent criminal behavior: murder, assault, assassination, rape, robbery, domestic violence, and drunk driving. Not only do such crimes cause physical, psychological, and economic harm; they also threaten the very quality of life by imprisoning the population in a state of fear. Occasional and conventional property crime are contrasted in Chapter 7. While the former is committed on a sporadic, irregular basis, the latter (such as burglary and larceny) constitutes a considerable involvement in crime.

Professional crime is the subject of Chapter 8. Such crimes are more sophisticated and range from con artists to professional "cannons" (pickpockets) and "boosters" (shoplifters). Chapters 9 and 10 were formerly a lengthy chapter on "white collar" crime but have been divided into "occupational crime" and "organizational/corporate crime." Such crimes are both the most costly to society as well as the least strictly enforced. Political crime, crime committed by and against the government for ideological reasons, is covered in Chapter 11, while Chapter 12 probes the changing world of organized (syndicate) crime. Chapter 13 details the area of public order crime often referred to as "vice-related" or "crimes without victims." Finally, the last chapter takes a speculative look at the future of crime and social policy.

While taking full responsibility for any shortcomings in the text, I would like to thank those who assisted in this endeavor. For their assistance with the first edition I once again thank Jonathan H. Turner, University of California, Riverside (Nelson-Hall Consulting Editor); Lawrence F. Travis III, University of Cincinnati; and George E. Evans, William Rainey Harper College (Illinois) for their critical reviews and suggestions. My gratitude is also extended to John Burian, Moraine Valley Community College, E. Ernest Wood, Edinboro University, and Sylvia Hill, University of the District of Columbia, who provided suggestions for the second edition. To my early professors Dan Koenig and Pierre Lejins, as well as colleagues Jim Calder, Dave Kozak, Bob Rhodes, and Ernest Wood, I express my appreciation.

I am also indebted to my colleagues at Mercyhurst College, particularly Peter Benekos, Vernon Wherry, and Shirley Williams, for their support. Finally, I would like to give my greatest appreciation to my wife Mary Ann, whose tireless and patient efforts in typing and editing, and whose moral support made completion of this project possible. I dedicate this edition to Mary Ann and our daughter Shannon.

Frank E. Hagan

1 Introduction

Criminology

A woman jogging in North Central Park in New York City is attacked, raped, bludgeoned, and left for dead by a group of young thugs. Small children are gunned down by a distraught man with an AK-47 automatic rifle while playing in their California schoolyard. Terrorist bombs kill all aboard a civilian airliner; and Wall Street, Madison and Pennsylvania Avenues join the South Bronx and Cabrini Green Housing Project in Chicago as bad crime neighborhoods. Wealthy drug cartels rival governments in power while environmental criminals threaten to make our next century mankind's last.

What all of these events have in common is that they refer to various forms of criminal behavior; and as we enter the twilight of the twentieth century, we can only guess what new, unforseen horrors await us. The field that addresses this issue of crime and criminal behavior and attempts to define, explain, and predict it is criminology.

While criminologists sometimes disagree regarding a proper definition of the field, *criminology* is generally defined as the *science or discipline which studies crime and criminal behavior.* Specifically, the field of criminology concentrates upon forms of criminal behavior, the causes of crime, the definition of criminality, and the societal reaction to criminal activity; related areas of inquiry may include juvenile delinquency and victimology or the study of victims. Applied criminology also claims what is labeled as the field of criminal justice: the police, the courts, and corrections. Criminological investigation may probe any or all of these areas. While there is considerable overlap between criminology and criminal justice, criminology shows a greater interest in the causal explanations of crime and criminal justice is more occupied with practical, applied concerns such as technical aspects of policing and corrections. In reality, the fields are highly complementary and interrelated, as indicated by overlapping membership in the two professional organizations representative of the fields: the American Society of Criminology and the Academy of Criminal Justice Sciences.

If you were to tell your friends that you are taking a course in criminology, many will assume that you are a budding Sherlock Holmes, a master detective trained in investigating crime scenes. That describes the field of *criminalistics* (the scientific evaluation of physical evidence), which is sometimes confused in the media and public mind with criminology. Criminology is more concerned with analyzing the phenomena of crime and criminality, in performing scientifically accurate studies, and in developing sound theoretical explanations of crime and criminal behavior. It is hoped that such criminological knowledge and scientific research can inform and direct practical public policies to solve some of the crime problems. The major concentration in this text will be upon the central areas of criminal behavior, research methodology, and criminological theory. Other areas will be included only to the degree that they impact upon these critical concerns.

Scientific Research in Criminology

Many, including practitioners in criminal justice, question the need and the usefulness of much criminology research, since, for instance, after all the myriad of research efforts, criminologists still are unable to answer the fundamental question, "What causes crime?" Many research results strike the layperson as irrelevant academic jargon, as intimidating and indecipherable statistics, or as confusing elaborations of what any person with common sense knows anyway. This view exists despite the fact that these research activities are conducted usually at great cost to the taxpayer, and at a time in which needed operational programs are being eliminated.

Some recent research findings are illustrative:

1. The elderly and females fear crime because they are the most heavily victimized of any age group.
2. Victims of crime seldom know or recognize their offenders.
3. The typical criminal offender is either unemployed or on welfare.
4. The larger the city, the greater the likelihood its residents will be victims of crime.
5. In general, residents of large cities believe that their police are doing a poor job.
6. Blacks and Hispanics are less likely than the population as a whole to report personal crimes to police.
7. Most residents of large cities think that their neighborhoods are not safe.
8. Blacks are overrepresented on death rows across the nation; however, this overrepresentation is more pronounced in the South than in the other regions.
9. Crime is an inevitable concomitant of complex, populous, and industrialized societies.
10. White collar crime is nonviolent.

11. Regulatory agencies prevent white collar crime.
12. The insanity defense allows many dangerous offenders to escape conviction.

One might respond to all of this by noting that common sense could have told us the same thing; however, sometimes common sense is nonsense. The above statements represent *myths* regarding crime (Bohm, 1987; Pepinsky and Jesilow, 1984; Walker, 1989; Wright, 1985; and U.S. Department of Justice, 1978), as we will discover in subsequent chapters in this text.

Women are one of the groups most fearful of crime. Many women are learning techniques of self-defense.

Unfortunately, those who criticize the need for scientific crime research tend to follow a line of argument in which, if the findings are agreeable to them and if after the fact they appear obvious, those findings are condemned as simply an example of common sense. On the other hand, if they disagree with the findings, these are viewed as unscientific or due to faulty research methods since common sense tells the critics so.

In following a scientific approach and seeking to isolate, define, and explain the critical features of crime and criminal behavior it will be one of the expressed purposes of this book to question such conventional wisdom or such common sense views. A major purpose of criminology is to supply, through the sound application of research methods, accurate and objective data regarding crime and criminal behavior. Despite the need for accurate criminological data, the per capita investment in justice research in the late eighties in the United States was eight cents, versus thirty-six dollars for health care research (Stewart, 1988, p. v).

The Emergence of Criminology

French sociologist Auguste Comte (1798–1857) viewed the *progression of knowledge* as consisting of *three stages*, from predominantly *theological* explanations to *metaphysical* (philosophical) approaches, to *scientific* explanations (Comte, 1877). Prior to the emergence of modern criminal law in the eighteenth century, religion was the primary basis of social control beyond kinship organization. Theological explanations (to be explored more fully in Chapter 4) used supernatural or other worldly reasons for understanding reality. Recall, for instance, the papal condemnation of Galileo for heretically questioning biblical descriptions of the earth and of astronomy. In the metaphysical stage, philosophy sought secular (worldly) events to provide understanding through a new spirit of inquiry—rationality and logical argument. The scientific stage combined this rational spirit of investigation with the scientific method, emphasizing empiricism or experimentation. The scientific orientation emphasized measurement, observation, proof, replication (repetition of observation), and verification (analyzing the validity of observations).

Systematic application of the scientific method enabled humankind to unlock many of the mysteries of the ages. At first, breakthroughs in knowledge took place in the physical sciences; more recently, changes have also begun to occur in the social sciences such as sociology and criminology. Since the scientific method provided major understanding, and ability to predict and control physical reality, the hope is that these same methods are applicable to and will prove useful in the social sciences. While many view criminology as a science, others, such as Sutherland and Cressey, view it as an art similar to medicine, a field based on many sciences and disciplines (Sutherland and Cressey, 1974, pp. 20–21).

Criminology as a field of inquiry had its beginnings in Europe in the late 1700s in the writings of various philosophers, physicians, physical scientists, sociologists, and social scientists. Much of the early theory was heavily couched in biological frameworks that have largely been abandoned by modern American criminology (Gibbons, 1982, p. 16). As will be described in greater detail in Chapter 4, criminology also emerged along with eighteenth-century criminal law. In fact, it was the early writings of Cesare Beccaria (1738-1794), especially his famous *Essay on Crimes and Punishment* (1764) which led to the reform of criminal law in Western Europe.

Despite its European roots, most of the major developments in modern criminology took place in America. It was closely linked with the development of sociology, gaining its place on the American academic scene between 1920 and 1940. Criminology has been largely a sub-discipline of sociology; and even though it is interdisciplinary in focus, sociologists have devoted the most attention to the issue of criminality. Once regarded as a prodigal child in sociology, criminology has contributed a surprising depth of theory and research. The earliest U.S. textbooks in the field were by Maurice Parmelee, John Gillin, Philip Parsons, and Fred Hayes; but it was the text and later writings of Edwin H. Sutherland, the acknowledged "dean of criminology," that received the most deserved recognition.

Crime and Deviance

Deviant behavior may refer to a broad range of activities which the majority in society may view as eccentric, dangerous, annoying, bizarre, outlandish, gross, abhorrent, and the like. It refers to behavior which is outside the range of normal societal toleration. One sociologist questioned a cross section of the public and asked them to list types of people they thought were deviant:

> The sheer range of response predictably included homosexuals, prostitutes, drug addicts, radicals and criminals. But it also included liars, career women, Democrats, reckless drivers, atheists, Christians, suburbanites, the retired, young folks, card players, bearded men, artists, pacifists, priests, prudes, hippies, straights, girls who wear makeup, the president, conservatives,

One survey found that some people considered working women to be deviant—along with bearded men, intellectuals, and Democrats.

integrationists, executives, divorcees, perverts, motorcyle gangs, smart-alec students, know-it-all professors, modern people, and Americans.—Simmons, 1969, p. 3.

Definitions of deviance are relative to time, place, and person(s) making the evaluation; and some acts are more universally defined than others. For instance, in the mid-nineteenth century in the U.S. bathing in a tub was considered immoral as well as unhealthy.

All societies have *cultural values*, practices, and beliefs which are prized or believed to be of benefit to the group. For instance, despite cultural relativity in defining deviance, anthropologists have identified a number of *cultural universals*, practices or customs that in general form exist in all known cultures. All cultures which have been studied look dimly upon indiscriminate lying, cheating, stealing, and killing. Societies protect their values by creating *norms* which are basically rules or proscribed modes of conduct.

Sumner's Types of Norms

Early American sociologist William Graham Sumner in his classic work *Folkways* (1906) identified *three types of norms*: folkways, mores, and laws. These norms reflect the values of a given culture; some norms are regarded by its members as more important than others. *Folkways* are the least serious of norms and refer to usages, traditions, customs, or niceties that are preferred, however not subject to serious sanctions. Manners, etiquette, dress patterns, and the like could serve as examples. The character Reb Tevye in the musical *Fiddler on the Roof*, when learning that his daughter had rejected the marriage mate chosen by the matchmaker, wailed, "Tradition—without our traditions life would be as precarious as a fiddler on the roof." Recognizing changing times or folkways, however, he shrugged and accepted his daughter's decision to choose her own mate. *Mores* refer to more serious customs which contain moral judgments as well as sanctions (rewards or punishments). The mores cover prohibitions against behaviors that are felt to be seriously threatening to a group's way of life. Our previous examples of lying, cheating, stealing, and killing are most certainly to be covered by the mores. Both the folkways and mores are examples of informal modes of social control and are characteristic of small, homogeneous cultures which feature simple technology and wide-scale consensus.

The evolution of normative controls to laws is described well by Thomas and Hepburn (1983, pp. 46–47): "Everywhere we find that the increasing complexity of social, economic, and political relationships erodes the ability of less formal methods of social control to ensure a reasonable level of stability, to mediate conflict and to protect the weak from exploitation." *Laws* represent formal modes of control, codified rules of behavior. If one were to accept the consensus model of law to be discussed shortly, laws represent an institutionalization of, or "crystallization of," the mores.

Mala in Se and *Mala Prohibita*

We already identified deviant acts as those which violate group expectation and crime as any act which violates criminal law. Crime and its definition are social products. Society (human groups) decides what is a crime and what is not.

Criminologists make the distinction between acts *mala prohibita* and acts *mala in se*. Acts which are defined as *mala prohibita* refer to those that are "bad because they have been prohibited." That is, such acts are not viewed as inherently bad in themselves but are violations because the law defines them as such. Traffic violations, gambling, and violating various municipal ordinances might serve as examples. Such laws are viewed as assisting human groups in making life more predictable and orderly, but disobedience carries little stigma other than (usually) fines. The criminalization of such acts might be viewed as institutionalization of folkways. On the other hand, acts *mala in se* are "acts bad in themselves," forbidden behaviors for which there is widescale consensus in the mores for prohibition. The universality of laws against murder, rape, assault, and the like, irrespective of political or economic systems, bears witness to the lack of societal conflict in institutionalizing such laws.

One can note that *not all deviant acts are criminal, nor are all criminal acts necessarily deviant*, assuming that many acts *mala prohibita* have a certain normality of violation.

Definitions of criminal activity may exhibit both undercriminalization and overcriminalization (to be explored more fully in Chapter 13). *Undercriminalization* refers to the fact that the criminal law fails to prohibit acts which many feel are *mala in se*. Elements of corporate violence, racism, structured inequality, and systematic wrongdoing by political officials represent such examples. *Overcriminalization* involves the overextension of criminal law to cover acts which are inappropriately or not responsibly enforced by such measures. Examples are the legislation of morality and attempts to regulate personal conduct that does not involve a clear victim, such as drug abuse, sexual conduct, and the like. Morris and Hawkins (1970) claim that the U.S. has one of the most moralistic systems of criminal law in history although one might suspect that ecclesiastical regimes such as Khomeini's Iran would more than give it a run for the money. They further state (Ibid., p. 2): "Man has an inalienable right to go to hell in his own fashion, provided he does not directly injure the person or property of another on the way. The criminal law is an inefficient instrument for imposing the good life on others. In short, the law has become too much of a moral busybody."

Social Change and the Emergence of Law

Western societies have undergone a long-term evolutionary development from sacred or *Gemeinschaft*-type societies to secular or *Gesellschaft*-type societies (Becker, 1950; Toennies, 1957). *Gemeinschaft* societies are simple, communal, relatively homogeneous societies that lack an extensive division of labor and are also characterized by normative consensus. Social control is assured by the family, extended kinship groups, and the community through informal modes of control, the folkways, and mores. Such societies lack and do not need formally codified laws since sacred tradition, the lack of change, and cultural similarity and isolation assure a degree of understanding and control. *Gesellschaft* societies are complex, associational, more individualistic, and heterogeneous (pluralistic); and are characterized by secularity, an extensive division of labor, and in free societies by a variety of moral views and political pressure groups. The assurance of social control is attempted by means of formal controls, codified laws administered by bureaucratic agencies of the state. Utilizing Sumner's notions of norms, as a society industrializes, urbanizes, and becomes more bureaucratic, complex, and pluralistic, the likelihood of clear consensus with respect to the mores as a means of social control becomes less likely. Complex societies must rely more and more upon formal controls — laws. As the mores of informal modes of control become weaker, the need for laws becomes greater. For example, as the family as an agent of social control becomes weaker, much of its responsibility is passed on to the state (see Shelley, 1981).

In a modern pluralistic society that has many conflicting values and norms, laws may reflect the values of only one particular group, usually one which has the power and resources to pressure the state and legislatures to put their interests first on the social agenda. This conflict perspective of law, to be discussed in more detail shortly, points out that laws may not have the full support or consensus of all members of society and may in fact be detrimental to the interests of some.

Sumner (1906) suggested a general maxim: in general, if laws do not have the support of, or are not in agreement with the mores of a particular culture, they will be ineffective. The story is often told of the Christian missionaries in the South Sea Islands who, having been shocked by the unabashed nudity of the natives, ordered that all females must henceforth wear blouses. They were dismayed the next day to discover that, though all of the females abided by this new rule, they had strategically cut openings in their new clothing so as to display their breasts.

The introduction of changes or new laws in society can be explored by Merton's classic concepts of manifest and latent functions (Merton, 1961, p. 710). The classic example is what has been described as "the noble experiment," the Prohibition era in the United States. *Manifest functions* are intended, planned, or anticipated consequences of introduced changes or of existing social arrangements. In perhaps the last gasp of rural Protestant religious power in the U.S. one group managed to pressure Congress into passing the Prohibition Amendment. Alcohol abuse was and still is a major problem, and the well intended goal was that it could be stamped out by totally forbidding alcohol consumption by law. *Latent functions* entail unintended or unanticipated consequences, ones which may have either positive or negative outcomes. The latent functions of Prohibition included increased corruption, disobedience, and public disrespect for the law. By eliminating legitimate suppliers of a commodity in high public demand, the state in effect created a monopoly for illegitimate entrepreneurs. It was Prohibition that converted small, localized gangsters into large, powerful, and wealthy regional and even national organized criminal syndicates.

Laws are by no means the most efficient means of social control; the passage of more and more laws may indicate that social solidarity and more effective informal modes of control in the society are weakening. The police and criminal justice system become a necessary agent or agencies of last resort. Many people view crime as an evil intrusion into an otherwise healthy society whereas, in fact, increased crime levels may be latent functions of increased freedom, affluence, competition, and otherwise desirable manifest functions in society. Sociologist Durkheim (1950) suggested that crime may in fact be a normality, a positive product, a functional necessity to a healthy society. To present once again the quote from Durkheim with which we began this chapter:

> Imagine a society of saints, a perfect cloister of exemplary individuals. Crimes, properly so-called, will there be unknown; but faults which appear venial to the layman will create there the same scandal that the ordinary offense does in ordinary consciousness. If then, this society has the power to judge and punish, it will define these acts as criminal and will treat them as such (Ibid., pp. 68–69).

Thus wrongdoing or crime serves to force societal members to react, condemn, and thus establish the borders of and reconfirm societal values. It is this organized resentment which upholds social solidarity.

Viewing crime as a normality is not to say that criminologists perceive it as a desirable prospect. Gibbons (1982, pp. 10–11) puts it succinctly: "When sociologists speak of the normality of crime, they often have in mind the broad claim that lawbreaking arises out of root causes or criminogenic conditions that are part and parcel of the social structure of societies." It is indeed, a possibility that rising crime rates in a society may serve as an indicator of modernization, growing affluence, and rising standards and expectations of morality.

Consensus vs. Conflict Model of Law

The *consensus model* of the origin of criminal law envisions it as arising from agreement among the members of a society as to what constitutes wrongdoing. Reflecting the "social contract theory" of Locke, Hobbes, and Rousseau, criminal law is viewed, as in our previous discussion of Sumner, as a "crystallization of the mores," reflecting social values which are commonly held within the society. The *conflict model*, on the other hand, sees the criminal law as originating in the conflict of interests of different groups. In this view, the definition of crime is assumed to reflect the wishes of the most powerful interest groups who gain the assistance of the state in opposing rival groups. The criminal law then is used primarily to control the behavior of the "defective, dependent and delinquent," the dangerous classes (Skolnick and Currie, 1988, p. 2); the crimes of the wealthy are very often not even covered. While the consensus model views criminal law as a mechanism of social control, the conflict approach sees the law as a means of preserving the status quo on behalf of the powerful. While both of these models will be explored in greater scope in Chapter 5, the criminal law appears to reflect both patterns. As Thomas and Hepburn (1983, p. 51) indicate, ". . . nobody would be too elated at the prospect of being murdered, raped or assaulted"; such prohibitions clearly reflect the consensus model. And Schafer (1976, p. 25) describes the conflict view dramatically: "While ordinary criminals use a gun or knife to make the victim an ever-silent witness, the white-collar criminals substitute for the gun or the knife their political or economic power to avoid appearing in the crime statistics."

Crime and Criminal Law

A purist *legal view* of crime would be to define it as violation of criminal law. No matter how morally outrageous or unacceptable an act, it is not a crime unless defined as such by criminal law. Fox (1976, p. 28) indicates: "Crime is a sociopolitical event rather than a clinical condition. . . . It is not a clinical or medical condition that can be diagnosed and specifically treated." In this view, which is technically correct, unless an act is specifically prohibited by criminal law, it is not a crime.

There are *four characteristics of criminal law:*

1. It is *assumed by political authority.* The state assumes the role of plaintiff or the party bringing forth charges. Murder, for example, is no longer just an offense against a person, but against the state. In fact, the state prohibits individual revenge in such matters; perpetrators must pay their debt to society, not to the individual wronged.
2. It must be *specific,* defining both the offense as well as the proscribed punishment.
3. The law is *uniformly applied.* That is, equal punishment and fairness to all, irrespective of social position, is intended.
4. The law contains *penal sanctions* enforced by punishments administered by the state. (Sutherland and Cressey, 1974, pp. 4–7)

Criminal law has very specific criteria: "Crime is an intentional act or omission in violation of criminal law (statutory and case law), committed without defense or justification, and sanctioned by the state as a felony or misdemeanor" (Tappan, 1960, p. 10). Some *specific criteria* that must be met in the American criminal law *in order for an act to be considered a crime* include:

1. The *act is prohibited by law* and contains legally prescribed punishments. "Nullum crimen sine lege" ("no crime without law") is the Latin expression, which can also be added to with the notion that "ex post facto" (after-the-fact) laws are also inappropriate. The act must be forbidden by law in advance of the act.
2. A criminal act, "actus reus" (the act itself or physical element), *must take place.*
3. *Social harm* of a conscious, voluntary nature is required. There must be injury to the state or people.
4. The act is *performed intentionally* (although some elements of negligence and omission may be exceptions). *Mens rea* (criminal intent or "guilty mind") is important in establishing guilt. A person who may have obviously committed a criminal act (for example, John Hinckley shooting President Reagan) may be found not guilty under such conditions.
5. The voluntary misconduct must be *causally related* to the harm. It must be shown that the decision or act did directly or indirectly cause harm.

Crimes were originally considered simply private matters: the offended party had to seek private compensation or revenge. Later, only offenses committed against the king and, still later, the king's subjects, were considered crimes. When compensation developed, fines were levied on behalf of the king (the state), thus evolving into the state as wronged party.

In addition to being defined by legislative statute (*statutory law*), criminality may also be interpreted by means of case law (*common law*). In contrast to laws enacted by legislatures, common law is based upon judicial decision, with its roots in precedence or previous decisions. In addition, *administrative law*, as enforced by federal regulatory agencies, may bear criminal penalties for offenders. Thus criminal law provisions may be contained in statutory law, common law, and administrative law. Vantage Point 1.1 describes some typical legal definitions of crimes in the United States.

Who Defines Crime?: Sociological Definitions of Crime

Since crime was previously defined using the legal view as any violation of criminal law, should criminologists restrict their inquiry solely to acts which are so defined? Should the subject matter of criminology be decided by lawyers and politicians? To do so would relegate the field of criminology to a status quo handmaiden of political systems. Hitler's genocide or Stalin's purges were accepted conduct within their political ideological systems. Criminologists must study the deviants, the criminals, as well as the social structural contexts which define them. Skolnick and Currie (1988, p. 11), in examining the analysis of social problems, state:

> In spite of its claim to political neutrality, the social science of the 1960s typically focused on the symptoms of social ills, rather than their sources: criminals, rather than the laws; the mentally ill, rather than the quality of life; the culture of the poor, rather than the decisions of the rich; the "pathology" of the ghetto, rather than problems of the economy.

A *sociological view* of crime does not restrict its concept of criminality only to those convicted of crime in a legal sense. Allen et al. (1981, pp. 19–20) indicate:

> In a simplistic way, one can say that a criminal is one who commits a crime. Such a definition, however, makes no distinction between one time and the habitual offender, and thus makes no provision for the temporary application

Crimes are defined by law

In this report we define crime as all behaviors and acts for which a society provides formally sanctioned punishment. In the United States what is criminal is specified in the written law, primarily State statutes. What is included in the definition of crime varies among Federal, State, and local jurisdictions.

Criminologists devote a great deal of attention to defining crime in both general and specific terms. This definitional process is the first step toward the goal of obtaining accurate crime statistics.

To provide additional perspectives on crime it is sometimes viewed in ways other than in the standard legal definitions. Such alternatives define crime in terms of the type of victim (child abuse), the type of offender (white-collar crime), the object of the crime (property crime), or the method of criminal activity (organized crime). Such definitions usually cover one or more of the standard legal definitions. For example, organized crime may include fraud, extortion, assault, or homicide.

What is considered criminal by society changes over time

Some types of events such as murder, robbery, and burglary have been defined as crimes for centuries. Such crimes are part of the common law definition of crime. Other types of conduct traditionally have not been viewed as crimes. As social values and mores change, society has codified some conduct as criminal while decriminalizing other conduct. The recent movement toward increased "criminalization" of drunk driving is an example of such change.

New technology also results in new types of conduct not anticipated by the law. Changes in the law may be needed to define and sanction these types of conduct. For example, the introduction of computers has added to the criminal codes in many States so that acts such as the destruction of programs or data could be defined as crimes.

What are some other common crimes in the United States?

Drug abuse violations—Offenses relating to growing, manufacturing, making, possessing, using, selling, or distributing narcotic and dangerous nonnarcotic drugs. A distinction is made between possession and sale/manufacturing.

Sex offenses—In current statistical usage, the name of a broad category of varying content, usually consisting of all offenses having a sexual element except for forcible rape and commercial sex offenses, which are defined separately.

Fraud offenses—The crime type comprising offenses sharing the elements of practice of deceit or intentional misrepresentation of fact, with the intent of unlawfully depriving a person of his or her property or legal rights.

Drunkenness—Public intoxication, except "driving under the influence."

Disturbing the peace — Unlawful interruption of the peace, quiet, or order of a community, including offenses called "disorderly conduct," "vagrancy," "loitering," "unlawful assembly," and "riot."

Driving under the influence — Driving or operating any vehicle or common carrier while drunk or under the influence of liquor or drugs.

Liquor law offenses — State or local liquor law violations, exept drunkenness and driving under the influence. Federal violations are excluded.

Gambling — Unlawful staking or wagering of money or other thing of value on a game of chance or on an uncertain event.

Kidnaping — Transportation or confinement of a person without authority of law and without his or her consent, or without the consent of his or her guardian, if a minor.

Vandalism — Destroying or damaging, or attempting to destroy or damage, the property of another without his or her consent, or public property, except by burning, which is arson.

Public order offenses — Violations of the peace or order of the community or threats to the public health through unacceptable public conduct, interference with governmental authority, or violation of civil rights or liberties. Weapons offenses, bribery, escape, and tax law violations, for example, are included in this category.

What are the characteristics of some serious crimes?

Crime	Definition	Facts
Homicide	Causing the death of another person without legal justification or excuse, including UCR crimes of murder and nonnegligent manslaughter and negligent manslaughter.	■ Murder and nonnegligent manslaughter occur less often than other violent UCR Index crimes. ■ 58% of the known murderers were relatives or acquaintances of the victim. ■ 20% of all murders in 1985 occurred or were suspected to have occurred as the result of some felonious activity.
Rape	Unlawful sexual intercourse with a female, by force or without legal or factual consent.	■ Most rapes involve a lone offender and a lone victim. ■ About 32% of the rapes recorded by NCS in 1985 were committed in or near the victim's home. ■ 73% of the rapes occurred at night, between 6 p.m. and 6 a.m. ■ 58% of the victims of rape in 1985 were under 25 years old.
Robbery	The unlawful taking or attempted taking of property that is in the immediate possession of another, by force or threat of force.	■ Robbery is the violent crime that most often involves more than one offender (in almost half of all cases in 1985). ■ About half of all robberies reported by NCS in 1985 involved the use of a weapon.

table continues

Table continued

Crime	Definition	Facts
Assault	Unlawful intentional inflicting, or attempted inflicting, of injury upon the person of another. Aggravated assault is the unlawful intentional inflicting of serious bodily injury or unlawful threat or attempt to inflict bodily injury or death by means of a deadly or dangerous weapon with or without actual infliction of injury. Simple assault is the unlawful intentional inflicting of less than serious bodily injury without a deadly or dangerous weapon or an attempt or threat to inflict bodily injury without a deadly or dangerous weapon.	■ Simple assault occurs more frequently than aggravated assault. ■ Most assaults involve one victim and one offender.
Burglary	Unlawful entry of any fixed structure, vehicle, or vessel used for regular residence, industry, or business, with or without force, with the intent to commit a felony or larceny.	■ Residential property was target in 2 out of every 3 reported burglaries; nonresidential property accounted for the remaining third. ■ In 1985, 42% of all residential burglaries occurred without forced entry. ■ About 37% of the no-force burglaries were known to have occurred during the day between 6 a.m. and 6 p.m.
Larceny-theft	Unlawful taking or attempted taking of property other than a motor vehicle from the possession of another, by stealth, without force and without deceit, with intent to permanently deprive the owner of the property.	■ Less than 5% of all personal larcenies involve contact between the victim and offender. ■ Pocket picking and purse snatching most frequently occur inside nonresidential buildings or on street locations. ■ Unlike most other crimes, pocket picking and purse snatching affect the elderly about as much as other age groups.
Motor vehicle theft	Unlawful taking or attempted taking of a self-propelled road vehicle owned by another, with the intent of depriving him or her of it, permanently or temporarily.	■ Motor vehicle theft is relatively well reported to the police. In 1985 89% of all completed thefts were reported. ■ The stolen property is more likely to be recovered in this crime than in other property crimes.
Arson	The intentional damaging or destruction or attempted damaging or destruction by means of fire or explosion of property without the consent of the owner, or of one's own property or that of another by fire or explosives with or without the intent to defraud.	■ Single-family residences were the most frequent targets of arson. ■ 16% of all structures where arson occurred were not in use.

SOURCE: BJS *Dictionary of Criminal Justice Data Terminology,* 2nd edition, 1981. BJS *Criminal Victimization in the U.S.,* 1985. FBI *Crime in the United States 1985.*

How do violent crimes differ from property crimes?

The outcome of a criminal event determines if it is a property crime or a violent crime. Violent crime refers to events such as homicide, rape, and assault that may result in injury to a person. Robbery is also considered a violent crime because it involves the use or threat of force against a person.

Property crimes are unlawful acts with the intent of gaining property but which do not involve the use or threat of force against an individual. Larceny and motor vehicle theft are examples of property crimes.

In the National Crime Survey a distinction is also made between crimes against persons (violent crimes and personal larceny) and crimes against households (property crimes, including household larceny).

How do felonies differ from misdemeanors?

Criminal offenses are also classified according to how they are handled by the criminal justice system. Most jurisdictions recognize two classes of offenses: felonies and misdemeanors.

Felonies are not distinguished from misdemeanors in the same way in all jurisdictions, but most States define felonies as offenses punishable by a year or more in a State prison. The most serious crimes are never "misdemeanors" and the most minor offenses are never "felonies."

SOURCE: Bureau of Justice Statistics, 1988b, *Report to the Nation on Crime and Justice*, 2nd edition, Washington, D.C.: Government Printing Office, March, pp. 2–3.

of the label of criminal. It does not take into account the difference between the convicted criminal, the fugitive, and the individual whose crime is known only to himself. Nor does it provide a guideline for the classification of someone believed by prosecutors, police and researchers to be guilty but found not guilty by a court of law (for example, Lizzie Borden, well-known defendant widely believed guilty in a case in which she was accused and exonerated of murdering her father and stepmother).

Many "white collar crimes" that we will discuss differ from other crimes only in the implementation of the law, which segregates white collar criminals administratively from other criminals. Reiman (1984, p. viii) indicates that many acts that are not treated as criminal acts are as great or more a danger to society than acts that are. "Thus, the disproportionality between our heavy-handed response to crime and our kid-glove response to noncriminal dangers continues to need explanation" (Ibid.). Were we to restrict analysis of crime solely to the legal definition in most countries, we would discuss primarily "crime in the streets" and ignore "crime in the suites." We would study the poor, dumb, slow criminal and conclude that low IQs and inferior genetics cause crime and ignore the fast, smart, and slick violator, and that maybe Ivy League educations and working on Wall Street or for the defense industry cause crime. Hyperbole (exaggeration) is useful at times for effect and obviously we must not loosely throw around the label criminal, but neither should we confine our analysis to ignoring the dangerous acts which do great harm, simply because the criminal justice system chooses to ignore them.

The Crime Problem

Radzinowicz and King (1977, pp. 3–5), in commenting upon the relentless international upsurge in crime in the later decades of the twentieth century, indicate: "No national characteristics, no political regime, no system of law, police punishment, treatment, or even terror, has rendered a country exempt from crime. . . . What is indisputable is that new and much higher levels of crime become established as a reflex of affluence." Despite rival explanations such as problems with statistics (to be discussed in Chapter 2), there has been an obvious increase in crime.

Recent estimates indicate that credit card fraud costs over $500 million a year.

It is difficult, if not impossible, to measure the *economic costs of crime*. Estimates of the actual financial operation take us into the "megabucks" range where notions such as "give or take a few billion dollars" stagger the imagination and numb us to the reality of the amounts we are really talking about. Vantage Point 1.2 provides some estimates of the cost of crime.

While recent estimates rank narcotics as the criminal world's greatest source of income, there is a problem with such assessments. These estimates to not even begin to measure the full impact of corporate price-fixing and other criminal activities. Added to these costs are economic costs incurred by victims of crime and costs of running the criminal justice system.

Not considered at all in these economic estimates are the *social and psychological costs* to society and to crime victims. Fear, mistrust, a curtailing of public activity, and a decline in the quality of life are but a few of the inestimable impacts of crime upon society. And horror stories abound of the impact of crime on the forgotten figure in the criminal justice equation—the crime victim. Aggregate statistics and trends fail to sensitize us to the psychological and emotionally crippling effects of crime upon some of its victims (see Moore and Trojanowicz, 1988). The writer is reminded of a conversation between two lawyers in which the first, a professor, was deriding the other who was an assistant district attorney: "Why, I remember when you were concerned with the downtrodden and concerned with defending and protecting the rights of the little people." The assistant D.A. replied, "I still am; the victims of crime are the downtrodden."

Hopefully, this brief introduction has served as a "sneak preview" of what criminology is and what criminologists are concerned with. Since crime is a popular focus of media exploitation and vicarious entertainment, it is quite important that criminologists base their analysis not on popular stereotypes or the latest rediscovery of a crime wave, but on accurate, objective data. This will be the subject of the next chapter.

Criminology is a fascinating and interesting study of the darker side of the human saga. To paraphrase Robert Browning, come along with me for the best is yet to come.

Summary

Criminology is the science or discipline which studies crime and criminal behavior. Major areas of investigation include criminal behavior, etiology (or theories of crime causation), the sociology of law and societal

VANTAGE POINT

The total cost of crime to society has been estimated, but the actual figure is unknown

There will never be a simple, single answer to the seemingly simple question, "What is the total cost of crime to society?" Some estimates have been made. For example, Wharton Econometric Forecasting Associates, Inc., recently estimated the total gross receipts from criminal activity to be between $26.9 billion and $136.9 billion in 1986 dollars.[1] Where the actual total lies within this $110 billion range is unknown because many of the component costs cannot be measured directly.

Although fairly accurate figures exist for some of the component costs of crime, many of the components cannot easily be measured.

- Some costs are difficult to measure, such as the higher costs for consumers from organized crime involvement in legitimate industries.
- Other costs of crime are difficult to quantify, like the pain and suffering of crime victims, their families and friends.
- Many crimes are undetected, such as successful fraud, embezzlement, and arson-for-profit.
- Some crimes go unreported because victims are afraid to report (blackmail), are embarrassed (con games), or are involved in the illegal activity (gambling).

What would be included in the total cost of crime to society?

Some of the direct costs of crime include—

- medical costs because of injuries suffered in victimization
- lost productivity because of death and medical or mental disabilities resulting from crime
- time lost from work by victims of crime
- damage to property
- lower property values because of crime in the neighborhood
- the cost of operating the criminal justice system
- the costs of private security services and devices, such as locks and burglar alarms.

In addition to direct costs, "involuntary transfers" occur when resources are taken from one person or organization and acquired by another, but they remain within society. For example—

- The dollar value of cash and property lost through robberies, burglaries, theft, embezzlement, and fraud is "transferred" to the offender.
- Additional costs of goods and services to consumers are charged by manufacturers and retailers to cover their losses from crime.

- Income tax evasion victimizes the government and other taxpayers who must pay higher taxes as a result.

A third type of economic cost of crime to society occurs in what is often called the "underground economy." This consists of consensual crimes where both parties agree to participate in the illegal activity. Examples of the underground economy are illegal gambling, prostitution, drug purchases, knowingly buying stolen property, and so on.

Some costs of crime have been measured

Most estimates of the *total* cost of crime to society are made by summing estimates of its individual components. Some of these recent estimates are—

Personal crimes of violence and theft and the *household crimes* of burglary, larceny, and motor vehicle theft cost their victims $13 billion in 1985.

- In 1981 most losses were from theft of property or cash (92%); 6% were from property damage and 2% from medical expenses.[2]
- $3.9 billion (36% of all losses) were recovered or reimbursed within 6 months after the offense.

Net losses from robbery, burglary, and larceny of banks was estimated at $37 million in 1982 by Abt Associates, Inc., using FBI data.[3] The losses from commercial robberies and burglaries can be estimated using FBI data at $1.1 billion in 1982.

Drug abuse costs to American society were estimated by Research Triangle Institute to be $59.7 billion in 1983:[4]

- Half the cost is in lost productivity by drug users.
- A third is crime-related (the cost to the criminal justice system and the private security industry attributable to drug-related crimes, property damage by drug users, and lost employment of crime victims).
- Social welfare expenditure such as disability payments, unemployment compensation, workers compensation, public assistance, and food stamps resulting from drug abuse were estimated at another $115 million.
- Health care services related to drug abuse and drug abuse treatment programs cost an additional $2 billion, and medicare reimbursements resulting from drug abuse were $100 million.

Credit and charge card fraud may cost as much as $500 million according to Federal Trade Commission 1984 estimates.[5]

Automated teller machine fraud in 1983 lost banks between $70 million and $100 million, a BJS study estimated.[6]

Counterfeit notes and currency valued at a total of $71.8 million by the U.S. Secret Service either were passed to the public or were seized before they could be passed.[7] Of this, close to $64 million were seized before they could be circulated, but $7.8 million found their way into general circulation.

Drunk driving caused motor vehicle crashes costing $13.2 billion in 1983 according to Research Triangle Institute estimates.[8]

Federal income tax evasion was estimated by the Internal Revenue Service at $81.5 billion in 1981, including failure to report income and overstatement of deductions.[9]

Private security costs for 1980 were estimated to be $21.7 billion by *Security World* magazine.[10]

The *criminal justice system* cost the Federal, State, and local governments $45.6 billion in 1985, according to BJS.[11]

Notes

1. Wharton Econometric Forecasting Associates, Inc.—Sima Fishman, Kathleen Rodenrys, and George Schink, "The income of organized crime," in President's Commission on Organized Crime, *The impact: Organized crime today* (Washington: USGPO, April 1986), pp. 413–439.

2. BJS National Crime Survey and *Economic cost of crime to victims*, BJS Special Report, NCJ-93450, April 1984.

3. Abt Associates, Inc., *Unreported taxable income from selected illegal activities*, prepared for the Internal Revenue Service, September 1984.

4. Hendrick J. Harwood, Diana M. Napolitano, Patricia L. Kristiansen, and James J. Collins, *Economic cost to society of alcohol and drug abuse and mental illness: 1980* (Research Triangle Park, N.C.: Research Triangle Insitute, June 1984).

5. "Facts for consumers: Credit and charge card fraud," Federal Trade Commission, November 8, 1984.

6. *Electronic fund transfer fraud*, BJS Special Report, NJC-96666, March 1985.

7. United States Secret Service, U.S. Department of the Treasury, in BJS *Sourcebook of criminal justice statistics, 1984*, NCJ-96382, October 1985, p. 540.

8. Research Triangle Institute in U.S. Department of Health and Human Services, *Toward a national plan to combat alcohol abuse and alcoholism: A report to the United States Congress*, September 1986, table 2-4.

9. *Income tax compliance research: Estimates for 1973–81*, Internal Revenue Service (Washington: USGPO, July 1983).

10. Security World magazine, "Key market coverage, 1981," in Cunningham and Taylor, *Private security and police in America: The Hallcrest report* (Portland, Oreg.: Chaneller Press, 1985).

11. BJS *Justice expenditure and employment in the U.S. 1985*, NCJ-104460, March 1987, table 2.

SOURCE: Bureau of Justice Statistics, 1988b, *Report to the Nation on Crime and Justice*, 2nd edition, Washington, D.C.: Government Printing Office, March, p. 114.

reaction; related areas include juvenile delinquency and victimology. Criminology also shares with the field of criminal justice the areas of policing, the courts, and corrections. Debunkers of the relevance of the scientific approach to criminology often substitute common sense, which they should beware of, since it often becomes nonsense.

Knowledge is defined as man's understanding of reality. This understanding is made possible through the creation of symbols or abstractions. Comte identified three stages in the progression of knowledge: the theological, metaphysical (philosophical), and scientific. Science combines the spirit of rationality of philosophy with the scientific method, which is characterized by the search for empirical proof. Criminology and sociology are more recent applicants to the scientific throne already enjoyed by the physical sciences. Having its origins in the eighteenth century in Europe, particularly in the writing of Beccaria, who was influential in codifying modern continental law, criminology has largely become a twentieth-century American discipline. This is particularly reflected in the work of Sutherland, who has been identified as "the dean of criminology."

Deviant behavior refers to activities which fall outside the range of normal societal toleration. Definitions of such activities are relative to time, place, and persons. *Values* are practices or beliefs that are prized in society and that are protected by *norms,* which are rules or proscribed modes of conduct. Sumner in his classic work, *Folkways,* identifies *three types of norms:* folkways, mores, and laws. While *folkways* are less serious customs or traditions, *mores* are serious norms which contain moral evaluations as well as penal sanctions. Both folkways and mores are examples of informal modes of control. *Laws,* codified rules of behavior, represent formal methods of attempting to assure social control.

Acts *mala in se* refer to acts which are "bad in themselves," such as murder, rape, and the like; acts *mala prohibita* are ones which are "bad because they are prohibited," such as laws regulating vagrancy and gambling. While not all criminal acts are viewed as deviant, neither are all deviant acts criminal. Undercriminalization involves the failure of the law to cover acts *mala in se*, while *overcriminalization* entails overextension of the law to cover acts which may more effectively be enforced through the mores. As societies undergo transition from *Gemeinschaft* (communal, sacred societies) to *Gesellschaft* (associational, secular societies), they must rely more upon formal agencies of control. In order to be effective, laws require the support of the mores.

Manifest functions are intended or planned consequences of social arrangements, whereas *latent functions* refer to unintended or unanticipated consequences. While the manifest function of Prohibition was to eliminate alcohol abuse, its latent functions were to encourage corruption, organized crime, and public disrespect. Durkheim viewed *crime as a normal condition* in society which served a positive function by the reactions it developed to encourage reaffirmation of values. *Crime,* a violation of criminal law, is characterized by politicality, specificity, uniformity, and sanctions. In explaining the origin of criminal law, the *consensus model* views the criminal law as reflecting agreement or public will, while the *conflict model* claims that it represents the interest of the most powerful group(s) in society. In reality, criminal law reflects elements of both models.

For official purposes *crimes* are identified as being felonies, misdemeanors, and, in some states, summary offenses. Although there is variation by state in the actual assignment to categories, a *felony* refers to more serious crime which bears a penalty of at least one year in a state prison, while a *misdemeanor* is a less serious offense subject to a small fine or short imprisonment.

The issue of "who defines crime?" should not be answered simply by accepting the current definitions, since to do so would permit others to define criminology's subject matter. The crime problem is a growing international problem; the costs of crime are economic (which can only be estimated), psychological, and social in nature. The full social costs are inestimable.

KEY CONCEPTS

Criminology
Stages of Progression of
    Knowledge
Two Features of Science
Crime
Deviance
Cultural Values
Norms
Folkways
Mores
Laws

Mala in Se
Mala Prohibita
Undercriminalization
Overcriminalization
Gemeinschaft
Gesellschaft
Manifest Functions
Latent Functions
Durkheim's "Crime as
    Functional Necessity"
Criminal Law

Characteristics of Criminal
    Law
Statutory Law
Common Law
Administrative Law
Consensus vs. Conflict Model
    of Law
Felony
Misdemeanor
Costs of Crime

2

Research Methods in Criminology

Theory and Methodology

Two critical features of any discipline are its theory and its methodology. *Theory*, which will be the subject of Chapters 4 and 5, addresses the questions of "Why?" and "How?"; *Methodology (methods)*, on the other hand, is concerned with "What is?"

Theories involve attempts to develop reasonable explanations of reality. They are efforts to structure, summarize, or explain the essential elements of the subject in question. What causes crime? Why do some individuals become criminal? Why are some nations or areas more criminogenic than others? Theories represent the intellectual leaps of faith that provide fundamental insights into how things operate; they attempt to illuminate or shed light upon the darkness of reality. Without the generation of useful theoretical explanations, a field is intellectually bankrupt; it becomes merely a collection of "war stories" and carefully documented encyclopedic accounts. It fails to explain, summarize, or capture the essential nature of its subject matter. A field devoid of theory would be akin to reading a good mystery novel without the author ever telling us "whodunit" and how and why they did it.

Methodology involves the collection and analysis of accurate data or facts. With respect to criminology this would concern information regarding: How much crime is there? Who commits crime? How does crime commission or definitions vary? and the like. If the facts regarding crime as provided by defective models are in error, then certainly theories or attempted explanations of this incorrectly described reality are most certainly to be misdirected.

In the social sciences there at times exists a chasm between those who are primarily interested in theory or broad conceptual analysis analogous to philosophy and those who are viewed as methodologists. Theory devoid of method, explanation without accurate supportive data, is just as much a dead end as method devoid of interpretive theory. The former resembles armchair theorizing, the latter a fruitless bookkeeping operation. In reality, in order to realize mature development, criminology needs both incisive theory and sound and accurate methodology.

The purpose of this chapter is to alert and sensitize the reader to the variety of research methods that are employed in criminological research. Many readers of lengthy prose in textbooks are relatively oblivious to sources that are cited by authors. But writers cite supportive references so the reader may consult them for further information on any given issue. Thus, a textbook, rather than representing a compendium of unsupported opinion, attempts to convey the latest thinking and research. Such a presentation, particularly in social science disciplines such as criminology, is, of necessity, tentative and can represent only our current state of understanding of reality. The purpose of this chapter on methodology is to identify the research base upon which the findings presented in this book are to be weighed with respect to the relative strengths as well as shortcomings.

The Research Enterprise of Criminology

Objectivity

A basic canon of scientific research is that researchers attempt to maintain *objectivity*. This requires that the investigators strive to be "value free" in their inquiry (Weber, 1949) and, in a sense, to permit the findings to speak for themselves. A researcher may occasionally find the attitudes, behavior, or beliefs of a group he or she is studying repugnant or immoral; however, the researcher is trained not to judge but rather objectively to record and determine what meaning these findings have for the field of criminology and the development of its knowledge base.

Ethics in Criminological Research

Because it is part of the social sciences, the subject matter of criminology is different in kind than that of the physical sciences. While the latter concentrates upon physical facts, criminology's subject matter—crime, criminal behavior, victims, and criminal justice system—is concerned with human behavior, attitudes, groups, and organizations. Like physical science investigations, criminological inquiry must also be concerned with its potentially adverse impacts upon human subjects.

The researcher in criminology of necessity often wears many hats: those of a researcher, a practitioner, a citizen, and a humanitarian. These roles obviously at times conflict, raising potential moral dilemmas. To mediate these potentially conflicting roles, the researcher must enter the investigation with eyes wide open. Important decisions, such as one's commitment to the research undertaking as well as clarifications of possible role conflicts, must be considered beforehand. While there are no hard and fast rules and each research endeavor has its own unique qualities, the researcher's primary role is that of scientist. This does not mean that the scientist role should in all cases take total precedence over other agenda; however, the investigator should address these issues of subject accountability and limits and priorities as soon as possible prior to embarking upon a study.

Ultimately, ethical conduct in research is an individual responsibility tied into deep moral judgments; a blind adherence to any checklist grossly oversimplifies a very complex decision. Although no code of ethics specifically appropriate to criminology or criminal justice exists other than those detailed by government agencies or parent professions such as the American Sociological Association or American Psychological Association, *some general principles of ethical conduct* can be derived. Researchers should, as a matter of professionalism:

- avoid procedures which may harm subjects,
- honor commitments to respondents and respect reciprocity,
- exercise objectivity and professional integrity in performing and reporting research,
- protect confidentiality and privacy of respondents (Hagan, 1989a, p. 358).

In the name of research, criminologists should have no interest in behaving as "mad scientists," in which science is inhumanely pursued for its own sake. In most research, informed consent of participants based upon knowledge of the experiment should be a goal. If some form of deception is necessary, it is even more incumbent upon the researcher to prevent harm and, where possible, debrief, reassure, and explain the purposes of the project afterwards. Obviously, criminology cannot afford to limit its inquiry to volunteers.

Reciprocity involves a system of mutual trust and obligation between the researcher and subject. Subjects are asked to share of themselves in the belief that this baring of information is not to be used in an inappropriate, harmful, or embarrassing manner.

A basic tenet of any scholarly research is the dictum that the investigator maintain objectivity and professional integrity in both the performance and the reporting of research. The researcher first and foremost is an investigator and not a hustler, huckster, salesperson, or politician. Researchers should avoid purposely choosing and reporting only those techniques which tend to shed the best light upon their data, or "lying with statistics" (Huff, 1966).

Related to these issues is the fact that the researcher should take steps to protect the *confidentiality* and privacy of respondents. One procedure for attempting to protect the identity of subjects, organizations, or communities is through the use of *pseudonyms*, aliases, or false names. Names such as "Doc," "Chic," "The Lupollo Family," "Vince Swaggi," "Deep Throat," and "Wincanton," just to mention a few, have become legend in criminology.

Pure vs. Applied Research

Many disciplines in the social sciences have experienced academic guerrilla warfare between two camps: those primarily interested in pure research and those who espouse applied research. *Pure research* is concerned with the discovery of knowledge, even that which may have no present applicability, in order to contribute to the development of a science or discipline. *Applied research* deals with finding answers in order to direct policy analysis on present problems. In reality, the division between pure and applied research is in part stereotypical, since there is in fact much overlap between the two types (Rabow, 1964). Often the most obscure and abstract research, that which critics might call "ivory tower" research, will in the long run produce the critical breakthroughs which may have more direct payoffs than many premature applied projects: Pasteur, Einstein, and Galileo were not applied researchers. On the other hand, even though critics of applied researchers may describe them at times as shamans or quacks attempting to provide advice or guide policy without adequate theoretical or methodological support, many existing projects require immediate policy decisions which cannot wait and must represent the best we have to offer at the present time.

Who Is Criminal? ————————————————————

To illustrate the importance of methodological precision, let us examine the basic, but deceptively complex questions, "Who is criminal?" and "How much crime is there?" While an initial response to these questions might be, "Why, of course, we know," the answers are not as obvious as they seem.

Taking what would appear to be the easiest question, "Who is criminal?" most would agree that long-term recidivists (repeaters) who have continually been found guilty are criminals. Yet some ideologues (those committed to a strict adherence to a distinctive political belief system) might even on this point maintain that some of these "career criminals" are in fact not criminals, but, using the conflict perspective, political prisoners, victims of an unfair class system, or a politically oppressive system (Quinney and Wildeman, 1977, and Turk, 1982).

Additionally, not all apprehended individuals or persons accused of crime are guilty; and what about those who commit crime but who are not arrested?

It becomes apparent that the manner in which the *variable* "criminal" is *operationalized* will have a major influence upon the definition of the concept of criminal. A variable is a concept that has been operationalized or measured in a specific manner and that can vary or take on different values, usually of a quantitative nature. Operationalization involves the process of defining concepts by describing how they are being measured; the notion of operationalization can practically be explained in completing the statement, "I measured it by _____."

Later, in Chapters 4 and 5 we will describe many theories which assumed excess criminality among lower class groups based upon official statistics. However, what methodological problem and bias in addressing this issue is introduced by relying solely upon one measure of crime?

Official Police Statistics—The Uniform Crime Report (UCR)

Internationally, until relatively recently the major source of information regarding crime statistics was official police statistics. Gathered for government administrative purposes with only secondary attention paid to their usefulness for social science research, these data tended to be uneven in quality and were not gathered or recorded in any systematic manner. Basically, criminologists had no efficient statistics to consult in order to answer even basic questions such as whether crime was increasing or decreasing.

Since 1930 the U.S. Department of Justice has compiled national crime statistics, the *Uniform Crime Report (UCR)*, with the Federal Bureau of Investigation (FBI) assuming responsibility as the clearinghouse and publisher. Although participation in the UCR program by local police departments is purely voluntary, the number of departments reporting and the comprehensiveness of the information has steadily improved over the years, with police departments from large metropolitan areas historically being the best participants (see Banas and Trojanowicz, 1985).

Sources of Crime Statistics

Returning to our question, "How much crime is there?" an examination of the UCR and its relationship to sources of data on crime and criminals is useful. Figure 2.1 illustrates the relationship between crime committed and the sources of crime statistics, including the UCR. It is unclear whether an accurate estimate of the amount of crime committed is possible, for several reasons. Not all crimes that are committed are discovered. For example, some crimes may be known only to their perpetrators, in which case the victim is unaware of loss, or perhaps there is no identifiable victim, such as in a gambling violation. The further a source of statistics is away from the "crimes committed" category, the less useful it is as a measure of the extent of crime. While obviously

Figure 2.1: Sources of Crime Statistics: The Flow of Offenders through the Criminal Justice System

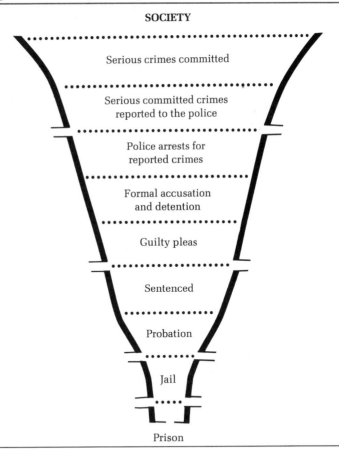

SOCIETY

Serious crimes committed

Serious committed crimes reported to the police

Police arrests for reported crimes

Formal accusation and detention

Guilty pleas

Sentenced

Probation

Jail

Prison

SOURCE: Adapted from the President's Commission on Law Enforcement and the Administration of Justice, 1967a, *The Challenge of Crime in a Free Society,* Washington, D.C.: Government Printing Office, pp. 262–63.

Motor Vehicle Theft is one of the eight major felonies that occurs most frequently and is viewed as more serious than nonindex offenses.

not all crimes are discovered, even if they are discovered, not all of them are reported to the police. Similarly, not all crimes reported are recorded by police.

In addition, although, as we will see, some law enforcement agencies may purposely conceal recorded crimes, a number of purported crimes may be *unfounded* or defined by investigating officers as not constituting a criminal matter.

Despite this problematic relationship between crimes recorded and crimes committed, the UCR until recently represented the best statistics available on crime commission and, as will be discussed later in this chapter, still represents one of the best sources. Again in Figure 2.1, once we move beyond crimes recorded as a measure of crime commission, we are getting farther removed from the accurate measurement of crime commission. Thus arrest statistics, indictments, convictions, incarcerations, and other dispositions such as probation and parole are not as useful. Such statistics have much more to do with police efficiency or allocations to the criminal justice system and general societal policies toward crime control policy than they do with measuring the extent of the crime problem.

Most media accounts of changes in the crime rate are based upon the annual summary presented in the UCR. While the UCR contains many qualifying remarks regarding the meaning of these statistics, in most instances the press tends to report these data uncritically and often in an alarmist manner. Obviously, the researcher who chooses to utilize UCR data must become as familiar as possible with any shortcomings or sources of bias in these statistics.

The FBI receives its information for the UCR from local police departments. Considerable variation exists in state penal codes regarding criminal offenses and their definitions, although participating departments receive instruction in uniform crime recording in order to standardize their reports into a comparable nationwide document.

In the majority of states there are UCR systems in which states require that all local departments report their statistics to the state. These data are then shared with the FBI. In the late eighties about 98 percent of the U.S. population living in Metropolitan Statistical Areas (MSAs),* 94 percent in "other cities," and 90 percent of rural departments participated. The Census Bureau estimates that about 97 percent of the total national population was covered by the report.

The Crime Index

The UCR is divided into two parts:

Part I crimes consist of the index crimes, major felonies which are believed to be more serious, to occur more frequently, and to have a greater likelihood of being reported to the police. *The index offenses are:*

1. Murder and non-negligent manslaughter
2. Forcible rape
3. Robbery
4. Aggravated assault
5. Burglary
6. Larceny/theft
7. Motor vehicle theft
8. Arson

The original index and the one used for historical comparison consist of the first seven offenses. Arson was added as a result of a law passed by the U.S. Congress in October 1978. As we will see shortly, the crime rate is calculated with the index offenses.

Part II crimes are nonindex offenses and are not used in the calculation of the crime rate. This includes twenty-two other crimes (twenty-one, excluding arson) such as simple assault, vandalism, drunkenness, gambling, and the like.

---

*An MSA includes a central city/cities (over 50,000 pop.) and contiguous counties that are functionally integrated, economically and socially, with the core city/cities.

Issues and Cautions in UCR Data

An extensive literature has accumulated regarding shortcomings of UCR statistics.* While the UCR has steadily improved and been refined since its inception in 1930, researchers utilizing these data should exercise caution and be aware of certain limitations. Some primary shortcomings of the UCR include the following:

1. The recorded statistics represent only a portion of the true crime rate of a community. Victim surveys suggest that there is possibly twice as much crime committed as appears in official statistics.

2. The big increase in the crime rate beginning in the mid-sixties may be explained in part by better communications, more professional and more efficient police departments, and better recording and reporting of crime. Larger, improved, and professionalized police departments appear to be positively related with rising crime rates. This was particularly the case in larger urban areas. In the seventies, while the official crime rate increased dramatically, victim surveys and self-report surveys showed a fairly stable crime rate during that period.

3. Increased citizen concern and awareness of crime, higher standards of expected public morality, and greater reporting of and response to ghetto crime may all have had impacts on increasing the recorded crime rate.

4. Most federal offenses, "victimless" crimes, and white-collar crimes do not appear in the UCR. Analysis of age, racial, and sexual characteristics of those arrested shows that the UCR concentrates on "crime in the streets," the inept and poor criminal, and fail to include "crime in the suites," elite crime.

5. Changes in record keeping procedures such as computerization, transition in police administrations, and political shenanigans can have major impact upon crime recording. The FBI attempts to monitor and control abuses; in 1949 it refused to publish New York City Police Department data. With "improved" recording, the robbery rate jumped 800 percent the next year. Changes in police practices showed similar leaps elsewhere: 61 percent in Chicago in 1961 when the chief was changed, 202 percent in Kansas City in 1959 due to departmental reform, and 95 percent in Buffalo in the early sixties (President's Commission, 1967, p. 25). Similar dramatic drops in the crime rate have taken place when required for political purposes. Nixon's targeting of

---

*See, for example, Beattie (1955); Black (1970); Hartjen (1974); Hindelang (1974); Kitsuse and Cicourel (1963); Lejins (1966); Savitz (1978); Seidman and Couzens (1974); Sellin (1957); Skogan (1974); U.S. Department of Justice (1979); and Wolfgang (1963). These represent only a sampling of the extensive literature on this subject.

the District of Columbia for a crime-busting program showed such a decline, which was more likely simply a matter of classifying crimes out of the index. Until 1973, grand larceny of $50 or more could be classified as under $50 and thus unrecorded as one of the index crimes from which the crime rate is calculated.

6. In interpreting UCR statistics, keep in mind what arrest statistics do or do not include:

    a. Arrests do not equal crimes solved or suspects found guilty.
    b. Many potential crimes are unfounded by police.
    c. In the situation of a multiple offense, only the most serious offense is recorded for UCR purposes.
    d. The majority of crimes committed are not index offenses.

7. The crime index is primarily made up of property crimes. Auto theft, a less serious and highly reported and cleared offense, artificially inflates this index and perhaps should be dropped from Part 1 designation (Savitz, 1978). Inflation causes bicycle thefts to become larceny, an index offense; while after 1973, all larcenies were included in the index, thus increasing the crime rate (Rhodes, 1977, p. 168). Greater insurance coverage further encourages reporting of property loss.

8. The crime index is an unweighted index; it is a simple summated scale in which a murder counts the same as a bicycle theft. Surprisingly, most bodily injury crimes are "nonindex" offenses (Savitz, 1978).

9. The existence of the "crime index" may encourage concentration by police agencies on these offenses at the expense of others.

10. The crime rate is calculated on the basis of dicennial census population figures. Rapidly growing cities of the Southwest would, under this system, have worse-appearing rates since, for example, 1979 crimes would be divided by a 1970 population base.

11. Demographic shifts may provide partial explanations for changing crime rates. Some criminologists had prophesied a *crime dip* (a decline in the crime rate trend) in the 1980s based upon a general aging of the baby boom generation (children born in the post-World War II era, from 1946 through the mid-fifties). This larger-than-normal population cohort overwhelmed hospital nursery wards, elementary and secondary schools, and later colleges. These establishments now have extra space as the last of the baby boom moved through. Similarly, the criminal justice system was overwhelmed by a larger-than-normal proportion in the maximal crime-committing ages (15–24), as the job market and housing industry inherits this now "middle-age boom." Barring other factors, as this group ages, the criminal justice system should find itself with a more manageable situation, although Blumstein and Cohen (1987) expect an "echo boom" in the 1990s. This involves higher crime rates by the children of the baby boomers. The researcher who decides to make use of official statistics such as the UCR must become familiar with such inadequacies in order to avoid the drawing of inappropriate conclusions or analyses. Despite the shortcomings that have been identified, the UCR remains an excellent source of information on police operations. Treatment of actual UCR data and trends using the crime index offenses and the crime rate will be deferred until the next chapter and the discussion of variations in crime.

The Crime Rate

$$\frac{\text{number of crimes}}{\text{population}} \times 100,000 = \text{Crime Rate}$$

The crime rate is a calculation which expresses the total number of index crimes per 100,000 population. The purpose of an *index* (like the Dow-Jones Industrial Average or the Consumer Price Index) is to provide a composite measure, one which does not rely too heavily upon any one factor. An index also enables control for population size, thus permitting fair comparisons of different-sized units. As previously indicated, it is this UCR crime rate that one reads about in the newspaper, with accounts of crime either rising or falling by a given percent. A principal difficulty with the UCR crime rate as an index of crime in the United States is that it is an *unweighted index*. That is, each crime, whether murder or bicycle theft, is added into the total index without a concern or weight given for the relative seriousness of the offense. Thus no monetary or psychological value is assigned. For instance, a city with 100 burglaries per 100,000 population and one with 100 homicides per 100,000 population would have the same crime rate.

One alternative that has been proposed is for the calculation of a weighted index using results of crime seriousness scales (Sellin and Wolfgang, 1964; and Rossi et al.; 1974). In a weighted crime index, criminal incidents are assigned weights on the basis of variables such as amount stolen, method of intimidation, degree of harm inflicted, and similar salient factors.

Redesign of the UCR Program

In 1982, in response to the criticisms and limitations of the UCR program, the Bureau of Justice Statistics and FBI formed a joint task force and contracted a private research firm (Abt Associates, Inc.) to undertake revisions in the UCR program, the first in the program's more than fifty years of existence (Poggio, et al., 1985; and Rovetch, Poggio, and

Rossman, 1984). On the basis of recommendations of a steering committee made up of police practitioners, academicians, and the media, suggestions for changes in the UCR included:

- A *new two-level reporting system* in which most agencies continue reporting basic offense and arrest data similar to the present way of reporting (Level I), while a small sample of agencies report more extensive information (Level II).
- The entire UCR system is to be converted into *unit-record reporting* in which police agencies report on the characteristics of each criminal incident (for example, location, time, presence of weapon) and on the characteristics of each individual arrest.
- Distinguish attempted from completed offenses.
- Distinguish between crimes against businesses, against individuals or households, and crimes against other entities.
- Institute ongoing audits of samples of participating UCR agencies to check for error in the new program.
- Support better user services particularly in making data bases more available to outside researchers. (U.S. Department of Justice, 1988, p. 82)

It is believed that these revisions in the program will overcome a number of past criticisms as well as provide a data base that will be more useful both for researchers and policy makers.

Crime Clocks

Figure 2.2 presents a summary device which is displayed in the UCR with proper cautionary statements: an illustration called a crime clock. Despite UCR warnings to readers, the media and others tend to either misunderstand or misuse this graphic device in summarizing trends in crime. The crime clock device is the poorest graphic device for analyzing crime change due to the fact that it fails to control for population growth and uses a constant fixed unit of comparison—time. Relative to population growth, a community could be experiencing a per capita decline in crime and the crime clock would still show an increase. Suppose, for example, that a community in 1960 had a population of one million and 100 serious crimes and in 1990 had a population of two million and 200 serious crimes. The crime rate would be ten in each period, but the crime clock would have shown an increase. The crime clock graphic device serves little function with growing populations other than to misleadingly alarm the public. In fact, companies peddling burglar alarms and security devices are particularly fond of reproducing these figures in their advertising.

Figure 2.2: Crime Clock, 1987

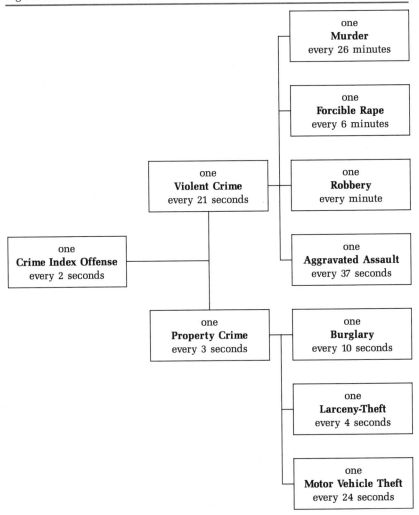

one
Murder
every 26 minutes

one
Forcible Rape
every 6 minutes

one
Robbery
every minute

one
Violent Crime
every 21 seconds

one
Aggravated Assault
every 37 seconds

one
Crime Index Offense
every 2 seconds

one
Property Crime
every 3 seconds

one
Burglary
every 10 seconds

one
Larceny-Theft
every 4 seconds

one
Motor Vehicle Theft
every 24 seconds

The crime clock should be viewed with care. Being the most aggregate representation of UCR data, it is designed to convey the annual reported crime experience by showing the relative frequency of occurrence of the Index Offenses. This mode of display should not be taken to imply a regularity in the commission of the Part I Offenses: rather, it represents the annual ratio of crime to fixed time intervals.

SOURCE: Federal Bureau of Investigation, 1988, *Crime in the United States, 1987*, Washington, D.C.: U.S. Government Printing Office, p. 6.

The nineteenth-century British Prime Minister Benjamin Disraeli has often been cited as having remarked, "There are three types of lies: lies, damn lies and statistics." Obviously, caution must be exercised in examining graphic devices and statistical reports (Huff, 1966; and Zeisel, 1957).

Alternative Data Gathering Strategies

Official crime statistics published by national governments have their uses; however, criminologists would be remiss in their duty as scholars and scientists if they were to restrict their inquiry and sources of statistics to data gathered for administrative purposes by government bodies. In some totalitarian regimes, for instance, there would be nothing to study, since the official government ideology might simply hold that there is no crime in the people's paradise. Even in open societies, official statistics seldom cover crimes of the elite.

Fortunately, criminologists have at their disposal a veritable arsenal of techniques whose application is limited only by the researcher's imagination and skill. Figure 2.3 offers a model or paradigm (schema) with which to consider and compare the alternative data gathering strategies which can be employed in criminal justice and criminological research.

As an illustrative device, Figure 2.3 is an attempt to broadly describe the relative advantages and disadvantages of the different data gathering strategies. The model suggests that, as we move up the list of techniques or vertical arrows to experiments, we tend to obtain *quantitative measurement* (which lends itself to sophisticated statistical treatment), *greater control* over other factors which may interfere with one's findings,

Figure 2.3: Alternative Data Gathering Strategies

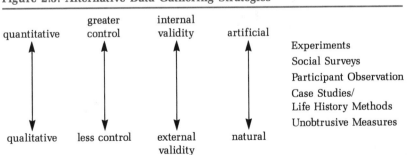

SOURCE: Frank E. Hagan, 1989a, *Research Methods in Criminal Justice and Criminology*, 2nd edition, New York: Macmillan, p. 67.

increased *internal validity* (or accuracy in being certain that the variable[s] assumed to be responsible for one's findings are indeed the causal agent[s]), but at the expense of *artificiality.* The latter point suggests that, as a result of controlling for error, the researcher may have created an antiseptic or atypical group or situation which no longer resembles the "real world" that one is attempting to describe.

Generally, as one proceeds down the vertical arrows or list of techniques, the methodology which is employed becomes more *qualitative.* Qualitative techniques involve less of a commitment on the part of the researcher to quantitative measurement, more of an engagement with field and observational strategies, and less direct means of obtaining information. Generally, as one moves down the list, one has less control over manipulating the research setting and rival causal factors. However, such procedures increase *external validity* (the ability to generalize to larger populations) as well as present the opportunity to study subjects in more natural settings. Implicit in this model is the fact that each method has its own relative strengths and weaknesses, and often the very strength of one technique is the weakness of another and vice versa. No one technique has an a priori superiority over any other means of obtaining data.

Criminologists, as other researchers, tend to favor their own particular methods of data gathering; this is to be expected. However, at times academic battles break out among those who claim that their preferred method contains some inherent superiority over other procedures. Such *methodological narcissism* (or methodologism) is a fanatical adherence to a particular research method, often at the expense of a concern for substance ("Martinson Attacks His Own Earlier Work," 1978, p. 4; Martinson, 1979; and Bayley, 1978). This "methods for methods sake" orientation ignores the fact that methodology is not an end in itself but a means to an end, the development of criminological knowledge. It is more useful to permit the subject to dictate the proper methodology rather than to assert that, unless a subject lends itself to deployment of one's favorite method, it is not worthy of study.

Experiments in Criminology

The *experiment* is the lodestone or benchmark for comparison with all other research methods. It is the most effective means of controlling for error or rival factors before the fact through the very design of the study (Campbell and Stanley, 1963).

While there are myriad variations of the experiment, the point of departure or prototype is the classic experimental design. *The Classic Experimental Design* contains three key elements:

- Equivalence
- Pre and Posttests
- Experimental and Control Groups

Basically, *equivalence* means assigning subjects to experimental and control groups in such a manner that they are assumed to be alike in all major respects. This can be done through either *random assignment* (where each subject has an equal probability of appearing in either group) or through *matching* (a procedure in which subjects with similar age, sex, and other characteristics exhibited by the experimental group are recruited for the control group).

The *experimental group* is the group that is to receive the treatment (X), while the *control group* is one which will receive no treatment but will be observed in order to compare it with the experimental group. Both groups are given *pretests* (preobservations in order to note conditions which exist prior to treatment) designated as 0_1 or observation time one and *posttests* or observations after the experimental treatment (X) has taken place. The logic of the experiment assumes that, since both groups were equivalent in the pretest period, any differences in the posttest observation must then be due to the fact that one group received a particular treatment and the other had not.

Increasingly, such experiments are being utilized in order to inform public policy decision-making. Such experiments are seen as giving answers which enable fairly clear policy direction (Kelling, 1988a; and Garner and Visher, 1988).

Some Examples of Experiments in Criminology

Candid Camera

In an attempt to increase both the apprehension and the conviction rates of robbers of commercial establishments, the Seattle Police Department created a field experiment using high-risk establishments, some of which were designated as the experimental group, others as the control group. The treatment for the experimental group involved installation of special hidden cameras that could be triggered by clerks during a holdup by pulling a "trip" bill from the cash drawer; prints of the photograph of the robber would be made available immediately. A posttest of the two types of sites found 55 percent of robberies in the experimental group cleared by arrest compared to 25 percent for control locations. (Clearance indicates that suspects have been arrested, charged, and turned over to the court for prosecution or the police feel that further investigation is unnecessary.) While 48 percent of the robbers at camera sites were convicted, only 19 percent of the control group brigands were found guilty (Hidden Cameras Project, 1978).

Scared Straight

Much fanfare was raised in the United States in the late seventies over a novel program intended to deter wayward juveniles from progression to more serious criminal activity by means of blunt, "heart-to-heart" talks in prison with specially selected inmates. Portrayed in a film, *Scared Straight*, the initial Rahway, New Jersey, prison project was intended to counteract the glamorized image associated with criminal life. Although many jurisdictions rushed to imitate what appeared to be the latest panacea in corrections, further research suggested that this optimism was premature (Finckenauer, 1982). Yarborough evaluated the JOLT (Juvenile Offenders Learn Truth) program at the Jackson State Prison, Michigan, by randomly assigning youths to experimental and control groups. He then measured their delinquency rates three and six months afterwards and found no significant differences between those who had attended the JOLT sessions (experimentals) and those who had not (controls) (Scared Straight Found Ineffective Again, 1979).

Obedience to Authority

Milgram's experiments, reported in *Obedience to Authority* (1974), raised many ethical problems like those we discussed at the beginning of the chapter. The experiments dealt with conditions under which people would commit immoral acts when instructed to do so by what they perceived as competent authorities. Volunteers were told they were participating in a learning experiment; they were to administer electric shocks to pupils (actually confederates who were in on the experiment) each time they gave an incorrect answer. Switches on a fake shock-generating machine ranged from small voltage to "XXX-Unknown." All of Milgram's subjects administered the mildest shocks, and a large proportion threw the most lethally labeled switches, despite screams and pleas from the pupils. They appeared to do so because they were assured by officials running the study that it was appropriate to do so.

While these experiments have been criticized as having problems with respect to artificiality and demand characteristics (participants willing to do the bidding of researchers because they wish to be good subjects), Milgram claims that the situation was real to the participants.

While some of the subjects experienced temporary psychological distress, follow-up studies demonstrated no lasting adverse impacts.

Mock Prison

Haney, Banks, and Zimbardo (1973) conducted a "simulated prison study" by creating a mock prison in which undergraduate volunteers were assigned roles as either guards or prisoners. The experiment had to be prematurely canceled when the guards, carried away with their roles, became increasingly brutal and aggressive and the prisoners displayed progressive hostility and passivity.

Evaluation of Experiments

Experiments are an excellent means of controlling for factors which may affect the internal validity of studies. Before the fact, through the very design of the study, the researcher is able to control for rival factors that may tend to invalidate a study. In most instances, experiments are also a relatively quick and inexpensive means of data gathering.

The Seattle Police Department ran a field experiment in 1978 they called "Candid Camera." Hidden cameras were triggered by pulling a special trip bill in the register.

The researcher can control the stimulus, the environment, and treatment time, as well as degree of exposure.

As discussed previously, the chief disadvantage of experiments is their potential artificiality. The very controls imposed in order to exclude rival causal factors often create atypical groups and conditions, thus impeding the ability to generalize to larger populations. Other difficulties relate to problems in obtaining proper subjects or conditions. Ethical issues are raised, since human subjects are involved. Random assignment in prison research might, for instance, constitute a violation of the right of due process or equal treatment under the law (Glaser, 1978, p. 775). *Experimenter effects* may also occur in which researchers unwittingly give cues to subjects as to desired results (Rosenthal, 1966). Experiments, therefore, are by no means the most effective or best strategy; and, depending upon one's research problem, some alternative research strategy may be desirable.

A particularly thorny issue affecting experimental work in criminology has been given the name "the *dualistic fallacy*" by Susan Titus Reid (1982, p. 657); she defines this as "the assumption that a population has two mutually exclusive subclasses, such as criminals and noncriminals." This problem presents itself in many studies which compare incarcerated populations, which are assumed to represent the criminal class, with the population at large, which is assumed to be purely noncriminal.

Surveys

Most readers are familiar with the use of surveys in public opinion polls, in voting-prediction studies, and in marketing research. Surveys are also used in criminology, particularly in analyzing victimization, self-reported crime, public ratings of crime seriousness, measurements of fear of crime, and attitudes toward the police and the criminal justice system. The principal methods employed in gathering data for surveys are variations of questionnaires, interviews, or telephone surveys. Just as experiments control for error and rival causal factors before the fact by the very design of the study, survey researchers attempt to control for these factors after the fact, through the use of statistical procedures.

A key issue that is often ignored when discussing the results of surveys is the fact that surveys are involved in measuring expressed attitude or claimed behavior and seldom the behavior itself. Another issue is that while some of the surveys such as the decennial U.S. Census involve a complete enumeration of the population, for economy reasons, most surveys entail some type of sampling. *Sampling* involves choosing a portion of the population usually in such a manner that the sample represents a microcosm of the population. The logic involved in probability sampling methods assumes that, if some equal probability of selection method (EPSEM) is employed, there is a very high likelihood that the sample will contain similar characteristics as the population, at a great savings in time and cost (Babbie, 1975).

Victim Surveys

One of the major shortcomings of such official police statistics as the UCR is that it fails to account for undiscovered or unreported crime; *the dark figure of crime* is the phrase early European criminologists used to refer to offenses which escaped official statistics. The assumption was that, for every crime that came to the attention of authorities, there was an unspecified number of undiscovered crimes: "the dark figure."

Victim surveys are specifically designed to record an estimate of claimed victimizations by a representative sample of the population. One major finding, beginning with the U.S. surveys of the late 1960s, was that overall about twice as much crime was reported to interviewers than appeared in official police records (Biderman et al., 1967; Ennis, 1967; and Reiss, 1967). Although now such surveys are conducted by many countries, the most ambitious and continuing victim survey program has been carried out since the early seventies by the Law Enforcement Assistance Administration (LEAA) of the U.S. Department of Justice. This effort is now under the auspices of the U.S. Bureau of Census. We will now briefly describe the National Crime Survey, some problems with such surveys, and some means that have been devised to attempt to control for errors in such surveys.

Clinard (1978, p. 222) traces the first victim surveys to household interviews conducted in Denmark in 1720. Despite this and other early efforts, it was not until the late 1960s that any major U.S. victim surveys were conducted in order to obtain a measure of crime. At that time, the President's Commission on Law Enforcement and the Administration of Justice commissioned studies by Biderman et al. (1967) in the District of Columbia, pilot surveys in Boston and Chicago (Reiss, 1967), and a national survey by the National Opinion Research Center (Ennis, 1967).

On the basis of the results of these surveys, a major victim survey effort was begun not only in the United States, but also in Belgium, Canada, Denmark, England, Holland, Norway, Sweden, Switzerland, and West Germany (Sparks, Genn, and Dodd, 1977, p. 3; Nettler, 1978, pp. 94–95; Mackay and Hagan, 1978). Among both private and government-sponsored surveys, by far the most ambitious and sustained effort has been conducted in the United States by the Law Enforcement Assistance Administration (LEAA). These are now conducted by the U.S. Census Bureau on behalf of the Bureau of Justice Statistics.

VANTAGE POINT

Vantage Point 2.1—Were You a Victim of Crime?

36. The following questions refer only to things that happened to YOU during the last 6 months— between _____ 1, 197___ and _____, 197___. Did you have your (pocket picked/purse snatched)?
☐ Yes—How many times?
☐ No _____

37. Did anyone take something (else) directly from you by using force, such as by a stickup, mugging or threat?
☐ Yes—How many times?
☐ No _____

38. Did anyone TRY to rob you by using force or threatening to harm you? (other than any incidents already mentioned)
☐ Yes—How many times?
☐ No _____

39. Did anyone beat you up, attack you or hit you with something, such as a rock or bottle? (other than any incidents already mentioned)
☐ Yes—How many times?
☐ No _____

40. Were you knifed, shot at, or attacked with some other weapon by anyone at all? (other than any incidents already mentioned)
☐ Yes—How many times?
☐ No _____

41. Did anyone THREATEN to beat you up or THREATEN you with a knife, gun, or some other weapon, NOT including telephone threats? (other than any incidents already mentioned)
☐ Yes—How many times?
☐ No _____

42. Did anyone TRY to attack you in some other way? (other than any incidents already mentioned)
☐ Yes—How many times?
☐ No _____

43. During the last 6 months, did anyone steal things that belonged to you from inside ANY car or truck, such as packages or clothing?
☐ Yes—How many times?
☐ No _____

44. Was anything stolen from you while you were away from home, for instance at work, in a theater or restaurant, or while traveling?
☐ Yes—How many times?
☐ No _____

National Crime Surveys (NCS)

Beginning in 1972, the National Crime Surveys were conducted. The NCS consisted of the Central City Surveys and the National Crime Panel Surveys. A National Academy of Sciences evaluation panel described

---

45. (Other than any incidents you've already mentioned) was anything (else) at all stolen from you during the last 6 months?

☐ Yes—How many times?

☐ No _____

46. Did you find any evidence that someone ATTEMPTED to steal something that belonged to you? (other than any incidents already mentioned)

☐ Yes—How many times?

☐ No _____

47. Did you call the police during the last 6 months to report something that happened to YOU which you thought was a crime? (Do not count any calls made to the police concerning the incidents you have just told me about.)

☐ No—SKIP to 48
☐ Yes—What happened?

_____

_____

_____

(058) ⊞⊞

48. Did anything happen to YOU during the last 6 months which you thought was a crime, but did NOT report to the police? (other than any incidents already mentioned)

☐ No—SKIP to Check Item E
☐ Yes—What happened?

_____

_____

_____

(059) ⊞⊞

Source: Adapted from National Crime Survey, 1977, "Basic Screen Questions," Form NJ-1, Washington, D.C.: U.S. Bureau of Census, April 19.

these as perhaps the most sophisticated and elaborate surveys ever conducted on such a large scale in the social sciences, particularly with respect to survey design, sampling, and estimating schemes (Panel for the Evaluation of Crime Surveys, 1976, p. 8). Full description of these schemes are beyond the intentions of this introductory sketch, but a brief picture hopefully will provide the reader with an appreciation of these surveys.

The Central City Surveys were essentially cross-sectional studies of households and commercial establishments in selected cities. Initially, probability samples of approximately 10,000 households and 1,000 to 5,000 commercial establishments were surveyed in twenty-six central cities. Residents twelve years of age and older were interviewed regarding victimization, victim-offender relationship, injury or loss suffered, time and place of incident(s), whether these crimes were reported to the police, victim demographic characteristics, and attitudinal items regarding crime, the police, and the criminal justice system (U.S. Department of Justice, 1974, 1975a, 1975b, 1976, and 1979).

The National Crime Panels employed a sophisticated probability sample of housing units and businesses throughout the United States. In contrast to the central city surveys, which were *cross-sectional* or studies of one time only, the panels were *longitudinal* in nature, that is, studies over time of a particular group. This enabled *bounding* of victim reports, the use of pretests in order to have a reference point for the survey reporting period; that is, the initial interview acted as a boundary or time period benchmark with which to compare future reported victimizations. Consisting of about 60,000 households to be interviewed every six months and 15,000 (later upped to 50,000) businesses, the national panels repeated the interviews twice a year in order to achieve the bounding feature previously described. Each housing unit remained in the sample for three years, while every six months a subsample of 10,000 was rotated out of the sample and replaced by a new group.

Some of the earliest findings of the first central city surveys were revealing not only with respect to differences between cities in victimization but also to variations within cities in regard to types of victimizations as well as the ratio of reported victimizations to official records in each jurisdiction. Detroit, for instance, had twice the victim rate of New York and three times the robbery rate of Dallas. Denver was found to have nearly four times more assault than Newark, while Cleveland led in auto thefts, Atlanta in commercial burglary, and Detroit in personal and commercial robbery. Most interesting was the finding that Philadelphia had 5 times the victim rate compared to official records, while Newark was only 1.4 to 1. These findings were heralded at the time as the first accurate statistics on crime; however, further analysis suggests that this conclusion may have been optimistically premature. Just as the UCR was found to have shortcomings, so any measure of crime, including victim surveys, can be found wanting in some respects.

Issues and Cautions in Victim Data

Some possible problems in victim surveys include, but are not limited to: the expense of large samples, false or mistaken reports, memory failure or decay, telescoping of events, sampling bias, over and/or underreporting, interviewer effects, and coding and mechanical errors.

1. While large-scale public opinion polls such as by Gallup or Roper can be conducted with sample sizes less than one thousand, the rarity

Table 2.1: Crime Victimization in 13 Selected Cities

| | Crime Victimization Rate per 1,000 Residents 12 and Over | | | | | Household Victimization Per 1,000 Households | | | Commercial Victimization per 1,000 Business Establishments | | |
	Crime of Violence	Rape and Attempted Rape	Robbery	Assault	Burglary	Household Larceny	Auto Theft	Burglary	Robbery	Ratio of Unreported Crime to Reported Crime
*Detroit	68	3	32	33	174	106	49	615	179	2.7 to 1
Denver	67	3	17	46	158	168	44	443	54	2.9 to 1
*Philadelphia	63	1	28	34	109	87	42	390	116	5.1 to 1
Portland, Ore.	59	3	17	40	151	149	34	355	39	2.6 to 1
Baltimore	56	1	26	28	118	100	35	578	135	2.2 to 1
*Chicago	56	3	26	27	116	77	36	317	77	2.8 to 1
Cleveland	54	2	24	28	124	80	76	367	77	2.4 to 1
*Los Angeles	53	2	16	35	148	131	42	311	47	2.9 to 1
Atlanta	48	2	16	30	161	102	29	741	157	2.3 to 1
Dallas	43	2	10	31	147	147	24	355	48	2.6 to 1
Newark	42	1	29	12	123	44	37	631	98	1.4 to 1
St. Louis	42	1	16	25	125	81	47	531	94	1.5 to 1
*New York	36	1	24	11	68	33	26	328	103	2.1 to 1

*Information for five largest cities covers 1972. Information for eight others is based on surveys carried out in July–October 1972 covering previous twelve months.

of some types of victimization such as rape requires large samples in order to turn up a few victims; for instance, hundreds must be surveyed in order to find one victim (Glaser, 1978, p. 63).

A parallel could be drawn with attempting to survey lottery winners on the basis of a sample of the general population. Many would have to be canvassed before turning up only a few winners. If the chances of winning the lottery are one in a million, in order to discover one winner by chance the researcher would have to interview one million players.

2. False or mistaken reports can result in error. Levine, for example, found inaccuracies in respondent reports regarding their voting behavior, finances, academic performance, business practices, and even sexual activity (Levine, 1976, p. 98). Should we assume greater precision in victim reports? Many respondents may also be relatively ignorant of the law, reporting as criminal incidents acts which the police would declare "unfounded" or not criminal matters.

3. Memory failure or decay tends to increase with the distance between the actual time of the event and the interview concerning the event (Panel for Evaluation, 1976, p. 21; Gottfredson and Hindelang, 1977).

4. Telescoping of events, a type of memory misfire, involves the moving of events which took place in a different time period (for example, before the reference period) into the time studied. A victimization of two years ago is mistakenly assumed to have occurred this past year. Subjects may even unconsciously telescope events in order to please interviewers (Biderman, 1967). Such *demand characteristics* or over-agreeability on the part of respondents can certainly bias victim studies.

5. Sampling bias may produce an underenumeration of the young, males, and minorities. These are the very groups that tend to be undercounted by the U.S. Census and are also more heavily victimized groups.

6. Overreporting in victim surveys generally involves subjects reporting incidents only to interviewers, acts which they normally would view as being too trivial or unimportant to call for police involvement. Much of the *dark figure* of crime consists of minor property crime, much of which could be considered unfounded by police (Black, 1970). Underreporting is particularly prevalent if the perpetrator is a friend, relative, or family member. Also, like the UCR, victim surveys fail to account for occupational, corporate, professional, political, and victimless crimes. Moreover, most victim studies are restricted to central city residents, thus underestimating tourist and commuter victims. In addition, police statistics are based upon the crime incident, while victim surveys look at individual victims: one robbery involving ten victims would result in two different measurements (Glaser, 1978, p. 64), ten incidents in victim counts, but only one in official incident counts.

7. Interviewer effects or bias can range from deception and exaggeration to the simple production of dema..d characteristics or agreeability in which respondents, wanting to appear helpful, may report incidents they otherwise would consider unimportant.

8. Coding and mechanical errors relate to human or machine errors in coding (assigning numbers to responses), keypunching, or analysis. Sussman and Haug (1967) have noted serious levels of such unchecked errors in large surveys.

Controlling for Error in Victim Surveys

Space does not permit a detailed analysis of the methodological controls that have been developed in victimization studies; however, a brief presentation should demonstrate that many of the problems that have been discussed can be controlled for. It is important to realize that no method of data gathering is without potential flaws, and that many of the shortcomings that have been described could apply equally to other means of obtaining information.

Some ways of controlling for error in victim surveys include, but are not limited to: the use of panels and bounding of target groups, evaluations of coding and other sources of human or mechanical error in data processing, reverse record checks of known groups, reinterviews of the same group, and interviews with significant others. Panels (longitudinal studies of the same group) were discussed previously as a means of bounding (establishing the time period during which events were recalled as having taken place), thus controlling for forward telescoping (the tendency to move prior incidents into the time frame being studied). Quality controls on coding, keypunching, and data management—such as rechecking calculations and double coding and verification in order to control for coding errors—can provide more accurate data (Crittenden and Hill, 1971; Ennis, 1967, p. 93; and Sussman and Haug, 1967). Reverse record checking of known groups involves studying a group whose behavior is already known, for example, known crime victims (Panel for the Evaluation, 1976; National Advisory Committee, 1976b, p. 146). Reinterviews of the same group in the National Crime Panel enables a tracking of reported crime incidents, and the checking of responses with significant others (those who know the respondent well) provides yet another measure of accuracy.

The primary benefit of victim surveys is that they provide us with another independent measure of crime, separate from official statistics. Neither official statistics nor victim surveys begin to tap the extent of occupational, corporate, and public order crime; and in that regard both measures seriously underestimate the extent of crime. For the types of "garden variety" or traditional crimes, the true rate is most likely somewhere between victim surveys, which overestimate by including minor property offenses, and official estimates, which underestimate crime. Victim studies provide us with a clearer picture of victims, their characteristics, and attitudes, as well as a better description of criminals and their operations. Such surveys can also be used to explore the fear of crime, reasons for not reporting crime, satisfaction with the criminal justice system, and the like. The National Crime Survey has undergone and continues to undergo revamping and redesign (Taylor, 1989). In addition to official statistics and victim surveys the third major primary source of information regarding crime commission comes from self-report surveys.

Self-Report Measures of Crime

A very interesting dilemma was presented to early experimental researchers who proposed to compare an experimental group of incarcerated criminals with a control group of the general population who were *assumed* to be non-criminal. By way of illustration, recall our earlier question, "Who is criminal?" Are you a criminal? (See Vantage Point 2.2)

As with victim surveys, self-report measures attempt to provide an alternative to official statistics in measuring the extent of crime in a

---

VANTAGE

POINT

Vantage Point 2.2—Self-Reported Delinquency Items

Please indicate if you have ever done the following:

1. Stolen items of small value (less than $50).
2. Stolen items of large value ($50 or more).
3. Destroyed the property of others.
4. Used someone's vehicle without his or her permission.
5. Hit or physically attacked someone.
6. Were truant from school.
7. Drank alcoholic beverages.
8. Used illegal drugs such as marijuana, heroin, or cocaine.
9. Indecently, sexually exposed self in public.
10. Were paid for having sexual relations.

society (see Menard, 1987). Criminologists ask individuals — as in the illustration in Vantage Point 2.2 — to admit to various crimes and/or delinquent acts. This may be achieved through anonymous questionnaires, surveys in which the respondent is identifiable that can be validated by later interviews or police records, signed instruments which can be checked against official records, validation through later interviews or threats of polygraph (lie-detector test), and interviews alone as well as interviews which are then checked against official records (Nettler, 1978, pp. 97–113).

Although most self-report surveys that have been conducted in the United States have been of "captive audiences," school or college populations (Hood and Sparks, 1971, p. 19; Glaser, 1978, p. 72), few studies have been done of the adult population. One of the earliest by Wallerstein and Wyle (1947) found 99 percent of their adult sample had committed at least one offense. Some of the percentages of admission for males and females, respectively, were: larceny — 89 and 83 percent; indecency — 77 and 74 percent; assault — 49 and 5 percent; grand larceny (except auto) — 13 and 11 percent; and tax evasion — 57 and 40 percent. These figures suggest a remarkable level of criminality on the part of an assumed noncriminal population.

Controlling for Error in Self-Report Surveys

Reliance upon self-reported data as a measure of crime commission poses a major question with respect to the relationship between claimed behavior and actual behavior. Nettler states that "asking people questions about their behavior is a poor way of observing it" (Nettler, 1978, p. 107). If people are inaccurate in reporting other aspects of their behavior, such as voting, medical treatment, and the like, it may be questionable to assume any greater accuracy in admitting deviant behavior. Some problems with self-report studies include: possible inaccurate reports, the use of poor or inconsistent instruments, deficient research design, and poor choice of subjects. While mistaken or inaccurate reports may impinge upon such surveys, Hood and Sparks (1971, p. 65) question the number of rather trivial offenses that are labeled delinquent in the U.S. and are included in such studies, pointing out that in Europe delinquency is a synonym for crime committed by the young. While small and unrepresentative samples are problematic, self-report surveys are also affected by possible lying, poor memory, and telescoping (Elliott and Ageton, 1980, p. 96).

A large body of literature has accumulated which suggests that, despite these criticisms, the self-report approach is a viable method of obtaining data on crime or delinquency commission (Elliott and Ageton, 1980;

Hardt and Hardt, 1977; Farrington, 1973; Hirschi, 1969; Gold, 1966; Clark and Tifft, 1966; Erickson and Empey, 1963; Dentler and Monroe, 1961; Nye and Short, 1956). Some means of checking for errors in self-report surveys include: comparison with official or other data, checking with other observers or peers, the use of threat of polygraph (lie detector), studies of known groups, the use of "lie scales" (measures of internal consistency), and the rechecking of reports using interviews.

A number of studies have been conducted that check self-report data with official reports such as police records, school records, and the like (Hardt and Hardt, 1977; Farrington, 1973; Erickson and Empey, 1963; and Voss, 1963); these studies, for the most part, have found agreement between self-report and official data. But Nettler (1978, p. 11) points out the paradox of critics of official statistics using these same data to validate what they claim is a superior self-report instrument. Hirschi (1969) and McCandless, Persons, and Roberts (1972) found underreporting in their samples, while researchers such as Gold (1966) interviewed associates of the respondents to check their claims. Short and Strodtbeck (1965) used confirming reports of detached workers. Threatening the use of a polygraph, Clark and Tifft (1966) found that fewer than 20 percent altered their response. Other researchers such as Voss (1963) and Short and Nye (1958) studied groups whose official transgressions were already known. While some discrepancies were found, Hardt and Hardt (1977) concluded that these may have been more of a problem with the instruments used rather than an inadequacy with the self-report method itself.

Another means of checking the validity or accuracy of the self-report survey includes the use of "lie scales" or "truth scales." These consist of a series of questions woven among the others that ask the respondent to admit to behaviors that would be inconceivable to assume any one person could have done, or similarly to deny behaviors with which most people would have been involved. A related procedure uses a measure of internal consistency of response by means of interlocking or contradictory questions; if a respondent is judged to be inconsistent in his or her responses, those may be discarded for analysis purposes (Edwards, 1957). Finally, subsequent interviewing of subjects may give an opportunity to double check the reliability or consistency of response.

In conclusion, while self-report surveys also have their problems, like victim studies, they provide us with another independent measure of crime commission.

Participant Observation

Participant observation involves a variety of strategies in which the researcher studies or observes a group through varying degrees of participating in the activities of that group. Ned Polsky's classic *Hustlers, Beats and Others* (1967) presents both a moving statement for the need for deployment of this strategy as well as sound advice in this regard.

Participant Observation of Criminals

Contrary to the advice given at one time in most criminology textbooks (Sutherland and Cressey, 1960, p. 69), uncaught criminals can be studied in the field. Early on, biologists noted that gorillas in a zoo act differently than gorillas in their natural habitat. It is imperative that criminologists break with their habit of studying the confined, slower, less intelligent, lower-class criminal. Polsky (1967, p. 147), in advocating field studies of criminals, states:

> Until the criminologist learns to suspend his personal distaste for the values and life-styles of the untamed savages, until he goes out in the field to the cannibals and headhunters and observes them without trying either to civilize them or turn them over to colonial officials, he will be only a veranda anthropologist. That is, he will be only a jailhouse or courthouse sociologist, unable to produce anything like a genuinely scientific picture of crime.

One of the reasons often given for discouraging such research is the belief that the researcher must pretend to be part of the criminal world. In fact, such a strategy would be highly inadvisable, not to mention unworkable, as well as possibly dangerous. Polsky suggests that the distance between criminal and conventional types is not as wide as many would suggest and the difficulty in gaining access to such subjects is highly exaggerated.

There are, of course, problems in studying criminals au naturel. The researcher must realize that he or she is more of an intruder than would be the case in a prison setting. Criminals have more to lose than those already in jail. And, being on their own turf, criminals are more free to put the researcher down or to refuse to be observed. Having successfully employed participant observation in studying uncaught pool hustlers, organized criminals, and drug addicts, Polsky (1967, pp. 117–149) offers some sage advice regarding procedures to employ in studying criminals in the field:

- Avoid using gadgets such as tape recorders, questionnaires, and the like. Construct field notes later, after leaving the scene for the day.
- Keep your eyes and ears open, but keep your mouth shut.
- Learn the argot, the specialized language or jargon of a group, but don't overuse it.

- You can often gain entry into the setting through common recreational interests, for example, card games, the track, or poolrooms.
- Do not pretend to be one of them. As soon as practicable, make them aware of your purposes.
- Be open to permitting the criminal(s) to study you as well and be prepared to be defined as "a right square," "a vicarious junkie," or "too scared to steal."
- Draw the line between yourself and the criminal. For instance, Polsky indicated that he did not wish to actually witness certain criminal acts.
- Use pseudonyms (fake names or aliases) in order to protect the identity of informants.
- Have a firm notion as to who you are, in order to avoid being maneuvered into an accomplice role. Polsky, for instance, was told he would make a fine "steerhorse" (someone who "fingers" the "mark") or wheelman (driver of a getaway car).
- While it is important not to pretend to be one of them, don't "stick out like a sore thumb." In studying heroin use and distribution, Polsky wore a short-sleeved shirt and an expensive watch.
- Be flexible; have few unbreakable rules.
- If you choose such field studies, be prepared for a very demanding, time-consuming, and at times very boring routine. Even criminals spend the bulk of their time in mundane activities.

Finally, Polsky raises a number of related issues to be considered in field studies of criminals. In some ways, researchers may be breaking the law or be considered accessories to the fact. Honoring reciprocity with respondents, observers must be prepared to be "stand-up guys" under police questioning. Although the actual legal status is unclear, social researchers have no guaranteed right to confidentiality or privileged information and are vulnerable to subpoena. While other field researchers such as Lewis Yablonsky (1965a, p. 72) feel that strict moral limits must be set in mediating the roles of scientist and citizen and that researchers should avoid nonmoralistic stances, Polsky argues that the scientist role is preeminent and that a few social scientists must take this stance in order to get a true picture of little understood subject matters.

Evaluation of the Method of Participant Observation

A researcher's decision to use participant observation as the primary means of gathering data represents an orientation toward a more qualitative and "sensitizing" approach, toward in-depth field studies in which the investigator attempts to obtain the "big picture" of a group by temporarily viewing the world from their eyes (Glaser and Strauss, 1967). In some instances, participant observation may represent the only viable means of data gathering (imagine, for instance, attempting a survey or experiment with volunteers from the ranks of organized crime). Participant observation is an excellent procedure for studying little understood groups.

Some examples of participant observation studies with criminological ramifications have been Whyte's *Streetcorner Society* (1955); Polsky's *Hustlers, Beats and Others* (1967); Yablonsky's *Synanon* (1965b) and *The Violent Gang* (1962); Ianni's *A Family Business* (1972); Albini's (1986) study of the Guardian Angels; and Humphreys' *Tearoom Trade* (1970) to mention just a few.

The major advantages of a participant observation relate to the qualitative detail that it can produce. Representing a sensitizing or *verstehen* strategy, the researcher is less influenced by prejudgments. The technique is very flexible and less artificial and enables the investigator to observe subjects in their natural environment. This technique has produced some of the most exciting and enthralling literature in the field, rivaling even some of the best of modern fiction. Examples from this genre will be presented in subsequent chapters.

Some potential disadvantages of participant observation include the very time-consuming nature of the technique; it may exact high demands upon the personal life of the observer (for example, see Carey, 1972). The observer faces the dual dangers of overidentification or aversion to the group being studied, often testing to the limits the researcher's commitment to objectivity. In addition to possible observer bias and the challenge of making sense of a mass of nonquantitative data, participant observation may pose major ethical dilemmas.

Life History and Case Studies

A classic illustration of the use of case study and life history in criminology was Edwin Sutherland's *The Professional Thief* (1937), based upon his interviews with an incarcerated professional thief given the pseudonym "Chic" Conwell. Like participant observation, *case studies / life histories* represent an interest in an in-depth close-up of only one or a few subjects in order to obtain a greater understanding or *verstehen* (Weber, 1949) that a more aggregate analysis might obscure. This method may employ diaries, letters, biographies, and autobiographies in order to attempt to capture a detailed view of either a unique or representative subject. Some more recent examples of the life history approach have been Chambliss's *Box Man* (1975); Klockars's *The Professional Fence* (1974); Steffensmeier's *The Fence* (1986); Shaw's *The Jack-Roller* (1930); and Snodgrass' *The Jack-Roller at Seventy* (1982).

Travis (1983, p. 46) notes an unfortunate decline in the coverage of case studies in criminology and criminal justice texts and their eclipse by more quantitative methods. The former involve oral and life histories, "recounts of events by participants" (Laub, 1983, p. 226). In *Criminology in the Making: An Oral History* Laub (1983) conducts in-depth interviews with major criminologists in order to construct a history of the field. Since many subjects may not be able to be analyzed through quantitative research, case studies can provide a view of the subjective elements of institutions (Kobrin, 1982; Bennett, 1981; Bertaux, 1981; and Hagan, 1989b).

Unobtrusive Measures

Unobtrusive measures entail clandestine, secretive, or nonreactive methods of gathering data (Webb, et al., 1981). Such techniques attempt to avoid *reactivity,* the tendency of subjects to behave differently when they are aware that they are being studied. This certainly has been a problem in much prison research, where the question might be asked whether research volunteers are indeed volunteers. Major types of unobtrusive methods include: physical trace analysis; the use of existing records like archives, available data, and autobiographies; simple and disguised observation, as well as simulation.

Physical trace analysis involves studying deposits, accretion of matter, and other remains of human activity, while archival and *existing records* contain information that may be useful in providing historical overviews of criminological issues. The uses of available data include procedures such as content analysis and secondary analysis. *Content analysis* refers to the systematic classification and study of the content of mass media, for example, newspapers, magazines, and the like. *Secondary analysis* consists of the reanalysis of data which was previously gathered for other purposes. The use of all of these types of data-gathering procedures represents an excellent, cost-effective means of obtaining data, particularly in a period of growing respondent hostility to studies.

Observation involves the researcher keeping participation with subjects to a minimum while carefully recording their activities; in *disguised observation* the investigator secretly studies groups by temporarily deceiving them as to his or her real purpose. For example, in order to study difficult subjects in the field, researchers have posed as "thieves and victims" (Stewart and Cannon, 1977), a "watch queen" (Humphreys, 1970), a "mental patient" (Caudill, 1958), "black panther supporters" (Heussenstamm, 1971), "a naïve international tourist" (Feldman, 1968), and "a caretaker" (Sherif and Sherif, 1966), among other roles.

Simulation entails research strategies which attempt to mimic or imitate a more complex social reality. For example, since actual research of jury deliberations is prohibited, researchers may set up simulated juries by reenacting the actual trial conditions in order to investigate the decision-making process.

While the obvious advantage of unobtrusive measures is the fact that they are nonreactive—that is, they avoid subject awareness of being observed and hopefully then escape reactivity—such techniques also have the strength of being more natural and of evading the overreliance upon attitudinal data. By making use of data that has already been gathered, researchers are able to exercise great economies in time and expense. Too many researchers assume that doing a study must necessarily involve the expense and time of gathering new data when, in fact, vast storehouses of potential information exist right under their noses, as close as the nearest library and scattered throughout public and private organizations.

On the debit side of the ledger, unobtrusive methods raise potential problems of privacy invasion. Does a researcher have the right to observe the private behavior of individuals without their permission? Compounding this ethical issue is the fact that criminological researchers have no state-recognized right to confidentiality or claim to privileged communication comparable to that in a doctor-patient relationship. In addition, nonreactive measures may yield atypical subjects, be time consuming, and be prone to observer bias.

Validity, Reliability, and Triangulation

In the introduction to this chapter, Hood and Sparks's (1971) view was quoted concerning the defective nature of much research methodology employed in criminology. Other writers have echoed these remarks. Bailey (1971), in a review of one hundred correctional research studies, pointed out that much of the research was invalid, unreliable, and based upon poor research design. In an analysis of the quality of publications in criminology, Wolfgang, Figlio, and Thornberry (1978) judged that the methodological sophistication was very poor and that a greater display of concern was needed for adequate research design and execution. Although later modifying his view and admitting methodological narcissism, Martinson (1974; 1978) blasted correctional research, claiming that in his review of the evidence of programs in corrections and their impact upon recidivism, he found that "nothing works." What is to be said of this sad state of affairs? If the data regarding "what is?" with respect to crime is defective, then what might we expect of the theories which are based upon this data? Fortunately, criminologists have plenty of methodological company with economists, psychiatrists, and meteorologists, just to mention a few. The problem of imprecise measurement is not a problem that is unique to the field of criminology and, furthermore, is not an insoluble one.

Validity is concerned with accuracy of measurement. It asks the question, "Does my measuring instrument in fact measure what it claims to measure?" "Is it a true and accurate measure of the subject in question?" *Reliability*, on the other hand, involves the consistency and/or stability of measurement. If repeated measures were made of the same entity, would stable and uniform measures ensue? Obviously, validity is a more crucial issue than reliability in that, if a measurement is inaccurate, the consistency of being inaccurate becomes a moot question.

The problem of inadequate methods in criminology arises not because of the inherent shortcomings of any particular method, but because a given method is used alone. It is foolhardy to concentrate upon the insufficiencies, the reliability, and/or validity of any one concept, measured at one time using one measure. *Triangulation* involves the use of multiple methods in measuring the same entity. Similar to the notion of corroborating evidence in law, if different measures of the same concept produce convergence or similar results, then we have greater confidence in the validity of an observation or finding.

Sanders in *The Sociologist as Detective* (1976) makes very clever use of Arthur Conan Doyle's fictional sleuth Sherlock Holmes as a means of illustrating the notion of triangulation. Holmes in attempting to answer the question "Whodunit?" employed multiple methods (triangulation) like those a social scientist might employ. In attempting to discover "who killed the lord of the manor," Holmes observed carefully, attempted reenactment of the crime (simulation), questioned suspects and witnesses, and carefully collected and evaluated the physical evidence at the crime scene. He collected some data through direct questioning, other data through astute observation. "Did the family dog bark the evening of the suspected murder?" If not, perhaps the murderer was a family member or friend. "Did any of the questioned suspects develop a nervous tic?" "Were there footprints or clues?" By combining these various methods, Holmes was able to make a reasonable guess as to which hypotheses to reject or accept (see also Truzzi, 1976).

This chapter has exposed the reader to a variety of methods that criminologists use in obtaining information on the nature of crime and criminals. The outcomes or findings as a result of the application of these methods will be presented in forthcoming chapters. Hopefully, the reader has been alerted to reading this material with a critical methodological eye, carefully weighing the sources of evidence for the materials presented.

Summary

Theory and methodology are the two critical features of any discipline, including criminology. Theory is an attempt to provide plausible explanations of reality and addresses the question "Why?" Methods (methodology) involves procedures for the collection and analysis of accurate data or facts and is concerned with the issue "What is?"

The research enterprise of criminology involves certain basic procedures. Objectivity, a commitment to a "value-free," nonbiased approach to the subject matter, is an essential canon of research. Despite conflicting roles, the criminologist's primary role is that of scientist. Some general principles of ethical conduct in criminology include that the researcher should avoid harmful procedures, honor commitments and reciprocity, exercise objectivity and integrity, and protect the privacy of subjects, as well as maintain confidentiality.

Pure research is concerned with expansion of the knowledge base of a discipline regardless of immediate societal concerns or problems. In contrast, applied research addresses present policy issues and represents an attempt to provide answers to present-day problems. Criminology requires both approaches.

The process of methodological thinking was illustrated by means of the research question "Who is criminal?" Until recently the primary source of information regarding crime statistics has been official police statistics, which represent crimes recorded by police. The *Uniform Crime Report (UCR)* presents such statistics for the U.S. Such statistics fail to account for unrecorded crime, "the dark figure of crime."

The UCR "crime index" from which the crime rate is calculated consists of *Part I crimes*: murder and nonnegligent manslaughter, forcible rape, robbery, aggravated assault, burglary, larceny/theft, motor vehicle theft, and arson. Researchers should be cognizant of shortcomings of official data such as the UCR. Crime clocks are the poorest graphic device for describing crime trends, since they fail to control for population growth and use a constant (time) as their base for comparison.

Other alternative measures of crime and criminal activity include crime seriousness measures, which attempt to provide a *weighted index* of crime. *Alternative data gathering strategies* include: experiments, social surveys, participant observation, case studies/life history methods, and unobtrusive methods. Each possesses relative strengths and weaknesses vis-à-vis the others with respect to quantitative/qualitative, control, internal/external validity, and artificiality/naturalness dimensions.

A key point is that, contrary to *methodological narcissism* (fanatical adherence to one's favorite method), no one method has any inherent superiority over any other. Methodology is a tool and not an end in itself.

For each method, the text provides descriptions as well as examples of the method's application in criminological research. For instance, *victim surveys* are a critical alternate measure of criminality. Similarly, *self-report surveys* are a useful means of tapping hidden criminality.

The basic strategy of *participant observation* (field studies), life histories, and case studies in criminology is delineated. A particularly moving pitch for the need for such studies emerges from Ned Polsky's research.

Unobtrusive (nonreactive) methods are a very cost-effective and neglected means of obtaining data. These include techniques such as physical trace analysis, use of archives/existing data (including content and secondary analysis), as well as autobiographies. Other procedures include simple and disguised observation and simulation.

Much of the criticism of criminological research is really questioning the *validity* (accuracy) and *reliability* (consistency/stability) of the methodology which has been employed. *Triangulation* (the use of multiple methods) is proposed as the logical path to resolve this issue.

KEY CONCEPTS

Theory	Unfounded Crimes	Victim Surveys
Methodology (Methods)	The Crime Index	Dark Figure of Crime
Objectivity	Part I Crimes	Self-Reports of Crime
Ethics in Research	Issues/Cautions in UCR	Crime Seriousness Measures
Code of Ethics for Research	The Crime Rate	Participant Observation
Reciprocity	Crime Clocks	Life History/Case Study
Confidentiality	Methodological Narcissism	Unobtrusive Measures
Pure vs. Applied Research	Classic Experimental Design	Reactivity
Concepts	Dualistic Fallacy	Simulation
Operationalization	Experiments	Validity
Variables	Surveys	Reliability
Uniform Crime Reports (UCR)	National Crime Surveys (NCS)	Triangulation
Sources of Crime Statistics	Sampling	

3 General Characteristics of Crime and Criminals

Caution in Crime Data

In Chapter 2 we treated at length the necessity of carefully examining the data base or sources of criminological research findings and conclusions. This advice is especially applicable to the material to be presented in this chapter. Descriptions of characteristics of crime and criminals can vary immensely, depending upon the sources of information—for example, official statistics, victim surveys, self-reports—as well as upon the type of crime or criminality that is being addressed, whether traditional crimes or crimes by the elite. The particular method chosen for analysis provides data which flavor the types of theories developed; likewise the theoretical framework for analysis may subjectively influence the methods of analysis. While the process of inquiry is seldom entirely value-free, triangulation assists in providing multiple assessments of the subject matter.

As previously indicated, statistics regarding crime and delinquency are not easily measured. Sutherland and Cressey (Ibid.) consider crime statistics the most difficult of all social statistics, as the chapter quotation indicates. Realizing the limitations of these statistics, we will attempt to avoid misleading and incorrect inferences.

An analysis of available data indicates that we have only a limited idea of the proportion of crime that is committed by any category of individuals or groups in a particular society. This is certainly the case if we rely entirely upon official statistics for our discussion. Two primary sources of crime information that have been discussed are the Uniform Crime Report (UCR) and the National Crime Survey (NCS). Vantage Point 3.1 on "Measuring Crime" compares the definitions of crimes utilized in these measures.

International Variations in Crime

Crime and criminality are not uniformly distributed throughout a society; they vary with respect to both perpetrators' and victims' demographic characteristics, as well as regard to effects of social institutions and other group affiliations. Variables such as age, sex, race, ethnicity, social class, type of family, region of residence, and economic trends all have impacts upon crime and criminality rates. Characteristics of the state or employing

VANTAGE

POINT

National crime statistics focus on selected crimes

The two sources, UCR and NCS, concentrate on measuring a limited number of well-defined crimes. They do not cover all possible criminal events. Both sources use commonly understood definitions rather than legal definitions of crime.

"Crime" covers a wide range of events. It isn't always possible to tell whether an event is a crime. For example, if your personal property is missing, you may not know for certain whether it was stolen or simply misplaced.

The UCR Index shows trends in eight major crimes

In 1927, the International Association of Chiefs of Police (IACP) formed a committee to create a uniform system for gathering police statistics. The goal was to develop a national system of statistics that would overcome variations in the way crimes were defined in different parts of the country.

Because of their seriousness, frequency of occurrence, and likelihood of being reported to the police, seven crimes were selected as the basis for the UCR Index for evaluating changes in the volume of crime. Arson was added as the eighth UCR Index offense in 1978.

The NCS adds information about victims and crimes not reported to police

In 1973, to learn more about crimes and the victims of crime, the National Crime Survey began to measure crimes not reported to police as well as those that are reported. Except for homicide (which is well reported in police statistics) and arson (which is difficult to measure using survey techniques), the NCS measures the same crimes as the UCR. Both the UCR and NCS count attempted as well as completed crimes.

The portraits of crime from NCS and UCR differ because they serve different purposes and are based on different sources

These are some of the more important differences in the programs, thought to account for a good deal of the differences in resulting statistics:

- The UCR counts only crimes coming to the attention of the police. The NCS obtains information on both reported and unreported crime.
- The UCR counts crimes committed against all people and all businesses, organizations, government agencies, and other victims. NCS counts only crimes against persons age 12 or older and against their households.

- The two programs, because they serve different purposes, count crimes differently, in some instances. For example, a criminal robs a victim and steals someone else's car to escape. UCR only counts the robbery, the more serious crime. NCS could count both; one as a personal crime and one as a household crime.
- Each program is subject to the kinds of errors and problems typical of its method of data collection that may serve to widen or narrow the differences in the counts produced by the two programs. For example, it is widely believed by analysis that the rise in the number of rapes reported to police stems largely from the special programs established by many police departments to treat victims of rape more sympathetically.

How do UCR and NCS compare?

	Uniform Crime Reports	*National Crime Survey*
Offenses measured:	Homicide Rape Robbery (personal and commercial) Assault (aggravated) Burglary (commercial and household) Larceny (commercial and household) Arson	Rape Robbery (personal) Assault (aggravated and simple) Household burglary Larceny (personal and household)
Scope:	Crimes reported to the police in most jurisdictions; considerable flexibility in developing small-area data	Crimes both reported and not reported to police; all data are for the Nation as a whole; some data are available for a few large geographic areas
Collection method:	Police department reports to FBI	Survey interviews: periodically measures the total number of crimes committed by asking a national sample of 60,000 households representing 135,000 persons over the age of 12 about their experiences as victims of crime during a specified period
Kinds of information:	In addition to offense counts, provides information on crime clearances, persons arrested, persons charged, law enforcement officers killed and assaulted, and characteristics of homicide victims	Provides details about victims (such as age, race, sex, education, income, and whether the victim and offender were related to each other) and about crimes (such as time and place of occurrence, whether or not reported to police, use of weapons, occurrence of injury, and economic consequences)
Sponsor:	Department of Justice Federal Bureau of Investigation	Department of Justice Bureau of Justice Statistics

SOURCE: Bureau of Justice Statistics, 1983b, *Report to the Nation on Crime and Justice: The Data,* Washington, D.C.: Government Printing Office, p. 6.

organization also have effects upon variations in individual criminality.

International or cross-cultural comparisons of crime statistics are hazardous given the different definitions of criminal activity, the quality of data, ideological considerations, and the sheer logistical problems of compilation. In a pioneering effort Archer and Gartner (1980 and 1984) constructed a "Comparative Crime Data File" based on data they had collected from 110 nations and forty-four major cities. Analysis of cross-cultural crime rates can produce some interesting conclusions. For instance, the inexorable rise in crime in the U.S. and other industrialized countries in the sixties was contradicted by a declining crime rate in Japan, thus denying the assumption that modernization inevitably produces increased criminality (Fenwick, 1982). Adler's *Nations Not Obsessed with Crime* (1983) and Clinard's *Cities with Little Crime* (1978) also indicate that crime is not a major concern in some countries of the world. Utilizing data from Interpol (The International Police Organization) and the World Health Organization, Brantingham and Brantingham (1984, p. 295) point out:

> At the world level of resolution, clearly different patterns emerge for crimes of violence against the person and for crimes against property. The highest overall crime rates were experienced by the nations of the Caribbean region during the mid-1970s, followed by the nations of Western Europe, North America, and Oceania. The highest levels of violent crimes against the person were experienced in the Caribbean, in North Africa and the Middle East, in sub-Saharan Africa, and in Latin America. Property crimes were highest in Western Europe, North America, and Oceania. Crime patterns appear to be closely associated with high economic development and with income inequality; and high levels of violent crimes against the person are associated with lack of economic development and with high income inequality. Modernization and urbanization are both associated with higher levels of property crime and lower levels of violent crime.

Similar patterns with respect to the impact of income inequality and the lack of economic development and high crime rates have been noted by others (Clinard and Abbott, 1973; and Krahn, Hartnagel and Gartrell, 1986).

A Bureau of Justice Statistics (Kalish, 1988, pp. 1–2) comparison of U.S. crime rates with those of other countries using United Nations, Interpol, and World Health Organizations (WHO) data found (see Table 3.1):

- The U.S. homicide rate per 100,000 population ranged from 10.5 using World Health Organization statistics for 1980 to 7.9 using 1984 Interpol data; the rate of homicide in Europe from all three sources was less than 2 per 100,000.

Table 3.1: Crime Rates in Selected Countries, 1984: Interpol Data

				Number of Crimes per 100,000 Population		
	Homicides					
Country	Actual	Including Attempts	Rape	Robbery	Burglary	Auto Theft
United States	7.9	—	35.7	205.4	1,263.7	437.1
Australia	—	3.4	13.8	83.6	1,754.3	584.7
Austria	1.3	2.4	5.3	29.8	805.8	16.9
Belgium	—	3.3	5.6	50.0	—	140.6
Canada	2.7	6.3	—	92.8	1,420.6	304.9
Chile	5.8	6.3	10.6	36.4	—	7.6
Colombia	—	2.5	4.4	32.8	—	14.2
Denmark	1.2	5.8	7.7	35.6	2,230.2	469.5
Ecuador	—	4.5	5.9	22.8	—	7.8
Egypt	1.0	1.5	—	.4	—	3.3
England and Wales	1.1[a]	1.4[a]	2.7[a]	44.6[a]	1,639.7[a]	656.6[a]
Finland	2.3	5.6	6.5	33.7	772.6	171.7
France	—	4.6	5.2	105.6	809.8	483.4
Germany (FRG)	1.5	4.5	9.7	45.8	1,554.1	118.0
Greece	1.0	1.8	.9	2.3	72.8	—
Hungary	1.9	3.7	6.1	15.5	211.0	4.0
Indonesia	—	.9	1.2	5.1	38.4	4.9
Ireland	.8	1.1	2.0	5.4	1,056.8	29.7
Italy	2.1[a]	5.3[a]	1.8[a]	35.7[a]	—	276.3
Japan	.8	1.5	1.6	1.8	231.2	29.4
Luxembourg	—	5.3	2.8	40.8	509.8	109.3
Monaco	—	—	—	43.2	500.0	176.3
Netherlands	1.2	—	7.2	52.9	2,328.7	155.9
New Zealand	1.7	2.5	14.4	14.9	2,243.1	—
Nigeria	1.5[a]	1.7[a]	—	—	—	—
Northern Ireland	4.0[a]	19.8[a]	5.0[a]	119.3[a]	1,360.7[a]	106.2[a]
Norway	—	.9[a]	4.2[a]	—	—	273.1[a]
Philippines	—	42.5	2.6	33.0	—	2.0
Portugal	3.0	4.6	2.0	21.6	99.7	61.3
Scotland	—	1.4	4.4	86.9	2,178.6	632.7
Spain	—	2.2	3.6	147.3	1,069.9	278.2
Sweden	1.4	5.7	11.9	44.1	1,708.8	460.0
Switzerland	1.1	2.2	5.8	24.2	276.8	—[b]
Thailand	—	16.6	5.3	10.0	8.7	2.0
Venezuela	—	9.9	17.4	161.0	—	85.9

—Not available.

[a] 1983 data.

[b] Auto theft in Switzerland omitted because it includes bicycles.

SOURCE: Carol B. Kalish, 1988, *International Crime Rates*, Bureau of Justice Statistics Special Report, May, p. 3.

- The U.S. rape rate was 36 per 100,000, roughly seven times higher than the average for Europe.
- U.S. rates for robbery at 200 per 100,000 compared to European rates of less than 50 per 100,000.
- For crimes of theft and auto theft, a comparison of U.S. rates to average European rates was roughly two to one.
- Burglary was the only crime examined for which the U.S. rates were less than double those for European countries.
- U.S. crime rates were also higher than that of Canada, Australia, and New Zealand, but the differences were smaller compared to Europe. For burglary and auto theft the rates were quite similar, and in 1984 Interpol data showed burglary rates about 40 percent higher for these countries than the U.S. rate.
- In the 1980s, while U.S. crime rates were dropping considerably, Europe, Canada, Australia, and New Zealand were experiencing sizeable increases.

The reader is reminded that due to unreliability in such statistics international comparisons are risky; however, we will return to more detailed international comparisons in later coverage of specific crimes. As an illustration of ideological influences on crime statistics, one need only look at the Soviet Union in the late eighties and the influence of Gorbachev's *glasnost* (openness) on crime statistics. In the first publication of crime statistics in more than half a century the Soviet Interior Ministry reported a sharp rise in crime of 18 percent for 1988 over 1987 ("Soviet Crime Rate Up," 1989). There does appear to be a relationship between heterogeneity of a nation's population and higher crime rates, although not a direct one as demonstrated by Switzerland's relatively low rates. The U.S. has been a nation of immigrants and is one of the most heterogeneous countries in the world. Indeed New York City is one of the largest Irish, Jewish, Puerto Rican, and black cities in the world; Chicago one of the largest Polish cities, and Miami the second largest Cuban city.

The Prevalence of Crime

Estimates of the extent of crime commission depend upon how far or wide one may wish to cast the net. Estimates of official statistics (UCR), victim surveys (NCS), and self-report surveys increase the estimate. Inclusion of other forms of nontraditional criminality, such as corporate crime or tax avoidance would make our estimate of crime even more pervasive.

Table 3.2 presents the UCR index of serious crimes, sometimes referred to as Part I offenses. Examination of crimes known to police in Table 3.2 underlines the point that the bulk of crime is made up of property crimes.

Table 3.3 reports the most frequent crimes of arrest. These data refer to persons arrested and not, as in the case of the index offenses, simply crimes known to police. Examination of these primarily Part II offenses indicates the extent to which policing is occupied with drunk driving, drunkenness, and disorderly conduct.

The National Crime Survey for 1987 (Bureau of Justice Statistics, 1988a) reported 34.7 million crimes or roughly three times more crime was recorded by official UCR statistics for index offenses. Menard (1987, p. 455) indicates that attempts to reconcile official statistics, victim surveys, and self-report studies seem unlikely to overcome the differences among the sources of such data.

Trends in Crime

As discussed in the previous chapter, official crime statistics represented by the UCR have risen dramatically since their first recording in the early thirties. Figures 3.1 and 3.2 present trends in these index crimes.

Table 3.2: Index of Crime, 1987

	Estimated Crime, 1987	
Offense	Number	Rate per 100,000 Inhabitants
Crime Index Total	13,508,708	5,550
Violent Crime	1,483,999	609.7
Property Crime	12,024,709	4,940.3
Murder	20,096	8.3
Forcible Rape	91,111	37.4
Robbery	517,704	212.7
Aggravated Assault	855,088	351.3
Burglary	3,236,184	1,329.6
Larceny-Theft	7,499,851	3,081.3
Motor Vehicle Theft	1,288,674	529.4
Arson[1]		

[1]Sufficient data are not available to estimate this offense.

SOURCE: Modified from Federal Bureau of Investigation, 1988, *Crime in the United States, 1987*, Washington, D.C.: Government Printing Office, p. 41.

Table 3.3: Number of Persons Arrested for the Ten Most Frequent Offenses, 1987

Offense	Number
1. Driving Under the Influence	1,286,587
*2. Larceny-Theft	1,175,775
3. Drug Abuse Violations	767,808
4. Drunkenness	672,097
5. Simple Assaults	628,316
6. Disorderly Conduct	558,888
7. Liquor Law Violations	463,875
*8. Burglary	350,235
*9. Aggravated Assault	282,001
10. Fraud	261,128

*denotes index crimes

SOURCE: Compiled from Federal Bureau of Investigation, 1988, *Crime in the United States, 1987*, Washington, D.C.: Government Printing Office, p. 63.

Figure 3.1: Trends in Crimes Against Persons, Rates Per 100,000 People Since 1933

SOURCE: President's Commission on Law Enforcement and the Administration of Justice, 1967a. *The Challenge of Crime in a Free Society*. Washington, D.C.: Government Printing Office, p. 23, updated with yearly Uniform Crime Report data.

Figure 3.2: Trends in Crimes Against Property, Rates Per 100,000 People Since 1933

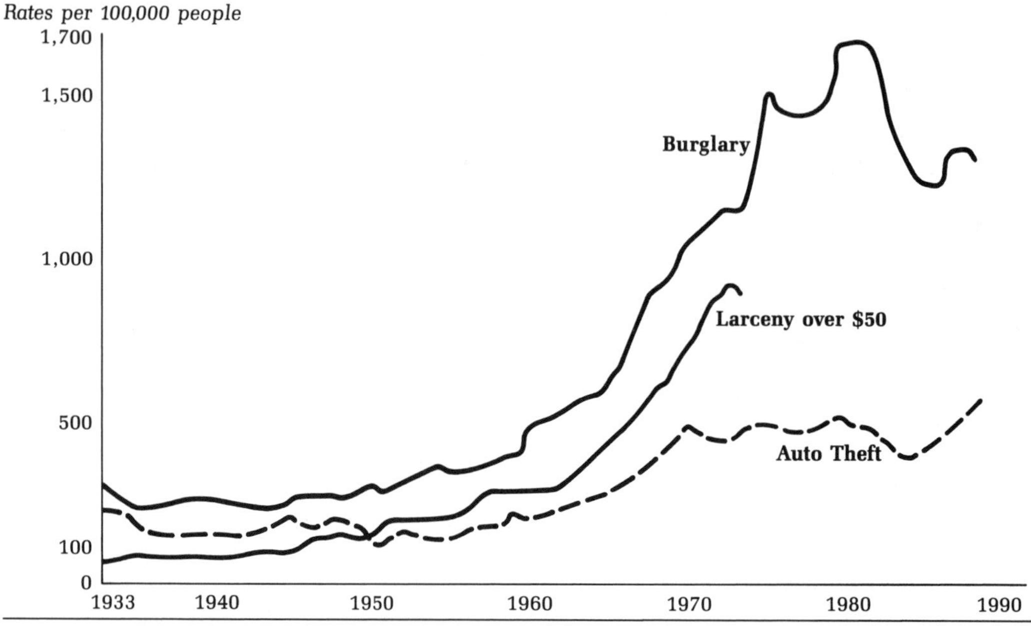

Rates per 100,000 people

SOURCE: President's Commission on Law Enforcement and the Administration of Justice, 1967a. *The Challenge of Crime in a Free Society.* Washington, D.C.: Government Printing Office, p. 23, updated with yearly Uniform Crime Report data.

Although, as we learned in Chapter 2, caution should be exercised in interpreting these statistics, these trend lines certainly dramatically depict an inexorable rise in officially recorded crime since the mid-sixties. Despite this rise in official rates, victim surveys for the seventies reported relatively stable rates, perhaps reinforcing the point that better recording and reporting may have in part accounted for some of the rise in official statistics.

The public alarm concerning the rapid rise in UCR crime statistics beginning in the mid-sixties was abetted by the fact that the decades of the 1940s and 1950s, particularly with postwar prosperity, demonstrated relative stability in many categories of crime. The new "crime wave" appeared particularly out of place. Historians of crime and violence in America remind us of our myopia in this regard and that waves of crime and violence, however difficult to measure, were characteristic of this land since colonial times, particularly in the post-Civil War era in the U.S. (This subject will be treated in greater scope in the later chapter on violence.) In 1968, the President's Commission on Law Enforcement and the Administration of Justice (1967a p. 101) addressed this historical issue:

There has always been too much crime. Virtually every generation since the founding of the Nation and before has felt itself threatened by the specter of rising crime and violence. A hundred years ago contemporary accounts of San Francisco told of extensive areas where "no decent man was in safety to walk the street after dark, while at all hours, both night and day, his property was jeopardized by incendiarism and burglary." Teenage gangs gave rise to the word "hoodlum"; while in one central New York City area, near Broadway, the police entered "only in pairs, and never unarmed." A noted chronicler of the period declared that "municipal law is a failure . . . we must soon fall back on the law of self preservation." And in 1910 one author declared that "crime, especially its more violent forms, and among the young is increasing steadily and is threatening to bankrupt the Nation."

In *Hooligans*, Pearson (1982) remarks upon the historical myth of a crime-free past in England and attributes this to the abundance as well as sophistication of modern statistics, a nostalgia for the past, and cultural amnesia. The relationship of crime with the early history of many countries can be illustrated by Australia, a country which in its early settlement acted as a penal colony for England. Gangs of "bushrangers" (horse rustlers) achieved notoriety, particularly the group led by Ned Kelly, whose reputation reached mythic proportions. This Robin Hood-like figure received support in opposing authority from small farmers who were nicknamed "cockatoos" or "cockys" because, like the bird, they scratched out a living from the ground. The cocky spirit was one of independence and defiance of authority as illustrated by Ned Kelly, who was obstinate until the end when he was hanged at age twenty-five. This spirit is illustrated in Australia's most beloved song about a vagabond who steals a sheep and commits suicide rather than be caught (Levathes, 1985, p. 261):

> Up jumped the swagman
> Sprang into the billabong
> "You'll never catch me alive," said he.
> And his ghost may be heard
> as you pass by that billabong,
> "Who'll come a-waltzing Matilda with me?"

Because systematic victim data is only available since the early seventies, a relative comparison with UCR data before 1973 is not possible. Figures 3.3 and 3.4, as well as Table 3.3, present information from the National Crime Survey (NCS) on victimizations.

Comparison of these trend lines with those from the UCR for the same period suggests similarities as well as differences. While the bulk of crimes for both measures are predominantly crimes against property rather than against person, the NCS did not demonstrate the same steep rise in offenses in the seventies that the UCR reported. In 1981 the U.S. Bureau of Justice Statistics developed a new crime indicator called "households touched by crime" on the assumption that the effects of crime are not limited to the victim alone but extend to and are felt by other members of the victim's household (Bureau of Justice Statistics, 1982, p. 1). Figure 3.5 presents an example of this NCS data.

In considering these figures it is important to realize that, if we were to consider the full range of economic crimes such as the impact of corporate price fixing, then in fact every household has been touched by crime. Similarly, casting a wider net were we to consider self report data, particularly minor offenses, the rate of criminality is pervasive. Despite problems in instruments used and in samples drawn, self-report studies provide much needed evidence of the extensiveness of hidden criminality and law violation; moreover, they support the notion

Figure 3.3: Victimization Trends, 1973–87

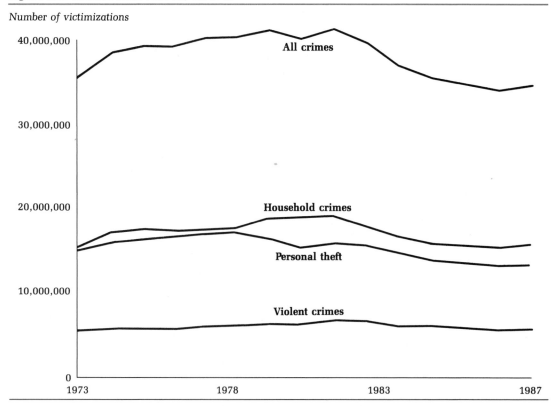

SOURCE: Bureau of Justice Statistics, 1988a, *Criminal Victimization 1987*, Bureau of Justice Statistics Bulletin, October, p. 1.

Figure 3.4: Trends in Victimization Rates of Personal Crimes, 1973–87

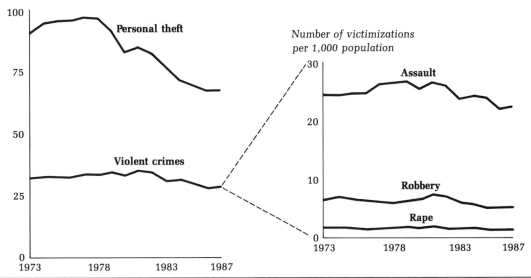

SOURCE: Bureau of Justice Statistics, 1988a, *Criminal Victimization 1987*, Bureau of Justice Statistics Bulletin, October, p. 4.

Table 3.4: Victimization Rates for Personal and Household Crimes, 1973–87

	Victimization Rates per 1,000 Persons Age 12 and Older or per 1,000 Households														
	1973	1974	1975	1976	1977	1978	1979	1980	1981	1982	1983	1984	1985	1986	1987
Personal Crimes	123.6	128.1	128.9	128.7	131.2	130.5	126.4	116.3	120.5	116.8	107.9	103.2	99.4	95.6	96.1
Crimes of Violence	32.6	33.0	32.8	32.6	33.9	33.7	34.5	33.3	35.3	34.3	31.0	31.4	30.0	28.1	28.6
Rape	1.0	1.0	.9	.8	.9	1.0	1.1	.9	1.0	.8	.8	.9	.7	.7	.7
Robbery	6.7	7.2	6.8	6.5	6.2	5.9	6.3	6.6	7.4	7.1	6.0	5.7	5.1	5.1	5.2
Assault	24.9	24.8	25.2	25.3	26.8	26.9	27.2	25.8	27.0	26.4	24.1	24.7	24.2	22.3	22.7
Aggravated	10.1	10.4	9.6	9.9	10.0	9.7	9.9	9.3	9.6	9.3	8.0	9.0	8.3	7.9	7.8
Simple	14.8	14.4	15.6	15.4	16.8	17.2	17.3	16.5	17.3	17.1	16.2	15.7	15.9	14.4	14.9
Crimes of Theft	91.1	95.1	96.0	96.1	97.3	96.8	91.9	83.0	85.1	82.5	76.9	71.8	69.4	67.5	67.5
Personal Larceny with Contact	3.1	3.1	3.1	2.9	2.7	3.1	2.9	3.0	3.3	3.1	3.0	2.8	2.7	2.7	2.6
Personal Larceny without Contact	88.0	92.0	92.9	93.2	94.6	93.6	89.0	80.0	81.9	79.5	74.0	69.1	66.7	64.7	64.9
Household Crimes	217.8	235.7	236.5	229.5	228.8	223.4	235.3	227.4	226.0	208.2	189.8	178.7	174.4	170.0	171.4
Household Burglary	91.7	93.1	91.7	88.9	88.5	86.0	84.1	84.3	87.9	78.2	70.0	64.1	62.7	61.5	61.3
Household Larceny	107.0	123.8	125.4	124.1	123.3	119.9	133.7	126.5	121.0	113.9	105.2	99.4	97.5	93.5	94.0
Motor Vehicle Theft	19.1	18.8	19.5	16.5	17.0	17.5	17.5	16.7	17.1	16.2	14.6	15.2	14.2	15.0	16.1

NOTE: Detail may not add to total shown because of rounding.

SOURCE: Bureau of Justice Statistics, 1988a, *Criminal Victimization 1987*, Bureau of Justice Statistics Bulletin, October,

77

Figure 3.5: Trends in Victimization Rates of Household Crimes, 1973–87

*Number of victimizations
per 1,000 households*

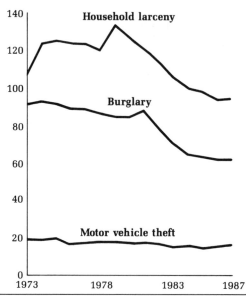

Source: Bureau of Justice Statistics, 1988a, *Criminal Victimization 1987*, Bureau of Justice Statistics Bulletin, October, p. 4.

of the "dualistic fallacy" discussed in the previous chapter in which one must exercise great care in comparing "criminals" and "noncriminals." One may control misunderstanding or overgeneralizations in referring to "criminals" by using operational definitions such as "those arrested" or "those identified by victims" or "those admitting to certain offenses."

Age and Crime

Most of those arrested are young. Vantage Point 3.2 presents data on ages of those arrested for particular crimes. The peak arrest age for property crime is sixteen, while age eighteen is the highest for violent crime. Overall, crime commission declines with age.

Particularly glaring is an involvement of younger groups in serious property crimes. It is important to note that, while most persons arrested and convicted as adult criminals were first arrested as juveniles, most juvenile delinquents do not become adult criminals.

Youthful offenders in urban areas are probably overrepresented in arrest statistics. Such areas have more efficient, formalized policing, while youth generally have less power than their elders to shield themselves from arrest. Juveniles also commit the types of crimes upon which municipal police departments tend to concentrate. Excluding common youth offenses such as curfew and runaway violations and assuming juvenile offenders are often handled and recorded differently depending upon police jurisdictions, the median age for arrested robbers, burglars, thieves, auto thieves, arsonists, and vandals is under twenty years of age, in all categories. Estimates of the average age of embezzlers, price-fixers, bribers, and the like considerably alter this age profile, however, since these crimes are committed by older criminals. The "graying of America," with large proportions of the population becoming elderly, has led to forecasts of an increase in older criminals (Wilbanks and Kim, 1984).

Age/Crime Debate

An intramural academic war of sorts has broken out in criminology which could be described as the "age/crime" debate. On the one side of the debate are Gottfredson and Hirschi (1986, 1987, 1988), who view the "maturing out of" crime or desistance from crime as individuals age as a *constant*. They indicate (1986, p. 219):

> Further, this distribution is characteristic of the age-crime relation regardless of sex, race, country, time or offense. Indeed, the persistence of this relation across time and culture is phenomenal. As long as records have been kept, in all societies in which such records are available, it appears that crime is an activity highly concentrated among the young.

They question the emphasis upon career criminal research, incapacitation, and the recent fetish for longitudinal research that justifies a search for groups of offenders (career criminals) whose criminality does not decline with age (Blumstein, Cohen, and Farrington, 1988a, 1988b; Cohen and Land, 1987; and Farrington, 1986). Blumstein and Cohen (1987) in a longitudinal study of those arrested for more serious crimes in the District of Columbia and Detroit in 1973 found that those who remained active in their twenties did not age out in their thirties, but only after age forty-five. Farrington (1986, p. 189) suggests that offenses of different types peak at different times and that this represents ". . . crime switching rather than replacement of one group of offenders by another." Steffensmeier (1989) finds variation by age-specific type over time with the offenders becoming younger and younger, and that some crimes such as embezzlement or fraud are less likely to decline with age.

VANTAGE POINT

Young people make up the largest proportion of offenders entering the criminal justice system

In 1985—

- Two-thirds of all arrests and three-quarters of all UCR Index arrests were of persons under age 30.
- Arrests of youths under age 21 made up half of all UCR Index property crime arrests and almost a third of all violent crime arrests.
- Arrests of juveniles (persons under age 18) made up 17% of all arrests and 31% of all UCR Index arrests.
- During 1976-85, the number of arrests of juveniles (persons under age 18) fell by 18%, reflecting the decline in the size of that age group and a 15% drop in their arrest rate.

Serious crime arrest rates are highest in young age groups

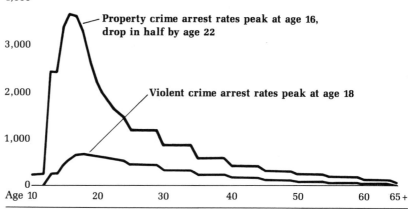

SOURCE: FBI Uniform Crime Reports, 3-year averages, 1983–85.

Participation in crime declines with age

Arrest data show that the intensity of criminal behavior slackens after the teens, and it continues to decline with age. Arrests, however, are only a general indicator of criminal activity. The greater likelihood of arrests for young people may result partly from their lack of experience in offending and also from their involvement in the types of crimes for which apprehension is more likely (for example, purse snatching vs. fraud). Moreover, because youths often commit crime in groups, the resolution of a single crime may lead to several arrests.

The decline in crime participation with age may also result from the incapacitation of many offenders. When repeat offenders are apprehended, they serve increasingly longer sentences, thus incapacitating them for long periods as they grow older. Moreover, a RAND Corporation study of habitual offenders shows that the success of habitual offenders in avoiding apprehension declined as their criminal careers progressed. Even though offense rates declined over time, the probabilities of arrest, conviction, and incarceration per offense all tended to increase. Recidivism data also show that the rates of returning to prison tend to be lower for older than for younger prisoners. Older prisoners who do return do so after a longer period of freedom than do younger prisoners.

Arrest rate trends vary by age group

Between 1961 and 1981—

- The most dramatic increases in arrest rates were for persons age 18 to 20.
- Smaller increases in arrest rates occurred for persons age 21 to 24 and age 25 to 29.
- For persons age 35 and older, arrest rates declined.
- Persons age 18 to 20 had the highest arrest rates followed by those age 21 to 24.
- Persons age 50 or older had the lowest arrest rates.

Arrests per 100,000 age-eligible population

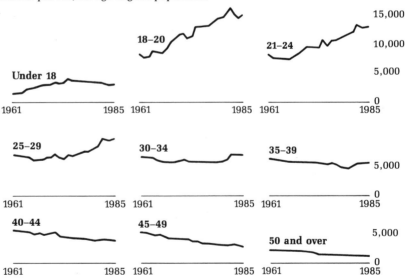

SOURCE: FBI Uniform Crime Reports, 1961–85, unpublished data.

Why do most criminals "mature out of" crime? Farrington (1986) suggests factors such as the influence of wives and/or girlfriends, the decline of gang or peer group support, increased penalties, as well as increased

---

Different age groups are arrested and incarcerated for different types of crimes

- Juveniles under age 18 have a higher likelihood of being arrested for robbery and UCR Index property crimes than any other age group.
- Persons between ages 18 and 34 are the most likely to be arrested for violent crimes.
- The proportion of each group arrested for public order crimes increases with age.
- Among jail and prison inmates, property crimes, particularly burglary and public order crimes, are more common among younger inmates.
- Violent crimes were more prevalent among older inmates admitted to prison in 1982 but showed little variation among jail inmates of different ages.
- Drug crimes were more prevalent among inmates age 25 to 44 in both prisons and jails.

Average age at arrest varies by type of crime

Most serious charge	Average age at arrest in 1985	Most serious charge	Average age at arrest in 1985
Gambling	37 years	Drug abuse violations	26 years
Murder	30	Stolen property	25
Sex offenses	30	Larceny/theft	25
Fraud	30	Arson	24
Embezzlement	29	Robbery	24
Aggravated assault	29	Burglary	22
Forcible rape	28	Motor vehicle theft	22
Weapons	28		
Forgery and counterfeiting	27		

SOURCE: *Age-Specific Arrest Rates and Race-Specific Arrest Rates for Selected Offenses 1965–85*, FBI Uniform Crime Reporting Program, December 1986.

Many older prison inmates had never been to prison before

Of all persons admitted to prison after age 40, nearly half were in prison for the first time.

Inmates whose most recent admission to prison was at or after age 40 were more likely to be serving time for a violent crime than inmates who had the longest, most continuous criminal careers. The seriousness of their offenses

legitimate opportunities as individuals reach their twenties. The outcome of this age/crime controversy is claimed by the disputants to have important consequences for career criminal research (Tittle, 1988).

---

alone probably explains why so many inmates were incarcerated for the first time at or after age 40.

Persons who were returning to prison at or after age 40 generally had prior criminal records rather than a current violent conviction. Given their records, these returnees did not have to commit a violent crime to bring them back to prison.

The average age of arrestees for most crimes remained fairly constant from 1965 to 1985

Some exceptions are that the average age of persons arrested for—

- murder declined
- forcible rape increased
- fraud declined
- embezzlement declined
- larceny/theft increased
- motor vehicle theft increased.

The greatest increase in average age was for persons arrested for arson.

Historically, studies have shown property crimes to be more typical of youths than of older offenders

In a historical assessment of offending patterns, Cline reviewed several studies. These studies indicated a change from property to violent crimes as adolescents moved into adulthood.

Adults commit more serious crimes than juveniles

In a study of delinquency over time in England, Langan and Farrington examined the relationship between age of offenders and the value of the property they stole. The study found that crimes committed by adults were much more serious when measured in terms of value of stolen property than those committed by juveniles. Findings showed that the average amount stolen increased with age.

SOURCE: Bureau of Justice Statistics, 1988b, *Report to the Nation on Crime and Justice*, 2nd edition, Washington, D.C.: Government Printing Office, March, pp. 32–33.

Sex Differences in Criminality

Of all demographic variables, sex is the best predictor of criminality: most persons arrested are males. In the United States, in the eighties, men represented about 83 percent of those arrested; and, with the exception of primarily female offenses such as prostitution (in which "Johns" or customers are seldom arrested), this difference holds for all criminal offenses. The male crime rate exceeds that of females universally, in all nations, in all communities, among all age groups, and in all periods of history for which statistics are available. Vantage Point 3.3 presents some data with respect to sex differences and arrest statistics. Whereas in some more traditional countries the crime-sex arrest ratio may be as high as two hundred to one or one thousand to one, in modernized societies the gap in sexual variation in crime has been closing. Why such variation? Sex per se is not the key variable so much as the particular culture's conception of sex. The female crime rate appears to be closer to the male level in countries in which females enjoy more equality and freedom and thus an increased opportunity to commit crime.

This universality of disproportionate male criminality can best be explained by the differential treatment of males and females. Traditionally, males are socialized to be dominant, active, and aggressive. In fact, chivalry and the law often require that the male take responsibility for what occurs. In many traditional societies it is the husband who is punished for any transgressions of his wife. Similarly, customary gender role socialization of females emphasizes passivity and subordination.

The traditional handmaiden of sexism has been paternalism, a sort of sexual noblesse oblige in which males felt that they were responsible for protecting the dependent female. This policy is reflected in the law and its administration, since females generally receive much lighter sentences for the same offense, are viewed more favorably by judges and juries, and seldom receive the death penalty.

Recent literature on the subject of sex and crime note the *androcentric* (male-centered) *bias* in many delinquency and crime theories (Chesney-Lind, 1989). Burnett (1986) also notes that women have been left out of criminological scholarship and that a new era was begun with publications such as Adler's *Sisters in Crime* (1975) and Adler and Simon's *The Criminology of Deviant Women* (1979). While writers such as Adler (1975) were arguing that a gender convergence or closing of the gap between male and female crime rates was taking place, others such as Steffensmeier (1978) and Steffensmeier and Allan (1988) found no such closing of the crime sex ratio. Vantage Point 3.3 explores the offense characteristic differences between men and women.

This woman was arrested as part of an investigation of international drug rings. The number of crimes committed by women has increased over the past decades, and many experts believe this is due to women's increased independence.

Self-report data on admitted offenses by sex show mixed results, with some demonstrating less of a gap between male and female criminality (Jensen and Eve, 1976; Hindelang, 1979; and Short and Nye, 1958). Other researchers indicate that the differences are similar to those that exist in official arrest statistics (Hindelang, Hirschi, and Weis, 1979; and Williams and Gold, 1972).

A major literature is developing regarding gender and crime. One example is a "power-control theory" of delinquency and gender (Hagan, Gillis, and Simpson, 1985 and 1987) which proposes that male and female children react differently to parental power sharing. They hypothesized that ". . . balanced family structure [shared power by spouses] reduces the disparities in delinquency between genders and that unbalanced family structures perpetuate those differences" (Singer and Levine, 1988, p. 643). Singer and Levine (1988) found little support for this theory. For further review of this literature the reader is referred to Nagel and Hagan, 1983; Mann, 1984; Moyer, 1985; and Rosenbaum, 1989b).

VANTAGE

POINT

Vantage Point 3.3—How Do the Offense Characteristics of Men and Women Differ?

Relatively few offenders are female

	Females in group
All arrests (adults and juveniles)	17%
Index crime arrests	21
Violent crime arrests	11
Property crime arrests	24
Larceny	31
Nonlarceny	8
Under correctional supervision	
Juveniles	20
Jail inmates	7
Prison inmates	5

For UCR Index Crimes, the rate of arrest of females is much lower than that of males, but it has risen faster

Males

Arrest rate per 100,000 resident population

Percent change (1971–85)

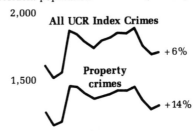

2,000

All UCR Index Crimes

+6%

Property crimes

1,500

+14%

1,000

Violent crimes

500

+4%

Females

Arrest rate per 100,000 resident population

Percent change (1971–85)

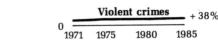

500 All UCR Index Crimes +37%

+25%

250 **Property crimes**

Violent crimes +38%

0

1971 1975 1980 1985

0

1971 1975 1980 1985

Offense patterns differ for males and females

UCR Index Crimes	Percent of all arrests	
	Males	Females
Murder and nonnegligent/manslaughter	88%	12%
Rape	99	1
Robbery	92	8
Aggravated assault	87	13
Burglary	93	7
Larceny-theft	69	31
Motor vehicle theft	91	9
Arson	87	13

- Men are more likely than women to be arrested for the more serious crimes, such as murder, rape, robbery, or burglary.
- Arrest, jail, and prison data all suggest that a higher proportion of women than of men who commit crimes are involved in property crimes, such as larceny, forgery, fraud, and embezzlement, and in drug offenses.

While all prison populations have been growing dramatically, the women's share has risen from 4% to 5% in the past decade

Over the past 10 years, the number of women in prison rose by 107% (from 11,170 in 1976 to 23,091 in 1985), while the number of men rose by 80% (from 266,830 in 1976 to 480,510 in 1985).

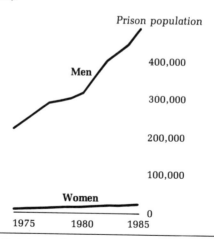

SOURCE: Bureau of Justice Statistics, 1988b, *Report to the Nation on Crime and Justice*, 2nd edition, Washington, D.C.: Government Printing Office, March, p. 46.

Social Class and Crime

Social class is not a category included in the Uniform Crime Report, yet the vast majority of those arrested or labeled as criminal are from lower social classes. Criminality for traditional crimes is higher among lower class individuals despite bias in statistics or the administration of justice. Part of the excess rate is likely to be due to their lack of power and sophistication in shielding themselves from formal litigation proceedings. Traditional explanations of crime and social class view them as involving an inverse relationship; that is, as social class becomes higher, the volume of crime commission decreases proportionately. Figure 3.6(a) attempts to depict this relationship schematically. Reckless (1967) proposes a bimodal theory of the distribution of crime commission in which the criminality curve has two modes (most frequently appearing cases) among the lower class and the upper class, though crimes of the latter are seldom reflected in national crime statistics. Figure 3.6(b) illustrates this relationship.

The relationship between social class and criminality remains a subject of debate. The early self-report surveys (Short and Nye, 1958; Nye, Short, and Olson, 1958) found no relationship other than that lower class offenders were more likely to be officially processed. Tittle, Villemez, and Smith (1978), in a literature review of major self-report studies, found no relationship between class and criminality. More recent research and reviews of self-report surveys suggest that much

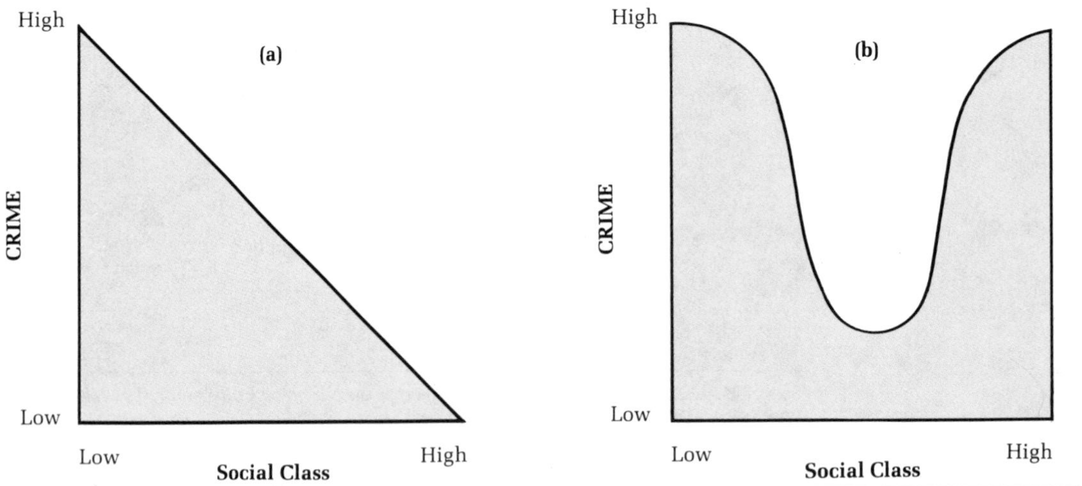

Figure 3.6: Models of the Relationship between Social Class and Criminality

of this lack of difference by class may have been due to the measuring instruments, which tended to concentrate on rather trivial offenses. Lower class youth were found to commit more serious crimes more often; and their offense profile was found to more closely follow that as presented by official statistics (Hardt and Hardt, 1977; Elliott and Ageton, 1980; and Hindelang, Hirschi, and Weis, 1979). It is important to caution, however, that official statistics undercount the typical crimes of upper socioeconomic groups so that, even if the lower class has higher official crime rates, this does not indicate that they necessarily have excess criminality.

Race and Crime

Race is a relatively arbitrary, socially defined status. For example, in an early study, Herskovits (1930, p. 177) estimated that of the total number of black persons classified as "Negro" in the United States, 15 percent were more "white" than Negroid, 25 percent were equally "white" and Negroid, and 22 percent were unmixed Negroid. Thus, the concept of "race" becomes more of a socially defined category rather than a taxonomically simple biological classification. As Sutherland and Cressey (1974, p. 132) point out: "There is no avoiding the fact that at least 80 percent of the offenders contributing to the 'black' crime rate are part 'white.'" The foregoing facts become important in light of cryptoracist theories rediscovered and received with some respectability in the 1970s which regenerated long-discredited hereditary theories of racial inferiority, for example, by William Shockley and Arthur Jensen, to explain why blacks, or African-Americans, despite social changes in the 1960s, had failed to succeed (Skolnick and Currie, 1988, p. 12). Such theories obviously ignore the black experience in a nation which until relatively recently practiced institutionalized racism against blacks. The long legacy of slavery, followed by "Jim Crow" laws (legalized or de jure segregation and discrimination) and then succeeded by de facto (in fact) discrimination, placed a generational burden upon black Americans that far exceeded the milder forms endured temporarily by other ethnic groups. Much of the discrepancy between black and white crime rates can perhaps be explained by the fact that African-Americans until relatively recently have been locked disproportionately into the lower class through a pseudocaste system.

In the late sixties through mid-eighties, roughly 27 percent of those arrested in the U.S. were black, while blacks made up only about 12 percent of the population. The disparity of rates between blacks and nonblacks was much greater for offenses of violence than for property offenses. This difference in arrest rates is generally taken to indicate equally disproportionate rates of crime commission. Most studies indicate that these differences are not a result of police discrimination.

Crime has in the past been primarily intraracial in nature; that is, for most crimes, whites mainly victimize whites and blacks victimize blacks. Utilizing UCR arrest data for the mid-eighties, blacks represented 62 percent of robbers and exhibited particularly disproportionate rates for murder, rape, and assault (Bureau of Justice Statistics, 1988b, p. 47). All of these crimes are relatively unsophisticated and command a great deal of police attention, see Vantage Point 3.4.

Wilbanks (1985, 1987) questions this intraracial nature of crime assumption as well as *The Myth of a Racist Criminal Justice System*. If crime is intraracial, it occurs within rather than between (interracial) races. He noted that the National Crime Survey for 1983 had included only one percentaged table to analyze the intraracial assumption and asked to what extent black or white victims had been victimized by black or white offenders. This showed an intraracial relationship; that is, 78 percent of whites were victimized by whites and 87 percent of blacks were victimized by blacks. Wilbanks argued, and the NCS agreed by adding such a table to their report, that the table should also be percentaged to answer the question, "To what extent do white or black offenders choose white or black victims?" (see Hagan, 1989a for detail). This showed that violent crime was interracial (occurs between races), blacks being more likely to commit violent crime against whites (roughly 55 percent) than against blacks (about 45 percent), while only 2 percent of the targets of white criminals were black. While Wilbanks' data were correct, some critics accused such an unexplained analysis of giving aid and comfort to the enemy; that is, without a broader understanding of demography such data could be used to perhaps justify racist conclusions. Assuming, for instance, that whites represent 85 to 90 percent of the population, then a color-blind choice of targets would find blacks choosing 85 to 90 percent of their targets as whites. Given a rate of nearly half that suggests a continuing intraracial preference (see O'Brien, 1987).

Statistics on crime by race are subject to countervailing pressures which may on the one hand overestimate and on the other underestimate the actual black crime rate. Blacks are more likely to be arrested, indicted, convicted, and imprisoned than are whites. If convicted, they are less likely to receive probation, parole, or pardon. These factors may tend to exaggerate the black crime rate. In the past, particularly, many crimes by blacks against other blacks were ignored by the criminal justice system. A certain proportion of the rising crime rate beginning in the sixties reflected a greater willingness on the part of the police to respond to ghetto crime, which previously had been overlooked.

Despite these offsetting trends, the crime rate of blacks is disturbingly disproportionate to that of the general population. Wolfgang's (1958) analysis of homicide in Philadelphia found the nonwhite, twenty-24-year-old male rate to be about twenty-five times that of the Caucasian rate. The few early self-report surveys suggested no significant differences by race with respect to admitted offenses (Gould, 1969; Hirschi, 1969; and Voss, 1963). However, more recent research (Elliott and Ageton, 1980; and Hindelang, Hirschi, and Weis, 1979) again points to the tendency of many early instruments to concentrate on trivial offenses. For more serious offenses, such as assault, robbery, and the like, black youths were significantly more persistent offenders, their rates in self-report surveys being similar to those in official statistics.

Reviews of studies argue that there is no discrimination in the administration of justice (J. Hagan, 1987; Myers and Talarico, 1987; Petersilia, 1983; and Klein, Turner, and Petersilia, 1988); however, the relationship is a subtle one as identified by other writers (Georges-Abeyie, 1984; and Sampson, 1985). Hawkins (1986a, 1986b, and 1987) found the racial differences between rates of arrest and imprisonment vary with the type of offense. The level of arrest failed to account for overincarceration of blacks for drug offenses, forgery, and driving under the influence, and an unexpected underincarceration for rape and robbery. Hawkins concludes that we must avoid the simplistic assumptions that blacks will be treated more severely than whites for all types of crime—the system of criminal justice is oppressive, but not without contradictions. On a final note it should be pointed out that the African-American crime rate for inside-trading, price-fixing and defense procurement rip-offs and other white-collar crimes is minimal.

Minority Groups and Crime

Race per se is not as crucial an explanatory variable in traditional crime commission as is social class. Until recently, a large percentage of blacks have been concentrated in lower socioeconomic class ghettos which have traditionally exhibited high rates of breakdown. African-Americans are disproportionately located in the very largest cities. Early research by the "Chicago school" of sociology, most notably that of Shaw and McKay (1942) and their utilization of Burgess's "concentric zone theory" (1925), serves as an illustration of this relationship.

In examining delinquency areas, Shaw and McKay report similar rates of delinquency in the same area of transition (zone II) despite changeover in racial, nativity, and nationality groups. Despite this

Vantage Point

The number of black criminals is disproportionately high

Blacks, who made up 12% of the U.S. population in 1980, accounted for—

- 27% of all arrests in 1985
- 34% of all UCR Index Crime arrests
- 47% of all arrests for violent crimes
- 40% of local jail inmates in 1984
- 46% of State prison inmates in 1984.

According to many researchers, the disproportionality of blacks in the prison population is mostly attributable to age, seriousness of crime, prior criminal record, and other legally relevant factors. This finding neither rules out nor confirms the possibility of some discrimination in the criminal justice system.

Victim reports confirm the pattern of arrests by race

The pattern of racial involvement in arrests shown in police records closely parallels that reported by victims of crime in the National Crime Survey.

	Percent of offenders who were black	
	Robbery	Burglary
NCS victim observation	63%	34%
UCR arrests	59	35

NOTE: Data exclude offenders under age 18 and of races other than black and white. NCS victims observed the offender in 92% of the robberies and 5% of the burglaries.

The lifetime chance of incarceration is six times higher for blacks than for whites

The likelihood that any adult male will have served time in a juvenile or adult jail or prison by age 64 is estimated to be 18% for blacks and 3% for whites. However, after the first confinement, the likelihood of further commitments is similar for white and black males. About a third of each group who have ever been confined will have been confined four times by age 64.

The proportion of black State prisoners in the South is more consistent with their share of the population than in other regions

	Blacks as a percent of prison population	Blacks as a percent of U.S. population	Ratio of prison proportion to U.S. proportion
United States	46%	12%	4 to 1
Northeast	51	10	5 to 1
Midwest	45	9	5 to 1
South	54	19	3 to 1
West	26	5	5 to 1

Blacks were more likely than whites to be violent offenders

Among UCR Index Crimes, the arrest rate of blacks was higher for violent than for property crimes:

	Whites	Blacks
All arrests	72%	27%
All Index Crimes	65%	34%
Violent crimes	52%	47%
Murder	50	48
Rape	52	47
Robbery	37	62
Aggravated assault	58	40
Property crimes	68%	30%
Burglary	70	29
Larceny-theft	67	31
Motor vehicle theft	66	32
Arson	76	23

NOTE: Percentages do not add to 100% because arrests of persons of other races are not shown.

In 1983 blacks accounted for 45% of all prison admissions and about 47% of all admissions for violent crimes. Of all blacks admitted to prison in 1983, 38% were admitted for violent crimes as compared to 31% of all whites. Eighteen percent of all blacks were admitted for robbery as compared to 11% of all whites.

The proportion of Hispanics in prisons and jails is greater than in the total U.S. population

Fifteen million Hispanics make up 6% of the U.S. population. This number is divided about equally between males and females.

Hispanics (both white and black)—

- accounted for 15% of all arrests for violent crimes and 11% of all arrests for property crimes in 1985
- made up 13% (27,423) of the male jail population and 11% (1,929) of the female jail population in 1984
- made up 10% (46,125) of the male prison population and 9% (1,781) of the female prison population
- were more likely than non-Hispanics to be in jail or prison for drug offenses in 1983 and 1984.

SOURCE: Bureau of Justice Statistics, 1988b, *Report to the Nation on Crime and Justice*, Washington, D.C.: Government Printing Office, March, p. 47.

assumption, Nettler (1982, vol. 2, p. 58) points out that Dutch, German, and Scandinavian settlers in the U.S. have had low crime rates in general, particularly for violent crimes. In addition, the low rates for Jews and Orientals challenge the assumption that racial visibility,

Figure 3.7: Burgess's Concentric Zone Theory

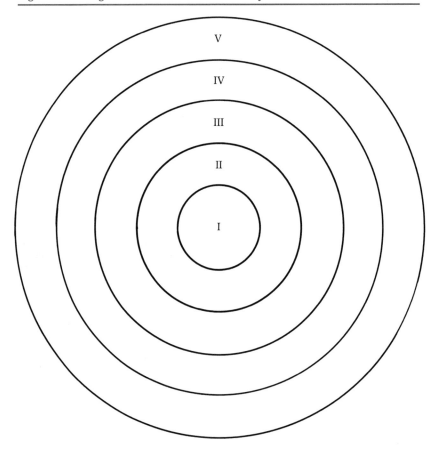

Zone
I. Economic Center (Central Business District)
II Zone of Transition
III Industry and Workingmen's Homes
IV Better Residential Areas
V Suburbs

SOURCE: Figure is based upon theoretical presentations in Ernest W. Burgess, 1925, "The Growth of the City," in *The City*, edited by Robert E. Park, Ernest W. Burgess and Robert D. McKenzie, Chicago: University of Chicago Press, pp. 47–62.

prejudice, and discrimination are sufficient explanations of criminality. It should be pointed out, however, that many of these groups were not lower-class immigrants, but instead had migrated during a period in which their craft, mercantile, and other skills were economically in demand (Flowers, 1988).

The excessive black violent crime rate in the U.S. stands in contrast to Hispanics who are poorer, less educated, and have more menial jobs, but who also have lower rates of violent crime. Silberman (1978) in analyzing New York City crime rates found the rate of black violent crime to be three times greater than the Hispanic rate and twice as high for homicide.

Since other minority groups who at one time were discriminated against were able to overcome difficulties and "rise from the ashes," so to speak, many ask the question: "Why haven't blacks been able to achieve the same success?" In 1968 in the aftermath of the worst series of urban riots in modern American history, the Kerner Commission, the National Advisory Commission on Civil Disorders, addressed this issue by suggesting four reasons for differences in the immigrant and black experiences:

1. *The Maturing Economy:* When the European immigrants arrived they gained an economic foothold by providing the unskilled labor needed by industry. Unlike the immigrant, the Negro migrant found little opportunity in the city. The economy, by then matured, had little use for the unskilled labor he had to offer.

2. *The Disability of Race:* The structure of discrimination has stringently narrowed opportunities for the Negro and restricted his prospects. European immigrants suffered from discrimination, but never so pervasively.

3. *Entry into the Political System:* The immigrants usually settled in rapidly growing cities with powerful and expanding political machines, which traded economic advantages for political support. Ward-level grievance machinery, as well as personal representation, enabled the immigrant to make his voice heard and his power felt.

   By the time the Negro arrived, these political machines were no longer so powerful or so well equipped to provide jobs or other favors, and in many cases were unwilling to share their influence with Negroes.

4. *Cultural factors:* Coming from societies with a low standard of living and at a time when job aspirations were low, the immigrants sensed little deprivation in being forced to take the less desirable and poorer-paying jobs. Their large and cohesive families contributed to the total income. Their vision of the future—one that led to life outside of the ghetto—provided the incentive necessary to endure the present.

   Although Negro men worked as hard as the immigrants, they were unable to support their families. The entrepreneurial opportunities had vanished. As a result of slavery and long periods of unemployment, the

Negro family structure had become matriarchal; the males played a secondary and marginal family role—one which offered little compensation for their hard and unrewarding labor. Above all, segregation denied Negroes access to good jobs and the opportunity to leave the ghetto. For them, the future seemed to lead only to a dead end.
—Kerner, 1968 p. 15.

Conklin correctly points out that differences in ethnic and racial crime rates do not reflect innate biological differences, but social, cultural, and economic differences. He further states that ". . . to argue that blacks and whites of similar backgrounds would have the same crime rates is to argue that centuries of discrimination have had no long-term effects on blacks which are linked to criminal behavior" (Conklin, 1981, p. 137). Austin (1987) argues that progress in racial equality is reducing the gap between black and white criminal violence.

Does minority group status itself produce higher crime rates? In general, the answer to this question is no. Much depends upon the particular minority group and its specific values and cultural traditions. In the United States, for instance, the crime rate among Japanese-Americans and Orientals in general is lower than that of the general population. Many newer immigrant groups in the United States such as Cambodians, Koreans, and Vietnamese have low crime rates in part due to close extended family ties, a strong work ethic, and merchant skills (Launer and Palenski, 1988; and Light and Bonacich, 1988). On the other hand the crime rates for Algerians in France or Finns in Sweden or Hispanics in the U.S. are higher than that of the general population.

Most immigrants to the U.S. have been from close-knit peasant societies; and the crime rate for this first-generational group is usually lower, with the exception of crimes which were peculiar to the area from which they migrated. For instance, for the first-generation Italian immigrant crime rates were lower, with the exception of murders and assaults. Since the areas of southern Italy and Sicily from which they came were experiencing at that time a wave of vendetta and violence, this pattern was carried over into the new world. Similarly Irish immigrants experienced higher rates for alcohol-related offenses, since in the nineteenth century Ireland reputedly had the highest alcoholism rates in the Western world.

It is not the parental group of immigrants that exhibits excess criminality; for many groups, it is the second generation who exhibit a marked upsurge in crime. Living in a strange, new land and often the victims of discrimination, the first generation often clings to old values. Moreover, they may fear deportation. Wishing to be Americanized, the second generation often rejects many of these ways and attempts to assimilate the general values of American culture. Unfortunately, in the milieu or area in which they live (zone II, for instance), they also assimilate the criminal values of a high crime area. Not being placed in such environments or possessing a higher parental social class explains the relative success of Vietnamese immigrants in the U.S.

Nettler (1982, vol. 2, pp. 48–62) in his four-volume work, *Explaining Crime*, does an excellent job of summarizing much of the international research on ethnic migrants and crime. Care must be exercised in examining these data, since many of the studies refer to *Gastarbeiter* (guest workers), who are not immigrants as such, but rather temporary workers in the host community. Studies in Switzerland found the crime rate higher for foreigners than natives, particularly for violent crime. Ferracuti (1968) claimed that the crime rate of foreign workers increased as their numbers increased, although many of their crimes went unreported. Nettler (1982, vol. 2, pp. 48–49) cites similar findings which suggest higher rates among Hungarians and Yugoslavs in Sweden; for Turks, Italians, Africans, and Mediterraneans in West Germany and Belgium; for Algerians in France; and for Irish, Asian, and West Indians in England. However, one chief problem in many of these studies is their failure to control for age and sex differentials, since many migrants consist of a heavier population of young, single males, a group with a higher crime commission potential.

Regional Variation in Crime

Not only do crime rates vary between nations, they also vary by region within a country (see Brantingham and Brantingham, 1984). In 1987 the South had the highest rates for murder and burglary and the West was highest for rape, aggravated assault, larceny, and vehicle theft. The Northeast was highest for robbery, while the Midwest (North Central states) was the lowest in four of the seven index crimes.

Urban-Rural Differences

Internationally, urban recorded crime rates are generally higher than rural crime rates; and, with few exceptions, this difference appears to have been the case since cities began. Although crime rates tend to increase with the size of the community, there are some important exceptions. Table 3.6 presents findings from the National Crime Survey, showing that for certain crimes the rates are higher in cities under one million population.

Table 3.5: Rates of Crime per 100,000 by Region of the United States, 1987

Offense	Northeast	Midwest (North Central)	South	West
Crime Index Total	4,838.9	4,907.6	5,893.0	6,460.0
Violent Crime	635.4	504.3	607.1	714.3
Property Crime	4,203.5	4,403.3	5,285.9	5,745.7
Murder	6.9	6.7	10.0	8.5
Forcible Rape	29.3	37.1	39.3	42.9
Robbery	283.7	173.2	191.9	223.2
Aggravated Assault	315.5	287.3	365.9	439.7
Burglary	1,031.0	1,088.1	1,565.0	1,523.5
Larceny-Theft	2,543.8	2,889.2	3,238.2	3,590.4
Motor Vehicle Theft	628.7	426.1	482.7	631.8
Arson				

NOTE: While Arson is included as a Part I crime, national figures are not available or included in the index calculation.

SOURCE: Data were adapted and compiled from Federal Bureau of Investigation, 1988, *Crime in the United States, 1987*, Washington, D.C.: Government Printing Office, pp. 44–51.

In contrast to this victim data, UCR statistics in general show a positive relationship in which, as size of community increases, the crime rate increases, with some exceptions such as for rape, assault, burglary, and larceny which were highest in cities of 250,000–499,999 population. (Table 3.7).

Even if one assumes less reporting and recording of rural crime rate, the difference between rural-urban rates persists. Yet, rural and suburban crime rates have actually been increasing faster than those of central cities since the sixties. Urbanism and its "way of life" is no longer confined just to cities. The advent of modern communications and transportation has effectively erased many of the distinctions between rural and urban life-styles, creating a truly urban society. The relatively high rates of violent crime in rural areas may be explained by certain criminalistic traditions in some areas that are much closer to frontier values; and a possible "subculture of violence," to be explored in Chapter 6 may explain high rural rates in the South as well as southern Appalachia. In contrast to the American pattern, Canadian murder rates are higher in rural than in urban settings (Schloss and Giesbrecht, 1972, p. 22).

Using their "Comparative Crime Data File," Archer and Gartner (1984, pp. 115–116) found that homicide rates were higher the larger the city between 1966-1970 in twenty-four societies, but found no support for the proposition that city size and homicide rates increase together. The city's size relative to its society is more important in determining homicide

Table 3.6: Victimization Rates by Place of Residence

Victimization Rates for Persons Age 12 and Older

Place of Residence and Population	Crimes of Violence	Crimes of Theft
Total All Areas	31	77
All Central Cities	43	92
50,000–249,999	38	90
250,000–499,999	39	85
500,000–999,999	48	105
1,000,000 or more	48	90
All Suburban Areas	29	82
50,000–249,999	25	72
250,000–499,999	30	79
500,000–999,999	30	88
1,000,000 or more	33	93
Nonmetropolitan Areas	22	58

NOTE: Rates are per 1,000 population age 12 and older. The population range categories shown under the "all central cities" and "all suburban areas" headings are based only on the size of the central city and do not include the population of the entire metropolitan area.

SOURCE: Bureau of Justice Statistics, 1985, *Locating City, Suburban, and Rural Crime*, BJS Special Report, December, 1985, reproduced in Bureau of Justice Statistics, 1988b, *Report to the Nation on Crime and Justice*, Washington, D.C.: Government Printing Office, March, p. 19.

Table 3.7: Crime Rates by Size of Community

	Number of UCR Index Crime Rates per 100,000 Population	
	Violent Crimes	Property Crimes
Metropolitan statistical areas (MSAs) Urbanized areas that include at least one city with 50,000 or more inhabitants, or a Census Bureau defined urbanized area of at least 50,000 inhabitants and a total MSA population of at least 100,000	658	5,262
Non-MSA cities Cities that do not qualify as MSA central cities and are not otherwise included in an MSA	319	4,262
Suburban areas Suburban cities and counties within metropolitan areas	341	3,883
Rural Areas	168	1,636

SOURCE: FBI, 1985, *Crime in the United States*, reproduced in Bureau of Justice Statistics, 1988b, *Report to the Nation on Crime and Justice*, 2nd edition, Washington, D.C.: Government Printing Office, March, p. 19.

rates than its absolute size. ". . . [A]ny jurisdiction more urban than its national environment will have a homicide rate higher than the national average" (Ibid., p. 116).

Institutions and Crime

Sociologists define *social institutions* as relatively stable social patterns that serve a broad range of crucial functions in society; examples are economy, family, church, state, and schools. In contrast, *associations* are special-purpose organizations which serve a narrow range of interests; examples are corporations, unions, and professional societies. The impact of associations upon criminality will be explored in Chapters 9 and 10, where criminogenic environments in organizations such as the oil, automobile, and pharmaceutical industries, may have a major impact upon predisposing individuals toward criminality. While this section has concentrated upon crimes by individuals, we will give greater coverage later to criminal organizations.

The Family and Crime

Much "conventional wisdom" suggests that the family is the cradle of crime; crime starts in the home or it is the parents' fault if a child goes wrong. While the family plays an important role in the socialization process and characteristics of the family do impact upon criminality, these assumptions are gross oversimplifications of a more complex reality. The family is the primary or most important agent of socialization, particularly during childhood. The family has exclusive contact with the child during the period of greatest dependency and plasticity. Despite considerable popular literature on the subject, there is little, if any, scientific evidence on the subject of child rearing. Advocates of permissive or restrictive socialization to the contrary, the key appears to be firm, but consistent discipline that is reinforced as well as understood by the child. One of the most important variables correlated with delinquency is probably poor home discipline, neglect, or indifference (Rosenbaum, 1989a).

Many American studies of delinquency include under that label a significant number of activities, such as truancy, incorrigibility, and the like, that would not be criminal had they been committed by an adult. In a review of family factors associated with delinquency, Sutherland and Cressey (1974, pp. 203–218) as well as Hirschi (1983, pp. 53–68) point to moderate-to-high correlations between delinquency and immorality or criminality or alcoholism of parents, absence of one or both parents, a lack of parental control, unhappy home life, subcultural differences in the home, and economic pressures. The general process of family influence relates to the fact that the parental social class determines the residence, school, and associates of their offspring. Parental transmission of criminogenic attitudes or failure to train the child may influence delinquency. Similarly, a poor home environment may force the youth into the streets seeking peer primary group support.

Statistics on broken homes, ordinal positions (birth order) of siblings, and number of siblings and their influence on crime and delinquency appear inconclusive (Rosen and Neilson, 1978; and Sutherland and Cressey, 1974, pp. 216–217). It would appear that the quality of family interaction instead of the family structure per se is important.

More sophisticated family studies of delinquents could be noted with early research by Sheldon and Eleanor Glueck (1950) who examined five hundred delinquents and five hundred nondelinquents and found roughly 50 percent of the delinquents were from broken homes compared with about 29 percent of nondelinquents. Delinquents were more likely to have families characterized by physical illness, mental retardation, mental disturbance, alcoholism, and parental criminality. Such parents exercised poor child rearing practices, either overly strict or overly permissive and inconsistent discipline. Thus defective family relations was perceived as a key causal variable in delinquency (Hagan and Sussman, 1988a and b).

In the longest longitudinal study of delinquents, the "Cambridge-Somerville study" begun in 1937, William and Joan McCord (1958) found delinquents characterized by poor or weak parental discipline as well as a quarrelsome home environment. Family structure, *broken or intact home, was less salient than the nature of family interaction.* All of the boys from quarrelsome environments had been convicted of crime (Wilson and Herrnstein, 1985, p. 232). West and Farrington's (1977) longitudinal study of London working class boys found the following associated with delinquency: low IQ, poor child rearing practices, criminality of father, large family size, and low family income. Similar findings with respect to defective parental supervision and socialization have been suggested by Hirschi (1969), Baumrind (1978), Patterson (1982), and Van Voorhis, et al. (1988).

Loeber and Loeber (1986) in an exhaustive analysis of the literature summarize the relationship between family and delinquency as exhibiting (1) the most powerful predictors: lack of parental supervision, parental rejection, and lack of parent-child involvement; (2) medium predictors: background variables such as parents' marital relations and parental criminality; and (3) weaker predictors: lack of parental discipline, parental health, and parental absence. Research by other scholars confirm these findings (Patterson and Dishion, 1985; Johnson, 1986; Farrington, Ohlin, and Wilson, 1986; and Laub and Sampson, 1988).

Wilson and Herrnstein (1985) and Hirschi (1983) express the view that the field of the family severed its connections with criminological matters beginning in the fifties for ideological reasons which favored examination of larger social institutions. Elliott Currie in *Confronting Crime* (1985, pp. 183–184) also indicates that interest in the relationship between the family and delinquency reflects broader ideological trends in society rather than the fruits of any new research breakthroughs.

Conservative writers who have more recently dominated the literature such as Hirschi (1983) and Wilson and Herrnstein (1985) seem to view material disadvantage and quality of family life as mutually exclusive explanations. Currie calls this belief, that what goes on in the family is somehow separate from outside social forces that affect the family, the "fallacy of autonomy" (Currie, 1985, p. 185). Those who commit this fallacy fail to view the family in a larger social context, have an obsessive concern with control rather than supportive social policies, and lend the impression of intractability of family problems, unresponsive to enlightened social policy.

Two influential works which challenge our criminological conception of family and crime are Daniel Moynihan's *Family & Nation* (1986) and Elliott Currie's *Confronting Crime* (1985). Moynihan reiterates his theme of the disintegration and siege of the American family, an issue which he claims should have concerned us in the sixties. He indicates that the individual has been the center of public policy in the U.S. rather than families. "This was a pattern almost uniquely American. Most of the industrial democracies of the world had adopted a wide range of social programs designed specifically to support the stability and viability of the family" (Moynihan, 1986, p. 5). While growth in federal entitlement programs since the sixties led to a major achievement—the virtual elimination of poverty among the elderly—by the 1980s the U.S. had achieved another unique distinction: it had become the first society in history in which a person is more likely to be poor if young rather than old.

The age bias of poverty is most pronounced affecting 24 percent of school age children. The principal correlate has been this change in family structure—the rise of female-headed households and the feminization of poverty. In 1984 nearly half of the poor in the U.S. lived in female-headed households (Ibid., p. 96). The percentage of such households nearly doubled from the 10 percent of all families in 1960. A flattening of the tax system and federal reduction in income maintenance programs constituted a federal family policy in reverse. While three-fourths of median family income in 1948 was exempt from federal tax (a powerful national family policy), by 1983 less than one-third of such income was exempt, although the new tax law promises to remove many low-income groups from the tax rolls.

While broken homes per se are an uncertain predictor of delinquency and crime, the stresses and lack of support systems that result in changed family functioning for the more impoverished and growing numbers of single mothers and children are of concern. Currie (1985, p. 219) states:

> The real issue is whether we regard the evidence on the persistence of family problems and the continuity of troubling behavior from childhood to adult life as indicative of predispositions that are largely unrelated to their social context and that we are virtually powerless to alter.
>
> One's marital status appears to have some effect upon propensity to arrest. Crime rates are lowest for married adults and highest for single and divorced adults. Much of this data, however, is based upon arrest and incarceration statistics, which tend to include younger persons and traditional crimes.

Education and Crime

The relationship between education (formal schools/schooling) and crime and delinquency is at least twofold. First, for adolescents in modern societies, schools, particularly high schools, represent a major force in their self-esteem at a very important stage in their lives. Secondly, there is an inverse (negative) relationship between the amount of formal schooling individuals possess and arrest rates for traditional crimes.

The fact that traditional crime commission decreases with the amount of formal education simply reflects the fact that legitimate opportunities increase with formal education as well as higher occupational and corporate criminal opportunities, which are less likely to be criminally stigmatizing. It is not formal education per se that causes or does not cause crime; rather, educational status reflects one's social class background, location of residence, and exposure to criminal and/or delinquent opportunity.

Research on crime and delinquency has come to focus most heavily upon family and education as critical variables (Hawkins and Lishner, 1987; and Wilson and Lowry, 1987). Moynihan (1986, p. 92) cites a study commissioned by the National Association of Elementary School Principals (1980) entitled, *The Most Significant Minority: One-Parent Children in the Schools*, in which one-parent kids were twice as likely to drop out and showed significantly lower achievement in school.

Fagan and Wexler (1987) argue that social influences outside the family are very strong, such as schools, peers, and community, and that the role of the family alone should not be overstated. Fagan, Piper, and Moore (1986) note that violent delinquents in inner cities differ from nondelinquents in their attachment to school, peers, and weak maternal authority among other variables. They indicate (Ibid., p. 463):

> Complex social, economic and political factors are contributing to the creation of a vast new class of poor persons who are younger, more poorly educated and more likely to give birth sooner. One of the predictable consequences of this phenomenon is the continuing isolation of inner-city communities and a hardening of the processes observed among these samples . . . These findings suggest that delinquency policy should be linked with economic development policy. The infusion of material and social resources into inner-city neighborhoods may strengthen social institutions including schools and families and alter the familiar correlates of serious delinquency by providing for the natural controls which characterize lower-crime neighborhoods.

Denno (1985) indicates that a major predictor of delinquency is misconduct in school. An example of a highly successful program is Head Start, a program for preschool enrichment. Schweinhart and Weikart

These children participated in a Head Start program in Mississippi, intended to both alleviate poverty by educating disadvantaged children, and promote racial integration.

(1980) in evaluating such a program for disadvantaged black children found better later elementary school performance, graduation from high school, employment, and less crime and delinquency (Farrington, Ohlin, and Wilson, 1986). Adler (1983) in a previously cited study of low crime nations analyzed forty-seven variables and found the only factor common to all low crime countries was strong social controls outside the formal system of justice. This well illustrates the fact that crime and justice matters are not to be treated in isolation from general societal conditions.

War and Crime

War, armed conflict between nations, has an impact on crime. Though it is an example of institutionalized violence, elements of war itself may be considered violations of international law, although the precarious state of the interpretation and enforcement of such laws will be discussed later (in the chapter on political crime). Viewed from this perspective, Hitler and Stalin were probably the largest mass murderers in history. Social conflict theorists such as Simmel (1955) and Coser (1956) tell us that conflict with an outside group tends to increase the internal solidarity within groups; that is, as conflict with outside enemies increases, conflict within groups decreases.

During major wars, the domestic crime rate on a whole tends to decline. This probably reflects increased social solidarity, group cohesion, against an outside enemy, and high employment. Juvenile delinquency tends to increase during such periods due to displacement of families and increased mobility. As noted earlier, female crime rates increase due to increased opportunity. A major form of crime that tends to increase during wartime is "white collar crime" such as black-marketing, profiteering, wartime trade violations, violations of wage-price freezes, and the like (Sutherland and Cressey, 1974, pp. 240–241).

Archer and Gartner (1984, pp. 79–81) using their "Comparative Crime Data File" found nations participating in World Wars I and II were more likely to experience postwar increases in homicide than control nations (those who had not participated). The differences are similar, but less pronounced, for smaller wars. They found their data supporting a "legitimation of violence model" (Ibid., p. 92) in which wars tend to legitimate the general use of violence in domestic society.

Economy and Crime

In summarizing the diverse literature on the relationship between economic trends and crime, Sutherland and Cressey (1974, pp. 225–226) draw the following conclusions:

- Serious crimes have a slight and inconsistent tendency to rise in periods of economic depression and to fall in periods of prosperity.
- The general crime rate does not increase significantly in periods of economic depression.
- Property crimes involving violence tend to increase in periods of depression; but property crimes involving no violence, such as larceny, show only a slight and inconsistent tendency to increase in depression periods.
- Juvenile delinquency tends to increase in periods of prosperity and to decrease during periods of depression.

Using data from the U.S., Canada, England, Scotland, and Wales, Brenner (1978) examined historical data for all major crimes since 1900 and their relationship to employment/unemployment, per capita income, inflation, and other economic indices. He found in all five political areas that the rate of unemployment showed strong and significant relationships to increases in *all* major categories of crime (Ibid., p. 562). There is a significant difference in these statistics for before and after World War II. There is a speeding up or a quicker reaction to unemployment since World War II, particularly an increase in violent crimes. The United States in particular demonstrated inverse (negative) correlations between employment and incarceration rates (see also Cantor and Land, 1985).

Currie (Skolnick and Currie, 1988, p. 471) argues that conservative criminologists tend to underemphasize the impact of economic forces on crime. He points out that, while little crime increase took place during the Depression, it rose during the more prosperous sixties. Currie feels there is a strong, although subtle, relationship and that those who underemphasize the economy ignore three factors (Ibid.):

> First, subgroups with high crime rates—such as young black males—do have high unemployment rates, even when overall unemployment is low. Second, unemployment has a different impact when it portends a lifetime of diminished opportunity. And finally, unemployment statistics do not reflect the *quality* of available work.

Mass Media and Crime

A subject of continual heated debate is and has been the role of the mass media in encouraging crime, particularly crimes of violence. Do comic books, newspapers, and magazines, movies, and/or television cause an increase in crime? This protracted debate is periodically fueled by crimes, particularly brutal ones, that appear to have some link with the media coverage or fictionalization of criminal events.

Two rival hypotheses exist with respect to media and violence: the *catharsis hypothesis* and the *precipitation hypothesis.* The former claims that exposure to media violence enables a vicarious letting off of steam and thus results in a calming effect. This notion comes to us from the Greek tragedies, in which it was assumed that audiences, as a result of identification with the travail and horrible experiences of the characters, would breathe an inevitable sigh of relief that, after all, it was only fiction. The precipitation hypothesis assumes that exposure to media coverage of violence, fact or fiction, will produce greater propensities to aggression and violence.

In a report entitled *Television and Behavior,* the Department of Health and Human Services (1982) concluded on the basis of a review of the research literature that there is an association between the viewing of television violence and aggression. One finding that seems continually to present itself is the image of society that television creates. In an American Broadcasting Company poll of viewers (ABC, 1983c) 51 percent thought television news gives too much coverage to crime and violence and that this distorts the public view of what is really going on in the streets; leads to the perception that crime is more rampant and a person more likely to be victimized than is, in fact, the case; and brainwashes us into fear, suspicion, and feelings of vulnerability. Glaser (1978, p. 236) indicates that television networks exert pressure against federal sponsorship of research on the impact of television on violence and for the suppression of reports on such research for fear of public boycotts (Cater and Strickland, 1975). The National Institute of Mental Health, in its review of the literature, concluded that violence on television was one factor in children's aggressiveness, although not necessarily in their violence (ABC, *20/20,* 1983b).

One key in explaining media precipitation of violence seems to lie in the fact that portrayals of violence appear to have different effects upon different viewers. Individuals vary in their vulnerability to suggestion (Belson, 1978), with physically aggressive boys both favoring watching televised violence as well as practicing it (McCarthy et al., 1975; Bandura, 1973; and Leftkowitz, et al., 1977). Nettler (1982, p. 265), in a review of such studies, concluded that "Evidence points to the possibility that persons in 'poor psychological and social health' are more vulnerable to lethal suggestions" (Liebert and Baron, 1972; and Comstock, 1975).

In the U.S., the Surgeon General's Scientific Advisory Committee on Television and Social Behavior (1972) sponsored twenty-three independent research projects to examine the impact of television upon violence. They claimed:

By the time the average American child graduates from high school he had seen on television some 18,000 murders and countless highly detailed incidents of robbery, arson, bombing, forgery, and torture. One hundred forty-six research articles based on 50 studies involving 10,000 children had all shown that viewing violence increased aggressive behavior in the young. A review of the literature on the subject did not reveal a single study which showed that violence did not have such an effect.

—cited in Haskell and Yablonsky, 1983, p. 199

In 1981 John Hinckley attempted to kill President Reagan because of his infatuation with Jodie Foster and the character she portrayed in the movie *Taxi Driver*.

In support of the precipitation hypothesis, Glaser (1978, p. 235) states: "The $30 billion spent annually in the United States on advertising—about $5 billion of it on television—suggests that many people have faith in the impact of mass communication on conduct."

The subject of the impact of mass media upon crime will continue to be a subject of hot debate. This writer agrees with the conclusions drawn by the Surgeon General's Committee (1972, p. 230) and although their suggestions were specifically intended for televised violence and children, these recommendations could be applied to studies of the media in general. More studies of the effect of television alone are not needed. What is needed are studies which identify predispositions of subgroups, reactions by age of subjects, the moderating influences of labeling, contextual cues, and other factors, as well as more longitudinal studies.

Copycat Crimes

The issue of differential impacts of the media upon different subgroups can be illustrated by means of the notion of "copycat crimes." The term "copycat" is an American slang expression for imitation; thus, "copycat crime" refers to fads in crime, those that are often stimulated by media coverage or portrayals. Haskell and Yablonsky (1983, p. 222) claim that "violent sociopaths seek out literary and historical materials that synthesize the violent fantasies they already harbor in their minds." While most observing such fictional portrayals are unaffected, the distorted few may find role models.

"I wish I could write a book and not have to make a living" (Nash, 1981, p. 125). Following his own advice, convicted Watergate criminal John Dean along with many other of his convicted Watergate conspirators began capitalizing on an American tradition: making money on describing how their crimes were committed. This practice, according to Nash (1981, p. 128), was begun by Henry Tufts who penned a manual for horse thieves in 1807 and by D. W. Griffith with the first gangster film, *The Musketeers in Pig Alley*, which employed actual gangsters (Nash, 1981, p. 157).

Clarke (1982, pp. 180–181) cites the case shown in the 1976 film *Taxi Driver* that starred Robert DeNiro and Jodie Foster. Richard Bremer, attempted assassin of presidential candidate George Wallace, had a love life which resembled that of Travis Bickle, the character portrayed by DeNiro, who attempts to develop a relationship with an attractive campaign worker and shocks her by taking her to a porno film. *Taxi Driver* was produced after the release of Bremer's diary and apparently the Bickle character was modeled in part on Bremer's personality. In an odd case of "fact imitating fiction which imitated fact," in 1981, John Hinckley, Jr., attempted assassin of President Ronald Reagan, revealed a love obsession with the teenage prostitute character portrayed by Jodie Foster in the film and an identification with the Bickle character who had expressed his love by means of violence. Ironically, after having attempted to assassinate Wallace, Bremer was cited as having stated: "How much do you think I'll get for my autobiography?" (Peter, 1977, p. 516).

The persuasive appeal of the media for some has been illustrated by imitative patterns in juvenile gangs in the films (*The Wild One*, *The Warriors*), Russian roulette (*The Deer Hunter*), prison escapes via helicopter, and other "copycat" patterns. Of particular concern are possible media "glorification" or "immortalization" of criminals as well as detailed instructions in the techniques of crime.

In order to prevent criminals from earning money publicizing their crimes, New York State passed the "Son of Sam" law (named after David "Son of Sam" Berkowitz, a serial murderer). Thirty-five other states had joined New York by the late eighties in putting the earnings from such books into escrow accounts and encouraging victims to civilly sue.

Criminal Typologies

One limitation of many discussions of crime and of theories of crime causation is the global manner in which the concept of crime is employed. To expect criminologists to address the question, "What causes crime?" is comparable to asking medical pathologists to answer the query, "What causes sickness?" "What *type* of sickness?" or "What *type* of crime?" are the next logical steps in attempting to approach these questions. While the only thing most sicknesses have in common is that they have produced an unhealthy biological state, the only thing most crimes hold in common is the fact that they are at a given point in time a violation of criminal law. Thus cancer, polio, and the common cold probably have about as much in common as shoplifting, embezzlement, and murder.

While it is important that the field of criminology continue with theoretical work to explain crime and criminal behavior as a whole, it is also important and perhaps more expeditious in the short run to explain particular criminal behaviors. Until an acceptable general theory is developed, is it desirable to delimit the specific areas to which a theory is applicable, to coordinate these theories, and hopefully build a general theory. We need both general as well as specific theories and must avoid confusing the two.

Criminal typologies refer to attempts to classify or derive types of crimes and criminals. These attempts may represent one of the oldest theoretical and practical approaches to crime. Although the work of Lombroso (to be discussed in greater detail in Chapter 4) is often pointed to as the beginnings of criminal typologies, the tradition of attempting to classify lawbreakers precedes him (Schafer, 1976, p. 104; 1969, pp. 140–182). Criminal typologies are based upon various criteria. Vantage Point 3.5 outlines a few of the better known efforts to develop typologies of criminals or criminal behavior.

A Critique of Typologies

Typologies can have two purposes: (1) to be used as a scientific classificatory system, or (2) to be utilized as a heuristic scheme. The former effort exists in taxonomical classifications in biology where life forms are sorted into categories such as phylum, species, and the like on the basis of physical characteristics. Related to this tradition are prison classification systems (Fox, 1976, pp. 345–361) which attempt to line up criminal offense records with treatment regimes. This effort has obviously been limited by inadequacies of offense records themselves for the purposes of classifying individuals. Many critics of the typological approach expect typologies to meet rigorous taxonomical refinement. Their critiques of typologies include:

- Specific offenses vary according to time and place.
- Some offenders exhibit great diversity, participating in more than one behavior system, or may in fact change their offense profile.
- No typology can contain purely homogeneous types.
- The number of career criminals specializing in one type of offense is smaller than has been suggested by the typologies developed thus far (Conklin, 1982, p. 354).
- Some typologies attempt to make types of crimes and criminals more distinct from each other than they really are, thus oversimplifying reality (Ibid., p. 16).
- No single typology is useful to group all offenders (Thomas and Hepburn, 1983, p. 262).
- Typologies overemphasize unique aspects and minimize similarities among types (Ibid.).

Feeling that the use of typologies as a taxonomical system is trivial, Gibbons, who has grown more skeptical of the typological approach, admits that many criminals "defy pigeonholing" (Gibbons, 1982 p. 263) and further states:

Typological systems that sort offenders into relatively homogeneous types do have *heuristic value* [italics mine], alerting us to broad categories of law-breakers that make up the criminal population. However, they put forth an oversimplified characterization of the real world of criminality and criminals. Many criminals are "situational casual" criminals who are involved in various forms of short-run criminality, such that they do not fall into any clear-cut type, syndrome, or role-career (Ibid., p. 232).

A Defense of Typologies

The real value of criminal typologies is their heuristic benefit in providing a useful, illustrative scheme, a practical device which, although subject to abstraction and overgeneralization, enables us to simplify and make sense of complex realities. Any ideal types are prone to over-

---

Vantage Point

Vantage Point 3.5 — Some Sociological Typologies of Criminal Behavior

Gibbons's "Criminal Role Careers"

1. Professional thieves
2. Professional "heavy" criminals
3. Semiprofessional property offenders
4. Naïve check forgers
5. Automobile thieves — "joyriders"
6. Property offenders —"one-time losers"
7. Embezzlers
8. White-collar criminals
9. Professional "fringe violators"
10. Personal offenders, "one-time losers"
11. Psychopathic assaultists
12. Statutory rapists
13. Aggressive rapists
14. Violent sex offenders
15. Nonviolent sex offenders
16. Incest offenders
17. Male homosexuals
18. Opiate addicts
19. Skid Row alcoholics
20. Amateur shoplifters

SOURCE: Don C. Gibbons, 1982, *Society, Crime and Criminal Behavior*, 4th ed., Englewood Cliffs, NJ: Prentice-Hall, p. 225.

Schafer's "Life Trend" Typology of Criminals

1. Occasional criminals
2. Professional criminals
3. Abnormal criminals
4. Habitual criminals
5. Convictional criminals

SOURCE: Stephen Schafer, 1976, *Introduction to Criminology*, Reston, VA: Reston Publishing Co., pp. 107–108.

simplification, but without them the categorical equivocations in discussing reality become overwhelming. Although critics of typologies have many good points, it would be interesting to have any of them attempt extensive discussion of crime or criminal behavior at any length without using implicit typologies often consisting of the very labels that have been rejected. Sanders (1983, p. 11) makes a cogent point:

> It is important to understand that criminologists cannot explain everything about every possible crime. Rather by looking at several crimes, either over a long period of time, committed by certain groups, committed in certain areas, or in comparison between different groupings, it is possible to learn about the typical and general patterns of criminal behavior.

The first purpose of typologies as classificatory systems requires empirical verification using actual quantitative research, while the

---

Lombroso's Types of Criminals

1. Born criminals   **3.** Occasional criminals
2. Criminaloids   **4.** Criminals by passion

SOURCE: Gina Lombroso-Ferrero, 1972, *Criminal Man According to the Classification of Cesare Lombroso*, Montclair, NJ: Patterson Smith, p. 100.

Abrahamsen's Types of Criminals

1. Acute criminals   **2.** Chronic offenders
   a. situational   **a.** neurotic
   b. associational   **b.** psychopathic
   c. accidental   **c.** psychotic

SOURCE: David Abrahamsen, 1960, *The Psychology of Crime*, New York: Columbia University Press, p. 14.

Glaser's Types of Crime

1. Predatory crime   **4.** Illegal consumption offenses
2. Illegal-performance offenses   **5.** Disloyalty offenses
3. Illegal selling offenses   **6.** Illegal status offenses

SOURCE: Daniel Glaser, 1978, *Crime in our Changing Society*, New York: Holt, Rinehart and Winston, p. 15.

second purpose recognizes that concepts or typologies as ideal types have qualitative, heuristic value. They sensitize or alert us to and are useful in explaining critical features of reality even though as ideal or constructed types they obviously oversimplify that same reality. McKinney (1966, p. 7) makes this point succinctly: "The constructed type is a special kind of concept in that it consists of a set of characters wherein the relations between the characteristics are held constant for the purposes at hand. Hence, the type is a pragmatically constructed 'system.'"

Criminal Behavior Systems

As an organizing, heuristic scheme, this text will make use of a variation of a typology of criminal behavior systems originally developed by McKinney (1966) and elaborated by Clinard and Quinney (1973) in their now classic work, *Criminal Behavior Systems: A Typology*. This typology is based upon constructed types "that serve as a means by which concrete occurrences can be compared and understood within a system of characteristics that underlie the types." Clinard and Quinney (1973, p. 250) identify nine types of criminal behavior:

1. Violent personal crime
2. Occasional property crime
3. Occupational crime
4. Corporate crime [which was added to the typology later]
5. Political crime
6. Public-order crime
7. Conventional crime
8. Organized crime
9. Professional crime.

These types are based upon four characteristics:

1. The criminal career of the offender
2. Group support of the criminal behavior
3. Correspondence between criminal behavior and legitimate behavior and
4. Societal reaction and legal processing of offenders.

Clinard and Quinney admit that there are undoubtedly other ways of delineating crime into types along these four characteristics; however, the typology serves useful purposes that permit the ordering of presentation of research on various forms of crime. Rather than using legal categories for the organization of materials, the purpose is to derive as few categories of crime, based upon behavior similarities, as possible in order to simplify analysis. Chapters 6 through 12 will concentrate upon crime and criminal activity making use of a variation of elements of this typology.

Summary

In examining descriptions and statistical accounts of crime and criminals it is important to examine the data base or source of findings and conclusions. Official statistics, victim surveys, self-reports, or other sources all will provide different pictures. Similarly, the type of criminal activity being addressed, whether traditional or elite, will provide different findings. Although they differ slightly in definitions of crime, concentrating upon the incident in the UCR and upon victims in NCS, the two measures are viewed as converging, with each providing certain information which the other lacks.

Estimates of the prevalence of crime depend upon the measure used, with the extent of crime increasing as we move from UCR to NCS to self-reports to estimates of corporate crime and other forms of criminality. The bulk of UCR Part I or *"index crimes"* consists of property crimes; the most frequent arrests among Part II crimes are for service functions. Trends in crime as measured by the UCR demonstrate a major crime wave in the United States since the mid-sixties. Comparison of trends using the NCS since the early seventies shows only a small increase, if not a stable pattern in criminal victimization. Despite the lack of good, representative self-report surveys of the general population, existing studies certainly suggest that crime is even more pervasive than is reported in the UCR and NCS.

Official statistics on crime indicate that most of those arrested are young (fifteen to nineteen years of age). This is particularly the case with serious property crimes. *Age* profiles obviously would be altered upward were we to have accurate estimates for corporate and "upperworld" violators. Of all demographic variables, *sex* is the best universal predictor of criminality: with the exception of prostitution, the male crime rate exceeds the female rate for all crimes, although the gap has been closing, particularly in developed societies. This difference in crime by sex can best be explained by cultural and socialization differences rather than by innate genetic ones. While some self-report studies demonstrate less of a gap, others indicate patterns like official data.

Official statistics show an inverse relationship between *social class* and criminality (as measured by arrests); that is, as social class increases, criminality decreases. This relationship remains a subject of debate. Most recent self-report surveys indicate that patterns of lower class admissions match those of official statistics. Such findings still do not belie the possibility of high upper class criminality, since their most typical offenses are not tapped by such sources.

In examining *race* and crime, the reader was informed of the precariousness of the scientific concept of "race" and that a goodly proportion of the "black" population in the U.S. might better be described as of "mixed" race. UCR arrest statistics indicate a black crime rate, particularly for violent crimes, that is in great excess of their proportion of the U.S. population. Despite countervailing biases in these statistics, it would appear that they are accurate descriptions of excess commission of these offenses. Most crime is intraracial in nature; that is, most whites victimize whites and most blacks victimize blacks. While self-report surveys show mixed results, more recent studies confirm higher rates among blacks for serious offenses.

Minority group status itself does not result in higher crime rates. Early research demonstrated high rates in the zone of transition despite turnover in the minority in residence. Some groups—Dutch and Japanese, for example—never appear to have had higher crime rates. The first generation of migrants generally has lower crime rates than the native population. It is their offspring, becoming Americanized to the lower class, who experience higher rates. Blacks have higher rates than other minorities in part due to: a maturing economy, the disability of race, late entry into the political system, and cultural factors. Crime patterns of European immigrants are similar to U.S. patterns, although many migrants are really temporary guest workers.

Official U.S. crime rates vary by *region*, with the South highest for murder and the West highest for rape, assault, burglary, and larceny and the Northeast highest for vehicle theft and robbery. International variations are difficult to determine due to inadequacies in crime statistics. Urban crime rates are generally higher than suburban and rural ones, particularly for property crimes. Recently, suburban and rural rates have been increasing more rapidly than urban rates.

While much has been written regarding the impact of the *family* on crime, with variables such as poor home discipline, neglect, indifference, parental criminality, and others identified as correlates, the key appears to be the quality of the family interaction rather than its structure as such. The impact of *education* and crime is highly intercorrelated with social class; however, track position in school was identified as a key variable in self-reported delinquency.

Major external conflicts (wars) appear to decrease internal conflicts (crime) with the exception of female crime, juvenile delinquency, and certain "white collar crimes." Studies of economic trends and crime show inconsistent results; however, since the end of World War II there has been a quicker crime increase, particularly in violent crimes, with dips in the economy.

The nature of the impact of *media u⃗* on crime is unresolved. While some propose a *catharsis hypothesis* (media violence as a vicarious tension-relieving function), others support a *precipitation hypothesis* (media violence as an encouragement of the acting out of fictional themes). Television portrayals of violence appear to create increased feelings of potential vulnerability on the part of the public. Surveys of the literature by the Department of Health and Human Services, the Surgeon General's Committee, and the National Institute of Mental Health all concluded that violence on television tends to increase aggressiveness in children. Media violence appears to have particular, although unpredictable, impacts on certain subpopulations of viewers. This point was illustrated by means of "copycat crimes," imitation crimes due to media portrayal.

Criminal typologies (attempts to classify criminals or criminal behavior) have two purposes: (1) a scientific classification system, and (2) a heuristic (practical) scheme. While many criticisms have been levied against such typologies as pure scientific classes, the heuristic benefit of using criminal typologies as organizing schemes for presentation or discussion purposes remains. After briefly reviewing other typologies, Clinard and Quinney's typology of "criminal behavior systems" was presented. This examines nine criminal behavior systems: violent personal, occasional property, occupational, corporate, political, public-order, conventional, organized, and professional crime from the standpoint of their criminal career, group support, correspondence with legitimate behavior, and societal reaction and legal processing.

KEY CONCEPTS

Crime Trends	**Urban/Rural**	**Copycat Crimes**
Variations in Crime	**Institutions**	**Criminal Typologies**
Age	**Family**	**Criminal Behavior Systems**
Sex	**Education**	**Age/Crime Debate**
Social Class	**War**	**Androcentric Bias**
Race	**Economy**	**Fallacy of Autonomy**
Minority Status	**Mass Media**	**Feminization of Poverty**
Region	**Catharsis Hypothesis**	
International	**Precipitation Hypothesis**	

4 Criminological Theory I: Early, Classical, and Positivistic Theories

In Chapter 1, *theory* was discussed as referring to plausible explanations of reality, a reasonable and informed guess as to why things are as they appear. Theorizing represents a leap of faith, an élan vital (vital force) with which to shed light upon the darkness of reality. The term "theory" is derived from the Greek "theoros," to observe and reflect upon the meaning of an event. Representatives from the city-states were sent to observe celebrations in honor of the gods and were asked to attempt to separate themselves from their personal views and try to conceive of what the gods wished. Without incisive theories, a field or discipline becomes a hopeless catalog of random and seemingly unrelated facts. However, theories are not laws or facts, though this is sometimes forgotten by those who become convinced of the correctness of a particular theory which they come to espouse. Thus, as powerful and persuasive as they may be, Freudian and Marxist theories, for example, are just that— theories: general or systemic models of how human personalities or societies function.

According to Turner (1974, p. 2):

> Theorizing can be viewed as the means by which the intellectual activity known as "science" realizes three principal goals: (1) to classify and organize events in the world so that they can be placed into perspective, (2) to explain the causes of past events and predict when, where, and how future events will occur, and (3) to offer an intuitively pleasing sense of "understanding" why and how events should occur.

Pure and Applied Theory

In Chapter 2, we distinguished between pure research, which is concerned with advancing the knowledge base of a discipline, and applied research, which is concerned with finding or prescribing solutions to immediate problems or needs. Similarly, *pure theory* is concerned with the search for cause and basic principles underlying phenomena, while *applied theory* attempts to provide practical explanations with which to guide existing policy. The rift that often exists between pure and applied researchers may also be evident between pure and applied theorists.

Often pure theorists' efforts to explain or understand crime causation—which account for most theories to be presented in this and the next chapter—are viewed as attempts to justify and excuse crime and/or as being wholly inadequate in guiding practical, existing social policy. Explanation of why or how things happen should not be confused with justification or defending why things happen lest we risk killing the messenger bearing bad news. The uninitiated find review and critique of these theories a futile exercise in self-flagellation in which criminologists parade their dirty laundry in bitter debates between warring camps of theorists. High hopes are raised for the discovery of a "key" to explaining all crime and criminality, though no such breakthroughs have occurred in the parent social sciences — sociology, psychology, political science, or economics — themselves, and many of the same competing schools persist in these fields. Those who are uncomfortable with such a theoretical morass might best be advised to study chemistry or biology or auto mechanics — fields in which the theoretical and empirical turf is tidier; the subject matter of the social sciences is infinitely more complex and not likely to yield to a general theory of universal acceptance in the near future.

In the meantime, what of the demands of applied theorists and practitioners for explanations with which to guide immediate policy? Some have abandoned pure theory as fruitless in providing guidelines for existing policy needs and then propose therapies, treatments, and policies which surprisingly are based upon one or the other of the pure theories they have rejected. In reality, criminology as an interdisciplinary field requires both pure and applied theory. The search for basic, underlying cause is important in itself for the mature development of the discipline, while obviously applied theories need not and cannot wait until ultimate laws are discovered before attempting to advocate existing policy programs. Fields are able to utilize workable applied theory without having resolved the issue of ultimate causal theory.

Much criminological theory, even the more modern variety, possesses a global or sensitizing quality which alerts us to critical issues but lacks the quality of containing formally testable, empirically verifiable propositions. It is to this same quality that Turner (Ibid., p. 9) refers when he states: "much of what is labeled sociological theory is, in reality, only a loose clustering of implicit assumptions, inadequately defined concepts, a few vague and logically disconnected propositions." Compared to the physical sciences, much theory in criminology also does not meet the formalized criteria in evaluating theory which is common in these fields.

Major Theoretical Approaches

This chapter will begin with an exploration of many early theories which represent the historical legacy of the field and will finish with a sketch of modern biological and psychological theories; the next chapter will explore more current sociological theories of crime. While many of the early theories have been discredited, their examination is warranted not only from the standpoint of gaining a sense of continuity of the discipline, but also because many expressions of these theories are resurrected in new forms in modern thinking.

Figure 4.1 presents an outline of the major theoretical approaches in criminology. The last type, sociological theory, will be subdivided and described in more detail in the following chapter. This division of criminological theories into types or schools of thought is primarily for convenient presentation purposes since, in fact, some theorists demonstrate evolution in their views and may in fact exhibit theoretical conceptions which meld different types or schools of thought. The primary theoretical approaches in criminology (Figure 4.1) are: the demonological, classical (neoclassical), ecological (geographic), economic, positivistic (biological and psychological), and sociological (which has many subtypes to be discussed in Chapter 5). Discussion will begin with the demon-

Figure 4.1: Major Theoretical Approaches in Criminology*

Theoretical School	Major Themes/Concepts	Major Theorists
Demonological	criminal as "evil," "sinner," "supernatural pawn"	traditional authority
Classical (Neoclassical)	criminal as "rational, hedonistic, free actor" "incapacitation, punishment, deterrence"	Beccaria, Bentham Wilson G. Becker
Ecological (Geographic)	"group characteristics, physical and social ecological impacts upon criminality" "geographical and climatic impacts upon criminality"	Quetelet & Guerry Lieber & Sherin
Economic	"capitalism, social class inequality and economic conditions cause crime"	Marx, Bonger
Positivistic Biological	"physical stigmata, atavism, biological inheritance causes criminality" "mental deficiency" "feeblemindedness" "physical inferiority" "somatotypes — mesomorphs" "brain disorders, twin studies, XYY syndrome, physiological disorders"	Lombroso, Ferri, Garofalo Goring Goddard Hooton Sheldon Moniz, Christiansen, Jacobs
Psychological	"unconscious repression of sexual instincts," "criminal personality," "extroversion," "inadequate behavioral conditioning," "IQ"	Freud, Eysenck, Skinner, Hirschi, Hindelang
Sociological	"anomie, subcultural learning, elite dominance cause crime"	Durkheim, Sutherland, Quinney

*See Figure 5.1 for greater detail regarding "sociological theory" in criminology.

ological or supernatural approach to explaining crime causation, a brief sketch of a superstitious and tradition-oriented past in which wrongdoers were perceived as controlled by otherworldly forces.

Demonological Theory

Demonological or supernatural explanations of criminality dominated thinking from early history well into the eighteenth century and still

The Salem Witch Trials in 1692 were one of the last times in America that demonic possession and supernatural forces were given as the cause of criminal behavior.

have modern remnants. In a system of knowledge in which theological explanations of reality were predominant, the criminal was viewed as a sinner who was possessed by demons or damned by otherworldly forces. Mankind was viewed as at the mercy of the supernatural: Fates, ghosts, furies, and/or spirits. Felonies (mortal sins) were viewed as manifestations of basically evil human nature reflecting either legion with the prince of darkness or an expression of divine wrath. The Salem Witch Trials in Puritan New England and the Spanish Inquisition serve as examples of the torture, burning at the stake, and other grim executions awaiting heretics, witches, and criminals. Such a world view perceived the violator's actions as deterministically controlled by forces beyond the individual's mastery. In Genesis (22:1–12) Abraham was ordered by God to sacrifice his son Isaac, although he was later released from this injunction. Appeasement of God or the gods, a world beyond human cognition and interpretable only by the clergy, the shaman, and other emissaries to the supernatural was supported by a traditional world view which looked to the "wisdom" of the past rather than a rational interpretation of the present for guidance (see Fox, 1976, pp. 7–12).

Application of the theological approach to crime control is not confined to the past but can be illustrated in the modern era by the ecclesiarchy (state-church fusion) in Iran under the Ayatollah Khomeini, in which criminals or opponents of the state are summarily subject to torture, death, or the "wrath of Allah." The primary challenge to theological approaches to explaining reality would present itself in the form of philosophical approaches to reality which would seek worldly, rational, secular explanations for human fate. The reasons for crime and criminality were to be found not in the supernatural, but the natural world.

Classical Theory

Prior to the formulation and acceptance of classical theory, the administration of criminal justice in Europe was cruel, uncertain, and unpredictable. In England alone in the early nineteenth century there were over one hundred crimes punishable by the death penalty (Heath, 1963, p. 98). Penal policy was designed to control the "dangerous classes," the mass of propertyless peasants, workers, and unemployed. Emerging liberal philosophies espoused by such writers as Locke, Hobbes, and Rousseau advocated the "natural rights of man" and reason as a guide to regulating human conduct. This Enlightenment of the seventeenth and eighteenth centuries questioned the power of the clergy and aristocracy and gave birth to the American and French revolutions.

Cesare Beccaria

Italian *Cesare Beccaria* (1738–1794), actually Cesare Bonesana, the Marquis of Beccaria, was, along with British philosopher Jeremy Bentham (1748–1832), the principal advocate of the classical school of criminological theory. Beccaria's (1963) essay entitled *On Crimes and Punishments*, originally published in 1764, had a profound impact upon continental European as well as on Anglo-American jurisprudence. His essential point is expressed in the concluding paragraph of this work (Ibid., p. 99):

> From what has thus far been demonstrated, one may deduce a general theorem of considerable utility, though hardly conformable with custom, the usual legislator of nations; it is this: In order for punishment not to be, in every instance, an act of violence of one or many against a private citizen, it must be essentially public, prompt, necessary, the least possible in the given circumstances, proportionate to the crimes, dictated by the laws.

Beccaria was appalled with the arbitrary nature of the European judicial and penal systems of his time, which were unpredictably harsh, which exacted confessions by means of torture, and which were completely subject to the whim of authorities. Since potential criminals had no way of anticipating the nature of the criminal law and its accompanying penalty if violated, punishment served little intended deterrent value. Beccaria was primarily interested in reforming the cruel, unnecessary, and unpredictable nature of punishment, feeling that it made little sense to punish lawbreakers with unjust laws (Vold and Bernard, 1986, p. 29). Beccaria was responsible for the abolition of torture as a legitimate means of exacting confessions. "Let the punishment fit the crime" is a succinct phrase by which to sum up Beccaria's argument.

Beccaria's British counterpart, Jeremy Bentham (1823), borrowed from Beccaria the notion that laws should provide "the greatest happiness shared by the greatest number" (Beccaria, 1963, p. 8). Bentham has been called an advocate of "utilitarian hedonism," or "felicific calculus" or "penal pharmacy." *Utilitarianism* is a practical philosophical view which claims "we should always act so as to produce the greatest possible ratio of good to evil for all concerned" (Barry, 1983, p. 106).

The classical theorists viewed individuals as acting as a result of "free will" and as being motivated by *hedonism*. The latter refers to a "pleasure principle," the assumption that the main purpose of life is to maximize pleasure while minimizing pain. Individuals are viewed as entirely rational in this decision-making process in which they will attempt to increase pleasure, even illicit desires, until the anticipated pain to be derived from a particular activity appears to outweigh the enjoyment to be derived. In a work entitled *Seductions of Crime: Moral and Sensual Attractions in Doing Evil*, Jack Katz's (1988) research based upon interviews with career criminals supports Beccaria's notion of the pleasure or thrill of evil outweighing punishment. Image, danger, glamour, the excitement of crime overshadows any desire for a successful life in straight society.

Critique of Classical Theory

The *classical school* and the writing of Beccaria in particular were to lay the cornerstone of modern Western criminal law as it became formulated from 1770 to 1812. The characteristics of modern Western criminal law—politicality, uniformity, specificity, and described penal sanctions—are in essence called for in Beccaria's essay. The French *Declaration of the Rights of Man* (Jacoby, 1979, p. 215), which was passed by the revolutionary National Assembly of France in 1789, included the statement: "The law ought to impose no other penalties but such as are absolutely and evidently necessary; and no one ought to be punished, but in virtue of a law promulgated before the offense, and legally applied." The Eighth Amendment to the U.S. Constitution, prohibiting "cruel and unusual punishment," was also a Beccarian legacy.

The revolutionary and liberating impact of the ascendancy of classical theory in reforming Western jurisprudence is now taken for granted, but without the fundamental changes which it introduced the remaining criticisms and subsequent modifications would not have been possible. However, classical theory contained the seeds of its own demise. While Justinia, the blind goddess of justice carefully weighing the evidence irrespective of the violator, is an appealing symbol, classical theory by its very insistence upon equality of punishment proposes inequality. Should minors or the insane be treated in the same manner as others? Should repeat offenders be accorded the same sanctions as first offenders for an equivalent act? Thomas and Hepburn (1983, p. 137) state:

> contemporary criminologists tend to assign little importance to its concepts and ideas. Perhaps the two major reasons are that it focuses our attention on criminal law rather than criminal behavior and that it is based on a speculative set of philosophical premises rather than a sound theory that could be verified or refuted by the collection of systematic empirical evidence.

Application of the pure classical theory would rob judges of discretionary power, and seems to rest upon a simplistic assumption of the ability to exactly measure individual conceptions of pain and pleasure.

Recent revivals in the United States of determinate sentencing and mandatory punishments for specific offenses are remnants of classical theory. Although theoretically appealing because of the essential cookbook application of graduated punishment reflecting the seriousness of crime, implementation becomes problematic for reasons already described: the quantification of such acts and their perpetrators defies such a simplistic scheme.

Neoclassical Theory

The neoclassical school basically admitted environmental, psychological, and other mitigating circumstances as modifying conditions to classic doctrine. The beginnings of this approach could be found as early as the later writings of Cesare Lombroso (1835–1909), himself and, more particularly, in those of his students, Ferri and Garofalo, to be discussed shortly. Beginning in the late sixties and particularly in the writings of economist Gary Becker (1968), James Q. Wilson (1983a and 1983b), and Ernest Van den Haag (1966), a resurgence in neoclassical doctrine can be noted. Becker advocated a "cost/benefit" analysis of crime, reminiscent of hedonistic doctrine. Disappointed with criminology's overconcern with the search for basic causes of crime, Wilson (1975) proposed a *policy analysis approach*, applied research which is less concerned with finding "causes" and more concerned with "what works." These writers have sparked an interest in the abandonment of treatment and rehabilitation and a call for the return to the classical punishment model. Often ignored by devotees of such theories are the very limited categories of crime such theorists in fact address. Wilson (Ibid.), for instance, quite clearly indicates that this call for incapacitation of offenders (criminals in jail can no longer victimize) is applicable to what we will describe as conventional property offenders or common burglars and thieves. Although a more practical, policies-oriented approach needs emphasis, what is disturbing in such theories is the relatively conservative ignorance of criminogenic, social structural conditions as well as an often cavalier disregard for theoretical approaches to crime causation. While the neoclassicists argue that less theory and more action is needed, they at times ignore the fact that the basic theoretical underpinnings of their own theories are rooted in assumptions of eighteenth-century hedonism, utilitarianism, and free will. On balance, however, they make a key point: that one need not have a basic explanation of cause or wait for one in order to meet pressing policy needs that cannot wait for final explanation.

Ecological Theory

While some would point to Cesare Beccaria and his writings as the beginning point of criminology, his primary interest was not so much in the analysis of crime and criminals as in the reform of criminal law and punishment. Others point to the writings of Cesare Lombroso, to be discussed shortly, and view the century between the works of the two Cesares as a criminological Dark Age. On the contrary, the writings and research of Frenchman A. M. Guerry (1802–1866) and Belgian Adolphe Quetelet (1796–1874) qualify them as the "fathers of modern criminology" (Vold and Bernard, 1986, p. 39; and Gibbons, 1982, p. 17). Thomas and Hepburn (1983, p. 138) best reflect this writer's view:

> It is hard to understand why so many criminologists persist in their apparent conviction that scientific criminology was not to be found until Lombroso. . . . Nevertheless, the wealth of scientific analyses published by those we can classify as members of the statistical [ecological] school are commonly ignored while the often absurd and poorly executed work of Lombroso is considered to be the first true criminological analysis.

Another explanation for the popularity and widespread acceptance of the Lombrosians and the relative obscurity of the early ecological theorists might be the fact that the latter were not translated into English until much later (Ibid., p. 152).

The ecological school of criminological theory is also referred to as the statistical, geographic, or cartographic. *Ecology* is that branch of biology that deals with the interrelationships between organisms and their environment. *Human ecology* deals with the interrelationship between human organisms and the physical environment. This school was called *statistical* because it was the first to attempt to apply official data and statistics to the issue of explaining criminality. The labels *geographical* and *cartographic* have been assigned due to the fact that writers in this group tended to rely upon maps and aerial data in their investigations.

A. M. Guerry and Adolphe Quetelet

Sometime after 1825, A. M. Guerry published what many regard as the first book in "scientific criminology" (Vold, 1979, p. 167). Guerry was more cartographic in his approach, relying exclusively upon shaded areas of maps in order to describe and analyze variations in French official crime statistics. Since he employed these sections of maps and used these as his principal unit of analysis, he is often viewed as the founder of the ecological or cartographic school of criminology (Thomas and Hepburn, 1983, p. 139). Another adherent of this school was Henry Mayhew (1862), who in his *London Labour and the London Poor* made extensive use of official statistics and aerial maps.

Quetelet (Lambert Adolphe Jacques Quetelet) was the first to take advantage of the criminal statistics that were beginning to become available in the 1820s (Radzinowicz and King, 1977, p. 64; and Beirne, 1987). He was the first scientific criminologist, employing an approach to his subject matter which was very similar to that of modern criminologists, and is the "father" of modern sociological and psychological statistics (Thomas and Hepburn, 1983, pp. 140, 145; Schafer, 1969, pp. 118–120; and Mannheim, 1965, pp. 96–98). Challenging the classical school's view that individuals exercise free will in deciding upon their actions, Quetelet insisted upon the impact of group factors and characteristics. In his *Treatise on Man and the Development of His Faculties* (1835, 1869) which was translated into English in 1842, Quetelet noted that there was a "remarkable consistency" with which crimes appeared annually and varied with respect to age, sex, economic conditions, and other sociological variables. This consistency in group behavior, in crime rates and the like, speaks against crime being solely a matter of individual choice. He argues (Quetelet, 1969, pp. 299–308):

> We can count in advance how many individuals will soil their hands with the blood of their fellows, how many will be swindlers, how many prisoners, almost as we can number in advance the births and deaths that will take place . . . Society carries within itself, in some sense, the seeds of all the crimes which are going to be committed, together with the facilities necessary for their development.

In a sense, the stage and script are provided by society and only the faces playing the individual characters change.

Some of Quetelet's findings included the propensity for crime among younger adults and males, and the tendency of crimes against persons to increase in summer and property crimes to predominate in winter. In what is called his famous "thermic law" of crime, he claimed that crimes against persons increase in equatorial climates while property crimes are most prevalent in colder climates (Fox, 1976, p. 64). Social conditions such as heterogeneity of population tended to be associated with increased crime as did poverty, although the latter not in the manner usually supposed. Noting that some of the poorest provinces of France also had very low crime rates, Quetelet anticipated the concept of "relative deprivation" by suggesting not absolute poverty but a gap between status and expectation as a variable in crime causation (Quetelet, 1969, pp. 82–96).

Critique of Ecological Theory

The work of Guerry and Quetelet took place nearly half a century prior to the writings of Lombroso, to be discussed shortly, who is often viewed ("the Lombrosian myth") as "the father of criminology" (Lindesmith and Levin, 1937). Lombroso's principal work *L'Uomo Delinquente* (the Criminal Man) first published in 1876 emphasized the notion of "born criminality." Rather than representing progress in criminological investigation, the dominance of the early positivists such as Lombroso may have put the field on over a half-century journey of using arcane and ultimately useless concepts. The superordination of the early positivists may have represented an ideological coup d'etat in which medical concepts and *psychologism* (a reduction of analysis solely to the individual level) temporarily retarded the early mainstream sociological efforts of the ecologists. Pointing the finger at the individual rather than social conditions as had Guerry and Quetelet was intellectually acceptable for the wealthy, who preferred to view criminality as an individual failing of the dangerous classes rather than a societal shortcoming (Vold and Bernard, 1986, p. 40; Lindesmith and Levin, 1937; and Radzinowicz, 1966).

On this point, Radzinowicz (Ibid., pp. 38–39) states:

> This way of looking at crime [the ecological school's approach] as the product of society was hardly likely to be welcome, however, at a time when a major concern was to hold down the "dangerous classes" . . . who had so miserable a share in the accumulating wealth of the industrial revolution that they might at any time break out in revolt in France. . . .
>
> It served the interests and relieved the conscience of those at the top to look upon the dangerous classes as an independent category, detached from the prevailing social conditions . . . a race apart, morally depraved and vicious. . . .

The social statisticians with their emphasis upon social facts, statistics, the use of official data, and external social factors were perhaps ahead of their time. Shortcomings in their analysis, such as lack of full awareness of the inadequacies of official statistics and appropriate use of statistics themselves, are excusable given their pioneering efforts and the state of knowledge of the time. The ecological school represented a critical transition from the philosophical and purely theoretical approach of Beccaria to the more scientific criminological approaches of the twentieth century.

Other Geographical Theories

The ancient origin of human interest in astrology and the assumed role of astrological bodies upon human behavior represent just one of many attempts to predict human emotion and activity on the basis of outside physical forces, the moon, the weather, climate, and the like. The word "lunatic," from the word luna, or moon, indicates the belief that human minds can be affected by phases of the moon. This is illustrated by legends and myths such as les lupins, werewolves in French folklore, which supposedly appeared on moonlit nights (Cohen, 1979, p. 87), and is dramatically presented in fiction in the introduction to the popular 1943 Universal Pictures film, *The Wolf Man*:

> Even a man who is pure in heart
> And says his prayers by night
> Can become a wolf when the wolfbane blooms
> And the moon is full and bright.

Cohen (Ibid., pp. 84–89) cites studies of mental hospital records which claim more admissions of mental patients during new and full moons, as well as a suicide prevention center and a coroner's study both indicating more successful suicides around the full moon period. The most frequently cited recent study of this type has been Lieber and Sherin's (1972) research on lunar cycles and homicides. They note that synodic cycles (phases of the moon) influence physical variables such as gravitation and atmospheric pressure which, in turn, influence human behavior. For instance, tidal periodicity is greatest at the period of new and full moon due to stronger gravitational influences. Assuming such forces may also affect human behavior, Lieber and Sherin analyzed homicide statistics for Dade County (Miami), Florida, and Cuyahoga County (Cleveland), Ohio, and found a statistically significant difference at full and new moon periods for the Dade County figures and a high, but not statistically significant, relationship for Cuyahoga County. Indicating that a lunar influence may exist, they explain the differences may be due to the fact that Florida is closer to the equator and would be more influenced by a stronger moon effect or gravitational pull. Other analyses of these same correlations, however, fail to support their hypothesis (Nettler, 1982, vol. 1, p. 31; Pokorny, 1964; and Pokorny and Jachimczyk, 1974). The bulk of such studies does not show a relationship and, although more replications are needed, criminological interest in this line of investigation has waned. Criminologists interested in geographical and ecological impacts upon criminality have focused their attention instead upon the social as well as manmade environment. "The Chicago school" of sociology and its contribution to American criminology will be detailed in the next chapter as an illustration of such an approach.

In examining a related line of inquiry, Fox (1976, p. 64) tells us that Quetelet's "thermic law" of crime was actually borrowed from Montesquieu, who claimed that criminality increases as one nears the equator, while drunkenness increases in proximity to the poles. Examination of official statistics both internationally and within the U.S., France, Great Britain, and Canada seems to generally support this hypothesis (see Brantingham and Brantingham, 1984, pp. 251–296). While statistical analysis of official crime reports such as the UCR indicates that rapes and other violent crimes are more prevalent in warmer months and that property crimes such as shoplifting are heaviest in December (Christmas season), these are more likely due to cultural rather than climatic effects (Cheatwood, 1988; and LeBeau, 1988). Brantingham and Brantingham (1984, p. 296), in analyzing spatial patterns in crime, indicate:

> Different crime patterns are associated with different demographic, economic, and social profiles. Homicide and assault are associated with high proportions of minority population, with poverty and low income, with low-status jobs and low education, and with income inequality. Robbery is highest in large, dense cities that rely on public transit and have high levels of pedestrian traffic. Burglary and theft rates are highest in cities with growing populations, with growing suburbs, and with low density.

In a related manner one can find that combinations of hot weather and foul air (polluted with airborne toxins such as ozone) may provoke violence, particularly family disputes.

> . . . the findings which link high levels of both pollution and crime do fit into the growing knowledge that, in the long run, many chemicals can cause nerve damage and behavioral changes.
>
> For example, scientists have known for years that mercury causes brain damage: the 19th century "mad hatters" stammered, twitched and trembled from inhaling mercury vapors in London hat factories. Today, many factories use masks and protective hoods to shield workers from the worst effects of chemicals (Londer, 1987, p. 6).

While recognizing that climate itself is not a major factor, but a precipitating or mitigating circumstance in deviant behavior, Lab and Hirschel (1988a and 1988b) emphasize studying the impact of the actual weather rather than seasonal or monthly data. Examining precipitation, humidity, temperature, and barometric pressure they indicate that, "Not a single text or journal article substantiates the lack of a relationship between weather and crime" (Ibid., 1988a, p. 282). They conclude that the potential for weather conditions playing a part in criminal activity is related to the perspective of "routine activities" (LeBeau and Langworthy, 1986) in which criminal behavior is viewed as part of normal, everyday behavior. These social ecological impacts upon criminal behavior will be discussed as well as critiqued in greater scope in the discussion of the "Chicago school" in the next chapter.

Forerunners of Modern Criminological Thought

The three thinkers who would have a critical impact upon the shaping of social ideas as well as criminological inquiry in the twentieth century did not even specifically address the issue of crime. Their ideas, however, would influence criminological theorists in a profound manner. The first figure was *Karl Marx* (1818–1883) whose *Communist Manifesto* (1848) and *Das Kapital (Capital)* (1867), the former coauthored with Friedrich Engels, emphasized the *economic* basis of societal conflict and would give birth to the economic school of criminology. The second was *Charles Darwin* (1809–1882) whose *Origin of Species* (1859) and *Descent of Man* (1871) and theories of *evolution*, natural selection, and survival of the fittest would heavily inspire the biological positivists, to be discussed shortly. Finally, the third was *Sigmund Freud* (1856–1939) whose many volumes dealing with *unconscious sexual motivation* would influence not only psychiatry, but the psychological positivists. These themes of economics, biology, and sex underlie a large number of the criminological theories to be discussed.

Economic Theory

Karl Marx

Karl Marx, the inspirational figure behind most economic criminological theories, was an economic determinist. He insisted that the economic substructure determines the nature of all other institutions and social relationships in society. In his view, the emergence of capitalism produces economic inequality in which the proletariat (workers) are exploited by the bourgeoisie (owners or capitalist class). This exploitation creates poverty and also is at the root of the existence of other social problems. Since Marx did not specifically address the issue of crime, Marxist criminologists draw upon his economic and philosophic writings and apply them to the crime issue.

Marx viewed the history of all existing societies as one of class struggle. Influenced by the writings of German philosopher Hegel, Marx described this conflict as a dialectical process in which thesis (existing ideas or institutions) spawn their opposites or antithesis until a final synthesis (new idea or social order) emerges. Thus for Marx,

Karl Marx's economic theories have been influential in the formulation of some criminological theories.

capitalism (thesis) breeds its own destruction by giving birth to a proletariat revolution (antithesis) and finally a new world order of socialism (synthesis). Since Marx applied Hegel's theory to the material world, this is often described as Marx's theory of dialectical materialism. For Marx the resolution of social problems such as crime would be achieved through the creation of a socialist society characterized by communal ownership of the means of production and an equal distribution of the fruits of these labors.

Willem Bonger

The foremost early Marxist criminologist was the Dutch philosopher Willem Bonger (1876–1940), whose most noted work was *Criminality and Economic Conditions* (1969), which first appeared in 1910. Bonger viewed the criminal law as primarily protecting the interests of the propertied class. In contrast to precapitalistic societies which he claimed were characterized by consensus and altruism, capitalistic societies emphasized egoism (selfishness). Capitalism was viewed as precipitating crime commission by creating unequal access to the necessities of life as well as by viewing success in economic competition as a sign of status (Turk, 1969b). Bonger's work provides a very detailed literature review of a large number of works of the time which examined the impact of economic conditions upon crime, a persistent theme since early times. In referring to the early Marxist orientation, Schafer (1969, p. 76) indicates:

> Napolean Colajanni, Enrico Ferri and Willem Bonger and a number of others in the last 150 years represented the same "new" trends that our radicals seem to claim as their invention. The classical authors presented these proposals in a scholarly fashion quite often superior to that of our modern radicals; in fact almost nothing is said today in this line that was not already written in criminology a century ago.

Greenberg (1981, p. 11) points out that a large number of early Marxist thinkers did not seriously consider the crime issue, viewing it with typical "Marxian contempt for the lumpen proletariat—the beggars, pimps and criminals" in capitalist society. Many writers with a distinctive Marxian and/or economic view of criminality are cited in the Bonger work (1969), although as Greenberg (Ibid.) correctly indicates, Bonger is often mistakenly viewed as the only early Marxist criminologist.

Some of the basic claims made by Bonger regarding criminality included (Turk, 1969b, pp. 7–12):

- Notions of what constitutes crime varies among societies and reflects existing notions of morality.
- Criminal law serves the interest of the ruling class in capitalist systems and is enforced by force rather than by consensus.
- Hedonism (pleasure seeking) is natural among people, but capitalism encourages egoism (selfish individualism) to an extreme and to the disadvantage of the society and the poor.
- All groups are prone to crime in capitalist society, but seldom are the crimes of the wealthy punished.
- Poverty resulting from capitalism encourages crime. The unequal distribution of rewards and encouragement of egoistic material accumulation encourages crime.
- Most crimes (other than those due to mental problems) would be eliminated in a socialist system in which the goods and wealth of a society would be equally distributed.

The writings of the early Marxist criminologists were more historical, analytic-inductive, and descriptive than empirical. The early Marxist theorists had the luxury of making theoretical predictions without empirical referents at the time. Marx and Bonger predicted the benefits of a socialist state which were compared hypothetically with the evils of early capitalism, which were a grim reality. Short-comings of socialism could not be observed. Modern radical and Marxist criminologists no longer have this luxury, as we will examine later in discussing the conflict and radical schools of criminology. As did Marx, Bonger insisted upon the conflict rather than the consensus model of criminal law, a dynamic rather than static conception of society. Despite the fact that Bonger's ideas contained the seeds of many potentially fruitful criminological conceptions, the positivistic detour inaugurated by Lombroso would lead to their relative dormancy in criminology until the 1970s. A critique of the Marxist approach will be undertaken in the next chapter when we discuss the modern conflict and radical, "Marxist" perspectives.

Positivist Theory

Positivism is a philosophical approach proposed by French sociologist Auguste Comte (1798–1857) and stated in the title of his work, *A System of Positive Polity* (1877), originally published in 1851. Comte proposed the use of empirical (quantitative) or scientific investigation for the improvement of society. Taylor et al. (1973, p. 22) indicate that the three basic premises of positivism are:

1. measurement (quantification)
2. objectivity (neutrality)
3. causality (determinism).

In applying Comte's approach, criminological positivists emphasize a consensus world view, a focus upon the criminal actor rather than the criminal act, a deterministic model (usually biological or psychological in nature), a strong faith in the scientific expert, and a belief in rehabilitation of "sick" offenders rather than punishment of "rational" actors. Stressing a scientific rather than philosophical orientation, there are three elements to the positivistic approach:

1. application of the scientific method
2. the discovery and diagnosis of pathology (sickness)
3. treatment (therapy or corrections).

Through the systematic application of the scientific method, the positivists seek to uncover the basic cause of crime and, once this is discovered, to prescribe appropriate treatments in order to cure the individual deviant. This section will examine precursors to positivism

Auguste Comte first proposed the Positivist approach. Positivism investigates the basic cause of crime through scientific methodology and uses the discoveries to cure individual deviants.

as well as the major types of positivism: early biological positivism, recent biological positivism, and psychological positivism.

Precursors to Positivism

Prior to and competing with emergent positivism were various popular pseudosciences, some of which had existed since ancient times. *Astrology* had been used much in the manner of modern newspaper horoscopes, to predict the fate of human behavior in terms of the alignment of the stars. The Copernican revolution and acceptance that the earth was not a fixed place in the universe discredited the basic premises of astrology, leaving it as a "hokum device" for fortune tellers and their superstitious clients.

Similar ideas whose time was rapidly passing were phrenology, physiognomy, and palmistry. *Phrenology* attempted to determine intelligence and personality on the basis of the size and shape of the skull and posited that certain areas of the brain corresponded to various psychological and intellectual characteristics. Writers such as Franz Gall (1758–1828) measured bumps on the head in order to identify brain development. Since sections of the brain do not completely govern specific personality characteristics and could hardly be detected by measuring configurations of skulls, phrenology was rapidly outpaced and replaced by the more scientific methods of emergent positivism.

Physiognomy involved measuring facial and other body characteristics as indicative of human personality, while *palmistry* was concerned with "palm reading," interpreting lines on the palm with which to predict future behavior. These theories have been discredited, simply due to the fact that they were unable to provide any proof of accuracy in their forecasts and were rapidly overtaken by developments in modern biology and the social sciences.

Biological Positivism

As previously indicated, the works of Charles Darwin, beginning in the mid-nineteenth century, had a profound impact upon theory in the social sciences as well as on criminology. Concepts such as evolution, natural selection, survival of the fittest, and human genetic connections to a savage past captured the imaginations of theorists in the young social sciences, including criminology.

Cesare Lombroso

Cesare Lombroso (1835–1909) sometimes, in this writer's and others' (Thomas and Hepburn, 1983; Mannheim, 1965, pp. 96–98; and Lindesmith and Levin, 1937) opinions, erroneously called "the father of criminology," was certainly the most influential figure in biological positivism. Although he is best known for his early work—which gives an overly simplistic picture of his later, more sophisticated writing— Lombroso's ideas are important due to the large number of adherents and subsequent research which he inspired. His most important work was *L'uomo Delinquente (The Criminal Man)*, first published in 1876. Lombroso was highly influenced by Darwin's theory of evolution, and this led him to the development of his theory of "atavism"—that criminals were "throw-backs" to an earlier and more primitive evolutionary period. Such born criminals could be identified by certain "physical stigmata," outward appearances, particularly facial, which tended to distinguish them from noncriminals. He claimed to have made his discovery almost by serendipity during the autopsy of a criminal, which he was performing in his duties as a prison physician (Lombroso, 1911, p. xiv, in Wolfgang, 1960, p. 184):

> This was not merely an idea, but a revelation. At the sight of that skull, I seemed to see all of a sudden, lighted up as a vast plain under a flaming

sky, the problem of the nature of the criminal—an atavistic being who reproduces in his person the ferocious instincts of primitive humanity and the inferior animals. Thus were explained anatomically the enormous jaws, high cheek-bones, prominent superciliary arches, solitary lines in the palms, extreme size of the orbits, handle-shaped or sessile ears found in criminals, savages, and apes, insensibility to pain, extremely acute sight, tattooing, excessive idleness, love of orgies, and the irresistible craving for evil for its own sake, the desire not only to extinguish life in the victim, but to mutilate the corpse, tear its flesh, and drink its blood.

Some examples of *physical stigmata* provided by Lombroso sound similar to characteristics Hollywood directors would search for in casting the villain on the silver screen: excessive jaw and cheek bones, eye defects, large or small ears, strange nose shape, protruding lips, sloped foreheads, and the like.

While Lombroso's early work was well received at the time, it is not seriously regarded today. What remains, however, was his emphasis upon observation, data collection, and the need to obtain positive facts to support theory. When his theories of atavism came under attack from mounting evidence to the contrary, Lombroso modified his theories, although still indicating that atavism existed in about a third of all criminals. His other categories were the insane criminal, the epileptic criminal, and the occasional criminal, hardly an exhaustive, comprehensive list of criminal types.

Lombroso's notions of *biological determinism* of criminality were very compatible with the ideological climate of the late nineteenth century in which the philosophy of social Darwinism provided intellectual backing to the harsh realities of emergent industrial capitalism. *Social Darwinism* claimed that there is a "survival of the fittest" in society, among men and social institutions. The success or failure of individuals in competing in society was not to be interfered with, since they were all part of a natural system of societal evolution. The Lombrosian model, minimizing the importance of social conditions such as inequality, and ignoring the extensive literature of the ecological school, pointed the blame for criminality at the individual rather than the society. This triumph of Lombrosian theory represented a "seizure of power of the medical profession who viewed criminology as a branch of medicine" (Lindesmith and Levin, 1937, p. 669; and, Bottomley, 1979, p. 44). Criminal behavior was viewed as a matter of "defective" individuals who were unable to adjust to an otherwise healthy society, the unfit in the struggle for survival.

The other two important figures in the Italian or continental school of positivists were Lombroso's students, Enrico Ferri (1856–1929) and

Raffaelo Garofalo (1852–1934). Ferri's *Criminal Sociology* (1917) was first published in 1878, and Garofalo's *Criminology* (1914) was originally published in 1884. Lombroso, Ferri, and Garofalo have been called "the holy three of criminology" by Stephen Schafer (1969, p. 123).

Enrico Ferri proposed four types of criminals: insane, born, occasional, and those who were criminal by passion. He proposed a multiple-factor approach to crime causation, admitting both individual and environmental factors. Often ignored in considering the diversity of Ferri's views was the fact that long before twentieth-century criminologists began to consider the shortcomings of official statistics, Ferri (1917, p. 77, cited in Vold, 1979, p. 173) proposed his "law of criminal saturation." Similar to a Parkinson's law of criminology, Ferri suggested that crime expands to fit the amount of control machinery assigned to it. Traveling widely as a visiting professor throughout Europe and South America spreading the evangelism of the new positivism, he later became a supporter of Mussolini. Vold (1979, p. 42) indicates: "The end of Ferri's career, ascent to Fascism, highlights one of the problems of positivistic theory, namely, the ease with which it fits into totalitarian patterns of government." Raffaelo Garofalo strongly advocated social Darwinism, the physical elimination of the "unfit" and their offspring, and also became a supporter of Mussolini's fascist regime.

Early positivism contributed theoretically to a scientific approach to criminology and inspired others to study the subject, but otherwise little remains of it in current criminological theory. Lombroso and his colleagues used poor sampling techniques, their findings were statistically insignificant, and they ignored the fact that physical stigmata were most likely an environmental defect (due to poverty and malnutrition). Moreover, modern genetics negates their atavism theory. Their findings have been refuted by later investigators, particularly by their earliest and most vehement critic, Charles Goring.

Charles Goring

Charles Goring (1870–1919) in 1913 published *The English Convict*, the results of a study begun in 1902 of 3,000 English convicts and comparison groups of college students, hospital patients, and soldiers. He compared these "criminals" with "noncriminals" with respect to physical characteristics, personal histories, and mental qualities. The only differences he was able to discover were that criminals were shorter and weighed less and, most importantly, were "mentally defective." While refuting Lombroso's physical stigmata, a distinctive physical criminal type, as a characteristic, he launched yet another search for hereditary mental deficiency as the cause of crime.

While Goring refuted Lombroso's notion of physical differences, his own methodology was critically flawed. Eschewing the then available Simon-Binet tests of mental ability, he used his own impressions in order to operationalize the mental ability of his subjects (Reid, 1982, p. 96). The nail in the coffin of Goring's theory was the advent of wide scale mental testing of American military conscriptees during World War I. Using Goring's definitions of feeblemindedness, nearly one-third of the draftees would have been so classified; the standards for such tests were modified as a result. Other studies just comparing mental age found no difference in performance by prisoners and the draft army, and one even found that the former performed better. As a result, feeblemindedness joined the graveyard of outmoded criminological concepts (Vold, 1979, pp. 85–87). However, we will examine shortly modern psychometric approaches to crime and current efforts to identify and measure the "criminal personality" which represent more sophisticated revivals of this line of inquiry.

The Jukes and Kallikaks

Other attempts to stress heredity as a source of criminality appeared in two case studies of generations of criminals who were claimed to be examples of degeneracy and depravity. Published only a year after Lombroso's *Criminal Man*, Robert Dugdale's (1841–1883) *The Jukes* (1877) was a case study of generations of an American family. Tracing over 1,000 descendants of Ada Jukes (a pseudonym), he found 280 paupers, 60 thieves, 7 murderers, 140 criminals, 40 venereal disease victims, 50 prostitutes, as well as other various deviants—proof positive, he claimed, of inherited criminality.

A similar case study was conducted by Henry Goddard in his *The Kallikak Family* (1912), which dealt with the offspring of one Martin Kallikak, a militiaman during the American Revolutionary War. Kallikak fathered a child out of wedlock to a "feebleminded barwench," a large number of the descendants of whom were feebleminded, or deviant. The offspring of his marriage to a "respectable" woman were, on the other hand, all of the highest moral and mental standards. Goddard took these findings as proof positive of the real cause of crime—feeblemindedness or low mentality. He also was the first to use the term "moron."

Smith (1985) took a close look at Goddard's Kallikak research and reported that the photographs included in Goddard's book of the "bad" Kallikaks were retouched to make them appear more evil, the methodology was unscientific, and the historical data simply not true (Haas, 1985). Rafter in *White Trash: the Eugenic Family Studies, 1887–1919*

(1988), as well as Gould's *The Mismeasure of Man* (1981), document Goddard's deceptions. Gould went to New Jersey and found some of the "bad" Kallikaks, who turned out not to be so bad after all.

The popularity of this type of research can be explained by the fact that " . . . it makes society's so-called superiors feel better about themselves" (Haas, 1985, p. 74). Fancher (1985) indicates " . . . the science of intelligence and its measurement has from the start been dominated by men who have been eager to show that the disenfranchised of society are at the bottom rung of the ladder because they are inherently inferior." (Haas, 1985, p. 74). A more detailed critique of biological positivism will follow shortly.

Earnest Hooton

Goddard attracted a major critic in the form of a neo-Lombrosian, Earnest Hooton (1887–1954), a Harvard anthropologist who in *Crime and the Man* (1939) claimed that, on the basis of a very detailed and extensive study of physical differences between criminals and non-criminals, he had discovered the causes of criminality: physical inferiority. His twelve-year study of 14,000 prisoners and 3,200 college students, firemen, and others led him to conclude (1939, p. 309):

> Criminals are organically inferior. Crime is the resultant of the impact of environment upon low grade human organisms. It follows that the elimination of crime can be effected only by the extirpation (eradication) of the physically, mentally, and morally unfit, or by their complete segregation in a socially aseptic environment.

Some physically distinguishing characteristics of Hooton's damned included: tattooing, thin beard and body hair, but thick head hair; straight hair; red-brown hair; blue-gray and mixed eye color; thin eyebrows; low and sloping foreheads; thin lips; pointed and small ears; and long, thin necks with sloping shoulders. These findings and their interpretations could be regarded with a tolerant, mild curiosity if they had appeared in Lombroso's 1876 work, but these were released in 1939 by a professor from one of America's finest universities. The totalitarian compatibility of positivism was again illustrated. In the same year that Hooton's work appeared, Hitler had already built experimental gas chambers in mental hospitals and in a two-year period "extirpated" (murdered) 50,000 non-Jewish Germans, a grim prophecy of what was in store for millions of Jews, Eastern Europeans, and groups the Nazis considered to be *Untermenschen* ('subhumans'). Since many criticisms of biological positivism apply in general to all such theories, a detailed critique will be presented at the conclusion of this section.

Body Types

Advocates of attempts to discover distinctive body types and relate them to crime include Ernst Kretschmer (1926), William Sheldon (1940), and Sheldon and Eleanor Glueck (1950). The best known of these efforts was Sheldon's (1940), in which he proposed three "somatotypes"—body builds which had relationships to personality characteristics (temperaments). Endomorphs have soft, round, and plump physiques and tend to be relaxed, easygoing, and extroverted; mesomorphs are hard and muscularly built and are aggressive, assertive, extroverted, and action-seekers; and ectomorphs are thin and fragile of form as well as introverted, sensitive, and subject to worrying. Comparing judgmental samples of "problem" youths with college males, Sheldon claimed that the problem youths tended to be mesomorphic.

Similar studies by the Gluecks (1956) found delinquents to be more mesomorphic than nondelinquents and suggested that this body type may be more suited to the delinquent role, while endomorphs were too slow and ectomorphs too frail to occupy it. Similar research by Cortés (1972) found 57 percent of his delinquent sample mesomorphic while only 19 percent of nondelinquents had such body builds, while McCandless, Persons, and Roberts (1972) were unable to find any such relationship between body type and self-reported delinquency.

Describing much of biocriminology as a "frightening slice of historical criminology," McCaghy (1976, p. 11) points out:

> Today scarcely a year goes by without some revelation concerning the possible connection between a biological characteristic and human behavior. In fairness to the scientists of today they are generally far less sweeping in their claims than were the researchers of a few decades ago. But the probing of every nook and cranny of the human system goes on. One can only sense the public's anticipation that someday a pill or a swipe of a scalpel will put an end to thievery, homosexuality, and all sorts of behavior.

The fact that the search goes on can be illustrated by means of a brief treatment of more recent examples of biological positivism. But first a critique of early biological positivism from Lombroso to the Gluecks is in order.

A Critique of Early Biological Positivism

Here are some common problems that nearly all of the early biological positivistic theories share:

- They suggest that one can genetically inherit a trait or propensity (to violate criminal laws) which is socially defined and culturally relative.

- Biological differences which are found are likely to explain only a minor proportion of criminal behavior compared to social and cultural factors.
- The biopositivists seem to share a conservative consensus world view, an unquestioned acceptance of official definitions of criminality, and the social class bias that crime is primarily to be found among "the dangerous class."
- Most of these studies reflect Reid's "dualistic fallacy" notion, which assumes the mutual exclusivity of criminals (defined as prisoners) and noncriminals (defined as nonprisoners).
- Most of their analyses are plagued by weak operationalization of key concepts such as "feebleminded," "inferior," and "crime."
- Not all biological differences are inherited, but may also be due to prenatal environment, injury, and inadequate diet (Vold, 1979, p. 99).
- Modern genetics has simply bypassed many of these simplistic theories. Most modern biologists speak against notions of the inheritance of acquired characteristics, emphasizing instead selective adaptation and mutation (Ibid., p. 100).
- Many of these studies are based upon small and/or inappropriate samples.
- As a result of the dominance of this approach, criminological theory was very likely led down the wrong path. The popularity of many of these theories related to their conservative and individualistic emphasis and their compatibility with authoritarian and simplistic solutions to the crime problem.

On balance, however, it should be pointed out that the early biological positivists made some important contributions:

- The commitment of the early positivists to testing their theories by means of experiments, the collection of empirical data, and the employment of statistics is a continuing feature of modern criminology.
- As the following discussion of neobiopositivism illustrates, one cannot rule out the biomedical approach simply because of this school of thought's association in the past with simplistic theories or the political abuse of such theories by fascist regimes. Sagarin (1980) views the exploration of many of these subject areas as unfortunately representing *Taboos in Criminology*, topics which have been viewed recently as "untouchable," fruitless, or "mined-out."
- The early positivist approach did influence Western criminal codes and led to modifications in the classical model. Special treatment of juvenile offenders, indeterminate sentences for career criminals,

extension of the insanity ruling, probation, corrections,and rehabilitation were all positivist contributions (Radzinowicz and King, 1977, p. 62).

Pierre Van den Berghe in an article entitled "Bringing the Beasts Back In" (1974) argues that modern criminology, in rejecting early positivism, had swung the other way and was ignoring the biological basis of human behavior. A brief examination of some of the research of modern biological positivists may provide some support for his point. Modern biological positivism replaces simplistic biological determinism with biological approaches which take into account the interplay of biological and socio-environmental factors (Shah and Roth, 1974). Whether criminality can be explained by human nature (genetics, inherited characteristics) or nurture (environment, learning, socialization) has been a continuing debate among criminological thinkers.

More Recent Biological Positivism

Shah and Roth (Ibid.) in their review of criminology's "nature-nurture" controversy (whether criminality is explained by genetics or environment) detail a variety of research including biochemical effects, brain disorders, endocrine and hormonal problems, nerve disorders, and other factors which can hardly be ignored at least in explaining a restricted number of individual cases of criminality (Marsh and Katz, 1985).

Brain Disorders

While the early phrenologists were convinced of their ability to map areas of the brain which controlled aspects of personality, modern attempts to probe the brain were begun by the Portuguese physician Antonio Moniz, who, beginning in 1935, performed prefrontal lobotomies (destruction of portions of the frontal lobes of the brain) as a last resort for nonresponsive mental patients. McCaghy (1976, p. 28) reports:

> His subjects were twenty mental patients who had been unaffected by other treatments; according to Moniz fifteen showed some degree of improvement as a result of the operation. One lobotomized patient was later to pump five bullets into Dr.Moniz, but the operation and variations of it were widely hailed as the answer to many behavioral problems.

Psychosurgery, surgical alterations of brain tissue in order to alter personality or behavior, became quite popular. Roughly 50,000 such operations were performed in the U.S. alone from the mid-thirties to mid-fifties (Ibid.). Lobotomized patients were indeed more controllable with respect to behavior, but were often described as resembling hollow shells of human beings, zombies, or human vegetables, devoid of a full range of normal emotions. As an illustrative case of the misapplication of such a drastic procedure, in the forties, actress Frances Farmer was forced into psychiatric treatment allegedly for alcoholism and other related problems. Her real "problem" was radicalism, which was "treated" with psychosurgery (Jenkins, 1984, p. 180).

Vernon Mark and Frank Ervin (1970) in *Violence and the Brain* proposed the use of psychosurgical procedures in order to control brain malfunctions, particularly those which may trigger aggressive behavior. Our discussion of "the terminal man" in chapter 11 vividly illustrates the irreversible and dangerous consequences of behavior brain engineering, although it has been known to produce some positive results (Brown et al., 1973). Biomedical and surgical approaches to criminality represent a last resort, a "quick fix" which, although applicable in rare, special cases, has little to offer as a general theory of crime causation.

Twin Studies

Studies of twins and adoptees are ingenious ways of attempting to address the "nature vs. nurture debate," that is, whether criminality is inherited or learned. Such studies are ex post facto in nature and begin with criminals who have a twin and then attempt to find the other twin in order to discover whether he or she is also criminal (Lange, 1931; Rosanoff, Handy, and Plesset, 1934; Christiansen, 1968; and Dalgard and Kringlen, 1975). Such studies often also compare monozygotic (MZ) with dizygotic (DZ) twins. Monozygotic (identical) twins are produced by a single egg and therefore exhibit the same hereditary environment, while dizygotic (fraternal) twins are produced by separate eggs and portray less biological similarity.

Although findings have been mixed, Dalgard and Kringlen's (Ibid.) study of all twins born in Norway between 1900 and 1935 concluded that the significance of hereditary factors in registered crime is nonexistent. They examined 33,000 twins in order to turn up 139 pairs where one or the other committed crime as measured by a national crime registry. Their study, as well as those of others, found greater concordance (similar patterns with respect to criminality) among monozygotic than among dizygotic pairs. A review of studies conducted from 1929 to 1961 by Mednick and Volavka (1980) found roughly 60 percent concordance among MZ twins and about 30 percent among DZ pairs. Christiansen's (1968) study of 3,586 male twins found 52 percent MZ concordance and 22 percent among DZs.

Twin studies provide unique opportunities for researchers to study the nature vs. nurture debate and try to determine if behavior is inherited or learned.

Adoption Studies

Related in design and execution to twin studies have been adoption studies. The assumption underlying such studies is that, if the behavior of children more closely matches that of their biological parents than that of their adoptive parents, this would lend greater support to the argument of a biological base of human behavior. Schulsinger (1972), for instance, found criminality in adopted boys to be higher when biological fathers had criminal records. Hutchings and Mednick (1977) studied 1,145 male adoptees born in Copenhagen between 1927 and 1941; they found 185 adoptees with criminal records and found the criminality of the biological father was a major predictor of the child's behavior. Crowe (1974), however, discovered no differences between adoptees and a control group, except that the former demonstrated a higher proportion of psychopathic personalities. However, he admits problems with small samples as well as the fact that other environmental influences may have been responsible for the higher psychopathy among adoptees.

Problems with Twin/Adoption Studies

There are a number of methodological problems associated with twin and adoption studies, despite painstaking research and admirable scholarship on the part of those who have conducted them:

- Most studies involve a small number of cases, since they attempt to combine two rare events: twin/adoptees and crime.
- Some studies are subject to unsystematic and uncontrolled samples (Dalgard and Kringlen, 1975, p. 230).
- Often the operationalization of DZ and MZ relies upon official records rather than blood-serum group samplings. The latter is a far more accurate means of noting identical vs. fraternal twin patterns.
- Official records are the major source of data on the dependent variable — crime commission.
- A shift of only a few cases (which may have been misdiagnosed) can erase the DZ-MZ differences.
- Higher concordance among MZs (identical twins) may still be due to more similar environmental treatment in which identical twins are more likely to be treated the same.

XYY Syndrome

In the late fifties in England, speculation began regarding males who possessed an XYY chromosome pattern — an extra male chromosome. Of the 46 chromosomes most humans possess, males receive an X chromosome from their mothers and a Y chromosome from their fathers, while females receive two X chromosomes, one from each parent. Beginning with papers by Patricia Jacobs et al. (1965), in which a large number of the 197 Scottish inmates they studied were found to be "double Ys," the hypothesis had been proposed of a "double male" or "super-male syndrome." This theory held that the possession of an extra Y chromosome caused males to be unusually tall, to suffer severe acne as children, and to become predisposed to aggressive and violent behavior. During the late sixties, defense attorneys for brutal murderers in France and in Australia and for Richard Speck, the murderer of eight Chicago nurses, employed as part of their defense the claim that their clients were XYYs. Only in the Australian case was the accused acquitted (Sarbin and Miller, 1970).

While early research suggested that a larger proportion of XYYs could be found in prisons than among the public, which exhibited less than one double-Y per one thousand live male births, further research has found no difference (Shah and Roth, 1974, p. 137; Witkin et al. 1976). Because of the relative rarity of the syndrome, studies demonstrating a large number of cases are difficult. A Danish study by Witkin et al. (Ibid.) did not support the aggression hypothesis and even found that incarcerated XYYs showed less aggression while in prison than did the other inmates. Earlier reviews of the research by Fox (1971) and Sarbin and Miller (1970) essentially agreed with these findings and found XYYs when institutionalized to have less serious offense records than others. While more research is required in this area, the negative findings have considerably lessened interest in the XYY syndrome as a cause of criminality.

Other Biological Factors

Further theoretical and empirical work in the tradition of biological positivism in criminology continues to raise interesting hypotheses and some explanation in individual cases of criminality.

In the 1970s ideas proposed by Edward Wilson (1975) in his book *Sociobiology* attracted adherents. Basically, the sociobiological perspective insists upon the genetic base of human behavioral differences. Individuals are born with different potentialities; their reactions to the social environment are modified by biochemistry and the cellular reactions of the brain. Each individual's unique genetic code and nervous system react differently to the same environmental stimuli (Jeffrey, 1978, p. 162). A variety of other biological factors have been explored, primarily by means of the limited case study approach, and require more study before definitive conclusions can be drawn.

Variables such as diet, environmental pollution, endocrine imbalance, and allergies have been claimed to have criminogenic influence. In our discussion of the "Twinkie defense" in Chapter 6, we see claims that sugar consumption (too little or too much) is a causal agent in crime. Hypoglycemia (low blood sugar) also has been claimed to be linked to impaired brain function and violent crime.

Explorations of endocrine imbalance have found an obvious connection with sexual functioning, but no clear relationship with crime. Theories of relationship between male hormones (testosterone levels) and criminality have been found inconclusive, although injection of the female hormone (estrogen) has been found to decrease male sexual potency (Mednick and Volavka, 1980). Dalton's (1961) study of "Menstruation and Crime" found that nearly half of the crimes of her sample of female inmates had occurred during menstruation or premenstruation.

Cerebral and neuroallergies to food substances have also been suggested as a potentially criminogenic factor (Wunderlich, 1978; and Schauss, 1980). In Schauss's study comparing nutritional differences of delinquents and nondelinquents, the surprising major difference found was that delinquents drank more milk. Similar investigations of environmental pollution upon aberrant behavior indicate that deadly substances such as lead, mercury, and other poisonous substances can adversely affect human behavior and life itself.

Neurological studies have suggested that criminals are more likely to exhibit abnormal electroencephalogram (EEG) patterns (a measurement of brain waves), although studies of association of such patterns with criminality have presented mixed findings (Moyer, 1976). Denno (1985, p. 713) indicates:

> Considerable evidence indicates that many biological and developmental disorders associated with delinquency (for example, learning and reading disabilities) may be attributable, in part, to minor central nervous system (CNS) dysfunction which is linked, most predominantly, to complications occurring before and after birth.

It is important that criminologists keep an open mind on this matter and not view such studies as a taboo area (Sagarin, 1980) nor mistake more modern biological studies for their more primitive Lombrosian ancestors. Ellis (1982, pp. 57-58), in his review of the genetics and criminal behavior literature of the seventies, offers prudent conclusions:

> Sensing the weight of this accumulating evidence, especially throughout the past decade, along with several other types of less direct evidence not treated in this article (e.g., the discovery of a growing number of neurological and neurochemical correlates of criminal and psychopathic behavior), many scientists have concluded since the start of the 1970s that some significant genetic factors are probably, or at least very possibly, causally involved in criminal behavior variability . . . However, it seems important to quickly insert and underscore the point that none of these scientists in any way excluded the possibility of environmental factors also being involved.
>
> In fact, nearly all of them specifically entertained hypotheses about what one or more of those environmental factors might be within the very same reports in which they acknowledge possible or probable genetic influences.

A literature review examining the link between learning disabilities and criminality commissioned by the Law Enforcement Assistance Administration concluded that no such connection had been proven (Murray, 1976). Some studies have claimed that brain dysfunction (damage) is associated with violence, suicide, and likelihood of processing by criminal justice authorities (Monroe, 1978).

Critique of Neobiological Positivism

While more recent biological positivistic research is more sophisticated and less grandiose than the early theories discussed previously, most examples given are of limited case studies. While illustrative cases can be found which show connections with criminality, often just as many cases of individuals with the same "claimed causative agent" can be brought forth whose behavior is normal. Much of this research is limited by small samples, is prone to the dualistic fallacy, is overreliant upon incarcerated subjects, and often employs poor sampling procedures. While undoubtedly biological factors have impact on particular individuals and their commission of certain crimes, biological explanations tend to be limited and appear to offer less exposition than social and cultural factors.

Neo-biological research which continues attempts to revive such literature into the criminological mainstream, such as Wilson and Herrnstein's *Crime and Human Nature* (1985), has not received the same laudatory reviews within criminology and criminal justice as it has in the popular press (Austin, 1986; and Gibbs, 1985). In support of the attempt to regenerate biological positivism, Herrnstein (1985, p. 2) claims:

> The bits of evidence may be individually disputed but, taken together, the case for genetic involvement in criminal behavior cannot plausibly be rejected. On the average, offenders are distinctive in physical constitution, they are more likely to have chromosomal abnormality, and they tend to occur in families with other offenders whether or not they were raised by their criminal relatives. Unwholesome environments are surely among the significant predictors of crime; they are just not the only predictors. But genes do not cause crime as such. Rather, the evidence suggests a more complex chain of connections: genes affect psychological traits which in turn affect the likelihood of breaking the law. Intelligence and personality are the two traits most strongly implicated in this chain.

Psychological Positivism

Various psychological, psychiatric, and psychoanalytic theories of criminality share in common the search for criminal pathology in the human personality. Although the approaches overlap, *psychology* is the study of the individual human mind, personality, and behavior, while *psychiatry* is a branch of medicine which deals with the diagnosis and treatment of mental disorders. *Psychoanalysis*, originally based upon the writings of Sigmund Freud, is an applied branch of psychological theory which employs techniques such as free mental association and dream therapy in order to diagnose and treat mental problems; the therapist assists the patient in probing the unconscious in search of sources of mental pathology. Most such theories tend conservatively to take for granted the existing social order and to scrutinize the human psyche for explanations of individual deviation. Much of this approach can be illustrated with the continual quest for "the criminal personality," measurable traits which enable the distinguishing of criminals from noncriminals. Many adherents of this approach also concentrate more upon applied therapy and rehabilitation of identified criminals and less upon pure theoretical explanations of crime causation (see Bartol and Bartol, 1986).

Freudian Theory

While Charles Darwin was the intellectual forefather to many biological positivistic theories, many early psychological and psychoanalytic approaches were based upon the writings of Sigmund Freud (1856–1939). While Freud did not address his writings specifically to the crime issue, his theories of personality as well as psychopathology have been applied to explanations of criminal behavior. He emphasized the instinctual and unconscious bases of human behavior.

Freud viewed the human personality as being made up of three parts: id, ego, and superego. The id is the instinctive, natural, or animalistic self. It is totally selfish and seeks to maximize pleasure. Expressions of this pleasure principle (or libido) are the life or love instinct (eros) as well as the death instinct (thanatos). The superego is the socialized component of the personality, the part developed in order to function and gain acceptance in human society. Repressing the pleasure-seeking instincts, the superego is in constant conflict with the id. The ego is the mediator or "referee" in this contest (Freud, 1930).

Psychoanalytic adherents of Freudian theory view much criminality as being unconsciously motivated and often due to the repression (hiding or sublimation into the unconscious) of personality conflicts and unresolved problems experienced in early childhood. Hostility to male authority symbols (the Oedipus complex) originates when the male child's id, desiring sexual relations with the mother, is blocked by the father. Overly harsh toilet training; premature weaning as a child; or other unpleasant, sexually related episodes contain the seeds of unconscious motivation for later adult criminality. Some hold that the inability to control instincts due to inadequate ego and superego development causes criminality (Friedlander, 1947). Crime represents a substitute response (displacement, reaction); that is, when original goals are blocked, they are sublimated (displaced) and expressed by means of substitute goals. Crime may be committed due to the unconscious desire to be caught and punished (an expression of the thanatos complex or death wish).

Relying extensively upon case studies, Freudians document examples of the operation of the Oedipus or Electra complex, the death wish, inferiority complex, frustration-aggression, birth trauma, castration fears, and penis envy, in which crime is a substitute for forbidden acts

(Vold and Bernard, 1986, p. 113). While it has had a profound impact upon Western thought, Freudian theory, dealing as it does with abstract notions of the human psyche, has not lent itself very well to empirical analysis. Most of his hypotheses have been neither verified nor refuted.

Psychometry

Psychometry refers to attempts to obtain measured psychological and mental differences between criminals and noncriminals. This search for the distinctive criminal mind or personality could also be described as often taking the form of a criminological "wild-goose chase." While having its origins in the work of Goddard, which was described earlier, modern and more sophisticated tests have been employed in the attempt to discern basic mental and psychological differences. In an early literature review, Schuessler and Cressey's (1953) examination over a twenty-five-year period of such studies was unable to find conclusive evidence of specific personality characteristics related to criminality. Later reviews by Waldo and Dinitz (1967) of the literature from 1950 to 1965 confirmed Schuessler and Cressey's conclusion, as does a later survey by Tennenbaum (1977).

In this tradition of mental testings, the Gluecks (1950) conducted a survey of 500 delinquent boys and 500 nondelinquent boys and found the former to be more assertive, defiant, destructive, hostile, and ambivalent toward authority. Even these differences were small and may be an illustration of post hoc error, where, since differences were observed after the fact (the official labeling of delinquency), they are assumed to be the cause of such behavior. Similarly, some research suggests that the incarcerated criminals suffer greater emotional disorders than the general population, a possible likely reaction to confinement, as illustrated by the "simulated prison" study discussed in Chapter 2. Other studies attempting to link "psychopathology" and crime have also been inconclusive.

Hans Eysenck

Hans Eysenck (1977) in *Crime and Personality* combines a number of streams in social scientific thought in proposing a theory of criminality. Borrowing from psychologist B. F. Skinner (1971) as well as from the classical school of criminology, he views human conscience and guilt as merely conditioned reflexes, simple reactions to the apprehension of pleasure and pain. Eysenck claims the extroverted (outgoing) personality is more delinquent or criminal than the introverted (inhibited) personality. His disciple, Gordon Trasler (1962), feels that conditioned anxiety reaction (fear of punishment) inhibits individuals from crime. Extroverts, however, are less responsive to this conditioning. Viewing the labeling of deviant acts as nonproblematic, Eysenck feels that society is too permissive in its child-rearing practices and unwilling to rationally apply the knowledge of modern psychology in the area of behavioral modification which attempts to encourage positive behavior through the application of pleasure and pain (Taylor et al., 1973, p. 49). Hindelang's (1971) self-report survey of 234 high school boys supported Eysenck's theory of extroverts being more delinquent, particularly among the most normal or middle-neurotic group.

B. F. Skinner

Perhaps the most influential proponent of a branch of applied theory called behavioral psychology is B. F. Skinner (1953), who in his *Science*

An influential proponent of behavioral psychology, B.F. Skinner, proposed ideas that are appealing as therapeutic strategies.

and Human Behavior views behavior as primarily a response to consistent conditioning or learning reinforced through expected rewards and punishments. Through behavioral modification (sometimes in laboratory settings, called operant conditioning), which is widely used in juvenile corrections, unacceptable behavior theoretically can be engineered toward acceptable behavior. While an apparently effective therapeutic strategy, Skinner's approach is a pure behaviorist approach: that is, it says "behavior causes behavior"; it is less concerned with addressing the issue of the underlying origin of crime, criminal law, or conditions in the social order which act as prior conditions to the transmissions of behavior. As an applied theory or therapeutic strategy, it represents an attractive scheme, despite its shortcomings in pure theory aspects.

Samuel Yochelson and Stanton Samenow

More recent advocates of the existence of a distinctive "criminal personality" are psychiatrist Samuel Yochelson and clinical psychologist Stanton Samenow (1976), who on the basis of their fourteen-year therapeutic work with 240 hard-core criminal and delinquent subjects at St. Elizabeth's Hospital for the criminally insane in Washington, D.C., claim to have challenged prevailing sociological and economic theories of crime causation. In a revival of early biological and psychological positivism, they argue that socio-environmental constraints on individual criminality are irrelevant, that there is a "criminal personality," and that such individuals freely choose to become criminal (Ibid., p. 199). Feeling that their criminal patients were conning them by using current theories in the social sciences to rationalize their criminality, they claim that criminals were victimizers of society rather than its victims (Vold and Bernard, 1986, p. 253).

Proposing a therapeutic treatment technique rather than a theory of crime causation, they make some of the following points:

- The criminal personality is imprinted at birth and is relatively unaffected by the family.
- Criminal personalities seek the excitement of the crime.
- They are exploitative and selfish in interpersonal relationships.
- They are amoral, untrustworthy, intolerant of others, manipulative, lack empathy, and are in a pervasive state of anger.
- They lack trust and refuse to be dependent.
- In all, Yochelson and Samenow claim to have discovered fifty-two criminal thinking patterns (Yochelson and Samenow, 1976).

Similar to programs such as Alcoholics Anonymous (AA), Synanon, the Delancey Street Foundation (Fox, 1985, p. 255), and that proposed by Glasser's (1965) "reality therapy," Yochelson and Samenow propose a treatment in which criminals must confront their antisocial thoughts. AA calls this a rejection of "stinkin' thinkin'," in which the subjects abandon past excuses and rationalizations. The criminal is expected to totally reject their former criminal personality and assume personal responsibility for their wrongdoing.

Despite having some promise as a behavioral therapy, Yochelson and Samenow's theory has a naive "old-wine-in-new-bottles" flavor about it; a revival of the "grunts and bumps" theories of the past. They cite little convincing empirical evidence of success for their treatment. They fail to refute evidence regarding environmental and social influences. Among their methodological problems, their operationalization of basic terms is unclear. In response to their claim that they have refuted criminological theory of environmental influences on crime, Vold (1979, p. 159) retorts:

> It does not appear, however, that the study demonstrates that point. It is certainly possible that providing a criminal with insight into the root causes of his behavior does not change that behavior. That is very different than saying crime does not have root causes.

Rather than restricting its focus to specific types of offenders, the search for "the criminal personality" of which Yochelson and Samenow's theory is the most recent example is too globally ambitious in trying to explain all types of criminals.

Intelligence and Crime

Hirschi and Hindelang (1977) charge that, due to the discrediting of much of the early work on intelligence and crime by Goddard and Goring and others, the field of criminology has ignored the strong evidence of a link between intelligence quotient (IQ) and crime. On the basis of an extensive literature review, they argue that the textbooks have been wrong on this subject and that:

- IQ is more important in predicting official delinquency among white boys than is social class.
- IQ is a better predictor of delinquency than is father's social class, especially among black boys.
- All other things being equal, the lower the IQ, the higher the recidivism.
- There is a roughly nine-point deficit in the IQs of delinquent compared to nondelinquents.

Unable to find contrary conclusions in current research, Hirschi and Hindelang (Ibid.) conclude that IQ is at least as good a predictor of delinquency as is race and social class. Wolfgang, Figlio, and Sellin's (1972) study found arrested juveniles in their Philadelphia cohort study to have lower IQs, but that race was a more important predictor, while the contribution of IQ to criminality, independent of race and class, was also indicated in a literature review of such studies by Herrnstein (1983). Research by Gordon (1987) similarly claims to have demonstrated that black-white differences in juvenile delinquency rates were best predicted by IQ rather than socio-economic variables.

Vold and Bernard (1986, p. 82) cite the rather seamy history of the IQ controversy, indicating that blaming low IQ for delinquency has a long tradition. In the 1820s the high delinquency of the Irish was attributed to their having inferior racial stock (Finestone, 1976, pp. 12–36), and at the turn of the century early IQ tests were utilized to show the inferiority of Southern and Eastern European immigrants. The IQs of Italian-American children with a median of 84 was 16 points below the national norm (Pinter, 1923), about the same as black children today.

Modern advocates of a relationship between IQ and delinquency and crime do not, as earlier writers, insist that intelligence potential is entirely inherited and view it as an acquired as well as inherited entity. Given criticisms of cultural bias in intelligence testing, they insist that, although no test is culture free, one obtains similar results with a variety of measures. IQ remains a critical variable in explaining traditional crime and delinquency and may even shed light on white collar crimes where perhaps higher IQ is likely. Little research, however, has taken place with respect to the latter.

A full and detailed account of modern psychological and psychiatric approaches to crime exceeds the intentions of this volume. Much of this literature, which has often been given short shrift by criminological theorists, is important, but it also has been of an applied theoretical or clinical nature, proposing treatment rather than being causal in intention. Schafer (1976, Chapters 8 and 9) provides excellent coverage of such work by Erik Erikson (1950) on identity crisis, family therapy, reality therapy (Glasser, 1965), gestalt therapy (Perls, 1970), and other important therapeutic approaches. Similarly Jacks and Cox (1984) provide an excellent anthology of psycho-criminology. On this point Fox (1976, p. 416) states:

> Crime is so complex that a single theory or small constellation of theories is difficult to operationalize and evaluate through controlled research. There is disagreement between the research and the clinical viewpoints, most graphically demonstrated by the demand for solid research by (pure research)

sociologists and experimental psychologists, on the one hand, and the more pragmatic clinical viewpoint (applied research) held by psychiatrists, clinical psychologists, and social workers on the other. . . . These disparate viewpoints will probably never become congruent. It is apparent that both are needed.

A Critique of Psychological Positivism

Some of the same shortcomings which plague biological positivism also impinge upon the psychological theories:

- Many of these theories focus almost exclusively upon the individual personality, ignoring social conditions and life situations. This has the quality of appearing to commit what Ryan (1971) calls "blaming the victim" (see Vold, 1979, p. 156; and Cohen, 1955, p. 55).
- Being more concerned with therapy than with measurement, many psychiatric theories in particular tend to be speculative rather than scientific.
- Many of these theories overemphasize the case study approach and are prone to observer bias.
- They often fail to use useful control groups, and the experimental groups are usually institutionalized populations.
- A number of studies have inadequate, unrepresentative samples and utilize unclear operationalization of concepts.
- Many of these theories fail to recognize crime as a socially or legally defined act, considering it almost a physical or clinical condition.

Vold and Bernard (1986, p. 107) best sum up the state of such theories by indicating that many of these theories may be correct with respect to particular types of criminals, but they ignore the conflict basis of criminal law.

It is important that, in explaining the forest (environmental and sociological influences, to be discussed in the next chapter), we do not ignore the individual trees (biological and psychological differences among individuals). Monahan and Splane (1980, p. 42) indicate: "What the field of criminology needs, it appears to us, are sociologists who use psychological intervening variables without embarrassment and psychologists who are aware of the social roots of the individual processes they study."

Multifactor Approach

A primary criticism of most theories that have been discussed is their tendency to attempt to associate crime with a single cause, for example, some biological or psychological defect. Critics of these approaches merely had to demonstrate the presence of these conditions in equal proportions among noncriminals in order to refute these assumptions. This single-factor deficiency has led some writers (Healy, 1915; and the Gluecks, 1950) to propose a *multifactor approach* in which crime is assumed to be produced by multiple factors—biological, psychological, and sociological—with different combinations of variables coming into play, depending upon the type of crime being examined. This approach is appealing in that multiple factors are indeed involved in any causal explanation of criminality; however, the identification of factors associated with a process does not constitute a causal theory. In that sense, the multifactor approach is atheoretical (without theoretical content).

Albert Cohen (1951) has provided a succinct critique of the multifactor approach, which may be paraphrased:

- Advocates of this approach confuse causal theories which employ a single variable with those which propose a single theory. Simply listing correlations of factors associated with crime does not represent a theory, while a single theory may utilize multiple factors.
- Due to the emergence of easily available, sophisticated statistical programs which enable the calculation of multiple correlations, researchers forget that correlation does not equal causation. Since variables account for a certain proportion of variance in crime, this does not mean that substantively they cause that amount of crime.
- This approach falls into the "evil causes evil" fallacy: evil outcomes require evil causes, which represents a conservative, consensus view of crime as an evil intrusion into an otherwise healthy society.

In the next chapter, discussion will focus upon sociological theories in criminology, beginning with classic theorist Emile Durkheim and mainstream sociological theories and ending with what has been called "critical criminology," viewpoints which claim to challenge conventional criminology.

Summary

Theory refers to plausible explanations of reality. While *pure theory* attempts to search for basic causes or underlying principles, *applied theory* is concerned with gaining explanations with which to guide practical social policy. Criminology as an interdisciplinary field requires both. *The major theoretical approaches in criminology are:* the demonological, classical, ecological, economic, positivistic (biological and psychological), and sociological.

The earliest theories of crime causation were *demonological* in nature, seeking supernatural explanations for criminality. The criminal was viewed as possessed, sinful, or evil. The *classical school* of criminological theory, which developed in the eighteenth century, was reflected in the writings of Beccaria, Bentham, and later Garafalo and Ferri. Seeking rational explanations, classical theorists viewed the criminal as exercising *free will*, as motivated by *hedonism* (pleasure-seeking), and as carefully weighing potential pleasure vs. pain to be derived by an activity. Attacking the cruel and unpredictable penal methods of the time, classical theory inspired the reform of Western criminal law. *Neoclassical theory* admits extenuating circumstances (insanity, age, and the like) to the equal treatment for equivalent offense notions of the classical school.

Ecological theory (sometimes called statistical, geographic, or cartographic) is concerned with the impact of groups and social and environmental influences upon criminality. The earliest writers, Guerry and Quetelet, could be regarded as the "fathers of modern criminology" in that they employed statistics and scientific analysis in the investigation of their theories. Quetelet's "thermic law" hypothesized that violent crimes predominate in warmer climates, while property crimes increase in colder weather zones. Since they extensively employed maps in their analyses, they are sometimes called the cartographic school. The work of this school was interrupted and for a time forgotten as a result of the popularity of the Darwinistically-motivated biological positivism of Lombroso. Other *geographic theories* relating to moon cycles, climate, weather, and the like have attracted considerable interest, but research verification has been inconclusive.

Three major thinkers who have inspired much criminological theory have been *Marx (economics)*, *Darwin (evolution)*, and *Freud (unconscious sexual motivation)*. Early *economic theories*, based upon Marx's writings, view crime as determined by the economic system in which capitalism creates inequalities which produce crime. Socialism is viewed as the solution to the crime problem. Bonger, a Marxist criminologist, suggests that egoism (selfishness), developed as a result of capitalism, causes criminality.

Positivistic theory was based upon three elements; (1) use of the scientific method in order to (2) diagnose individual pathology and thus enable the (3) prescribing of treatment. The criminal is viewed as sick. Precursors to positivism included astrology, phrenology, physiognomy, and palmistry, none of which is taken very seriously today.

Biological positivism proposed the notion of "the born criminal." Lombroso viewed criminals as "atavistic" beings (savage "throwbacks" to earlier human ancestors); he proposed the identification of *physical stigmata* as a means of identifying such persons. *Social Darwinism* is a philosophy which posits "a survival of the fittest in society" among human groups and their institutions. Ferri and Garofalo extended and modified the biopositivism tradition, which was well accepted by conservative and totalitarian political structures, since the blame for crime rested upon the individual and not society. The text presents a critique of early positivism. Goring's research, which was highly critical of Lombrosian theory, proposing instead "inherited mental deficiency"—*feeblemindedness*—as the explanation of crime, has been discredited by more sophisticated mental tests. Other biopositivist theories include: case studies of the Jukes and the Kallikaks, Hooton's notion of "physical and mental inferiority" of criminals, and Sheldon's "somatotypes" (body types). The text also presents a more detailed critique of early biological positivism.

More recent biological positivism is more sophisticated in addressing the "nature vs. nurture" argument; it generally views criminality as produced by a combination of genetics and environment. Such research includes variables such as brain disorders, biochemical effects, endocrine and hormonal abnormalities, and nerve disorders. *Twin and adoption studies* have produced mixed findings, but suggest that monozygotic (identical) twins are more similar (concordant) in their criminal behavior than are dizygotic (fraternal) twins. A critique of such studies includes the point that many twins experience similar environmental influences. The *XYY syndrome*, the supermale phenomenon, has been largely discredited. Other areas of inquiry in this tradition include sociobiology (which insists upon the genetic base of human behavior). A further critique is presented.

Psychological positivism reflects psychological, psychiatric, and psychoanalytic theory; much of the early work was based upon Freud's writings. The latter includes a tripartite personality system consisting of the id (instinctual self), ego (mediator), and superego (socialized self). According to *Freudian theory* as applied to criminology, the basis of deviance can be found in repressed sexual motivations deeply hidden in the individual's subconscious.

Psychometry (mental testing) attempts to discover personality characteristics of criminals. Various literature reviews of these efforts find the evidence inconclusive. Research by the Gluecks suggests that differences do exist between delinquents and nondelinquents, as does Eysenck's research, the latter attributing crime to extroverted personalities who lack adequate societal conditioning (training).

Skinner's theory of *behavioral modification* (modeling behavior by means of rewards and punishments) has had a major impact upon clinical programs in corrections. The continual search for a distinctive "criminal personality" is illustrated in the work of Yochelson and Samenow, who on the basis of their clinical work identify specific traits and propose a therapeutic technique similar to Alcoholics Anonymous in which criminals are challenged to take personal responsibility for their actions and to reject rationalizations. Although perhaps clinically useful, as a theory of crime causation the theory leaves much to be desired.

Hirschi and Hindelang revive the IQ controversy by insisting that on the basis of their literature review criminologists have been too unappreciative of the role of IQ in crime and delinquency.

The text provides a critique of psychological positivism along with a rejoinder that criminologists, while concerned with sociological forces in crime causation, cannot afford to ignore individual factors. The *multifactor approach* is a reaction to many single-variable theories, proposing instead that many variables cause crime. However, while rejecting any single variable as appropriate, the multifactor approach sometimes also rejects any single theory which may include multiple variables in its explanation.

KEY CONCEPTS

Pure Theory
Applied Theory
Demonological Theory
Classical Theory
Hedonism
Neoclassical Theory
Ecological Theory
Human Ecology
"Thermic Law" of Crime
Economic Theory
Proletariat
Bourgeoisie
Positivism

Basic Premises of Positivism
Astrology
Phrenology
Physiognomy
Palmistry
Biological Positivism
Atavism
Physical Stigmata
Social Darwinism
"Law of Criminal Saturation"
Feeblemindedness
Somatotypes
"Nature-Nurture" Controversy

Lobotomy
Monozygotic Concordance
XYY Syndrome
Psychological Positivism
Freudian Personality Theory
Psychometry
Behavioral Modification
IQ and Crime
Critiques of Each Theoretical
 School
Multifactor Approach

Criminological Theory II: Sociological Theories

The early classical, biological, and psychological traditions in criminology theory were similar in their relatively conservative view of society (the consensus model) as well as in their search for the cause of crime in either lack of fear of deterrence, defective individual genetics, or the psyche. The individual criminal was the unit of analysis. The only departures from this deviant behavior approach to criminality were found in the writings of the economic theorists (Marx and Bonger) and the ecologists (Quetelet and Guerry). Economic and ecological theories constitute the groundwork for the preeminence of sociological approaches to criminological theory beginning in the 1930s in the United States. Societal conditions, groups, social disorganization, and conflict have become additional units of analysis. Crime is perceived as a status (definition) as well as behavior (pathology), and sociological criminology in general takes a more critical stance toward the society itself as generator of criminal conduct.

Major Sociological Theoretical Approaches in Criminology

Figure 5.1 is a more detailed outline of the sociological theories which were briefly presented in Figure 4.1, *Major Theoretical Approaches in Criminology*. These include: *mainstream sociological theories* (anomie, social process, and social control) as well as *critical sociological theories* (labeling, conflict, and radical).

Discussion will begin with the mainstream tradition and the views of late nineteenth-century sociologist Emile Durkheim, and the "anomie theories" which he inspired. Other representatives of this approach are Robert Merton, Richard Cloward and Lloyd Ohlin, and Albert Cohen.

Anomie Theories

Emile Durkheim and "Anomie"

The writings of French sociologist Emile Durkheim (1858–1917) were in sharp contrast to the social Darwinistic, individualistic, and psychological and biological positivistic theories dominant in the late nineteenth century. The works of Durkheim represented a return to the thinking and orientation of the statistical/ecological theories advocated by Quetelet and Guerry,

Figure 5.1: Major Theoretical Approaches in Criminology (Sociological)*

Theoretical School	Major Themes/Concepts	Major Theorists
Sociological Mainstream	"crime reflects consensus model"	
Anomie Theory	"anomie (normlessness) lessens social control" "anomie (gap between goals and means) creates deviance" "differential social opportunity" "lower class reaction to middle class values"	Durkheim Merton Cloward and Ohlin Cohen
Social Process	"social disorganization and social conditions" "routine activities" "crime is learned behavior, culturally/subculturally transmitted" "focal concerns of lower class" "subterranean values, drift techniques of neutralization"	Shaw and McKay Cohen and Felson Sutherland Miller Matza
Social Control	"containment theory" "social bonds weakened reducing individual stakes in conformity"	Reckless Hirschi
Critical	"crime reflects conflict model"	
Labeling	"societal reaction theory" "dramatization of evil" "secondary deviance" "crime as label, status"	Tannenbaum Lemert
Conflict	"imperatively coordinated associations" "pluralistic model" "more powerful groups define criminal law"	Dahrendorf Vold Turk
Radical	"capitalism causes crime"; "neo-Marxist"	Quinney, Chambliss

*See Figure 4.1 for other theoretical approaches in criminology.

an approach that had been preempted by the popularity of Lombroso and the early biological positivists.

In his works—which included *The Division of Labor in Society* (1964), originally published in 1893, and *Suicide* (1951), first released in 1897—Durkheim insisted upon the primacy of groups and social organization as explanatory factors of human misconduct. As we said in Chapter 1, he viewed crime as a normal phenomenon in society because group reactions to deviant actions assist human groups in defining their moral boundaries. In his doctoral dissertation which was completed in 1893, *The Rules of Sociological Method* (1950), Durkheim insisted that sociologists' role is being the systematic observers of "social facts," empirically observable group characteristics which impact upon human behavior. Durkheim's analysis of suicide clearly demonstrated his hypothesis of group influences upon individual propensity to suicide. In *Suicide* (1951) he identified several types, which included: altruistic ("selfless" suicide), egoistic (self-centered suicide), and anomic (suicide due to "anomie" or a state of normlessness in society). The latter concept represents Durkheim's principal contribution to the field of criminology.

The term "anomie" appeared in the English language as early as 1591 and generally referred to a disregard for law (Fox, 1976, p. 115). "Anomie" as used by Durkheim involves a moral malaise; a lack of clear-cut norms with which to guide human conduct (normlessness). It may occur as a pervasive condition in society due to a failure of individuals to internalize the norms of society, an inability to adjust to changing norms, or even conflict within the norms themselves.

Emile Durkheim's concept of "anomie" influenced a number of criminological theories.

Social trends in modern urban-industrial societies result in changing norms, confusion, and lessened social control over the individual. Individualism increases and new life-styles emerge, perhaps yielding even greater freedom but also increasing the possibility for deviant behavior. The close ties of the individual to the family, village, and tradition (what Durkheim calls "mechanical solidarity"), though confining to the individual, maintained social control. In modern societies (characterized by "organic solidarity") constraints upon the individual weaken. In a theme which would influence many later criminological theories, Durkheim viewed anomie in modern societies as produced by individual aspirations and ambitions and the search for new pleasures and sensations which are beyond achievement even in times of prosperity (Durkheim, 1951, p. 256).

This notion of anomie would influence a number of criminological theories, constituting a theoretical school of thought within mainstream or conventional criminology that began with the work of Robert Merton in the late thirties and continued with Richard Cloward and Lloyd Ohlin and Albert Cohen in the post-World War II period. Chronologically preceding these later developments in the anomie tradition was the work of "the Chicago school" of sociology and another major approach: the social process school of thought. These theories were less concerned with the origin of crime in society and concentrated instead upon the social process (learning, socialization, subcultural transmission) by which criminal values were transmitted to individuals by groups to which they are affiliated.

Merton's Theory of "Anomie"

Robert Merton's (1910–   ) theory of "anomie" first appeared in 1938. Modifying Durkheim's original concept, Merton (1957, pp. 131–194) viewed anomie as a condition which occurs when discrepancies exist between societal goals and the means available for their achievement. This discrepancy or *strain* between aspirations and achievement has resulted in Merton's conception being referred to as "strain theory." According to this theory, American society is firm in judging peoples' social worth on the basis of their apparent material success and in preaching that success is available to all if they work hard and take advantage of available opportunities. In reality the opportunities or means of achieving success ("the American dream") are not available to all. Merton (1938, p. 78) states:

> It is only when a system of cultural values extols, virtually above all else, certain common symbols of success for the population at large while its social structure rigorously restricts or completely eliminates access to approved

modes of acquiring these symbols for a considerable part of the same population, that antisocial behavior ensues on a considerable scale.

Thus according to Merton's theory of anomie, antisocial behavior (crime) is produced by the very values of the society itself—in encouraging high material aspirations as a sign of individual success without adequately providing approved means for all to reach these goals. This discrepancy between goals and means produces various "modes of personality adaptation," different combinations of behavior in accepting or rejecting the means and goals. Given this high premium placed upon individual success without concomitant provision of adequate means for its achievement, individuals may seek out alternate (nonapproved) means of accomplishing this goal. American fiction, the Horatio Alger stories of "rags to riches," the media, and literature constantly pound home the theme of success. "Social Darwinism" (the theme that the capable or fit will succeed) and the "Protestant ethic" (the attachment of religious value to work) have been persistent philosophies. These values are generally accepted by persons of all social classes.

One of the essential premises of this approach is that organization and disorganization in society are not mutually exclusive, but rather that many of the cultural values which have desirable consequences ("manifest functions") often contain within them or produce undesirable consequences ("latent functions") (Merton, 1961).

Modes of Personality Adaptation

Merton describes five possible "modes of personality adaptation" which represent types of adjustments to societal means and goals: the conformist, the innovator, the ritualist, the retreatist, and the rebel. All except the conformist represent deviant responses. The *conformist* accepts the goals of success in society and also the societally-approved means of achieving this status such as through hard work, education, deferred gratification, and the like. Acceptance of the goals does not indicate that all actually achieve such ends to their satisfaction, but that they have faith in the system.

The *innovator* accepts the goal of success, but either rejects or seeks alternate (illegitimate) means of achieving these aims. Criminal activities such as theft or organized crime could serve as examples, although societally encouraged activities such as inventions could also provide illustrations. An interesting example is the case of Fred Demara, Jr., *The Great Imposter* (Crichton, 1959), a high school graduate, who was disappointed that people had to spend much of their existence preparing usually for only one occupation. Forging credentials and identities

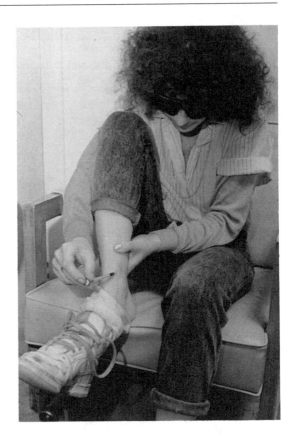

An intravenous drug user. Drug users are an example of a subculture alienated from society. Withdrawal into such a subculture is one response to a lack of opportunity in main-stream society.

he launched into careers as a college professor, Trappist monk, peniten-tiary warden, and surgeon in the Canadian Navy, just to mention a few.

The *ritualist* is illustrated by the "mindless bureaucrat" who becomes so caught up in rules and means to an end that he or she tends to for-get or fails to place proper significance upon the goal. The individual will compulsively persist with going through the motions with little hope of successful achievement of goals.

The *retreatist* represents a rejection of both societally approved means and ends. This adaptation might be illustrated by the advice of Timo-thy Leary, the prophet of psychedelic drugs in the sixties, who preached, "tune in, turn on, and drop out." Chronic alcoholics and drug addicts may eventually reject societal standards of jobs and success, and posit the goal of "getting high" with the means being by begging, borrow-ing, or stealing.

The *rebel* rejects both means and goals and seeks to substitute alter-nate ones which would represent new societal goals as well as new methods of achieving them, for example, through revolutionary activities aimed at introducing change in the existing order outside of normal, societally approved channels.

A Critique of Merton's Theory

Merton's theory, very well received in sociology and in criminology, became the basis of a number of subcultural theories of delinquency to be discussed shortly. Criticisms of the theory include that:

- His assumption of uniform commitment to materialistic goals ignores the pluralistic and heterogeneous nature of American cultural values.
- The theory appears to dwell upon lower class criminality, thus failing to consider the law-breaking among the elite. Taylor et al. (1973, p. 107) express this point: "Anomie theory stands accused of predicting too little bourgeois criminality and too much proletarian criminality."
- The theory is primarily oriented toward explaining monetary or materialistically oriented crime and does not address violent criminal activity.

While many writers (Hirschi, 1969; Johnson, 1979; and Kornhauser, 1978) have concluded that Merton's theory does not hold up empirically, recent research by Farnworth and Lieber (1989) argued in favor of its durability. They indicate that strain (anomie) theory combines psychological and structural explanations for crime and thus avoids purely individualistic explanations, and that the research of the critics failed to examine the gap or strain between economic goals and educational means. Farnworth and Lieber found this to be a significant educational predictor of delinquency in their sample of juveniles, and concluded that the theory is " . . . a viable and promising theory of delinquency and crime" (Ibid., p. 273).

Subcultural Theories

Merton's modification of Durkheim's notion of anomie began the "anomie tradition" in American criminology, with further influential theoretical work by writers such as Richard Cloward and Lloyd Ohlin and Albert Cohen, which directed itself toward subcultural theories of delinquency.

Merton's theory had a major impact upon many of the more sociologically-oriented theories of crime and delinquency. A major area of theoretical focus from the thirties through the sixties in American criminology related to juvenile gangs, as studies of citations in recent criminology textbooks (Schichor, 1982) and most frequently nominated books and journal articles (Wolfgang, 1980b) show.

Cloward and Ohlin's "Differential Opportunity" Theory

An extension of the works of both Merton and Sutherland, to be discussed, appeared in Richard Cloward and Lloyd Ohlin's (1960) *Delinquency and Opportunity: A Theory of Delinquent Gangs.* According to their theory of "differential opportunity," working class juveniles will choose one of another type of subcultural (gang) adjustment to their anomic situation depending upon the availability of illegitimate opportunity structures in their neighborhood. Borrowing from Merton's theme, Cloward and Ohlin view the pressure for joining delinquent subcultures as originating from discrepancies between culturally induced aspirations among lower class youth and available means of achieving them through legitimate channels. In addition to legitimate channels, Cloward and Ohlin stress the importance of available illegitimate opportunities, which may also be limited, depending upon the neighborhood. Neighborhoods with highly organized rackets provide upward mobility in the illegal opportunity structure. Individuals occupy positions in both legitimate and illegitimate opportunity structures, both of which may be limited. Illegitimate opportunities are dependent upon locally available criminal traditions.

Delinquent Subcultures

Cloward and Ohlin identified three types of illegitimate juvenile subcultures: the criminal, conflict, and retreatist. The criminal subculture occurs in stable slum neighborhoods in which a hierarchy of available criminal opportunities exist. Such a means of adaptation substitutes theft, extortion, and property offenses as the means of achieving success. Disorganized slums (ones undergoing invasion-succession or turnover of ethnic groups) are characterized by a conflict subculture. Such groups, denied both legitimate and illegitimate sources of access to status, resort to violence, "defense of turf," "bopping," "the rumble," as a means of gaining a "bad rep" or prestige. The retreatist subculture is viewed by Cloward and Ohlin as being made up of "double failures." Unable to succeed either in the legitimate or illegitimate opportunity structure, such individuals reject both the legitimate means and ends and simply drop out; lacking criminal opportunity, they seek status through "kicks" and "highs" of drug abuse. These subcultures become the individual's reference group and primary source of self-esteem. According to this theory, delinquent gang members do not generally reject the societal goal of success, but, lacking proper means, seek out other opportunities.

A Critique of "Differential Opportunity" Theory

Cloward and Ohlin's theory, building as it had upon other respected theories, was well received in the field of criminology. Criticisms of the theory have generally involved:

- This theory focused exclusively upon delinquent gangs and lower and working class backgrounds, ignoring, for instance, middle class delinquent subcultures.
- It is doubtful that delinquent subcultures fall only into the three categories they identified. In fact, much shifting of membership and activities among members appears common (Bordua, 1961; and Schrag, 1962).
- The orientations and specialization of delinquent gangs, even if the analysis was restricted to the United States, appear far more complex and varied than as identified by their theory.

Despite criticism, Cloward and Ohlin's ideas were very influential in the field and represented a broader theory than another in the anomie tradition, that of Albert Cohen (1955). Where Cloward and Ohlin viewed delinquency as an anomic reaction to goals, means discrepancy, and the particular form of adaptation dependent upon available illegitimate opportunities, Cohen had perceived delinquency as a reaction of lower class youth to unobtainable middle class values.

Cohen's "Lower Class Reaction" Theory

Albert Cohen's (1955) *Delinquent Boys* presents another theory in the tradition of lower class subcultural delinquency. According to his theory, delinquency is a *lower class reaction* to *middle class values*. Lower class youth use delinquent subcultures as a means of reacting against a middle class dominated value system in a society which unintentionally discriminates against them because of their lower class lifestyles and values. Unable to live up to or accept middle class values and judgments, they seek self-esteem by rejecting these values. Cohen (Ibid., p. 25) carefully compromises his remarks by indicating that this theory is not intended to describe all juvenile crime.

He views much lower class delinquency as nonutilitarian, malicious, and negativistic. Much theft, for instance, is nonutilitarian, performed for status purposes within the gang rather than necessarily out of need. Maliciousness is expressed in a general disdain for middle class values or objects and a negativistic reaction to such values. The delinquent gang substitutes its own values and sources of self-esteem for the middle class values it rejects. Some examples of middle class values include: ambition, individual responsibility, verbal skills, academic achievement, deferred gratification (postponement of rewards), middle class manners, nonviolence, wholesome recreation, and the like. The gang subculture represents a means of protection and striking back against values and behavioral expectations the lower class youth is unable to fulfill.

A Critique of Cohen's Theory

Major criticisms of Cohen's theory relate to:

- His overconcentration upon lower (working) class delinquency.
- His assumption that lower class boys are interested in middle class values (Kitsuse and Dietrick, 1959).
- Cohen as well as other subcultural theorists fail to address ethnic, family, and other sources of stress as well as the recreational ("fun") aspects of gang membership (Bordua, 1962).
- By emphasizing the nonutilitarian nature of many delinquent activities, Cohen tends to underplay the rational, for-profit nature of some juvenile criminal activities.

Cohen's theory fits into the "anomie tradition" in that he views lower class delinquency and gang membership as a result of strain or reaction to unfulfilled aspirations. A related subcultural theory by Walter Miller disagrees with this strain hypothesis and argues instead—in the social process tradition of Shaw, McKay, and Sutherland—that lower class delinquency represents a process of learning and expressing values of one's membership group. Miller's theory will be discussed in detail shortly.

Social Process Theories

Social process theories emphasize criminality as a learned or culturally-transmitted process and are represented as an outgrowth of the "Chicago school of sociology" in the works of Henry Shaw and David McKay, Edwin Sutherland, Walter Miller, as well as David Matza.

The Chicago School

In 1892 the first American academic program in sociology was begun at the University of Chicago, marking the inception of sociology's "Chicago school." Names associated with this school would represent a virtual Camelot of sociology: Park, Burgess, Wirth, Shaw, McKay, Thrasher, Zorbaugh, Anderson, Mead, Faris, Dunham, Thomas, Znaniecki, Cressy, and Sutherland, just to mention a few. Originally begun by sociologist Albion Small, the school would have a primary influence on the development of sociology as a distinctive American discipline in the twenties and thirties with Robert Park, Ernest Burgess, and Louis Wirth as the primary mentors. This group would develop a comprehensive theoretical system—urban ecology—which would generate a remarkable number of urban life studies (Stein, 1964, pp. 13–46).

Human Ecology

Like Durkheim, Park (1952) saw that freedom from group constraints often also entailed freedom from group supports. While Durkheim referred to this as anomie, Park used the notion of "individualization due to mobility." *Ecology* is a field which examines the interrelationship of organisms and environment. Park's theory was based upon *human ecology*, looking at humans and the environment and, more specifically, at *urban ecology*, viewing the city as a growing organism, heavily employing analogies from plant ecology. According to Park, the heterogeneous contact of racial and ethnic groups in the city often leads to competition for status and space and sometimes conflict, accommodation, acculturation, assimilation, or amalgamation, terms all quite similar to concepts in botany (plant biology) such as segregation, invasion, succession, and dispersion. One of Park's key notions was that of "natural areas," subcommunities which emerge to serve specific, specialized functions. They are called "natural" since they are unplanned and serve to order the functions and needs of diverse populations within the city. Natural areas provide institutions and organizations to socialize its inhabitants and to provide for social control. Such natural areas include: ports of embarkation, Burgess's "zone of transition" (discussed in Chapter 3), ghettos, bohemias, hobohemias, and the like. Burgess's (1925) "concentric zone theory," which views cities as growing outward in concentric rings, served as the graphic model for the Chicago school's theory of human ecology. Wirth's (1938) theory of "Urbanism as a Way of Life" viewed the transition from the rural to the urban way of life as producing social disorganization, marginality, anonymity, anomie, and alienation due to the heterogeneity, freedom, and loneliness of urban life. The Chicago school expressed an antiurban bias in their analysis and a nostalgia for the small Midwestern towns from which most of its theorists had originated.

Using Park's concept of "natural areas" as a building block, their students were enjoined to perform case studies of these areas in order to generate hypotheses as well as, hopefully, generalizations. Park (1952, p. 198) expressed the hope:

> The natural areas of the city, it appears from what has been said, may be made to serve an important methodological function. They constitute, taken together, what Hobson has described as "a frame of reference," a conceptual order within which statistical facts gain a new and more general significance. They not only tell us what the facts are in regard to conditions in any given region, but insofar as they characterize an area that is natural and typical, they establish a working hypothesis in regard to other areas of the same kind.

This empirical orientation, as opposed to armchair theorizing, was the chief contribution of the Chicago school. Among the students to be inspired to perform field research were Clifford Shaw and David McKay and Edwin Sutherland.

Shaw and McKay's "Social Disorganization" Theory

Ironically, although Clifford Shaw and David McKay are pointed to as members of the Chicago school, they never enjoyed faculty status at the University of Chicago but performed their research while employed by the Illinois Institute for Juvenile Research in Chicago. Snodgrass (1972) indicates that neither Shaw nor McKay received their doctorates due to foreign language requirements, but worked closely with many faculty and students from the University (Carey, 1975, pp. 84–92). The lasting contribution of Shaw and McKay's ecological studies in the thirties was their basic premise that crime is due more to social disorganization in pathological environments than it is to abnormal individuals committing deviant behavior (Gibbons, 1979, p. 45).

In the tradition of the statistical school of criminological theory, Shaw and McKay made extensive use of maps and official statistics to plot the ecological distribution of forms of social disorganization such as juvenile delinquency (Shaw, 1929; and Shaw and McKay, 1942). Using Burgess's "concentric zone theory" as a schema, as well as Park's notion of "natural areas," they were able to document the ecological impact upon human behavior. For instance, one transitional area (an area undergoing invasion/succession) was shown to exhibit very high crime rates despite considerable change in its ethnic makeup. Such areas breed criminogenic influences which predispose occupants to crime and social disorganization. In other research, Shaw utilized ethnographic and autobiographical field methods in order to provide case studies of criminals and delinquents (Shaw, 1930; and Shaw, McKay, and MacDonald, 1938). Imposing concentric circles on mapped areas of Chicago upon which rates of social disorganization had been plotted, Shaw (1930, pp. 198–204) was able to demonstrate the highest rates of truancy, crime, delinquency, and recidivism in Zone II (area of transition), while such rates declined as one moved further out the rings. Criminal attitudes and social pathology were viewed as culturally transmitted within the social environment.

A Critique of "Social Disorganization" Theory

The human ecologists' insistence upon ecological and social conditions having criminogenic impacts upon otherwise normal individuals would inspire later criminologists such as Sutherland. Their stress upon field studies and an empirical orientation would provide credibility to the fledgling disciplines of sociology and criminology and win them greater academic acceptance. A number of shortcomings, however, have been identified:

- Their theories at times border on ecological determinism: that an area or physical environment causes social pathology. Concentration upon the geophysical environment tends to make the social structure and institutions secondary.
- The attempt to borrow an organic analogy and adapt biological concepts such as competition, invasion, succession, and the like to criminology saddled the field with unnecessarily primitive concepts.
- Some of the studies tend to commit the "ecological fallacy" (Robinson, 1950) in which group rates are used in order to describe individual behavior. Aggregate statistics do not yield accurate estimates if the intended unit of analysis is the behavior of individuals.
- Although Shaw and McKay studied other cities, the theories and conceptions of the Chicago school (such as the concentric growth of cities) were perhaps applicable to Chicago, a city undergoing fantastic urbanization during the twenties and thirties, but may not apply to other urban communities, particularly since the post-World War II period.
- These theories assume stable ecological areas which in fact is not the case. Such areas disappeared in the post World War II decentralization of urban areas (Bursik, 1988, pp. 523–524; and Schuerman and Kobrin, 1986).

- Problems in operationalizing (measuring) key concepts such as delinquency rate and disorganization exist in which there is a heavy reliance upon official statistics (Pfohl, 1985, p. 167).
- There was an overemphasis upon consensus in community and an unappreciation of political conflict (Bursik, 1988, p. 524).

In defense of Shaw and McKay, Brantingham and Brantingham (1984, p. 312) point out that they were not as guilty of falling into the ecological fallacy trap as many of their followers, since they supplemented many of their statistical studies with case studies. This was illustrated by ethnographic works such as Shaw, McKay, and MacDonald's (1938) *Brothers in Crime* and Shaw's (1930) *The Jack Roller*. Focusing upon group or social process, the urban ecologists and Shaw and McKay in particular were influential in shifting criminological analysis from an overconcentration upon the individual deviant and instead upon criminogenic influences of social environments.

Routine Activities Approach

A resurgence and rediscovery of interest in the ecological and social disorganization theories of crime has been rekindled by formulations such as Cohen and Felson (1979) and Felson's (1983) "routine activities approach" to crime causation. This approach says, "the volume of criminal offenses will be related to the nature of normal everyday patterns of interaction . . . there is a symbiotic relationship between legal and illegal activities" (Messner and Tardiff, 1985, pp. 241–242). In summarizing the routine activities approach, Felson (1987, p. 911) indicates that:

> (1) It specifies three earthy elements of crime: a likely offender, a suitable target, and the absence of a capable guardian against crime. (2) It considers how everyday life assembles these three elements in space and time. (3) It shows that a proliferation of lightweight durable goods and a dispersion of activities away from family and household could account quite well for the crime wave in the U.S. in the 1960s and the 1970s without fancier explanations. Indeed modern society invites high crime rates by offering a multitude of illegal opportunities.

Other works which illustrate the reaffirmation of social disorganization theory are by Simcha-Fagan and Schwartz (1986) who include social disorganization and subcultural approaches in explaining urban delinquency. Similarly Byrne and Sampson (1986) indicate that the social-ecological model is based upon the premise that community has independent impacts on crime that are not disaggregable to the individual level. In "Deviant Places," Stark (1987), in arguing that "kinds of places" explanations are needed in criminology in addition to the "kinds of people" explanations, codifies thirty propositions from over a century of ecological explanations of both the Chicago school and the moral statisticians of the 19th century.

Stark identifies five aspects of high deviance areas: density, poverty, mixed use, transience, and dilapidation. These elements create criminogenic conditions for crime. His propositions include that density is associated with interaction between least and most deviant populations, higher moral cynicism, overcrowding, outdoor gatherings, lower levels of supervision of children, poorer school achievement, lower stakes in conformity, and increased deviant behavior. Crowding will increase family conflict, decrease the ability to shield wrongdoing and thus increase moral cynicism. While Stark's hypotheses are too numerous to cover here, his systematic extracting of propositions from over a century of social disorganization/ecological research represents a reaffirmation and resurgence of such literature.

Sutherland's Theory of "Differential Association"

Perhaps the most influential general theory of criminality was that proposed initially in 1934 by Edwin Sutherland (1883–1950) in his theory of differential association. Simply stated, the theory indicates that individuals become predisposed toward criminality due to an excess of contacts which advocate criminal behavior. Due to these contacts a person will tend to learn and accept values and attitudes which look more favorably upon criminality.

Sutherland's theory was strongly influenced by Charles Horton Cooley's (1902) theory of personality—"the looking-glass self." Cooley viewed the human personality as a "social self," one which is learned in the process of socialization and interaction with others. The personality as a social product is the sum total of an individual's internalization of the impressions he or she receives of the evaluation of others—"mirror of alters." "Significant others," people who are most important to the individual, are particularly important in this socialization process. Thus in Cooley's perception, the human personality is a social self, a product of social learning and interaction with others. Sutherland was also influenced by Shaw and McKay's (1942) notion of social disorganization and cultural transmission of crime, as well as by French sociologist Gabriel Tarde's (1912; originally published in 1890) concept of imitation as transmitter of criminal values. Similarly, in Sutherland's explanation of criminality, crime is a learned social phenomenon, transmitted in the same manner in which more conventional behavior and attitudes are passed on.

In explaining how he developed the theory, Sutherland indicated that he was not even aware that he had done so until, in 1935, Henry McKay referred to "Sutherland's theory": "I asked him what my theory was. He referred me to pages 51–52 of my book" (Sutherland, 1956, p. 14). The first edition of Sutherland's text was published in 1924; while the 1934 edition to which McKay referred contained the nexus of a theory, it was in the 1939 edition that Sutherland outlined its major propositions. These were slightly modified in the 1947 edition and have remained essentially the same in subsequent editions which have been coauthored or (since Sutherland's death in 1950) authored by Donald Cressey.

The nine propositions of the differential association theory are these (Sutherland, 1947, pp. 6–7):

- Criminal behavior is learned.
- Criminal behavior is learned in interaction with other persons in a process of communication.
- The principal part of the learning of criminal behavior occurs within intimate personal groups.
- When criminal behavior is learned, the learning includes (a) techniques of committing the crime, which are sometimes very simple; (b) the specific direction of motives, drives, rationalizations, and attitudes.
- The specific direction of motives and drives is learned from definitions of the legal codes as favorable or unfavorable.
- A person becomes delinquent because of an excess of definitions favorable to violation of law over definitions unfavorable to violation of law.
- Differential association may vary in frequency, duration, priority, and intensity.
- The process of learning criminal behavior by association with criminal and anticriminal patterns involves all of the mechanisms that are involved in any other learning.
- While criminal behavior is an expression of general needs and values, it is not explained by those general needs and values since noncriminal behavior is an expression of the same needs and values.

Differential association theory is not directed at the issue of the origin of crime in society, but concentrates instead on the transmission of criminal attitudes and behavior. It is a behavioristic theory—"previous behavior causes subsequent behavior"—and contains elements of a "soft social determinism," that is, exposure to groups does not cause but predisposes individuals to criminal activity or causes them to view it more favorably. Why, then, do not all with similar exposure become similarly criminal? Sutherland's notion of variations in contacts provides for individual reaction to social groups and exposures.

Contacts in differential association vary according to frequency, duration, priority, and intensity. *Frequency* deals with the number of contacts, *duration* with the length of time over which an individual is exposed to such contacts. The sheer length and volume of association with criminogenic influences has impact upon different people in divergent ways. Humans are not robots responding in a predictable manner to a given number of influences. *Priority* refers to the preference individuals express toward the values and attitudes to which they are exposed, while *intensity* entails the meaningfulness the human actor attached to such exposure. While Sutherland (Ibid.) admits an inability to reach a quantitative or exact measurement of these modalities, a very general example should illustrate their operation. What explains the good child in the bad environment? Despite a great frequency of and long duration of criminal attitudes, such individuals fail to prefer such values, and attach greater meaning to noncriminal attitudes which, although less frequently available, may be found in "significant others," perhaps role models such as teachers, coaches, peers, and the like.

A Critique of "Differential Association"

Due to its being a general theory of criminality and its relative compatibility with many other criminological explanations of crime, differential association theory enjoyed widespread acceptance in the field. It was not, however, without critics. Donald Cressey, Sutherland's coauthor, explains that since Sutherland's principal propositions are presented in only two pages in his textbook, the theory is often misinterpreted by some critics, most notably Vold (1958, p. 194). Among these claimed errors of interpretation, Cressey (Sutherland and Cressey, 1974, pp. 78–80) mentions the following:

- The theory is only concerned with contacts or associations with criminal or delinquent behavior patterns. (It actually refers to both criminal and noncriminal behavior, as demonstrated by the use of terms such as "differential" and "excess" of contacts.)
- The theory says persons become criminals due to an excess of associations with criminals. (It actually says that criminal attitudes can be learned from the unintentional transmission of such values by noncriminals.)
- Using the 1939 version of the theory, critics believe the theory refers to "systematic criminals." (This was modified since the 1947 version to refer to all criminal behavior.)

- The theory fails to explain why persons have the associations they have. (It does not pretend to do so.)

Cressey (1960) also addresses other criticisms which he feels are misinterpretations. However, a number of shortcomings have been identified:

- While Sutherland traces the roots of criminality to culture conflict and social disorganization, a comprehensive theory of criminality should provide more explanation regarding the origin of crime in the first place.
- Being a general theory, it is difficult to either empirically prove or disprove by means of research, and reformulations are necessary in order to permit testing (see Burgess and Akers, 1966; and DeFleur and Quinney, 1966).
- The theory fails to account for all forms of criminality.
- The theory fails to acknowledge the importance of non-face-to-face contacts such as media influences (Radzinowicz and King, 1977, p. 82).

Despite these and other criticisms, differential association remains important as a useful general theory of criminality even though it may fail to specify the process for each individual case of criminality. The theory of differential association remains one of the most cited theories in modern criminology and will probably remain so until a more acceptable general theory of criminality appears. It also has received support by recent research (Matsueda, 1988; and Orcutt, 1987).

Miller's "Focal Concerns"

Walter Miller's (1958) ideas appeared in an article entitled "Lower Class Culture as a Generating Milieu of Gang Delinquency." Miller qualifies the applicability of his theory to ". . . members of adolescent street corner groups in lower class communities" (Ibid., p. 5). Unlike Cohen, who viewed such delinquency as a lower class reaction to middle class values, Miller views such activity as a reflection of the focal concerns of dominant themes within lower class culture. These are ". . . areas or issues which command widespread and persistent attention and a high degree of emotional involvement" (Ibid., p. 7). Faced with a chasm between aspirations and the likelihood of their achievement, lower class youths seek status and prestige within one-sex peer units (gangs) in which they exaggerate focal concerns already in existence within lower class culture. Thus gang delinquency, rather than representing an anomic reaction to unobtainable middle class goals, represents, in the tradition of social process theory, a pattern of subcultural transmission or learning of values prevalent within the local environment.

The *focal concerns of lower class culture* emphasize: trouble, toughness, smartness, excitement, fate, and autonomy. Getting into *trouble* often confers prestige and a means of obtaining attention. The "class clown," the "bad dude" become attention attracting roles. *Toughness,* "macho," having physical prowess, or being able to handle oneself is a highly prized characteristic among lower class males. The "hard guy" is preferable to the "chump," "wimp," or "sissy." *Smartness* ". . . involves the capacity to outsmart, outfox, outwit, dupe, "take," "con" another . . . ." (Ibid.) This is illustrated by the "streetwise" game of "playin' the dozens," a highly ritualistic game of razzing, "ranking," "cappin' on someone's Mom" practiced by lower class black males in particular. Extremely foul insults are traded by two antagonists, the themes usually relating to sexual matters and female relatives of one's opponent. Such insults are rhythmically presented one-liners, the object being to have the opponent speechless or "humbled out." "Playin' the dozens" is also known as signification. Such activities, poetry of the streets, would be regarded in conventional society as having a "bad mouth."

The theme of *excitement* emphasizes the quest for skill, danger, risk, change, activity. The future, rather than being viewed as a subject of control and planning, is perceived as a matter of *fate,* luck, or good fortune. Gambling's popularity within lower class culture makes it the "poor person's stock exchange." The stress upon *autonomy* (independence) looms as a dominant concern within lower class culture, particularly among males, even though it is less likely to be achieved given their narrow occupational and life options. "Being one's own man" and free from authority, "the man," and external constraint is a strong value.

A Critique of Miller's Theory

- Similar to the other subcultural theories, Miller's theory also ignores middle and upper class delinquent/criminal activity.
- By focusing exclusively upon the lower class, Miller and others in this tradition are perhaps most responsible for the criticism of mainstream sociology as ignoring deviance of the powerful.
- Miller's theory rests very heavily upon the assumption of the existence of a distinctive lower class culture which holds values and attitudes distinct if not at odds with dominant middle class values. The pluralistic nature of American society makes it quite uncertain that such a distinctive value system solely based upon class is indeed the case.

Miller's theory views criminogenic influences as learned or transmitted as part of subcultural values. Similarly, the writing of David Matza views delinquency as part of a general social process of learning cultural values rather than an anomic reaction to unobtainable goals.

Matza's "Delinquency and Drift"

The theories of David Matza are presented in his book, *Delinquency and Drift* (1964), and in a coauthored article with Gresham Sykes (Sykes and Matza, 1957) entitled "Techniques of Neutralization." Matza's theories are an example of "soft determinism," which holds that, although human behavior is determined to some extent by outside forces, there still exists an element of free will or individual responsibility (Matza, 1964, pp. 5–7). Humans are neither entirely constrained nor entirely free, nor is the individual entirely committed to delinquent or nondelinquent behavior. Matza (Ibid., p. 28) explains the drift theory of delinquency: "The delinquent exists in a limbo between convention and crime responding in turn to the demands of each, flirting now with one, now the other, but postponing commitment, evading decision. Thus he drifts between criminal and conventional action."

Subterranean Values

Rather than being wholly committed to delinquency, most delinquents are dabbling with it and are acting out "subterranean values" of society (Ibid., pp. 63–64) which exist alongside more conventional values in a pluralistic society such as the United States. Conventional society attempts to control the expression of these values and reserve it for the proper time and place; in a sense, it is the practice of "morality with a wink." The delinquent, rather than being committed to goals which are alien to society, exaggerates society's subterranean values and acts them out in caricature. Sykes and Matza explain (1957, p. 717):

> The delinquent may not stand as an alien in the body of society but may represent instead a disturbing reflection or caricature. His vocabulary is different, to be sure, but kicks, big time spending and rep have immediate counterparts in the value system of the law abiding. The delinquent has picked up and emphasized one part of the subterranean values that coexist with other, publicly proclaimed values possessing a more respectable air.

Thus, while conventional mores disapprove of subterranean values, they often represent "hidden" patterns or themes within the culture. Illicit sexual behavior, slick business practices, a dislike of work, substance abuse, and media violence as a popular form of entertainment are examples. Delinquents simply have poor training and timing in confining the expression of subterranean values. The pervasiveness of subterranean values might be illustrated by the attempt of conventional members of "straight" society to appear "hip," "with it," and "streetwise." "Can you dig it?"

Techniques of Neutralization

Sykes and Matza's (Ibid.) term "techniques of neutralization" refers to rationalizations or excuses which juveniles use to neutralize responsibility for deviant actions. In drift situations, offenders can obviate their responsibility by exaggerating normal legal defenses (for example, self-defense or insanity) or by pointing to the subterranean values prevalent in society. They identify *five techniques of neutralization:*

1. *Denial of responsibility* such as appeals based upon one's homelife, lack of affection, and social class.
2. *Denial of harm to anyone* such as stealing being defined as "borrowing" or drug abuse as harming no one but the offender.
3. *Denial of harm to victim* in which the assault is justified since the person harmed was also a criminal.
4. *Condemning the condemners,* reversing the labeling process by claiming that authorities are more corrupt than the offender, as well as hypocritical.
5. *Appeal to higher authority* which claims that the offense was necessary in order to defend one's neighborhood or gang.

As an illustration of the techniques of neutralization, the "Gee, Officer Krupke" song from the musical *West Side Story,* finds members of the Jets gang arguing that they are victims of a social disease:

> "Dear Kindly Sergeant Krupke,
> You gotta understand,
> It's just our bringin' upke
> That gets us out of hand.
> Our mothers all are junkies,
> Our fathers all are drunks.
> Golly, Moses,
> natcherly we're punks!"
> (Stephen Sondheim)

Sykes and Matza (Ibid., p. 668) explain:

> The delinquent both has his cake and eats it too, for he remains committed to the dominant normative system and yet so qualifies its imperatives that

violations are "acceptable" if not "right." Thus the delinquent represents not a radical opposition to law abiding society but something more like an apologetic failure, often more sinned against than sinning in his own eyes. We call these justifications of deviant behavior techniques of neutralization; and we believe these techniques make up a crucial component of Sutherland's "definitions favorable to the violation of the law." It is by learning these techniques that the juveniles become delinquent, rather than by learning moral imperatives, values or attitudes standing in direct contradiction to those of the dominant society.

A Critique of Matza's Theory

A gang fight scene from the musical "West Side Story."

Matza provides a transition between Sutherland's social process theories and the social control theories to be discussed next. By combining deterministic models with the notion of free will, he avoids

the overly deterministic nature of many earlier theories and explains why the majority of individuals who find themselves in criminogenic settings do not commit crime. His concept of neutralization enables him to escape the problem inherent in previous subcultural theories of delinquency which rested on the premise that delinquent values were at variance with conventional values. Some possible shortcomings, however, of Matza's views include the following:

- While some research has shown offenders more prone to rationalizing their behavior (Regoli and Poole, 1978; and Ball, 1980), Hindelang (1970) found different value systems among delinquents. Obviously, more research is needed.
- In order for his theory to be correct, empirical evidence must demonstrate that Matza's neutralization takes place during the period of drift preceding the act, an issue which may be difficult to operationalize.

Hamlin (1988) argues that the notion of rational choice in neutralization theory has been misplaced and that such rationalizations are utilized after the fact only when behavior is called into question (see Minor, 1981 and 1984, for additional analysis).

The transitional nature of Matza's theories with social control approaches can be found in his notion of drift, in which individuals become temporarily detached from social control mechanisms. This release from group bonds is the basic unit of analysis in social control theories.

Social Control Theories

The final grouping of mainstream socio-criminological theories to be discussed are referred to as social control theories and are represented by the work of Walter Reckless and Travis Hirschi.

Social control theories address the issue of how society maintains or elicits social control and the manner in which it obtains conformity or fails to obtain it in the form of deviance. As Gibbons (1979, p. 113) points out, this once-major area in sociological investigation is still a viable area of investigation. While in one meaning, the concept dealt with penology or corrections, another usage, the subject of this discussion, was concerned with socialization and learning processes, the internalization of societal norms (inner controls) and external influences (outer controls) (Clark and Gibbs, 1965). Although a number of writers have contributed to social control theories, this presentation will concentrate primarily upon the formulations of Walter Reckless and his associates (1956, 1957a, 1957b, 1961; Reckless and Dinitz, 1967) and Travis Hirschi (1969).

Reckless's "Containment Theory"

One of the earliest and best known examples of social control theory was Walter Reckless's (1961) containment theory. Like his contemporary Sutherland, Reckless was a product of the "Chicago school" of sociology and one of the mainstream pioneers in American criminology (Gibbons, 1979, p. 115). Reckless wrote an early textbook called *The Crime Problem* in 1940, and in a much later edition began to state his theories. Containment theory basically holds that individuals have various social controls (containments) which assist them in resisting pressures which draw them toward criminality. This theory attempts to account both for social forces which may predispose individuals to crime as well as for individual characteristics which may insulate them from or further propel them toward criminality. Various social pressures, treated in previously discussed deterministic theories, exert pushes and pulls upon the individual; these pressures interact with containments (protective barriers), both internal and external to the individual, and these containments add the element of free will in resisting criminality. Thus the presence or absence of social pressures interacts with the presence or absence of containments to produce or not produce individual criminality.

The basic elements of Reckless's containment theory (Reckless et al., 1957a, 1957b; and Reckless and Dinitz, 1967) can be summarized:

- *Layers of Social Pressures:*

    External pressures push an individual toward criminality. Variables impinging upon an individual include: poor living conditions, adverse economic conditions, minority group membership, and the lack of legitimate opportunities.

    External pulls draw individuals away from social norms and are exerted from without by bad companions, deviant subcultures, and media influences.

    Internal pressures push an individual toward criminality; they include personality contingencies such as inner tensions, feelings of inferiority or inadequacy, mental conflict, organic defects, and the like.

- *Containments:*

    Inner containments refer to the internalization of conventional behavioral values and the development of personality characteristics which enable one to resist pressures. Strong self-concept, identity, and strong resistance to frustration serve as examples.

Outer containments are represented by effective family and near support systems which assist in reinforcing conventionality and insulating the individual from the assault of outside pressures.

Reckless and his colleagues (1957a) felt that the theory was helpful in explaining both delinquency and nondelinquency, as indicated by the title of one article, "The Good Boy in a High Delinquency Area." Individuals may become predisposed toward criminality due to strong external pressures and pulls and weak inner and outer containments, while others with these same pressures may resist due to a strong family or through a strong sense of self. Weak containments plus strong external pressures provide the conditions for individual criminality. The attractiveness of containment theory is its general ability to subsume variables discussed in other more specific theories as well as its attempt to link the deterministic and free will models and to intersect socio-economic factors with individual biography, biological, and psychological factors.

A Critique of "Containment Theory"

Reckless and associates (Reckless, Dinitz, and Murray, 1957a; Reckless, Dinitz, and Kay, 1957b; and Scarpitti et al., 1960) have attempted to verify his theory. In one study, they had teachers nominate "good boys" in a high delinquency area, then found strong self-images as well as more conventional behavior among this group four years later. But critics call for more research, indicating that poor operationalization and weak methodology have plagued these studies (Schwartz and Tangri, 1965; and Schrag, 1971). As a very general sensitizing theory that attempts to account for both criminogenic forces and individual responses, the containment theory is a useful descriptive model; but actual empirical specification of the process is problematic.

Hirschi's "Social Bond" Theory

Travis Hirschi (1969) in *Causes of Delinquency* presented his social bond theory, which basically states that delinquency takes place when a person's bonds to society are weakened or broken, thus reducing personal stakes in conformity. Individuals maintain conformity for fear that violations will rupture their relationships (cause them to "lose face") with family, friends, neighbors, jobs, school, and the like. In essence, individuals conform not for fear of prescribed punishments in the criminal law, but more from concern with violating the mores and the personal image of them held by important groups of which they are members. *These bonds to society consist of four components: attachment, commitment, involvement, and belief.*

Attachment refers to a bond to others such as family, peers, and important institutions such as churches or schools. Weak attachment to parents and family may impair personality development, while poor relationships with the school is viewed as particularly instrumental in delinquency. *Commitment* involves the degree to which an individual maintains a vested interest in the social and economic system. If an individual has much to lose in terms of status, job, and community standing, he or she is less likely to violate the law. Adults, for instance, have many more such commitments than do juveniles. *Involvement* entails engagement in legitimate social and recreational activities which either leaves too little time to get into trouble or binds one's status to yet other important groups whose opinion one does not wish to tarnish. Finally, *belief* in the conventional norms and value system and the law acts as a bond to society. Like Reckless's containment theory and Matza's delinquency and drift, Hirschi's social bond theory combines elements of determinism and free will; individual choice still enters the equation.

A Critique of "Social Bond" Theory

Social bond theory has been relatively well received because as a general theory it subsumes and is supported by many more specific findings with respect to relationships between crime/delinquency and particular variables. School performance, family relationships, peer group attachments, and community involvement as predictors of norm violation have been stock items in criminological research. Research by Hirschi (1969), a partial replication by Hindelang (1973), and review of studies by Bernard (1987) provide some strong support for control theory. Strong parental attachments, commitment to conventional values, and involvement in conventional activities and with conventional peers were found to be predictive of nondelinquent activity. While Agnew (1985) found that social control variables explained only 1 to 2 percent of future delinquency and that cross-sectional studies exaggerated the importance of Hirschi's theory, Rosenbaum (1987) found that the theory explained some types of delinquency better than others. The theory accounted for more female than male crime and more for drug use than for violent or property offending. Variations of social control theory have been offered by Briar and Piliavin (1965), in whose theory individuals evaluate the risk of being caught and punished once bonds are weakened, and Glaser (1978, p. 126), who combines elements of differential association, control, and classical theory. While Hirschi's social control appears to be quite useful in explaining the general process of commitment/noncommitment to delinquency, more research is certainly needed in order to specify and modify it. Hirschi's theory is not concerned with societal origins of crime, but with individual deviation from given societal norms.

Mainstream vs. Critical Criminology

The general characteristics of mainstream criminology, although subject to variation in individual anomie, social process, or social control theories, include the following (Gibbons, 1979, p. 77–79; and Gibbons and Garabedian, 1974):

- An emphasis upon criminal behavior rather than upon the criminalization of behavior. Emphasis had been upon the criminal rather than upon the social control machinery.
- A consensus world view in which the existing society and its operations are perceived as relatively viable or unquestioned.
- A critical, sometimes cynical stance with respect to societal institutions, combined with a liberal optimism in reform measures.
- A mild pessimism regarding the perfectability of the criminal justice system, but willingness to work within the established social order.
- Advocation of rehabilitation of offenders and their adjustment to the status quo.
- A positivistic orientation which stresses objectivity and empirical analysis.

Critical criminology consists of a variety of perspectives that challenge basic assumptions in mainstream criminology, espoused by a group of U.S. thinkers who emerged in the sixties and seventies and who have been variously labeled as representatives of "conflict," "radical," "new," "critical," or "Marxist" criminology. Inciardi (1980, p. 7) explains:

> The perspective is *new* and *radical* in that it departs somewhat from the mainstream or traditional criminological emphases on the nature and etiology of criminal behavior; it is *conflict* oriented and *critical* in that it focuses more fully on value and cultural differences, social conflicts, racism, and sexism as sources of crime and deviance in contemporary society; and it is *Marxist* in that a number of its representatives argue that law—and, by extension, crime—and the structure of individual and group interactions which support legal codes flow from the manner in which the relations of economic production are organized.

Critical criminology consists of three major types of theoretical approaches: the labeling *(societal reaction) perspective,* conflict theory, *and the* radical *(Marxist)* viewpoint. While each of these approaches will be detailed shortly, here are some common characteristics of critical criminology:

- Crime is a label attached to behavior, usually of the less powerful in society.
- More powerful groups in society control this labeling process in order to protect their vested interests.
- The conflict model rather than consensus model explains the criminalization process.
- Crime is often a rational response to inequitable conditions in capitalistic societies.

More extreme statements advocate a critical philosophy and practical revolutionary action (*praxis*) as opposed to value-free, scientific inquiry.

While views of critical criminologists diverge, making it difficult to identify unitary themes, they perceive themselves as making a radical break with a consensus, ameliorative, and essentially conservative world view. Critical criminologists view their mainstream counterparts as handmaidens or social technicians for the status quo and see themselves as champions of the underdog and sometimes as prophets of a new social order.

The discussion of critical criminology will begin first with the labeling (societal reaction) theories, followed by conflict and radical criminological theories.

Labeling Theory

"If men define situations as real, they are real in their consequences."
—W. I. Thomas (Thomas and Swaine, 1928, p. 572)

Although there were earlier precedents, labeling theory (sometimes called "the societal reaction perspective") became a major criminological approach in the sixties primarily in the United States. Labeling theorists base their point of view on symbolic interactionism, a school of thought that emphasizes the subjective and interactional nature of human experiences. Derived from the writings of George Herbert Mead and Charles Horton Cooley and expressed later in the work of Herbert Blumer, George Homans, and Harold Garfinckel, with variations called exchange theory, ethnomethodology, and role theory, the emphasis in symbolic interactionism is upon analysis of subjective meanings of social interaction as perceived from the standpoint of the actor. Individuals perceive the meaning of their activity through the reaction of others.

Labeling theory says that individuals are deviant mainly because they have been labeled as deviant by social control agencies and others. The notion of deviance is not inherent in the act itself, but rather in the reaction and label attached to the actor; that is, crime is a label and not an act. Frank Tannenbaum called the process of attaching a label to deviants "the dramatization of evil" (1938). He (Ibid., pp. 19–20) viewed this criminalization process as: ". . . a process of tagging, defining, identifying, segregating, describing, emphasizing, making conscious and self-conscious; it becomes a way of stimulating, suggesting, emphasizing, and evoking the very traits complained of. . . ." Along with Edwin Lemert (1951), Howard Becker (1963, 1964), and Edwin Schur (1969, 1971) and others, Tannenbaum and the labeling theorists attempted to shift criminological inquiry from the deviant act to the social control and societal reaction machinery. In a sense, this reverses the usual process of analysis: rather than assuming that criminal behavior causes societal reaction, it posits that societal reaction causes criminal behavior.

Schrag (1971, pp. 89–91) summarizes some of the basic assumptions of labeling theory:

- No act is intrinsically criminal.
- Criminal definitions are enforced in the interest of the powerful.
- A person does not become a criminal by violation of the law, but only by the designation of criminality by authorities.
- Due to the fact that everyone conforms and deviates, people should not be dichotomized into criminal and noncriminal categories.
- The act of "getting caught" begins the labeling process.
- "Getting caught" and the decision making in the criminal justice system are a function of the offender as opposed to offense characteristics.
- Age, socioeconomic class, and race are the major offender characteristics that establish patterns of differential criminal justice decision making.
- The criminal justice system is established on a free will perspective that allows for the condemnation and rejection of the identified offender.
- Labeling is a process that eventually produces identification with a deviant image and subculture and a resulting "rejection of the rejectors."

Lemert's "Secondary Deviance"

Two important concepts in labeling theory are Edwin Lemert's (1967, p. 17) notions of "primary deviance" and "secondary deviance." *Primary deviance* refers to the initial deviant act itself, while *secondary deviance* is concerned with the psychological reorganization the individual experiences as a result of being caught and labeled as being a deviant. Once this stigma or discrediting mark or status is attached, the individual may find it very difficult to escape the label and may come to identify with this new deviant role.

Deviant behavior, then, is viewed as having been created in society by control agencies representing the interest of dominant groups (Piven, 1981, p. 490). For Lemert, the usual approach to analyzing deviance can be reversed. He states (Lemert, 1967, p. v):

> This is a large turn away from the older sociology which tended to rest heavily upon the idea that deviance leads to social control. I have come to believe that the reverse idea, i.e., social control leads to deviance, is equally tenable and the potentially richer premise for studying deviance in modern society.

Sociologist Howard Becker (1963) has coined the term "moral entrepreneurs" with which to refer to agents or officials who are concerned with creating and labeling new categories of deviance in order to expand the social control function of their organization. In Becker's view, deviance, rather than being inherent in the quality of the act, is so designated only by societal reaction and the subsequent labeling or stigmatization process.

A Critique of Labeling Theory

Some of the criticisms of the labeling perspective include the following:

- Labeling theory is overly deterministic and denies individual responsibility. Akers (1967, p. 46) very dramatically states:

> Those of this school come dangerously close to saying that the actual behavior is unimportant. . . . One sometimes gets the impression from reading this literature that people go about minding their own business, and then— "wham"—bad society comes along and slaps them with a stigmatized label. Forced into the role of deviant the individual has little choice, but to be deviant. This is an exaggeration of course, but such an image can be gained easily from an overemphasis on the impact of labeling.

Violators of societal rules are not passive robots of societal reaction.
- Some acts are universally regarded as intrinsically "wrong" (Wellford, 1975, p. 334). While labeling theorists have concentrated upon

public order crimes where the model may be more appropriate, they tend to generalize to all forms of deviance. Murder, forcible rape, aggravated assault, and robbery are more universally regarded as *mala in se*. Schur (1971, p. 14) observes: ". . . borderline forms of deviance seem to be especially good candidates for labeling analysis and those deviations on which widespread consensus exists less promising candidates."

■ If deviance is solely a matter of public reaction, then are "secret deviants," those who are uncaught, deviant (Taylor et al., 1973, p. 149)? While deviance has been traditionally viewed in criminology as involving rule-breaking of normative expectations and even the relativistic nature of definitions of deviance is widely shared, to define it solely in terms of reaction to the deviance is narrowly focusing upon only one part of this process.

■ The societal reaction approach pays inadequate attention to the causes of the initial deviant act, almost as if to say that the social control agencies cause crime.

■ While labeling theorists citing self-report surveys argue that nearly everyone commits crime, their argument seems to suggest that labels are attached capriciously, almost randomly. In fact most offenders involved in serious crimes are more likely to be labeled.

■ Wellford (1975, p. 343), on the basis of a review of Schrag's assumptions and the existing empirical evidence in criminology and the social sciences concluded, ". . . the assumptions underlying the theory are at significant variance with the data as we now understand it, or are not crucial to the labeling perspective."

By focusing primarily upon the social control machinery, labeling theory has obvious inadequacies as a general theory of criminality; but this focus upon societal reaction corrected an overly conservative, positivistic approach to criminological theory—a tradition to be even further challenged by conflict criminology. While critics are correct that studies of the enforcement and administration of traditional crimes (murder, rape, and the like) do not indicate bias (Wellford, 1975), this does not therefore repudiate the labeling point of view since it still does not speak to the conflict perspective that crimes committed by the poor are more likely to be labeled criminal than those of the wealthy. Labeling theory appears to have some validity with respect to areas of deviant behavior such as mental illness and in highlighting the lack of stigmatization of many areas of organizational and occupational crime, but it has clearly been repudiated when attempts have been made to apply it to traditional and universally condemned crimes such as murder.

Conflict Theory and Conflict Criminology ————————

Conflict theory in sociology has a long tradition, beginning as early as Georg Simmel (1955) in his *Conflict and the Web of Group Affiliations*, originally published in English in 1908. Criminological expressions of this tradition can be traced to Marx and Bonger, discussed in Chapter 4, and more recently to Ralf Dahrendorf (1959) and George Vold (1958). In Chapter 1 we made a distinction between the consensus model, which views criminal law as originating in agreement of the majority, and the conflict model, which points to a conflict of interest among groups in which the dominant group controls the legal machinery of the state. The initial edition of Vold's *Theoretical Criminology* was the first to be extensively based upon the conflict approach. Thorsten Sellin's (1938) notion of "culture conflict" as an explanation of crime also is part of this tradition. Sellin viewed criminal law as originating in cultural or normative conflict in which more powerful groups in society are able to have the laws reflect their norms and values.

Ralf Dahrendorf

Ralf Dahrendorf (1959) reformulated Marxian theory in *Class and Class Conflict in Industrial Society*, proposing a more pluralistic conflict theory in which numerous groups compete for power, influence, and dominance. His concept of "imperatively coordinated associations" holds that social control in society rests upon stratified or hierarchical relationships characterized by superordinate/subordinate associations. Borrowing from Marx and Hegel's notion of dialectics (in which each thesis or existing state produces an antithesis or opposition state until a new synthesis is formed), Dahrendorf viewed every society as characterized by coercion of some groups by others (Ibid., p. 48). The unequal distribution of authority produces social conflict, in which dominant groups impose their will and subordinate groups act to oppose it. While Dahrendorf did not specifically speak to the crime issue, his theoretical work influenced much of the conflict tradition in criminology.

George Vold

George Vold's (1958) *Theoretical Criminology*, subsequent editions of which were posthumously updated by Thomas Bernard (Vold, 1979; and Vold and Bernard, 1986), is a highly regarded classic in the conflict criminology tradition. Building upon the work of Dahrendorf, Vold proposed that society is made up of a variety of continually competing interest groups and that conflict is one of its essential elements (Vold, 1979, p. 204), with more powerful groups able to have the state formulate laws in their interest. In Vold's view, many criminal acts represent challenges by subordinate groups to the existing dominant group's control, although he seems to restrict this explanation to issues related to political-ideological conflicts such as political reform movements, union conflicts, civil rights disputes, and the like. Crime, then, can be explained as a product of intergroup conflict that expresses the political struggle of these groups. While Vold's theory does not adequately explain irrational, personal, violent acts, his emphasis upon the conflict basis of criminal law had a profound impact upon later theories.

Conflict Criminology

As indicated previously, a number of tags are used to refer to the "new" or emergent conflict criminology in the seventies. It is at times difficult to distinguish between "conflict" criminology—which, like Vold and Dahrendorf, proposes a pluralistic model with a variety of competing groups—and "radical" criminology—which generally espouses an orthodox, neo-Marxian, ideological view. Austin Turk has been one of the more persistent advocates of conflict criminology. Many figures to be discussed, particularly William Chambliss and Richard Quinney, demonstrate theoretical evolution from early conflict-orientation to later, more Marxian conceptions. The pluralistic conflict approach assumes that different class, racial, ethnic, and subculturally distinct interest groups vie for political dominance and the assistance of the legal machinery of the state in order to protect their interests (Hills, 1971). Unlike the Marxian model, no one group dominates completely.

Austin Turk

Austin Turk (1969a, 1972, and 1980) has been a prolific writer in the conflict perspective. His basic position can be summarized in the following propositions (Turk, 1980, pp. 82–83):

- Individuals are different in their understandings and commitments.
- Divergence leads to conflict.
- Each conflicting party tries to promote his or her own views.
- This leads to a conscious struggle over the distribution of resources.
- People with similar beliefs tend to join forces and develop similar understandings and commitments.
- Continuing conflicts tend to become routine and develop into stratification systems.

- Such systems exhibit economic exploitation, sustained by political domination in all forms.
- The relative power of conflicting parties determines their hierarchical position as well as changes in the distribution of power.
- Convergence in understandings and commitments is due to sharing of experiences in dealing with "insiders," "outsiders," and the environment.
- Human understandings and commitments are dialectical, characterized by continual conflict.

Turk's theory, while abstract, alerts us to the political nature of criminal law as well as to the pluralistic conflict basis of such norms.

William Chambliss and Richard Quinney— Conflict Theory

Other leading statements of conflict theory are in the early works of William Chambliss (with Robert Seidman, 1971) and Richard Quinney (1970); their later writings would evolve into more radical perspectives. Chambliss and Seidman viewed criminal law as representing the interests of the most powerful forces in society and deviance as a political rather than moral question (Chambliss and Seidman, 1971, p. 4). Richard Quinney (1970, pp. 15–23) in *The Social Reality of Crime* presented six propositions describing the relationship between crime and the social order:

- Crime is a definition of human conduct created by authorized agents in a politically organized society.
- Criminal definitions describe behaviors that conflict with the interests of segments of society that have power to shape public policy.
- Criminal definitions are applied by segments of society that have power to shape the enforcement and administration of criminal law.
- Behavior patterns are structured in segmentally organized society in relation to criminal definitions, and within this context persons engage in actions that have relative probabilities of being defined as criminal.
- Conceptions of crime are constructed and diffused in the segments of society by various means of communication.
- The social reality of crime is constructed by the formulation and application of criminal definitions, the development of behavior patterns related to criminal definitions, and the construction of criminal conceptions.

Critics of Quinney's formulations argue that his propositions oversimplify reality and that many represent statements rather than necessarily empirically-supported propositions (Manning, 1975). A more detailed critique will be provided at the conclusion of this chapter.

Jeffrey Reiman

In *The Rich Get Richer and the Poor Get Prison*, Jeffrey Reiman (1984) argues a conflict perspective which includes:

- Acts that are not treated as crimes pose at least as great a danger to the public as those that have been criminalized.
- Acts that are criminalized are generally those of the poor.
- The system often fails to even treat as criminal the dangerous acts of the wealthy and powerful.
- The failure of the criminal justice system in fighting street crime conveys an important ideological message — the greatest danger to the average citizen is from below him or her on the economic ladder.
- Crime in the suites should be prosecuted in the same manner as crime in the streets and all acts should be prosecuted in proportion to the actual harm they produce.

Reiman (1984, p. 162) concludes: ". . . every step toward economic and social justice is a step that moves us from a system of *criminal* justice to a system of criminal *justice*."

Radical "Marxist" Criminology ———————————

Richard Quinney — Radical Criminology

Perhaps the foremost spokesperson of radical criminology is the same Richard Quinney who was at one time a more moderate conflict theorist. For Quinney — now an orthodox Marxist — crime is the result of capitalism and the crime problem can be resolved only by the establishment of a socialist state (Quinney, 1974a, 1974b, 1974c, 1977). In his critical theory of crime control in America, he provides the following propositions:

- American society is based on an advanced capitalist economy.
- The state is organized to serve the interests of the dominant economic class, the capitalist ruling class.
- Criminal law is an instrument of the state and the ruling class to maintain and perpetuate the existing social and economic order.

- Crime control in capitalist society is accomplished through a variety of institutions and agencies established and administered by a governmental elite, representing ruling class interests, for the purpose of establishing domestic order.
- The contradictions of advanced capitalism—the disjunction between existence and essence—require that the subordinate classes remain oppressed by whatever means necessary, especially through the coercion and violence of the legal system.
- Only with the collapse of capitalist society and the creation of a new society based on socialist principles will there be a solution to the crime problem.

For Quinney and other Marxist criminologists, crime is viewed as a necessary outcome of inequality in capitalistic societies. Criminal law originates in conflict of interest in which the most powerful ruling class (capitalists or bourgeoisie) makes the laws and controls the criminal justice machinery. Marxist criminologists often reject the positivistic tradition of analyzing crime causation through objective and empirical analysis, advocating, instead, an ideological commitment to Marxist philosophy wherein their task is to provide descriptive and analytical examples to serve as evidence for a preconfirmed social reality—that capitalism causes crime.

William Chambliss

Radical criminologists argue that, by concentrating upon the crimes of the poor rather than upon racism, imperialism, and inequality, criminologists become conservative handmaidens of state repression (Platt, 1974). Advanced industrial capitalism creates "surplus people" (Spitzer, 1975), an underclass that is unneeded in the system of production. Among William Chambliss's (1975b) later views regarding capitalism and crime are these:

- As capitalist societies industrialize and the gap between the bourgeoisie and the proletariat widens, penal law will expand in an effort to coerce the proletariat into submission.
- Crime diverts the lower classes' attention from the exploitation they experience and directs it toward other members of their own class rather than toward the capitalist class or the economic system.
- Crime is a reality which exists only as it is created by those in the society whose interests are served by its presence.
- Crime is a reaction to the life conditions of a person's social class.

- Socialist societies should have much lower rates of crime because the less intense class struggle should reduce the forces leading to the functions of crime.

Similar perspectives have been enunciated by many others including Gordon (1973), Krisberg (1975), and Taylor et al. (1973, 1975). In their *Critical Criminology* Taylor and associates (1975, p. 49) called for the use of Marxism as the method of analysis in a "materialistic criminology" whose purpose is to expose the basis of social control in capitalistic societies. The tenets of Marxist theory, rather than representing subjects for empirical analysis, now become foregone conclusions, ideological dictates requiring illustration and reification.

Radical or Marxist criminologists view *praxis*, practical critical action, as more important than the objective analysis of their theoretical formulations. "They view 'intellectualism' as a negative quality due to the 'academic repression' and 'elitism' associated with intellectuals. Praxis is then the most important factor in the struggle to replace capitalism with socialism" (Pelfrey, 1980, p. 96).

Conflict vs. Marxist Criminology

While the two are often confused, conflict criminology posits a pluralistic conflict model (a diversity of conflicting parties), places less emphasis upon capitalism alone as the source of crime, favors objective research, does not reject the legal order, and advocates reform rather than revolution (Friedrichs, 1980b, p. 39; and Bohm, 1982). Marxist or radical criminology, on the other hand, advocates a singularistic conflict model (capitalistic class control), names capitalism and inequality as the sources of crime, holds Marxist theory as a fact to be illustrated rather than a subject for empirical investigation, rejects the legitimacy of the existing legal order, and advocates revolutionary overthrow of the system.

Critiques of Conflict and Radical Criminology

While conflict criminology has done much to reverse overconcentration upon criminal actors and unquestioned acceptance of the consensus model of criminal law and to point to the criminal justice system as a possible transgressor, it has been criticized for ignoring the consensual basis of much criminal law and for assuming rather than demonstrating discrimination in traditional law enforcement.

Radical (Marxist) criminology has attracted a barrage of critics. In Geis and Meier's (1979) survey of leading criminologists, nearly 40 percent of the respondents indicated the emergence of Marxist ideology in criminology as a "less healthy development" in the field. Comments such as "ideology whether in theory or method is pretentiously seen as 'new paradigms,' 'theories,' 'methods'"; "the substitution of ideology for science"; "nonscientific voices"; "Marxist rhetoric and ideological narrowness" (Ibid., pp. 180–181) were offered. In the previous chapter we cited Toby's (1980) statement that much of "the New Criminology is the Old Baloney," that this tradition ". . . far from being new, is the explicit assertion of a relativism and a sentimentality that is as old as sympathy for members of the oldest profession." Sparks (1980) criticizes radical criminologists for the lack of attention to solid research which would critically test their theoretical assumptions.

Klockars's Critique

The definitive though most controversial critique of Marxist criminology appears in Carl Klockars's (1979) "The Contemporary Crisis of Marxist Criminology," which in turn has stirred considerable commentary (Akers, 1980; Mankoff, 1980; and Friedrichs, 1980a). Klockars's critique can be paraphrased into the following points:

- Marxist criminology resembles an untrustworthy social movement, since it ignores Russian gulags (Solzhenitsyn, 1975), Cuban domestic repression, and other abuses within socialist states. By giving a social movement a higher priority than academic inquiry, they abandon science for ideology and are untrustworthy as objective scholars.
- Marxist criminology as a social movement takes on predictable, orthodox lines. After class, the legal order and capitalism are blamed for everything; these themes are reiterated ad nauseam.
- In their subjective zeal for advocating social revolution, Marxist criminologists find evil in everything associated with the American state, legal, and economic system, ignoring good laws. In their mystical transcendence of reality, they destroy their academic credibility.
- They dramatize and attack issues—e.g., that politicians are corrupt or businesses dishonest—as if these were startling revelations, insulting the intelligence of the general public.
- All of the problems of justice are collapsed into the economic interest of classes.
- American Marxist criminologists criticize society from ". . . a *moral ground set so high* [italics mine] and so far removed from any extant social reality that it loses all perspective" (Klockars, 1979, p. 484).

- They elevate Marx from a social philosopher to the status of prophet or saint. By describing the ideal of Marxism, they avoid responsibility for the present depredations of existing Marxist states.
- Marxist criminology resembles a new religion in which its "true believers" are unwilling to test, evaluate, or objectively examine their theories or beliefs.

While the Klockars critique pulls no punches, it is difficult to apply these points to all writers within the Marxist tradition, although his criticisms appear on target on the whole. As Akers (1980, p. 138) states:

> Compared to a socialist ideal system, the real American system looks unjust, repressive, and controlled by a tiny capitalist elite. Compared to the Soviet Union, China, Vietnam, North Korea, East Germany or Cambodia, to name some socialist alternatives, or to Iran, South Korea or Chile, to name some nonsocialist alternatives, American society looks pretty good.

While some versions of radical criminology appear to constitute ideology rather than objective inquiry, their insistence upon the economic base of the social structure and human behavior is an important challenge to individualistic and consensus views of social order. Even though some theories appear biased in overlooking shortcomings within socialistic systems, the impact of economic inequality upon conventional and corporate crime in particular is crucial to modern criminology.

Theoretical Range and Criminological Explanation

This presentation of theories in criminology can only introduce major themes and schools of thought, leaving more formalized and sophisticated exposition to upper-level theory texts (see Vold and Bernard, 1986); detailed explication of the general theories' applications to types of criminal behavior would require far more space than is possible in this volume. However, to summarize the interrelationship between descriptions, criminal behavior typologies, and general theory, some final points may prove fruitful.

Theoretical range, or scope in this writer's view, refers to the unit(s) of analysis and levels of explanation which may be sought in a particular theory. In their *The New Criminology,* Taylor et al. (1973, pp. 270–278) provide an example of theoretical range when they describe the formal requirements or scope of a general theory in criminology. Such a model must describe:

1. The wider origins of the deviant act.
2. Immediate origins of the deviant act.
3. The actual act.
4. Immediate origins of the societal reaction.
5. Wider origins of deviant reaction.
6. The outcome of the societal reaction on deviant's further action.
7. The nature of the deviant process as a whole.

Harry Allen et al. (1981, p. 39) address this issue of theoretical range:

> . . . what has been, and is, remiss in theoretical criminology in the opinion of many, is the spurious attempt to explicate all crime on the basis of one unitary, universal theory. Any theory that attempts to explain all crime, it is charged, cannot escape being a general theory of all human behavior, because criminal behavior encompasses a wide and divergent body of conduct. A general theory of crime would have to explain too much and therefore would explain too little. The essential questions are: what kinds of criminals and what kinds of circumstances, result in the commission of what kinds of crime? In short, the development of criminal typologies, in this view offers the most plausible approach to the etiology of crime.

The Global Fallacy

Williams and McShane (1988, p. 134) point out:

> The sheer variety of behavior defined as criminal also presents a problem. When we use the term "crime," the reference is often to a wide range of illegal behavior. The individual criminal acts, though, may have very little in common except that someone, at some time, disliked each of them enough to have a law passed against them. Murder and petty theft, for example, have about as much in common as a rock and an orange. Thus, theories of crime and criminal behavior must encompass a wide range of human activity. This is the reason that some criminologists advocate the limiting of theories to a very specific behavior.

A long recognized limitation of many discussions of crime as well as theories of crime causation, particularly early ones, relates to the global (or broad) manner in which the concept of crime is employed. The only thing most crimes hold in common is the fact that they are at a given point in time defined or viewed as violations of criminal law. The "global fallacy" refers to the tendency to attempt to generalize relatively specific explanations to all types of crimes (Hagan, 1987c). Many individual theories are not invalid in themselves, but are either too globally ambitious or interpreted as such. A perfectly appropriate theory for explaining burglary may not apply at all to inside trading nor should it be expected to do so.

The range of theories may be at the general (macroscopic) level, addressing a broad issue such as "How does crime originate in society?" or at the specific (microscopic) level, which might ask "What causes specific individuals to commit specific crimes?" Merton (1968, p. 45) advocates development of "theories of the middle range," proposing explanations aimed at describing specific activity between macroscopic and microscopic levels. All of the major theoretical views in criminology in these last two chapters were seen as subject to certain shortcomings; in many instances, the criticisms were as much due to what the theories failed to cover as they were with what they did address.

Figure 5.2 presents a summary schema which compares the major theoretical views in criminology in terms of whether they address the following range of activities:

1. Origin of crime in society
2. Immediate factors of transmission of criminal values
3. Individual criminality
4. Prevention of individual criminality
5. Prevention of crime in society.

In addition, Figure 5.2 indicates the types of criminal behavior to be discussed in this book to which each theory is addressed. While the author's analysis of presence or absence of features of each theory may be debated, and you can judge for yourself as we examine each type of criminal behavior, none of the general theories applies to all of the types of criminal behavior. Many specific theories to be discussed — such as Wolfgang and Ferracutti's "subculture of violence" or Cressey's "theory of embezzlers" — represent "theories of the middle range," more of which are needed to build more crime-specific explanations. Until more all-encompassing, all-purpose theories concerned with all types of crimes are developed, more middle range, crime-specific theories appear to be a fruitful direction. In the discussion of typologies it was suggested that the answer to "what causes crime?" is "what type of crime?" Perhaps a criminological Einstein or Galileo will yet arrive to provide an acceptable general theory. Until then, more Sutherlands, Mertons, and Hirschis will hopefully provide needed "middle range" theoretical explanations.

Summary

Theory is necessary for capturing the essence of criminology. The *major sociological theoretical approaches in criminology* are: mainstream theories (anomie, social process, and social control approaches) and critical theories (labeling, conflict, and radical [Marxist] theories).

Emile Durkheim is the father of the "anomie tradition," which also includes Merton's notion of "anomie and personality adaptations," Cloward and Ohlin's "differential social organization," and Cohen's theory that delinquency is a "lower class reaction" to middle class values. While Durkheim viewed *anomie* as a state of normlessness, a moral malaise experienced by individuals when they lack clear-cut guidelines, later theorists such as Merton adapted the theory to refer to a situation

Figure 5.2: Range of Major Theoretical Views in Criminology*

Range	Demonological	Classical	Ecological	Economic	Positivist Biological/ Psychological	Sociological — Anomie Theories	Social Process	Social Control	Labeling	Conflict	Radical
(1) Origin of Crime in Society				X		X				X	X
(2) Immediate Factors of Transmission			X		X	X	X	X	X		
(3) Individual Criminality	X	X	X		X	X	X	X	X		
(4) Prevent Individual Criminality	X	X			X			X	X		
(5) Prevent Crime in Society				X		X				X	X
Types of Criminal Behavior Addressed											
Organizational/Occupational							X			X	X
Violent	X		X		X	X					
Conventional Property	X	X	X	X	X	X	X	X		X	X
Occasional Property	X	X	X	X	X	X	X	X		X	X
Public Order	X					X			X		
Political	X					X				X	X
Organized						X					
Professional							X				

*an X indicates that a particular theory addresses a particular explanatory range as well as a particular type of criminal behavior.

SOURCE: Frank E. Hagan, 1985, *Theoretical Range in Criminological Theory*, paper presented at the Academy of Criminal Justice Sciences Meetings, Las Vegas, Nevada, April.

experienced due to a gap between societal goals and the means provided to achieve these ends. This results, according to Merton, in "modes of personality adaptation": conformity, innovation, retreatism, ritualism, or rebellion. Cloward and Ohlin argue that the type of juvenile subculture gang response to anomie depends upon the "differential social organization" (legal and illegal opportunity structures) in the neighborhood. Depending upon the type, one of three juvenile delinquent subcultures may emerge: the criminal, conflict, or retreatist. Cohen's theory of delinquency views it as "lower class reactions to unobtainable or rejected middle class values" such as ambition, verbal skills, nonviolence, and the like. He views much delinquency as nonutilitarian, malicious, and negativistic.

The *social process tradition* concentrates upon learning, socialization, and subcultural transmission of criminal values. Originating in the work of the "Chicago school" of sociology in the twenties and thirties, and in particular with the works/ideas of Burgess ("concentric zone model"), Park ("natural areas"), and Wirth ("urbanism as a way of life"), *human ecology* was seen, at least initially, as an organizing perspective. This approach examines the interrelationship between humans and the physical/social environment. Included among better known Chicago school criminologists are Clifford Shaw and David McKay and Edwin Sutherland.

Making extensive use of maps and official statistics, Shaw and McKay viewed delinquency as reflecting the "social disorganization" of areas in which individuals lived, with delinquency less a matter of individual abnormality and more a matter of "cultural transmission" or social learning. Concern that Shaw and McKay committed the "ecological fallacy" (attributed group characteristics to individuals) may be alleviated by the fact that they performed a number of case studies of criminals. Cohen and Felson's (1979) "routine activities approach" views crime as related to everyday, normal activities such as the proliferation of consumer goods and the lack of guardians. Sutherland's "differential association theory," the most popular theory in American criminology, states that individuals become predisposed toward criminality due to an excess of contacts which advocate criminal behavior, *contacts that vary according to frequency, priority, intensity, and duration.* Differential association aims at describing the process by which crime is transmitted but does not address itself to origins of crime. Miller's theory of delinquency views it as reflecting "the focal concerns of the lower class" such as an emphasis upon trouble, toughness, smartness, excitement, fate, and autonomy.

David Matza's "delinquency and drift" theory claims that individuals are often in a limbo or uncommitted status between delinquent and nondelinquent behavior. He and Gresham Sykes view delinquents as acting out "subterranean values" (underground values which exist along with more conventionally approved values) and utilizing "techniques of neutralization" (rationalizations) in order to justify their behavior.

Social control theories argue that individuals deviate when *containments* (Walter Reckless) or *social bonds* (Travis Hirschi) are removed or weakened. Reckless's "containment theory" views individuals as resisting or giving in to various pressures based upon social controls (self-concept or near support systems). Hirschi's "social bond theory" states that delinquency takes place when bonds to society are reduced and the individual has fewer stakes in conformity. *These bonds consist of: attachment, commitment, involvement, and belief.*

Mainstream criminology (anomie, social process, and social control theories) has been viewed as emphasizing study of the criminal rather than social control agencies, stressing positivism, a consensus world view, and liberal reformism. In response to this, in the sixties and seventies in the U.S. "critical criminology" emerged, which *consists of the labeling, conflict, and radical perspectives.* Critical criminology stresses the conflict model, inequality, the process of assigning criminal labels, and, in some cases, ideology.

Labeling theory (societal reaction approach) is derived from symbolic interactionism (a stress upon subjective meanings of social interaction). Labeling theory assumes that individuals are criminal because they have been labeled as such by social control agencies; i.e., societal reaction causes criminality. Schrag's summary of the basic assumptions of this school of thought was presented along with Lemert's concept of "secondary deviance"; the latter refers to continued deviance once an individual has been caught and labeled.

Conflict theory advocates a "pluralistic conflict model" of criminal law and is represented in the writings of Dahrendorf, Vold, and, in conflict criminology, in the works of Austin Turk, the early work of Richard Quinney and William Chambliss, and that of Jeffrey Reiman. According to conflict criminology, a variety of groups compete for control of the law making and enforcement machinery in order to protect their vested interests. *Radical "Marxist" criminology,* as presented in the later writings of Quinney and Chambliss, views crime as a result of capitalism, with the criminal law representing the interests of the capitalist class. The Marxist prescription for solving the crime problem is the collapse of capitalism and the creation of a socialist state. Major critiques of radical criminology as well as each of the other theoretical approaches were presented throughout this chapter.

Theoretical range refers to the units of analysis and level of explanation which may be sought in a particular theory. This range may focus upon the macroscopic level—for example, general theories of the origin of crime—to the microscopic—explanations of individual criminality. Merton's concept of "theories of the middle range" argues for explanations aimed at describing specific activity between the macro- and microscopic.

The "range of major theoretical views" (Figure 5.2) attempts to summarize the theoretical range (origins, immediate factors, individual criminality, individual prevention, and societal prevention) of each theory and its ability to address different types of criminal behavior. This illustrates the view that the answer to the question, "What causes crime?" must first be specified by the question, "What type of crime?" The answer to the first question awaits the development of an acceptable general theory of criminology.

KEY CONCEPTS

Anomie
Human Ecology
"Chicago School"
Natural Areas
Social Disorganization Theory
Ecological Fallacy
Differential Association Theory
"Looking-Glass Self"
Merton's "Anomie" Theory
Modes of Personality Adaptation
Subcultural Theories

"Differential Opportunity" Theory
Cohen's "Lower Class Reaction" Theory
Miller's "Focal Concerns"
Delinquency and Drift
"Soft Determinism"
Subterranean Values
Techniques of Neutralization
Social Control Theory
Containment Theory

Social Bond Theory
Labeling Theory
Secondary Deviance
Conflict Criminology
Radical "Marxist" Criminology
Imperatively Coordinated Associations
Praxis
Theoretical Range
Routine Activities Approach
The Global Fallacy

6

Violent Crime

Violence by human beings against other human beings has scarred history from earliest times. In addition to hundreds of smaller conflicts, this century has already witnessed two major world wars with casualties in the millions and devastation, such as that at Hiroshima and Nagasaki, that is unparalleled in human history. Mass genocide of populations by the Nazis, human purges in which millions disappeared as in Stalin's Russia, and continuing torture of political opponents in many countries throughout the world has made this a frightening century indeed.

While writers such as Konrad Lorenz (1966) and Robert Ardrey (1963) argue that humans have a "killer instinct," a natural predisposition toward violence and aggression, most social scientists reject this view, arguing instead that individuals learn violence, like nonviolence, through socialization. Anthropological studies have discovered wide variations in the degree of violence prevalent in human cultures, with a few cultures in which violence is unknown. Japan's transition from a violent, warlike society before and during World War II to a pacifistic society in the postwar period suggests that violence is not an inevitability. Just as violence can be learned and assumed to be a natural part of a culture, it probably also can be unlearned.

History of Violence in America

In their report to the National Commission on the Causes and Prevention of Violence entitled *Violence in America: Historical and Comparative Perspectives,* Hugh Davis and Tedd Gurr (1969) indicate that we ignore history when we view our present levels of violence as unusual. They claim that violence in America is rooted in *six historical events* which are deeply imbedded in our national character (Ibid., pp. 770–774):

1. Revolutionary doctrine expounded in the Declaration of Independence.
2. A prolonged frontier experience, which tended to legitimize violence and vigilante justice.
3. A competitive hierarchy of immigrants that has been highly conducive to violence.
4. A pervasive fear of governmental power, which "has reinforced a tendency to define freedom negatively as freedom *from*" (Ibid., p. 772).

5. The Industrial Revolution and the great internal migration from countryside to city, which has produced widespread social dislocation.

6. Unmatched prosperity combined with unequal distribution and unequal opportunity, which has produced a "revolution of rising expectations" in which improved economic rewards can coincide with *relative* deprivation that generates frustration and violence.

Glaringly absent from this list is the bitter legacy of slavery and subsequent racially-motivated violence against blacks. The burning cross of the KKK (Ku Klux Klan) symbolized the bombings, lynchings, murders, shootings, arsons, mutilations, and other violent tactics used against African-Americans as well as others. In the fifties and sixties the bombing of churches and murders of civil rights workers, often in collusion with local police officers, aroused a nation to oppose racism (Wade, 1987; and Revell, 1988, p. 10).

Historian Richard Brown (1969, pp. 69–70) sums much of this up by indicating:

> Violence has formed a seamless web with some of the noblest and most constructive chapters of American history: the birth of the nation (Revolutionary violence), the occupation of the land (Indian wars), the stabilization of frontier society (vigilante violence), the elevation of the farmer and the laborer (agrarian and labor violence), and the preservation of law and order (police violence). The patriot, the humanitarian, the nationalist, the pioneer, the landholder, the farmer, and the laborer (and the capitalist) have used violence as a means to a higher end.

Violence may indeed reflect a society's values. For example, Americans value "life, liberty, and the pursuit of happiness," while their less violent, next-door neighbors, the Canadians, reflect a less revolutionary view of society and applaud "peace, order, and good government." America has inherited a violent cultural tradition; but as a relatively young country, its tradition may not be that much different than the early histories of older civilizations of Europe or Asia. It has been less than 100 years since 1890, the date that historian Frederick Jackson Turner (1975) earmarked as signifying the closing of the American frontier. Moreover, as discussed in Chapter 3, the United States' assimilation of culturally divergent populations has not been a smooth process, as Canada and England are beginning to realize first hand. Racial violence and a history of institutionalized racism until just a generation ago have made this the very first generation of Americans to attempt to provide justice to the nation's oldest immigrant minority—blacks. Yet despite high rates of domestic violence, America has not been characterized by the large-scale genocide, the torture of political opponents, or the patterns of governmental violence apparent in other parts of the world.

Fads and Fashions in Violent Crime

Violent crime refers to any criminal act which results in the threat of or actual physical harm to a victim. The violent crime to be discussed in this chapter will specifically be concerned with homicide, assault, robbery, rape, and family violence. In later chapters we will discuss political crime involving state violence as well as corporate violence. Even though these forms may kill far more people than the primarily interpersonal violence discussed here, these are omitted from this section merely for organizational/instructional purposes and not because they are not examples of violent crime.

In Chapter 3 we briefly discussed a criminal phenomenon which was called "copycat crime," in which criminals seem to imitate publicized patterns of criminal activity. Related to this phenomenon are various changes in criminal activity, much of them brought about by social and technological changes in the society itself. There are a variety of crimes which were of major concern in the past which appear in modern societies only in old reruns on the late show. Train robbery, piracy, stagecoach robbery, cattle rustling, gunfights such as at the OK Corral, and grave robbery have some modern remnants, but for the most part have disappeared. Some of these practices have reappeared in different forms. In the seventies, South Vietnamese "boat people" attempting to escape from their homeland were robbed, raped, and murdered by Thai pirates. Brinks trucks have replaced stagecoaches, and semi trucks full of prepared beef are hijacked instead of herds of live cattle. Post-Civil War gangs of Wild West robbers with members such as Doc Holliday, the Earp brothers, Jesse James, the Dalton gang, Black Bart, the Younger brothers, and Butch Cassidy disappeared with the settlement of the frontier only to reappear on wheels during the Depression of the thirties with infamous names such as Dillinger, "Pretty Boy" Floyd, the Barrows, Bonnie Parker, and the Ma Barker gang. Mobile, organized gangs of bank robbers have largely faded into a quaint, unsavory history.

Skyjacking, a very big problem in the sixties, virtually had been eliminated as a result of better security measures, only to reappear in the U.S. in the early eighties as Cuban refugees attempted to use this method as a means of returning home. Kidnapping, a major crime of concern in the U.S. in the thirties, as illustrated by the famous Lindbergh case, is not as much of a concern today despite highly publicized cases such as the Patty Hearst kidnapping, or the rash of child kidnappings by their own noncustodial parents. On the other hand, in Italy since the seventies, kidnapping has become a major crime, as best illustrated by the highly publicized kidnapping of billionaire John Paul Getty's grandson; the kidnappers mailed one of his ears to police to impress upon them the seriousness of their intentions. Nostalgic views of the past tend to color over bygone violence or suppress its memory. Particularly forgotten are conditions of the past which more than match any chronicle of horrors of the present.

Murder and Mayhem

The Old Five Points Brewery (1792–1852)

Situated in the old Five Points section (due to the convergence of five streets) in Manhattan was a five-story, cavernous old brewery which, in 1837, was converted into a 100-room tenement. Journalist Jay Robert Nash claims that (1975, vol. 1, pp. 296–298) Irish immigrants lived on the top floors while blacks lived in the basement rooms. The old brewery had an estimated one murder per night for fifteen years and the police dared not enter in numbers less than fifty. Strangers foolish enough to enter the building were marked for death and those attempting to leave were just as likely to be attacked by citizens fearing contamination from these barbarous inhabitants. When demolition of the building occurred in 1852, it is claimed that workmen removed a hundred sacks of human bones from between the walls and under the floors.

Murder Castle

Until recently, it is believed, the all-time champion multiple murderer in the United States, excluding war-related genocide, was one Herman Mudgett, who, until the time of his execution in 1896, was described by Nash (Ibid., p. 266) as ". . . the criminal of the nineteenth century, the archfiend of America and the all-time mass killer who slaughtered by the dozen. And he was the nicest man you'd ever want to meet." A former medical student and small-time swindler, Mudgett tortured and murdered over two hundred female victims during the Chicago World's Fair of 1893. In what sounds like a plot from a Boris Karloff movie, he would lure young secretaries with offers of employment to his house of horrors, a mysterious castle-like mansion on the city's South Side. After first wooing them with promises of marriage and having them sign over insurance policies to him, Mudgett drugged them with chloroform and murdered them.

The Leopold-Loeb Case

In 1924, Nathan Leopold and Richard Loeb, the "genius" sons of wealthy Chicago businessmen, planned the "perfect crime." Both boys were described as precocious and compulsive perfectionists. Leopold had graduated from the University of Chicago at age 18; at that time, he was the youngest to do so and was estimated to have an IQ of 200. Leopold was interested in homosexual activity; Loeb was interested in committing perfect crimes. They signed a pact agreeing to accomplish both and then planned and carried out the murder of fourteen-year-old Bobbie Franks, a distant relative of Loeb. They were caught, however, and given lengthy sentences.

While cases such as these attract much public attention in the same vein as that which fascinates devotees of detective magazines, such crimes are relatively rare and make up only a very small proportion of the incidents of violent crime. Media, fictional, and popular accounts of violent crime tend to focus upon the dramatic, tales of murder and mayhem that make our blood curdle as much as the latest Stephen King Gothic novel. The post-World War II period has had no shortage of material for such chronicles.

The Texas Tower Incident

In 1966, former Eagle Scout leader and engineering honor student Charles Whitman murdered his wife and mother and then, with a small arsenal of weapons and ammunition, climbed to the top of a tower at the University of Texas. With deadly accuracy he randomly killed sixteen persons and wounded another thirty before being killed himself by police.

The Manson Family

On August 8, 1969, devotees of a cult mesmerized and run by Charles Manson brutally murdered pregnant actress Sharon Tate and four other guests at her home and two days later murdered two members of the La Bianca family in an apparently bizarre attempt to foment a race war. Particularly frightening in the incident was Manson's Rasputin-like ability to obtain undying devotion from his followers, most of them young female drifters.

In 1924 "boy geniuses" Richard Loeb and Nathan Leopold failed in their attempt to commit the perfect crime. They were convicted of the murder of fourteen-year-old Bobby Franks.

Wayne Williams

Wayne Williams, age twenty-three and himself black, terrorized the black community of Atlanta, murdering an estimated twenty-eight young blacks over a two-year period ending in 1981. Hating poor young blacks, whom he regarded as racially inferior, Williams lured them into his company with promises of fame in the entertainment business and then murdered them when they agreed to perform homosexual acts (see Detlinger, 1983).

Types of Multiple Murders

Holmes and DeBurger (1988, p. 19) estimate that between 3500 and 5000 persons may be slain per year in the U.S. by multiple murderers, and that even though such killings are not new, they do appear to have increased since the sixties. Much of the gap in our academic knowledge of multiple murder is being addressed by recent scholarship (Egger, 1984; Fox and Levin, 1985; Hickey, 1986; Jenkins, 1988; and Leyton, 1986).

Although there is no consistency in terminology or agreement regarding types, at least *three different types of multiple murders* exist: "serial murder," "mass murder," and "spree murder" (Bureau of Justice Statistics, 1988). "Serial murder" involves killing several victims in three or more separate incidents over weeks, months, or even years. Herman Mudgett, Juan Corona, Wayne Henley, John Wayne Gacy, Ted Bundy, and David "Son of Sam" Berkowitz are just a few of the "Jack the Rippers" who have shocked us in modern times.

Serial murderers can be illustrated as well by the still-at-large (as of 1989) "Green River Killer" (near Seattle), who is believed to be responsible for over two hundred murders since 1982. In April, 1989, the thirteenth victim of cult slayings was discovered in Matamoros, Mexico, the work of cult "godfather" Adolpho de Jesus Costanzo and cult "witch" Sara Aldrete, who allegedly ritualistically sacrificed victims in order to "provide a 'magical shield' for members of a drug-smuggling ring" (13th Victim, 1989, p. A-1). In a case reminiscent of the play *Arsenic and Old Lace*, in 1988 Dorothea Puente, a boardinghouse landlady in Sacramento, California, was charged with poisoning at least eight of her elderly boarders and collecting their social security checks. Finally, in Philadelphia in 1987, police arrested Gary Heidnik and an accomplice charging them with running "A Little House of Horrors" (Johnson, 1987, p. 29). Heidnik, who had a history of psychiatric problems, attracted women to his house and imprisoned, tortured, sexually abused, murdered, and cannibalized them. Police have accounted for at least six victims.

The "mass murder" involves killing four or more victims at one location (en masse) within one event. Richard Speck, the murderer of eight Chicago nurses, Charles Whitman, or James Huberty serve as examples. In 1984 Huberty killed twenty-one and wounded a dozen others at a McDonald's restaurant in San Ysidro, California. The restaurant was torn down rather than serve as a reminder of what was described as the worst mass murder in U.S. history.

A variation of the above is the "spree murderer," who kills at two or more locations with almost no time break between murders. In February, 1985, Daniel Remeta and accomplices robbed and killed the manager of a restaurant, an hour later shot a sheriff's deputy, then shot a grain elevator manager and killed two hostages before his capture (Bureau of Justice Statistics, 1988, p. 4).

As previously indicated, while bizarre and mass murders attract media and public attention, they represent the rare and dramatic rather than the typical violent crime.

Victim Precipitation

Victimology is the study of victims of crime, a group that in the past has been neglected by the criminal justice system. In examining violent crime,

Lombroso was one of the first to note that passionate criminals often acted under the provocation of victims. In many violent crimes such as assault and voluntary manslaughter, a flip of the coin separates the victim from the offender, with both parties being active participants. In many violent crimes, victims contribute to their own harm (Von Hentig, 1948). Benjamin Mendelson (1963), one of the pioneers of victimology, developed a *typology of victims* in terms of their degree of guilt in the perpetration of crime:

- The *completely innocent victim*, such as a child or an unconscious person.
- The *victim with minor guilt*, such as a woman who provokes a miscarriage and dies as a result.
- The *victim as guilty as offender*, such as in cases of suicide and euthanasia.
- The *victim as more guilty* than the offender, such as those who provoke someone to commit a crime.
- The *victim as most guilty*, such as the aggressive victim who was killed in self-defense.
- The *simulating or imaginary victim*, such as paranoids, hysterics, or senile persons.

Wolfgang (1958, p. 252), in his study of criminal homicide in Philadelphia, viewed victim-precipitation as present in incidents in which the victim initiated the altercation by being the first to use and/or threaten the use of violence. Victim-precipitation is common in murder and assault; it may also be common in other crimes.

Typology of Violent Offenders

John Conrad (Spencer, 1966; Vetter and Silverman, 1978, p. 65) has proposed a very useful *typology of violent offenders:*

- culturally violent offenders
- criminally violent offenders
- pathologically violent offenders
- situationally violent offenders.

Culturally violent offenders are individuals who live in subcultures (cultures within a culture) in which violence is an acceptable problem-solving mechanism. The "subculture of violence" thesis, to be explored shortly, is used as a means of explaining the greater prevalence of violent crime among low income minorities from slum environments of large central cities.

Criminally violent offenders use violence as a means of accomplishing a criminal act, such as in robbery. Mental illness or brain damage characterize the *pathologically violent offenders*. (Discussions later in this chapter focusing upon psychiatry and the law and psychopathy will further elaborate upon the mentally-disturbed violent criminal.)

Finally, the *situationally violent offenders* commit acts of violence on rare occasions, often under provocation, such as in domestic disputes which get out of hand. These incidents are often described as "crimes of passion," in which the individual temporarily loses control and often expresses regret for the actions later.

Yet another typology of violent crime has been proposed by Haskell and Yablonsky (1983, p. 207), who identify the *basic patterns of violence* as:

1. Legal, sanctioned, rational violence (e.g., war, police)
2. Illegal, socially sanctioned, rational violence (e.g., killing spouse's lover)
3. Illegal, nonsanctioned, rational violence (e.g., syndicates, robbery)
4. Illegal, nonsanctioned, irrational violence (e.g., murder "for kicks").

Our discussion throughout this chapter will primarily concentrate upon the most common form of violence, type 2, illegal, socially sanctioned, rational violence and, to a lesser extent, on type 4, illegal, nonsanctioned, irrational violence. However, this typology calls attention to the fact that the state or agents of the state commit violence and that "contract" killings also exist. Murder by agents of the state will be covered later, in our chapter on political crime, while murder-for-hire will be touched upon in the organized crime chapter.

Legal Aspects

Vantage Point 6.1 provides a brief outline of the key legal features of violent crimes. Although violent crimes were at one time treated under tort law as a matter of private wrong to be settled by the parties involved, today the state has assumed authority and jurisdiction in cases of harmful, violent personal behavior. Private revenge is forbidden and is replaced with retribution in which the violent act is viewed as a threat to the well-being of the society and the culprit must pay his or her debt to society.

Psychiatry and the Law

In order for an individual to be held guilty or responsible for violating the criminal law, he or she must exercise mens rea or proper criminal

VANTAGE POINT

Vantage Point 6.1—Legal Aspects and Definitions of Violent Crime in the U.S.

Assault—involves offering to give bodily harm to a person or placing him or her in fear of such harm. Assault is an attempted, but uncompleted battery.

Battery (Aggravated Assault)—is "an offensive, uncontested to, unprivileged and unjustified offensive bodily contact." Battery includes mens rea, where the contact was intentional or resulted from wanton misconduct and in which bodily harm takes place.

Forcible Rape—Forcible and unlawful sexual relations with a person against her or his will. Rape is defined in common law as "carnal knowledge of a female forcibly and against her will."

Statutory Rape—Sexual relations with a victim under age of consent.

Murder—A killing which is "calculated, in cold blood" or with "malice aforethought" (or a guilty mind).

First Degree—includes the following:
(1) an intent to effect death with "malice aforethought"
(2) deliberate act
(3) premeditated act

Second Degree—includes:
(1) an intent to effect death, "malice aforethought"
(2) without deliberation or premeditation. In essence, in most states second degree murder is any murder which is not defined as first degree.

Felony Murder Doctrine—if in the act of committing a felony the death of one of the victims is brought about, this is murder and it is not necessary to demonstrate intent, deliberation, or premeditation.

Manslaughter—homicide which lacks malice aforethought:
Voluntary—(non-negligent) intentional killing without "malice aforethought"; often described as homicide "in hot blood" and often takes place due to provocation.
Involuntary—(negligent) unintentional killing without "malice aforethought," for example, vehicular homicides.

For additional detail on legal definitions and the nature of the criminal law, see Katkin (1982) *The Nature of Criminal Law* or any text on criminal law.

SOURCE: Adapted from Bureau of Justice Statistics 1983b, *Report to the Nation on Crime and Justice: The Data*, Washington, D.C.: Government Printing Office, pp. 2–3; and Federal Bureau of Investigation, 1984, *Crime in the United States, 1983*, Washington, D.C.: Government Printing Office, p. 342.

intent. Exceptions to this rule are cases of negligence or strict liability, such as the felony murder doctrine. Anglo-American common law is based upon the classical theory of criminology which assumes that individuals are rational actors and thus will respond in kind to threats of punishment. Individuals are to be held responsible for their conduct, but what if the individual is insane?

Basic Decisions

The M'Naghten rule is named after an 1843 English decision regarding Daniel M'Naghten, an individual who, suffering from severe delusions of persecution (paranoia), attempted to shoot Sir Robert Peel (the famous founder of the London police, who were nicknamed "Bobbies" in his honor). M'Naghten missed and killed Peel's secretary. This decision held that individuals who are insane, unable to distinguish between right and wrong, cannot be held responsible for their actions. The M'Naghten rule became the basis of psychiatric justice in Anglo-American criminal law, such individuals being held "not guilty due to insanity." Sometimes referred to as the "right-wrong test" or the *NGRI defense* (not guilty by reason of insanity), individuals who are successfully defended under this rule are usually institutionalized for long-term psychiatric treatment. In 1897 the Federal courts as well as many states added a modification called the "irresistible impulse" test to the "right-wrong" test. The accused could not be found guilty if he had a mental disease which prevented him from controlling his conduct (Morris, 1987, p. 1).

The Durham decision was a 1954 decision in the U.S. Court of Appeals, District of Columbia, regarding Monte Durham, a burglar who had been found guilty in a lower court when psychiatrists indicated there was no clear evidence Durham could not tell right from wrong, even though he had a long history of psychotic and deranged behavior. The appeals court overturned the previous decision and ruled that individuals are not guilty due to insanity if their acts are the *product* of mental disease or defect. This rule was utilized in the Federal system from 1954 to 1972.

The Brawner Test

In 1972 the Federal system rejected Durham and adopted a standard suggested by the Model Penal Code. This is used by half of the states, although subject to increasing restriction in the wake of the Hinckley trial. John Hinckley, the attempted assassin of President Reagan, had been tried under what is called the Brawner test (United States v. Brawner), which holds:

A person is not responsible for criminal conduct if at the time of such conduct as a result of mental disease or defect he lacks *substantial capacity* [italics mine] either to appreciate the wrongfulness of his conduct or to conform his conduct to the requirements of the law (Morris, 1987, p. 2).

Although the Brawner test dominated Federal and State practice until the Hinckley trial, after the adverse reaction to this trial a new standard resembling the original M'Naghten rule was adopted, which placed the burden of proof of insanity upon the defendant. Figure 6.1 summarizes these insanity defense standards.

Guilty but Mentally Ill

At least nine states as of April 1983 (Ibid.) had abolished the NGRI defense and substituted the "guilty, but mentally ill" rule in which convicted individuals undergo civil commitment until cured and still must

Figure 6.1: Insanity Defense Standards (Tests)

Test	Legal Standard Because of Mental Illness	Final Burden of Proof	Who Bears Burden of Proof
M'Naghten	"didn't know what he was doing or didn't know it was wrong"	Varies from proof by a balance of probabilities on the defense to prove beyond a reasonable doubt on the prosecutor	
Irresistible Impulse	"could not control his conduct"		
Durham	"the criminal act was caused by his mental illness"	Beyond reasonable doubt	Prosecutor
Brawner Test	"lacks substantial capacity to appreciate the wrongfulness of his conduct or to control it"	Beyond reasonable doubt	Prosecutor
Present Federal Law	"lacks capacity to appreciate the wrongfulness of his conduct"	Clear and convincing evidence	Defense

Source: Norval Morris, 1987, "Insanity Defense," *Crime File,* National Institute of Justice, p. 3.

serve out their time in jail. Other states such as Oregon have established psychiatric review boards both to determine release as well as monitor continuous follow-up counseling. Over half of the states have joined the federal government in tightening insanity defense standards.

The Twinkie Defense

"You are what you eat!" "Beware that you do not eat too many Twinkies or else you may become a killer!" There was a gay riot in San Francisco when under a "diminished responsibility" argument a jury found Dan White not guilty of first-degree murder in the 1978 killing of that city's Mayor Mosconi and Harvey Milk (a gay city supervisor). Despite the fact that White gave a full confession, psychiatrists convinced the jury that his over-indulgence in junk food (Twinkies and Cokes) diminished his reponsibility to premeditate (NBC, 1983).

Growing steroid (synthetic growth hormone drugs) abuse by athletes and bodybuilders in order to "bulk up" has led to the growing documentation of adverse side effects including "bodybuilder's psychosis." This involves bizarre and violent behavior as a result of steroid abuse and has led some to speculate regarding yet another tool for defense attorneys—"the dumbbell defense" (Monmaney and Robins, 1988, p. 75).

Despite the bizarre nature of this case and similar ones and the media attention it arouses, the reader should be aware that such cases are rarities and attract interest for that very reason. Morris (1987, p. 1) points out that another reason for the rare use of the insanity defense is that a person found not guilty by reason of insanity may be held in a mental hospital longer than if he or she were convicted and sent to prison. For additional information on the insanity defense, the reader is referred to Hermann, 1983; Moran, 1985; Morris, 1987; and Simon and Aaronsen, 1988.

The Psychopath

The "psychopath," "sociopath," and "antisocial personality" are all terms referring to the same phenomenon, the inadequately socialized personality. While at one time such persons were viewed as having innate psychological defects, the concepts of psychopath, sociopath, and antisocial personality imply that such personalities are learned through socialization. Harrington (1972, p. 15) describes the roots of psychopathy in the following manner:

> Persons diagnosed as psychopathic begin as rejected, cruelly or indifferently treated children, or may possibly have suffered early brain damage, detected

or not. They strike back at the world with aggressive, unrestrained, attention-drawing behavior. (Why one person emerges from a disordered childhood inhibited and neurotic and another, the psychopath, with the opposite tendencies remains unclear.) Since conscience is instilled by early love, faith in the adults close by, and desire to hold their affection by being good, the child unrewarded with love grows up experiencing no conscience. Uncared for, he doesn't care, can't really love, feels no anxiety to speak of (having experienced little or no love to lose), does not worry about whether he's good or bad, and literally has no idea of guilt.

A psychopath never really develops the full range of human emotions. Some general characteristics linked with the phenomenon include the lack of inhibition, guilt, fear, conscience, or superego. Such individuals' lack of empathy is illustrated by mass killers such as Charles Manson, who was described as viewing others as moving furniture or objects in the world around him.

Hervey Cleckley (1976), in *The Mask of Sanity*, identifies the following traits as characteristic of psychopathy: unreliability, insincerity, superficial charm, inability to learn from mistakes, impersonal sexual behavior, and an incapacity to love. The background of Charles Manson is instructive. Manson was born to a sixteen-year-old prostitute who did not know the identity of the father. She was sent to prison when he was four and he spent the next four years with relatives who gave little love or affection. She finally returned and took up her old ways. At the age of either nine or twelve, he was sent to a reform school; until age thirty-two, he had spent nearly his entire life in correctional institutions in which he had been exposed to a considerable amount of violence. He had become totally institutionalized to prison. When finally eligible for release on parole, he pleaded with officials to permit him to remain in prison (Scheflin and Opton, 1978, pp. 28–29). While Manson attracted a small, devoted following, imagine a sociopath operating in a larger arena.

The following description of Adolf Hitler by Albert Speer, his armaments minister, illustrates both the shallowness as well as inexplicable charm of the psychopath:

> . . . Hitler could fascinate, he wallowed in his own charisma, but he could not respond to friendship. Instinctively, he repelled it. The normal sympathies that normal males and females enjoy were just not in him. At the core, in the place where the heart should be, Hitler was a hollow man. He was empty . . . the man's drive—his iron will, his demonism—fascinated even while it repelled . . . I was enthralled.
>
> —cited in Harrington, 1972, p. 32.

The actual definition and diagnosis of psychopathy is elusive; there is considerable disagreement and confusion within the psychiatric profession itself regarding the concept. Many critics view it as a "waste-basket concept," a catchall, a diagnosis of convenience or of last resort. If some inexplicably horrible crime is committed by an individual that defies our sensibilities, then such a person is labeled a psychopath.

Homicide and Assault Statistics

Nearly all murders represent some form of aggravated assault and, although the latter generally is not taken as seriously as murder, in fact there is a thin line separating the two. Both offenses entail the use of violence as a means of resolving some grievance, except that in the case of murder the victim dies. In our previous discussions of the short-comings of crime statistics, it was pointed out that official police statistics such as the UCR underestimate the actual rate of crime commission. While this is true, the accuracy of these statistics varies according to the type of crime, with homicide statistics being one of the best (see Reidel and Zahn, 1985).

Generally, homicide is regarded as the most serious of crimes; a body is present, as are witnesses, and, as a result, such a crime is far more likely to be reported to the police. In addition, homicide is the type of crime that the public, the media, and the police place a high priority on solving. Due to all of these factors, homicide has the highest "clearance by arrest" (solved) proportion of all UCR offenses. Clearance means that, as far as the police are concerned, the person responsible for the crime has been accounted for either through arrest or incarceration.

Assault statistics are less accurate, while figures on rape have been notoriously poor until relatively recently. In fact, police and criminal justice professionals have applauded the recent rise in the rape rate, not because of greater rape victimizations but because of a greater willingness on the part of victims to report the crime to the police. The least accurate violent crime statistics relate to categories of intrafamily violence such as spouse abuse, child abuse, and incest. Such offenses, which are to be described in detail shortly, have been regarded as family secrets until relatively recently.

Figure 6.2 portrays the overall trend with respect to homicide statistics in the United States, while Table 6.1 provides comparative United Nations figures on the rate of homicide in selected countries. While the willful homicide rate declined from its peak in 1933 only to be surpassed again in the seventies, this dip may be misleading. Faster ambulances, better communications, transportation, and emergency room service meant better treatment for seriously injured persons, so that many who previously would have been homicide statistics were

Figure 6.2: Homicide Rate in the United States Since 1900

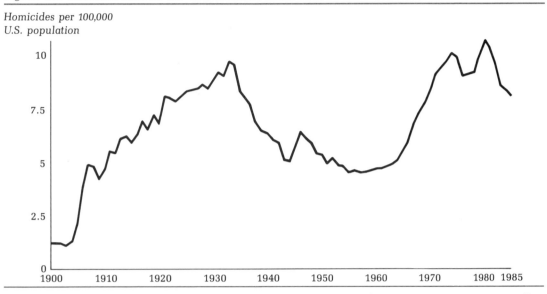

Homicides per 100,000
U.S. population

Source: Bureau of Justice Statistics, 1988b, *Report to the Nation on Crime and Justice*, Washington, D.C.: Government Printing Office, March, p. 15.

surviving. By the seventies, however, the sheer volume of violence had surpassed extraordinary means of patching up such victims. It also is important to note that, although prior to the thirties the U.S. had no national statistics, fragmentary information suggests that at the turn of the century we had violent crime rates equal to present levels. In 1916 Memphis had a homicide rate seven times greater than its rate in 1969 and Boston, Chicago, and New York during and after World War I had higher rates than in the first published national statistics in 1933 (National Commission, 1969, p. 20). Despite problems of measurement, there is little denying that there was a precipitous increase in violence, particularly for homicide in the United States beginning in the sixties.

Table 6.1 shows that the United States has the highest homicide rate of economically developed countries, with figures far higher than those of most European countries, although much lower than those of many Latin American or African countries whose statistics are not shown in this table. Comparative rates in the seventies were: Chile, 47.7; Guatemala, 20.8; Mexico, 31.0; and Philippines, 27.7. The frightening level of such violence can be illustrated by the fact that an American boy born in 1973 is more likely to die from murder in his lifetime than

Table 6.1: Homicide in Selected Countries, Rates for 1980: Comparison of Data Sources

	Number of Homicides per 100,000 Population				
	Actual Homicides			Attempted and Actual Homicides	
Country	World Health Organization	Interpol	United Nations	Interpol	United Nations
United States	10.5	10.0	10.1	—	—
Australia	1.2	2.5	—	3.1	—
Austria	1.2	2.5	—	3.1	—
Canada	2.1	2.6	2.1	6.0	5.4
Chile	2.6	5.7	—	6.1	5.8
Costa Rica	5.8	4.5	2.7	6.5	5.8
Czechoslovakia	1.1[a]	—	—	.2[a]	.7
Denmark	1.3	1.4	1.5	4.5	4.6
Ecuador	6.0[a]	—	—	.2[a]	—
Egypt	.9	2.1	—	2.2	—
England and Wales	.8	1.3	1.2	1.6	1.6
Finland	3.3	2.4	2.4	5.3	5.3
France	1.0	—	—	3.9	—
Germany (FRG)	1.2	1.4	1.4	4.4	4.4
Greece	.7	.7	—	.9	1.2
Hungary	2.6	—	—	3.5	—
Ireland	.7	—	.4	.6	.6
Italy	1.9[a]	1.4[a]	2.0	3.3[a]	3.5
Japan	1.0	.8	—	1.4	—
Netherlands	1.3	1.7	—	2.2	—
New Zealand	1.3	1.7	—	2.2	—
Norway	1.1	—	—	.8	.8
Panama	2.2	—	—	—	9.6
Portugal	1.3	1.6[a]	1.8	3.2[a]	3.7
Scotland	1.6	—	1.1	1.3	6.6
Spain	1.0	—	—	1.2	.1
Sweden	1.2	1.6	1.6	4.7	4.7
Thailand	25.1	—	—	18.3[b]	—
Venezuela	9.7[a]	—	—	13.5	—
Yugoslavia	1.7	—	—	—	6.0

NOTE: Homicide excluding attempts was recalculated from original data whenever possible.

—Not available.

[a]1981 data.

[b]1983 data.

SOURCES: World Health Organization, *World Health Statistics Annual*, vols. 1982–86; Interpol, *International Crime Statistics*, vols. 1979–80, 1981–82, 1983–84; United Nations, Second United Nations Crime Survey; U.S. Census Bureau, *Statistical Abstract of the United States, 1987*, in Carol Kalish, 1988, *International Crime Rates*, Bureau of Justice Statistics Special Report, May, p. 5.

an American soldier was likely to die in combat during World War II (Barnett and Kleitman, 1973). In the 1980s, murder was the leading cause of death among black males in their twenties in many American cities. The estimates for being a murder victim in one's lifetime in the U.S. in 1985 were 1 of 21 black males, 1 of 104 black females, 1 of 131 white males, and 1 of 369 white females (Langan and Innes, 1985).

Patterns and Trends in Violent Crime

The National Commission on the Causes and Prevention of Violence (1969, pp. 21–29) provided the following profile of violent crime:

- Violent crime in the United States is primarily a phenomenon of large cities.
- Violent crime in the city is overwhelmingly committed by males.
- Violent crime in the city is concentrated especially among youths between the ages of fifteen and twenty-four.
- Violent crime in the city is committed primarily by individuals at the lower end of the occupational scale.
- Violent crime in the cities stems disproportionately from the ghetto slum where most low income blacks live.
- The victims of assaultive violence in the cities generally have the same characteristics as the offenders: victimization rates are generally highest for males, youths, poor persons, and blacks. Robbery victims, however, are very often older whites.
- Unlike robbery, the other violent crimes of homicide, assault, and rape tend to be acts of passion among intimates and acquaintances.
- By far the greatest proportion of all serious violence is committed by repeaters. In the Wolfgang, Figlio, and Sellin (1972) Philadelphia study, 627 of the 10,000 boys were chronic offenders. Though they represented only 6 percent of the boys in the study, they accounted for 53 percent of the police contacts for personal attacks—homicide, rape, and assault—and 71 percent of the contacts for robbery.
- Americans generally are no strangers to violent crime. A comparison of reported violent crime rates in this country with those in other modern, stable nations shows the United States to be the clear leader.

Despite the association of crime with urbanization, crime was basically a rural rather than urban problem during ancient times and the Middle Ages. Walled cities were built in order to provide protection from marauding highwaymen (Fox, 1976, p. 41). In the United States it was not until the sixties that urban rates for homicide exceeded those of rural areas (Glaser, 1978, p. 210) and in Canada the rural homicide rate still exceeds the urban rate (Schloss and Giesbrecht, 1972, p. 22).

Racial disparity in arrest rates is highest for crimes of violence. The black arrest rate for homicide is about eight times that of the white rate. Wolfgang's (1958, pp. 33, 66) classic study *Patterns in Criminal Homicide* found the overall murder rate for white males in Philadelphia was 1.8 per 100,000 and, for white males age 20 to 24, 8.2 per 100,000. These same rates for black males were 24.6 and 92.5, respectively. In the Northeast and Midwest, the highest rates are to be found among recent black migrants from the South to large cities. Internationally, lower class slum backgrounds are significantly associated with high rates of violence.

Nettler (1982, vol. 2, pp. 32–39) found that a number of studies indicate that countries with greater inequalities in income distribution have higher murder rates. International homicide statistics are questionable, however, since totalitarian regimes don't report statistics for government murder of citizens. Studies by Messner (1980) and Atkinson (1975) found moderate relationships between inequality in income distribution and homicide rate (r = .40 to .59).

Suppose you have been tipped off that you are likely to be the victim of a violent crime. Whom would you avoid? When? Where? Surprisingly, you are most likely to be stabbed, shot, beaten, or abused in your own home or in the home of one of your friends, relatives, or acquaintances. Saturday nights are lethal, as is the month of December, when all the friends and relatives get together and drink; summer months are even more lethal. Alcohol is a contributing factor in the majority of homicides, assaults, and rapes; it serves is a deinhibitor, causing individuals to have less rational control over their emotions as well as less awareness of the consequences of their actions (see Collins, 1981). In the U.S., drunk drivers kill far more people every year than all recorded homicides.

The American cultural tradition of violence, combined with certain subcultures in which resort to aggression is legitimized, presents a strong predisposition to violence in the United States. These are the raw materials of typical interpersonal homicides. The spark that sets off this kindling could be any number of interpersonal conflict situations, such as arguments over money, love triangles, threats to masculinity, and the like. While ordinarily such disputes do not lead to violence, the addition of two other fuels to the fire can spell danger: alcohol and guns.

Guns

Plastic guns, automatic weapons, exploding bullets which penetrate bullet-proof vests, and practically instant drive-through, take-out service

Police recover a cache of guns used by New York City gang members.

for purchasers of such "sports equipment" appear to constitute a recipe for disaster, and it is.

As testimony to the power of the National Rifle Association, the U.S. House of Representatives in 1988 voted to eliminate the waiting period language from an existing omnibus antidrug bill and require instead the development of an on-the-spot determination by gun dealers as to whether a purchaser was a felon. The defeated seven-day waiting period to purchase a handgun had been called the "Brady bill" after White House Press Secretary, Jim Brady, who had been shot and seriously injured during the 1981 assassination attempt on President Reagan (Policy Lobbying, 1988, p. 1). Much emotion surrounds the gun control debate, with opponents of control arguing that regulation would hurt only the law-abiding who would be unable to protect themselves from the criminal. It is the law-abiding, however, that are also of concern. The very weapon which was probably purchased in order to protect the family against outside intruders all too often becomes the intimate enemy's tool to effect the death of a loved one. Morris and Hawkins (1970, p. 72) view the issue quite succinctly. A major precipitating condition of murder in the United States is the possession of a gun. They state "easy access to weapons of this kind may not merely facilitate violence, but may also stimulate, inspire, and provoke it."

Why such continuing opposition to handgun control, despite clear public support for such measures? The National Rifle Association is probably the single most powerful lobby in Washington, representing a $2 billion per year business with a very generous campaign donation policy (Haskell and Yablonsky, 1983, p. 199). Yet more Americans have been killed with guns by their fellow citizens in this century than have been killed in all of the wars this nation has ever fought, from the Revolutionary War through the Vietnam War.

A popular defense of the progun lobby in the United States is: "Guns don't kill people, people kill people." In fact, people with guns (particularly handguns) do kill people and it is no coincidence that the United States has both the highest homicide rate by far of any developed nation and the highest civilian-armed population in the world. This widespread ownership of firearms combined with a culture as well as subculture of violence foments lethal combinations. *The National Commission on Violence* (1969, p. 40) indicates:

> The frequency of violent themes in myriad forms in the media tends to foster permissive attitudes toward violence. Much the same can be said about guns in American society. The highest gun-to-population ratio in the world, the glorification of guns in our culture, and the television and movie displays of guns by heroes surely contribute to the scope and extent of urban violence.

Conklin (1981, pp. 314–316) reports that states with restrictive gun laws have smaller percentages of murders by firearms than states with lax gun laws. This relationship also may be due, however, to nonviolent, antigun attitudes in strong gun control states. Conklin concludes: "Tight firearm controls might reduce the number of robberies and murders; even if offenders continued to commit crime, crimes without firearms would be preferable to crimes with firearms" (Ibid., p. 316). Surprisingly, however, the chances of an individual's suffering harm in robbery are decreased if the perpetrator uses a gun rather than another or no weapon. In such instances, the intimidation of the victim is more complete and thus the perpetrators' resort to physical means is less necessary. But a major problem with analyses of the impact of tighter gun controls in the U.S. is experimental contamination, in which neighboring states undermine policies of states with greater control.

Opponents of gun control point to the Second Amendment of the U.S. Constitution and the right to bear arms as an inviolate principle, arguing that gun control measures would take guns away from everyone but criminals. While heated arguments continue from opponents and proponents of gun control, more research is needed on the potential impacts of various policy options (Zimring, 1987). As an example, a large survey of convicted felons by Wright and Rossi (1986) suggested the following:

- Rather than reducing crime in violent urban neighborhoods through gun control, the violence endemic to such impoverished areas must be reduced, thus reducing the need for carrying weapons.
- The theft of firearms must be reduced.
- The informal market for guns must be interdicted.
- Mandatory sentences for crimes with guns are ineffective and do not serve as a deterrent.
- The control of "Saturday night specials" (cheap handguns) would simply encourage criminals to switch to more lethal weapons (Bonn, 1987).

Clarke's Typology of Assassins

In *American Assassins: The Darker Side of Politics,* James Clarke (1982) is highly critical of the popular assumption that all or most assassins suffer from some mental pathology, that they are insane or deranged, and that this causes them to become assassins. Because sources incestuously cite each other's works and rely upon inaccurate secondary literature, Clarke feels that this pathological myth about assassins is continually repeated, in leading works such as those by Donovan (1952), Hastings (1965), Kirkham (1969), and the Warren Commission (1964). Much observation of assassins' pathological symptoms may result from "post hoc error," the false assumption that since one variable or outcome follows another in time, it must be the cause of that outcome. Clarke believes that most of major works on assassins simply fail to consider the political context of assassinations (Ibid., p. 7).

Clarke identified five types of assassins (the names have been provided by this writer):

1. Political assassins
2. Egocentric assassins
3. Psychopathic assassins
4. Insane assassins
5. "Atypical" assassins.

Type 1

Political assassins commit their acts (they believe) selflessly, for political reasons. Some examples of such assassins and attempted assassins are: John Wilkes Booth (Lincoln), Leon Czolgosz (McKinley), Oscar Collazo and Griselio Torresola (Truman), and Sirhan Sirhan (Robert Kennedy). Booth committed his crime in support of the Confederacy, Czolgosz's was in support of a class revolt, Collazo and Torresola were Puerto Rican nationalists, and Sirhan felt his act would help the Arab cause.

Type 2

Egocentric assassins are "persons with an overwhelming and aggressive egocentric need for acceptance, recognition and status" (Ibid.). They appreciate the consequences of their act and do not exhibit cognitive distortion characteristic of delusion or psychoses. Some examples are: Lee Harvey Oswald (John Kennedy), Samuel Byck (Nixon), Lynette ("Squeaky") Fromme (Ford), and Sara Jane Moore (Ford). Such assassins seek attention, which they feel they have been denied, and seek to place a burden upon those they feel have denied or rejected them. It would appear that John Hinckley, attempted assassin of Ronald Reagan, would fit this Type 2 description. Oswald and Byck projected their personal difficulties into political extremism. Oswald wanted to prove himself to the Cuban government and to his wife, neither of whom took him seriously. In February of 1974, Byck died in an attempt to hijack a jetliner which he planned to crash dive into the White House in order to kill Nixon. Although "Squeaky" Fromme resembled a Type 1 assassin, her devotion was to a man (Charles Manson) and not a cause (Ibid., p. 262). Moore wished to demonstrate her commitment to radicals who had rejected her when they discovered she was an FBI informant; she also wished to obtain protective custody.

Type 3

Psychopathic assassins, unable to relate to others, are emotional cripples who direct their perverse rage at popular political figures. In describing Guiseppi Zangara (Franklin Roosevelt) and Arthur Bremer (Wallace), Clarke indicates ". . . their motives were highly personal: they wanted to end their own lives in the most outrageous display of nihilistic contempt possible for a society they hated" (Ibid., p. 167). Both transferred resentment for their emotional deprivation in childhood to public figures. Bremer targeted Wallace after other presidential candidates he had stalked did not lend the proper opportunity.

Type 4

Insane assassins have documented histories of organic psychosis, a type of mental illness which is due to physiological factors, either environmentally or genetically induced. They exhibit severe emotional and cognitive distortion of reality, such as paranoia, one characteristic of which might be delusions of grandeur. Such psychotic assassins include: Richard Lawrence (Jackson), Charles Guiteau (Garfield), and Joseph Schrank (Theodore Roosevelt). Guiteau and Lawrence both believed they had been selected by God to perform His will, while Schrank irrationally believed that he was avenging McKinley's assassination and that Theodore Roosevelt had been the culprit.

Type 5

Atypical assassins are those who defy classification, such as Carl Weiss (Huey Long) and James Earl Ray (Martin Luther King, Jr.). Weiss was a successful physician who apparently killed Long because he felt he was protecting the lives and political jobs of his relatives. Although obviously racism was behind the King assassination, Ray, an unsuccessful career criminal, appeared to be primarily motivated by an alleged $50,000 payment for the assassination (Ibid., p. 246).

Clarke concludes his analysis by indicating that since 1963, Type 2 and 3 assassins have shared a strong desire for media notoriety and that restriction of such coverage could help discourage some attempts. He also feels that there is less need for additional surveillance of suspects than for analysis of information already in the possession of organizations such as the FBI. For instance, the FBI was aware of Byck, Fromme, Hinckley, Moore, and Oswald and even covered up information after the fact regarding the Oswald and Ray cases. (This, by the way, has led to a variety of conspiracy theories with respect to the King and John Kennedy assassinations.) Additionally, fourteen of the sixteen assassins used handguns, whose possession conservatives continue to insist is an inalienable constitutional right.

Rape

Susan Estrich, a rape victim herself, maintains in her book, *Real Rape: How the Legal System Victimizes Women Who Say No* (1987), that little has changed in the way most rape cases are handled by the courts and that judges still use their personal views to decide the victim's claim (Berger, 1988). This all depends upon whether the rape is viewed as "real rape" or "simple rape." "Real rape" is aggravated rape involving violence, weapons, attackers, and is recognized as rape by the courts. "Simple rape" is everything else, including date rape, and is dismissed as not "real rape." Victims of simple rape are viewed with suspicion, as not really victims, particularly if the victim did not physically resist. "The reasonable woman, it seems, is not a school boy 'sissy'; she is a real man" (Berger, 1988, p. 65). Vantage Point 6.2 illustrates some inter-

---

Vantage Point

Vantage Point 6.2—International Rape Rates

Rape

Interpol defines a sex offense category that includes rape as follows: "Each country should use the definitions in its own laws to determine whether or not an act is a sex offense; rape shall always be included in this category." It then asks countries also to report rape separately, but it does not define the term. Interpol leaves the matter of statutory rape to each country. The UN defines rape as "sexual intercourse without valid consent," which includes statutory rape.

Few individual countries provided explanatory notes for rape. None provided any to Interpol. Egypt reported sexual offenses including rape but did not provide separate figures for rape. Norway and the United States reported to the UN that their figures did not include statutory rape; Belize noted that rape included indecent assault; and Greece reported that the rape category included "lewdness, sodomy, seduction of a child, incest, prostitution, and procuring."

Nine European countries and the United States reported identical rates for rape in 1980 to both the UN and to Interpol (table 6). It appears that in both cases they simply reported their official rape statistic for that year. If the official number corresponded to the UN definition, it included statutory rape.

The eight other countries that reported to both the UN and Interpol tended to report higher rates to the UN, suggesting that they did not include statutory rape in the number they reported to Interpol.

In any comparison of rape rates, two underlying factors must be noted, even though they cannot be quantified. One is the degree of freedom and independence women have within a society and, consequently, the degree of exposure they have to the possibility of rape. Another is the extent to which stigma still attaches to a rape and the consequent reluctance victims may have to report the crime to authorities. The first factor may actually affect the volume of rape from one country to another. The second will not affect the total volume of rape but will affect the proportion of rape cases reported to the police. Both of these factors will tend to raise the reported rate of rape in developed countries, compared to some less developed nations.

SOURCE: Carol B. Kalish, 1988, *International Crime Rates*, Bureau of Justice Statistics Special Report, May, pp. 4–5.

national comparisons with respect to rape, although caution must be exercised due to unreliability of measurement.

The women's movement has been largely instrumental in altering public and official views of rape and rape victims. Susan Brownmiller (1975) in *Against Our Will: Men, Women and Rape* claims, correctly or incorrectly, that the criminalization of rape took place with the emergence

Rape in Selected Countries, Rates for 1980: UN and Interpol Data

Country	Number of rapes per 100,000 population		Country	Number of rapes per 100,000 population	
	UN	Interpol		UN	Interpol
United States	36.0	36.0	Indonesia	—	1.5
Australia	—	7.7	Ireland	1.4	1.4
Austria	7.5	5.2	Italy	3.3	1.1*
Belgium	—	.7	Japan	—	.2
Belize	17.7	—	Netherlands	5.6	5.6
Canada	9.6	14.1	New Zealand	—	9.6
Chile	34.2	12.1	Nigeria	—	4.3
Colombia	8.6	6.0	Northern Ireland	3.1	4.2
Costa Rica	13.5	9.9	Norway	3.2	3.2
Czechoslovakia	2.9	—	Panama	10.2	—
Denmark	6.3	7.0	Peru	—	2.3
Ecuador	—	.6*	Philippines	—	1.2
England and Wales	2.5	2.5	Poland	4.4	—
Finland	7.7	7.7	Portugal	1.2	1.5*
France	3.5	3.5	Scotland	5.9	3.2
Germany (FRG)	11.2	11.2	Spain	2.5	2.3
Greece	5.3	1.0	Sweden	10.6	10.6
Hungary	—	4.4	Venezuela	—	15.6
India	—	.7	Yugoslavia	8.5	—

—Not available.

*1981 data.

SOURCES: United Nations, Second United Nations Crime Survey; U.S. Census Bureau, *Statistical Abstract of the United States, 1987*; Interpol, *International Crime Statistics*, vols. 1979–80.

of a money economy, in which violation of virginity posed potential economic hardship for the family since the future bride was now tainted goods. Statistics regarding the extent of rape have been notoriously poor. Women have been reluctant in the past to report rapes for a variety of reasons, including:

- The stigma attached to rape victims, which alleges that they either invited the attack or cooperated in it.
- Sexist treatment given to many women, who are in effect mentally raped a second time by the criminal justice system (the police, prosecutors, and judges).
- Legal procedures that in the past have permitted courtroom prosecutors to probe the victim's sexual past, which can be both humiliating and embarrassing.
- The burden of proof that often has been shifted to the victim, to assure that the attack was forced and against her will and that she resisted the assault.

For these and other reasons, only recently have a significant proportion of rape victims been willing to report rapes and undertake prosecution of their attackers. The growth of rape crisis centers, featuring counseling and supportive services to victims, has been instrumental in this greater willingness to prosecute.

Other factors which account for an increase in the tendency to report rape include:

- More women police officers.
- Better training of police in sensitive handling of rape cases.
- Changes in rape laws in many states, eliminating barriers such as forbidding prosecutors from probing into the victim's prior sexual behavior.

Rape was the fastest growing of all UCR index crimes in the seventies, increasing 85 percent from 1970 to 1979. However, the NCS victim data that was available for part of this same period shows virtually no change in the rape rate. The increase in the seventies rape rate was primarily due, not to an increase in the number of rapes, but rather to a growth in the willingness to report such crimes.

Convicted and arrested rapists generally present the same demographic profile as other violent and conventional property criminals; that is, for the most part, they are fifteen to twenty-four years old, unmarried, from lower class and minority backgrounds (particularly black), and choose a victim of the same race. Amir (1971) in his Philadelphia study of forcible rape found that most rapists had backgrounds in property offenses rather than in violent criminal activity. He examined 646 cases in 1958 and 1960 and found rape twelve times higher among blacks than among whites. Amir's research was based solely upon official police reports, however, and for that reason has been subject to dispute.

Date Rape

While official data suggests that about half of all rapes involve strangers, this is partially offset by the victims' greater willingness to report stranger-precipitated incidents. Victimization surveys suggest that over 80 percent of rapes and attempted rapes are by strangers (McDermott, 1979). Amir (1971, p. 143) found that 58 percent of single offender and 90 percent of group rapes were planned rather than spontaneous events and that rape by more than one attacker took place in over 40 percent of the cases. But studies of attempted rapes reported in anonymous surveys by high school and college women indicate that many of these incidents are unlikely to be reported even to other household members, let alone to victim survey interviewers. Such potential "date rapes" do not meet the stereotype of the attacker being a stranger on a dark street. Contrary to Amir's research, these findings suggest that attacks by intimates and acquaintances make up the majority of rapes (Kirkpatrick and Kanin, 1957; and Christensen and Gregg, 1970).

McCaghy (1976b, p. 136) summarizes the *factors in the typical rape in the United States as follows:*

1. General values supporting violence in our society.
2. Values supporting the male as sexual aggressor (e.g., machismo, no sexual control, and so on).
3. The image of women as legitimate victims (i.e., they need, deserve, or want to be raped).
4. Situations conducive to rape (for example, the dating game, misinterpretations of intentions, and the like).
5. Presence of alcohol.

Given the general backdrop of a culture and subculture of violence, popular sexist images of females provide rationalizations for many rapists. Women may be viewed as legitimate targets of rape on the basis of past reputations or patterns of dress. They are viewed as secretly desiring to be dominated by a male. Many of these rapes may constitute date rapes in which misinterpretations and confused expectations in the male dating game in American society may create situations in which males are expected to press for greater degrees of sexual intimacy and females to set the limits. Much confusion exists as to when "no" really means "no." The presence of alcohol as a disinhibitor serves as a further predisposing factor in anywhere from one-third to one-half of the cases (Amir, 1971, p. 98).

Rape-Trauma Syndrome

Burgess and Holmstrom (1974) coined the term "rape-trauma syndrome" to refer to the adverse psychological impacts rape victims continue to suffer long after the incident. It includes sexual anxiety, a pervasive fear of violence, avoidance of relationships with the opposite sex, problems in interpersonal relationships, and a general feeling of unhappiness. Thus, mental scars often remain long after the incident has occurred.

Amir vs. Brownmiller

Chappell and Fogarty (1978) in a literature review on *Forcible Rape* indicate that two major landmark works preempt the field. Menachem Amir's (1971) *Patterns in Forcible Rape* and Susan Brownmiller's (1975) *Against Our Will: Men, Women and Rape.* Amir's work, the most widely cited source in the rape literature, espouses a now controversial *theory of victim precipitation,* in which the victim's behavior contributes to the incident. This theory was viewed as perpetrating many of the myths regarding rape that are quite common in society. Brownmiller's work espouses a theory that rape is "nothing more or less than a conscious process of intimidation by which *all* men keep *all* women in a state of fear" (Ibid., p. 15). While one critic found this theory simple facetious, another questioned the accuracy of the anthropology which Brownmiller had employed (Wilson, 1975, and Tiger, 1976 cited in Chappell and Fogarty, 1978, p. 2). Chappell and Fogarty indicate that while much of the pre-1972 literature such as MacDonald's (1971) *Rapists and Their Victims* suffered from male chauvinistic biases prevalent at the time, some recent literature reflects an equally unbalanced, strong feminist view lacking the backing of substantial research. Medea and Thompson's (1974) *Against Rape* is one such work. More objective works with a feminist perspective include Gager and Schurr's (1976) *Sexual Assault* and Russell's (1975) *The Politics of Rape.* Such works involve systematic interviews with rape victims.

Rape as a Violent Act

Rape is often perceived primarily as a sexually-motivated act, but most authorities on rape identify it *as primarily a violent act* in which sexual relations are merely a means of expressing violence, aggression, and domination. While our discussion will give consideration to arguments as to whether rapists are sexually or violently motivated or both, the classification of rape as a crime of violence looks not at the motivation of the offender, but the perception of the act by victims. Similar to the argument that robbery is really a property crime, sex (rape) or money (robbery) may be the motivation, but the tool employed and perceived by victims is violence or threats of violence and intimidation. For this reason the author views rape as a crime of violence. On the basis of their study of over five hundred convicted rapists, Groth and Birnbaum (1979) in *Men Who Rape* identified three types of rape:

- The *anger rape*, in which sexual attack becomes a means of expressing rage or anger and involves far more physical assault upon the victim than is necessary. Groth and Birnbaum claimed that 40 percent of their subjects were anger rapists.
- The *power rape*, whose assailant primarily wishes to express his domination over the victim. Since rape is viewed as an expression of power rather than a means of sexual gratification, the rapist generally uses only the amount of force necessary to exert his superordinant position. The majority, about 55 percent, of Groth and Birnbaum's offenders were of this type.
- The *sadistic rape*, whose perpetrator combines the sexuality and aggression aims in psychotic desires to often torment, torture, or otherwise abuse his victim. About 5 percent were of this type.

Gebhard et al. (1965, pp. 197–205), on the basis of interviews with 140 rapists, distinguished the following types: assaultive, amoral, drunken, explosive, double-standard, mentally defective, and psychotic. Glaser (1978, p. 364) correctly indicates that the attributes utilized for classifying rapists into such schemes are often not mutually exclusive and proposes an interesting typology of rapists based upon their wish or desire for affection from their victim as well as their respect for her autonomy. Glaser's four categories of rapists are: naïve graspers, meaning stretchers, sex looters, and group conformers (Ibid., pp. 365–367).

"Naïve graspers" are usually sexually inexperienced youths who possess an unrealistic conception of female erotic arousal. Awkward in relating to the opposite sex, they hold high expectations that their crude advances will be met with affection by their victims. They possess a high desire for affection but little respect for their victim's autonomy in resisting such advances. "Meaning stretchers" are involved in the most typical rape, the "date rape." They stretch the meaning of or misinterpret a woman or date's expressions of friendliness and affection as indicating that the female desires coitus even when she says no. "Sex looters" have a low desire for affection or low respect for the victim's autonomy and callously use women as sex objects. This type figures in the stranger-precipitated rape that is most likely to be reported to the police. "Group conformers" participate in group rapes or "gang bangs," often following the leader, a sex looter, out of a felt sense of conformity and a perverted notion of demonstrating their masculinity. The 1989 "Lord of the Flies" or "wilding" rape of a female jogger in Central Park by a gang of youths may serve as an example.

In an examination and criminal profiling of forty-one convicted "serial rapists" (defined in the project as those having committed ten or more rapes), Hazelwood, Burgess, and associates (Hazelwood and Warren, 1989; Hazelwood and Burgess, 1987; and Burgess et al., 1987) found 76 percent had been sexually abused as children. The majority of the claimed serial rapes had not been reported to authorities.

Such typologies may not accurately reflect the motivations of typical rapists at the time of the offense. They are based upon ex post facto case studies of incarcerated offenders and interviews with offenders which makes them prone to post hoc error. They are also unnecessarily steeped in psychiatric assumptions regarding offender motivations. In addition, incarcerated rapists are more likely to be of the "stranger" variety and perhaps either more violence-prone or willing to use violence than the nonstranger rapists.

Perhaps an overly macho image of rapists has been drawn. Sanders (1983, pp. 273–274) provides a very unflattering view of "the rapist as wimp." A "wimp" is contemporary American slang referring to a male who is weak, "a sissy," one who is deficient in masculine identity and performance. Sanders suggests that since rape involves violence against females, it violates male role expectations. He continues (1983, p. 273):

> In effect, they "hit girls" and that is something only wimps and sissies do. This conceptualization of rapists is less flattering than that of their being truly "violent men"—men to be taken seriously, dangerous men not to be trifled with. It is also a good reputation for rapists since it scares the victims into submission. However, it is inaccurate. The greater the resistance of women in rapes, the more likely rapists will run off. In the world of violent men, rapists are considered punks and generally low life. . . . Thus while rapists loom large as fiends and overpowering monsters to women, they loom small to men, more mice than monsters.

A study of violent rapists being treated at Atascadera State Hospital, California, by the Queen's Bench Foundation (1976), although plagued with the same after-the-fact-analysis discussed previously, indicated the following:

- The majority demonstrated poor relations with women, including a general inability to develop interpersonal relations, a lack of self confidence, and a negative self-concept.
- 51 percent indicated they were seeking power or dominance over their victims.
- The majority had planned to have sex that day and 92 percent said rape was their intention.
- Not one of the 75 subjects indicated a lack of sexual outlet as a reason for the crime.

Advice on victim resistance appears to be mixed. While resistance as Sanders proposes (particularly screaming rather than physical defense) increases the likelihood of escape, it also increases the possibility of injury. "The Criminalization of Forced Marital Intercourse" (Sigler and Haygood, 1988), or "marital rape," underscores the view of rape as a violent rather than sexual crime. In *State vs. Rideout* (1978) an Oregon court challenged the marital immunity defense; that is, the husband's right to force involuntary intercourse.

Robbery

Vantage Point 6.3 provides some international comparisons in robbery rates. *Robbery* involves theft by the use or threat of violence. Until recently, the biggest score on an individual robbery was the great Boston Brinks' robbery which involved theft of about $2 million dollars. Later, the Lufthansa airport robbery in New York City netted $4 million (Clinard and Yeager, 1980, p. 8). In 1983, the largest American take in a robbery escalated to $11.1 million, when cash was taken from a Sentry Armored Car warehouse in New York City. Nine months later, a Wells Fargo armored car guard pulled a gun on his fellow worker and boss, tied them up, injected each with a drug to put them to sleep, and carted away a cool $7 million in cash (Wells Fargo, 1983). In November, 1983, British robbers made off with a record $37 million in gold and diamonds from a Brinks warehouse at London's Heathrow Airport.

Cook (1983, pp. 1–2) describes robbery as the "quintessential urban crime":

> The six largest cities (with 8 percent of the population) experienced 33 percent of the robberies in 1980. New York City alone had more than 18 percent. Robbery is more highly concentrated in large cities than any other of the major crimes. The 56 cities with populations exceeding 250,000 in 1980 (which contained 19 percent of the U.S. population) reported 60 percent of all robberies, as compared with 46 percent of all criminal homicides

and 30 percent of all burglaries . . . Controlling for population density, there is no pronounced regional pattern to urban robbery.

Robbery of commercial establishments has particularly experienced an explosion. There were 278 bank robberies in the U.S. in 1957; by 1980, there were 6,515. (This rise was believed to be primarily due to increased "target availability" or growth in branch banks.)

The typical robbery is rather minor. Most robberies are of individuals rather than of commercial establishments and for amounts considerably

Vantage Point

Vantage Point 6.3—International Robbery Rates

Robbery

The Interpol definition of robbery is "robbery and violent theft." The UN definition is "the taking away of property from a person overcoming resistance by force or threat of force."

The United States defines robbery as "the taking or attempting to take anything of value from the care, custody, or control of a person or persons by force or threat of force or violence and/or putting the victim in fear."

England and Wales reported to Interpol that their definition of aggravated theft, which is the sum of robbery and burglary, includes the crime of "going equipped for stealing." It is not clear if this crime is included in robbery or in burglary or is divided between the two.

Czechoslovakia reported to the UN that robbery and crimes of theft refer only to crimes against individuals and individually owned property. Robbery or theft in Czechoslovakia involving socially owned property is classified in a separate category. As a result, robbery and theft rates in Czechoslovakia are strikingly lower than those for other countries.

The robbery rate reported to the UN for Chile, 403, is extremely high, while its reported theft rate, which includes minor offenses, is rather low, 404 (appendix table). The fact that they are also practically the same suggests the possibility of error. This possibility is enhanced by the fact that the robbery rate Chile reported to Interpol for 1980 was 24 per 100,000. Although its reported rates are less than half those of Chile, Colombia also reported a higher rate for robbery than for theft, but it did not report whether minor theft was included in the theft rate.

Aproximately one-fourth of the countries reported the same or nearly the same robbery rates both to Interpol and to the UN.

Source: Carol B. Kalish, 1988, *International Crime Rates*, Bureau of Justice Statistics Special Report, May, pp. 5–6.

less than the millions as described in our examples. According to the UCR (FBI, 1988, p. 18), the average loss per robbery incident was $631. Bank robbery averaged $3,013 (although Cook [1983, p. 3] puts the figure at $7,000), and street or highway robbery netted a $414 average take. A disproportionate number of robbers are young, black males, while a large proportion of victims are white males over twenty-one. The unusual interracial nature of robbery, unlike other violent crimes, can be explained by the fact that robbers are primarily interested in money and adult white males are perceived as being good targets. Haran (1982)

Robbery in Selected Countries, Rates for 1980: UN and Interpol Data

Country	No. of robberies per 100,000 population UN	Interpol	Country	No. of robberies per 100,000 population UN	Interpol
United States	240.9	244.0	Indonesia	—	8.2
			Ireland	39.2	33.4
Australia	—	56.6	Italy	7.6	18.6*
Austria	12.6	30.5	Japan	—	1.9
Belgium	—	32.5	Monaco	—	11.1
Belize	29.9	—			
Canada	102.1	103.7	Netherlands	30.0	30.1
			New Zealand	—	9.0
Chile	403.4	23.5	Nigeria	—	4.3
Colombia	191.8	36.7	Northern Ireland	—	84.2
Costa Rica	82.2	21.6	Norway	8.3	—
Czechoslovakia	5.3	—			
Denmark	28.3	28.5	Panama	14.3	—
			Peru	—	19.3
Ecuador	—	6.9*	Philippines	—	13.9
England and Wales	30.2	30.5	Poland	.7	—
Finland	39.1	40.9	Portugal	16.5	18.3*
France	9.0	65.8			
Germany (FRG)	38.5	39.3	Scotland	72.3	72.2
			Spain	73.2	63.6
Greece	.8	.7	Sweden	41.2	41.2
Hungary	—	9.6	Venezuela	—	149.0
India	—	3.5	Yugoslavia	4.5	—

—Not available.

*1981 data.

SOURCES: United Nations, Second United Nations Crime Survey; U.S. Census Bureau, *Statistical Abstract of the United States, 1987*; Interpol, *International Crime Statistics*, vols. 1979–80.

in an examination of armed robberies in New York City found that in the 1960s 60 percent of the robbers were older, white males, but that in the seventies 61 percent were black males with 58 percent under age 26. But Glaser (1978, p. 254) points out that official statistics overlook both juvenile offenders and victims. More people are serving time in U.S. prisons for robbery than for any other single crime category (Bureau of Justice Statistics, 1983, p. 31).

Perhaps the biggest victim apprehensiveness in robbery is the fear of personal harm in street robberies. Roughly one-third of victims are harmed to some degree, with 2 percent requiring inpatient hospital care. In 1988 FBI statistics claimed that about 20 percent of murders were due to robbery, arson, or other felonious circumstances. "In New York City, for example, 24 percent of the criminal homicides in 1980 were classified as robbery-related, amazingly, a majority of slayings of whites in New York City resulted from robberies" (Cook, 1983, p. 4).

Feeney and Weir (1975) indicate that while resistance greatly increases the possibility of suffering injury, screaming and yelling may cause the robber to quit and does not increase the likelihood of harm. Many armed robbers are primarily interested in intimidating the victim and in fact may employ unloaded or even fake weapons, whereas unarmed robbers are far more likely to attack their victims (Conklin, 1972, pp. 113–116).

Conklin's Typology of Robbers

Conklin (1972) developed a *typology of robbers* based upon interviews with sixty-seven convicted robbers in Massachusetts prisons as well as ninety victims. He classified them as:

1. The professional robbers
2. The opportunist robbers
3. The addict robbers
4. The alcoholic robbers

Professional robbers have a long-term commitment to crime, their major source of livelihood. They are very rational about crime and plan their operations carefully. (This type of criminal will be discussed in detail in Chapter 8 on professional crime.) The most common type of bandits are the *opportunist robbers*. Having little commitment to or specialization in robbery, they are all purpose property offenders. Their engagement in robbery is infrequent and relatively unplanned. Often young and from lower class, minority backgrounds, such offenders often operate in groups. *Addict robbers* are addicted to substances such as heroin or other drugs and commit robbery to support their expensive habits. Most drug abusers are interested in safe and quick criminal gain and are less likely to be involved in robbery than in burglary and sneak thievery. Such offenders were less likely to use weapons and therefore more likely to use physical force as a means of intimidation. *Alcoholic robbers* have little commitment to robbery; they engage in unplanned robberies on occasion in order to support their habits. Many claim to be intoxicated at the time of their offense.

Perhaps the most feared type of robber, even though not a separate type, is the *mugger*, a "strong-armed" robber who generally does not use a weapon. Many muggers are semiprofessional in that they do some planning and specialization, though not to the extent of the professional robber. *Mugging*, as an American slang term for robbery, may refer to everything from purse-snatching to brutalization or murder of the victims. Working in groups, muggers may start by carefully surveying the scene as well as the mark (victim). The actual techniques employed vary from the "yoke," a method of grabbing the victim from behind around the neck, to the use of knives or guns to scare the victim. Young and black offenders are more likely to commit purse snatches and street robberies, netting small amounts, while adult, white offenders are more likely to participate in commercial robberies (Dunn, 1976, p. 12).

McClintock and Gibson (1961, p. 16) classify robberies into five types, taking into account both the location and role of the victim in the crime. Table 6.2 presents their types and the percentages of robberies in London

Table 6.2: Types of Robbery Incidents in London and Philadelphia (In Percent)

Robbery Group	London[a] (N = 749)	Philadelphia[b] (N = 1,732)
I. Robbery of persons who, as part of their employment, were in charge of money or goods	35.9	25.8
II. Robbery in the open following sudden attack	36.0	52.2
III. Robbery on private premises	10.0	7.3
IV. Robbery after preliminary association of short duration between victim and offender	14.3	10.2
V. Robbery in cases of previous association of some duration between victim and offender	3.7	4.5
Total[c]	100.0	100.0

[a]Source: McClintock and Gibson, 1961, p. 16, Table 6. These percents are derived from the total of robberies in 2 years (1950, 1957).

[b]Source: Normandeau, 1968, p. 120. Table 41. These percents are derived from data for a 7-year period, 1960–1966.

[c]Percentages may not sum to 100 percent because of rounding.

SOURCE: Christopher S. Dunn, 1976, *Patterns of Robbery Characteristics*, Washington, D.C.: National Crime Justice Information and Statistics Service, Analytic Report 15, p. 11.

for 1950 and 1957 that fit these groupings; for comparison, the table also shows Normandeau's (1968) distribution for Philadelphia from 1960 to 1966 using this classification.

High robbery rates are not an inevitable product of urbanization in advanced capitalistic societies, as can be illustrated in Japan. In the late seventies, New York City had eleven thousand robberies per million residents while Tokyo had about forty robberies per million population (Nettler, 1982, vol. 2, p. 34).

Violence in the Family

In our previous discussion, we indicated that one stands the greatest chance of being kicked, stabbed, shot, or otherwise brutalized within the refuge of one's own home. *Child abuse* may include excessive physical assault, neglect, and/or sexual molestation. (The last topic will be discussed in a later chapter.) *Spouse abuse* usually involves physical assaults by husbands against their wives, although the reverse is not unheard of.

Child Abuse

On January 30, 1989, a jury in New York City convicted lawyer Joel Steinberg of manslaughter in the killing of his illegally adopted six-year-old daughter, Lisa, and sentenced him to the maximum eight and one-third to twenty-five years in prison. Steinberg had systematically battered his live-in lover, Hedda Nussbaum, and had so controlled her that she would not even call an ambulance as battered Lisa lay comatose on their bathroom floor while Nussbaum freebased cocaine with Steinberg. Even more chilling was the total lack of remorse on the part of Steinberg, who indicated: "I understand the meaning of remorse. I have remorse about losing my life" (Steinberg Sentenced, 1989, p. 4-B). Adults are literally like gods to small children; they are bigger and smarter, they provide necessities, and they explain and negotiate the bewildering world out there. But, for many of these adults, particularly parents, the child is the safest target they can choose to vent their frustrations and aggression. While corporal punishment is an approved-of disciplinary practice in society—as epitomized in the expression "spare the rod and spoil the child"—*child abuse* is defined as excessive mistreatment, either physically or emotionally, of children beyond any reasonable explanation (Kempe and Kempe, 1978).

Bakan (1975, p. xi) in *The Slaughter of the Innocents* relates the following grisly anecdote: "When I was a child I was told that the story of the fall of man had a hidden secret: the fruit of the tree of knowledge which Adam and Eve ate was a baby." In this rather dramatic manner, he introduces the question of historical silence on the torture and murder of children. In a nationwide survey of 2,143 families, Gelles (1978) discovered that, during the previous year, over 20 percent of children had been assaulted by their parents by having objects thrown at them or being hit with them, being kicked or bitten, or hit with fists.

The child batterer strikes against the defenseless, against people who cannot defend themselves; historically, he or she is exercising a traditional prerogative of parents. Infanticide was a parental privilege in many ancient societies and childhood was simply not regarded as a particularly important stage in life. Ironically, it was not until 1866 that state protection of abused children was begun, then using SPCA (Society for the Prevention of Cruelty to Animals) authority for the removal of a child from an abusing household.

The extent of homicide and brutal assault and torture vented up child victims was illustrated by a study by Raffali (1970). Following up on 302 battered children as reported by some New York City hospitals, it was discovered that one year later 35 had died and 55 suffered permanent brain damage due to their injuries. A study by Gil (1971) estimated serious physical abuse of children under eighteen at about 9 per 100,000 or comparable to the homicide rate at that time. The fact that most instances are never reported to police or come to the attention of authorities would suggest a large "dark figure" of child abuse. Estimates by the National Center on Child Abuse figure that about a million American children are mistreated each year, with as many as 200,000 physically assaulted, up to 100,000 sexually abused, and the remainder subject to neglect. Gelles and Straus (1979) put this statistic at as many as 1.9 million per year who are physically abused. Abusive activities seem to take place more often in families which have a foster or stepparent present (Zalba, 1971), with boys more frequently the targets than girls until age twelve, after which girls are more subject to attack.

A virtual statistical epidemic in reports of child abuse has occurred since the sixties, primarily due to increased efforts at detection and reporting. Emergency room personnel, for instance, receive special training in spotting the "battered child syndrome," which includes a variety of symptoms including lethargy, fear of parents, subdural hematoma (blood and swelling next to bones or skull), multiple broken bones demonstrating various stages of healing (thus multiple incidents), suspicious bites, bruises, and the like which cannot be reasonably explained by parents (Fontana, 1973, pp. 28–29). Between 1976 and 1985 reports of child abuse grew from 669,000 reports per year to 1.9 million.

 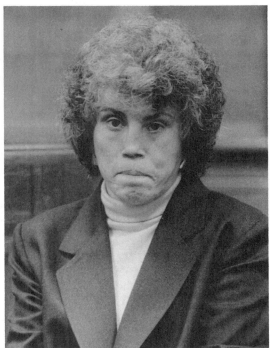

Joel Steinberg and Hedda Nussbaum are unfortunate reminders of the fact that a person stands the greatest chance of being abused within his or her own home.

The flip side of this increased reporting was that more than half of the latter figure were unfounded; that is, determined not to have taken place (Whitman, 1987, p. 39). In a reversal of previous rulings, the U.S. Supreme Court in *Coy vs. Iowa* ruled that children in sexual abuse cases must confront their alleged abusers "face-to-face" (Lauter, 1988, p. 6-A). Such a ruling may discourage prosecutions of real batterers.

Studies of spouse and child batterers suggest a frightening, although not inevitable link in which former child abuse victims grow up to become child or spouse abusers themselves. Perhaps a behaviorist analogy would illustrate the point. Suppose you had a small puppy and every day, in a highly unpredictable manner, would beat it unmercifully with a stick. It would not be at all unexpected that a couple of years later you would have one mean dog on your hands. With humans this analogy is not as straightforward in that not all abused children become scarred irreparably or future abusers, but, not surprisingly, many do (see Koski, 1988). In addition to a history of abuse, some other characteristics of child abusers include family isolation from helping resources in periods of crisis, disappointment with the child, and some crisis which precipitates maltreatment (Kempe and Kempe, 1978, p. 24).

Most parents are aware of the unbelievable demands small children make upon parental time; even strong, coping parents are at times at wit's end. If you add poverty, isolation, the parents' own childhood abuse, and few resources to obtain help, some parents will strike out, unfortunately, against the easiest target available and one which often cannot even complain. Child abuse cuts across ethnic and class lines; however, like other crimes of violence, it appears to be overrepresented in lower class families, even controlling for bias in statistical reporting (Pelton, 1978).

According to Bakan (1975, p. 100) hostility toward children is generally associated with two age-maturity distortions. First, the adult may ascribe to himself the role of a person younger than he actually is. Second, he may ascribe to the child a maturity beyond the child's years. Studies of child abusers and their personality characteristics, however, are often plagued by post hoc error, the assumption that since one variable follows another in time, it must be the cause of that outcome. Gelles (1977) indicates that often psychological conditions that are identified as being present after an abuse incident tend to be viewed as the cause of the incident. Abusers are often described as being depressed and paranoid. These conditions could be results of the incident rather than its cause.

Child battering may represent assault or even homicide, but most cases in the United States are handled in family or juvenile courts as categories of child neglect or abuse. Such courts have an orientation toward rehabilitation rather than toward imposing penalties or imprisonment (Glaser, 1978, p. 246). Often children are removed from the home for their own protection and temporarily placed in foster homes until their parents are adjudged fit, but a major objective in the past has been to maintain the family unit. This could account for the later one-third death and brain damage result in Raffali's (1970, p. 301) study.

Spouse Abuse

Straus, Gelles, and Steinmetz (1980) "claim" that husbands and wives are equally likely to batter each other, although most others find the male as the major aggressor. Descriptions such as "The Marriage License as a Hitting License" (Ibid., 1982) and "The Family as a Cradle of Violence" (Steinmetz and Straus, 1978) illustrate the intimate nature of intrafamily violence, particularly with respect to spouse abuse. The same difficulties in estimating child abuse are applicable here.

In their self-report survey of 2,143 husbands and wives, Straus, Gelles, and Steinmetz (1982, pp. 274–275) indicated that one out of every six couples admitted one of the following in the past year: threw something at spouse, pushed, grabbed, shoved, slapped, kicked, bit, hit with fist or other object, beat up, threatened with or used a knife or gun against the spouse. In line with our earlier discussion of victim-precipitation in many assaults, they found the most common situation was one in which both spouses used violence, although husbands employed the most dangerous and injurious forms of violence and were greater repeaters. Often family members (women, older persons), who are generally thought of as victims, become assailants and spontaneously strike back, sometimes with lethal consequences (Kratcoski, 1988; and Kuhl, 1985).

As in the history of child abuse, traditionally in Western society "a man's home was his castle" and wife-beating has been the prerogative of the "master of the house." Many traditional societies approved of husbands murdering their wives for serious transgressions such as adultery, although the "double standard" did not permit reverse action of this type. Until the women's movement and until new occupational options became available for females, most women had little choice but to continue being a grim imitation of a punching bag, particularly if support of children weighed as an additional consideration.

Although the list is subject to post hoc error, Newman (1979, pp. 145–146) identifies the following as characteristic of wife abusers: alcohol abuse, hostility dependence on their wives, excessive brooding over trivial events, belief in societal approval of battering, economic problems, a sudden burst of anger, present military service, and having been a battered child.

In the past, the degree of danger to police in handling domestic disputes has been exaggerated. The frequently cited police deaths at "disturbance calls" failed to break down the category which included the very lethal bar room fights. The number killed in family quarrels was actually smaller than the number shot accidentally by fellow officers (Sherman, 1987; and Garner and Clemmer, 1986). Robbery calls were consistently the most dangerous.

A study by the Police Foundation (1977) found that, in the two years preceding a domestic assault or homicide, the police had been at the address of the incident five times or more in half of the cases. In the *Minneapolis Domestic Violence Experiment* (Sherman and Berk, 1984) a randomized field experiment demonstrated that arrested domestic offenders were about half as likely to commit repeat violence than nonarrested offenders. While care must be taken in replications in specifying this policy, the experiment certainly illustrated that there are things police can do in intervening and preventing family violence (Berk and Newton, 1985; and Binder and Meeker, 1988).

Drunk Driving

In May, 1988, a drunken driver in Kentucky drove his pickup truck the wrong way on an interstate highway and crashed head-on into a school bus carrying sixty-seven passengers, killing twenty-four teenagers and three adults, as the bus's gas tank ruptured, engulfing the interior in flames (Highway Safety, 1988). In March, 1989, the oil tanker *Exxon Valdez* ran aground and ruptured, releasing 10 million gallons of oil and creating the worst oil spill in North America. The captain was alleged to have been drunk and below deck, leaving the craft in the hands of an untrained third mate. On January 4, 1987, a speeding Conrail freight locomotive piloted by an engineer high on marijuana ran a stop signal and collided with an Amtrak train near Baltimore. The toll was 16 killed and 170 injured in the worst accident in Amtrak history. While one of our examples involved marijuana, rhetoric regarding a war on drugs tends to overlook the fact that alcohol abuse remains the Western world's number one drug problem.

Drunk driving has been a very neglected area of violent crime in American society until relatively recently. But more Americans are killed or injured every year by drunk drivers than are murdered or assaulted in standard violent criminal behavior. The National Highway Traffic Safety Administration estimates that as many as a quarter of a million persons were killed in alcohol-related motor vehicle accidents between 1978 and 1988 in the United States, with 650,000 persons

In the U.S. drunk drivers kill more people than murderers do. This drunk driver smashed into a Students Against Driving Drunk display in California.

injured annually and an annual cost in property damage estimated at $24 billion (Greenfeld, 1988, p. 1). Excluding traffic citations, DUI (Driving Under the Influence) arrests were the highest category of arrests in the UCR. In 1986 there was one DUI arrest per eighty-eight licensed drivers (Greenfeld, 1988, p. 1). Despite this fact, the likelihood of a drunk driver on any given evening being stopped by police is small. Even chronic abusers slip through the cracks, often until it is too late and they maim or kill someone. In the past, drunk driving simply was not taken very seriously, until political pressure groups (such as MADD, Mothers Against Drunk Drivers), particularly the families and other survivors of such victimization, began to apply pressure to legislatures for stricter laws.

Beginning in the seventies, many states passed more stringent laws in an effort to cut down the carnage on American streets and highways. These laws included mandatory jail sentences for offenders and temporary suspension of licenses as well as DWI or DUI (Driving While Intoxicated or Driving Under the Influence) schools which the offender had to pay to attend. A 1983 survey of state law enforcement by the U.S. Transportation Department found that, despite these strict laws, judges were unwilling to impose jail terms on first offenders (Why So Few, 1983). In addition, arrested drivers were tying up the courts, which led to greater plea bargaining and thus lesser penalties. The required jail sentence also placed an even greater burden on overcrowded jails. But policies such as the immediate seizure of licenses, longer suspensions, and the impounding of vehicles of habitual offenders promise success in reducing fatalities. In addition, civil and criminal suits against negligent bartenders and public service work for offenders offer some additional hope. While some researchers have not been very impressed with the impact DUI laws have had in deterring drunk driving (Kingsworth and Jungsten, 1988; and Wheeler and Hissong, 1988), others point out the need for continuing research on this matter (Jacobs, 1988). The federal Department of Transportation was exploring whether or not to begin urine testing of airline pilots, bus and truck drivers, and others involved in public transportation in 1990.

Criminal Careers of Violent Offenders

Most violent offenders, such as murderers, assaulters, and forcible rapists, generally do not have criminal careers or extensive backgrounds in and commitment to violent crime as a major component of their lives. Most do not view themselves as criminals nor associate with other criminals. The major exception to this are people incarcerated for robbery who, with the exception of the violence, resemble conventional property criminals (to be discussed in Chapter 6).

As seen in Chapter 3, various cultural and subcultural values and attitudes regarding violence have an impact upon the relative frequency of violent crimes and their propensity in various countries, regions within countries, urban/rural differences, social classes, races and ethnic groups, as well as ages and sexes.

Culture of Violence

Entire cultures can have a predisposition to the use of violence to resolve grievances. Given a lack of centralized law enforcement, in the last century areas such as Sardinia and Sicily were characterized by vendetta, which required personal revenge for wrongs against oneself or kin; in some cases, whole families killed each other off, responding in kind to the need to avenge past harm to relatives. Additionally, in the 1950s the nation of Colombia experienced what has been called "violencia Colombiana," in which during a ten-year period two hundred thousand persons were killed in a nation of only ten million, a fantastic rate of one out of every fifty Colombians. Moreover, Wolfgang and Ferracuti (1967, p. 280) claim that the risk of death from homicide was greater in Mexico City in the sixties than the risk of death from bombing during the London blitz in World War II. Machismo is a typical Latin American emphasis upon masculinity which includes an expression of violence.

Subculture of Violence

Marvin Wolfgang and Franco Ferracuti (1967) in their now-classic *The Subculture of Violence* refer to a "culture within a culture," mainly among some ethnic and lower class groups that demonstrate favorable attitudes toward the use of violence as a means of resolving interpersonal grievances. In such subcultures, violence is viewed as a necessary measure to uphold one's masculinity. "Quick resort to physical combat as a measure of daring, courage, or defense of status appears to be a cultural expectation, especially for lower socioeconomic class males of both races." (Ibid., p. 189).

The National Commission on Violence (1969, pp. 39–40) expresses the matter succinctly:

> Violence is actually often used to enable a young man to become a successful member of ghetto society. In the subculture of violence, proving masculinity may require frequent rehearsal of toughness, the exploitation of women,

and the quick aggressive responses that are characteristic of the lower-class adult male. Those who engage in subcultural violence are often not burdened by conscious guilt, because their victims are likely to belong to the same subculture or to a group they believe has exploited them. Thus, when victims see their assaulters as agents of the same kind of aggression they themselves represent, violent retaliation is readily legitimized.

The Southern U.S. has higher rates of homicide than other regions of the country. This has led some to view the region as reflecting a subculture of violence. Not coincidentally the South also has the highest rates of firearm ownership. Another rival explanation for the higher murder rates in the South may be related to the fact that poorer emergency medical services exist there than in other regions of the country (Doerner and Speir, 1986; and Doerner, 1988).

A basic tenet of the "subculture of violence" thesis is that, within such subcultures, violence is not viewed as undesirable conduct, and little guilt or disapproval is experienced when aggression is used. Erlanger (1974), in an empirical assessment of this concept, indicated the surprising lack of examples in the ethnographic literature, citing Liebow's (1967) *Tally's Corner* and Whyte's (1955) *Streetcorner Society* as examples. Other such literature that he does not cite certainly does lend credibility to the theory, for example, Allen's (1977) *Assault with a Deadly Weapon*, and Brown's (1964) *Manchild in the Promised Land*. In a reanalysis of data which had originally been gathered for the President's Violence Commission, Erlanger (1974) concluded that on attitudinal measures of approval/disapproval of violence, lower class and minority groups were no different than general society. He concludes that the social and economic deprivation experienced by these groups is primarily a result of social structural factors, for example, poverty and racism, rather than the product of group pathology. In essence, while there is no greater attitudinal approval of violence, the lack of sophistication with respect to other means of resolving grievances results in higher rates of violent behavior. Other researchers have indicated that blacks and Hispanics had lower tolerance of violence than the general population. "Demographic and residential variables explained more of the variance in violence tolerance and experiences with violence than did ethnic background" (Shoemaker and Williams, 1987, p. 464).

Machismo, the code of conduct requiring that males defend their sense of honor, is particularly virulent in Latin American culture. In Brazil, for instance, some courts until recently refused to convict husbands of killing unfaithful wives, although the reverse did not apply. The view is that a man should not be punished for defending his honor.

Bourgois (1988) described a "culture of terror" in the underground drug economies of American central cities in which regular displays of violence are necessary for success in the street-level drug-dealing world. What outsiders view as senseless violence may be viewed as public relations, "a curriculum vita (resumé) that proves their capacity for effective violence and terror" (Ibid.).

Most violent criminals are not career criminals. Some are, and the impact that a small number of career criminals can have upon crime rates simply in terms of the quantity of crimes they commit can be illustrated by means of the "Marielitos," refugees from the 130,000-person Cuban freedom flotilla that embarked from Mariel, Cuba, in the spring of 1980. Law enforcement officials estimated that, among the majority of decent Cubans permitted to emigrate, about 1 percent were the very worst of Cuban career, violent criminals. The sign of a seasoned Cuban criminal included a lip tattoo from prison and a hand tattoo indicating the criminal specialty as well as other self-administered tattoos. Such violently antisocial types apparently were primarily responsible for a 20 percent increase in the Miami crime rate, while the Havana crime rate for the same year decreased by 30 percent (NBC, 1983).

Career Criminals/Violent Predators

Most violent offenders do not make a career out of murdering, assault, and the like. Those who do are professional or organized criminals (to be discussed in detail in later chapters). A small number of violent offenders may be classified as *career criminals* since their patterns of offense occur frequently and over a sustained period of time, and cause them to spend a considerable period of time in prison. Petersilia, Greenwood, and Lavin (1977), based upon interviews with 49 incarcerated robbers, found that such individuals committed roughly 214 offenses apiece, although these crimes were nonspecialized and were as likely to involve conventional, nonviolent property crime. They divided *career criminals* into *two types*: the *intensives* and the *intermittents*. Intensives have continuing criminal involvement since an early age and have committed on the average 51 crimes per year. Intermittents are irregular in their offense patterns, committing 5 crimes per year, generally with lower takes from their victims.

In a previously discussed longitudinal study of Philadelphia delinquents by Wolfgang, Figlio, and Sellin (1972), it was indicated that roughly 61 percent of the 1945 male birth cohort were "chronic offenders," accounting for 52 percent of all the crimes committed by this group. FBI computerized studies of criminal histories of arrested offenders found the highest recidivism rate in 1972 was for burglaries,

Figure 6.3: Types of Career Criminals

Adolescence: ages 7-17	Young adulthood ages 18-39	Middle age: age 40+	Type	Percent of inmates
Criminal	Criminal ⟶ Criminal		1	14.0
	Noncriminal ⟶ Criminal		2	1.2
NonCriminal	Criminal ⟶ Criminal		3	38.2
	Noncriminal ⟶ Criminal		4	46.6

SOURCE: Patrick A. Langan and Lawrence A. Greenfeld, 1983, "Career Patterns in Crime," *Bureau of Justice Statistics, Special Report,* Washington, D.C.: Bureau of Justice Statistics, June, p. 2.

but the next highest were for robbery, motor vehicle theft, rape, and aggravated assault (Conklin, 1981, p. 350).

Chaiken and Chaiken (1982) in *Varieties of Criminal Behavior* used self-reports and official records in a survey of 2,200 inmates in California, Michigan, and Texas in which they identified "violent predators" who commit a highly disproportionate amount of crime, consisting of a combination of robbery, assault, and drug-dealing. They began taking drugs as juveniles, committed violent crimes before age sixteen, were addicted to multiple drugs, and perpetrated an exceptionally high level of robberies, property crimes, and assaults in order to support their addictions. Most were unmarried, had few other family obligations, and were characterized by irregular employment. Their distinctive characteristic was multiple drug use, for example, heroin with barbiturates or alcohol, or amphetamines with alcohol. The California inmates who had been addicted admitted, on the average, thirty-four robberies, sixty-eight burglaries, and seventy-two thefts per year, while the same figures for those without drug use were two, three, and eight per year.

Langan and Greenfeld (1983), in a retrospective national study of a random sample of 11,397 male and female state prison inmates, propose a typology of criminal career types, Figure 6.3. Figure 6.3 "identifies career types according to the absence or presence of criminality during three of life's major stages: adolescence (seven through seventeen), young adulthood (eighteen through thirty-nine), and middle age (forty and over) . . . Type 1 offenders were criminal in all three periods—adolescence, young adulthood and middle age; Type 2, in all but young adulthood; Type 3, in all but adolescence; and Type 4 in middle age only" (Ibid., p. 2).

In examining the data in Table 6.3, keep in mind that we are looking at middle-aged incarcerated offenders on a retrospective or after the fact basis. Nevertheless the career patterns by type of offender as well as type of crime were quite revealing. Of these middle-aged offenders, nearly half were of the Type 4 pattern. They were most likely to be serving time for the gravest offenses. Type 1 offenders, even though they had the longest criminal careers, were least likely to be serving time for violent crime. Type 4 offenders accounted for about 65 percent

Table 6.3: Number of Offenses for which Currently Imprisoned, and Percent Distribution of Offenses by Type of Criminal Career

Offense	Number of Offenses[1]	Career Type Percent Distribution				Total
		1	2	3	4	
Violent	15,494	11.6	1.0*	35.7	51.7	100%
Murder	3,920	6.2	1.6*	27.6	64.7	100
Attempted Murder	537	16.4	0.0*	45.4	38.2	100
Manslaughter	2,382	10.5	1.1*	33.7	54.7	100
Kidnapping	315	17.5	0.0*	27.1	55.4	100
Rape, Sexual Assault	1,892	11.8	0.0*	30.3	57.9	100
Lewd Act with Child	554	0.0	0.0*	25.5	74.5	100
Robbery	2,763	23.2	0.0*	46.6	30.3	100
Assault	2,959	9.0	2.2*	41.6	47.2	100
Extortion	57*	0.0	0.0*	47.4	52.6	100
Other Violent	114*	24.3	0.0*	51.3	24.3	100
Property	7,410	23.9	2.4*	44.2	29.5	100
Burglary	2,542	32.9	1.2*	37.6	28.3	100
Forgery, Fraud	1,721	13.3	1.7*	57.1	27.9	100
Larceny-Theft	1,792	26.8	4.9*	40.1	28.2	100
Arson	279*	10.0	10.0*	30.1	50.1	100
Other Property	1,076	18.4	0.0*	50.1	31.9	100
Drug	2,713	16.7	1.0*	54.8	27.6	100
Trafficking	1,369	16.4	0.0*	48.0	35.6	100
Possession	1,139	20.0	2.5*	60.2	17.4	100
Other Drug	205	0.0	0.0*	69.8	30.7	100
Public Order/Other	3,776	10.6	0.7*	32.4	56.4	100
Weapons	934	13.0	2.9*	27.7	56.4	100
Traffic	1,233	4.5	0.0*	28.0	67.4	100
Other	1,609	13.8	0.0*	38.5	47.9	100

NOTE: Detail may not add to total because of rounding. Estimated values of less than about 300 are based on too few cases to be statistically reliable.

[1]The number of offenses is greater than the number of inmates because some inmates were imprisoned for more than one offense.

*Estimate based on 10 or fewer cases is statistically unreliable.

SOURCE: Patrick A. Langan and Lawrence A. Greenfeld, 1983, "Career Patterns in Crime," *Bureau of Justice Statistics, Special Report*, Washington, D.C.: Bureau of Justice Statistics, June, p. 3.

of murders, 55 percent of manslaughters, and 58 percent of rapes and sexual assaults, and were highly representative of offenders imprisoned for public-order crimes. The biggest surprise of the study was that "inmates with the shortest records—the Type 4s, imprisoned only in middle age—constitute the single most prevalent type of middle-aged inmate" (Ibid., p. 7).

Societal Reaction

As our discussion has suggested, most violent crime is intimate; a large proportion of violent offenders are not career criminals and reflect situational or subcultural reactions to interpersonal disputes. The analysis of Type 4, middle-aged offenders, was instructive in this matter. Studies indicated that a high proportion of crimes are committed by a small portion of the criminal population, the chronic or career offenders, so social policies to identify and specially process these career criminals holds much promise. The creation of special career criminal bureaus by police departments and district attorney offices, using computerized information on up-to-date offense records that are shared with the courts, can assist in preventing such career felons from slipping through the cracks in the system. In a sense, they can be "red flagged" as if to say, "Do not overlook this one; give it priority prosecution."

In our discussion of Type 4 offenders, we described "late blooming violent criminals." As previously cited, a Police Foundation (1977) survey in Kansas City found that in the two years preceding an assault or homicide, police had answered previous calls for domestic disturbances in 85 percent of the cases and at least five times in half of the cases. Thus, early use of crisis intervention teams could help reduce the high rates of domestic violence. Langan and Greenfeld's (1983) study of middle-aged prisoners also found that two-thirds had participated in alcohol treatment programs at one time. Therefore, social programs related to substance abuse as well as family crisis intervention address two key components of the violence equation.

In 1985 the FBI began its VICAP program, the Violent Criminal Apprehension Program. VICAP is a nationwide data information center designed to collect and analyze data submitted by police departments regarding special crimes of violence. Local police departments fill out a separate data form in circumstances involving unsolved or solved homicides involving abduction, series victimizations, or random, motiveless, or sexually oriented themes. It is also used for special missing person reports where foul play is suspected or for unidentified dead bodies. VICAP can analyze such cases for possible linkages, for example, in the case of serial murderers (Howlett, Hanfland, and Ressler, 1986).

A key explanatory variable in explaining the very high interpersonal violence rates in the United States compared to other developed countries is the widespread, easy availability and ownership of handguns. Although the majority of the population favors stricter legislation and control, the public has remained relatively passive in this regard. Until strong, active public pressure is felt, Americans will continue to murder one another at a rate that bewilders most of the civilized world.

One problem with U.S. crime control is that much of the attempted social control for most crimes rests in the hands of state and local governments. Since crime is a national problem, what, if anything, can the federal government do to improve crime control? Among some of the recommendations of the Attorney General's Task Force on Violent Crime (1981) were the need for the National Institute of Justice and other branches of the Department of Justice to conduct more research on career criminals and violent juvenile offenders. The task force called for priority to be given to testing programs to reduce violent crime and disseminating such information, the articulation of a clear, coherent, and consistent drug enforcement policy, stricter gun control measures particularly over automatic weapons, and increased federal involvement in dealing with youth gangs.

Justifications for Punishment

Society responds to each of the types of criminal behavior by desiring punishment (Newman, 1978); the particular reaction varies with the specific form of criminal activity. One highly controversial response to murder has been the death penalty, the appropriateness of which, although ultimately a moral question, varies with the specific justification for punishment which advocates or critics assume. For example, while the argument for use of the death penalty for deterrence of others is weak, its use as the ultimate retribution may be strong.

The punishment of criminals has at least four justifications; retribution, deterrence (including incapacitation), rehabilitation, and protection and upholding the solidarity of society (Sutherland and Cressey, 1974, pp. 325–330). *Retribution* is the societal counterpart of individual revenge. When criminal laws were formulated, the state assumed responsibility for punishing offenders and forbade victimized parties from taking the law into their own hands. Criminals must pay their debt to society, not to the harmed party. Having its origins as early as *lex talionis* (the law of the talons) in Hammurabi's code, "an eye for an eye and a tooth for a tooth," criminals are viewed as having to suffer in some way for justice to be served. Retribution is a moral motive for punishment, not simply a utilitarian one. Nettler (1982, vol. 4, p. 14) states: ". . . response to crime is not produced by an economic calculation of how much crime is deterred by how much punishment of which sort. Response to crime is strongly motivated by a people's sense of justice which like all else, is subject to change." Nazi hunters, who are still searching for war criminals decades after World War II, when asked, "What good does it do?" reply that "It does justice." So public sentiment and outrage are the guideposts for enforcement, rather than having a direct effect upon future crime commission.

Deterrence refers to the belief that perceived punishment will serve as a warning and inhibit the convicted criminal (*specific deterrence*) as well as others (*general deterrence*) from involvement in criminal activity. Based upon the classical school of criminology and the writings of Cesare Beccaria (to be discussed in Chapter 11), the deterrence model assumes that if the pain (clear, swift, and certain punishment) outweighs any pleasure to be derived from the criminal act, then crime will be prevented. This assumes, of course, that individuals are aware of criminal penalties and are capable of mens rea, which does not always appear to be the case (Zimring and Hawkins, 1973, p. 5). *Incapacitation*, the prevention of crime by keeping criminals behind bars for longer periods, is an additional example of special deterrence. In a revival of classical criminology, large and impressive literature has begun to accumulate on the issue of specific deterrence which, although inconclusive at this point, suggests the potentially positive impacts of selective incapacitation of career criminals upon lowering crime rates (Bowker, 1981; Clarke, 1974; and Greenberg, 1975).

Rehabilitation, which has been the watchword in the U.S. in the post-World War II period, assumes that the purpose of punishing criminals is to reform or resocialize them to conventional, law-abiding values. Even name changes indicated this philosophical shift: The field of penology is now called corrections and prisons became correctional facilities. But a "rose by any other name is still a rose" and there appeared to be more talk in prisons about rehabilitation than programs. The addition of threat of punishment was assumed to assist reformation. Martinson (1974), in "What Works?—Questions and Answers about Prison Reform," examined a large number of correctional programs and their claims of rehabilitation success, as well as their recidivism (repeating of crime) rates; he felt that there was little evidence of any significant programs in corrections that had an important impact upon reducing recidivism. Only later (Martinson Attacks His Own Earlier Work, 1978; and Martinson, 1979) did he retract this devastating critique by admitting that he may have suffered from "methodological fanaticism" in which substance was overlooked in the name of method and that some of the programs did have positive outcomes. With estimates of recidivism and reincarceration rates as high as 65 percent (Greenberg, 1975, p. 551), there seemed to be a decline in the liberal optimism of the possibility of the success of the rehabilitation model (Bayer, 1981). However, in defense of rehabilitation, some feel that it never has been given a decent chance. Badillo and Haynes (1972) indicate that in the early seventies only about 5 percent of correctional budgets was used for rehabilitation programs and it has often been more a matter of talk than action.

Protection and the upholding of social solidarity as a goal of punishment reflects Durkheim's (1950) point made in Chapter 1, that a society reaffirms its values in reacting to and punishing wrongdoers. In this justification the purpose of punishment is not to obtain revenge or deter or change the criminal, but a bottom-line intent to protect the society from such criminals and in so doing to reinforce group solidarity.

The Death Penalty Debate

The subject of capital punishment has fueled heated debate both by criminologists and by the public at large.

Arguments in favor of the death penalty include:

- It is sanctioned in the Bible as well as by historical tradition as a culturally-approved manner of dealing with heinous offenders.
- It is an effective deterrent in preventing cold-blooded murder.
- It is more economical than the permanent, lifelong warehousing of the most dangerous criminals.
- It is the ultimate specific deterrence.
- In terms of retribution, those who kill innocent persons in cold blood deserve similar punishment.
- Enactment of the death penalty where appropriate discourages private revenge and vigilantism.

Arguments against capital punishment include:

- The death penalty is irreversible; thus, the rare execution of an innocent party cannot be undone.
- No matter what the reason for execution, the state becomes a murderer, a cold-blooded killer.
- Use of the death penalty is a savage practice and has no place in civilized society. The society becomes as inhumane as the condemned.

- The general deterrence ability of the death penalty has not been proven.
- The adjudication of cases involving the death penalty is far more costly and raises difficulties in finding juries which are willing to find defendants guilty.
- The enactment of capital punishment has always been discriminatory. In the U.S., the majority of those executed have been black (Bowers, 1974) and in 1982 blacks still represented over half of the death row population.
- All countries whose values resemble those of the U.S. have eliminated the death penalty.

The research on capital punishment has indicated that the enactment of the death penalty is no more of a deterrent than life imprisonment (Schuessler, 1952; Sellin, 1959; Reckless, 1967; and Bowers and Pierce, 1975). Ultimately, the capital punishment debate is a moral one that is likely to continue to be heated (Van den Haag and Conrad, 1983).

In the next chapters, we will explore other types of criminal activity. But violent crime, particularly by strangers, has had a profound impact upon American urban life. In many respects urban wastelands—including some downtown areas in the evening—are grim reminders of an erosion of the urban vitality that is the hallmark of civilized societies. Until society can control violent crime, our culture will fail to realize its full potential.

Summary

Violence has enjoyed an ignominious career in the history of civilization, particularly in the twentieth century. Some writers claim that violence is instinctual in humans, but most social scientists view it as a *culturally learned* phenomenon. The Violence Commission identified *six factors which may explain the high level of violence in the U.S.:* the Declaration of Independence, the frontier experience, immigrant competition, fear of government power, movement from rural to urban/industrial centers, and relative deprivation amidst affluence. Violence has been intimately tied to major historical changes throughout American history, although other young countries had similar experiences.

Social and technological changes have impact upon various *fads and fashions* in crime, many of which, such as train robbery, cattle rustling, and grave robbing, have now largely disappeared. Brief accounts of murder and mayhem of the past—such as in the Five Points Brewery, Mudgett's "murder castle," and the famous Leopold-Loeb case—indicate that horrible violent criminals of the present such as Whitman, Williams, or Manson are not mere modern aberrations. Multiple murders consist of *serial murder, mass murder,* and *spree murder.*

Victim-precipitation is quite common in many violent crimes. Mendelson's types of victims include the completely innocent victim, one with minor guilt, one that is as guilty as the offender, the more and most guilty victim, and the imaginary victim. *Conrad's typology of violent offenders* includes: culturally violent offenders, criminally violent offenders, pathologically violent offenders, and situationally violent offenders. Haskell and Yablonsky's types include violence by the state as well as by syndicates, both of which will be discussed in later chapters. Vantage Point 6.1 provides general legal definitions of violent crimes.

The discussion of *psychiatry and the law* details the *M'Naghten rule* (NGRI—not guilty by reason of insanity or "right-wrong test"), the *Durham decision* (innocent because of mental defect), as well as the "irresistible impulse test" (mental disease at time of act), and the "substantial capacity test" (lack of capacity to appreciate criminality of the act). Many states, in reaction to cases such as the Hinckley case, are passing *guilty, but mentally ill* laws and abolishing NGRI. The "Twinkie defense" (poor nutrition obviates guilt) was briefly discussed as yet another bizarre defense. The concept of *psychopath-sociopath-antisocial-personality* is used as a catch-all constructed to describe individuals who exhibit a variety of characteristics including lacks of: empathy, guilt, fear, conscience, and super-ego. Actual diagnosis of psychopathy has been unreliable and of questionable validity.

The *close relationship between homicide and assault* was described, in which the same components are present; in the case of the former, the victim dies. Homicides enjoy the highest clearance rate by police due to their serious nature, the presence of witnesses, and the high priority they are given. Rape statistics have been notoriously underreported, but have improved as a result of better support for victims.

The *overall trend in homicide* in the U.S. has been a decline from a peak in 1933 and a rise in the sixties, to new highs in the seventies. The dip in the forties and fifties may actually have been due to better medical treatment procedures, which masked a rise in potentially lethal violent assaults. Fragmentary historical evidence suggests even higher rates prior to 1933. The U.S. possesses by far the highest homicide rate of economically-developed countries, although this rate is lower than those of many lesser developed countries. Domestic homicide in the U.S. in this century exceeds the combined fatalities of every war the country has ever fought.

Patterns of violent crime indicate perpetration and victimization associated with: large cities, males, youths, lower class, and ghetto blacks. Unlike robbery, most violent crime occurs between intimates. A large proportion of violent crimes are committed by repeaters. Some relationship between social inequality and homicide rates is suggested. Surprisingly one's own home is the most likely setting for one's demise and intimates/acquaintances are the most likely perpetrators. *Alcohol consumption* has a high association with violent crimes such as homicide, assault, and rape and particularly with vehicular homicide. *Factors associated with the typical homicide* include a backdrop of cultural/ subcultural traditions of violence, personal dispute, alcohol, and guns, the last being the most telling. The U.S. has the *largest civilian armed population* in the world and a relationship between firearm possession and homicide rate is highly suggested.

Clarke addresses the myth of the *assassin* as mentally pathological and suggests five types which could be named: political, egocentric, psychopathic, insane, and "atypical." Estrich distinguished between "real rape" (aggravated, involving violence) and "simple rape" (all other types) in which the latter is still not recognized in the courts.

The *reluctance to report rape* has been due to: stigma, sexist treatment by the criminal justice system, prosecutorial privacy invasion, and the burden of proof resting upon the victim. *Increased reporting* has been spurred by: victim centers, female officers, better trained police, and changes in the law. While UCR data show a precipitous rise in rape in the seventies, victim data find no such increase. Rapists are generally young, lower class, unmarried, and disproportionately black. Other analysis suggests that victims *underreport rapes* by offenders that they know, in which case rape may more closely resemble most other violent crimes. Factors involved in most rapes are: violent values, machismo, sexist views of women as legitimate victims, conducive dating-game circumstances, and alcohol. *Rape trauma* continues to plague victims long after the incident. While *Amir* views rape as a sexual and sometimes *victim-precipitated act*, *Brownmiller* views it as entirely a method of male intimidation and *violence against women*. While both authors express an extreme, there is little argument that *rape is a violent crime*, regardless of offender motivation. Many typologies of rapists suffer from after-the-fact analysis and post hoc error. More research is needed.

Robbery rates show great recent increases using the UCR, but stability using victim surveys. Robbery is more likely to be interracial and involve strangers than other violent crimes, although official statistics overlook large numbers of juvenile offenders and victims.

The majority of robberies do not involve direct physical harm, although "strong-armed" robbery (mugging) and victim resistance (other than screaming) increases its likelihood. *Conklin's typology of robbers* includes: professional, opportunist (the most common), addict, and alcoholic robbers. Other research and types by McClintock and Gibson are presented.

Recent research has demonstrated that domestic disturbances in homes is not as dangerous to police as previously supposed and that arrest of domestic assaulters can deter repeat offenses.

Drunk drivers kill more Americans yearly than are killed in homicides; only recently have stricter laws attempted to address this problem. Such laws may not be enforced as vigorously as had been intended. *The largest dark figure of violent crime has been spouse and child abuse;* there has been a virtual statistical epidemic in such estimates since the sixties. Although post hoc error also operates in this area, it appears that those abused as children are likely to become future abusers.

Most violent offenders do not make a career of such violations and have little commitment to crime. *Cultures/subcultures of violence* may serve to reinforce predispositions to use of violence in resolving grievances. Wolfgang and Ferracuti's *subculture of violence* thesis is used to explain the disproportion of such crimes among certain lower class minorities and high rates in the South. Violent predators who are persistent offenders are labeled career criminals; they are responsible for a disproportion of crimes of violence. Programs to identify, isolate, and expedite incarceration of such offenders are viewed as a promising strategy for decreasing the violent crime rate. Recent research suggests a variety of types and patterns of *career criminality.* Better programs in family crisis, alcohol treatment, and career offender areas are viewed as trends in societal reaction.

The *four justifications for punishment* are: retribution, deterrence (including incapacitation), rehabilitation, and protection and maintenance of social solidarity. Arguments in favor of and against implementation of the *death penalty* are briefly presented.

KEY CONCEPTS

Victim-Precipitation
Types of Violent Offenders
Assault
Battery
Forcible Rape
Statutory Rape
Murder, 1st Degree
Murder, 2nd Degree
Felony Murder Doctrine
Manslaughter
M'Naghten Rule
Durham Decision
Twinkie Defense

NGRI
Psychopath-Sociopath-Antisocial
   Personality
Patterns/Trends in Violent Crime
Real Rape
Serial Murder
Mass Murder
Gun Control
Types of Assassins
Factors in Rape
Rape as Violent Act
Rape-Trauma Syndrome
Types of Robbers

DUI
Child Abuse
Spouse Abuse
Post Hoc Error
Culture of Violence
Subculture of Violence
Types of Career Criminals
Justifications for Punishment
Death Penalty, Pro and Con
Minneapolis Domestic
   Violence Experiment

7

Property Crime: Occasional and Conventional

Introduction

Offenses against property were among the first to be punished under formal legal systems. The basic offense, theft, was referred to under English common law as *larceny*, defined simply as the taking of the property of another without the owner's consent. Although the specific legal definition varies by country and state, the various forms of larceny include: embezzlement, the receipt of stolen goods, shoplifting, employee theft, burglary (breaking and entering with intent to steal), robbery (stealing by means of force or threat of force), forgery (the fraudulent use of commercial instruments), auto theft, vandalism, and arson (the willful burning of a dwelling or property). More specific legal definitions of property crimes are presented in Vantage Point 7.1.

Larceny can be committed by a variety of criminal types, ranging from the most amateur to the most highly organized or professional criminal. Figure 7.1 depicts the range of criminals involved in property offenses (though actual placement on the continuum is obviously more problematic than suggested by a simple schema).

At the far end of the continuum is the career criminal. The notion of *career criminality* is explained by Clinard and Quinney (1973, p. 57):

> The characteristics of a fully developed criminal career include identification with crime and a conception of the self as a criminal. There is group support for criminal activity in the form of extensive association with other criminals and with criminal norms and activities. Criminality progresses to the use of more complex techniques and frequent offenses, and ultimately crime may become a sole means of livelihood. Those who have careers in crime generally engage in some type of theft of property or money.

White collar property offenses will be covered in Chapters 9 and 10, and professional criminality and organized (syndicate) criminality will be detailed in Chapters 8 and 12. This chapter will concern itself with comparing and discussing *two different types of criminal behavior systems: occasional property criminality and conventional property offenders.*

Occasional offenders are the opposite of career criminals; conventional criminals are usually unsuccessful aspirants to careers in crime (Ibid., pp. 57, 132). *Occasional property criminals* steal or injure property on an infrequent basis. They

VANTAGE POINT

Burglary

"the unlawful entry of a structure to commit a felony or theft. The use of force to gain entry is not required to classify an offense as burglary. Burglary in this Program [UCR] is categorized into three subclassifications: forcible entry, unlawful entry where no force is used, and attempted forcible entry."

Larceny-theft

"the unlawful taking, carrying, leading, or riding away of property from the possession or constructive possession of another. It includes crimes such as shoplifting pocket-picking, purse-snatching, thefts from motor vehicles, theft of motor vehicle parts and accessories, bicycle thefts, etc., in which no use of force, violence, or fraud occurs. In the Uniform Crime Reporting Program, this crime category does not include embezzlement, 'con' games, forgery and worth-less checks. Motor vehicle theft is also excluded from this category inasmuch as it is a separate crime index offense."

Motor vehicle theft

"the theft or attempted theft of a motor vehicle. This definition excludes the taking of a motor vehicle for temporary use by those persons having lawful access."

Arson

"any willful or malicious burning or attempt to burn, with or without intent to defraud, a dwelling house, public building, motor vehicle theft or aircraft, personal property of another, etc. Only fires determined through investigation to have been willfully or maliciously set are classified as arsons. Fires of sus-picious or unknown origins are excluded."

Forgery and counterfeiting

"making, altering, uttering or possessing, with intent to defraud, anything false which is made to appear true. Attempts are included."

Fraud

"fraudulent conversion and obtaining money or property by false pretenses. In-cluded are larceny by bailee and bad checks, except forgeries and counterfeiting."

Vandalism

"willful or malicious destruction, injury, disfigurement, or defacement of any public or private property, real or personal, without consent of the owner or persons having custody or control."

SOURCE: Federal Bureau of Investigation, 1984, *Crime in the United States, 1983*, Washington, D.C.: Government Printing Office, pp. 342–343.

Figure 7.1: Range of Career Criminal Involvement in Property Crime

Noncareer (Amateur) Criminality			Career Criminality
Occasional Property Crime	White-Collar Crime (Occupational and Corporate)	Conventional Property Crime	Organized and Professional Crime

account for most, but not all, auto theft, shoplifting, check forgery, and vandalism (see Hepburn, 1984). These offenses are committed relatively irregularly and rather crudely, involving little skill or planning. In contrast, *conventional criminals* tend to commit crimes of theft-larceny and burglary on a more regular basis and, although they are at the bottom rung of the ladder or continuum of career criminality, they exhibit elements of career criminality.

In Figure 7.1, occasional property criminals represent the noncareer end of the continuum; organized and professional criminals most exhibit characteristics of career criminality: conventional offenders exhibit the rudiments of such characteristics; and white collar and occupational offenders, due to their commitment to the conventional world, fall closer to the noncareer criminality pole of the continuum.

UCR index offenses statistics show that property crimes outnumbered violent crimes 9 to 1. Vantage Point 7.2 details relative differences in victimization comparing property crimes with violent crimes.

Occasional Property Criminal Behavior

Most occasional property criminals lack a past official history of criminality. They exhibit little progressive knowledge of criminal techniques or of crime in general. In contrast to career criminals or even conventional criminals, crime is not their sole or major means of livelihood and they do not view themselves as criminal. Not identifying with criminal behavior, they have little of the vocabulary or "street sense" of the conventional criminal.

Under the category of occasional property offenses, discussion will center upon most shoplifting, vandalism, motor vehicle theft, and check forgery. (Professional crimes of these types will be discussed later.) Surprisingly, there have not been many studies that focus attention upon occasional and ordinary property offenders (Hepburn, 1984; and Shover, 1983).

Shoplifting

The polite term for shoplifting used by the retail trade industry is "inventory shrinkage," quite literally, goods which have disappeared or shrunk from the total of accountable inventory. The slang term "five-finger discount" is a less polite term for this same process. While shoplifting is perhaps as ancient as the existence of merchants, the post-World War II emergence of a consumer society and of large, retail chains has created both a greater desire as well as an opportunity for retail theft. Inventory shortage costs in the U.S. for the early eighties are estimated at $8 billion per year, accounting for about 2 percent of retail sales; the actual proportion may be considerably higher depending upon location, product, and clientele (Bremer, 1980; Rupe, 1980; and Cherrington and Cherrington, 1982).

The classic study on shoplifting is Mary Owen Cameron's (1964) *The Booster and the Snitch: Department Store Shoplifting*, which was based upon store records and arrest data in the late 1940s; more recent research by Cohen and Stark (1974) supports her findings. Cameron distinguished between "boosters" (or "heels")—professional shoplifters—and "snitches," amateur shoplifters. *Boosters* (to be discussed in detail in Chapter 8), are like other professional criminals in carefully planning and skillfully executing their thefts, and in concentrating upon expensive items which can be quickly converted to cash by prearrangement with a fence (dealer in stolen goods). On a continuum of shoplifters between the booster and the snitch are "shadow" professionals (Stirling, 1974, p. 120; and Hellman, 1970), individuals who in an avocational manner supplement their legitimate incomes by stealing for friends. The majority of shoplifters are "snitches," amateurs or individuals who do not view themselves as criminals. According to Cameron most are females and the vast majority have no official history of previous recorded criminal involvement. Most "snitches" steal small, inexpensive items for their own personal use. In most instances they have on their person sufficient funds to cover the stolen items. Such snitches come from all walks of life. Nettler (1982, vol. 3, p. 106) indicates, for instance, that: "theories of poverty and low education and shoplifting would surprise store owners in university towns who experience three times the amount of theft as stores in other neighborhoods."

Most snitches simply do not anticipate being caught. In the past when snitches were apprehended, most stores avoided lawsuits or possible adverse publicity by releasing the offenders after brief admonishment. Upon apprehension, most snitches attempt to rationalize or excuse their behavior. For the middle class offender with a psychological bent, "kleptomania," a compulsion to steal, becomes a handy rationalization.

VANTAGE POINT

In 1985 violence or theft touched about a fourth of all households

According to the NCS more than 22 million households were victimized by at least one crime of violence or theft.

- Almost 16 million households, or 18% of those in the Nation, were victimized by at least one theft during the year.
- Almost 5 million, or 5%, were burglarized at least once.
- About 1% were victimized by the theft or attempted theft of a motor vehicle.
- 5% of all households had members who were victims of at least one violent crime of rape, robbery, or aggravated or simple assault.

A violent crime by strangers and/or a burglary struck 8% of all households in 1985

Public opinion polls show that burglaries and violent crime by strangers are high on the list of the greatest public concerns and fears. According to NCS, 7 million U.S. households were touched by one or more of these crimes in 1985—the household was burglarized and/or one or more of its members were raped, robbed, or assaulted by a stranger. These high-concern crimes affected 1 in 13 households in the Nation.

35 million victimizations occurred in 1985 according to NCS data

Personal Crimes	
Crimes of Violence	
Rape	138,000
Robbery	985,000
Aggravated Assault	1,605,000
Simple Assault	3,094,000
Crimes of Theft	
Larceny with Contact	523,000
Larceny without Contact	12,951,000
Household Crimes	
Burglary	5,594,000
Larceny	8,703,000
Motor Vehicle Theft	1,270,000
Total	34,864,000

SOURCE: *Criminal victimization, 1985*, BJS Bulletin, October 1986.

Adventure, excitement, need, greed, or simply available opportunity or inadequate security may prove more likely as reasons. Cameron claims that most snitches, upon apprehension and faced with an unacceptable criminal self-image, cease future shoplifting activities.

Most retail thefts involve employees pilfering goods. Inventory shrinkage is thought by retail experts to be 60 percent due to employee theft, 30 percent to outside shoplifters, and 10 percent to paper errors (Rupe, 1980). Far more research on shoplifting is required in order to gain a more definitive picture of its varieties.

Property crimes outnumbered violent crimes by 9 to 1

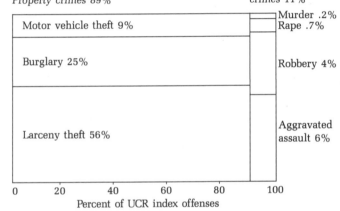

Property crimes 89%

Violent crimes 11%

Motor vehicle theft 9%

Burglary 25%

Larceny theft 56%

Murder .2%
Rape .7%

Robbery 4%

Aggravated assault 6%

Percent of UCR index offenses

NOTE: Percents do not add to 100% becausing of rounding.
SOURCE: FBI *Crime in the United States 1985.*

12 million UCR Index Crimes were reported to police in 1985

Violent Crimes	1,327,440
Murder	18,980
Forcible Rape	87,340
Robbery	497,870
Aggravated Assault	723,250
Property Crimes	11,102,600
Burglary	3,073,300
Larceny/Theft	6,926,400
Motor Vehicle Theft	1,102,900
Total	12,430,000

NOTE: Offenses may not add to totals because of rounding.

SOURCE: FBI *Crime in the United States 1985.*

Businesses reported almost 1 million burglaries and over 100,000 robberies in 1985

The UCR shows that more than half the 956,096 nonresidential burglaries reported to the police in 1984 occurred at night. Eighteen percent were known to have taken place during the day. (In 31% the time of day was not known.)

In 1985 more than 100,000 completed or attempted robberies were reported to the police by stores, gas stations, banks and other commercial establishments. Convenience stores were subjected to 26,000 robberies—about 1.7 times the number of gas station robberies and 4 times the number of bank robberies.

SOURCE: Bureau of Justice Statistics, 1988b, *Report to the Nation on Crime and Justice,* 2nd edition, Washington, D.C.: Government Printing Office, March, p. 12.

Vandalism

Vandalism involves the willful destruction of property without the consent of the owner or agent of the owner. The term is derived from the Vandals, a barbaric Teutonic tribe that sacked Rome in the fifth century, senselessly destroying many priceless works of art. Clinard and Quinney (1973, p. 59) explain:

> Vandalism or the willful destruction of property is widespread in American society. It constitutes one of the largest categories of juvenile delinquency but occurs at all ages. It is associated with affluence for it virtually never occurs in less developed countries (except as a part of rioting) where the destruction of goods in limited supply is inconceivable. Vandalism in the United States is widespread against schools, parks, libraries, public transportation facilities, telephone and electric company facilities, traffic department equipment and housing. In one year, the public school system of Washington, D.C., reported a loss of 28,500 window panes, replaced at a cost of $118,000.

Graffiti adorning a subway car. Graffiti is perhaps the most common type of vandalism.

Wade (1967) identifies *three basic types of vandalism: wanton, predatory, and vindictive. Wanton vandalism* refers to destructive acts which have no monetary gain or purpose in mind. These are the most common acts of vandalism, "senseless" destruction practiced by juveniles "just for the hell of it" or for fun. *Predatory vandalism* involves destructive acts of gain, such as "trashing" or destroying vending machines in order to gain their contents. *Vindictive vandalism* is undertaken as an expression of hatred, such as of a particular racial or ethnic group; swastikas painted on synagogues, Ku Klux Klan attacks on black churches, or antibusing groups' assaults upon school buses serve as illustrations.

Most acts of wanton vandalism are committed by juveniles, who regard their activities as an extension of play activity, "goofing off," "raising hell." In some American communities the evening before Halloween and "trick or treat" is called "devil's night" in which juveniles play tricks which may not be simply restricted to throwing eggs at houses or soaping windows. Wade (1967) describes the typical pattern of wanton vandalism as consisting of:

- hanging around waiting for something to happen
- an initial exploratory gesture of vandalism by one member
- mutual conversion of others to participate
- an escalation of destructive behavior from minor to major property damage
- after the fact, feelings of guilt, remorse combined with naughty pleasure

Such vandalism is rationalized by the offenders as not really being criminal since they did not plan, intend, nor realize any monetary gain. Often urban public facilities, for example, some large city subway systems, are "graced" with the unrequested graffiti of freelance "artists" or anyone who can afford a can of spray paint. In some cities "tagging" is practiced in which gangs tag or mark their territory with their colors, nicknames, club names, and symbols. This type of vandalism in most instances could be viewed as an extension of wanton vandalism. Such senseless vandalism is not restricted to juveniles. The price of winning a Superbowl, World Series, or NCAA championship sometimes includes drunken fans of the winner "trashing" downtowns as part of the celebration. Recent football (soccer) "hooliganism" in England has cost not only property, but human lives. In 1989 a mob of frenzied fans overturned a cab, smashed windows, and uprooted street signs in Ann Arbor, Michigan, celebrating the University of Michigan Wolverines' NCAA basketball championship.

A variation of predatory vandalism and theft involves "bibliotheft" and destruction, in which students intentionally steal and destroy library reference materials. Rather than take notes or make copies of materials, students tear out the needed information thus raising the cost of library materials and denying others of the opportunity to use such references.

Motor Vehicle Theft

Nearly 1.3 million motor vehicles were stolen in the U.S. in 1987. The thieves' top picks that year were Pontiac Firebirds and Chevrolet Camaros. While two-thirds of all stolen vehicles are recovered, most are returned in damaged condition. The highest rates for vehicle theft continues to be in the Northeast with the District of Columbia, Massachusetts, New York, and New Jersey the leading states ("Havens," 1989). While Western states with 632 thefts per 100,000 population were highest, the rate per vehicles was highest in the Northeast with 1 of every 107 registered vehicles. An estimated 1 of every 144 motor vehicles were stolen nationwide in 1987 (FBI, 1988, p. 34). Vantage Point 7.3 shows some international audio theft rates, with England and Wales exhibiting the highest rates.

McCaghy, Giordano, and Henson (1977) have proposed a *typology of auto thefts* which includes:

- Joyriding—the temporary "borrowing" of an automobile, usually by juveniles, not for theft purposes, but for temporary adventure and enjoyment.
- Short-term transportation—the vehicle is stolen as a temporary means of transportation and then abandoned.
- Long-term transportation—the car is stolen for the purpose of providing a relatively permanent means of transportation for the thief.
- Profit-motivated—this type is represented by highly organized auto theft rings which permanently alter the vehicle's identity, by "chop shops" which cannibalize the auto for parts, and by "auto strippers" who abandon the hulk after removing parts of value.

While allegations have been made that theft of motor vehicles by professional thieves is on the rise, analysis of NCS data from 1973-1985 found a fairly stable percentage of vehicles recovered, thus suggesting no change (Harlow, 1988, p. 3). During this period, motor vehicle theft rates declined by 33 percent. Due to state laws requiring auto insurance, as well as insurance regulations requiring police reports for reimbursement, auto theft represents the most highly reported of larcenies (about 90 percent reported to police).

Vantage Point 7.3—International Auto Theft Rates

Auto Theft

Since the U.N. groups all of its crimes of theft into one category, it has no statistics for auto theft. Interpol defines auto theft as "theft of motor cars." The U.S. definition includes theft of any motor vehicle that is self-propelled and runs on a surface instead of rails. This includes motorcycles, motor scooters, and the like; however, the overwhelming number of U.S. motor vehicle thefts are thefts of autos or trucks. Probably the most important factor in the rate of motor vehicle theft is the number of motor vehicles per capita in the country. Developed nations in which automobile ownership is widespread generally had the highest rates of auto theft.

Auto Theft in Selected Countries, Rates for 1984: Interpol Data

Country	Number of auto thefts per 100,000 population	Country	Number of auto thefts per 100,000 population
United States	437.1	Ireland	29.7
		Italy	276.3
Australia	584.7	Japan	29.4
Austria	16.9	Luxembourg	109.3
Belgium	140.6	Monaco	176.3
Canada	304.9		
Chile	7.6	Netherlands	155.9
		New Zealand	—
Colombia	14.2	Nigeria	—
Denmark	469.5	Northern Ireland	106.2[a]
Ecuador	7.8	Norway	273.1[a]
Egypt	3.3		
England and Wales	656.6[a]	Philippines	2.0
		Portugal	61.3
Finland	171.7	Scotland	632.7
France	483.4	Spain	278.2
Germany (FRG)	118.0	Sweden	460.0
Greece	—		
Hungary	4.0	Switzerland	—[b]
		Thailand	2.0
Indonesia	4.9	Venezuela	85.9

—Not available.

[a]1981 data.

[b]Auto theft in Switzerland omitted because it includes bicycles.

SOURCE: Interpol, *International Crime Statistics*, vols. 1983–84, cited in Carol B. Kalish, 1988, *International Crime Rates*, Bureau of Justice Statistics Special Report, May, p. 3.

Joyriding is occasional property crime. It is committed almost exclusively by juveniles and on an unplanned, unskilled, and sporadic basis. A car is stolen, either by "hot wiring" (jumping the ignition) or because the keys were left in the ignition. The car is then temporarily used for cruising and abandoned when it runs out of gasoline. The intent is not to strip the vehicle of parts or permanently possess it. Most offenders view their activity as a prankish adventure and rationalize that, since they had not intended to actually steal the car and that they were simply borrowing it, their behavior was not really criminal.

In contrast to the occasional property criminal, profit-motivated offenders are for the most part either conventional criminals or professionals. Such profit-oriented auto thieves may range from sporadic amateur thieves (the hubcap crooks) to full-time professionals in auto theft rings. The amateur thieves are responsible for scenes like the abandoned automobiles in high crime areas of New York City; after 48 hours, only the carcasses remain, as individuals help themselves to needed parts. Most items are stolen by such thieves either for their own personal use or sold to used parts dealers.

Check Forgers

As defined in the UCR, *forgery* involves "Making, altering, uttering or possessing, with intent to defraud anything false which is made to appear true." *Fraud* involves the conversion or obtaining of money or property under false pretenses. Both fraud and forgery may vary from the simple, to be discussed in this section, to the most elaborate professional "con" games, to be examined in Chapter 8.

The classic study on check forgery was that of Edwin Lemert (1953), "An Isolation and Closure Theory of Naïve Check Forgery," in which he makes the distinction between "naïve check forgers" and "systematic check forgers." The majority of check forgers, those passing bad checks, are *naïve check forgers*. Faced with a financial crisis, such as an alcoholic binge, gambling debts, or creditors demanding immediate payment, they resolve this crisis by writing checks for which there are no covering funds. Closure is what Lemert calls this use of bad checks in order to solve personal problems, since it is a reduction of other possibilities for solving the financial crisis. In his study of naïve check forgers, Lemert found that such offenders did not identify themselves as criminals nor associate with criminals. While most amateur forgers were from middle-class backgrounds, many were also unemployed, divorced, or alcohol abusers, conditions which tended to isolate them and bring about closure.

In contrast to the amateur, the *systematic check forger* or "paper hanger" is a professional, making a good portion of his or her living passing bad checks. Most check artists work alone and associate very little with other criminals.

While there are different types of vandals, auto thieves, check forgers, and shoplifters, the majority of these offenders are described as occasional property offenders because, in contrast to conventional property offenders (to be discussed next), most commit their crimes sporadically, infrequently, and crudely. They also lack identity with criminal life-styles.

Conventional Property Criminals

Conventional property criminals are those who commit crimes of theft-larceny and burglary on a fairly persistent basis and whose activities constitute rudimentary forms of career criminality. Most such offenders identify with criminal behavior and associate with other criminals. Often described as "semiprofessionals" or "minor leaguers" in the world of crime, they represent about half of the prison inmates in the United States (Bureau of Justice Statistics, 1983 p. 31). They begin their careers in crime as juvenile delinquents and, even though most juvenile delinquents do not graduate to adult criminality, conventional property criminals do. Most conventional offenders exhibit a diversified offense record including theft, larceny, robbery, burglary, and the like. Lacking the skill and organization of more successful career criminals, they are more likely to be eventually arrested and imprisoned. The majority will retire from conventional crime in their mid-twenties.

Burglary

Burglary, the unlawful entry of a structure in order to commit a felony or theft, may include actual forcible entry, unlawful entry where no force is used, or attempted forcible entry. In 1987 there were an estimated 3.2 million burglaries in the U.S., accounting for 24 percent of the crime index total, and 27 percent of all property crime (FBI, 1988, p. 25). As a general rule, burglars are nonviolent and choose this particular brand of thievery as a relatively safe, nonconformative means of obtaining booty. Vantage Point 7.4 presents international

Burglary

For most crimes U.S. rates are much higher than European rates. Burglary is the only crime examined in the Bureau of Justice Statistics' comparison for which U.S. rates were less than double those of European countries. For burglary the combined group of Canada, Australia, and New Zealand had a higher rate than the U.S. Since the United Nations groups all of its theft into one category, it has no statistics for burglary. The Interpol definition of burglary is "breaking and entering." The U.S. definition is "the unlawful entry of a structure to commit a felony or theft. The use of force to gain entry is not required to classify an offense as a burglary."

Burglary in Selected Countries, Rates for 1984: Interpol Data

Country	Number of burglaries per 100,000 population	Country	Number of burglaries per 100,000 population
United States	1,263.7	Ireland	1,056.8
		Italy	—
Australia	1,754.3	Japan	231.2
Austria	805.8	Luxembourg	509.8
Belgium	—	Monaco	500.0
Canada	1,420.6		
Chile	—	Netherlands	2,328.7
		New Zealand	2,243.1
Colombia	—	Nigeria	—
Denmark	2,230.2	Northern Ireland	1,360.7[a]
Ecuador	—	Norway	—
Egypt	—		
England and Wales	1,639.7[a]	Philippines	—
		Portugal	99.7
Finland	772.6	Scotland	2,178.6
France	809.8	Spain	1,069.6
Germany (FRG)	1,554.1	Sweden	1,708.8
Greece	72.8		
Hungary	211.0	Switzerland	276.8
		Thailand	8.7
Indonesia	38.4	Venezuela	—

—Not available.

[a] 1981 data.

SOURCE: Interpol, *International Crime Statistics*, vols. 1983–84, cited in Carol B. Kalish, 1988, *International Crime Rates*, Bureau of Justice Statistics Special Report, May, p. 3.

burglary comparisons with the Netherlands and Denmark having the highest rates.

Burglars of the Pharaohs

Burglars were ingeniously plying their trade in ancient society; even the pharaohs' treasures were stolen, despite elaborate security precautions (Rosberg, 1980, p. 28). "Tomb robbers," who might better be described as burglars, were systematically plundering the great tombs in the Valley of the Kings before 1100 B.C., as related by a papyrus collection from the period of Ramses IX (1140–1121 B.C.). This document describes a "tomb-robbery" trial which took place three thousand years ago. The burglars gave the following depositions (Ceram, 1967, p. 159):

Burglaries account for 27 percent of all property crime and 24 percent of the crime index total.

We opened their coffins and their coverings in which they were. We found the august mummy of this King. . . . There was a numerous string of amulets and ornaments of gold at its throat; its head had a mask of gold upon it; the august mummy of this King was overlaid with gold throughout. . . . We stripped off the gold, which we found on the august mummy of this god, and its amulets and ornaments which were at its throat, and the covering wherein it rested. We found the King's wife likewise; we stripped off all that we found on her likewise. We set fire to their coverings. We stole their furniture, which we found with them, being vases of gold, silver and bronze. We divided and made the gold that we found on these two gods, on their mummies, and the amulets, ornaments, and coverings, into eight parts.

Although the defendants were found guilty and harshly dealt with, this did little to halt the systematic looting of treasure by "tomb robbers, traitorous priests, bribed officials, corrupt magistrates and highly organized gangs of thieves recruited from all levels of the social scale" (Ibid., p. 160).

Types of Burglars

Marilyn Walsh (1977), in *The Fence*, provides an interesting *typology of burglars* which resembles a continuum ranging from most organized to least organized. The types of burglars are: professionals, known burglars, young burglars, juvenile burglars, and junkies. The *professional*, "skilled," or "master" burglar exhibits the characteristics of professional criminal behavior. Such offenders are highly skilled, undertake extensive planning, and concentrate on "big jobs," since burglary is often their sole livelihood. *Known burglars* are far less sophisticated, professional, or successful at their operations, even though burglary may represent a major source of their livelihood. Their operations are generally much more crude and are less reliant upon organizations with other specialists. Being older and more experienced than other amateur burglars, the known burglars are so-called since they are known to the police; this suggests the fact that they are less successful than professionals. They are an excellent illustration that "practice does not always make perfect" (see Shover, 1973; and Rengert and Wasilchick, 1985).

Young burglars are usually in their late teens or early twenties, have less planning or organization in their operations than professionals, and are well on their way to becoming professional or known burglars. *Juvenile burglars* are under sixteen years of age and prey upon local neighborhood targets which are chosen by chance or occasion; such juveniles often operate under the supervision of older fences and burglars. Finally, *junkies* are simply opportunist burglars and are also the least skilled of such thieves.

Other analyses of burglars have basically supported Walsh's distinctions; Scarr (1973), for example, classified burglars into professionals and drug abusing "casual burglars." Excluding from discussion professional burglary, which will be examined in Chapter 8, other analyses of conventional burglars have been provided by Repetto (1974), and Pope (1980). Although not constituting a distinct typology as such, Repetto's case study of ninety-seven burglars provides some interesting profiles. Juvenile offenders were generally unskilled, concentrated on local easy targets of small gain, and viewed crime as more of a game than a commitment to a way of life. The eighteen to twenty-five-year-old offenders, despite previous convictions, continued to burglarize because they found targets involving low risk and low danger. Many in this group were drug users. Their targets were more likely outside their neighborhood and produced higher gains; they made more extensive use of fences. Older offenders (over twenty-five) had extensive incarceration histories, continued at burglary due to its low risk nature, exercised better planning, and had fewer, but higher quality targets. Such individuals were more highly committed to criminal careers. Drug users were likely to make more burglaries than nonusers, but were more likely to concentrate near their own neighborhood and to be more reckless or unplanned in their operation. In contrast, the non-drug user made fewer, but better planned burglaries. In a statistical analysis of burglaries in California, Pope (1980) found that those with no criminal record concentrated upon nonresidential targets while those with a record preferred residential sites. He concluded that "unlike violent crimes in which there is an interactive pattern [between type of burglar and type of burglary], burglary and other property crimes as well, may reflect more opportunity than choice" (Ibid., p. 50).

Characteristics of Burglary

In the United States in the late eighties, burglary rates were highest in the South and West with the lowest rate in the Northeast. The highest months for burglary were July and August. Some recent statistics on burglary (Bureau of Justice Statistics, 1988, p. 6) indicate that:

- About 45 percent of burglaries are nonforcible entries.
- Burglary is more likely to occur during warmer months perhaps due to a greater tendency to leave windows and doors open creating an opportunity for easy entry.
- Burglars often enter through an unlocked window or door or use a key (for example, a key "hidden" under a doormat).
- 48 percent of burglaries occurred during the daytime.

- Burglary victims suffered losses of an estimated $3.2 billion in 1987 and the average dollar loss per burglary was $975.
- In 1987, 14 percent of the burglaries brought to police attention were cleared.

Figure 7.2 presents recent trends in burglary based upon official statistics. However, since only half of all burglaries are reported to the police, trend estimates using official data are hazardous (Bureau of Justice Statistics, 1983a, p. 24).

The Fence

Of great importance in the crime of burglary as well as other property crime is the burglar's connections with *fences*, dealers in stolen property. "Professional or master fences," full-time specialists in stolen property, are essential to the operation of professional burglars and are detailed later in Chapter 8. Amateur burglars and less professional burglars are more likely to deal with a "neighborhood fence" or an "outlet fence" (Blakey and Goldsmith, 1976, pp. 1530–1535). Usually a small merchant, the "neighborhood fence" occasionally buys and deals in stolen goods while the "outlet fence" adds stolen merchandise to his or her usual stock. Smaller fencing operations may also be operated out of a neighborhood home with a room or two devoted to a display storeroom(s) of "hot merchandise," some still bearing the original price tags.

Sting Operations

Because conventional burglars shop around for fences, "sting operations," police antifencing programs, have been relatively successful. In these efforts, the police pose as dealers in stolen goods. These operations, first introduced at the federal level in 1974, have obtained a 98 percent conviction rate and produced a subsequent decline in property crimes in the areas in which they have operated.

An interesting early sting operation was PFF, Inc., which was run for five months in Washington, D.C., in 1975 (The Sting, 1976). PFF, Inc., stood for Police-FBI Fencing, Incognito, and was headquartered in an abandoned warehouse. They hung *Playboy* centerfolds at the entrance; behind them, a camera photographed entering customers and videotaped each transaction. Their customers assumed the proprietors were mafiosi, and one subject filled out an application for a "hit man" job in which he supplied information on a hitherto unsolved murder. Running out of "buy money," funds with which to purchase the stolen

Figure 7.2: Trends in Burglary

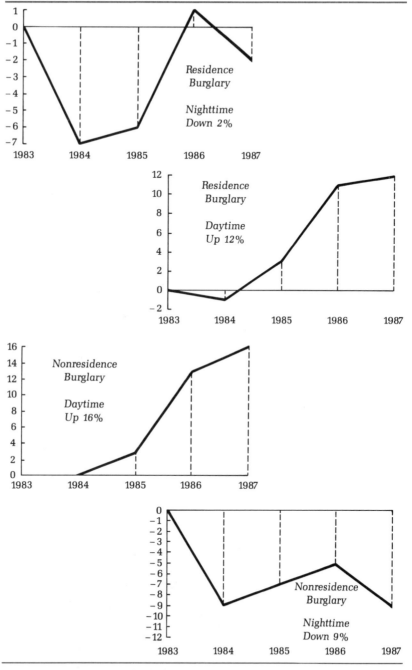

Burglaries of unknown time of occurrence are not included.

Source: Federal Bureau of Investigation, 1988, *Crime in the United States, 1987*, Washington, D.C.: Government Printing Office, p. 19.

property, PFF announced a formal party and celebration to which they invited their good customers. The customers checked their guns at the door and upon entering were arrested and escorted out the back door to jail.

Larceny-Theft

Most conventional property offenders tend to hustle or be generalists in theft. While some may prefer and concentrate on burglary operations, they also are opportunists, taking advantage of a given occasion to commit any variety of larceny-theft.

The broad category of larceny-theft includes shoplifting, pocket-picking, purse-snatching, thefts from motor vehicles, thefts of motor vehicle parts and accessories, bicycle thefts, and the like. Excluded from this category in the UCR are crimes involving the use of force or violence as well as fraud, embezzlement, confidence games, forgery, and motor vehicle theft.

ABSCAM. FBI agent Anthony Amoroso (far left) meets with Congressman Michael Myers, Angelo Errichetti, and Mel Weinberg. The FBI agents claimed to represent a group of wealthy Arabs, and gave bribes to several members of Congress—all on videotape.

August was the peak month for larceny and February the least frequent. The West had the highest rate of larceny-theft in 1987 and the Northeast had the lowest. Larceny-theft makes up the largest proportion of the crime index, Vantage Point 7.2, with the largest categories being theft from motor vehicles, theft of motor vehicle accessories, theft from buildings, and shoplifting, Figure 7.3. Twenty percent of the reported larceny-thefts were cleared nationwide in 1987 (FBI, 1988, pp. 30–32).

Larceny-theft as a category in the UCR has been correctly described as a "garbage can" (McCaghy, 1980, p. 164), a "wastebasket concept," a catch-all for miscellaneous property crime. It covers a large variety of offenses and lumps together relatively minor offenses with major professional operations. Peter Lejins (1966) suggests that the UCR

Figure 7.3: Larceny Analysis, 1987

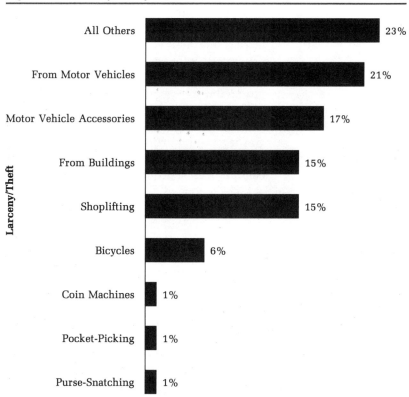

SOURCE: Federal Bureau of Investigation, 1988, *Crime in the United States, 1987*, Washington, D.C.: Government Printing Office, p. 31.

category should distinguish between joyriding by juveniles and theft for stripping or sale of the vehicle. Including theft of small value with major or grand larcenies confuses the assessment of any offense's seriousness. Compared to other categories of offenses, this makes it difficult to describe specific characteristics of offenders. Figure 7.4 provides some recent UCR estimates of trends in various categories the FBI includes under larceny-theft; however, it must be borne in mind that much larceny-theft escapes official record. From 1979 to 1983 pocket-picking, purse-snatching, shoplifting, theft from motor vehicles, and theft from buildings were up while theft of motor vehicle accessories, of bicycles and from coin machines decreased.

Juvenile Gangs

Judging from arrest records, property crime in general is more characteristic of youthful offenders under the age of eighteen. Youths are far more likely than adults to commit their crimes in groups. This is a primary difference between juvenile and adult offenders—gang membership and group criminal activity (Bureau of Justice Statistics, 1983a, pp. 32–33).

The study of juvenile gangs and theories relating to such gangs was a major focus if not fetish of criminological inquiry in the post-World War II period, particularly in the fifties and sixties. A review of such literature (Bookin-Weiner and Horowitz, 1983) pointed out that concentration upon juvenile gangs was so dominant during this period that at times it appeared to be synonymous with the study of juvenile delinquency, with the writings of Cohen (1955), Miller (1958), and Cloward and Ohlin (1960) dominating the field. Walter Miller's (1975, 1980) research on youth gangs estimates that such groups were responsible for over half of all juvenile crimes and that such groups are particularly active in the larger cities such as New York, Philadelphia, Chicago, and Los Angeles. Even though by the seventies criminological attention had shifted from the analysis of juvenile gangs, it is unclear that this change in focus was in any way related to an abatement in such criminality. Definitions of gang or gang activity also varied among sociologists, police, social workers, and other analysts.

Bookin-Weiner and Horowitz (1983) view much of the shift in inquiry as ideologically inspired. The 1950s and 1960s reflected a centrist view and an emphasis upon subcultural and interactionist theories of gangs, while the seventies, characterized by ideological polarization, focused analysis upon either individual or socioeconomic structure in which

Figure 7.4: Trends in Larceny Theft, 1979–1983

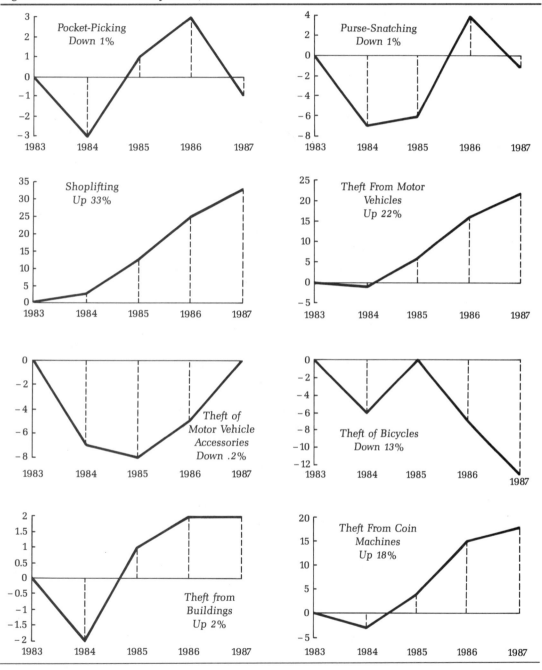

Source: Federal Bureau of Investigation, 1988, *Crime in the United States, 1987*, Washington, D.C.: Government Printing Office, p. 30.

gangs were of little interest. A right-wing shift in the eighties rekindled interest in individual explanations. Bookin-Weiner and Horowitz (Ibid., p. 599) indicate:

> Since the right views crime to be the result of the failures of social institutions, inadequate deterrence, and insufficient incapacitation, we would expect that funds available for research would be allocated to such areas. Studies using a deterrence model will not focus on the dynamics of gang interaction but on police and probation activities and reports on the violent activities of gangs. Efforts will be made to understand how to prevent individuals from joining gangs and how to stop violent activities. Because the right is concerned with types of people, we would expect interest in offender types and characteristics rather than situational or structural factors, such as Hirschi and Hindelang's (1977) concern with intelligence tests, Shah and Roth's (1974) biological research, and Wolfgang's (1972) cohort studies that examine individual differences in criminal involvement.

The Graveyard, the DMZ, and Beirut are all names that have been used to describe urban no-man's-lands such as the Cabrini-Green Housing Project (Chicago), where gangs compete for "trophies" to join their group. "Trophies" are what gang members call young boys who are living in the housing projects. Supposedly the term comes from the fact that they are the products of fathers who brag about how many unclaimed children they have (CBS, 1989b). In Los Angeles, crack-dealing gangs such as the Crips and the Bloods were responsible for over two hundred killings in 1988. These gangs are also spreading their drug operations to other cities. Gang activity, particularly of a drug-related variety, will be further detailed in Chapter 12 (see Stafford, 1984; and Vigil, 1988).

Arson—A Special Category Offense

It is an irresistible although admittedly bad joke to say that arson is a hot topic or a burning issue, but only since the late seventies have U.S. law enforcement officials devoted attention to this matter to any degree related to its seriousness. Defined by the UCR as "any willful or attempted malicious burning of a structure, vehicle, aircraft, or property of another," arson was added to the crime index (Part I crimes) in 1979 due to congressional statute. Since arson differs from other crimes, statistics are acquired from fire services and the insurance industry as well as from law enforcement agencies. Since fires of suspicious or unknown origin are not included in the statistics and only those determined through investigation are included, the actual number

Arson was added to the crime index in 1979 but estimates of the damages caused by such activity range from $1 billion to $15 billion a year.

of arsons is probably higher than is recorded in the UCR. For the year 1987, 102,310 arson offenses were reported (FBI, 1988, p. 37).

One fire department official calls arson "the cheapest crime in the world to commit. All you need is a box of matches" (Arson, 1977, p. 22). While the actual cost of arson in the U.S. per year can only be estimated, such guesses have ranged from $1 billion to $15 billion. The full cost of arson increases when we include (National Criminal Justice Reference Service, 1979):

- Death and injury to innocent citizens and firefighters.
- Increased insurance premiums.
- Increased taxes to support fire, police, and court services.
- Inferior education facilities during reconstruction of burned-out schools.
- Erosion of tax base as property values fall.
- Loss of jobs at burned-out factories and businesses.
- Lost revenue to damaged stores and shops.

In the eighties about 16 percent of arsons were cleared by arrest, with roughly 36 percent of these consisting of people under age eighteen, a higher percentage of juvenile involvement than for any other index crime. Arson is viewed as a special category offense due to the varying motives of its perpetrators. Based upon these motives of arsonists described by Boudreau and others (1977) and Inciardi (1970), McCaghy (1980) proposes a typology of arson which includes: profit-motivated arson, revenge arson, vandalism arson, crime concealment arson, sabotage arson, and excitement arson.

Profit-motivated arson is illustrated by insurance fraud, in which structures are purposely torched in order to collect on their insured value. Insurance companies themselves in the past have encouraged such practices by insuring suspicious properties in high amounts as well as by not performing sufficient investigation before honoring claims. Arson often serves as an index of urban decay in which owners unload their deteriorating properties on the companies which insure them. An excellent example of citizen action against a white collar arson ring that threatened to destroy their neighborhood is provided by the "Case of Boston's Symphony Road area":

> On September 12, 1976, a young boy died in an apartment house fire in Boston's Symphony Road area. That same night, residents met and decided to investigate the pattern of fires that had devastated their neighborhood. They started by tracing the history of burned buildings—who owned them, their value, what they were insured for. The results of this neighborhood effort are now well known: information provided by the Symphony Road

residents helped authorities to uncover and prosecute an arson for profit ring responsible for as many as 25 fires that destroyed $6 million worth of property (National Criminal Justice Reference Service, 1979).

In the chill, predawn darkness one day last week [October 24, 1977], 80 Massachusetts state police fanned out through Boston and its suburbs, ringing doorbells, rousing residents and hauling off to jail 22 surprised and discomfited citizens. Among those indicted: six attorneys, eleven real estate operators, four public insurance adjustors, one police officer and a retired fire chief. By week's end a total of 26 men had been arraigned in Suffolk County superior court on charges as varied as fraud, bribery and murder. But all of them were alleged to have committed one crime: arson. They were accused of contracting with landlords, financially troubled shopkeepers, warehouse owners and others to burn down their buildings for the insurance, with the arsonists taking a percentage of the claim (Arson, 1977, p. 22).

Revenge arson may take place due to spite or jealousy, as a means of getting even. The burn-for-hate category can be illustrated by fired employees gaining revenge against employers, or by cases like the one in which a jealous suitor burned down a night club in which his girlfriend was dating someone else. This category could also serve as an example of vindictive *vandalism arson*, in which arson is employed as a means of expressing hatred toward a particular group or individual. Vandalism accounts for most arsons in deteriorating urban areas. Any structure may be torched in an extension of play activity, but abandoned properties are particular targets. *Crime concealment arson* takes place as a way of hiding murder victims or physical evidence such as records or in order to draw attention from a crime being committed elsewhere. *Sabotage arson* may be illustrated by fires set during labor or racial strife, prison riots, or other civil disturbances.

Excitement arson may also be a motivation. The term "pyromaniac" refers to an individual who has a morbid fascination with setting and observing fires. Freudians would even associate a sexual basis to pyromania, in which such individuals experience erotic satisfaction by means of arson.

As a type of property crime which may also result in violence, arson cuts across many of the criminal behavior systems discussed in this text. Profit-motivated arson is most often committed by "white collar criminals," occupational and corporate offenders, often in conjunction with professional torch artists. This category may also be committed as in New York City by welfare recipients seeking city assistance in gaining better accommodations or by drug addicts or even by conventional criminals called "mango hunters" by New York City police. These offenders burn structures in order to expose and facilitate the stealing of fire resistant plumbing and fixtures (Ibid., p. 22). Revenge arsonists resemble violent personal criminals, but arson for crime concealment may involve conventional property offenders or corporate or organized offenders. Arson as sabotage resembles political criminality, and vandalism-inspired arson fits the occasional property offender. Finally, pyromania opens up the area of the psychotic or psychopathic offender.

Criminal Careers of Occasional and Conventional Property Criminals

The distinction between occasional and conventional offenders is not made because of the legal categories of the offenses which they commit, but because of the manner in which the crimes are committed and the degree of the offender's identification with the criminal world. Most snitches, amateur shoplifters, wanton vandals, joyriders, and naïve check forgers do not view their activities as criminal, have short or no official criminal records, do not commit crime as a means of livelihood, and are not "streetwise" or "crimewise" in terms of using the language of the criminal life. On the other hand, most conventional property offenders may be viewed as exhibiting minor levels of career criminality. Many have early histories of truancy, vandalism, street fighting, delinquent gang membership, and contact with the law (Clinard and Quinney, 1973, p. 149).

The criminal careers of most conventional criminals peak in the late teens and rapidly decline after they reach their mid-twenties. Reaching ages where the full weight of criminal penalties falls upon them as adult offenders and not being particularly skilled enough to make a living at crime, most simply curtail their level of criminal involvement. Middle age and maturity, rather than any specific rehabilitation regimen, eventually reform the conventional criminal. Werthman (1967, p. 170) indicates:

> After a few years of this existence [street hustling], these boys are really at the end of their "delinquent" careers. Some get jobs, some go to jail, some get killed, and some simply fade into an older underground of pool rooms and petty thefts. Most cannot avoid ending up with conventional jobs, however, largely because the "illegitimate opportunities" available simply are not that good.

Occasional property offenders do not require criminal associations in order to commit their crimes. Their crimes are fairly easy to commit, requiring little training or skill. In contrast, the conventional property offenders often operate in groups or gangs in which many of the techniques of crime are learned from their peers. While most occasional offenders maintain their commitment to conventional society, rejecting criminal identities, conventional offenders are only partially committed to legitimate society.

Societal Reaction

The societal reaction toward occasional property offenders is relatively mild. Since most offenders lack a previous criminal record, charges are usually dismissed, or the individual is given immediate probation or a suspended sentence. In contrast, societal reaction toward conventional property offenders is relatively strong and, until recently, even stronger than that against more professional, organized, and corporate criminals (Cullen et al. 1982b). Conventional offenders are of a different social class than those who make and enforce the law. This may in part explain the stronger legal processing of such offenders when compared with that of corporate offenders.

Occasional property offenders strongly identify with middle class societal values and reject criminal identification. Because of this, most offenders are deterred from future activity once confronted with legal action or arrest. Relative leniency with offenders is often justified, since few have previous criminal records of any substance and most are unlikely to progress into a career of crime. Since many such offenders come from the same social class as those who make and enforce the laws, they fail to fit popular public stereotypes of criminals. Diversion of such offenders into restitution programs or accelerated rehabilitation dispositions also relieves the courts of caseload burdens.

Most conventional criminal offenders tend to identify with criminal behavior and are less likely to be deterred by the threat of arrest or the stigmatization of the label of criminal. For some, criminal processing enhances their reputation on the street as "bad." The attachment of the criminal label and record may also begin a criminalization process which isolates the individual from more conventional associates and reinforces a criminal identity. Because of their relative lack of skill and organization, most conventional criminals are eventually arrested and a large proportion imprisoned. About half of all prison inmates in the United States are conventional criminals. It is to this population that the term "revolving door of justice" has been applied in that some end up doing the equivalent of life terms on the installment plan; conventional rehabilitation plans are claimed to be relatively unsuccessful with this group of offenders (Martinson, 1974). Most of these offenses are outgrowths of deprived lower class environments and subcultures and legal processing appears to have only minimal effects.

Conservatives such as James Q. Wilson (1975 and 1983b) call for incapacitating through imprisonment larger proportions of serious conventional offenders, while liberals suggest that preventive social programs aimed particularly at reducing inequality are necessary in order to erase the family and social conditions which breed the next generation of losers—semiprofessional criminals.

Recent anthropological field studies of juvenile conventional criminals, directed by the Vera Institute of Justice in New York City, provided some insights into such behavior that are often missed in more aggregative statistical studies, which are conducted after the fact (Press, 1983). The predatory street crime pattern involves juveniles committing such offenses for years, then ceasing such activity due to a combination of threats of jail, conventional job opportunities, and simple maturity. One researcher, Mercer Sullivan, claims that solutions calling for employment programs and/or of "getting tougher" with such offenders are too simplistic and that the campaign for selective incapacitation particularly misses the mark; most offenders are not identified as serious offenders until they are at least twenty years old—"over the hill in terms of street crime" (Ibid.). A strategy to treat such individuals earlier as hard-core, career criminals and to incapacitate them through imprisonment, assuming that 5 to 8 percent account for over 50 percent of juvenile crime (OJJDP, 1983, p. 1), ignores the fact that most teen crime careers are short in duration, thus such policies risk incarcerating them at the very time when most would be ending their criminal careers.

Comparing white, black, and Hispanic juveniles, Sullivan says that they begin as conflict-oriented gangs preying only upon each other. Growing older, white teenagers were able to obtain part-time jobs through their parents' contacts. These jobs occupied their time and supplied money; continued street robberies would not be tolerated by the local neighbors. Blacks and Hispanics lacked such employment contacts, and many became the self-employed of the streets, experimenting with muggings and burglaries, the fruits of the latter sometimes being purchased by neighbors. Local muggers, since they tended to operate close to home, were not tolerated, and most were eventually arrested.

While the crimes of occasional property offenders point out the pervasiveness of violations among those otherwise respectable in society, offenses of conventional property offenders and the relative lack of success of correctional efforts with such offenders continues to disappoint crime control policy patterns. Conventional property offenders fail to respond to the very policies, such as threat of jail and stigmatization, which appear to work very well in discouraging occasional property offenders. Conservative approaches that aim to reform individuals without concomitant efforts related to social reform are likely to continue to fail.

Summary

Offenses against property, among the first to be punished under formal legal systems, include a wide variety of violations usually labeled larceny (theft). These offenses can be committed by a variety of criminal types, two of which are discussed and contrasted in this chapter: *occasional property criminals* and *conventional property criminals*. *Career criminality* is characterized by: identification with crime, criminal self-concept, group support and association with other criminals, progression in criminality, and crime as a sole means of livelihood. While occasional property offenders are the antithesis of career criminals, conventional property violators are on the bottom rung of the ladder or continuum of career criminality. Occasional property offenders commit their crimes relatively infrequently, irregularly, crudely, and without identifying with criminality. Conventional criminals commit their offenses more regularly and tend to aspire more toward career criminality.

Occasional property criminal behavior includes most, but not all shoplifting, vandalism, motor vehicle theft, and check forgery. Cameron distinguishes between two types of shoplifters: boosters (professionals) and snitches (amateurs). The majority of snitches have no previous criminal history, do not identify with criminality, and are deterred from future activity when threatened with formal legal processing. *Vandalism*, the willful destruction of the property of others, has been identified by Andrew Wade as consisting of three types: wanton (senseless), predatory (criminal), and vindictive (hateful). Wanton vandalism by juveniles is the most common type and usually represents an extension of play activity. Motor vehicle theft also consists of a variety of types: joyriding, short-term transportation, long-term transportation, and profit purpose. Joyriders, who borrow a car for temporary adventure, illustrate well the occasional property criminal.

Check forgers have been distinguished by Lemert as consisting of two types: "naïve check forgers" and "systematic check forgers." The former, who are occasional property criminals, write bad checks as a means of resolving a temporary crisis. The bad check writing is a result of closure or reduction of other possibilities by which to solve this problem.

Conventional property criminals are those who commit larceny-theft and burglary on a fairly persistent basis, constituting a rudimentary form of career criminality. Such offenders are less skilled and organized than their professional counterparts and represent about half of the prison inmates in the U.S. Most will eventually reduce or cease their "careers" by their mid-twenties. *Burglary* involves the unlawful entry of a structure in order to commit a felony or theft. This may include actual forcible entry, unlawful entry without force, or attempted entry. As a rule, burglars attempt to avoid violence. Walsh (1977) identifies *types* of burglars. These include: professionals, known burglars, young burglars, juvenile burglars, and junkies, each type representing, in decreasing order, less sophistication and organization. Other characteristics of burglars and burglary by Scarr (1973), Repetto (1974), and Pope (1980) were elaborated. Indispensable to property criminals and particularly burglars is the fence, a dealer in stolen property. Successful police "sting" or anti-fencing operations were described. Most conventional offenders are nonspecialists; they "hustle" or take advantage of various criminal opportunities.

Larceny-theft, which includes a broad category of property crimes, makes up over half of the index offense total and as a category constitutes a "wastebasket concept," a catch-all. Property offenses are more characteristic of youthful offenders, who tend to commit crimes in groups. Criminological research on youth gangs, a problematic concept, was described as very much reflecting ideological climate. *Arson*, which has since 1979 been included as a UCR index offense, involves any willful or attempted malicious burning of another's property. Arson is described as a special category property offense because of the variety of motivations involved including: profit-motivated, revenge, vandalism, crime concealment, sabotage, and excitement. The "Symphony Road, Boston, Case" illustrates the white collar nature of much arson.

Comparisons of criminal careers of occasional vs. conventional property criminals demonstrates that only the latter exhibit any level of commitment to criminality, and even they consist of many youthful offenders whose property criminality peaks at age sixteen, halves by age twenty, and declines thereafter. *Societal reaction* to occasional offenders is relatively mild while relatively strong against conventional property offenders. Recent anthropological field research suggests that programs designed for identifying and getting tough with "career criminals" must be careful in examining the interplay between employment, threatened incarceration, and aging of offenders lest they get tough at the very time that most will mature out of crime (Shover, 1983).

KEY CONCEPTS

Career Criminality	Snitch	Burglary
Occasional Property Criminality	Types of Vandalism	Fences
Conventional Criminality	Motor Vehicle Theft	Larceny-Theft
Shoplifting	Naïve Check Forgers	Arson
Booster	Systematic Check Forgers	Types of Arson

8

Professional Crime

The Concept of "Professional Crime"

In sociology, the *concept of profession* refers to occupations or their incumbents which/who possess various traits, including (a) esoteric, useful *knowledge* that requires lengthy training, as well as (b) a claimed *service* orientation and a code of ethics that permit occupations to attempt to obtain (c) *autonomy* or independence of operation and various concomitants such as high prestige and remuneration (Hagan, 1975). This knowledge-service-autonomy dimension of the professions model makes it inappropriate to criminals or criminal activity; Mack (1972) prefers the term "able criminal," while Klein (1974) suggests the concept "grifter" (professional theft) as more appropriate constructs. However, the application of the tag "professional" to certain types of criminals is widespread in the literature, which justifies its treatment as a separate category even though our treatment will be somewhat critical. Cressey (1969, p. 45) warns that many of these skilled criminals are simply slightly better than other crooks at lying, cheating, and stealing and we should be careful in calling this "professional." Studies of career criminals by Petersilia and associates (1977) suggest the term "intensives" for those who commit more sophisticated crimes and face a lesser chance of arrest or conviction. Therefore, while the professional criminal is not truly a professional in the sociological sense, the term is appropriate in referring in a slang manner to those who earn a considerable portion of their livelihood in criminal pursuits.

Characteristics of Professional Crime

The benchmark in the U.S. for analysis of professional criminal behavior was Edwin Sutherland's (1937) *The Professional Thief*, a work based upon interviews and a detailed case study of a professional thief/confidence man with the pseudonym "Chic Conwell." In his original formulation Sutherland saw the professional thief as characterized by: crime as a sole means of livelihood, careful planning, reliance upon technical skills and methods, and a migratory life-style. They have a shared sense of belonging, rules, codes of behavior, and a mutual specialized language (Sutherland, 1956, pp. 3–4).

Professional crime is a sociological rather than legal construct. What distinguishes professional crime from other crimes is not the legal definition of the behavior, but the way in which the crimes are performed. Clinard and Quinney (1973, p. 246) identify the following features of professional crime:

1. Crime is the criminal's sole livelihood and is engaged in for economic gain.
2. There is a highly developed criminal career.
3. There is considerable skill involved.
4. High status in the criminal world is bestowed upon professional criminals.
5. Professional criminals are more successful at avoiding detection and imprisonment.

Argot

Acts of professional criminals differ from those of less professional criminals only in the distinctive manner in which they are committed. Professional crime primarily involves the relatively safe and consistent stealing of large sums of money on a systematic, rational, planned, skillful, and nonviolent basis. Professional criminals attempt to avoid "heat," or the daring and bravado characteristic of many amateur criminals which tends to attract public attention and often subsequent police action. Distinctive *argot* or specialized language also is characteristic of the world of professional crime. Arthur Judge's *The Elizabethan Underworld* (1930), Henry Mayhew's *London's Underworld* (1862), and McMullan's *The Canting Crew: London's Criminal Underworld 1550–1700* (1984) provide some of the argot of seventeenth-century Elizabethan professional criminals (see also Taylor, 1984). Sutherland's informant, "Chic Conwell," provides us with the argot of early twentieth-century America (Sutherland, 1937).

Elizabethan Underworld Argot (1600s, England)

Black art: picking locks
Cony: dupe, victim (literally rabbit)
Curb: hook used to steal from open windows
Rookeries: criminal districts in Victorian times
Santar: outside accomplice of one who robs shops
Sharper: card cheat

Early Twentieth-Century American Argot

Cannons: professional pickpockets
Heels: sneak thieves who operate in stores and offices

Boosters: professional shoplifters
Pennyweighting: stealing from jewelry stores by substituting fake lookalikes
Hotel prowling: stealing from hotel rooms
The con: confidence games
Hanging paper: passing bad checks, money orders, and other commercial paper
The shake: extorting money from others who are criminally involved

Maurer (1964, p. 55) quotes an interesting example of a professional pickpocket's argot when he was asked to explain in court what he had done:

> Well, Judge, your honor, I was out gandering around for a soft mark and made a tip that was going to cop a short. I eased myself into the tip and just topped a leather in Mr. Bates' left prat when I blowed I was getting a jacket from these two honest bulls. So I kick the okus back in his kick and I'm clean. Just then this flatfoot nails me, so here I am on a bum rap. All I crave is justice, I hope she ain't blind.

A Model of Professional Crime

Figure 8.1 depicts a continuum model of professional crime. Like the "organized crime continuum" in Chapter 12, the purpose of this continuum model is to underline the fact that there are no hard-and-fast divisions between professional and amateur crime; the professionalism of criminal activity is a matter of degree rather than of kind. Thus, the greater extent to which an individual's criminal activity involves key factors — crime as a sole livelihood, an extensive criminal career, skill, high status in the criminal world, the successful avoidance of detection and/or immunity from prosecution, and a criminal subculture and organization — the greater the likelihood that such activity can be labeled "professional crime." The concept, however, is an "ideal type," a heuristically useful overgeneralization which is unlikely to exist in pure form.

Professional crime is similar to legitimate occupations such as entertainment or professional sports in that it is a "skyrocket profession." For those who succeed, it can be a glamorous life of fast living; however, it shares another characteristic with these fields, and that is "many are called, but few are chosen." Many semiprofessional criminals who might occupy a middle ground on the continuum are unable to perform crime as their sole livelihood — they are not good enough. Most eventually leave the world of crime because they simply cannot make a living at it: they are less skillful, enjoy less status in the criminal

Figure 8.1: A Model of Professional Crime

Amateur Crime		Professional Crime
Occasional	(Sole Livelihood)	Full-time
Short Duration	(Extensive Career)	Lifelong
Little	(Skill)	Extensive
Low	(High Status)	High
Unsuccessful	(Avoidance Detection)	Successful
None	(Criminal Subculture)	Extensive
None	(High Degree of Planning)	Extensive
No	(Employment of "the Fix")	Yes

world, and are less successful at avoiding detection. Although they belong to criminal subcultures to a degree, these subcultures lack the network of talent and successful contacts which the more professional criminal enjoys. Finally, such less professional offenders generally commit crimes which require or involve less planning and have less success in avoiding prosecution and incarceration.

Crime Pays?

In Chapter 7 career criminality was said to include characteristics such as identification with crime, extensive association with other criminals, progression and specialization in crime, as well as crime as a sole means of livelihood. Professional and organized criminals best fit this model, though differences between these types are often a matter of degree rather than kind. Similarly, criminal pursuits such as video-tape/motion picture pirating, drug sales, prostitution, and pimping are pursued by criminals of various degrees of sophistication, with career criminals being generally more persistent and successful in their activities. Professionals tend to "freelance" or be less tied to relatively permanent criminal organizations than their organized crime counterparts. In the last analysis, however, criminologists have not arrived at a consensus in categorizing these activities.

Edelhertz's Typology

Edelhertz (1970) has developed a typology of white collar crime. Figure 8.2 presents one of Edelhertz's categories of white collar crime, which is more professional than it is occupational or corporate in nature. The main distinction between professional crime and occupational/corporate crime is that in the former the sole purpose of the business is to perform criminal activity, while in the latter crime is incidental to a legitimate business or professional service. Some offenses listed in Figure 8.2 are not simply professional crime but, following the model, become so the more and the degree to which they involve the characteristics of professional criminal activity.

Scams

"Scam" is a criminal slang term used to refer to various criminal techniques, "hustles," or operations. Many criminal operations that may be described as examples of professional crime or sometimes even as white collar crime—since they are committed by stealth, nonviolently, and by persons of apparent respectability—are in fact semiprofessional in nature. They involve little skill and prey upon gullible victims. *Confidence (con)* games meet this definition. These are called "confidence" because they rely upon winning the confidence of the victim in order to steal from him or her. Another possible origin for the term *con* is "cony," the dupe or victim. Sometimes called "flim flam" or "bunko" or "short cons," such scams come in an infinite variety, although some of the more common ones are disturbingly familiar in their repetition and success. Surprising to many is the fact that most short con artists at the present time are women, as are most of their victims.

The *pigeon drop* is one of the best known of simple confidence swindles. Here is a description of an actual pigeon drop that has been repeated hundreds of times with remarkable success:

> A 61-year-old widow (the "mark" or victim) gave her $3,596 in life savings to two con artists in a downtown five-and-dime with the assumption that she would receive this back and $6,000 besides. A woman (one of the con artists—the "catch woman") approached the widow while she was shopping in a department store, began talking to her and a few seconds later a third woman (accomplice) appeared. The third woman said she had found a wallet

Figure 8.2: Edelhertz's Categories of White-Collar Crime (Professional Crime)

White-collar crime as a business, or as the central activity.

1. Medical or health frauds.
2. Advance fee swindles.
3. Phony contests.
4. Bankruptcy fraud, including schemes devised as salvage operation after insolvency of otherwise legitimate business.
5. Securities fraud and commodities fraud.
6. Chain referral schemes.
7. Home improvement schemes.
8. Debt consolidation schemes.
9. Mortgage milking.
10. Merchandise swindles:
    a. Gun and coin swindles.
    b. General merchandise.
    c. Buying or pyramid clubs.
11. Land frauds.
12. Directory advertising schemes.
13. Charity and religious frauds.
14. Personal improvements schemes:
    a. Diploma Mills.
    b. Correspondence Schools.
    c. Modeling Schools.
15. Fraudulent application for, use and/or sale of credit cards, airline tickets, etc.
16. Insurance frauds:
    a. Phony accident rings.
    b. Looting of companies by purchase of over-valued assets, phony management contracts, self-dealing with agents, inter-company transfers, etc.
    c. Fraud by agents writing policies to obtain advance commissions.
    d. Issuance of annuities or paid-up life insurance, with no consideration, so that they can be used as collateral for loans.
    e. Sales by misrepresentation to military personnel or those otherwise uninsurable.
17. Vanity and song publishing schemes.
18. Ponzi schemes.
19. False security frauds, i.e., Billy Sol Estes or De Angelis type schemes.
20. Purchase of banks, or control thereof, with deliberate intention to loot them.
21. Fraudulent establishing and operation of banks or savings and loan associations.
22. Fraud against the government:
    a. Organized income tax refund swindles, sometimes operated by income tax "counselors."
    b. AID frauds, i.e., where totally worthless goods shipped.
    c. F.H.A. frauds
       (1) Obtaining guarantees of mortgages on multiple family housing far in excess of value of property with foreseeable inevitable foreclosure.
       (2) Home improvement funds.
23. Executive placement and employment agency frauds.
24. Coupon redemption frauds.
25. Money order swindles.

SOURCE: Herbert Edelhertz, 1970, *The Nature, Impact and Prosecution of White-Collar Crime*, National Institute of Law Enforcement and Criminal Justice, Washington, D.C.: Government Printing Office, pp. 73–75.

with $20,000 in cash and a note saying that the money should be delivered to Castro in Cuba. She showed them some loose twenties (the rest of the roll of money actually consists of a "Michigan bankroll" of phony money), and the three women discussed the situation for a while. Then the woman with the wallet convinced them that she would phone "Attorney Burger," a fictitious man, who she said worked in City Hall.

After a fake phone conversation with him, she reported that he asked all three to put up some money to show good faith ("good faith deposit") until the money could be divided three ways, with $2,000 for the lawyer. The woman who had first spoken to the victim said she could come up with $4,000 from a recent insurance claim, and she supposedly went to get it. Then the other woman took the victim to a bank for her life savings, which she turned over to them in the ladies' room of a five-and-dime. She was told to report to "Attorney Burger at City Hall" at 4:30 P.M. She arrived at the appointed time and came to the grim realization that she had been duped. "I've read about that one in the papers, but I never thought it could happen to me," she told police (Con Game, 1972, p. 11-A).

Many victims are so humiliated that they do not even report their victimization to the police. Short cons such as the pigeon drop usually prey upon not the affluent, but the middle-aged, retired, and widowed working-class types, particularly females.

The *badger scam* also preys upon the naïveté of victims.

An alert teller at a savings and loan association alerted police when an obviously distressed 81-year-old man withdrew his life savings of $10,622 — in cash. He had been visited on a number of occasions by a 19-year-old girl who had indicated that she represented a Bible Institute. During the last visit, a man feigning the role of an outraged father burst into the apartment and accused the victim of having illicit relations with his daughter. His paternal rage could, however, be forgotten for the right price (Langway and Smith, 1975, p. 67).

In the *bank examiner's scam,* swindlers pretend to be government investigators who are seeking the cooperation of the victim in order to catch a dishonest bank teller. The mark (victim) is asked to withdraw money and turn it over to the investigators, who will mark it in order to apprehend the dishonest employee. Obviously, government agencies are not so "hard up" that they have to use the money of private citizens in order to conduct their undercover operations.

The "too good to be true" opportunity for easy money, something for nothing, to "get rich quick" lures would-be victims. The following examples are illustrative:

- A wealthy Eastern industrialist was contacted by a group posing as Texan inventors who indicated that for a large investment he could own part of the patent rights to their new invention—a process which makes it possible to *extract gold from water.* In fact, such a distillation is possible but economically cost-ineffective, since more must be spent in extraction than the value of that which is produced. The suspicious industrialist contacted the FBI who, posing as his agents, met with the con artists, who were arrested and convicted of multiple charges, including fraud.

■ The *Spanish prisoner's scam* (so-named because it originated during the Spanish Civil War, although the theme is continually updated to reflect current conflicts) involves the victim being approached with a tale of a wealthy prisoner who is being held captive without access to his riches. The victim is convinced to give money to be used to bribe the rich prisoner to freedom, after which he or she will be handsomely rewarded. Obviously, such a prisoner never existed and gullible victims may bid their money adieu.

■ The *Murphy* involves promising to deliver an illegal commodity (prostitute's services, drugs, and the like) and then skipping with the prepayment. In one Murphy operation, the "shyster" took those seeking drugs to an apartment house and obtained prepayment; then while the "mark" waited in the lobby, slipped out the back door. Such victims are unlikely to report to the police that they were "ripped-off" trying to buy illegal drugs. In 1972 in Hamburg, West Germany, Dieter Glocke, a bar owner, advertised for men to serve as heterosexual prostitutes in a bordello he claimed to be opening in order to service women. Each applicant had to pay a $10 registration fee as well as to file a three-page questionnaire on their sex lives. More than 2,000 applied for the job, but Glocke never opened or planned to open such an establishment. Not surprisingly, to date no charges have been filed against him, since Glocke had in his possession some very revealing information.

■ *Postal fraud* is widespread including: skipping with payments for orders, precollected fees for fake franchises, and offers to arrange a "guaranteed" business loan or employment for an "advance fee" which fails to deliver as promised. Beware of paying advance fees for: estates that have been left to you by people unknown to you, chain letters, work-at-home schemes, and far-off land sales.

■ *Circus grifting* (dishonest carnival games) is another example of a "short con." Grifters will often work with a "shill," or plant, who pretends to be a winning customer. Such "con games" were quite common in traveling carnival shows which worked Midwestern county fairs. Hidden pedals for gambling wheels; switched rings for the ring toss; loaded dice for the "crap" game; fake "two-headed" ladies or half-man, half-ape; and willing customers ever too eager to part with their money certainly provide substance to P.T. Barnum's slogan, "There's a sucker born every minute."

- In this same vein of "short cons," readers should certainly beware of *snake oil* salespersons or offers to increase breast size, sexual prowess, or to sell bogus diplomas (Stewart and Spille, 1988). In one home repair scam which targeted the elderly, the swindler would short out electric wires, start fires near furnaces, or release bugs or mice in order to create problems in need of solution. Claiming to be waterproofing the customer's roof with a clear silicone-based liquid, he would spray water on their roof (Home Repair Scam, 1986).

Peter Maas (1975) in *King of the Gypsies* describes the elaborate gypsy con game of *boojo* in which superstitious victims, usually visitors to fortune-telling parlors, are conned into turning over their life savings in cash in order to have a "curse" removed. The gypsy con artist removes the cash instead.

According to Maas (1975, pp. 59–112) the vast majority of boojo cases are unreported because the victims are embarrassed that they had been so gullible. Such cons begin in a gypsy fortune-telling establishment (*ofisa*), when a likely victim is identified and asked to tell the fortune teller what it is that is troubling him or (usually) her. The misfortune is identified as being due to "cursed" money, and the victim is instructed to return the following day with money so that it can be checked out in order to see if in fact it is cursed. With different variations, the boojo woman demonstrates that the money is cursed. For example, in one con she has the victim bring an egg along with the money and "with expert sleight-of-hand, places a tiny, carved devil's head or a pinch of hair in the yolk, a rather awesome sight" when cracked and shown to the mark as an evil omen. The victim now asks what is to be done. The remaining steps also vary: for example, having the evil money handed over to the boojo woman to be sewn into a sack (by now the money has been switched for paper) to be slept on and opened later or burned. Or perhaps the money must be buried, while the customer is naked, at midnight in a cemetery, and, since the victim is too modest, the boojo woman will "reluctantly" act as her surrogate. The money also may be burned on the spot, although it is first switched and replaced by worthless paper. When the heat is on, gypsies simply move on to greener pastures. In one boojo operation a Warren, Missouri, farm couple were warned that the darkness or hex upon them had been placed by their family and not to talk to them. A long string of evil omens and misfortunes were forecast, including fatal cancer and gangrene. Each could be removed by paying the gypsy women money. Until they finally wised up, the family lost over $150,000 in the scam (O'Connor, 1987, p. 41).

In the Gypsy con game "boojo," fortune-tellers remove "evil curses" from gullible victims—along with the victim's money.

The most successful gang of professional con artists in the U.S. is the *Williamson clan,* an extended-family band of traveling con artists who dupe thousands of people every year, primarily in the Midwest. They peddle fake repair work on driveways and roofs and other phony products, and then move on before their victims discover they have been taken.

Many scams are on the edge of slick business practices. Used car dealers have been known to leave spouses alone to talk over the deal in a "bugged" office. Or after the agreement seems to be made and the papers are almost filled out, they use "the close and bump." Pretending to take the papers with the agreed-upon price to the boss in the back room, the salesperson then says that the boss wants $100 more. Some may even roll back odometers. If the one-tenth-mile digit vibrates while the car is moving, the odometer has probably been rolled back (Bennett and Clagett, 1977, p. 142).

Big Cons

Ivar Kreuger, the king of fraud, stole roughly $500 million from investors between 1917 and his death by suicide in 1932. He had legitimately made his first million and more in the match business in Sweden. Later he used bribery to establish monopolies over match production in other countries, eventually owning the International Match Company, which operated in thirty-eight countries. Not satisfied with his honestly gained riches, Kreuger began to use huge sums of cash for his own purposes, switching assets to cover nonexistent assets and creating dummy firms in order to hide personal bank accounts. Then, in a strategy that will become all too familiar, he began to pay out large dividends in order to attract investors. The 1929 Stock Market Crash caught him with no money to cover the clamor for funds. After his attempt to forge $142

Ivar Krueger, receiving an honorary degree from Syracuse University, before his fraudulent schemes were discovered.

million in Italian government bonds failed, Kreuger's paper empire failed and he killed himself in 1932 (McCaghy, 1976, p. 223).

Maurer's *The Big Con*

David Maurer (1964; 1940) in *Whiz Mob* and *The Big Con* describes the following steps in the big con (Ibid., 1964, pp. 15–16):

1. Putting up the mark (investigating and locating likely victims).
2. Playing the con (gaining the confidence of the victim).
3. Roping the mark (steering him to meet the inside man).
4. Telling the tale (showing him how he can make big money dishonestly).
5. Giving the convincer (permitting him to make a profit).
6. Having him invest further.
7. Sending him after more money.
8. Playing him against the big store and fleecing him.
9. Getting him out of the way.
10. Cooling out the mark (having him realize that he cannot turn to the law), and
11. Putting in the fix (bribing or influencing action by the law).

While not all big confidence games involve all of the procedures Maurer describes, each example to be discussed demonstrates variations of these steps. Wealthy marks—such as business executives, entertainment personalities, and, recently, wealthy professionals such as doctors and dentists who are hunting for "tax shelters" or even greater affluence—are ideal targets for those on the lookout for "fingering the score."

"Yellow Kid" Weil—Master Swindler

One of the most famous American swindlers of all time was Joseph "Yellow Kid" Weil, who was given the nickname from a popular cartoon strip character of the 1890s. Elaborately attired and exuding success by his lavish life-style, Weil made an estimated $8 million in nearly forty years of the big con. Weil made his money peddling worthless oil stocks to bankers (Nash, 1975, vol. 2, pp. 410–414). Just one example of "Yellow Kid's" ingenious frauds involved his belief that people would trust anything in print. He located an article concerning an investor who had made a fortune from purchasing an abandoned gold mine. Next he had a friend who was a printer reproduce facsimiles of the article, with Weil's own picture in place of the investor's. Weil's first stop in each town was the local library, where he switched the fake copy for the original and then assured doubting victims that they could check out his credentials in the local library. After fleecing his victims, he was always careful to replace the original in the library before moving on to the next town (Ibid., pp. 411–412).

Pirate's Inheritance

- Could you be an heir to Sir Francis Drake's fortune?
- Would you like to buy exclusive rights to Adolf Hitler's diary or the authorized Howard Hughes biography?
- Could I interest you in buying the Brooklyn Bridge?

While few fools have fallen for the last offer, some highly reputable victims have been hoodwinked by the other two. Prior to World War I, Oscar Merrill Hartzell conned seventy thousand "heirs" of Sir Francis Drake (Wade, 1976, pp. 21–27). Hartzell founded the Sir Francis Drake Society, the supposed purpose of which was to force the British crown to release the $22 billion impounded estate of the infamous pirate. He contacted people in Europe and America who possessed the Drake surname, indicating that he needed money from them to press the legal case; in return, they would share in the fortune. Swearing them to secrecy, he promised $5,000 for each $1 invested. As many as three thousand members rented halls for meetings in some cities, and one minister denounced Britain from the pulpit for its lack of cooperation. Even though the statute for probate of the estate had expired under British law over three hundred years ago, Hartzell continually journeyed to England, from which he could send correspondence to the members. As part of what he claimed was an international conspiracy to prevent him from claiming the Drake fortune, he was deported from England and eventually tried in the U.S., where he was found mentally incompetent and civilly committed until his death in 1943. Nothing remained of the over $2 million which he had bilked from his victims.

Hitler's Diary

If you were approached by someone attempting to peddle Karl Marx's *Das Kapital* in the original Russian language, you would be justifiably skeptical, since Marx wrote only in the German language and knew very little Russian. Similarly, though the language was German, skepticism should have been exercised by *Stern* magazine (a West German publication) when its publishers were approached in 1981 and enticed to pay somewhere between $1 million to $3.75 million for Hitler's "personal diary" (Watson, Moreau, and Westerman, 1983, p. 39). *Stern* felt that the handwritten documents would rewrite Nazi history, not to mention dramatically increase its own weekly circulation. The documents, according to one account, were allegedly lost in an airplane crash during the close of the war and later discovered in a hayloft in East Germany. But expert document examiners became suspicious of entries around July 1944, a time when Hitler, complete with a mangled arm gained in surviving an assassin's bomb, was apparently unable to even write his name. However, the diary entries during that period showed no signs of this handicap. The fake diary was apparently the workings of one Konrad Kujau, a seller of Nazi memorabilia in Stuttgart, and a man with a long history of selling forged documents (Harris, 1986).

The Hughes Biography

Author Clifford Irving (Fay et al., 1972) gained some previous notoriety as the result of writing a best-selling book entitled *Fake*, which detailed the career of a professional art forger (Irving, 1970). Apparently, Irving learned some things from his research on that book when, in the early seventies, he forged letters, checks, and a book contract allegedly signed by the reclusive millionaire Howard Hughes. Irving obtained a half-million-dollar advance from the McGraw-Hill Book Company for a phony manuscript which he claimed was Hughes' authorized biography. When the hoax became apparent and Irving was jailed, he admitted that the entire thing was a fraud.

Ponzi Schemes

Perhaps the most legendary swindler of all times was Charles "Get Rich Quick" Ponzi, whose modus operandi has now inherited his name — Ponzi schemes. A *Ponzi scheme* involves paying off early investors with money obtained from later investors in a nonexistent enterprise. In 1919 Ponzi discovered that postal return coupons could be purchased overseas and redeemed in the U.S. at anywhere from 100 to 300 percent profit. He offered investors 40 percent profit on their investment in ninety days. He then paid off his first investors sooner and with larger dividends than promised, and once the word got around, they were beating down his door. Many preferred to reinvest rather than to withdraw their money. As investors multiplied, he ran out of the product (coupons) and simply operated a *pyramid scheme* in which early customers were paid off with money obtained from later ones. Ponzi was living like a king and was rumored to have taken in over $15 million.

When later it was discovered that Ponzi had a criminal record which included forgery, the stack of cards fell. Investors demanded their money, but of course he had spent it all. After serving various sentences, he eventually died in 1971 in a Brazilian charity ward, but the legacy of Ponzi's technique lives on. Ponzi schemes prey upon victims who are greedy, who want something for nothing (Nash, 1975, vol. 2, pp. 337–341).

Pyramid Schemes

A pyramid scheme resembles the familiar chain letter which asks you to send a dollar to the first name on the list, add yours to the bottom, duplicate four copies of the new list, and recruit four new members to continue the chain. Assuming the chain is not broken, you could reap, for example, $256 in return for your original dollar investment. You earn $256 if the four people you recruited obtain four others each (16), and they secure four each (64), and they in turn find four others (256) who now all mail $1 to you (the name at the top of the list). The problem with such schemes is that they generally break down before reaching the bottom of the pyramid and usually provide rewards only to the initial organizers.

"Dare to Be Great"

In 1967 a sharecropper's son named Glenn Turner began a cosmetics firm which was called Koscot Interplanetary (Kosmetics for the Communities of Tomorrow) and became the messiah of a get-rich-quick pyramid scheme that eventually cost over one hundred thousand investors upwards of $44 million. The real problem with Turner's, as with most pyramid schemes, is that it assumed an infinite progression of new prospects. Maxa (1977, pp. 24–25) explains:

> . . . if the Koscotter brought one new salesman into the business a month, or 12 per year—a frequent figure given by Koscot executives—and each of these 12 brought in another 12, after a dozen such sets, the total number of cosmetics salespersons would be 8,916,100,448,256. Or more than 2,000 times the population of the world.

The selling of products was secondary to recruiting new salespersons. Turner would pick up the tab for round-trip flights and weekends for prospective "distributors" at one of his adventure seminars, which graduated in price from $300 to $400 to $1,300 to $3,000. Complaints from disgruntled investors finally forced most states to ban Turner's operations.

ABSCAM's Mel Weinberg

In the FBI sting operation ABSCAM, U.S. congressmen were caught red-handed in accepting bribes from what they thought were foreign interests (Greene, 1981). The man responsible for setting up these operations was a convicted swindler named Mel Weinberg, age fifty-five at the time, who had spent most of his life as a professional con artist. One of his "marks" had been singer Wayne Newton, whom Weinberg took for about $200,000 (The Man, 1980, p. 1–A). Prior to his conviction for fraud and participation in ABSCAM, he jet-setted around the world with a phony Lady Evelyn Knight, whom he introduced as one of the ten richest women in the world, whose family was in Swiss banking. Headquartered out of a rented office, his London Investors Limited "operated" on four continents. Wearing lavish clothes and claiming access to his private jet, Weinberg would offer to process loan applications for supposed millions in Arab oil money to which he claimed access. He charged up to $3,750 for processing each loan. Of course, no such arrangements were ever available, but Weinberg had only promised to "attempt" to arrange them.

Options Scam

Supervisors in Superman or gorilla costumes prowled the room lined with telephone salespersons urging them on, and bells or cheers rang out, as at a high school football rally, to greet each announcement of a sale (An Option to Run, 1978, p. 24). The scene was not a college telethon, but rather a Boston commodity options firm which had a clean bill of health with Dun & Bradstreet and the Better Business Bureau, and eleven branch offices throughout the U.S. It was also one of the biggest scams in history, grossing as much as $75 million, in a little over eighteen months, from hapless victims (Options Scam in Boston, 1978, p. 49) and run by a career criminal who had previously escaped from a New Jersey correctional facility, having been incarcerated for security scams. Alan Abrahams, using the name of James A. Carr, president of Lloyd, Carr, and Company, sold commodity option futures which he claimed were bought on the London Stock Exchange. Investors could buy futures of coffee, soybeans, and the like with the hope that the price would go up by harvest time. Carr apparently did not even bother to buy any futures on the London market, pocketing the money instead.

From "Maggot Mile" (in Fort Lauderdale, Florida) to "Con Man's Coast" (in Orange County, California) some highway corridors are strung with telephone swindlers who are getting rich playing "Dial-a-Dupe" (Cary, 1987). Operating telephone sales operations (called "boiler rooms") and employing ten to fifty slick talkers (known as "slammers"), they make their pitch very effectively. One California firm, Capital Trust, stole $50 million from two thousand persons. Advance fees to collect a "free" travel prize, oil and gas, gems and coins are all popular investments. Many "churn and burn" investors by constantly switching from one investment to another to collect broker fees (Ibid.).

Billie Sol Estes

In the early eighties the name Billie Sol Estes was once again in the news, along with the latest tales of large-scale financial swindles. Estes was still on probation for a 1965 conviction in an estimated $22 million rip-off of some of the top finance companies in the U.S. (Wade, 1976, pp. 78–88). A close friend of former President Johnson in the sixties, Estes had secured loans on the basis of false collateral: phony fertilizer tanks which he claimed he owned in Texas. Estes had farmers purchase the storage tanks on installment payments and then lease them back to him at the same price. He then sold the installment notes to finance companies, although less than two thousand of the thirty thousand claimed tanks existed. When inspectors arrived, he switched tanks and serial numbers so quickly that inspectors saw several tanks a number of times at different locations without knowing it. The latest charges against Estes accuse him of running a phony oil field steam-cleaner rental operation. On the previous conviction, he had served six years of a fifteen-year term.

Religious Cons

Today, a new source of big money in professional crime appears to be found in burgeoning religious cults. Although most are probably sincere operations, a number appear to be interested in capturing the minds, bodies, as well as assets of their members. The son of L. Ron Hubbard (1963), author of *Dianetics* and father of Scientology, a pseudo-religious movement, claimed recently that the organization was simply a front or con for the private aggrandizement of Hubbard, who used most of the organization's money to buy drugs (Scientology Fraud, 1983).

Hubbard employed his own private police force, the "guardians organization," to attack and harass enemies as well as defectors from the organization. His son also claimed that the guardians on one occasion broke into an IRS office in an attempt to steal records on people. Some of these religious groups recruit naïve young people, indoctrinate them often through classic resocialization techniques, keep them incommunicado from friends and relatives, and exploit their labor in order to build financial empires. Critics of many of these groups often resort to extreme measures themselves. One of the most controversial is Ted Patrick (1976), author of *Let Our Children Go*, who used unusual deprogramming tactics himself with former followers of such cults, and claims ". . . the groups we are talking about are not religious groups. These are plain crooks . . . 'con artists' . . . This is a multibillion dollar racket."

In this era of Elmer Gantry evangelism, mystic cults, charlatans, channelers, spoon-benders, and faith healers, psychics are

> . . . joined by people whose honesty is difficult to assess because they appeal to messages from supernatural sources to justify their asking for our money . . . [One] evangelist . . . told Americans that God would "take" him to another world if he did not receive $4.5 million in donations by April, 1987 (Nettler, 1989, p. 73).

In 1986 magician James Randi exposed psychic spoon-bender Uri Geller as a faker and also debunked faith healer Peter Popoff as using the old trick of "calling out" to people in an audience and listing their names, occupations, ailments, and other surprising personal information. Randi showed an audience on the Johnny Carson show how Popoff simply used confederates beforehand to garner information and transmit it to him into a tiny earpiece (Randi, 1988). Randi (in Jaroff, 1988, p. 72) indicates:

> Popoff says that God speaks directly to him because he's an anointed minister. Three things amaze me about that. First of all, it turns out that God's frequency—I didn't know that he used a radio—is 39.170 MHz, and that God is a woman and sounds exactly like Popoff's wife Elizabeth.

The PTL Scandal

In 1987 a major scandal broke, which would topple the PTL Ministry empire of televangelist Jim Bakker and his wife, Tammy Bakker. The Bakkers were charged by the IRS with drawing $9.3 million in excess pay and by other sources (ABC, 1987) with perpetrating the biggest

Jim and Tammy Bakker's PTL empire toppled when Bakker was convicted of defrauding his followers of millions of dollars.

religious fraud in history, with as much as $100 million of the church's funds siphoned off for their personal use. The high lifestyle was complete with an air-conditioned dog house. The last straw in the collapse of the Bakker operation was related to charges of sexual scandal. Bakker was removed from the ministry and defrocked (Carey, 1988).

Boosters

While con artists represent the "aristocracy of the professional criminal world," "boosters" (professional shoplifters) or "heels" represent the bottom. Among professional criminals, boosting is viewed as requiring less skill or talent and thus enjoys less status. One confidence man said of a booster: "While he is undoubtedly a professional thief, I should have been ashamed to be seen on the street with him. . . . My reputation would have suffered in the eyes of my friends to be seen in the company of a booster" (Adams, 1976, p. 76). Mary Cameron Owen's (1964) classic *The Booster and the Snitch,* distinguishes between the booster (professional) and snitch (amateur) shoplifter. Boosters carefully plan their operations for big "scores" in such a manner that they minimize risks and are able to sell their booty to a fence (dealer in stolen property). Snitches, on the other hand, often commit their crimes in a spur-of-the-moment fashion, with little planning, and take enormous risks in order to "five-finger discount" relatively inexpensive items for their own personal use.

Boosters often rely upon a variety of equipment and special paraphernalia such as "booster boxes" (ones with slots or removable sections for easy stealing), special scissors or razor blades for removing labels, and special "booster bags, coats, pants, skirts" with hidden compartments. Fat shoplifters may employ the "crotch walk" in which goods are actually held in suspension between their legs, hidden by long coats or dresses.

Professional shoplifters usually work in groups, with each individual having an assigned role. The stall "throws a hump" or creates a commotion in order to attract the attention of the store personnel, while the "clout" is the actual thief who may turn over the goods to a "cover" who may actually carry out the booty. Cameron describes the long-standing nature of such techniques by means of an English shoplifting expedition of 1597:

> The higher degrees and gentleman-lifts have to the performance of their facility three parties of necessity, the lift, the marker and the santar. The lift, attired in the form of a civil country gentleman, comes with the marker

into some mercer's shop . . . and there he calls to see a bolt of satin, velvet, or any such commodity . . . "Sirrah, reach me that piece of velvet" . . . and whilst the fellow turns his back he commits his garbage [stolen goods] to the marker. . . . The marker gives a wink to the santar, that walks before the window. . . . "Sir, a word with you . . . " "Truly sir," says the santar, "I have urgent business in hand, and as at this time I cannot stay." "But one word, and no more," says the marker, and then he delivers to him whatsoever the lift was conveyed to him; and then the santar goes on his way, who never came within the shop, and is a man unknown to them all" (cited in Adams, 1976, p. 78).

In what sounds like Charles Dickens' Fagin in *Oliver Twist*, a school for shoplifters, complete with a "how-to-do-it" manual, was discovered by police in New York City. About seventy-five boys ages eleven to fourteen were believed involved. They were trained in avoiding security at suburban shopping malls and sent on expeditions with shopping lists in hand (Hamilton, 1987). Since accurate statistics on shoplifting are poor, an estimate of the proportion perpetrated by professionals is hazardous. However, it is clear that professionals account for a small proportion.

The Cannon

Professional pickpockets (sometimes called "cannons" or "dips") require exceptional dexterity, quickness of hands, and awareness of the art of misdirection. Most pickpockets work with a "stall" who "puts up" (sets up) the "mark" (victim). This is usually accomplished by tripping against, bumping, or otherwise distracting the subject, while the "tool" or "claw" or "mechanic" actually hooks or steals. According to Stirling (1974, p. 105), authorities on the subject claim South Americans are the world's most skillful pickpockets. In the late eighties some large airports in the U.S. were plagued by gangs of thieves who specialized in pickpocketing and stealing from luggage-laden strangers. Speculation was that the theft gangs were graduates of the infamous "School of the Seven Bells," a shoplifting school of crime in Colombia. In order to graduate, students must steal items from the instructor's coat to which seven bells are attached. If a bell rings, the student flunks (Fry, 1986, p. 7-D). Since ancient times pickpockets have worked crowds, any event in which there is a large gathering of people, such as parades, carnivals, sporting events, and the like. In medieval Europe even during public executions of pickpockets, cannons "worked the crowds." Today, Derby day, Super Bowl week, and World's Fairs all attract a large influx of cannons.

The next time you attend a large sporting event, see if, with the practiced eye of a bunko squad detective, you can spot the possible cannons in the crowd. Look for the people who are continually watching the crowd rather than the event. Unless they are security personnel, they may very likely be cannons attempting to "set a mark."

Pickpockets usually work in groups of two, three, or four, with a specific role for each. One may select "marks" (victims), another locate the valuables or money on the person ("fanning") maneuvering him into position, then the theft and the passing off of the stolen item (Inciardi, 1977, 1983, and 1984).

Related to, but less skillful than pickpockets are "cutpurses," those who attempt to surreptitiously steal women's purses by cutting the purse straps. If such a theft involves rough stuff, such as shoving or physical force, the "cutpurse" has crossed the boundary from pickpocket to strong-armed robber or mugger. A related sneak thief is a "moll buzzer" who attempts to steal unattended purses in public places. Robert Dale (1974, pp. 73–74), a "cutpurse," relates:

> One friend of mine, known as Wimpy, does nothing but drift around the country, working fairs, holiday crowds, centennial celebrations, and various annual observances such as the Indianapolis 500 and the Kentucky Derby. He was in Chicago for the fair in 1933, in New York for the fair in 1939. . . . Like many another once-honored trade, the traditional art of the cutpurse has fallen upon evil times. The profession is now overrun with amateurs, heavyhanded louts of small talent and even smaller character who would be better employed on a rock pile.

Expert or class cannons have been estimated to have considerably declined in numbers from the pre-World War II period, when they numbered in the thousands, to as few as less than a thousand today (Inciardi, 1975, p. 21).

Professional Burglary

Shover (1973) interviewed 143 successful career burglars, some of whom were professionals. Such burglars typically worked in groups, although there may be constant turnover in the members from job to job. Critical connections for a professional burglar's success are tipsters, fixers, and fences. Tipsters provide information on likely targets in return for a portion of the take, while fixers are attorneys and bondsmen who use bribery to fix or ward off any prosecutions against the burglar. Fences or criminal receivers readily convert the burglar's booty into more portable cash. Many burglars rationalize their activities by claiming that most people are insured anyhow and that often, when they read of reports of their burglaries, the amount lost is inflated by the victim in order to cheat the insurance company.

Picking a lock is just one of the many skills of an able burglar. The best pick men may practice daily and are the first to buy and master the latest "burglar-proof" locks when they become available. Some take the locksmith correspondence courses that one sees advertised in magazines, and some are even licensed locksmiths. On entering premises, the skilled burglar will often jam a small object such as a match stick into the lock so that it will jam if the occupants unexpectedly return and insert their key.

While no clear criteria exist to distinguish professional from nonprofessional burglary, specific cases are the unmistakable work of skilled or able burglars. For example, Plate (1975, p. 20) describes some burglaries of jewelry firms in Manhattan in the seventies which involved feats such as breaking through two concrete walls and opening two huge safes without leaving even a fingerprint. In one job, the front windows were sprayed with black paint and in another the main cable serving a protection service alarm system was cut, affecting thousands of Manhattan customers.

"Chic Conwell," the professional thief in Sutherland's 1937 book, used the term "hotel prowler" to refer to burglars who specialize in stealing from hotel rooms. Such sneak thieves are particularly active in convention towns; they may pay off hotel employees who act as accomplices. One hotel prowler told Plate (Ibid., p. 50) that after first obtaining a master key from an accomplice, he would wait until 2:00 A.M., maintaining that at that hour few of the conventioneers were in their rooms sleeping and, if they were, they were so "bombed" they would not notice his presence. The only town he had problems in was Philadelphia, where he claimed the town was so dead at night that conventioneers stayed in their rooms and drank.

The Box Man

At the top of the hierarchy of burglars are safecrackers or "box men." Chambliss's (1975a) edition of professional safecracker Harry King's autobiography, *Box Man* (reissued as *Harry King: A Professional Thief's Journal* [King and Chambliss, 1984]), reveals that King ranks professional safecrackers, although a dying breed, with the big con artists as a high status calling within the professional criminal hierarchy.

The history of safe cracking has involved a constant escalation of technology, first to secure safes and second, in reaction, to develop better ways to "open" them. Box men are really professional burglars who specialize in breaking into safes. Between 1890 and 1940 professional burglary gangs flourished, hampered only by the newly developed burglar alarm. Telephones and automobiles were also beginning to narrow the apprehension gap (Rosberg, 1980, pp, 44, 52). As more and more sophisticated safes were developed, the methods employed to break into them improved. Since dynamite often damaged the safe contents, a core drill (a diamond-tipped construction device) provided more sophisticated means of entry, as did burning bars (an oxygen lance which burns up to temperatures of seven thousand degrees Fahrenheit).

The Professional Fence

The dilemma of a thief who makes a "big score" but who lacks ready connections of disposing of the goods was brought home to the author one evening in Cleveland while walking across a parking lot of a neighborhood shopping center. Two shady-looking characters blocked my path with their car, and the driver said, "Hey, sport, I have a bunch of cashmere sport coats in the back; and if we can find one that fits ya, I'll give you one helluva deal." Sure enough, glancing into the back seat I could see at least twenty boxes with a recognizable name in men's clothing on them. When I indicated a lack of interest, they shrugged, saying, "Suit yourself, sport," and drove off. Such amateurs without connections are not only in the business of stealing, but the even riskier business of soliciting unscreened customers in order to dispose of "hot" goods. More experienced and professional thieves would have disposed of the property soon after the offense with a reliable fence or receiver of stolen property.

A *fence* is an individual who buys and sells stolen property. Legitimate operators of pawnshops, second-hand antique shops, junkyards, and other general merchandisers may knowingly add stolen goods to their inventory, but a professional fence does this on a regular, persistent basis. Hall (1952) distinguishes between the "lay receiver" (customer), the "occasional receiver" (a rare buyer), and the "professional receiver" (a specialist in stolen property). Professional burglars could not operate on a long-term basis without reliable relationships with fences who are willing to buy large quantities of stolen property on short notice. Klockars (1974) describes how "Vince Swaggi," the professional fence he studied, was able to sell a lot of factory seconds and other legitimate merchandise to customers who assumed the goods were "hot" (stolen) and thus a bargain. Similar findings caused Steffensmeier (1986) to entitle his case study, *The Fence: In the Shadow of Two Worlds.*

Fences and other professional criminals also may obtain a certain degree of immunity of operation by acting as informants to the police. The importance of the fence to property criminals and sneak thieves is well illustrated by the relative success of police fencing sting operations which, after being set into operation for only a short time, are able to arrest large numbers of thieves.

The classic professional fence was an Englishman (by the name of Jonathan Wild), who operated in the early eighteenth century (Ibid., 1974). Wild took advertisements in the newspaper and claimed that he was a "thief-taker," that he could recover stolen goods. Wild paid thieves higher-than-usual fence prices for their booty and then sold the goods to the victims at considerable profit. Wild was a "double-dealer," building quite a reputation for turning in thieves as well as for fencing their goods. Finally, when some thieves accused him of being a fence, he was tried, found guilty, and hanged in 1725.

Blakey and Goldsmith (1976, pp. 1530–1535) identify four types of fences: the "neighborhood fence," the "outlet fence," the "professional fence," and the "master fence," each representing a more sophisticated form. The "neighborhood fence" is usually a small merchant who occasionally deals in stolen goods, while the "outlet fence" regularly sells "hot" merchandise along with legitimate stock. While using a legitimate company as a front, the "professional fence" is a major distributor of stolen articles. The "master fence" is involved at all levels, from organizing the theft to contacting customers in advance to distributing the goods; theft of art and museum masterpieces and their sale to wealthy private collectors may serve as one example. Plate (1975, p. 65) tells us that most fences determine the pricing for items they buy and sell by using the Sears and Roebuck wholesale catalog or, if pressed, calling the manufacturer directly, pretending to be an interested customer.

Paper Hanging

"Paper hanging" (passing bad checks and other documents) is a persistent form of professional crime. In the U.S., cash is becoming the poor man's credit card. A larger proportion of transactions are conducted by means of checks and credit cards, which create a ripe situation for the forger. Lemert (1958) distinguishes between "naïve check forgers" and professionals or "systematic forgers": the former are amateurs and only occasional offenders (as discussed in Chapter 7), while the latter make an illegal business of forging checks (see Klein and Montague, 1977). Lemert also found that forgers often operate independently and are less a part of the world of professional criminals than some other offenders (Lemert, 1958). Sutherland (1937) also claimed that forgers and counterfeiters were considered marginal in professional crime. One reason might be that such operators are often "loners" or "technicians" and thus do not share the professional criminal subculture (see Bloom, 1957).

Edward Wuensche of Philadelphia, a major fence in stolen securities, described his operations in testimony before the U.S. Senate Subcommittee on Investigations (cited in Pennsylvania Crime Commission, 1980, p. 175):

> I started in a life of crime at the approximate age of 23 . . . in the numbers business and advanced to other forms of criminal activity. . . . As I became more and more active in hustling stolen merchandise, passing bad checks, and so forth, I naturally gravitated to and became associated with other criminals. . . . I became so proficient at passing bad checks that I was nicknamed "The Paper Hanger". . . . The same people . . . who know each other and who traffic in stolen securities also deal with counterfeit or fraudulent securities. . . . From my experience, there may be as many as 500 persons in this country who are major suppliers or passers or fences of stolen securities who, among themselves, form an intricate and complicated web. . . .
>
> I have personally used the following methods to convert stolen securities to cash:
>
> 1. I have resold stolen securities through brokerage firms.
> 2. I have placed or caused to be placed stolen securities in banks as collateral for loans.
> 3. I have personally taken stolen securities, especially U.S. Treasury notes, outside the United States to Switzerland and other countries where they were placed in banks and other financial institutions.
> 4. I know of situations where stolen securities were placed in insurance company portfolios, both inside the United States and abroad. . . .
>
> In the late '50s, thieves never had any regard for paper. They used to throw it away, discard it, as if it were worthless rubbish. Then they found out they could get 10 or 15 percent for this paper, and then, of course, they went after it. . . .
>
> To the best of my knowledge, the bigger thefts in the securities field didn't start until the early 1960s. Prior to that time, we were in the business of counterfeiting them.

Perhaps one explanation for a decline in professional counterfeiting was related to journalist Tom Plate (1975, p. 163) by Mickey Cohen, a retired organized crime figure. When asked to react to the opinion that some crimes are reasonably secure and others are not, since they are too much an affront to authorities, Cohen responded: "That's right. If you go into anything that has to do with counterfeiting, for example, you have to contend with the Secret Service, not to mention the FBI and everyone else, you understand."

A growing area of professional fraud and counterfeiting relates to phony credit cards, records, tapes, and spare parts. The latter are produced in foreign factories and are reasonable facsimiles of the real thing. These pose few problems for those who purchase phony, inexpensive, "hot" watches from "Duke the Goniff" at the Greyhound station. They present major problems if they happen to be unsafe parts for airlines, elevators, and manufacturing machinery.

Law enforcement of the future is faced with an increasing sophistication in this area. For example, how do businesses control checks which an hour or two after being cashed decompose and disappear? A growing racket is that of "credit doctors," those who sell clean credit references to people with bad credit (Reibstein and Drew, 1988). Using computers, credit thieves can steal your good credit, identify and sell it to someone who has a similar name but now with your all-important social security number and good credit references. The latter, of course, will not remain "good" for long.

"Video Piracy," the massive production of fake video tapes, became a burgeoning industry of the late eighties. We are not talking here of people making tapes for their own personal use, but of well organized syndicates that can often hit the market with "knock-off copies" before the original manufacturer, with the latter losing an estimated $1 billion a year as a result. An estimated 15 percent of the movie videos on display in American stores are illegal (Pauly, Friday, and Foote, 1987).

Another example of the dangers of counterfeit products was the accusation in 1987 (Anderson and Van Atta, 1987) that bogus bolts made of cheaper alloys have either been found in or are believed to be in the nation's airliners, buildings, bridges, nuclear power plants, and military hardware.

In 1873 archeologist Heinrich Schliemann discovered the ancient remains of fabled Troy. Many of the treasures "found" at the site were later determined to be hoaxes, bought from dealers or brought from other sites. Art is now a major item of investment, but "art forgery" is not clearly defined in the the law (Haywood, 1987, p. 7). Besides estimates by Interpol, the U.S. Treasury Department and the New York Police Department's Fine Arts Squad, of some ten thousand stolen works of art on the market, the identication of forgeries has found even major art museums in confusion (Dutton, 1983; and Savage, 1976).

Professional Robbers

Professional robbers differ from most other professional criminals in that they threaten and are willing to use force if necessary. Also, in contrast to others, they need little specific training or skill to be a "stick-up artist." Professional "heavy" criminals of the present-day (Gibbons, 1977, p. 2), such as robbers, tend to band together for particular jobs, but only on a short-term basis. This is in sharp contrast to the Jesse James-type gangs of the Wild West or the Depression-era Bonnie-and-Clyde-type groups.

The most successful type of robbery today is most likely the hijacking of trucks (Glaser, 1978, p. 446). Writers such as Abadinsky (1983), Teresa (1973), and Walsh (1977) have all indicated increasing cooperation between professional and organized criminals particularly in the area of truck hijacking. Close relationships between crime syndicates and master and professional fences as well as syndicate infiltration of legitimate businesses enables a quick disposal of massive quantities of stolen goods (Blakey and Goldsmith, 1976, p. 1541). It appears that many hijackings are preplanned from the point of departure, using syndicate planning and professional robbers and fences as operatives. Blakey and Goldsmith (Ibid., p. 1547) also contend, as does Plate (1977), that most hijackings are actually "give ups," that is, the drivers, according to previous arrangement, deliver the truck to the thieves and then report it hijacked. Also according to Plate (Ibid.), contrary to popular impression, most hijackers do not wear masks. If the hijacking has not been prearranged, they will also take the driver's license or operating tag number, indicating that they will know where to get him if his memory is too good.

One major difference between amateur robbers and professional robbers is that the former tend to rob individuals while the latter tend to concentrate upon commercial establishments. Letkemann (1973), as a result of interviewing bank robbers, describes how many, in planning their jobs ("casing the joint," as they used to say in gangster English), were aided by the fact that many branch banks were architectural clones of each other. Such a similar layout plus practiced impression management, a persona that the robbers would utilize to verbally intimidate bank personnel and customers, made many "stick-ups" routine. Showing they meant business hopefully incapacitates resistance and enhances cooperation. In short, no one gets hurt. Professional robbers, in contrast to most other criminals, do not require as extensive subcultural support of other professional criminals in order to acquire skill and technique or in order to plan and execute their operations.

Professional Arsonists

Most arson is committed by amateurs or individuals who do not make a career out of burning down structures. However, there are professional arsonists. In the late seventies, Morris Klein was a member of a ring of torch artists who boasted, "I can make concrete burn" (Karchmer, 1977). Klein's ring, which sold a complete package of arson services to businesses, was responsible for hundreds of fires in several states. For a percentage of the insurance settlement, he could mobilize a team of engineers, torches, and insurance experts. He was "a fire broker who scouted around for troubled firms to sell. . . . If the business kept fumbling, Klein would approach the owner with an arson scam proposal. . . . He informed clients that their buildings were burning with the code message, 'The sky is red.'" (Ibid.)

Professional Auto Theft Rings

While most of us carefully guard and secure our valuables, one of our most expensive investments, an automobile, is often sitting unguarded on the streets or in a parking lot. While most automobiles are stolen by amateur juveniles for joyriding purposes, a significant number are stolen by auto theft rings and either chopped up for parts or refinished, complete with new papers and serial numbers, and sold to a waiting market. While professionals organize such rings, the greatest risk— actually stealing the cars—is done by young car thieves who may even be given shopping lists for specific makes or models (Savitz, 1959).

Some car thieves are professionals who may possess standard burglary tools and master keys. Plate (1975, p. 28) indicates that Porsche master keys may go for several thousand dollars. Master keys may be duplicated from those bought from showroom employees, for instance. Another tool is a "slam hammer" or "bam bam" instrument, which is usually used to pull dents out of cars. Thieves can use this tool for heisting a car by inserting one end of the small hammer over the door lock of a car, which enables the entire door lock to be removed in seconds. Looking at the code number on the lock and using an auto code key book and key cutter, the thief can prepare the exact key for the auto in less than two minutes (Ibid., pp. 29–30).

The thief's job ends when the car is left at the drop-off spot, usually a local shopping center. Runners or "gophers" (go-fors) transport the car to the shop. New plates can easily be obtained from states with lax inspection laws. Using a die tool, new numbers can be etched into the vehicle identification number, which can be found die-cast to various parts of the car. Dishonest junk yards can also furnish registration cards which can serve as false ownership credentials. Other auto theft rings operate "chop shops," where the stolen auto is immediately cannibalized for parts and sold to legitimate repair shops which can now, due to low overhead, underbid competitors on repair work. Obviously, professional auto thieves vary in their operations, sophistication, and organization.

The Youngstown Gang

It has been suggested throughout this text that the types of crime studied are "ideal types," heuristic overgeneralizations, and that in fact most criminals, including professional criminals, do not restrict their criminal operations to their preferred specialty. Our example of the "Youngstown Gang" provides such an illustration.

The all-purpose nature of professional criminals is provided in an examination of a professional theft ring that operated in Youngstown, Ohio, in the sixties and seventies (Pennsylvania Crime Commission, 1980, pp. 168–169). The Youngstown Gang was primarily involved in burglaries but also took part in armed robbery, burglary, bank robbery, hijacking, counterfeiting, forgery, and the sale of stolen credit cards and money orders. According to informant and former member James Wardrop, the ring was aided by police officers as well as members of the La Rocca (Pittsburgh) syndicate. The "working crew" was generally stable and spent little time planning operations, due to excellent tipsters and setup men and reliable fences. Composed of twenty to thirty professional criminals, eight to ten crews committed three to four burglaries and robberies per month.

Primary targets were furs, frozen meats, guns, securities, televisions, gold, silver, rare coins, and—most of all—cash. Using police scanner radios to monitor police calls and walkie-talkie contacts between burglars and lookouts, the gang exercised considerable caution in their operation. Wardrop claims the police acted as tipsters in about half of the thefts which his ring committed. Describing a job in Aliquippa, Pennsylvania (near Pittsburgh), he indicated (Ibid., 1980, p. 168):

> The chief of police of a local municipality took us and showed us the township building. . . . He showed us a warehouse full of copper. He showed us a TV store—none of which we liked, but they had a house in Aliquippa, and the owner also owned a tire shop and he told us the owner bought truckloads of hot tires and he kept—I think the sum was $20,000 in the house at all times to buy truckloads of hot tires.
>
> So he took us down and showed us the house and told us how many people to expect and which night it had to be hit because the tires were purchased on a certain night of the week.

The chief received 10 percent of the $11,000 in cash gained in the burglary. Interestingly, Wardrop indicates that almost all of the fences and tipsters they dealt with were members of the "Outfit" (organized crime). Many professional criminals operate closely with or have permission of organized crime groups in their area (see Teresa, 1973b).

Professional Killers

Professional assassins, "hit men," are a popular subject of fiction and undoubtedly a few do in fact exist, for instance, in the shady world of international espionage. Most organized crime executions appear to be assignments to members in addition to their ordinary tasks. Even members of *Murder Inc.* did not spend most of their criminal time in executions. While undoubtedly professional murderers exist, the literature is either scant or unreliable in providing a reasonable picture.

Poachers

Poachers are those who violate game laws and kill animals, many of which are on the protected list or are quickly becoming extinct. Black bears, coyotes, elk, eagles, mountain lions, and desert big horn sheep are hunted to near extinction usually for sport or their trophy value. In Africa endangered species such as rhinoceros are gunned down with AK-47s and their horns cut off with chain saws. Elephant poachers, also after horns, utilize rocket-launchers and grenades. Professional rings of poachers kill not only animals, but game wardens. Kenya has lost 98 percent of its rhino population since 1970 (Ransdell, 1989). Ivory and rhino horn are highly prized for medicinal and believed aphrodisiac qualities in the Orient.

Criminal Careers of Professionals

Reviews of the use of the term "professional criminal" in the field of criminology (Staats, 1979; and Winslow, 1970), point at the heavy reliance upon case studies and popular sources. Anthologies such as Bruce Jackson's (1972) *In the Life* and Duane Denfeld's (1974) *Streetwise Criminology* are illustrative. These provide firsthand accounts, primarily by incarcerated criminals, of their lives in crime. While these are revealing, it is unclear as to how typical such accounts may be. Given this methodological limitation, much of the description of criminal careers

A survey team inspects an elephant killed by poachers. Ivory poachers are driving the African elephant to the brink of extinction.

of professional criminals is limited and certainly requires more investigation.

Indicating that professional criminals may not be specialists in any one area of crime, Plate (1975, pp. 7–10) identifies ten characteristics of professional criminals:

1. They seek anonymity.
2. They are often on speaking terms with police as informants, bribers, or simply as those who share a similar area of work.
3. They are not necessarily members of organized crime, although they cooperate in some cities.
4. They are usually not drug addicts.
5. They take arrests and prisons in stride, often putting money away for a rainy day.
6. They do not leave fingerprints.
7. When possible, they will run through a crime (practice it) beforehand.
8. They are well aware of the law and police clearance rates.
9. Most avoid gaudy display or conspicuous consumption.
10. Many are stable, family men.

While some professional criminals, such as hired killers or professional robbers, are into "heavy" crimes, most attempt to avoid rough stuff, to avoid "heat," to operate through wit, guile, cunning, technical skill, and "grifting." Most professional criminals look with disdain upon the tactics and senseless violence of amateur criminals. Professionals plan and carefully choose their victims in order to maximize the score and minimize risks.

A criminal does not usually simply decide one day that he or she is going to be a professional criminal. Recognition, skill, and contact with other hustlers and professionals is a prerequisite; without this contact, the required knowledge and experience for a successful move into professional crime is less likely. Recruits into the world of professional crime may come from the ranks of hotel workers, waitresses, and cab drivers as well as pimps, fences, and promising conventional property criminals. While in early history, professional training schools such as Fagin's in *Oliver Twist* did, in fact, exist, today the training appears to be much more informal, although the nation's prisons appear to operate as a major training ground for some.

A leading explanation of professional criminality is Sutherland's (Sutherland and Cressey, 1978, pp. 80–83) "differential association" theory. In explaining patterns of professional criminality, the theory would point to the criminal contacts (values and attitudes) as essential in the learning process. Some professional criminals, particularly cannons, con artists, and professional burglars, participate in an informal apprenticeship of jobs, learning very specific skills and make the indispensable contacts with fixers and fences without which they would have great difficulty in operating. Letkemann (1973) sees this "crime as work" orientation among professional criminals as involving not only the learning of technical skills, but just as importantly social and organizational skills such as victim management. An important component of professional criminality is the shared subculture which requires frequenting common haunts (bars, restaurants, and the like) in order to discover "what's going down" or "what's happening."

Compared with other categories of criminal activity, professional crime is rare and perhaps becoming more rare. Generally, most professional criminals come from better economic backgrounds than conventional or organized criminals. Many begin their careers at a later age. This varies, however, with the area of criminality. Safecrackers and bank robbers, for instance, appear to require early juvenile crime experience (Conklin, 1981, p. 265). Maurer (1964) describes the professional criminal as one who approaches crime in a businesslike manner, expecting to earn his or her living from it. Professional criminals are known to and know other professional criminals. Such criminals highly identify with criminal activity and are proud that they are good at their work. Many professional criminals rationalize their activity, feeling that all people are crooked or involved in what Al Capone called "the legitimate rackets." As Mel Weinberg, the ABSCAM consultant, put it: "I'm a swindler . . . the only difference between me and the congressmen I met on this case is that the public pays them a salary for stealing" (The Man Behind ABSCAM, 1980, p. 1–A). Con artists justify their behavior on the basis of the dishonest behavior of many of their victims, who may be trying to avoid taxes or buy stolen goods.

Informants from the ranks of professional crime as early as Sutherland's (1937, pp. 2–42) "Chic Conwell" have indicated that, while cannons tend to restrict their criminal activities to their specialty of pickpocketing, most others "hustle" or engage in a variety of offenses, even though they may prefer their specialty. Boosters and paper hangers appear to be more similar to cannons in attempting to stick to their specialty.

While there is specialization within professional crime, most "hustle" or continually explore a variety of opportunities to make a "score." Journalist Tom Plate (1975), for example, relates the story of an occasion in which he was having lunch with a very wealthy and successful professional criminal during which Plate excused himself to make a telephone call. Upon returning he happened to mention that the pay phone had erringly given him back his dime. The criminal shot up and began to mercilessly beat on the phone in hopes of additional coins. Plate viewed this as the epitome of the criminal mind. On the basis of his case studies of "uncaught professional criminals," Plate (Ibid., p. 108) claims that:

> There is now a generation gap in the criminal world. The traditional career paths to profitable positions in the profession are being scrapped by youngsters with get-rich-quick schemes. The primary short cut is through illegal drugs. As long as the dope industry is a relatively wide-open game, their path will become a well-traveled route to the pot of gold at the end of the rainbow.

Societal Reaction

Most experts on the subject see professional criminality as declining since its heyday during the Depression. This decline may simply represent an increase in semi-legal enterprises (Roebuck and Windham, 1983). Bank robbery for the most part has passed into the hands of amateurs. There appear to be fewer big-time con artists around than previously. Pickpockets, although still around, have been replaced by muggers. Female involvement in bunko operations has increased considerably in the post-World War II period. Inciardi (1975) suggests that the decline of professional crime began in the 1940s with the application of modern communication and scientific identification in the field of criminal investigation. Computerized information, fingerprints, regional cooperation in law enforcement, and greater professionalization of criminal justice "raised the ante" for a career in crime.

As previously described, most professional criminals attempt to commit crimes which are difficult to track and their operations are often characterized by use of specialists for each element of the job. Since most criminals, even the best, are eventually caught, the more sophisticated professionals will attempt to forestall action by victims or the criminal justice system (put in the fix) by gaining the cooperation of corrupt officials: crooked judges, court administrators, lawyers, or police officers; the latter, for instance, could convince victims of the futility of attempting to proceed with a case and offer immediate compensation. According to the President's Commission on Law and the Administration of Justice (1967, p. 154), two essential elements which explain the success of professional crime are "the fix" and "the fence." Yet another element should be added: a steady demand for stolen goods. Without a ready market, much professional theft would dry up.

The traditional public view of burglary and thievery is that the perpetrators of these crimes are unorganized and are reduced to crime to support a drug or gambling habit. However, 90 percent of the dollar value of objects taken is stolen by crime rings, although those rings are responsible for only 10 percent of the incidents of burglary (Pennsylvania Crime Commission, 1980, p. 167).

Many professional criminals charge that the high price of legal representation contributes to the high crime rate in the United States. They claim that many criminals have to commit additional crimes to afford the high legal fees, as well as other costs, like "the fix." While the operations of professional criminals, too often celebrated in fictional accounts, continue to fascinate, it appears unlikely that this line of criminality will again rival its heyday during the Great Depression.

Most discussions of white collar crime by organizations such as the U.S. Chamber of Commerce or federal law enforcement such as the FBI concentrate upon areas we have discussed in this chapter as professional crime, particularly the work of confidence artists. This would suggest that the most serious white collar crimes are committed by "hustlers," "fast buck artists," actors who are clearly foreign to standard business practices. In fact, such operations, although a serious concern, are relatively minor compared to pervasive and economically more costly operations which are incidental sidelines of legitimate business enterprise where many of the same tactics are employed.

Summary

In sociology, *profession* refers to occupations which possess useful knowledge and a claimed service orientation for which they are granted autonomy. In this light, the term "professional" may be an inappropriate tag with which to designate skilled, able grifters, or intensive career criminals. However, it is so widely used in the literature that not to use the concept would be more confusing than to employ it. Sutherland's classic work on the subject, *The Professional Thief* (1937), describes some characteristics of professional criminals as including: crime as sole livelihood, planning, technical skills, codes of behavior, high status, and an ability to avoid detection. Professional crime is a sociological rather than legal entity.

The argot (specialized jargon) of the professional world was described, using both Elizabethan and Depression-era American terms. Some examples of the latter included: cannons (pickpockets), heels (sneak thieves), boosters (shoplifters), the con (confidence games). A continuum *model of professional crime* views crime as being more professional the greater the degree to which it possesses the following chracteristics: sole livelihood, extensive career, skill, high status, avoidance of detection, criminal subculture, planning, and "the fix." "*The fix*" refers to the ability to avoid prosecution by compromising the criminal justice process. *Scam* refers to various criminal techniques or hustles. Professional crime differs from occupational/corporate crime in that in the case of the former, crime is the sole purpose of a business. Some examples of professional crime from Edelhertz's typology were presented, most of which tend to be examples of fraud.

Some professional crime might be described as *semiprofessional* in that it involves less skill and planning. Sometimes called "*bunko*" or "*flim flam*" or "*short con*" operations, these scams include: the pigeon drop, the badger scam, the bank examiner's scam, the Spanish prisoner's scam, the Murphy, various postal frauds, circus grifting, "boojo" (a gypsy con game), and various home improvement frauds practiced by groups such as the Williamson clan.

The "*big con*" involves far more skill, elaborate planning, higher-status victims, as well as much larger rewards for the criminal. Examples were provided of Ivar Kreuger, "Yellow Kid" Weil, Hartzell's "Drake Society" swindle, a fake Hitler's diary, and a fake Hughes biography. *Ponzi schemes* are frauds in which early investors in a nonexistent product are paid high dividends on the basis of money obtained from later investors. *Pyramid schemes* involve schemes by which investors must seek and continue a chain of other investors in order to reap a promised high return. Glenn Turner's "Dare to Be Great" organization serves as an example, as does the "circle of gold." Other examples of big con operations included Weinberg of ABSCAM fame, the options scam, Billie Sol Estes, and religious cons.

Various professional criminal trades were described, such as those of boosters, cannons, professional burglars, the box men, fences, paper hangers, robbers, arsonists, and auto thieves. The lack of specialization or tendency of professional criminals to "hustle" was illustrated by means of the Youngstown gang.

Descriptions of criminal careers of professional criminals is methodologically limited by the need to rely upon case studies and popular sources for many accounts. Most professional criminals seek anonymity, know the police and members of organized crime, are very deliberate in plying their trade, and avoid conspicuous consumption. They avoid rough stuff and "heat" and attempt to minimize risks. Requiring skill and contact with others, most seek subcultural support as suggested in Sutherland's "differential association" theory. *Professional criminals are a rare and a dying species.*

The professionalization of criminal justice has appeared to reduce many of the previous opportunities available in professional crime. The President's Commission on Law Enforcement and the Administration of Justice (1967) points to the importance of two essential elements which explain the success of professional crime: "the fence" and "the fix." The high cost of legal defense also may in fact be responsible for a portion of such crime.

KEY CONCEPTS

Professional Crime	Paper Hanging	Ponzi Schemes
Profession	Model of Professional Crime	Pyramid Schemes
Features of Professional Crime	Scams	Boojo
Argot	Pigeon Drop	Options Scam
Cannon	Confidence Games	Grifting
Heel	Badger Game	Box Man
Booster	Bank Examiner's Scam	Fence
Pennyweighting	Spanish Prisoner's Scam	The Fix

9

Occupational Crime

White Collar Crime—the Classic Statement ———

Although previously discussed in the popular literature, the concept of *white collar crime* was first introduced in the social sciences by Edwin Sutherland in a 1939 presidential address to the American Sociological Association. Defining white collar crime as "a crime committed by a person of respectability and high social status in the course of his occupation" (Sutherland, 1940), Sutherland's address was important in that it was the first major statement on white collar crime in academic criminology. Volk (1977, p. 13) describes Sutherland's pioneering effort as "the sign of a Copernican revolution in Anglo-Saxon criminology," a radical reorientation in theoretical views of the nature of criminality. Mannheim (1965, p. 470) felt that if there were a Nobel Prize in criminology, Sutherland deserved one for his effort. It certainly represented, to use Kuhn's (1962) notion, "a paradigm revolution," a new model that served to radically reorient future theoretical and empirical work in the field.

Sutherland's (1949) investigation using records of regulatory agencies, courts, and commissions found that of the seventy largest industrial and mercantile corporations studied over a forty-year period, every one violated at least one of the laws and had an adverse decision made against them related to false advertising, patent abuse, wartime trade violations, price-fixing, fraud, and intended manufacturing and sale of faulty goods. Many of these corporations were recidivists with an average of roughly eight adverse decisions issued for each. On the basis of his analysis, it becomes obvious that, although he used the general label of "white collar crime," Sutherland was in fact primarily interested in organizational or corporate crime.

Sutherland maintained that while "crime in the streets" attracted headlines and police attention, the extensive and far more costly "crime in the suites" proceeded relatively unnoticed. Despite the fact that white collar crimes cost several times more than other crimes put together, most cases were not treated under the criminal law. White collar crime differs from lower class criminality only in the implementation of criminal law which segregates white collar criminals administratively from other criminals (Ibid.). Furthermore, "white collar crime" is a sociological rather than legal entity. It is the status of the offender rather than legal uniqueness of the crime which is important.

Related Concepts

One of the earliest scholars to discuss types of behaviors that later would be described as white collar crime was Edward Ross (1907) in an article that appeared in *The Atlantic Monthly*. Borrowing a term used by Lombroso (Lombroso-Ferrero, 1972), Ross referred to "criminaloids" as "those who prospered by flagitious [grossly wicked] practices which may not yet come under the ban of public opinion" (Ross, 1907, p. 46). Describing the criminaloid as "secure in his quilted armor of lawyer-spun sophistries" (Ibid., p. 32), Ross viewed such offenders as morally insensible, and concerned with success but not with the proper means of achieving it. C. Wright Mills used a similar notion, "*the higher immorality*," to characterize this moral insensibility of the power elite. Mills felt this was a continuing, institutionalized component of modern American society, involving corrupt, unethical, and illegal practices by the wealthy and powerful (Mills, 1952).

In a literature review, Italian criminologists di Gennaro and Vetere (1977) addressed the problem of arriving at an adequate international concept and appropriate definition of white collar crime. They discovered that serious and negligible acts by the powerful were often lumped together with terms such as "criminality of barons," "criminal capitalists," "criminality of gentlemen," "occupational crimes," "criminality of corporations and bureaucracies," "white-collar delinquents," "business crime," "economic crime," and "gilded crime." They also found that international councils such as the Council of Europe and the United Nations had been unable to arrive at satisfactory conceptual or definitional agreement (Ibid.).

Sutherland's (1949, p. 9) initial concept of "white collar crime," defined as "a crime committed by a person of respectability and high social status in the course of his occupation," has been criticized on a number of points, mainly relating to: the unclear importance attached to the status of the offender, the exact meaning of the status of the offender, and the fact that such "crime" includes deviant behaviors which are not necessarily illegal (Quinney, 1964, p. 285). All of these criticisms are on target; however, the importance of Sutherland's concept lies not in its scientific utility but rather in its sensitizing quality. It alerted us to a phenomenon and, as a result, the field of criminology will never be the same. Vantage Point 9.1 outlines the Pandora's box of definitions that have appeared to describe elements of this "white collar crime phenomenon."

Chapters 9 and 10 concentrate on two key types of criminal activity: occupational criminal behavior and corporate (organizational) criminal behavior. *Occupational crime* refers to personal violations that take place for self-benefit during the course of a legitimate occupation, while *corporate (organizational) criminal behavior* refers to crimes by business or officials that are committed on behalf of the employing organizations. Though organizational crime refers to crime on behalf of the organization, it becomes corporate (business) crime when done for the benefit of a private business. Thus much of what ordinarily would be branded as corporate (business) crime in a free enterprise economy is labeled organizational crime when committed by state bureaucrats in

---

Vantage Point

Vantage Point 9.1—"White Collar Crime": Varieties of Definitions

Sutherland's initial concept of "white collar crime" has been found unscientific. But the many proposed substitutes, synonyms, variations, and related terms are confusing, too. Here are some of them:

Avocational crime is crime which is deterrable by the prospect of public labeling as a criminal, committed by one who does not think of himself as a criminal and whose major source of income or status is something other than crime (Geis, 1974a, p. 273)

Corporate crime consists of the offenses committed by corporate officials for their corporations and the offenses of the corporation itself (Clinard and Quinney, 1973, p. 188).

Economic crime refers to any nonviolent, illegal activity which principally involves deceit, misrepresentation, concealment, manipulation, breach of trust, subterfuge, or illegal circumvention (American Bar Association, 1976).

Occupational crime consists of offenses committed by individuals for themselves in the course of their occupations and of offenses of employees against their employers (Clinard and Quinney, 1973, p. 188).

Organizational crime involves illegal actions taken in accordance with operative organizational goals that seriously (physically or economically) harm employees, consumers, or the general public (Schrager and Short, 1978, pp. 411–412).

Professional crime is illegal behavior for economic gain or even for economic livelihood which involves a highly developed criminal career, considerable skill, high status among criminals, and fairly successful avoidance of detection (Clinard and Quinney, 1973, p. 246).

Upperworld crime refers to lawbreaking acts committed by those who, due to their position in the social structure, have obtained specialized kinds of occupational slots essential for the commission of these offenses (Geis, 1974b, p. 114).

socialist systems. The organizational, economic crimes discussed in this chapter are also distinct from political crimes by government, which will be discussed in Chapter 11; the latter have more to do with efforts to maintain power, ideology, and social control than with economic advantage.

The Measurement and Cost of Occupational Crime

In totalitarian societies, the problem of measurement of elite, organizational, and many economic crimes is resolved quite simply: the government denies their existence and fails to keep any such crime records. Even in societies that permit a measure of freedom of information, the collection of accurate data on most occupational and corporate crimes is difficult. Our primary sources of data (discussed in Chapters 2 and 3), such as official statistics (the UCR), victim surveys (the NCS), and self-reports, generally do not include much information on corporate or upper-level occupational crimes.

Problems faced by researchers who attempt to examine occupational crime include:

1. The higher professions are self-regulating, and very often codes of silence and protectionism rather than sanctions greet wrongdoers.
2. Many employers simply ask for resignations from errant workers in order to avoid scandal and recrimination.
3. Occupational crime statistics simply are not kept on a systematic basis by criminal justice agencies or by professional associations.
4. Probes of occupational wrongdoing by outsiders are usually greeted by secrecy or a professional version of "honor among thieves."

For all of these reasons, estimates of the cost of "white collar crime" (which includes corporate crime as well as much occupational crime) are hazardous. This remains an area where criminologists still rely upon anecdotes and secondary sources, primarily because much of the hard data simply is not readily available. Estimates of the cost of white collar crime do not appear in standard official reports such as the UCR.

Figure 9.1 provides an example of one attempt to appraise the cost of white collar crime in 1976. In the pie chart, the revenues estimated by the Senate Subcommittee on Investigations are broken down into percentages of the total. By this reckoning, the largest source of criminal income is derived from consumer fraud (Senate Permanent Subcommittee, 1979, p. 372). While these were conservative total estimates of roughly $36 billion in 1976, estimates for the early 1980s place the figure at $50 billion and upwards, a costly sum considering that FBI estimates for all UCR property crimes such as burglary, larceny, and robbery were in the $10 billion range in the early 1980s (Webster, 1984). Much higher white collar crime revenue estimates have been made by the Judiciary Subcommittee on Antitrust and Monopoly, which put the figure between $174 billion and $231 billion annually in the late seventies

Figure 9.1: White Collar Crime Revenues

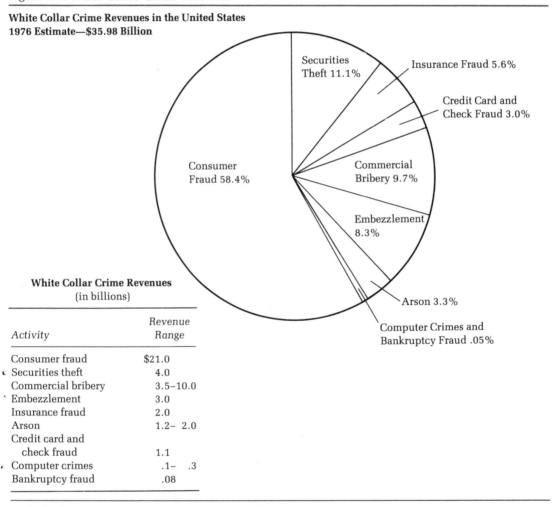

White Collar Crime Revenues in the United States
1976 Estimate—$35.98 Billion

Securities Theft 11.1%

Insurance Fraud 5.6%

Credit Card and Check Fraud 3.0%

Consumer Fraud 58.4%

Commercial Bribery 9.7%

Embezzlement 8.3%

Arson 3.3%

Computer Crimes and Bankruptcy Fraud .05%

White Collar Crime Revenues
(in billions)

Activity	Revenue Range	
Consumer fraud	$21.0	
Securities theft	4.0	
Commercial bribery	3.5–10.0	
Embezzlement	3.0	
Insurance fraud	2.0	
Arson	1.2– 2.0	
Credit card and check fraud	1.1	
Computer crimes	.1–	.3
Bankruptcy fraud	.08	

Source: Testimony of Jack Key before the Senate Permanent Subcommittee on Investigation, Committee on Governmental Affairs, 1979, 96th Congress, First Session, December 7, 11, 12, 13 and 14, p. 372. (Key is a staff person for the subcommittee.)

(Clinard and Yeager, 1980, p. 8). Rather than quibble over a few billion dollars here or there, the point is that the cost of white collar crimes far exceeds the cost of traditional crimes as recorded in official police statistics and as previously presented in Chapter 1.

The History of Corporate, Organizational, and Occupational Crime

Current publicity and concern with corporate, organizational, and occupational crime sometimes creates the false impression that such activities did not exist in the past. Nothing could be further from the truth. In fact, history is replete with examples of past corporate wrongdoing; current business climates probably have higher moral expectations than in the past.

The early annals of capitalism and the Industrial Revolution found fortunes made by unscrupulous "robber barons," who viewed the state and laws as negotiable nuisances. Cornelius Vanderbilt, the U.S. railroad magnate, when once asked whether he was concerned with the legality of one of his operations, was quoted as having stated: "Law! What do I care about Law! Hain't I got the power?" (cited in Browning and Gerassi, 1980, p. 201). Though conflict criminologists have tended to concentrate upon corporate and occupational crime in capitalist societies, organizational and occupational crimes most likely have accounted for the bulk of crime in society, East or West, capitalist or socialist, since ancient times. The political murders of millions to force the acceptance of new economic arrangements in Stalin's Russia serve as but one example.

Journalistic "muckrakers" or specialists in exposing what Becker calls "sex, sin and sewage" (Becker, 1954, p. 145) preceded criminologists in analyzing abuses in high places. Works such as Lincoln Steffens's *The Shame of the Cities* (1904) and Upton Sinclair's *The Jungle* (1906) dramatically focused upon and aroused public attention to corruption and abuse in public and private organizations. Galbraith tells the story of John D. Rockefeller, the founder of the family fortune, and a lecture he was fond of giving to Sunday school classes: "The growth of a large business is merely the survival of the fittest . . . The American Beauty rose can be produced in the splendor and fragrance which bring cheer to its beholder only by sacrificing the early buds which grow up around it" (Peter, 1977, p. 87). Browning and Gerassi (1980) in *The American Way of Crime* claim that the period between the Civil War and World War I was probably the most corrupt in American history and describe this time as a "dictatorship of the rich." No one valued private property

Cornelius Vanderbilt,
U.S. railroad baron, was
an early example of a
corporate leader who
believed power and
influence superseded
the law.

more than the industrial magnates who were stealing it (Ibid., p. 210). Jay Gould, a captain of industry, gobbled up railroads through stock manipulation, rate wars, the falsifying of profit records, and the intimidation of competitors by means of hired thugs such as the Hell's Kitchen mob (Ibid., pp. 133–136). Myers (1936, pp. 13, 17) in his *History of Great American Fortunes* reports an episode in which Russel Sage and business associates masterminded a swindle against their creditors; after it succeeded, Sage conned his own partners out of their proceeds from the caper.

Political corruption, bribery, kickbacks, and influence-peddling among political officeholders—federal, state, and local—has been rife since the very beginnings of the republic. The widespread acceptance of such corruption has given rise to a number of humorous comments, for example, the description of Mayor Curley of Boston as having been so crooked that when they buried him, they had to screw him into the ground. Another cynical remark claims that it was so cold the other day that the politicians had their hands in their own pockets.

In the post-Civil War period in the U.S., political machines were epitomized by "Boss" Tweed's Tammany Hall (New York City's Democratic Party) in which widespread vice and corruption were combined with political favors and voting. More than one political election has been won with stuffed ballot boxes or the graveyard vote. Ross (1988) in *Fall From Grace: Sex, Scandal and Corruption in American Politics From 1702 to the Present* documents the fact that political scandal has struck in nearly every decade since before the American Revolution.

Foremost conservative economist Milton Friedman, in his *Capitalism and Freedom* (1962, pp. 133–136), makes the point that business has no social responsibility beyond making profits for its members and stockholders; it is up to the rest of us to regulate and control this single-mindedness by pressuring legislatures to pass laws to prevent abuse. What, however, is the public to do if they lack the power and funds that special interest groups possess to bend the ear or grease the palms of politicians?

Typologies of "White Collar Crime"

One useful typology of occupational and organizational crime is that suggested by Bloch and Geis (1970, p. 301), who distinguish between offenses committed:

1. by individuals as individuals (for example, lawyers, doctors, and so forth);
2. by employees against their employers (for example, embezzlers);
3. by policy-making officials for the employers (for example, antitrust cases);
4. by agents of the corporation against the general public (for example, in false advertising); and
5. by merchants against customers (for example, in consumer frauds).

Another widely cited typology of "white collar crime" is proposed by Edelhertz (1970, pp. 19–20). He identifies:

1. crimes by persons operating on an individual ad hoc basis (for example, income tax violations, credit card frauds, bankruptcy frauds, etc.);
2. crimes committed in the course of their occupations by those operating inside business, government, or other establishments, in violation of their duty of loyalty and fidelity to employers or clients (for example, embezzlement, employee larceny, payroll padding, and the like);
3. crimes incidental to, and in furtherance of, business operations, but not central to the purpose of the business (for example, antitrust violations, commercial bribery, food and drug violations, and so forth);

4. white-collar crime as a business, or as the central activity. (This is covered in this text under the label "professional crime"; it refers to activities such as medical and health frauds, advance fee swindles, and phony contests).

Eliminating Edelhertz's item 4 as more appropriately an example of professional crime and combining elements of both Bloch and Geis, and Edelhertz, Figure 9.2 proposes an *"Occupational/Organizational Crime Grid"* which classifies the crimes in terms of both perpetrators and victims. Goff and Reasons (1986) have proposed a similar model for organizational crime.

Figure 9.2: The Occupational Organizational Crime Grid

		Criminal *Crime Committed by:*		
		Individuals *(Public, Consumer)*	*Employee*	*Organization* *(Corporation, State)*
Victim Crime Committed against	Individuals (Public, Consumer)	(1) Merchant vs. Consumer Professional vs. Client	(2) Individual Corruption, Payoffs	(3) Production of Unsafe Products Deceptive Advertising
	Employee	(4)	(5) Sweetheart Contracts	(6) Occupational Health and Safety Violations Environmental Hazards on Job
	Organization (Corporation, State)	(7) Insurance Fraud Tax Fraud	(8) Embezzlement Inside Trading	(9) Industrial Espionage Unfair Competition Patent Violations

Type	Description
(1)	Individual vs. Individual (Public)
*(2)	Employee vs. Individual (Public)
(3)	Organization vs. Individual (Public)
*(4)	Individual vs. Employee
*(5)	Employee vs. Employee
(6)	Organization vs. Employee
*(7)	Individual vs. Organization
(8)	Employee vs. Organization
(9)	Organization vs. Organization

*These crimes may not have direct corporate or occupational ramifications.

The types of occupational/organizational crime are:

- *Type 1 — Individual vs. Individual Crime.* These refer only to crimes committed in relationship to one's occupation, such as merchants cheating consumers or professionals taking illegal advantage of clients.
- *Type 2 — Employee vs. Individual Crime.* These are crimes by an employee against individuals such as the receipt or payment of bribes and payoffs for the personal benefit of the employee and to the disadvantage of the public or individuals.
- *Type 3 — Organization vs. Individual Crime.* These are organizational crimes against individuals such as deceptive advertising, the production and sale of unsafe products, and the like. (The public and consumers are included in the notion of individuals.)
- *Type 4 — Individual vs. Employee Crime.* This type may not exist with respect to occupational crime, in that crime by the individual need not be occupationally or organizationally related.
- *Type 5 — Employee vs. Employee Crime.* This involves crime by employees against fellow employees. Sweetheart labor contracts, to be discussed, could serve as one example.
- *Type 6 — Organization vs. Employee Crime.* Crime by organizations against employees may involve threats to the health and safety of an organization's workers.
- *Type 7 — Individual vs. Organization Crime.* This includes crimes by individuals, merchants, or professionals against organizations. Insurance or tax fraud related to one's occupational role may serve as examples. The state is included as an organization which may be victimized.
- *Type 8 — Employee vs. Organization Crime.* This concerns any situation in which any employee violates the trust bestowed upon her or him within an organization, such as by embezzlement or inside trading.
- *Type 9 — Organization vs. Organization Crime.* This refers to situations in which an organization commits an offense to the detriment of other organizations or the state such as industrial espionage or unfair trade practices.

While examples can be found for types 2, 4, 5, and 7, these categories are less useful since many of the offenses are not uniquely occupationally or organizationally related. As pointed out in our discussion of typologies in Chapter 3, such classifications are intended as heuristic devices for explanatory purposes, since many crimes in fact defy placement into mutually exclusive, homogeneous categories. These types will be used as a useful scheme for organizing the presentation of occupational crime in this chapter as well as organizational/corporate crime in the next chapter.

Legal Regulation

Occupations and the Law

In Western societies, the legal regulation of occupations is often "self-regulation." Although laws and codes of ethics exist purportedly to protect the public from harmful occupational activity, much self-governance has been used instead to protect the interests of members of the occupation. The more developed *professions* claim and attempt to convince legislatures that they possess highly sophisticated, useful, esoteric knowledge; that they are committed to serving societal needs through a formal code of ethics; and that they therefore should be granted autonomy, since they and only they are in a position to evaluate the quality of their service. In fact, the actual legal codes that control occupational practice tend to be formulated by the occupations themselves in order to dominate or monopolize a line of work. Playwright George Bernard Shaw (1941, p. 9) in *The Doctor's Dilemma*, has one of his characters state that "all professions are a conspiracy against the laity." The original source for Shaw's statement was the eighteenth-century conservative economist Adam Smith (1953, p. 137), who claimed, "Seldom do members of a profession meet, even for trade or merriment, that it does not end up in some conspiracy against the public or some contrivance to raise prices."

More developed occupations (professions) virtually control the law-making machinery affecting their work. Professional organizations and their political action committees are quite effective in blocking legislation which may be detrimental to their interests. An excellent case in point was the effective lobbying campaign orchestrated by the American Bankers Association in 1983 to block proposed legislation which would have required banks to withhold interest paid on accounts for federal income tax purposes. Although this would have represented more work for banks, the Internal Revenue Service lost an effective weapon with which to collect unpaid taxes; it could have increased federal revenues an estimated $8 billion dollars.

Another example of professional power is the AMA (American Medical Association), which Friedson (1970) describes as "professional dominance" or Harmer (1975) as *American Medical Avarice*. The AMA as a lobbying organization appears more concerned with guarding profit, competition, and private enterprise in the business of medicine than in supporting legislation that would improve the equality of medical care delivery. According to the *Report of the National Advisory Commission on Health Manpower* (1968, p. 268), the health statistics of certain groups in the U.S., particularly the poor, resemble the health statistics in an underdeveloped country.

Occupational crime may be controlled by professional associations themselves, by traditional criminal law, by civil law, and by adminstrative law. Actions by professional ethics boards may include suspensions, censure, temporary or permanent removal of license and membership, and the like. Traditional criminal prosecution also may occur, such as for larceny, burglary, and criminal fraud; civil actions by the government may include damage and license suspension suits. Administrative proceedings may call for removal of license, seizure of illegal goods, and fines.

The FBI in its early history was involved primarily in investigating and enforcing white collar crimes such as false purchases, security sales violations, bankruptcy fraud, and antitrust violations and only later became so preoccupied with its gangbuster image (Lowenthal, 1950, p. 12). As late as 1977, however, the House Judiciary Subcommittee charged that the FBI was soft on white collar crime and that its idea of white collar crime was small scale fraud (Simon and Swart, 1984).

This issue of legal processing of corporate and occupational offenders will be further explored at the end of this chapter. But first we should explore the nature and types of such crime.

Occupational Crime

Crimes by Employees

In the "occupational/organizational crime grid" (Figure 9.2) *crimes by employees can theoretically take three forms:*

1. *Against individuals or public* (type 2 in Figure 9.2), such as through bribery and corruption.
2. *Against other employees* (type 5 in Figure 9.2). This may be a null case since this type does not represent a major area of concern in occupational/organizational crime.
3. *Against organizations (corporations)* (type 8 in Figure 9.2), such as embezzlement or employee pilferage. Much computer crime (really a description of a technique by which crime is committed rather than a type of crime) involves employees "ripping off" employers.

Although there are cases of overlap, both "crimes by employees" and "crimes by individuals" are examples of occupational crime—that committed in the course of a legitimate occupation for one's own benefit. While the types of activities to be discussed in this section are executed by employees (those who work for someone else), those to be examined in "crimes by individuals" will primarily be crimes by professionals.

Edelhertz's Typology

One attempt to delineate "white-collar crime" was the widely cited typology and examples provided by Edelhertz (1970, pp. 73–75; see Vantage Point 9.2). While Edelhertz had two other types in his classification,

---

Vantage Point

Vantage Point 9.2—Edelhertz's Typology of White-Collar Crime

Edelhertz's typology of white-collar crime details a variety of offenses:

A. Crimes in the course of their occupations by those operating inside business, government, or other establishments in violation of their duty of loyalty and fidelity to employer or client.
   1. Commercial bribery and kickbacks, i.e., by and to buyers, insurance adjusters, contracting officers, quality inspectors, government inspectors and auditors, etc.
   2. Bank violations by bank officers, employees and directors.
   3. Embezzlement or self-dealing by business or union officers and employees.
   4. Securities fraud by insiders trading to their advantage by the use of special knowledge.
   5. Employee petty larceny and expense account fraud.
   6. Frauds by computer, causing unauthorized payments.
   7. "Sweetheart contracts" entered into by union officers.
   8. Embezzlement or self-dealing by attorneys, trustees, and fiduciaries.
   9. Fraud against the government.
      a. Padding of payrolls.
      b. Conflict of interest.
      c. False travel, expense or per diem claims.
B. Crimes incidental to and in furtherance of business operations, but not the central purpose of the business.
   1. Tax violations.
   2. Antitrust violations.
   3. Commercial bribery of another's employee, officer or fiduciary (including union officers).
   4. Food and drug violations.
   5. False weights and measures by retailers.

many of those listed in his "crimes by persons operating on an individual basis" are not necessarily occupational in nature, except that the victims often happen to be organizations (business or the state). Some examples that he gives that are occupationally based include bankruptcy frauds and violations of Federal Reserve regulations by pledging stock for further purchases, flouting margin requirements. His category of "white-collar crime as business, or as the central activity" better fits the definition of professional crime. Edelhertz's category A best fits our discusion of "occupational crime," while category B better fits our definition of "corporate crime."

A. **6.** Violations of Truth-in-Lending Act by misrepresentation of credit terms and prices.
   7. Submission or publication of false financial statements to obtain credit.
   8. Use of fictitious or over-valued collateral.
   9. Check-kiting to obtain operating capital on short term financing.
   10. Securities Act violations, i.e. sale of non-registered securities, to obtain operating capital, false proxy statements, manipulation of market to support corporate credit or access to capital markets, etc.
   11. Collusion between physicians and pharmacists to cause the writing of unnecessary prescriptions.
   12. Dispensing by pharmacists in violation of law, excluding narcotics traffic.
   13. Immigration fraud in support of employment agency operations to provide domestics.
   14. Housing code violations by landlords.
   15. Deceptive advertising.
   16. Fraud against the Government:
      a. False claims.
      b. False statements
         1) to induce contracts
         2) AID frauds
         3) housing frauds
         4) SBA frauds, such as SBIC bootstrapping, self-dealing, cross-dealing, etc., or obtaining direct loans by use of false financial statements.
      c. Moving contracts in urban renewal.
   17. Labor violations (Davis Bacon Act).
   18. Commercial espionage.

SOURCE: Herbert Edelhertz, 1970, *The Nature, Impact and Prosecution of White-Collar Crime,* National Institute of Law Enforcement and Criminal Justice, Washington, D.C.: Government Printing Office, pp. 73–75. Edelhertz's remaining categories were detailed previously in Figure 8.2.

Crimes by Employees against Individuals (the Public)

Self-aggrandizing *crimes by employees against the public* (type 2 in Figure 9.1), take the form of political corruption by public servants or office-holders (public employees), or commercial corruption by employees in the private sector. These activities are distinguished from corporate or organizational criminal activities of the same type by the fact that in this case the employee personally benefits by the violation.

> There is no distinctly American criminal class except Congress.
> —Mark Twain (1899, p. 98)

Public Corruption

"Cigar smoke, booze, and money delivered in brown paper bags" is the description Hedrick Smith gives in *The Power Game* (1989) in characterizing the popular image of lobbyists and the backroom world of politics. The list of occupationally related crime on the part of political employees or office-holders may include: furnishing favors to private businesses such as illegal commissions on public contracts, issuance of fraudulent licenses, tax exemptions, and lower tax evaluations (Clinard and Quinney, 1973, p. 189). As an example, health inspectors in New York City (City Inspectors, 1988) turned the Department of Health into the Department of Wealth and doubled or tripled their salaries by extorting payments from restaurants, threatening to cite them for health code violations if they did not pay up.

Police Corruption—The Knapp Commission. In 1972 the New York City Knapp Commission issued its report regarding corruption in that city's police department. Corruption was found to be widespread in the police department, particularly in the plainclothes division assigned to enforce gambling laws. These officers participated in a "pad," regular biweekly or monthly payments in amounts as high as $3,500 per gambling establishment. The "nut" or monthly share per man ranged from $300 to $400 in Manhattan to $1,500 in Harlem. Corruption in the narcotics division was less organized than in the gambling division, but their "scores" (pads or payoffs) were generally higher. Uniformed patrolmen received payments in smaller but more numerous amounts from after-hours clubs, bottle clubs, tow trucks, motorists, cab drivers, parking lots, prostitutes, and defendants wanting to fix cases.

Corrupt superior officers used patrol officers as "bagmen" (collectors). Corrupt police fall into two categories: "meat-eaters" and "grass-eaters." "Meat-eaters," the smallest group, actively misuse their powers for personal gain; while "grass-eaters" simply accept the payoffs that come their way. A code of silence exerts pressure on honest officers not to become "whistleblowers" as had Officer Frank Serpico (Maas, 1973).

Investigations of police corruption take place regularly, about every twenty years, drawing similar findings and resulting in no substantial change in conditions. Police corruption is mirrored in other agencies of government, in industry, in labor, and in the professions. While public preoccupation with police corruption is viewed defensively by police, symbolically, for most people, the police officer is the law (Barker and Carter, 1986). Coleman (1985, p. 93) explains that "Police officers simply have more opportunities to receive illegal payments than other public employees" since they are asked to enforce inadequate vice laws which take place within very profitable black markets. This certainly was the case with the Miami Police Department in 1987 (Miami Police, 1987), when nearly one hundred officers (one in eighteen officers) were believed involved in serious corruption and misconduct, most of which was related to drug trafficking. Some officers were involved in stealing drug shipments and trafficking in drugs themselves. In *Buddy Boys*, McAlary (1987) explains how some New York City police would chase off drug traffickers from an apartment and continue selling drugs themselves. Since the transactions were conducted through a hole in the door, the officers were careful to roll up their sleeves lest they scare off customers.

Investigations in other cities have found similar patterns, with much corruption associated particularly with the enforcement of public order crimes such as gambling, drug, and vice enforcement. Probes of the Philadelphia police department in the early seventies, for instance, found ongoing, widespread, systematic corruption in every district and among officers at all ranks involving receipt of improper payments in cash, merchandise, "carnal favors," and meals (Pennsylvania Crime Commission, 1974).

Another former New York City police officer and informant, William Phillips, in a revealing autobiographical work *On the Pad* (Schecter and Phillips, 1973), provides the following anecdote:

> I know fellows made up to fifteen, eighteen thousand on DOA's [dead on arrivals]. If you get to these people's apartments first and all this cash is laying around, why it's just a matter of putting it in your pocket and keeping your mouth shut. In fact, when you receive a call for a DOA, radio cars race to the scene. You get there first, whatever you find, you tell the sergeant half. That way he gets only a quarter.

In 1988 an undercover investigation in Philadelphia city jails (Jacoby, 1988) found correctional officers (over thirty guards) involved in, among other offenses, smuggling drugs, money, and weapons into the prison, helping inmates escape, and taking bribes from reputed mobsters.

Judgescam—"Operation Greylord."   In 1983, Federal Bureau of Investigation agents posing as lawyers and criminals, revealed that for three years they had been running a "sting" operation on the Cook County, Illinois, criminal justice system. The "sting" was code-named "Operation Greylord" (referring to the powdered wigs historically worn by judges.) This was the largest and most successful investigation into judicial misconduct in U.S. history and as of fall, 1987, resulted in convictions of sixty-one persons including eleven judges, police officers, lawyers, and court officials with additional trials and indictments ongoing (Bensinger, 1987). (As we saw in Chapter 8, some crime is caused by criminals allegedly having to earn money in order to pay for high legal expenses and fixing of cases; Judgescam lends some credibility to this claim.)

Watergate.   Perhaps no one event evokes images of official corruption, deceit, and subterfuge as does Watergate. This event involved the discovery of the illegal break-in of the Democratic National Committee Headquarters located in the Watergate complex in Washington, D.C. by agents in the employ of Richard Nixon.

> "I am not a crook."
>
> —Statement by then-President Richard M. Nixon
> in the wake of the Watergate investigations

Richard Nixon certainly was not the first U.S. president to be involved in crooked practices (see Chambliss, 1988). But he was the first to be driven from office in disgrace because of the extent of his activities and the first to be saved from certain criminal prosecution through the issuance of a full pardon before-the-fact by his successor, President Gerald Ford. At the time, President Nixon's attitude toward the probe appeared in one of the later-to-be-released "missing tapes": "I don't give a shit what happens. I want you to stonewall it. Let them plead the Fifth Amendment, cover up, or anything else if it'll save the plan" (cited in Peter, 1977, p. 317).

 The Watergate events contain many features of "political crime" that will be discussed in Chapter 11. The bulk of the offenses, however, involved traditional corruption, "occupational crime" committed by Nixon and associates for personal, nonideological purposes, primarily the preservation of personal power. Among the offenses of the Watergate team were: burglary, illegal surveillance, attempted bribery of a judge (Ellsberg case), selling ambassadorships in return for illegal

G. Gordon Liddy helped to organize the Watergate burglary during Richard Nixon's 1972 political campaign. He is shown here with members of the private anti-terrorist squad he formed upon his release from prison.

campaign donations, maintenance of an illegal "slush fund," destruction of evidence by plans of "dirty tricks" in political campaigns by the FBI director and the President, the U.S. Attorney General Mitchell (the nation's top law enforcement officer) requesting IRS audits on opponents, use of the CIA and FBI to attempt to halt the investigation, perjury, withholding information, altering evidence, and deliberate lying to the American public by the nation's top officeholder (Simon and Eitzen, 1982, pp. 197–198).

A public already cynical about politics and politicians was further outraged by the Watergate revelations.

ABSCAM.

> Tony, you're going—let me just say this to you—you're going about this the right way. I'm going to tell you something real simple and short. *Money talks in this business and bullshit walks* [italics mine]. And it works the same way down in Washington (Green, 1981, p. 11).

This statement was not made by a "hip" lower class street hustler but by ex-U.S. Congressman Michael Myers of Pennsylvania to Amoroso, a phony Arab in the FBI ABSCAM (Arab or Abdul Scam) sting operation, in which agents posing as rich oil sheiks bribed a number of members of the United

States Congress. *Bakseesh* (Middle East), *bustarelle* (Italy), *pot de vin* (France), *mordida* (Latin America), or just plain bribe (North America), kickbacks, and corruption are apparently both widespread and international in scope. Individuals in their occupational roles may give or receive bribes for their own personal benefit (occupational crime) or for the benefit of the organization/corporation (organizational/corporate crime). Bribery, influence-peddling, and corruption are acceptable patterns of international commerce, and are not even illegal in many countries throughout the world.

Particularly revealing in the ABSCAM operation was the relative ease with which foreign agents were able to bribe members of the U.S. Congress. Though many regard such federal sting operations as entrapment (causing a crime to happen which would not have if the stimulus had not been put there by the government), others perceive such "aggressive tactics" as the only means of ferreting out "upper-world crime." In 1988 *Pravda* charged that corrupt officials in the Soviet Union, including the son-in-law of former Soviet Premier Leonid Brezhnev, stole over $6.5 billion from the Uzbekistan Republic. This involved extortion, bribery, and other criminal enterprises (Scandal Traced, 1988). Brezhnev's son-in-law was spared the firing squad and sentenced to twelve years in a labor camp.

Private Corruption

Commercial bribery and kickbacks   in which the individual personally benefits can take place in a variety of manners similar to those already outlined under corporate crime and political corruption. Buyers for large retail chains may accept gifts or cash in return for placing orders. Insurance adjusters, contracting officers, and quality control inspectors may all be willing to accept bribes in return for overlooking their duties to employers and, in the form of higher prices, at the expense of the general public.

Auto Dealers and Sharp Practices.   In analyzing what they call "coerced crime," Leonard and Weber (1970) describe how the four major domestic auto producers pressure their roughly thirty thousand dealers (who are technically independent proprietors) into bilking their customers. These dealers commit "coerced crime" because in order to retain their franchises they must meet minimum sales quotas, and in order to meet these, they must often employ "shady practices." The latter include: forcing accessories, service gouging, high finance charges (at times even employing loan sharks), overcharging for parts, misuse of "book time" (preset and inflated charges for labor time on repairs), and odometer (mileage meter) tampering.

Crimes by Employees against Employees

Sweetheart Contracts

While a variety of crimes like theft may be committed by an employee against another employee for personal benefit (type 5 in Figure 9.2), many such violations would not necessarily be occupationally related and therefore would not be appropriate examples for the "Occupational/ Organizational Crime Grid." But one type of violation that would certainly fit is the *sweetheart contract* in labor-management negotiations, which involves labor officials and negotiators secretly making a deal with management to the disadvantage of the workers whom the labor officials supposedly represent. For example, the union president and representatives might make a deal with management to take a bribe of fifty thousand dollars. They then might indicate to the workers that they have examined the company books and found that management can afford only a twenty cents per hour raise rather than the fifty cents originally promised. Depending upon the size of the workforce, management could save millions of dollars.

Operation Brilab

In *Operation Brilab* (for bribery-labor), an FBI "sting" operation, federal investigators uncovered evidence of corruption in the awarding of labor union health and welfare insurance plans. FBI men posed as insurance agents willing to pay bribes and kickbacks to obtain favorable treatment from government and union officials responsible for awarding insurance contracts (Dozens of Officials Implicated, 1980, p. 1). In this, employees (who are now union officials) betrayed the trust of and sold out their fellow employees for their own personal gain.

Crimes by Employees against Organizations

Organizations are vulnerable to a variety of offenses which employees can commit against them (type 8 in Figure 9.2). In this section we will briefly focus upon employee pilferage, computer crime, and embezzlement; but employee crimes obviously include many types of offenses discussed under crimes against the individual (public), corporate bribery, and the like.

Embezzlement

One form of stealing from one's employer is through *embezzlement*, which basically consists of theft from an employer by an individual who has reached a position of financial trust. The classic work on the subject was Donald Cressey's *Other People's Money* (1953) which involved interviews with 133 incarcerated embezzlers. He proposed the following explanation of why trust-violators steal:

1. Individuals who have achieved a position of trust are faced with what they conceive of as a nonsharable financial problem.
2. They feel they can resolve this problem by violating their position of trust, that is, by "temporarily borrowing" from their employer.
3. This rationalization of "borrowing" eventually breaks down as embezzlers realize they have been discovered and cannot make repayment in time (Ibid., p. 30).

Gambling, sexual affairs, and high living are often the factors behind the unshareable nature of the financial problem.

The typical embezzler does not fit the typical stereotype of criminal. Most are middle-aged, middle class males who have lived relatively respectable lives and lack a past history of criminal or delinquent activity.

Cressey's analysis of embezzlers has been criticized by Schuessler (1954, p. 604), who claimed that it was limited to an ex post facto (after the fact) study of only caught embezzlers and that his descriptions may not be characteristic of most embezzlers. Nettler's (1974) study found embezzlers to be motivated by greed and temptation as well as possessing the opportunity to commit the crime. Unlike Cressey, Nettler was unable to find the existence of a nonshareable problem as a necessary component of the embezzlement process.

Allison and Henderson in their book *Empire of Deceit: Inside the Biggest Sports and Bank Scandal in U.S. History* (1985) describe the embezzlement of an estimated $21 million from Wells Fargo Bank by one of its loan officers, Harold Smith. The case, which became public in 1981, described how Smith had used the bank's money to prop up very unwise boxing matches sponsored by Muhammed Ali Professional Sports. The organization's only connection to the ex-champ was that it had gained his permission to use his name in previous amateur sports promotions. It consistently lost money while financing bad deals and high living with Wells Fargo's money courtesy of Smith. Increasingly, embezzlement is aided by computer and electronic fund transfers to be discussed shortly in our section on computer crime.

Employee Pilferage

We are all perhaps familiar with the old joke about the pay for a job hauling garbage being "ten dollars per day and all you can eat." Many employees regard theft of their employer's property as a fringe benefit or sometimes a necessary supplement to inadequate pay; thus, many jobs are viewed by employees as paying "X dollars per day plus all you can steal." Not all occupational crime is white collar in nature; it may be blue, gray, pink, or tuxedo. Smigel and Ross (1970) in *Crimes against Bureaucracy* indicate that individuals and particularly employees feel less guilt the larger the size of the victim organization. Many individuals who would consider themselves criminals were they to steal from other persons, rationalize their theft from large, impersonal organizations by saying that "they can afford the loss."

According to Smigel and Ross (Ibid.), the very size, wealth, and impersonality of large bureaucracies, whether governmental or business, provides a rationalization for those who wish to steal from such organizations. The "Robin Hood myth" holds that theft from such organizations really hurts no one, since the victim is a large, wealthy organization. Combined with this is a certain public antipathy toward the large corporation or big government. Obviously, the Robin Hood rationalization breaks down when we consider the higher cost of goods consumers must pay as a result of "inventory shrinkage."

In a National Institute of Justice-sponsored survey (Satisfied Workers, 1983, pp. 6–7) conducted in three metropolitan areas, one-third of the employees of the forty-seven corporations studied admitted stealing company property. Almost two-thirds indicated "counterproductive workmanship" practices such as abuse of sick leave, substance abuse on the job, and other misconduct such as extra-long lunch and work breaks. The estimated $5 billion to $10 billion price tag on employee pilferage, while controllable through better security controls, was found to be strongly affected by the workers' perception of job satisfaction and feelings about employers' concern for their interests. Unhappy workers engaged in more counterproductive behavior and were also found to be more likely to be involved in pilferage.

Cameron (1964) in her classic piece on retail theft, *The Booster and the Snitch,* suggested that "inventory shrinkage" (loss of goods) in retail establishments was primarily a matter of employee theft rather than of shoplifting. Store security personnel concur, estimating that as much as 75 percent of such loss is due to employee theft. A familiar story relates to security personnel who suspected that an employee was "ripping off" the company since everyday he left work with a wheel barrow full of packages. Everyday they carefully checked the packages to no avail. When finally discovered, the employee had stolen over a thousand wheel barrows. Employees are quite ingenious in illegally supplementing their wages at the expense of their employer.

Some common techniques in employee retail theft include:

1. Cashiers who ring up a lower price on single-item purchases and pocket the difference, or who ring up lower prices for "needy" friends going through the checkout.
2. Clerks who do not tag some sale merchandise, sell it at the original price, and pocket the difference.
3. Receiving clerks who duplicate keys to storage facilities and who return to the store after hours.
4. Truck drivers who make fictitious purchases of fuel and repairs, and who split the gains with truck stops.
5. Employees who simply hide items in garbage pails, incinerators, or under trash heaps until they can be retrieved later (McCaghy, 1976b, p. 179).

Some employers, anticipating employee theft, purposely pay employees less, assuming they will make up the rest through theft; however, the double bind feature is that employees often do not make up the difference between what they are paid and a fair wage. In addition, if they are caught stealing, they are fired (Liebow, 1967, pp. 37–38).

A retired police captain from a large Eastern city told the author that in the 1950s, city administrators frankly told him and a police negotiation team that the reason they were unwilling to grant a fair wage increase was their assumption that the police made more than enough through widespread graft. Abuse of expense accounts, travel allowances, and company cars are additional means by which employers are robbed of organizational income.

Computer Crime

In 1978 Stanley Rifkin used a computer to transfer $10.2 million from a bank in California to a trust company in New York City and then to a Swiss bank. He used these funds to buy 42,000 carats of Russian diamonds, which he then attempted to smuggle back into the U.S. when he was caught (Lieberstein, 1979 p. 80). This case is one example of the burgeoning crime of the latter third of the twentieth century, computer crime.

The First National Bank of Chicago nearly lost $69 million in 1988 when an $18,000-a-year clerk attempted to electronically transfer money from accounts such as Merrill Lynch and United Airlines to those of his accomplices set up under assumed names in Vienna, Austria banks. Part of the scheme included the knowledge of code numbers, a phony Chicago "bank," fake letters of credit, and other elaborate ruses (Bock

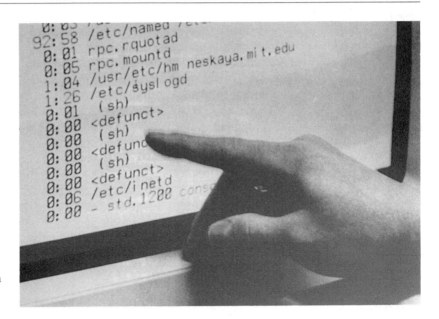

A computer "virus." The computer file labeled "(sh)" is a virus program that spread itself through the ARPANET computer network in 1988.

and McWhirter, 1988). Electronic payment systems (wire transfers) and credit cards have replaced bank vaults as the banks' weak spot. About the same time as the Chicago caper, $32 million was nearly transferred from another bank to a Swiss bank before being intercepted (Baris, 1988).

In 1983 the film *War Games* presented a scenario in which a young "hacker" (computer junkie) managed from his home terminal to gain access to Department of Defense computers. This brought about an alert which nearly precipitated a nuclear holocaust. Though the film exaggerated the ease of access to such facilities, it dramatically illustrated the fact that actual illegal access has been gained for sport by juveniles to corporate, university, and government computer banks. Practical jokes and juvenile pranks now have far more dangerous potential than could be previously imagined.

However, in August 1983, a loose-knit group of "hackers" known as the 414s (the area code number for Milwaukee) were linked with electronic break-ins at Los Alamos National Laboratory, Security Pacific Bank, the Sloan-Kettering Cancer Center, among others (Marbach, Conant, and Rogers, 1983, p. 45). The most serious computer crimes are not committed by juveniles, but the middle-aged respectables.

Rogue programs or computer viruses also struck recently as a new computer problem. A *computer virus* is a set of instructions or a program on a floppy disk that can copy itself into the computer's master software or operating system, usually without being noticed. The instructions could be a harmless message or instructions for the destruction of data in the computer's memory. The instructions can be passed to additional computers (Markhoff, 1988). In 1988 a Cornell graduate student was convicted of unleashing a virus as a prank that clogged thousands of computers nationwide, particularly those used by universities, industry, and government (Associated Press, 1989). One strain originating in Pakistan contained a phone number in Pakistan that could be called in order to obtain an antidote. Other viruses have infected military computers and NASA through burgeoning networks that electronically connect thousands of computers.

The Bureau of Justice Statistics (1979, pp. 353–378) manual on *Computer Crime* cites cases which give us a taste for the variety of computer crimes:

- A clerk who put invoices on the computer invented a few fraudulent names. His friend was an accountant in charge of reconciling checks. They collected $217,000 over an eight-month period. Both were laid off pending investigation.
- An employee dismissed from a small catalog sales firm retaliated by programming the computer to erase its files, resulting in $20,000 damage. Although there is circumstantial evidence (this employee was the only one with a key to log on), the firm does not think they will prosecute.
- False medical claims were processed at Blue Cross which were made out to real and fictitious doctors, mailed to private homes, and cashed by those involved in the scheme. The checks were for the cost of medical procedures which were never performed.
- An employee at the University of Maryland hospital was charged with malicious vandalism when $100,000 damage was done to the hospital's computer. Wires and the master switch had been ripped out.
- In New Jersey, Exxon Corporation filed a multimillion dollar suit against a former New Jersey state senator, his father, two of their family businesses, and others, alleging a conspiracy to defraud Exxon's Bayway Refinery of 16 million gallons of fuel oil over a six-year period. The scheme involved pumping more fuel oil than authorized records showed and maintaining the deception through juggled computer records and rigged oil tank gauges.
- A rival company was charged with theft of trade secrets and unfair competition when they stole and used the computer programs of the plaintiff to operate their company.
- In West Germany, nine persons were arrested for disclosing secrets about Western electronic data processing techniques (IBM technical

information) to an East European secret service. Charges filed included theft, fraud, bribery, offenses against embargo rules, and right of competition. Computer crime may include destruction of property, theft of intellectual property by deception, or actual confiscation, financial deception, or theft, as well as unauthorized use of service.

Argot of Computer Crime.   Like other areas of crime, computer-related crime has developed its own argot (specialized jargon). Depending on the meaning of the data, kinds of services, or purpose of the programs, the acts themselves range over many known types of crime. Some types of computer crime (Ibid., pp. 9–29) include: data diddling, Trojan horse, salami techniques, superzapping, trapdoors, logic bombs, asynchronous attacks, scavenging, data leakage, piggybacking, and impersonation, wiretapping, and simulation and modeling.

Data diddling, the simplest and most common method, involves changing data before or during its input to computers. For example, a data clerk could enter false data to cause the computer to increase his or her own salary.

Trojan horse involves covert placement of computer instructions in a program so the computer will perform unauthorized functions while still performing its intended purposes. This is common in computer program-based frauds and sabotage.

Salami techniques entail the theft of small amounts of assets from a large number of sources (taking small slices without noticeably reducing the whole). For example, a fraction of a percentage of thousands of customer savings accounts could be transferred into the thief's personal account. In the "round down" fraud, all remaining fractions on accounts which are rounded down to the nearest cent are retained for the thief's account.

Superzapping derives its name from superzap, similar to a master key, a macro/utility program designed for use in emergencies, to bypass all controls in order to modify or disclose any of the contents of the computer. Using the superzap, criminals can change data files to their advantage.

Trapdoors are debugging (error elimination) aids which provide breaks in the code for the insertion of additional code and intermediate output capabilities. These spaces are usually eliminated in final program editing but may be overlooked. Engineers in Detroit discovered a trapdoor in a commercial time-sharing service in Florida that allowed thieves to search uninhibitedly for privileged passwords which included copies of trade-secret computer programs that they proceeded to use free of charge.

Logic bombs are computer programs executed at appropriate or periodic times in a computer system that determine conditions or states of the computer. These also can be used in order to facilitate an unauthorized, malicious act. For example, in one case, secret computer instructions (a Trojan horse) were inserted, to be executed periodically. At a given time—for example two years later at 3:00 P.M.—the time bomb, a type of logic bomb, would go off and trigger the printout of a confession of crime on all of the 300 computer terminals on-line at that time and then would cause the system to crash. This was timed long after the perpetrator had departed.

Asynchronous attacks take advantage of the sequential functioning of a computer operating system in which jobs are performed in the order in which resources are available to fit the request or according to an overriding priority indication. Therefore, rather than executing requests in the order they are received, the system performs them asynchronously, based on resources available; in very long computer runs the program contains intermediate stopping points. Unscrupulous operators may gain access to the checkpoint restart copy of the program and to data and system parameters, and then change instructions in order to gain unauthorized or privileged data.

Scavenging is a method of obtaining information that may be left in or around a computer system after the execution of a job. Such data can be of great value to commercial competitors.

Data leakage refers to a wide range of computer-related crimes involving removal of data or copies of data from a computer system or computer facility. It has been reported that hidden in the central processors of many computers used in the Vietnam War were miniature radio transmitters capable of broadcasting the contents of the computers to a remote receiver.

Piggybacking and impersonation basically refer to unauthorized usage, which may occur physically or electronically. Physical access to a computer facility may be gained by sneaking through doors opened by authorized users. Electronic piggybacking can be accomplished by connecting a hidden computer terminal to the same line as an authorized user, using telephone switching equipment. Impersonation involves assuming the identity of another. In one case, a person stole magnetic strip credit cards that required secret personal identification numbers associated with each card for use. He called each card owner by telephone, claiming to be a bank official who had discovered the theft of the card; he said that he needed the secret number in order to protect the owner and to issue a new card. Invariably the number was supplied. He then used the numbers in automatic teller machines to steal the owners' money.

Wiretapping involves cutting and tapping into the wires involved in data communications. While there are no verified examples of data communications wiretapping, the potential grows as computers are connected to communication facilities. Presently there are easier ways of obtaining and modifying data.

Simulation and modeling entails use of a computer as a tool or instrument for planning or control of crime. An existing process can be simulated (imitated) on a computer or a planned method for carrying out a crime could be modeled to determine its possible success. In one case involving a million-dollar manual embezzlement, an accountant simulated his company's accounting and general ledger system on his computer in order to determine the effects of the embezzlement on the general ledger.

The computer simply represents a tool which can be utilized in order to effect a wide variety of crimes. Computer crime is expected to be an area of continuing growth for the remainder of this century.

Crimes by Individuals (or Members of Occupations)

The "occupational/organizational crime grid" (Figure 9.2) identifies three types of crimes by individuals (or occupational incumbents):

1. *Against individuals* (type 1 in Figure 9.2), which includes the public, consumers, and other professionals. Examples of such offenses would be merchant against consumer as well as professional against client.
2. *Against employees* (type 4 in Figure 9.2), may, for all practical purposes, represent a null case. Many of these violations are not necessarily occupationally related.
3. *Against organizations* (type 7 in Figure 9.2), which may include businesses as well as the state. Examples would include insurance and tax frauds.

Sutherland's original notion of "white collar crime" was seen as applying to crimes by the elite. Today it is viewed by most criminologists as expanded to include crimes by members of any occupation, irrespective of status; white collar crime will be viewed in this section primarily as "occupational crime." Utilizing Clinard and Quinney's (1973, p. 188) conception, this is viewed as "a violation of the criminal law in the course of activity in a legitimate occupation."

Crime in the Professions

Medicine. Medical quackery and unnecessary operations may very well kill more people every year in the United States than other crimes of violence. A House Subcommittee estimated that the American public was the victim of 2.4 million unnecessary surgical procedures per year, which resulted in a loss of $4 billion as well as 11,900 deaths (Coleman, 1985, p. 113). Americans may be becoming overdoctored, having twice the per capita number of surgeons, anesthesiologists, and operations as England and Wales, yet higher mortality rates (Ibid.). Jesilow, Pontell, and Geis (1985) estimate that American physicians defraud federal and state medical assistance programs up to 40 percent of all program monies.

Charges have been levied that Medicare (an American medical program for the elderly) is beginning to resemble a welfare program for doctors. Until recently, weak monitoring of medical claims has invited cheating, as the following case illustrates:

In 1981 Dr. Richard Kones of Pound Ridge, N.Y., testified before a Senate Finance and Aging Committee after having pleaded guilty to defrauding the government and health insurance companies of $500,000 under the Medicare program. From November 1977 until the fall of 1980 he submitted over $1.5 million worth of false claims for services never performed. Medicare patients were asked to fill out false claim forms, and Kones filed outrageous requests for reimbursement that he claimed "begged discovery." Claiming the system invites being "ripped off," he described a Social Security scheme he perpetrated in which he had himself admitted to a hospital, claiming a massive heart attack which was verified by blood test results he brought with him. Later, against his doctor's advice, he checked out of the hospital and took a tennis lesson after which he contacted yet another doctor to evaluate a fake stress test he misrepresented as his own. This enabled him to collect $1,000 per month disability for nineteen months. Being sued in various jurisdictions, as a condition of his federal plea, he agreed to resign his medical license in ten states where he was licensed and repay the U.S. government $500,000 (Cheating Medicare, 1981).

Some of the medical pilfering of Medicare funds includes: nursing-home purchases of boats and trips to Hawaii, laboratory kickbacks for new accounts, charges for fake services, unnecessary or unadministered treatments, laboratory tests, and operations.

Some other violations which physicians may become involved in include practices such as *fee splitting* (in which doctors refer patients to other doctors for further treatment and split the fee with them). "Ping-ponging" involves doctors referring patients to other doctors in the same office; "steering" entails directing patients to particular pharmacies; and "gang visits" involve billing for unnecessary multiple services (White-Collar Crime, 1981). In 1988 the Department of Health and Human Services established a nationwide computer bank to monitor malpractice suits and disciplinary actions against doctors and dentists in order to keep track of incompetent practitioners (Estill, 1988).

Law. Illegal and unprofessional activities by lawyers may include "ambulance chasing," i.e., soliciting and encouraging unnecessary lawsuits (such as fraudulent damage claims) in order to collect commissions (Freedman, 1976; Reichstein, 1965). Describing the practice of law as sometimes constituting a "con game" against clients, Blumberg (1967) mentions activities in which the lawyer collects fees for defense of clients in which cases are simply "plea-bargained" to expedite the cases, with little concern for the client's well-being.

Carlin (1962), Ladinsky (1963), and Wood (1967) have all pointed to the fact that lawyers who attended less prestigious law schools (often due to poor, ethnic backgrounds) and who were in "solo" practice were more likely to be stuck with the dirty work of the profession—fixing cases, bribing officials, and other "occupational fringe violations" (Gibbons, 1982, pp. 328, 333). On the other hand, graduates of more prestigious institutions spend much of their time, not in tasks portrayed by television-stereotype Perry Mason, but in defending corporate criminals and violators.

Other legal rackets include home closings (in which regular fees are collected for very little work) as well as the collection of contingency fees on liability cases (in which lawyers receive a percentage of anything won) (Merry, 1975, p. 1).

Until recently bar associations published minimum fees and sanctioned attorneys who charged less, even though the Sherman Anti-Trust Act made no exceptions for professional associations in prohibiting price-fixing (Coleman, 1985, p. 30). Recent increases in the number of lawyers in the U.S. (from 119,000 in 1965 to well over 600,000 today) has placed more pressure on lawyers to be "innovative" in finding work; this is creating an over-litigious society and may precipitate greater occupational violations.

In their *Defending Business and White Collar Crimes*, F. Lee Bailey and Henry Rothblatt (1969) outline a variety of tactics to be employed in defending white collar criminals. Defense recommendations revolve around any technical flaw that can be found in the prosecution's case: trial tactics are intended to either confuse or dazzle the jury. Little mention is made, however, of ethical considerations. The concentration of legal talent in the defense of wealthy and corporate violators and the underconcentration in representing their victims (the state and public) raise questions regarding the ethics of the legal profession itself.

Other Occupations. Quinney's (1963) analysis, "Prescription Violations by Pharmacists," reveals higher numbers of violations among pharmacists who see themselves as business persons rather than as professionals. If clients (whom the professional views with concern for their health and the provision of ethical service) are seen as customers (whose greater consumption equals greater profit), then greater numbers of occupational violations were likely to ensue.

Examples of crimes against consumers by professionals, merchants, and members of other legitimate occupations are numerous:

- The "greasy thumb on the scale" or short-weighting customers and overcharging for products.

Ivan F. Boesky leaves court after pleading guilty to violating federal securities laws.

- "Bait 'n' switch" techniques by small merchants, in which the product advertised is unavailable and a more expensive product is pushed on the customer.
- Phony or unnecessary repair work on products.
- Security violations by stockbrokers, such as misleading clients or inside-trading (making use of inside information for personal benefit).
- Abuses in the nursing home industry in which private owners often place profit ahead of the health and safety of elderly residents. Such practices are described by Mendelson (1975) as *Tender Loving Greed.*
- While not a blanket indictment of the profession as a whole, Mitford's (1963, p. 8) *The American Way of Death* describes illegal or unethical activities of funeral directors, including: misuse of the coroner's office in order to secure business, bribery of hospital personnel to "steer" cases, the reuse of coffins, and duplicate billings in welfare cases.

Brokers and financial agents are in positions of trust with their client's money. Sometimes they violate this trust for their own personal gain. Some of these violations may include:

- An investment fund manager bought a large volume of stock from a broker, who repaid the favor by tipping off the manager on "hot" stock issues which the manager purchased for his own benefit.
- Company officials and accountants conspired to falsify company earnings and assets in order to raise the price of its stock in order to sell at a high profit.
- Company officials split profits with outsiders who traded securities of little value for top-rated company bonds, which are then sold. The proceeds of the sale are used to purchase controlling interest in the firm—in a sense, buying the company with its own money (New Style, 1973, p. 53).
- "Churning" by stockbrokers refers to the practice of collecting high commissions by running up sales with unnecessary buy-and-sell orders.

Insider Trading Scandal

"Inside trading" involves agents, brokers, and company officials who, aware of pending developments, make use of this privileged information to buy and/or sell stocks before the public becomes aware of these events. In the mid to late eighties a major Wall Street scandal was uncovered in which brokers and traders were caught systematically manipulating stock prices to their own personal gain. Ivan Boesky, *Fortune* magazine's "Crook of the Year" in 1986, had been chief of Wall Street's largest arbitrage firm, a business which thrived on rumors of takeover bids. He was found guilty of violating the Security and Exchange Commission's insider-trading rules and agreed to pay a fine of $50 million and establish a fund with another $50 million to pay back cheated investors. In March of 1989 Michael Milken, the junk-bond king, along with accomplices was charged with manipulating stock prices and cheating shareholders and clients. Charging Milken with racketeering, the U.S. sought $1.8 billion in forfeiture. An innovator in the use of junk bonds (low-rated, high-yield bonds) for financing and buying out companies, Milken had earned an estimated $1.1 billion in four years. Some of this, however, illegally involved using insider information to the disadvantage of other investors. On March 23, 1989, Milken's employer Drexel, Burnham, Lambert Inc. pleaded guilty to federal charges of rigging the market and agreed to pay a $650 million fine (a record for a securities case) (Friday and Pauly, 1989; Pauly, et al. 1987).

Criminal Careers of Occupational and Organizational Offenders

Occupational and corporate offenders generally do not view their activities as criminal; their violations usually are part of their occupational environment. Such offenders maintain a commitment to conventional society while violating some of its laws because their activities often are supported and informally approved of by occupational or corporate subcultures or environments (see Frank and Lombness, 1988).

Sutherland (1956, pp. 93–95) sees many parallels between the behavior of corporate criminals and that of professional and organized criminals:

1. They are recidivists, committing their crimes on a continual and frequent basis.
2. Violations are widespread, with only a relatively few ever being prosecuted.
3. Offenders do not lose status among their peers or associates as a result of their illegal behavior.
4. Like professional thieves, business people reveal contempt for government regulators, officials, and laws which they view as unnecessarily interfering with their behavior.

The corporate or executive offenders involved in what gangster Al Capone used to call "the legitimate rackets" differ from professional criminals in that they do not view themselves nor are they usually perceived by others as criminals.

Since occupational offenders and corporate/organizational offenders share much in common, examination of societal reaction to occupational criminals will be deferred until the end of the next chapter.

Summary

The formative statement on "white collar crime" was made by Sutherland in 1939. He defined it as "crime committed by a person of respectability and high social status in the course of his occupation." Despite the much greater cost of widespread corporate violations, the criminal justice system finds it more politically expedient to concentrate upon traditional crimes. Related to Sutherland's notion is Ross's (1907) notion of criminaloids as "those who prospered by flagitious practices which may not yet come under the ban of public opinion" and Mills's the higher immorality or moral insensibility by the power elite. The concept of white collar crime has been criticized as being too global in nature and a variety of other terms have been suggested. Particularly important are the concepts of "occupational," "organizational," and "corporate" crime. *Occupational crime* refers to violations which take place for self-benefit during the course of a legitimate occupation, while *organizational crime* refers to crimes by business or officials on behalf of the employing organization. Organizational crime becomes *corporate crime* when undertaken on behalf of a private business or organization.

The reasons for the lack of research on occupational and corporate crime were detailed, indicating that criminologists, due to the lack of readily available data, still rely upon many secondary sources. Data and figures from various sources were presented in an attempt to measure the cost of white collar crime. Conservative estimates in 1976 placed the figure at $36 billion, while more liberal estimates would place the cost for monopolistic practices by 1980 in the $174 billion to $231 billion range. Any of the cost estimates far exceed those for traditional crimes.

Myopia must be avoided when viewing current white collar crime, since historical analysis suggests that similar activities may have been even more prevalent in the past. Analysis of legal regulation of occupational practice points out that the more developed professions have been granted a mandate for self-governance even though such self-policing has been less than impressive.

While different typologies of white collar crime have been offered (Bloch and Geis; Edelhertz), the author suggests an "Occupational/Organizational Crime Grid" as a heuristic device for presentation purposes in this chapter. This results in nine theoretical types based upon the criminal (individual, employee, or organization) and the victim (individual, employee, or organization).

Crimes by employees may include a variety of offenses as detailed in Edelhertz's typological examples. *Crimes by employees against individuals/the public* were portrayed by means of public corruption (the Knapp Commission, Judgescam, Watergate, and ABSCAM) as well as private corruption and sharp practices by auto dealers. *Employee vs. employee crime* was examined by means of "sweetheart contracts" and "Operation Brilab," while *crimes by employees against organizations* were depicted with descriptions of embezzlement, employee fraud, pilferage, and computer crimes (including the argot of electronic "hackers"). *Crimes by individuals* (or members of occupations) were delineated by telling about crooked practices in medicine, law, and pharmacy, as well as in business-related trades and occupations.

The *criminal careers* of occupational and corporate criminals entail little identification with crime; these offenders enjoy subcultural support and employ rationalizations to explain away responsibilty for wrongdoing.

KEY CONCEPTS

White Collar Crime
Criminaloid
Higher Immorality
Occupational Crime
Organizational Crime
Corporate Crime
Occupational/Organizational
  Crime Grid
Reasons for Lack of
  Occupational Crime Research

Costs of White Collar Crime
Judgescam
ABSCAM
Operation Brilab
"Coerced Crime"
Sweetheart Contracts
Embezzlement
Computer Crime
Argot of Computer Crime
Watergate

Trojan Horse
Salami Techniques
Logic Bombs
Churning
Insider Trading
Computer Virus

10 Organizational/ Corporate Crime

Corporate Crime

Organizational crime refers to crime committed on behalf of and for the benefit of a legitimate organization. *Corporate (business) crime* is a type of organizational crime committed in free enterprise economies and thus involves criminal activity on behalf of and for the benefit of a private business or corporation. *Organizational/corporate crime may take three forms,* as suggested in the "Occupational/Organizational Crime Grid" (Figure 9.2):

1. Crimes by organizations against the public, individuals, or consumers, type 3.
2. Crimes by organizations against their employees, type 6.
3. Crimes by organizations against other organizations (which include the state), type 9.

In actuality, it is difficult to categorize offenses purely into these categories. For instance, a crime such as price fixing affects not only the consumer but also other businesses, the state, and the competitive state of the economy.

In societies which possess elements of a free enterprise economy organizational crime often takes the form of corporate criminal behavior, while in socialist or controlled economies, it takes the form of public sector organizational crime. While in free enterprise systems corporate crime is generally committed to further the profit of the organization, in controlled economies it often takes the form of what Simis (1982, p. 128) calls "pripiska," a common practice in the Soviet Union of "cooking the books," that is, including false information in the official accounts of an enterprise. This practice, which may include bribing inspectors and auditors, may exaggerate the volume of work which has been completed, or may list projects as finished which have not even been done. Due to official policy of silence regarding such criminality, no official data exists.

Corporate crime takes many forms, including price fixing, kickbacks, commercial bribery, tax violations, fraud against government, and crimes against consumers, to mention a few (see Hochstedler, 1984). Sutherland's studies of white collar criminality in the 1940s set a tone and sparked other studies during that initial period. Surprisingly, however—with the exception of a few scholarly works, investigative journalistic pieces, and consumer studies particularly by Ralph Nader and

Ralph Nader, consumer advocate, testifies before a House subcommittee. Nader exposed the dangers of GM cars in his book *Unsafe at Any Speed.*

associates—there was a considerable hiatus of research activity in this area until the middle to late seventies. In 1977 Geis and Meier (1977, p. 1), in revising their classic reader on white collar crime originally published nine years previously, found that they were able to add less than a third new material. With the exception, then, of works by Sutherland (1940, 1941, 1945, 1949, and 1956), Clinard (1946 and 1952), Hartung (1950), and Nader and associates (Nader 1965, 1970, 1973), "white collar crime" was ripe for the research picking.

A new renaissance in studies of "white collar crime" took place in the late seventies with publications by Clinard and Yeager and associates: *Illegal Corporate Behavior* (1979) and later *Corporate Crime* (1980). Other than Sutherland's pioneering effort, which was modest by comparison, the research conducted by Clinard and Yeager and their colleagues represents a landmark: the first large-scale, comprehensive investigation of corporate crime. With a large grant from the Law Enforcement Assistance Administration, they conducted a systematic analysis of administrative, civil, and criminal actions either filed or completely by twenty-five federal agencies against 477 of the largest manufacturing corporations in the U.S. during 1975–1976. In addition, they performed a less comprehensive survey of 105 of the largest wholesale, retail, and service corporations (Ibid., p. 110). Among their findings:

- 60 percent of the large corporations had at least one action initiated against them during the period.
- The most deviant firms (multiple violators) accounted for 13 percent of those charged (8 percent of all corporations studied) and accounted for 52 percent of all offenses. The average for these corporations was 23.5 violations per firm, while the average for all corporations was 4.2.
- Large corporations were the chief violators, with oil, pharmaceutical, and automobile industries the biggest offenders and the most often cited. These three groups alone accounted for almost one-half of all the violations.
- The general leniency with which corporate violators are treated, noted over forty years previously by Sutherland, appears to continue.

The Measurement of Corporate Crime

Among others, Clinard and Yeager (1978, pp. 255–272) and Geis and Meier (1977, p. 3–4) suggest that there are a number of *reasons for the lack of research on corporate crime* in the past:

1. Many social scientists are inexperienced in studying corporate crime, which often requires some sophistication in areas of law, finance, and economics.
2. Corporate violations often involve administrative and civil sanctions to which criminologists have limited exposure.
3. Enforcement is often carried out by state and federal regulatory agencies rather than by the usual criminal justice agencies.
4. Funds for such studies have not been generally available in the past.
5. Corporate crime is complicated by the very complexity of the corporation.
6. Research data is not readily available due to the imperviousness of the corporate board room.
7. Corporate crime raises special problems of analysis and research objectivity.

Despite these obstacles, rising public concern about corporate wrongdoing has encouraged accelerated research into corporate crime.

Legal Regulation

Organizations and the Law

A corporation is a legal entity which permits a business to make use of capital provided by stockholders. Although the federal government has had the power of federal chartering of corporations since the 1791 *McCulloch v. Maryland* decision, it is rarely used; most chartering is done by the states. Corporations have been considered legal "persons" since a Supreme Court decision of 1886 (Clinard and Yeager, 1980, pp. 25–28).

In the United States, beginning in the nineteenth century, certain business activities were defined as illegal. These included: restraint of trade, deceptive advertisements, bank fraud, sale of phony securities, faulty manufacturing of foods and drugs, environmental pollution, as well as the misuse of patents and trademarks (Clinard and Quinney, 1973, p. 207). In the late nineteenth century, concern grew about the development of monopolies, which threatened to control economies, stifle competition, and thereby threaten the very philosophy of free enterprise markets.

The *Sherman Antitrust Act* (1890) was the first of many regulatory laws passed to control corporate behavior. This law forbids restraint of trade or the formation of monopolies; it currently makes price fixing a felony, with a maximum corporate fine of $1 million, and authorizes private treble (triple) damage suits by victims of price fixing. For the most part, the policing of corporate violations is done by federal regulatory agencies, for example, the Federal Trade Commission (FTC) which was set up in 1914 at the same time as the Clayton Antitrust Act and the Federal Trade Act. There are over fifty *federal regulatory agencies* with semipolicing functions with respect to corporate violations. Among these agencies are: The Civil Aeronautics Board (CAB), Environmental Protection Agency (EPA), Federal Communications Commission (FCC), the Food and Drug Administration (FDA), Federal Power Commission (FPC), Interstate Commerce Commissionl (ICC), National Labor Relations Board (NLRB), Nuclear Regulatory Commission (NRC), Occupational Safety and Health Administration (OSHA), and the Securities and Exchange Commission (SEC). Some areas regulated by these agencies and to be discussed in this chapter are: air safety, air and water pollution, unfair advertising, safe drugs and healthy food, public utility services, interstate trucking and commerce, labor-management practices, nuclear power plants, health and safety in the workplace, and the sale and negotiation of bonds and securities.

Regulatory agencies have a number of sanctions which they can use in order to attempt to assure compliance with their orders: warnings, recalls, orders (unilateral orders, consent agreements, and decrees), injunctions, monetary penalties, and criminal penalties (Clinard and Yeager, 1980, p. 83). In addition to criminal proceedings, acts such as the Clayton Act (Section 4) permit "treble damage suits" by harmed parties. Guilty companies, with their batteries of lawyers and accountants, generally have more expertise, time, and staff to devote to defense than the Justice Department, under its Anti-Trust Division, has for prosecution. Indefinite delays and appeals are not uncommon.

If the government appears to have a solid case, corporations are permitted to plead nolo contendere—no contest to charges. This is not an admission of guilt, and thus enables corporations to avoid the label of criminal. Consent decrees amount to a "hand slap"; that is, the corporation agrees to quit violating the particular regulation for which it was charged.

A number of *criticisms have been levied against federal regulatory agencies* and their efforts against corporate crime:

1. Lacking sufficient investigative manpower, the agencies are often reliant upon the records of the very corporations they are regulating to detect wrongdoing.
2. The criminal fines authorized by law are insignificant compared to the economic losses incurred by corporate crime and in effect become a minor nuisance, "a crime tax," "a license to steal," but certainly not a strong deterrent.
3. Other criminal penalties such as imprisonment have been rather rare and, when they do occur, tend to reflect a dual system of justice: offenders are incarcerated in "country club" prisons or are treated in a far more lenient manner than traditional offenders.
4. The enforcement divisions of many regulatory agencies are critically understaffed and can be cut back, as in the Reagan administration's plans for the EPA and other agencies, to inoperable levels.
5. The top echelons of agency commissions are often held by leaders from the very corporations or industries that are to be regulated, presenting much potential conflict of interest.
6. Relationships between regulators and regulated are often too compatible, with some agency employees more interested in representing the interests of the corporations they are supposed to be regulating than they are the public well-being. The fact that many former agency employees upon retirement are hired by the formerly regulated companies lends support to this argument.

In reviewing the state of regulation of illegal corporate activity, Clinard and Yeager (1980, p. 96) state: "One may well wonder why such small budgets and professional staffs are established to deal with business and corporate crime when billions of dollars are willingly spent on ordinary crime control, including 500,000 policemen, along with tens of thousands of government prosecutors and officials." Gross (1980) in his book *Friendly Fascism* answers their question by letting us in on what he calls "*the dirty secrets*":

> We are not letting the public in on our era's dirty little secret: that those who commit the crime which worries citizens most—violent street crime—are, for the most part, products of poverty, unemployment, broken homes, rotten education, drug addiction, alcoholism, and other social and economic ills about which the police can do little if anything. . . . But, all the *dirty little secrets* fade into insignificance in comparison with one *dirty big secret:* Law enforcement officials, judges as well as prosecutors and investigators, are soft on corporate crime . . . The corporation's "mouthpieces" and "fixers" include lawyers, accountants, public relations experts and public officials who negotiate loopholes and special procedures in the laws, prevent most illegal activities from ever being disclosed and undermine or sidetrack "over zealous" law enforcers. In the few cases ever brought to court, they usually negotiate penalties amounting to "gentle taps on the wrist."
>
> —Gross, 1980, pp. 110, 113–115

Crimes by Organizations/Corporations against Individuals (the Public)

Included in the discussion of *crimes by organizations against individuals (public)* are multinational bribery, money laundering, corporate fraud, price-fixing, manufacturing and sale of faulty or unsafe products, inequitable taxes, and environmental crimes, just to mention a few.

Multinational Bribery

Embarrassed by the public disclosure and international scandal of American-based multinational corporations' expending millions of dollars to bribe foreign officials, U.S. Congress passed the *Foreign Corrupt Practices Act (1977)*. This law forbids the payment of bribes in order to obtain business contracts. Some specific incidents which prompted the passage of this legislation included the following:

- In the early seventies, multimillion dollar bribes by Lockheed to Japanese Prime Minister Kakuei Tanaka caused his resignation, toppled his government, and threatened Japanese-American relations. Similar payments by Lockheed caused scandal in the Netherlands and Italy. Ironically in 1989 Japanese Prime Minister Noboru Takeshita also was forced to resign in an "influence peddling" scandal, although this time the corrupters were Japanese.

- The Communist Party in Italy scored impressive electoral support as a result of campaigning on a corruption issue, involving Exxon's disbursing over $50 million to Italian politicians.
- The same laundered funds from secret offshore account "slush funds" that are used to bribe foreign officials are also used domestically for illegal political campaign donations. About three hundred corporations admitted making such "donations" to Richard Nixon's campaigns in 1968 and 1972, using the same "laundered" money from which bribes of foreign officials were made (Anderson, 1983, p. 7–A).

"Laundering" Dirty Money

"Laundering" refers to making clean or washing "dirty money" (illegal funds). A classic task of organized crime syndicates has been to somehow convert the large amounts of illegally gotten funds they obtain into usable money that appears to come from legitimate sources. Similarly, corporations, rather than pay their fair share of taxes, find it far more feasible to make comparatively smaller investments in politicians who will return the favor more than tenfold in favorable legislative treatment.

An excellent description of the laundering process is contained in Clark and Tigue's (1975) *Dirty Money: Swiss Banks, the Mafia, Money Laundering and White Collar Crime.* Various countries, most notably Switzerland, the Bahamas, Panama, and other "tax havens" have created bank secrecy laws which generally forbid the disclosure of the financial affairs of account holders. This practice apparently was begun in Switzerland with numbered accounts to protect the finances of those whose holdings were being confiscated in Nazi Germany.

The laundering process involves these steps:

1. Hidden funds are smuggled or deposited by check in a secret Caribbean or Swiss account.
2. Such funds are altered in nature or origin by means of phony business transactions (to be discussed shortly).
3. The now "clean money" can be repatriated and invested, enjoyed, or used for bribery. Transferring it to branches of the "tax haven" banks in Montreal or Toronto is but one ploy (Ibid., 1975, p. 91).

One means of altering funds is through the practice of *double invoicing* (or overpricing) in which companies keep two invoices (bills): a secret bill which contains the true price of a product and an inflated, fraudulent bill that enables the smuggling of illegal profits out of the

Japanese Prime Minister Takeshita was forced to resign as a result of an "influence peddling" scandal in 1989.

country. In a classic example both of double invoicing and of "*influence peddling*" (a practice in which public officials sell or deny service on the basis of personal payment), American Airlines claimed that they were threatened with unfavorable regulatory agency decisions unless they made illegal donations to Nixon's CREEP (Campaign to Re-Elect the President). So first the airline ordered five thousand airplane seats from one of its European subsidiaries and paid a prearranged inflated price. The difference between the real and fake price was untaxed, secret money which then was deposited by the subsidiary in a secret account and used as a slush fund for bribes and illegal campaign donations. Not only are funds like these untaxed, but also donations made can be written off as an expense (Ibid., pp. 105–107). In a sense, bribes become tax deductible. Along with seventeen other corporations American Airlines pleaded guilty to making illegal campaign donations. Fines ranged from $1,000 to $25,000 (Jaworski, 1977, pp. 344–345). Recognizing the seriousness of such activity, Congress passed the Money Laundering Act of 1986, which made money laundering a federal crime with substantial penalties (Weinstein, 1988).

Corporate Fraud

In 1989 an FBI undercover sting operation of commodities traders at the Chicago Board of Trade discovered traders who overcharged customers, did not pay them the full proceeds of sales, used their knowledge of customer orders to "inside trade" for their own benefit, and executed orders at fictitious prices (Berg, 1989). Such fraud may come in many forms from the Chrysler Corporation admitting that they rolled back odometers on cars used by their executives and sold them to unwary customers to the following famous insurance fraud case.

The Equity Funding Corporation Scandal.   Perhaps one of the biggest swindles by computer in history, amounting to an estimated $2 billion, came to light in 1973 with the bankruptcy of the Equity Funding Corporation of America; this case illustrates the overlap between professional crime (wherein the entire purpose of the organization is illegal gain) and corporate crime (where the crime develops incidentally to legitimate corporate activities). The Equity Funding scandal is described under corporate crime because, at least in the beginning, it appears that the corporation was involved in legitimate services although it clearly evolved into a pure swindling organization.

Executives at Equity Funding's life insurance subsidiary used the company computer to create roughly 56,000 phony or "ghost" policies (about 58 percent of all policies the company held). Reinsurers who bought the rights to the dummy policies were out millions of dollars; stockholders alone lost over $100 million. Using computer records rather than hard copy records, the Equity Funding executives mixed geniune and phony policies in the master tape files; thus printouts showed that the company had nearly 100,000 policies. When auditors took samples to check against hard copies, they were held off for a day or two during which phony hard-copy records were produced (Conning, by Computer, 1973). The president and twenty-four other employees and officers were indicted. While the former received an eight-year sentence, the others received shorter terms (Blundell, 1978). Convicted of complicity in the case, outside auditing firms were ordered to pay $39 million to former equity shareholders (Ermann and Lundman, 1982, pp. 43–48).

The Savings and Loan Rip-Off.   As part of the deregulation of banking and savings and loans in the U.S. in the eighties, many high risk, questionable investments and loans took place which led to the largest number of failures of savings and loans since the Great Depression. Much of the failure of these institutions was not due to bad business cycles, but fraud. In order to prevent the savings and loans from failing it is estimated that it will eventually cost the taxpayers anywhere from $90-$300 billion. Much of the money lost through the fraud is not recoverable. Some, for instance, had been invested in inflated real estate that is now worthless. Those convicted in such complex financial cases have been receiving on average less than a twelve-month sentence, fines, or community service (Bartlett, 1989). By way of analogy the cost of this rip-off equals six to eleven times the cost of all property crime in the U.S. in a given year as estimated by the National Crime Survey.

Price Fixing

The Great Electrical Industry Conspiracy.   In May 1959, Julian Granger, a reporter for the Knoxville *News Sentinel,* did not particularly look forward to working on a Saturday, particularly his task of sorting through mimeographed press releases from local organizations and a weekly newsletter from the Tennessee Valley Authority (TVA). Out of a sense of duty, he persisted and was just about to discard the TVA bulletin when something caught his eye:

> On this bidding for a transformers contract which was awarded to Westinghouse in the amount of $96,760 Allis Chalmers, General Electric, and Pennsylvania Transformer quoted identical prices of $112,712.
>
> —Fuller, 1962, p. 9.

Reading on, Granger noted that two other firms quoted the same prices on a $273,000 contract and that another contract for conductor cable attracted seven identical bids down to the penny of $198,438.24 (Ibid., p. 10). Incredulous, he asked himself how, under a system of sealed bids, it was possible for independent contractors to quote identical prices. He was on the track of what would become at that time the largest antitrust case in U.S. history. Collusion and price fixing to set artificially high prices had become the norm in the electrical industry, with the firms taking turns (rotational bidding) submitting the lowest bid. This cost the American public untold millions, perhaps billions, of dollars in higher prices.

In February 1961 seven of the highest executives in the electrical industry, from firms such as General Electric and Westinghouse, were given jail sentences of thirty days, an unprecedented benchmark decision that sent a warning to corporate price fixers, bid-riggers, and market-slicers. In addition, General Electric was fined $437,500 and Westinghouse $372,500. In all, twenty-nine companies and forty-five executives were convicted in bid-rigging and price fixing estimated at approximately $2 billion (Herling, 1962). The conspirators were well aware of the illegality of their activities: they met under fictitious names in hotel rooms, called their meetings "choir practice," and referred to the list of participants as "the Christmas card list."

Plumbers Fix More than Leaks.   In 1975 the U.S. Justice Department filed an antitrust suit against three plumbing manufacturers (American Standard, Borg Warner, and Kohler) and three executives for conspiring to fix prices on $1 billion worth of bathroom fixtures. The case actually began in 1966 with seventeen corporate and individual co-conspirators named. The others pleaded "no contest" to the charges got short jail terms and were fined a total of $370,000 (U.S. Begins Price-Fixing Prosecution, 1975). One billion dollars stolen by these organizations from the public dwarfs by far the more "mundane" criminal activity that gains so much media attention. For instance, the big Boston Brinks robbery netted only $2 million and the largest robbery as of 1980 in U.S. history—that of the Lufthansa airport warehouse in New York City—scored only $4 million (Clinard and Yeager, 1980, p. 8). This was superseded in 1983 by the $11 million robbery of a Sentry Armored Car warehouse in New York City (Wells Fargo, 1983). Thus the "great plumbing equipment rip-off," which is far less dramatic and well-known, cost the American public the equivalent of five hundred great Brinks robberies.

In 1980 the Energy Department filed suit against fifteen major refining companies and charged them with more than $10 billion in possible pricing violations. As part of some out-of-court settlements, several of the corporations agreed to reimburse overcharged customers, pay the government, give rebates on past charges, cut prices, and accelerate investment in refining, exploration, and production (Lyons, 1980). Many feel, however, that the big oil companies "got off easy" considering the extent of their activities.

Panasonic Price-Fixing Scheme.   In 1989 the Japanese electronics giant, Panasonic, settled out of court and agreed to pay $16 million in rebates to over 665,000 U.S. consumers for overcharges as a result of an aborted price-fixing scheme. Although such price setting is legal in Japan, the firm had illegally threatened to cut off supplies of their VCR camcorders and cordless telephones unless retailers agreed to sell these items at prices dictated by Panasonic. Such a scheme would have cost consumers hundreds of millions of dollars (Panasonic, 1989).

The Great Oil Scam. *Scam* is a slang term explored in greater detail in the chapter on professional crime; it refers to various illegal hustles, swindles, or techniques of crime. The fact that legitimate organizations can "hustle" with the best confidence artists in the professional criminal world is well illustrated by the following examples.

In his sociological classic, *The Power Elite*, (1956), C. Wright Mills alleged that, contrary to high school civics class descriptions of the manner in which decisions are made in the United States, most major decisions were made by a small, interlocking power elite consisting of two hundred to five hundred individuals who represented the corporate, political, and military elite. Rather than checking and balancing each other's power, these elites often acted in unison, with much movement of members from one sector to another. It was in part this phenomenon that prompted President Dwight Eisenhower to warn the nation as he left office (1961) to beware of the development of a powerful "military-industrial complex," which might not be working in the national interest.

In 1972 David Rockefeller of the Chase Manhattan Bank initiated a meeting of world leaders from Western Europe, North America, and Japan which a year later became the *Trilateral Commission* with Zbigniew Brzezinski as its first director. Some other former members of this commission were later key members of the Carter Administration: Walter Mondale and Cyrus Vance, for example. The Rockefeller family, through Chase Manhattan, had top voting interests in Exxon, Mobil, Standard Oil of Ohio and Indiana, and Texaco. Cook (1982, p. 30) in *The Great Energy Scam* explains it:

> It is only through an understanding of this cartel structure of Big Oil, added to the potential influence at the top by the Trilateral Commission's fraternal ties, that one can begin to make sense of the manner in which crude oil supplies were manipulated and multibillion-dollar ripoffs were allowed to run unchecked — indeed, were protected — during the years of the Carter presidency.

Chase Energy Information Systems would supply through third parties the data the government would use to decide energy policy, and oil industry consultants actually designed our new National Energy Policy of 1977 (Ibid., pp. 31, 35).

"I think we may have stumbled on the greatest criminal conspiracy in American History."

—U.S. Representative Albert A. Gore, Jr., of Tennessee,
"NBC Nightly News," May 30, 1979

Cook (1982) maintains the following as a result of his investigations of the great oil price increase of the 1970s:

- The decontrol of oil (having Congress lift price controls) was supposed to spur competition, but actually resulted in higher, noncompetitive prices.
- The shortage that had precipitated the crisis was a myth. Wells were capped and storage tanks bulging until prices were forced upwards. Supplies were deliberately withheld from market.
- Why was fuel oil (which was cheap to produce) being marketed at the same price as gasoline? In 1978 price rises in fuel oil were uniform, across the board, no matter which refinery produced it.
- In the spring of 1979 during contrived shortages, refineries bought Saudi, OPEC oil at $13.35 per barrel but used the "spot market price" (as high as $23) to justify raising prices, yielding a huge profit on existing inventory.
- The Department of Energy was so infiltrated it was practically owned by Big Oil interests.

Daisy Chain Scam.   One means of camouflaging oil supplies and price manipulation was the "daisy chain." The *daisy chain scam* refers to a practice in the 1970s by the large oil companies in which phony paper transactions enabled the companies to claim that old oil (that which was produced from old wells and which was lower priced due to regulation) was new oil (which was unregulated and more than double the price). The companies simply created a chain of middlemen to buy and resell the oil to each other, increasing the price each time. This racket continued unhindered by the Department of Energy, the Federal Bureau of Investigation, or the Justice Department. A General Accounting Office investigation (cited in Cook, 1982, p. 56) concluded:

> . . . statistics, collected at the wellhead and then at the refinery indicated that over 300,000 barrels per day of old crude were converted to new crude during the month of March, 1977. As of September, 1977, the rate declined to over 139,000 per day. At the lower September rate, DOE stated that over $800,000 per day was being unlawfully taken from customers. At the $8 per barrel difference, the March, 1977, conversion rate indicates over $2.6 million per day may have been taken.

Even if the scheme operated for only twenty days, the take—assuming as Cook (Ibid., p. 56) does "that even thieves take weekends off"—amounted to $52 million in just one month. It was during this period that comedian Johnny Carson remarked, "If Jesse James were alive today, he'd work for Exxon." The "daisy chain" operated year after year with apparent approval of the regulators until "the greatest criminal conspiracy in American history died without a whimper—without the arrest and conviction of any of the major conspirators involved" (Ibid., pp. 56–57). It was later revealed that the Department of Energy had arrived at its conclusion that the oil industry had not conspired to fix prices on the basis of data that these same industries supplied. The 1981 hearings of the Dingell Subcommittee (U.S. Congress, 1981) further claimed that, as of March 1981, the DOE discovered roughly $13 billion in violations, $9.5 billion of which was accounted for by the fifteen major refiners. As of March 1981, eleven firms and thirty-nine individuals had been found guilty or claimed nolo contendere in "daisy chain" scams equaling $2 billion in settlements. The remaining cases are not likely to be pursued due to DOE budget cuts.

Sale of Unsafe Products

"Pinto leaves you with that warm feeling"

The Ford Pinto Case.   In the early sixties, in order to compete with compact foreign imports, the Ford Motor Company rushed the compact Pinto model into production. Since retooling for the assembly line was already a costly investment, the company chose to proceed with production despite the results of their own crash tests, which indicated that the gas tank exploded in rear-end collisions. Choosing profit over human lives, the company continued to avoid and to lobby even eight years later against federal safety standards which would have forced modification of the gas tank (Dowie, 1977; and Cullen, 1984a).

An estimated five hundred persons were burned to death due to the firetrap engineering of the tanks. Once the word spread, Ford withdrew their commercial that the car gave one a "warm feeling." *Mother Jones* (an investigative magazine) collected documents and called to public attention Ford's wrongdoing (Dowie, 1977; and Cullen, Makestad, and Cavender, 1987). While the company estimated that it could have made the necessary modifications for about $11 per car, *Mother Jones* estimated the changes at half that (Ibid.). Using the National Highway Traffic Safety Administration estimate of the cost per fatality (assuming law-suits) of roughly $200,000, Ford had, in a company memorandum, performed a cost/benefit analysis of the problem. Paying for

This Ford Pinto's owner died in 1978 when the car burst into flames upon being hit from behind. Ford Motor Company was apparently aware of the danger, but sold the cars anyway.

deaths, injuries, and damages without changing the tanks was guessed to cost about $49.5 million, while the cost of modifying the 12.5 million vehicles would run $137 million. It was "cheaper" to ignore the problem and face the lawsuits.

In May of 1978 the Department of Transportation finally recalled all 1971 to 1976 Pintos and, although it was the biggest auto recall until that time, the decision amounted to too little too late for the conservatively estimated five hundred dead, maimed, and scarred victims (Ermann and Lundman, 1982, p. 18). The Ford Pinto case was also a landmark, representing the first time in U.S. history that a corporation was indicted for murder. In 1978, Indiana prosecutors charged Ford with homicide after three people were burned alive in a Pinto (Browning and Gerassi, 1980, p. 406). Even though Ford was acquitted, the trial of a corporation for murder may have served as a signal that the public reaction to corporate crime was changing (Swigert and Farrell, 1980). When asked what fate Lee Iacocca, then president of Ford, deserved, one person sarcastically suggested that someone buy him a Ford Pinto complete with Firestone 500 tires (the latter was yet another dangerous product whose manufacturer hid its defects until an unacceptable number of human sacrifices sparked federal action).

X-Cars = Brand X. Brand X has never been a favored label for a product. It perhaps was prophetic that GM chose this name for what appears to have been a real brand X product. The National Highway Traffic Safety Administration (NHTSA) filed suit on August 3, 1983, against General Motors, alleging that the corporation with full knowledge had sold 1.1 million X-model cars with faulty brakes that later killed fifteen and injured seventy-one persons. The government has charged that the company knew of these problems and purposely withheld information that the rear brakes, due to a defect, tend to lock. To lend further complexity to the case, the Congressional General Accounting Office (GAO) has accused the NHTSA of a "cover-up" and of failing to follow usual procedures in alerting the public to a known danger.

The suit sought a recall on all 1980 X-cars, and $4 million in civil penalties. The former alone would be expected to cost GM about $300 million. At Congressional hearings on the issue, Representative Timothy Wirth charged, "They [the NHTSA] have been trying to protect GM all the way down the line" (Washington vs. GM, 1983, p. 9). On March 30, 1983, 240,000 X-cars were recalled (Coleman, 1985, p. 41).

Reminiscent of Mills's (1952) "higher immorality" notion, Heilbronner et al. (1973) in their book *In the Name of Profit: Profiles in Corporate Irresponsibility* maintain that the people who run our supercorporations are not merely amoral, but positively immoral. They and other authors cite examples like these:

- B. F. Goodrich plotted to sell defective air brakes to the U.S. Air Force by faking test records and falsifying laboratory reports. National security and the lives of fighter pilots appeared to be of little concern.
- In order to avoid heavy financial loss as a result of investment in a defective drug, the William S. Merrell Company submitted false records to the FDA in order to make the drug marketable.
- General Motors deliberately stalled in correcting dangerous defects in school buses. When consumer advocate Ralph Nader began to apply pressure, they attempted to blackmail him. Nader sued GM and collected $500,000 in an out-of-court settlement.
- In the early 1970s a General Dynamics engineer warned his superiors of dangerous defects in DC-10 cargo doors. They ignored this warning. A DC-10 two years later crashed in France when the cargo doors opened in flight, killing all 346 passengers (Nader, Green, and Seligman, 1976).

The National Consumer Product Safety Commission estimates that 20 million serious injuries and thirty thousand deaths a year are caused by unsafe consumer products (Coleman, 1985, p. 7). When Richardson-Merrell's (MER/29), a cholesterol inhibitor, was tested, all the rats died; nevertheless, the company falsified their data and marketed it. When over five thousand users had serious side effects, it was withdrawn from the market and the company received a minor fine (Ibid., p. 43). In 1988 the Cordis Corp. pleaded guilty in federal court to concealing defects in thousands of pacemakers (these are implanted in heart patients to regulate their heartbeat). The company agreed to a fine of $264,000 plus court costs. Executives were charged separately (4 Indicted, 1988).

In 1986 executives of Beech Nut Nutrition Corporation were indicted for marketing phony apple juice. Although the drink for babies was labeled apple juice, it was actually mostly flavored sugar water. Although executives and those involved were convicted, their case was overturned on a court jurisdictional technicality in 1989 (Doyle, 1989). The company had made over $3.5 million in sales from the scam.

Inequitable Taxes

Lekachman (1982, p. 61) points to the "eye-glazing complexity of the tax code" as a means of protecting wealth, since only affluent individuals and skilled professionals in the employ of large corporations are able to even begin to comprehend it. Tax fraud, hidden benefits, the abuse of expense accounts, and other tax loopholes raise the cost of living for the general public, rob the treasury of vitally needed funds for neglected social programs, and create and perpetuate the inequalities which act as the incubator for the types of street crimes which attract the bulk of media attention. To give but one example of tax benefits for the rich, Simon and Eitzen (1982, p. 46) comment:

> The late Nelson Rockefeller, while governor of New York, set up a Government Affairs Foundation. Between 1961 and 1964 the governor gave $310,469 to the Foundation, but it paid out exactly zero dollars in charitable causes. Instead Frank Moore was paid 120,000 dollars in salary and 40,000 dollars in expenses, and acted largely as Rockefeller's political liaison in various state matters. Essentially, Rockefeller had gained a full-time political liaison at costs which were tax deductible.

U.S. Representative Charles Vanik (D-Ohio) estimated that due to the political power of large corporations the one hundred largest corporations in the U.S. pay taxes only half as high as smaller firms (Coleman, 1985, p. 25).

Environmental Crime

In 1962, the publication of Rachel Carson's *Silent Spring* (1962) signaled the beginning of the age of environmental awareness. Specifically attacking toxic chemicals and pesticides, Carson's work very dramatically called attention to the irreversible and final genetic and biological harm the poisoning of the environment could bring about. According to Regenstein (1982, p. 132), "The accuracy and validity of *Silent Spring* was no inhibition to the chemical industry's attacking and attempting to discredit it, a vicious campaign which started even before the work was published and continues today."

Three Mile Island.   Ironically in a film, *The China Syndrome* (so-named because of the fictitious belief that a nuclear meltdown in the United States would bore through the earth to the other side—China), a character indicates that a nuclear mishap could render an area the size of Pennsylvania uninhabitable. Almost prophetically, after the release of the film, the worst potential nuclear plant disaster in history occurred at Three Mile Island, Pennsylvania. The accident released radioactivity into the surrounding area and required the temporary evacuation of young children and pregnant women from the immediate vicinity.

On November 7, 1983, a federal grand jury indicted Metropolitan Edison, the owners of the TMI facility, on criminal charges of faking safety test records before the accident. The indictment alleges that the company attempted to conceal from the Nuclear Regulatory Commission the rate of leakage in the main cooling system in which water passes over the reactor's radioactive core (Feds Indict, 1983). Allegations had been made that the corporation was anxious to have the reactor on-line by a certain date in order to take advantage of certain tax benefits.

In April, 1984, Metropolitan Edison pleaded guilty to knowingly using inaccurate and meaningless testing methods and agreed to pay a $1 million fine. The company also pleaded no contest to six other criminal counts including manipulating test results, destroying records, and not filing proper notice of cooling system leaks (Judge Agrees to TMI Plea Bargain, 1984).

Toxic Criminals.   Potential environmental hazards created by new technologies require that corporations and businesses exercise a higher level of ethical behavior than that depicted in the Ford Pinto incident or other cover-ups and deceptions of the public and government regulatory agencies. Bhopal (India), Love Canal, Times Beach, Seveso (Italy) have all represented well known environmental disasters. In 1979 the EPA estimated there were 109 very hazardous dumpsites and 32,254 sites where hazardous wastes were buried. That latter figure was subsequently raised to 51,000, with "significant problems" existing in between 1,200 and 34,000 (Brown, 1982, p. 305).

Medical waste is removed from a Staten Island Beach during a period of illegal disposal of hazardous wastes in the late 1980s.

In 1983, the U.S. Justice Department and six congressional committees were all investigating conflict of interest and malfeasance in the EPA. Allegations included conflict of interest, "sweetheart" deals, and use of the superfund cleanup program for political purposes. It is estimated that U.S. industry generates roughly 88 billion pounds of toxic wastes every year and that about 90 percent of this is improperly disposed of (Storm over the Environment, 1983). Midnight dumping, abandoning trucks loaded with lethal chemicals, spilling dangerous wastes on highways or even mixing them with fuel oil and selling them in New York City are just a few illustrations of the problem.

In the late 1980s beaches in various parts of the U.S. had to be closed because illegally dumped medical wastes were washing ashore. Blood gushing out of trash compactors and body parts found in trash piles illustrate the ghoulish proportions of such hazards. Each year about three hundred health-care workers die from hepatitis B after exposure on the job (Anderson and Van Atta, 1988a). Such wastes also expose the public to possible harm.

In 1983 Rita Lavelle, former director of the EPA's toxic-waste cleanup program or "superfund" as it was called, was indicted by a federal grand jury on five felony charges which included obstruction of congressional investigations and perjury. The latter charge was related to her testimony in which she claimed that she had disqualified herself from involvement in an EPA decision regarding cleanup costs at a California dump site involving her former employer, Aerojet-General Corporation. Lavelle is also charged with lying before the Congressional committee when she claimed superfund grants were not being awarded on political grounds. In December of 1983 Lavelle was convicted of obstruction of congressional inquiry and three felony counts of perjury.

Nuclear Dumping.   On the ABC news program *20/20* (1983b), it was reported that EPA investigators of nuclear dumping in the oceans discovered ninety thousand barrels of nuclear waste, many of them leaking and many dumped where they were not supposed to have been deposited. Many boat owners, rather than dumping the barrels far out to sea as contracted, scattered them all over the place on the continental shelf, including commercial fishing grounds. These fish will, of course, be eaten up through the food chain. One fisherman stated, "These people crap in their own plate and then eat dinner out of it."

The Great Kyshtym Disaster.   Reports of nuclear mishaps such as occurred at Three Mile Island are public information, or else an independent press raises a storm of controversy and publicity. This is not the case in more secretive societies in which news is carefully managed. Imagine in the United States if a strange explosion obliterated and wiped off the map hundreds of square miles, converting it into a wasteland. Just such an incident was believed to have taken place in the Soviet Union in the late 1950s. Although the exact cause of the incident is still in dispute, some scientists believe that improperly buried radioactive wastes produced a chain reaction that spread a volcano-like cloud of lethal dust over a wide area. Recent Soviet maps no longer display many towns which previously appeared in the Ural Mountains Kyshtym area (Wellborn and Chrysler, 1983, p. 24) — a "silent spring" indeed.

U.S.A. versus Allied Chemical.   In 1976, Judge Robert Merhige (Richmond, Virginia) fined Allied Chemical $13.2 million after it pleaded nolo contendere to 153 charges of conspiracy to defraud the EPA and Army Corps of Engineers. Allied had polluted the James River and had deceptively blocked the efforts of these agencies to enforce water pollution control laws. In justifying the largest fine ever imposed in a single environmental case, the judge stated, "I don't think that commercial products or the making of profits are as important as the God-given resources of our country" (Beachamp, 1983, p. 97).

Much of the work social scientists or federal agencies should have been doing in investigating corporate crime has until relatively recently been shouldered by investigative journalists and consumer advocates, the latter represented by Ralph Nader and his associates. A partial list of such studies and their subject matter includes:

Cox, Fellmuth, and Schulz (1969), a report on the Federal Trade Commission.
Esposito and Silverman (1970), *Vanishing Air*, on air pollution regulation.
Turner (1970), *The Chemical Feast*, on the Food and Drug Administration.
Wellford (1972, *Sowing and Wind*, on health and environmental hazards.
Green et al. (1973), *The Monopoly Makers*, on antitrust activity.
Page and O'Brien (1973), *Bitter Wages*, on occupational safety and health.

In addition to these, Nader and his associates have generated numerous other investigations and reports (Nader, 1965, Nader, Petkas, and Blackwell, 1972; 1973; Nader and Green, 1973; Nader, Green, and Seligman, 1976). In the foreword to Esposito's *The Vanishing Air*, Nader (1970, p. viii) states:

> The efflux of motor vehicles, plants and incinerators of sulfur oxides, hydrocarbons, carbon monoxide, oxides of nitrogen particulates, and many more contaminants amounts to the *compulsory consumption of violence* by most

Americans. There is no full escape from such violent ingestions, for breathing is required. This damage perpetuated increasingly in direct violation of local, state and federal law, shatters people's health and safety, but still escapes inclusion in crime statistics. "Smogging" a city or town has taken on the proportions of a massive crime wave, yet federal and state statistical compilations of crime pay attention to "muggers" and not "smoggers." In testament to the power of corporations and their retained attorneys, enforcement scarcely exists. Violators are openly flouting the laws and an Administration [Nixon] allegedly dedicated to law and order sits on its duties.

Related to environmental and health assaults upon consumers, Simon and Eitzen (1982, Chapter 5) describe some cases of "corporate dumping," the practice of corporations selling products overseas which have been deemed unsafe in this country by the EPA, FDA, or other federal agencies (Vantage Point 10.1).

Toxic crime may indeed be the ultimate and most insidious of crimes. Birth defects, long-term genetic damage and mutation, congenital heart defects and disorders in children—many of these effects may turn up twenty to thirty years later and be difficult to link to the original causative agents or toxic criminals. In that sense, those who commit environmental crimes may represent the first "intergenerational criminals," where the victimized may have not even been born at the time the crime is perpetrated and where the criminal may be deceased at the time the victimization takes place.

Radiation Leaks.   In 1988 in the wake of the Chernobyl disaster in the Soviet Union, investigations began to reveal massive cover-up by the U.S. federal government of the dangers and harm its nuclear facilities and testing program had posed to unwarned workers and neighbors. Fallout from atomic tests in the 1950s and 60s resulted in little warning by the Atomic Energy Commission of exposure hazards such as birth deformities, cancer, and early death (McGrory, 1988). The Department of Energy runs federally owned nuclear plants which produce the fuel for the nation's nuclear weapons. These obsolete plants have worse safety features than most privately owned plants. Some of the revelations included:

- That arms plants in Ohio and Washington regularly released vast amounts of radioactive particles into the air.
- Radioactive wastes were dumped haphazardly polluting surrounding areas.
- Managerial negligence and poor operating rules resulted in shutdown of Savannah River Plant, in South Carolina.
- Radiation leaks went unchecked for decades rather than the government paying for costly clean-up (Morganthau, *et al.*, 1988).

Unsafe Food—"Where's the Beef?"   In one of the most successful commercials of the mid-eighties a little elderly woman travels around to various fast food restaurants asking, "Where's the beef?" She was questioning the size of hamburger patties, but consumers would do well to echo her in questioning the chemical contents and condition of the processed meats and other foods which they consume. More and more of our food is processed and packaged by large corporations and, if recent investigations are believed, the food processors have not improved much since Upton Sinclair's (1906) exposés in *The Jungle*. Despite a 1906 federal Meat Inspection Act and a 1967 Wholesome Meat Act, abuses continue. In a Hormel plant in 1969, a Department of Agriculture inspector was bribed $6,000 annually for overlooking their production of "Number 2" meat (McCaghy, 1976b, p. 216).

VANTAGE POINT

Vantage Point 10.1—Corporate Dumping

- When *Dalkon Shield IUDs* (intrauterine devices) killed seventeen women in the U.S., the product was withdrawn from the U.S. market, but continued to be advertised and sold overseas (Mintz, 1987).
- Children's garments containing *Tris* fire retardant (a known carcinogen) were pulled off the domestic market by the Consumer Products Safety Commission (CPSC). These garments were then shipped and sold overseas.
- *Lomotil* is an antidiarrhea medicine which is sold only by prescription in the U.S. because it can cause death when consumed in amounts exceeding those recommended. It is sold off the shelf in countries such as Sudan and advertised with the slogan, "used by astronauts." In such countries it is recommended for children as young as twelve.
- *Depo Provera*, a contraceptive produced by Upjohn, is known to cause malignant tumors, but is sold in seventy other countries and even used in U.S.-sponsored population control programs.
- Many U.S. *asbestos* manufacturers, faced with stricter safety regulations, have simply moved to Mexico.
- The lack of effective international standards found the Nestlé Corporation marketing *baby formula* in Third World countries. Their advertising encouraged mothers to use such mixes rather than nurse their own infants. Many infants died when their mothers could no longer afford the formula or dangerously stretched the limited supply of formula by adding water, tea, or chocolate drink (Lappé and Collins, 1977). The sad part of all this is that had the mothers not been influenced to let their own milk dry up, the infants would have received the best possible nutrition from their mother's milk. Due to public pressure, Nestlé discontinued this marketing practice in 1984, but in 1988 resumed such practices (Griffin, 1989).

When the original customers returned the meat to Hormel, they used the following terms to describe it: "moldy liverloaf, sour party hams, leaking bologna, discolored bacon, off-condition hams, and slick and slimy spareribs." Hormel renewed these products with cosmetic measures (reconditioning, trimming, and washing). Spareribs returned for sliminess, discoloration, and stickiness were rejuvenated through curing and smoking, renamed Windsor Loins and sold in ghetto stores for more than fresh pork chops.

Corporate Violence.   From what has been said so far it should have become clear that, while the general public tends to view corporate crime as nonviolent, we might be more persuaded by Hills, who in *Corporate Violence* (1987, p. vii) describes ". . . 'respectable' business executives who impersonally kill and maim many more Americans than

- Lethal pesticides that are prohibited in this country are exported overseas. Products sprayed with such poisons are nevertheless imported into the U.S. and consumed by an unknowing public (Simon and Eitzen, 1982, Chapter 5).
- In 1983 it was revealed that Eli Lilly Company had continued to sell the drug Orãflex even though it was aware that the drug had deadly side effects. FDA investigators found in Lilly's possession reports of deaths which they had purposely hidden from the agency. Although the drug was finally withdrawn from the market, there was no prosecution (ABC, 1983b).

Dowie (1987, pp. 49–50) explains a number of methods employed for circumventing regulatory agencies at home and importers abroad including:

- "The Name Change"– if bad publicity takes place in the American market, change the name of the product.
- "Last Minute Pullout"– if the EPA threatens not to pass a chemical, the manufacturer pulls the application for approval and labels it "for export only." The manufacturer is not required to notify the importing country that the chemical is banned in the U.S.
- "Dump the Whole Factory"– move overseas where regulations are easier.
- "Change the Formula"– by simply adding or subtracting inert ingredients.
- "The Skip"– if target country says the drug or product must be approved in exporting country, export first to a country with looser laws, then export to target country.
- "The Ingredient Dump"– if the product is banned, export the ingredients separately, reassemble, and dump.

street muggers and assailants." He notes that the tools of such violence include (Ibid.):

> . . . exploding autos, defective medical devices, inadequately treated drugs and other hazardous products that are manufactured and marketed despite knowledge by corporate officials that such products can injure and kill consumers. There are reports of toxic chemical dumps that have poisoned drinking supplies, caused leukemia in children and destroyed entire communities; of cover-ups of asbestos-induced cancer, and the gradual suffocation of workers from inhaling cotton dust; of radioactive water leaking from improperly maintained nuclear reactors; of mangled bodies and lives snuffed out in unsafe coal mines and steel mills—and other dangers to our health and safety.

Crimes by Organizations against Employees

Organizational (corporate) crime against employees (type 6 in Figure 9.2) may take many forms; the most insidious relates to purposive violation of health and safety laws that may not only threaten the worker's life, but may genetically damage their offspring.

During World War II, I. G. Farben, a large German manufacturing corporation, worked captive workers (slave labor) to death in their factories. While most modern manufacturers do not directly kill their workers, health and safety violations by corporations and organizations against their employees can take many forms (see Frank, 1985). Some occupational exposure to injury and disease may be a necessary part of employment; but unnecessary, preventable hazards and their disregard by employers is regulated by the Occupational Safety and Health Administration (OSHA) and can incur criminal penalties. Terms such as black lung (due to coal exposure), brown lung (due to cotton mill exposure), and white lung (due to asbestos exposure) have become familiar to American workers. The sheer number of new chemicals to which workers are exposed and their long-term impact is enormous. The fact that occupational hazards are not new is illustrated by the fact that in 1812 in Lawrence, Massachusetts, sweatshop conditions in the textile mills produced death in one-third of the workers by the age of twenty-five (Browning and Gerassi, 1980, p. 237).

Just to cite one example of corporate negligence and coverup, an examination of the asbestos industry is enlightening. Carlson, appearing before a Congressional Subcommittee on Compensation, Health, and Safety (Carlson, 1979, pp. 25–52) indicated:

■ Examination of corporate memos, letters, and other documents from as early as 1934 showed that senior executives at Johns-Manville and Raybestos-Manhattan (two of the biggest asbestos producers) not only knew of, but covered up company-sponsored research findings that demonstrated asbestos-caused diseases.

- Asbestos industry-sponsored research in the 1930s and 1940s also showed asbestos dangers, and researchers were prevented from publishing their results.
- One company, Philip Carey Company, fired its medical consultant when he warned of possible lawsuits from workers exposed to asbestos.
- Years before the companies acknowledged any awareness of asbestos dangers, documents demonstrated that they had quietly settled injury and death claims from workers who had handled asbestos.
- Johns-Manville purposely did not notify employees of the results of their medical examinations which showed asbestosis, despite executives' knowledge that the disease was progressive and fatal unless treated in an early stage.

In 1988 OSHA fined meatpacker John Morrell and Co. $4.33 million for having forced hundreds of injured workers in its Sioux Falls, S.D., plant to keep working even right after surgery. This was the largest fine against a single employer in the agency's history. Workers in this industry chronically suffer from carpal tunnel syndrome and tendinitis in which joints stiffen due to the erosion of soft tissue (Meatpacker, 1988).

Larry Agran (1982) in "Getting Cancer on the Job" documents that the cancer epidemic has been primarily fed by many industries' systematic unconcern for workers' health, in which company physicians cover up evidence of unsafe exposure to carcinogenic substances. He concludes that the government regulatory agencies are either too timid to enforce the law or lack staff resources with which to protect workers.

Certain corporate occupational subcultures require conformity to prevailing wrongdoing: "sharp practices" are cynically viewed as the way of the world; the only way to do business. In these environments, anyone opposing such views is regarded as a naïve, unworldly, "boy scout" or "girl scout" type. Isolation of such figures in corrupt occupational environments has been well described by former officer David Serpico (Maas, 1973) of the New York City Police Department, who was ostracized when he refused to participate in extorting money from vice operators.

John F. Kennedy's (1957) *Profiles in Courage* very movingly describes the personal courage, heroism, and sacrifice of political figures who were willing to buck the tide and vote with their consciences. If there are any heroes or heroines in the world of corporate crime, they can

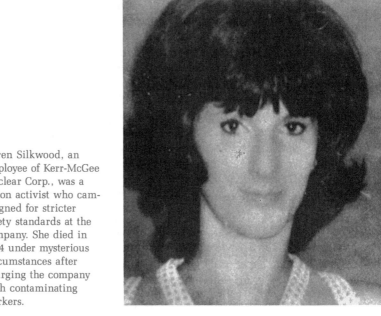

Karen Silkwood, an employee of Kerr-McGee Nuclear Corp., was a union activist who campaigned for stricter safety standards at the company. She died in 1974 under mysterious circumstances after charging the company with contaminating workers.

be found among the ranks of "whistleblowers," employees who are willing to step forth, usually at great personal sacrifice, to reveal wrongdoing on the part of their employers (see Westin, 1981). "You don't bite the hand that feeds you," states the old adage. The decision to inform on organizational violations has often meant firing, family disruption, ostracism from friends and former coworkers, as well as the end of one's career, as employers retaliate against the "squealer" or "stool pigeon."

In extreme cases an employer may even threaten one's life. While the following horror story is by no means typical, it profiles a true heroine in the fight against corporate crime.

The Karen Silkwood Case

Congressional hearings (U.S. Congress, 1976) and Rashke's (1981) *The Killing of Karen Silkwood* describe the Silkwood episode. She was an employee of the Kerr-McGee nuclear plant in Guthrie, Oklahoma. The company used plutonium, one of the most lethal of substances, in its plant. A union activist for stricter safety at the company, Silkwood had gathered considerable information documenting the firm's negligence of health and safety measures for employees as well as dangerous defects in the plutonium compounds being used. Then a medical examination revealed that Silkwood had been contaminated by the substance. Subsequent investigation discovered high radioactive readings in her apartment, food, and personal belongings.

On the evening of November 13, 1974, Silkwood was enroute with documents to a meeting with a union official and a reporter from *The New York Times,* when suspiciously her auto crashed into a ditch, killing her. Further suspicion was raised when the documents which had been observed at the scene by state troopers disappeared, when the normal wrecker service was called off by Guthrie police even though it was near the scene, and when an investigator hired by the union found evidence of another car's metal on Silkwood's rear bumper, which could explain her swerving off the road.

In a subsequent trial investigating her contamination, Kerr-McGee lawyers portrayed Karen as a drug abuser, as a person who may have purposely contaminated herself in order to paint the company in a bad light. Nevertheless, Kerr-McGee was found guilty of negligence in health and safety as well as criminally liable in Silkwood's contamination. The Atomic Energy Commission found the company in violation of the majority of the union complaints, including the contamination of seventy-three employees in seventeen safety lapses over a five-year period (Rose, Glazer, and Glazer, 1982, p. 407). The jury also ordered the company to pay Silkwood's estate $10.5 million in damages (Silkwood Vindicated, 1979, p. 40). The company appealed the case, and in January 1984, the decision was upheld by the U.S. Supreme Court.

Environmentally dangerous occupations include those of chemical and insecticide workers, miners and shipyard workers who deal with asbestos, petrochemical and refinery workers, coal miners, coke-oven workers, textile and lead workers, medical radiation technicians, and those employed in the plastic industry. The exposures and risks are enormous; since most workers cannot easily switch jobs, they are even more dependent on federal regulatory agencies to protect their health and safety. Occupational hazards may be a necessary evil in modern industrial societies, but corporate subterfuge in unnecessarily exposing workers to such threats is not.

In the mid-eighties, five executives from Film Recovery Systems, Inc., were charged with murder and two with manslaughter in the death due to cyanide poisoning of Stefan Golab, a Polish immigrant and employee of their company. They knowingly failed to advise him of the extreme hazards and necessary precautions in working with dangerous chemicals. In the *first recorded case of employers charged with murder for the work-related death of an employee,* each defendant was sentenced to twenty-five years in prison and the corporation was fined $25,000 (Frank, 1987).

Crimes by Organizations (Corporations) against Organizations (Corporations)

Criminal activity by organizations against other organizations (type 9 in Figure 9.2) may take many forms, including private corporations against the state (e.g., wartime trade violations, cheating on government contracts, or income tax violations) and crimes by corporations against corporations (e.g., industrial espionage and illegal competitive practices). Many crimes related to antitrust activity, which were previously covered as "organization vs. individual (public) crimes," obviously also impact upon firms who are cut out of markets as a result of competitors' illegal activities.

Wartime Trade Violations

Because of their international structure, multinational corporations can sometimes play both sides of the fence in wartime. In *Trading with the Enemy*, Higham (1982) raises eyebrows with the following accusations:

- While gasoline was being rationed in the U.S., managers of Standard Oil of New Jersey were shipping fuel through Switzerland to the Nazis.
- Ford trucks were produced for German occupation troops in France with authorization from Ford executives in the U.S.
- Chase Manhattan Bank did business with the Nazis during the war.

An early, classic study of "white collar crime" by Marshall Clinard (1969), originally published in 1952, was entitled *The Black Market*. Using records of federal regulatory agencies during World War II, Clinard examined wartime trade violations on the part of businesses. He found extensive violations of rationing, price-ceiling offenses, tie-in sales, and quality control. In a study conducted about the same period, Hartung (1950) found a large number of violations of wartime economic regulations in the Detroit wholesale meat industry.

While it is not uncommon for victors to demand that losing countries pay reparations or war debts for damages, it is surprising to realize that the U.S. paid for damages to U.S. multinational plants that were ruined during Allied bombing of Nazi-occupied Europe. Parenti (1980, p. 76) describes such postwar payments to General Motors (GM) and International Telephone and Telegraph (ITT). ITT had produced Nazi bombers and received $27 million for damages, while GM had produced Nazi trucks and obtained $33 million in compensation. Public furor took place after World War II when it was revealed that many oil companies had collaborated with the Nazis during the war. Although President Truman ordered that the Justice Department investigate and prosecute, the case was finally settled after fifteen years of litigation with a minor consent decree (Coleman, 1985, p. 178).

Industrial Espionage

Until recently, *Industrial espionage* has been a relatively neglected area of investigation by criminologists. Much of the work in this area has either appeared in trade magazines or has been done by journalists (see Barlay, 1973; Engberg, 1967; and Hamilton, 1967). Such *espionage* (literally spying, or the acquiring of information through deceptive or illegal forms) is performed by three different groups: (1) intelligence agencies, (2) competing firms, and (3) disloyal employees. While espionage by intelligence agencies will be discussed later (under political crime, in Chapter 11), commercial espionage by foreign powers can be illustrated by the Soviet KGB Directorate T, the scientific and technological bureau whose primary task is to steal information and commercial secrets. This section of the text will concentrate upon commercial espionage by competing firms, although disloyal employees often steal ideas for sales to competing firms.

Bergier's (1975, p. 51) highly readable *Secret Armies* tells the story of an industrial-espionage agent who traveled from office to office of a corporate headquarters with a pushcart telling everyone that he was doing a check on secret documents, which he then proceeded to wheel away. The documents and their collector were never seen again.

Industrial spying goes back at least as far as the stealing of industrial and commercial secrets (relating to silkworms and porcelain) from China around 3000 B.C. In the Middle Ages, it was so widespread that it led to patent laws. Bergier (Ibid., p. 15) claims that piracy by industrialists and governments was a significant factor in the spreading of the Industrial Revolution. From 1875 to World War I, Japan had the best industrial spies, after which Nazi Germany and the U.S.S.R. dominated European spying. In the recent Hitachi case, a Japanese corporation attempted to steal "state-of-the-art" computer secrets from International Business Machines (IBM). Some examples provided by Bergier include:

- A 1967 survey of leading American corporations found one-third of the respondents indicating that they used industrial espionage.

- One large Detroit company found nine television transmitters hidden in the air vents of their main drafting room; these were probably transmitting their latest drawings to their competition.
- A telephone tap discovered in Manhattan covered 60,000 phone lines, presumably to pick up useful market tips, blackmail information, and the like.
- Several cases in England involved spies posing as typewriter repairmen and removing them for "repair" in order to peruse used ribbons.
- Cars of important figures are stolen only to be quickly recovered — the aim is to bug them.
- The fictional "Spectre"-type organization of Ian Fleming's James Bond novels may actually exist. Bergier (Ibid., p. 74) calls it "Spies Inc." and describes it as a nonpolitical group which sells its services, which include execution, to the highest bidder.

In free societies, about 95 percent of industrial information is available in the trade and popular publications. Sources of information on American industry range from legitimate to illegal, as described by the *Wade System of Sources of Information on American Industry* (Hamilton, 1967, pp. 222–223) (Vantage Point 10.2). The first seven sources are usually legal and ethical, while the remainder, as one descends the list, become less so, depending upon the particular means which are employed.

The Hitachi Case

In 1982 three executives of Hitachi, Ltd., of Japan were arrested for their attempt to steal classified information from IBM. In all, twenty-one individuals and two corporations were indicted by the U.S. Department of Justice (DOJ). Japanese industry had rapidly industrialized itself earlier in the century through such borrowing and counterfeiting of Western technology (Ogata, 1983, p. 3), but rather than following the usual method of "reverse engineering"— obtaining, breaking down, and copying a competitor's finished product—Hitachi attempted to speed up the process and save millions of dollars in time-consuming research and development by directly buying the plans for a new computer technology. The breaking of the Hitachi case was primarily the result of the efforts of IBM's own security personnel. Many corporations criticize the lack of federal efforts in guarding trade secrets.

Corporate complaints requesting greater federal protection from industrial espionage has a "just deserts" quality to it as well as a "hollow ring"—"just deserts" because many of the victims of commercial spying are also the criminals, a "hollow ring" because it might not be a sincere request for more strict enforcement. It is hard to believe that the same organizations that lie, cheat, and steal, block regulatory laws, and push passage of protective legislation for their own benefit suddenly cannot effect legislation which would be in their interest.

Pentagon Procurement Scandal

In 1988 Hertz, the rental car company, admitted overcharging customers and insurance companies $13 million for accident repairs in which employees forged repair bids (Hertz, 1988). This was minor fraud compared to the operations of defense firms.

Vantage Point

Vantage Point 10.2—The Wade System of Sources of Information on American Industry

1. Published material and public documents.
2. Disclosures made by competitors' employees which are obtained without subterfuge.
3. Market surveys and consultant reports.
4. Financial reports and brokers' research surveys.
5. Trade fairs, exhibits, and competitor's brochures.
6. Analysis of competitor's products.
7. Reports of your salesman and purchasing agents.
8. Legitimate employment interviews with people who worked for a competitor.
9. Camouflaged questioning and "drawing out" of a competitor's employees.
10. Direct observation under secret conditions.
11. False job interviews with competitor's employee (i.e., where there is no real intent to hire).
12. False negotiations with competitor for license.
13. Hiring a professional investigator to obtain a specific piece of information.
14. Hiring an employee away from the competitor to get specific information.
15. Trespassing on competitor's property.
16. Bribing competitor's supplier or employee.
17. "Planting" your agent on competitor's payroll.
18. Eavesdropping on competitors (e.g., via wire-tapping).
19. Theft of drawings, samples, documents, and similar property.
20. Blackmail and extortion.

SOURCE: Peter Hamilton, 1967, *Espionage and Subversion in An Industrial Society*, London: Hutchinson, pp. 222–223.

In 1988 the FBI launched a major investigation of massive fraud, bribery, and bid-rigging in defense industry bids on Pentagon contracts. The investigation included the alleged sale of secret information by Pentagon officials to defense contractors, which enabled them to fix prices and assure contracts. ITT pleaded guilty in October 1988 to treating Air Force employees to meals, golf greens, liquor, and baseball tickets to obtain inside information on contracts worth $180 million. An ITT spokesman stated, "Quite frankly, while we don't condone what the (ITT) employee did, it was fairly minor in the scheme of things" (ITT, 1988). In a probe culminating two years of undercover work and wiretaps, federal investigators served search warrants on fifteen companies and on a half-dozen Defense Department officials. Particularly under attack was "the revolving door," a system in which defense company executives serve stints as Pentagon officials and then return to the industries they previously oversaw as contract officers. Such obvious conflict of interest might be viewed as "deferred bribes" in which cooperative defense contract officers will be later rewarded with defense industry jobs. The losers, of course, are the nation's armed forces and the nation's taxpayers (Waldman, 1989).

Criminal Careers of Organizational Offenders

Corporate Environment and Crime

Corporate crime does not occur in a vacuum, but is affected by characteristics of an organization and its market structure. For instance, in an analysis of auto makers, Leonard and Weber (1970) found that price fixing requires two market forces: a few suppliers and inelastic demand (i.e., a steady need or demand for a product irrespective of a rise or fall in cost). Summarizing these forces, Conklin (1977, pp. 51–52) lists six environmental situations which are conducive to corporate crime:

1. *Seller concentration.* If a few producers hold a large share of the market, this leads to possible monopolization of markets or antitrust violations.
2. *Buyer concentration.* A small number of buyers or wealth concentrated in a few buyers may lead to bribes and kickbacks from sellers.
3. *Price elasticity of demand.* When price increases do not affect the demand for goods or services, price fixing is likely.
4. *False product differentiation.* When there are few differences in the product, false advertising may be used to create fraudulent distinctions.
5. *Entry barriers.* These may be created by discriminatory pricing or dumping in order to eliminate competitors.

6. *Slow growth rate of demand.* This may encourage deceptive advertising.

Corporate Concentration

The marketplace in postindustrial or advanced capitalistic societies has moved from competitive capitalism of companies to shared monopolies controlled by huge corporations and conglomerates. Green, Moore, and Wasserstein (1972, p. 7) define a market as a "shared monopoly" when four or fewer firms control half or more of the market. U.S. products over which such control exists include: automobiles (the Big Four—GM, Ford, Chrysler, and American Motors), aluminum (Alcoa, Kaiser, and Reynolds), tires (Goodyear, Firestone, Goodrich, U.S. Rubber), soaps (Proctor and Gamble, Colgate, Lever Brothers), cigarettes (Reynolds, American, Phillip Morris, Liggett and Myers), and light bulbs (GE, Westinghouse, Sylvania. Similar monopolies exist for cereals, bread and flour, fluid milk and dairy products, processed meats, sugar, canned goods, and soups. The growing concentration of markets can be demonstrated by the fact that in 1960 450 U.S. firms controlled about 50 percent of all manufacturing assets and made 59 percent of all profits. By 1979, 79 percent of the assets were controlled by these firms, and 72 percent of the profits (Simon and Eitzen, 1982, p. 71).

Overpricing of products is more likely to occur when four or fewer companies control a market. As a result of such shared monopolies, the FTC estimates that prices are 25 percent higher than they should be, and that such concentrated market firms enjoy profits which are 50 percent higher than less concentrated industries (Ibid.). In size, complexity, assets, and power, these large corporations dwarf most states and most national governments. Their wealth and their power in elections, in private foreign policy, and in the international economy makes public sector regulation increasingly difficult.

"It's a Free Country"

Many corporate and occupational offenders, when pressed for explanations regarding their wrongdoing, all but express a common saying among juveniles in the United States—"It's a free country." At face value, this is a simple statement regarding political freedoms; exaggerated, it becomes a license for corporate and occupational crime and translates into "I can do whatever I damn well please and the government or anyone else has no right to tell me what to do." Such offenders rationalize their behavior, neutralize any harm done, express indifference and hostility toward government regulations and regulators, and see enforcement of the laws as an unfair changing of the rules compared with nonenforcement in the past. In an often cited example, during the "Great Electrical Conspiracy" trial an attorney asked one executive whether he realized his price fixing meetings with competitors were illegal. The executive replied:

> Illegal? Yes, but not criminal. I didn't find that out until I read the indictment. . . . I assumed that criminal action meant damaging someone, and we did not do that. . . . I thought that we were more or less working on a survival basis in order to try to make enough to keep our plant and our employees.
>
> —cited in Geis and Meier, 1977, p. 122–123.

Rationalizations

Having little or no criminal self-concept, offenders view violations as part of their work. Among the rationalizations, or ways of explaining away responsibility, for white collar criminality are (Clinard and Yeager, 1980, pp. 69–72):

- Legal regulations of business are government interference with the free enterprise system.
- Such regulations are unnecessary and reduce profits.
- Such laws are too complex, create too much paperwork, and are incomprehensible.
- Regulatory laws are not needed and govern unnecessary matters.
- There is little deliberate criminal intent (mens rea) in corporate violations.
- "Everybody is doing it" and I have to keep up with competitors.
- The damage and loss is spread out among large numbers of consumers, thus, individually, little loss is suffered.
- If corporate profits do not increase as a result of the violation, there is no wrong.
- Violations are necessary in order to protect consumers.

Most occupational and corporate violators relate their offenses to their occupational environments. They view laws and regulations as nuisances, "no way to run a railroad"; these are to be stretched, loopholed, gotten around, or bribed away. The prevailing view in some occupational milieus seems to be "all is fair in love, *business*, and war," "the end (profit) justifies the means," that slick, Machiavellian, manipulative practices are the expected manner of carrying out one's occupational duty.

Ethics and Subcultures

Beauchamp (1983) and Beauchamp and Bowie (1983) provide examples that while there are books on business ethics, this type of literature has obviously not been on the business best seller list. In a 1975 survey, Silk and Vogel (1976) found that the majority of the fifty-seven top corporate executives they interviewed felt that unethical conduct was prevalent throughout industry and an expected part of everyday business.

In examining occupational and corporate violators, the role of "occupational subcultures" is quite apparent. Executives, professionals, or workers tend to associate with others of their trade and to desire to conform, to succeed, to be viewed as team players. "Shaking the bush" (informing on wrongdoing) is viewed as deviant, as we saw in some of our "whistleblower" examples. Moreover, the risks and possible stigmatization for wrongdoing are small, the penalties are insignificant, and fines, when levied, are often uncollected, as we shall see shortly.

Societal Reaction

The Bureau of Justice Statistics estimates that property crimes such as robbery, burglary, and larceny cost American society nearly $13 billion. Federal investigators estimate that the federal government is being ripped off by at least $50 billion a year, primarily through fraud. In terms of threat and damage to property, health, theft, and corruption of law enforcement agencies, corporate crime therefore, is the "big leagues." The "oil scam" price fixing of the 1970s was estimated at $10 billion, while the celebrated "Great Brink's Robbery" only netted $2 million. The latter is much better known and has received more publicity than the former even though five thousand Brink's robberies would be required to equal the "oil scam's" take.

Despite growing pressure for more severity in the treatment of higher occupational and corporate offenders, the likelihood of prosecution and conviction remains small. When offenders are convicted, the penalties remain rather miniscule, considering particularly the economic loss to society. High recidivism rates among such criminals continue. Many are even "deadbeats" in paying assessed fines. The "big, dirty secret" remains true: judges and government agencies are "soft" on corporate crime.

Why the Leniency in Punishment?

If "white collar crimes" are economically the most costly crimes to society, why are such acts seldom punished? A number of reasons have been suggested:

- Many acts were not made illegal until recently. For example, many environmental and occupational health and safety regulations are of post-World War II vintage, and not until the twentieth century were false advertising, fraud, misuse of trademarks and patents, and restraint of trade considered criminal matters.
- American business philosophy has been dominated by beliefs in laissez-faire economics (government noninterference in business) as well as by caveat emptor ("let the buyer beware").
- Public concern with corporate crime is of recent vintage. Once this resentment becomes organized, public pressure against "white collar crime" and pressure for legislation and enforcement can be expected. A recent national survey suggests the general public regards white collar crimes as even more serious than conventional crimes such as burglary, robbery, and the like (Wolfgang, 1980a, p. E.21). Thus, lenient treatment of elite offenders is not supported by the public.
- In the past, white collar crimes were given less media publicity; sometimes the media were owned by businesses which themselves were violators (Snider, 1978). Fear of loss of major advertising revenue may also have an impact.
- White collar criminals and those who make and enforce the laws share the same socioeconomic class and values. They fail to match the public stereotype of the criminal. Vilhelm (1968) also suggests that the general public doesn't oppose such crime because they themselves often violate many of these same laws on a modest scale.
- Political pressure groups often block effective regulation or enforcement, for often some of the biggest campaign contributors are also the biggest violators. Funding for exerting this pressure can be obtained through previous tax avoidance, laundering, and other shady practices. Since such criminals are seldom prosecuted, many officially are first offenders and thus are treated with leniency.
- It is easier for politicians and public officials to concentrate attention upon the crimes of the young and lower class, groups which lack political clout.
- The long-term nature of corporate violations and court delays make sanctions difficult.

We have indicated that asbestos manufacturers had full knowledge that they were killing their workers, as Johns-Manville did, for instance, when they estimated dust control equipment installation and operation at $17 million and only $1 million for Workmen's Compensation payments, and judged that it was cheaper to infect workers (Brodeur, 1974, p. 128). But those responsible are hard to punish. Ermann and Lundman (1982, pp. 71–72) point out an often overlooked problem:

> The reason why executives are not sanctioned is quite straightforward. As was true of asbestos decisions, there frequently is such a gap between decision and consequence that corporations find it difficult, if not impossible, to sanction executives responsible for long-term blunders. Executives who make these decisions are promoted, retired, or dead which makes them invulnerable to corporate penalties. Others, therefore, pick up the pieces left in the wake of serious mistakes.

As we've said, a variety of other recent studies have demonstrated that the general public now regards many types of white collar crime as more serious than most traditional crime. Braithwaite (1981), in a reanalysis of Rossi, et al.'s (1974) study of public rankings of the seriousness of 140 offenses, found that public disapproval of actual or potentially violent white collar crimes was stronger than that for traditional crimes. This pattern has been further documented in studies by Schrager and Short (1980) as well as by Cullen et al. (1982b) and Sinden (1980). In analyzing public reactions Cullen et al. (1982a, pp. 19–20) concluded:

- While traditional crimes were assigned longer sentences, respondents also were quite punitive toward violent white collar crime and embezzlement.
- Among white collar crimes there was a call for harsher penalties against violent white collar crime and violations of financial trust and more leniency expressed for property crimes by or against corporations.
- There was little support for coddling "respectable" offenders. The sample favored prison sentences in the majority of white collar crimes.

Professional and Trade Associations

In an excellent review of "Court and Regulatory Agency Processing of Trade and Professional Association Law Violators," Lesieur and Esposito (1982, p. 9) cite the following reasons for the lax to nonexistent enforcement of ethical codes by associations: inadequate budgeting and staffing; conflict of interest in that the regulators come from the ranks of the regulated; fear of alienating the membership; apathy and hostility toward the procedures, resulting in underreporting of offenders; and fear of antitrust actions as a result of enforcing the code.

In their examination of federal cases involving trade or professional associations from 1976 to 1980, Lesieur and Esposito (1982, pp. 27–31) conclude:

- "Officers from only 2 out of 18 associations with guilty or nolo pleas went to jail and these were atypical cases." When given, fines against associations were small.
- "There appeared to be little effort on the part of judges to disgorge profits or enforce remedial action against offenders."

Sentencing

Mann et al. (1980), p. 482) found in a survey of judges' opinions of white collar sanctions that they were strong believers in sentencing for deterrence, which they viewed as more important than sentencing as a rationale for incapacitation, rehabilitation, or punishment. In order for this deterrence model to work, however, there must be a reasonable certainty of offenders being caught as well as being seriously punished (Yoder, 1978, pp. 46–47). In white collar offenses, the low risk of apprehension and negligible penalties when apprehended appear to negate the deterrence model (Orland, 1980; and McCormick, 1977; Hagan and Palloni, 1986; and Cullen, Makestad, and Cavender, 1987)).

Recent research continues to document relative laxity and leniency in corporate and higher level occupational crime enforcement (Benekos, 1983; Clinard et al., 1979; Hagan et al., 1980; and Snider, 1982). Hagan et al. (1980, p. 818) point out the overlooked fact that much white collar prosecution requires defendant cooperation, which is likely to lead to more lenient sentences. Pleas of nolo contendere, consent decrees, warnings, and cease and desist orders continue to remind us of the separate status accorded such offenders. Wickman and Whitten (1980, p. 367) sarcastically put the matter this way:

> Corporations that have been involved in polluting the environment sign consent decrees with the EPA and announce that they are working on the problem. Imagine the public reaction if a common street criminal were to be dealt with in this fashion. Here's the scene: Joe Thug is apprehended by an alert patrolman after mugging an eighty-five-year-old woman in broad daylight on the streets of Paterson, New Jersey. Brought down to police headquarters, he holds a press conference with the assistant police chief. While not admitting his guilt, he promises not to commit any future muggings and announces that he is working on the problem of crime in the streets.

The major reason for the use of consent decrees (in which the corporation promises not to violate the same regulation again) is the simple fact that understaffed and underfinanced legal staffs of the regulatory agencies cannot litigate most cases (Clinard and Yeager, 1980, p. 97). The antitrust division of the Department of Justice has filed relatively few criminal cases; and, even when convictions are won, they typically result in weak penalties which lack deterrent effect. Since December 1974, increased authorized penalties in the law and upgrading of violations to felony stature opened the door for more strict reactions (Ibid., pp. 144, 150).

McCormick's (1977) study of sentencing and convictions in antitrust cases by the Department of Justice from 1890–1969 shows that of the 2 percent of corporate violators who served prison sentences, most were for labor violations. Benekos's (1983) study, which compared cases reported in the *Wall Street Journal* in 1971 and 1981, found that criminal sentencing in 1981 was more severe for white collar criminals than in 1971. He also discovered that even though the total and average amounts of fines imposed upon individuals had increased, controlling for inflation, the 1981 fines were smaller than the 1971 fines. As Benekos points out, this may have been due to the greater use of incarceration and longer sentencing, both of which may indicate an emerging greater severity in penalizing the white collar offender.

Simon and Eitzen (1982, pp. 125–126) state:

> The probusiness approach argues that risks are inherent in living, the consumer is the ultimate arbiter. He or she may choose. If he or she doesn't buy the dangerous or wasteful products, then the corporations will provide alternative products to suit the wishes of the consumer. Or, the worker in an asbestos plant or a cotton mill can change jobs if he or she feels the current one is unsafe. Companies also argue that it is no business of the government what goes on in the marketplace.
>
> We argue, to the contrary, that the government must provide a watchdog function. We also argue that individuals do not have the options that the corporations suggest. We buy the products that are available. Our attitudes are shaped by advertising. Employees cannot shift from one job to another when most of the plants in the industry for which they are trained have similar problems and when the unemployment rate is high. . . .

Retrenchment of Consumer Legislation

In the early eighties, a more conservative business climate and the Reagan administration appeared to threaten some of the important gains in consumer legislation (Isaacson and Gorey, 1981, pp. 22–23):

- The White House cancelled laws requiring companies to list chemicals to which their workers are exposed on the job, that required drug manufacturers to list possible risks of the medicine they sell, and for hotdog manufacturers to warn consumers if their product contained ground bone.

- The administration moved to reduce crash speed for bumper protection on automobiles from 5 m.p.h. to 2.5 m.p.h.
- The number of OSHA inspectors was cut by 11 percent, and the Consumer Product Safety Commission's budget was cut by 30 percent.
- The FTC's antitrust division had been cut back in both funding and powers and has become less aggressive.
- To assist corporate dumping the administration relaxed regulations requiring labels and warnings on products exported overseas which are banned due to potential safety hazards in this country.

David vs. Goliath

If you were a probation officer, you would expect lawbreakers to reform and to abide by the conditions of their probation. However, what if, among your caseload of 157 probationers was Standard Oil of California, in 1971 the nation's fourteenth largest industrial corporation? In 1970, Standard Oil was convicted of an oil spill in San Francisco Bay and was fined $500 and placed on one year probation. When the probation officer complained that the company was not following the terms of its probation, the judge levied another fine of $1,000 (the maximum permitted) and extended probation to two years due to another spill; he also ordered Standard to modify their tankers to prevent spills and to provide a liaison man to work with the probation officer. Despite this order, the probation officer, when investigating thirty-nine oil spills over a four-year period, was given continual runarounds; when one of the company's tankers dumped fifteen to thirty thousand gallons of crude oil in the bay, he was kept at the company gate for nearly an hour before being permitted to investigate. A company attorney, when queried regarding the impact of all of this, indicated: "Standard intends to be as good a citizen as it can and get along with law enforcement in Contra Costa County. . . . I doubt there's been any change as a result of the activities of the probation department" (Ecology, 1971, p. 34).

White Collar Criminal "Deadbeats"

"Deadbeat" is an American slang term for someone who does not repay a debt which he or she owes. In August 1983, hearings before the Senate Governmental Affairs Subcommittee (1983) indicated that the federal government had collected only 55 percent of all criminal fines over the last sixteen years and a mere 34 percent in the last eighteen months prior to the hearings. As subcommittee staff director William Strauss indicated, a two-and-a-half-year study discovered that most of the thirty-two thousand unpaid cases of criminal fines involved white collar crimes, primarily fraud and income tax evasion. In the majority of cases, criminals had paid no portion of their fines. Similar investigations of nonpayment in the college student loan program, which runs in the billions, found that a large proportion of the violators were now successful doctors and professionals who could more than afford to repay their loans.

The "higher immorality" of criminaloid corporations and "upperworld crime" create greater inequalities and an underclass in society and indirectly foster "crime in the streets." Indifference to prosecution of society's most expensive forms of criminal activity supports the "dual system of justice" in the conflict model of criminal law, which argues that there are two systems of justice—one for the wealthy and one for the poor. This is a serious indictment of the fundamental equity of law upon which our system of criminal justice is morally and philosophically based. Any attempt at law and order that leaves untouched the pervasive criminality of respectable society is a travesty of justice.

Finally, in reading the remaining chapters of this text, keep in mind that we could end our discussion of crime with this chapter alone, and we would have covered the largest, most costly category of crime. All other forms of criminal behavior together do not equal the costs of occupational and organizational (corporate) crime.

Summary

Reasons for the lack of studies of corporate crime were detailed. In the U.S. the legal governance of business organizations began in the nineteenth century, particularly with the Sherman Antitrust Act (1890). Much regulation of corporate activity takes place through federal regulatory agencies such as the FCC, ICC, and SEC. These agencies can utilize civil and criminal as well as administrative means of assuring compliance, but they seldom do. Most agencies are "outgunned" by the industries they are supposed to control, and, in fact, they are sometimes controlled by these industries. Gross characterizes this non-enforcement and soft-gloves treatment of elite criminals as "the big dirty secret."

Studies by Clinard and Yeager and associates signaled a new renaissance in studies of corporate criminality—the first large-scale, comprehensive study of corporate crime. In examining *crimes by organizations against individuals/the public,* detailed examples were provided such as multinational bribery, "laundering dirty money," and case examples such as the "Equity Funding Scandal," the "Great Electrical Industry Conspiracy," and the "Great Oil Scam." Other important illustrations presented included the Ford Pinto case, toxic criminals, environmental violations, and corporate dumping of unsafe products.

Crimes by organizations against employees primarily relate to threats to the health and safety of workers, as dramatically illustrated by the tragic Karen Silkwood case. *Crimes by organizations against organizations* were illustrated by means of examples of wartime trade violations, industrial espionage (such as the "Hitachi Case"), and corporate fraud against government particularly on the part of defense contractors.

Characteristics of the corporate environment, such as supply and demand, and corporate concentration, such as the number of producers of a product, are predisposing factors in corporate criminality. *Societal reaction* to higher-level occupational and corporate crime has in the past been characterized by leniency. A number of reasons were provided for such indulgence, including policies of laissez-faire economics and a caveat emptor philosophy prevalent in the past. Recently, public reaction to such crimes has hardened and now rivals or exceeds that for traditional crimes. Recent research suggests some improvement in punishing elite offenders but still not in concomitance with the quantity, prevalence, and cost of such activities. Some retrenchment in regulatory activities may be occurring in response to a more conservative, probusiness political climate. The *toleration of white collar criminals and deadbeats* raises a major challenge to claims of equitable standards of justice and indirectly fosters crime in the streets through the perpetuation of inequality.

KEY CONCEPTS

Reasons for Lack of Corporate Crime Research	**The Great Oil Scam**	**Reasons for Leniency with White Collar Offenders**
Nolo Contendere	**"Daisy Chain" Scam**	**White Collar "Deadbeats"**
The Big Dirty Secret	**Corporate Dumping**	**Karen Silkwood Case**
Laundered Money	**Revolving Door**	**Ford Pinto Case**
Double Invoicing	**Whistleblowers**	**Equity Funding Scandal**
Influence Peddling	**Industrial Espionage**	
The Power Elite	**Corporate Environment and Crime**	

11 Political Crime

Ideology

The twentieth century and particularly the post-World War II period has been described as the "age of ideology," a period characterized by a war of words and ideas in which even the purpose of warfare is viewed as an attempt "to win the hearts and minds of the people." *Ideology* refers to distinctive belief systems, ideas, and abstract ideals which are perceived as providing the true meaning of life. Communism, capitalism, fascism, Islam, Judaism, Christianity, fundamentalism, and the like all may represent uniting political, religious, or economic belief systems that are conceived by their adherents as providing underlying meaning and purpose to life's mysteries. It is indeed fitting that a characteristic type of criminal activity, political crime, would become prevalent in this "age of ideology."

Schafer (1971, 1974) uses the term "convictional criminals" when referring to politically-motivated criminals. Such a criminal is "convinced of the truth and justification of his own beliefs" (Schafer, 1976, p. 138). The actual crimes committed by political criminals may be traditional crimes such as kidnapping, assassination, blackmail, robbery, and the like. It is not the crimes themselves that distinguish political criminals but their motivations, their views of crime as a necessary means to a higher ideological goal. Some political criminals, particularly human rights advocates, have committed no crime but have merely expressed their political views in authoritarian or totalitarian societies which forbid individual expression or criticism of the states, or even in free societies where civil disobedience may be viewed with suspicion.

Political Crime: A Definition

Political crime refers to criminal activity which is committed for ideological purposes. Rather than being motivated by private greed or benefit, such offenders sincerely believe they are following a higher conscience, a higher morality which supersedes present society and its laws. Such political criminals may possess social-political reasons (Robin Hood), moral-ethical motivations (anti-abortion activists), religious causes (Martin Luther), scientific beliefs (Copernicus, Galileo), or political concerns (Nathan Hale, Benedict Arnold) (Schafer, 1976). Such crime *may take one of two forms: crime by government or crime against the government.*

418

Crimes by government include violations of human rights, civil liberties, and constitutional privileges as well as illegal behavior that occurs in the process of enforcing the law or maintaining the status quo. Secret police violations, human rights abuses, genocide, crimes by police as well as illegal surveillance, disruption and experiments are just some of the examples of governmental crime to be discussed in this chapter.

Crimes against the government may range from protests, illegal demonstrations, and strikes to espionage, political whistleblowing, assassination, and terrorism. "One person's terrorist is another's patriot" is a common expression that suggests the relative nature of such political crime. In revolutions, the victors' beliefs become the status quo and they inherit the power and privilege by which to brand the acts of their enemies as criminal.

There is a surprising paucity of literature on political crime in criminology (Hagan, 1986; and Martin, Haran, and Romano, 1988). Fewer than ten works in the field appear to have specifically addressed this issue (see Ingraham, 1979; Kelman and Hamilton, 1988; Kittrie and Wedlock, 1986; Proal, 1973; Roebuck and Weeber, 1978; Schafer, 1974; Schur, 1980; and Turk, 1982). In his classic *Political Crime*, which was originally published in 1898, Louis Proal (1973, p. 28) indicates:

> Political passions have bathed the earth in blood; kings, emperors, aristocracies, democracies, republics, all governments have resorted to murder out of political considerations, these from love of power, those from hatred of royalty and aristocracy, in one case from fear, in another from fanaticism.

While political crimes may be committed by or against the government, seldom do governments or government officials choose to acknowledge their own lawlessness. Sagarin (1973, p. xiv) very aptly points out that political crime includes the tyrant as well as the assassin. At the close of World War II Hitler was not around to be prosecuted along with his fellow Nazis for war crimes, but Emperor Hirohito of Japan was. In the name of expediency of postwar reconstruction the Allies ignored the Emperor's complicity in war crimes, what Bergamini (1971, p. 1) called *Japan's Imperial Conspiracy*. In fact, the Allies were recognizing the sacredness of the powerful or the "doctrine of sovereign immunity" in which authorities of the state cannot be held responsible for wrongdoing.

> The Emperor is sacred and inviolable (Constitution, Art. 3). He cannot be removed from the Throne for any reason, and he is not to be held responsible for over-stepping the limitations of law in the exercise of his sovereignty. All responsibility for the exercise of his sovereignty must be assumed by

> the Ministers of State and other organs. Thus, no criticism can be directed against the Emperor, but only against the instruments of his sovereignty. Laws are not to be applied to the Emperor as a principle especially criminal laws, for no court of law can try the Emperor himself and he is not subject to any law.
>
> —*Japan Yearbook,* 1944, in Bergamini, 1971, p. 1.

An Example of Political Crime?

A group of heavily armed guerillas with arms supplied by a foreign power attack a provincial capital, blowing up the power station and killing fifty government troops, as well as thirty advisors from a friendly nation whose assistance had been requested by the central government. After destroying two bridges on the main highway, they retreat into the mountains. Airplanes from the friendly government attack the rebels, using various anti-personnel weapons which have been banned through international agreement. Government troops round up and execute citizens who were believed to have aided the rebels.

Did any of these incidents involve political crime or are they examples of incidents in a civil war in which "all is fair"?

Which incidents are to be condemned?

Does it make a difference if the setting is Nazi-occupied Europe, Eastern Europe, Northern Ireland, South Vietnam (1960s), Cambodia (1980s), Afghanistan, Lebanon, Nicaragua, El Salvador, or Namibia?

This example hopefully illustrates the relativistic nature of attempts to obtain international consensus on the identification and condemnation of political crime. Individuals who are identified as traitors or cold-blooded terrorists in one country are often decorated as heroes or martyrs in another. Governments or antigovernment dissidents roundly condemn such activities of their ideological foes while remaining curiously silent about the questionable activities by those whose views they support.

Legal Aspects

Crelinstein, Laberge-Altmejd, and Szabo (1978, p. xi) correctly point out:

> Historically, all crimes were "political," the separation of the legislative, executive, and judicial powers being a major achievement of modern statehood. One can say that nineteenth- and twentieth-century social evolution resulted in the "depoliticization" of the judicial system. . . . The responsiveness of the holders of political power to the aspirations of the general public for material well-being and and civil liberties tended to rule out violent means as a viable method for challenging the established rules of the social order.

While conflict theorists would argue that all crimes are political (Chambliss and Seidman, 1971; and Quinney, 1970), since crime is a creature of criminal law that is politically defined, the usage of the term *political crime* will be restricted in this presentation to a more specific meaning: crimes committed for ideological purposes.

In the United States, various laws have existed that are intended to protect the government from the clear and present or probable danger of disruption or overthrow. Laws such as the Alien and Sedition Act, the Espionage Act, Voorhis Act, Smith Act, Internal Security Act, and McCarran-Walter Act are such examples. The 1940 Voorhis Act requires registration of agents of foreign powers, while the Smith Act (1940), which was later struck down by the Supreme Court, outlaws advocating the overthrow of the government. The Internal Security Act (McCarran Act) calls for registration of Communists and Communist-front organizations, while the McCarran-Walter Act (1952) provides for deportation of aliens who espouse disloyal beliefs or have such associates (Clinard and Quinney, 1973, p. 155).

Other countries have similar laws. In the Soviet Union, Article 190–1 of the Soviet penal code forbids anyone to participate in "deliberate slander" against the state. Since "the state can do no wrong," Soviet courts have never acquitted anyone charged with violating this article (Whitaker et al., 1983, p. 42). Cuba and Soviet bloc countries possess criminal laws forbidding propaganda against the state, complaining about social conditions to foreigners, and attempting to publish works which are not authorized by the state. Many of these laws and their enforcement bear an uncanny resemblance to George Orwell's *1984* and his descriptions of the Minitrue (Ministry of Truth) in which thought criminals become political criminals or enemies of the state.

Under Anglo-American legal traditions, political crime and political criminals are not recognized as such, and these types of offenders are dealt with under traditional or nonpolitical laws. Anglo-American criminal law considers intent, but not motive. The motive, whether good or bad, has no bearing on guilt. Sagarin (1973, p. ix) points out: "At one time it was against the law in some parts of this country to preach freedom and abolition of slavery to slaves, or even to free men; it was often against the law to organize into trade unions; at various times political parties have been driven underground and their leaders jailed."

Kittrie and Wedlock in *The Tree of Liberty* (1988) provide historical documents related to elements of political criminality either by the state or by persons accused of such offenses:

■ The important Peter Zenger trial of 1735 for false, scandalous, and seditious libel which established the "freedom of the press" doctrine.

- The "crime of being black or Indian," e.g., the "Trail of Tears" of the Cherokee Nation, the Abolitionists, the underground railroad, and harboring fugitive slaves.
- Subjugation of blacks through private conspiracies and terrorism.
- Genocide against Indians.
- Voter registration drives and Freedom Rides during the Civil Rights struggle.
- Imprisonment of Japanese-Americans in internment camps during World War II.
- Anti-war protest, burning draft cards and records.
- Arson, bombing and other violations against abortion clinics.
- "Sanctuary activists" hiding Central Americans who they consider to be political refugees.

The Nuremberg Principle

After World War II, the victorious Allies held a tribunal and convicted Nazi war criminals. The Nuremberg trials were unprecedented in the fact that defeated war leaders were held responsible in an international legal area for activities which were legal, even encouraged, by their governments at the time they were committed. Defenses such as "I was just following orders" were rejected and held to be unjustifiable explanations for Nazi atrocities. Kelman and Hamilton (1988) refer to this as an example of a "crime of obedience." Offenses defined by the international tribunal included (Smith, 1977; Maser, 1979; and Nuremberg Principle, 1970, p. 78):

War Crimes

Violations of law or customs of war which include, but are not limited to murder, ill treatment, or deportation to slave labor or for any other purpose of civilian population of or in occupied territory, murder or ill treatment of prisoners of war or persons on the high seas, killings of hostages, plunder of public or private property, wanton destruction of villages, towns, or cities or devastation not justified by military necessity.

Crimes against Humanity

Murder, extermination, enslavement, deportation, and other inhumane acts committed against any civilian population, before or during the war, or persecutions on political, racial, or religious grounds, . . . whether or not in violation of the domestic law of the country where perpetrated.

The Universal Declaration of Human Rights

The concept of human rights is an outgrowth of the period of Enlightenment in Western society and is expressed in such documents as the Magna Carta, the English Bill of Rights, the American Declaration of Independence, the French Declaration of the Rights of Man and of the Citizen, and the United Nations Universal Declaration of Human Rights (1948). All of these documents support the notion of inalienable rights and freedoms which supersede those of government (Vantage Point 11.1).

The Nuremberg trials after World War II were the first time a nation's leaders were tried and executed because of atrocities committed under their regime.

END OF THE ROAD
SEPTEMBER 30, 1946

International Law

Since much political criminality is international in scope, it theoretically falls under the jurisdiction of international law, the power of which is limited. This covers fairly nonproblematic diplomatic and commercial customs between nations; agreements such as treaties that are drafted in international conventions; as well as international courts such as the International Court of Justice which was sponsored by the United Nations. Using precedents (past decisions), customs, and general principles of law, international law is theoretically binding upon any signatories to inter-

---

VANTAGE
POINT

Vantage Point 11.1—The Universal Declaration of Human Rights

The Universal Declaration of Human Rights, which was adopted unanimously by the U.N. General Assembly on December 10, 1948, is a proclamation, but not a treaty or international agreement. The basic elements of these human rights, which were the cornerstone of the Carter administration's foreign policy, *consist of three principles: integrity of persons, basic human needs, and civil and political liberties. Integrity of persons* is addressed in the following articles of the Universal Declaration (1948):

Article 3. Everyone has the right to life, liberty, and security of persons.
Article 5. No one shall be subjected to torture or to cruel, inhuman, or degrading treatment or punishment.
Article 9. No one shall be subjected to arbitrary arrest, detention, or exile.
Article 10. Everyone is entitled in full equality to a fair and public hearing by an independent and impartial tribunal, in the determination of his rights and obligations and of any criminal charges against him.

Basic human needs are addressed specifically in the following articles:

Article 25. (1) Everyone has the right to a standard of living adequate for the health and well-being of himself and of his family, including food, clothing, housing, and medical care and necessary social services, and the right to security in the event of unemployment, sickness, disability, widowhood, old age, or other lack of livelihood in circumstances beyond his control.
(2) Motherhood and childhood are entitled to special care and assistance. All children, whether born in or out of wedlock, shall enjoy the same social protection.

national treaties, although it may also through custom be held to be binding upon those who have not ratified the treaties. Stipulations of the Geneva Convention of 1929 regulating wartime conduct serves as an example.

While international bodies past or present, such as the World Court, the League of Nations, and the United Nations, have the facade of law, they lack the crucial power to enforce their decisions, ultimately through force if necessary (Kidder, 1983, p. 34). The closest entities to international police organizations are specially created U.N. police units, which are intended to temporarily block hostile armies, or Interpol, which is a

---

Article 26.   Everyone has the right to education. Education shall be free, at least in the elementary and fundamental stages. Elementary education shall be compulsory. Technical and professional education shall be made generally available and higher education shall be equally accessible to all on the basis of merit.

Some articles of the Universal Declaration dealing with *civil and political liberties* include:

Article 13.   (1) Everyone has the right to freedom of movement and residence within the borders of each state.
(2) Everyone has the right to leave any country, including his own, and to return to his country.

Article 19.   Everyone has the right to freedom of opinion and expression; this right includes freedom to hold opinions without interference and to seek, receive, and impart information and ideas through any media and regardless of frontiers.

Article 20.   (1) Everyone has the right to freedom of peaceful assembly and association.
(2) No one may be compelled to belong to an association.

Article 21.   (1) Everyone has the right to take part in the government of his country, directly through freely chosen representatives.
(2) Everyone has the right of equal access to public service in his country.
(3) The will of the people shall be the basis of the authority of government; this will be expressed in periodic and genuine elections which shall be by universal and equal suffrage and shall be held by secret vote or by equivalent free voting procedures.

SOURCE: Congressional Research Service, 1978, *Human Rights Conditions in Selected Countries and the U.S. Response*, Report prepared for the House Committee on International Relations, 95th Congress, 2nd Session, Washington, D.C.: Government Printing Office, July 25, pp. 10–14.

criminal intelligence-sharing organization with membership primarily made up of the Western democracies and former British Commonwealth nations.

Essentially, international law lacks teeth, the authority and power to assure compliance. A case of government-sponsored terrorism and the futility of any action by means of international law can be illustrated by the seizure and holding of American hostages in Iran. "Not only was there no means of enforcing what the United States took to be a violation of international law, but there was no consensus about whether there existed an established method for determining whether Iran violated the law in the first place" (Ibid., p. 18). Levi (1980, p. 552) notes:

> Fundamentally and ultimately, the absence of a community on the international scene is responsible for the role of power making and the political system inadequate to perform its normal function of maintaining social order . . . Moreover, the weakness . . . of the other social controls in the international society, places an intolerable burden upon the social control function of international law.

Crime by Government

The first major category of political crime to be discussed is crime by government. These are crimes or violations of human rights which are committed for ideological reasons by government officials or their agents. The government political criminal is motivated not by self-interest so much as by a commitment to a particular belief system, feeling that he or she is defending the status quo or preserving the existing system. Since many such violations are not formally recognized or enforced by the criminal law within most states, the concept of political crime by government is more *a sociological than political entity*. At times, it is difficult to determine whether crimes by government officials are ideological or occupational crimes (personally benefiting the offender either in terms of power or monetary reward). For this reason, the Watergate events were described primarily as occupational crime, though Nixon and his accomplices claimed the offenses were committed in order to preserve national security. In fact, most such offenses contain elements of both ideological and personally beneficial motivations.

Secret Police

All countries require some type of secret police for clandestine intelligence and internal security. Plate and Darvi (1981, p. 8), who have done extensive research on the subject, define secret police as "official or semi-official organs of government. They are units of the internal security police of the state, with the mandate to suppress all serious, threatening political opposition to the government in power and with the mission to control all political activity within (and sometimes even beyond) the borders of the nation-state." Secret police are often involved in the extraordinary means of illegal surveillance, searches, detention, and arrest; as a matter of practice, they may violate or border on the violation of human rights. According to Plate and Darvi (Ibid., pp. 14–17):

> Only democratic societies agonize over security forces; repressive regimes of the left or right take them for granted. . . . Even in the most open democracies, of which there are few, there can be no argument against the need for certain measures of clandestine intelligence activity to protect society from the enemies of the state. Free societies, as well as closed ones, need to have secret services; otherwise we run the risk that the closed ones will take over the free ones.

In totalitarian societies the effectiveness of secret police in deterring illegitimate violence (crime in the streets) occurs through legitimate violence (crime by the state). The specter and practices of such infamous secret police as Hitler's Gestapo, Stalin's OGPU (now KGB), or Haiti's Tonton Macoutes, and midnight raids, tortures, and disappearances are frightening, indeed. While one may not argue with the need for some secret police function even in democratic societies, abuse of such powers in culling legitimate dissent or in harassment of peaceful political opponents or public celebrities, such as by Hoover's FBI, certainly exceeds the limits of necessary surveillance in the interest of national security.

Austin Turk (1981) prefers the term "political policing" to refer to secret police operations. In "Organizational Deviance and Political Policing," Turk (Ibid., pp. 238–239) provides a number of illustrations:

- Assassination or maiming of political figures, e.g., Steve Biko, civil rights leader in South Africa.
- "Geneva Offenses" such as germ warfare, letter bombs, or use of cattle prods in order to torture political prisoners. The Geneva Convention originally forbade the mistreatment of sick or wounded soldiers.
- The torture of political detainees, such as those listed by Amnesty International.
- Character assassination, such as the Jean Seberg case (to be discussed shortly).
- Intervention in conventional politics, such as the FBI campaign against Martin Luther King.

- Violations of civil or human rights, for example, from illegal surveillance to mental institutionalization of political dissidents in the USSR.
- Economic or political harassment of dissident groups.
- Use of "agent provocateurs," informants, and spies in order to manipulate public institutions.
- Subversion of economic or other institutions, e.g., overthrow of Chilean government of Salvador Allende by the Central Intelligence Agency.

Human Rights Violations

Perhaps the most dramatic illustration of crimes by government is the pervasive international violation of human rights. Thousands of "political prisoners"—individuals who have committed no crimes other than their espousal of political ideas—are tortured, murdered, or abandoned and exiled to the "Gulag Archipelagos" throughout the world. It is difficult, due to governmental secrecy, to gain an accurate count of such prisoners, although human rights organizations such as Amnesty International provide rough figures for 1983 such as 10,000 in the USSR; 15,000 in Turkey; as many as 100,000 each in Pakistan, Afghanistan, Iran, Iraq, Philippines, Taiwan, China, and South Korea; 2,000 in Poland; 10,000 in Africa; and 5,000 in South America, Cuba, and Haiti (Whitaker et al., 1983, p. 40). Authoritarian and totalitarian regimes of the left and right are the biggest violators and least tolerant of dissent. These countries most resemble George Orwell's 1984, in which the state is preeminent. Soviet Article 190–1 of the penal code prohibits slander against the government, and violators are often committed to mental hospitals and subjected to involuntary therapy and treatment. Enforcement of this code began to ease in the late eighties.

While Savak (the Iranian secret police) under the Shah was a recognized brutal force, in the subsequent theocracy created by Khomeini in Iran, as many as 60,000 political prisoners have been held and over 25,000 executed as of 1984, including a systematic extermination of members of the Baha'i religion. According to a report by Amnesty International (Lippman, 1987), torture is routinely practiced on detainees in order to extract confessions. Beatings, floggings, suspension by limbs, and mock executions are common. Amputations are given in accordance with Islamic law for thefts. The death penalty is given for acts ranging from adultery and repeated lesbianism to wine drinking (see Elias, 1986). Beginning in 1975, the Pol Pot regime in Cambodia embarked upon a system of mass genocide that destroyed a large portion of that small nation's population. In Latin America right-wing governments and private government-related "death squads" kidnap and/or torture and murder individuals whom they feel threaten the state. Amnesty International estimates that ninety-eight countries practiced torture during the eighties primarily as a tool for repression rather than to extract information (Satchell, 1988, p. 38).

Soh Sung, a Korean graduate student, has been in prison in South Korea since 1971 for allegedly violating that country's Anti-Communist and National Security Laws. He was accused of being a North Korean spy, and shortly after his arrest had severe burns over 45 percent of his body and went into a coma for a month. "In fall 1971, Soh Sung was sentenced to death based on a confession he had signed (by a toe print while he was in a coma). The sentence was later reduced to life imprisonment" (Howery, 1988, p. 14). Amnesty International has expressed the concern that, as a result of international attention focused upon the plight of political prisoners, many governments may have turned to execution of dissidents (Whitaker, et al., 1983, p. 52), assuming that "dead men tell no tales."

In South Africa racist policies of apartheid (racial separation) and their enforcement has led to systematic violations of the human rights of black and "colored" South Africans by the white government. As of February 1989, Civil Rights groups estimate that more than thirty thousand people have been detained at some point since an emergency law of June 12, 1986 (Battersby, 1989, p. 4). In Ethiopia, Somalia, and Sudan large-scale starvation of civilian populations was used as a political weapon.

Genocide

Genocide, the mass destruction or annihilation of human populations, is the ultimate violent crime by government. The term was coined by jurist Raphael Lemkin (1944), who defined *genocide* as the destruction of a nation or of an ethnic group. Genocidal conflicts have a long history, from the Crusades, Roman persecutions, Genghis Khan, and medieval pogroms against European Jews up to the horrors of this present century. Kuper (1981, pp. 17–18) explains that modern totalitarian political ideologies replace religious justifications for genocide:

> The major examples of the genocidal potentialities of these ideologies in our day are provided by the Nazi regime with its conception of a brave new world of racially tolerated and ordered societies under German hegemony; the Soviet regime, under Stalin, with the Gulag Archipelago receiving, as a sort of "rubbish bin of history," the successive blood sacrifices of the communist utopia; and the recent Pol Pot regime in Cambodia, freely and righteously exterminating in total dedication to a starkly elemental blueprint for living. . . . It

is a massive toll of genocidal conflict, if one adds to the civil wars of decoloni-
zation, the destruction of scapegoat groups, and the ideological, ethnic and
religious massacres. And it is a particularly threatening scourge of our day
and age, facilitated by international concern for the protection of the sovereign rights of the state, by international intervention in the arming of contending sections, and by United Nations *de facto* condonation, which serves
as a screen for genocide.

In the late eighties as part of the Iran-Iraq war, Iraq used chemical
weapons on civilians as well as on the Iranian military. Such a practice has been outlawed by international conventions (the 1925 Geneva
Protocol) since after World War I.

Condemnation of political criminals may be compromised for other
political reasons. In July 1987 the French government convicted Klaus
Barbie, "the butcher of Lyons," of crimes against humanity which he
had committed as a Gestapo (SS) commander during World War II. He
directed the torture, death, and deportation to concentration camps of
thousands of Jews, Resistance fighters, and others. Barbie had been hidden from the French after the war by the Americans, who had used
him for intelligence purposes (Misner, 1987). Similar charges were
levied against former United Nations Secretary-General and Austrian
President Kurt Waldheim. The charges levied were that Waldheim,
while a young German lieutenant in the Balkans during World War
II, knew about war crimes. Investigations of Waldheim's involvement
were inconclusive.

Pol Pot's "Hell on Earth"

Massive genocide did not end with Hitler's pogrom against the Jews.
In the late seventies, unbelievable horrors were practiced by Pol Pot's
Khmer Rouge regime upon its own people. If one were to imagine a
country ruled by the Charles Manson family, one would be close to
picturing the raw terror of Angka (the organization of Khmer Rouge)
in Cambodia. Of all the Cambodian refugees who fled the country and
its invasion by Viet Nam, interviews and observations showed the most
devastated to be Khmer Rouge refugees (Cambodia, 1979). The Angka,
in an effort to create a radically new society overnight, had tortured,
terrorized, and murdered their subjects to the point that many of them
exhibited zombi-like behavior devoid of many normal human emotions.

Since they represented potential opponents under the regime, intellectuals were slaughtered. One woman, whose intellectual husband and
family were murdered before her eyes, said she could not cry, since
such emotion would have demonstrated disapproval of Angka policy

The 1984 film *The Killing Fields* dramatized the brutality of the Pol Pot regime in Cambodia.

and would have spelled her own doom. The Khmer Rouge refugees were forbidden to mourn for their deceased loved ones; they exhibited an indifference to life or death. They laughed when told the following true story: A married man and a pregnant woman were caught committing adultery, a forbidden offense; for this, they were executed in front of their fellow workers. The woman's stomach was cut open and the wailing child held by its heels. The workers were asked if any would take the baby, and all refused since agreement would signify approval of adultery and their own death warrants. The guards dashed the baby to the ground, killing it, and removed, fried, and ate its liver. The refugees' callous reaction to this story is the result of prolonged brutalization and terror.

In 1948 the United Nations passed a *Convention on Genocide* in which they defined genocide as a crime (Kuper, 1981, p. 19):

In the present Convention, genocide means any of the following acts committed with intent to destroy, in whole or in part, a national, ethnical, racial or religious group, as such:

(a) Killing members of the group;

(b) Causing serious bodily or mental harm to members of the group;

(c) Deliberately inflicting on the group conditions of life calculated to bring about its physical destruction in whole or in part;

(d) Imposing measures intended to prevent births within the group;

(e) Forcibly transferring children of the group to another group.

Despite the concerns expressed in this document, the U.N. has been less than a consistent force in condemning genocide, whether it be the Pol Pot regime in Cambodia, Idi Amin's Uganda, or Khomeini's Iran.

Crime by Police

In democratic societies the government is expected not only to enforce the law but also, in doing so, to obey the law itself. In the United States, the government is obliged and accountable to certain constitutional guarantees of individual rights such as freedom of speech, due process, and the right to privacy. Despite this, federal and local law enforcement agencies, being more interested in bureaucratic efficiency in law enforcement, have often ignored and violated these rights in the process of prosecuting their mandate. The Skolnick (1969, p. xxv) Report to the National Commission on the Causes and Prevention of Violence, entitled *The Politics of Protest*, which analyzed U.S. violence in the sixties, indicates:

> Police response to mass protest has often resulted in an escalation of conflict, hostility, and violence. The police violence during the Democratic National Convention in Chicago (1968) was not a unique phenomenon. We have found numerous other instances where violence had been initiated or exacerbated by police actions and attitudes, although violence also has been avoided by judicious planning and supervision.

Prior to the success of the civil rights struggle, local and state officials in the southern U.S. systematically violated federal law in maintenance of a racist, caste system. Murder, lynchings, beatings, and institutionalized denial of constitutional guarantees were all committed in the name of "law and order." It was to the destruction of this de jure or discrimination by law that the civil rights movement was directed; this will be discussed in detail later in this chapter.

Other abuses by government officials may include illegal surveillance of citizens, disruption of the conventional democratic process, and clandestine experiments with the public serving as unknowing subjects.

Illegal Surveillance, Disruption, and Experiments

Operation CHAOS

In 1967, during the height of dissident activity in America, President Johnson directed the Central Intelligence Agency (CIA) to investigate and determine the extent of foreign influence in domestic protest activity. This special operations group, Operation CHAOS, in surveillance activities of domestic groups, violated the CIA's initial charter, the National Security Act, which clearly excluded its activities from the domestic arena, although pressure for the expansion of activities were ordered by both President Johnson and later Nixon. Operation CHAOS and a related Project 2 placed agents in radical groups and collected thirteen thousand different files, over half of which were on American citizens. The Rockefeller Commission (1975) investigated the impropriety of the CIA's encroaching upon the domestic field of espionage, sabotage, and provocation. In activities related to these operations, the CIA and FBI in its operation Cointelpro committed 238 break-ins (black bag jobs) and later attempted to destroy records of such activities. In the early seventies, military intelligence organizations were discovered to be involved in investigating the private lives of prominent politicians, including Adlai Stevenson III. In addition, as part of Operation Leprechaun in 1970–1973, the Internal Revenue Service (IRS) hired twenty to twenty-five operatives to spy on political opponents of Nixon in Florida (Rosenberg, 1977).

Cointelpro

The misuse of power by intelligence agencies was further illustrated in hearings conducted by the U.S. Select Committee to Study Government Operations (1979), which revealed that civil rights organizations had been investigated for over a twenty-five-year period in order to uncover possible Communist influences.

> Dr. Martin Luther King, Jr., was harassed by anonymous letters, his telephone was tapped, his speaking engagements were disrupted by false fire alarms—all as a strategy to discredit him and his organization. In addition it is apparent that the FBI and various state police departments used *agents provocateurs* to infiltrate dissenting groups, radicalize the members, secure the weapons and explosives necessary for violent confrontations, and plan the target of attacks as a means to discredit dissident groups.
> —Karmen, 1974, in Thomas and Hepburn, 1983, p. 280.

As part of Cointelpro, the FBI's counterintelligence program to harass and disrupt legitimate political activity such as the Socialist Worker's Party and various black nationalist groups, the FBI employed false letters accusing people of being informants in order to foment internal warfare (Blackstock, 1976, p. 9). The difficulty of separating ideologically motivated actions from personal corruption and vendetta is illustrated in examinations of J. Edgar Hoover's personal files, some of which have been released in the 1980s under the Freedom of Information Act. In his nearly fifty years in office Hoover kept personal files replete with gossip and defamatory information on the personal lives of public figures, particularly those whom he happened to dislike either politically or due to racial bigotry. Eleanor Roosevelt, John and Robert Kennedy, and Martin Luther King were just a few of the political figures on whom Hoover harbored revealing information. In addition to surveillance on Dr. King, it is alleged that the FBI sent threatening letters and a tape to Coretta King regarding her husband's enjoying a sexual tryst. The opening quotation to this chapter suggests an attempt by the FBI to blackmail King into committing suicide (Garrow, 1981).

Character Assassination

Actress Jean Seberg at one point had helped to raise funds for the Black Panthers (*The FBI vs. Jean Seberg*, 1970). In 1969 Seberg committed suicide, apparently in response to FBI tactics which were designed to defame her character. According to FBI documents, the bureau had fed the rumor that a Black Panther leader had fathered the then pregnant actress's baby. Distraught, Ms. Seberg had a miscarriage, suffered adverse psychotic symptoms, and finally killed herself.

In 1988 civil liberties groups released FBI documents, which they had obtained under the Freedom of Information Act, indicating extensive investigation of CISPES (Committee in Solidarity with the People of El Salvador) and one hundred other organizations associated with CISPES in some way. Concern was expressed that such investigations were reminiscent of 1960s operations and constituted unnecessary harassment of legitimate opposition groups because of their political beliefs. CISPES was opposed to Reagan administration policy in Central America, although the administration charged the group was communist inspired (Messinger, 1988; and Jacoby, Sandza, and Parry, 1988).

Oliver North and Enterprise: Hero or Criminal?

America has the habit from time to time of televising modern versions of pageant plays; Congressional hearings from McCarthy and Kefauver to Watergate have fascinated and mesmerized millions. Such was certainly the case in the late eighties with the televised Iran-Contra Hearings and subsequent coverage (which was not televised) of the trial of Lt. Col. Oliver North, former White House aide during the Reagan administration.

Col. North, along with former national security advisor John Poindexter, and others were indicted on charges that they conspired to divert Iranian arms sales profits to the Nicaraguan Contras. Among the charges filed by the grand jury was that North and others had "deceitfully and without legal authorization" organized, directed, and concealed "a program to continue funding of and logistical and other support for military and paramilitary operations in Nicaragua by the Contras" at a time in which U.S. law forbade such activity (Ledeen, 1988).

The indictment also charged that North and William Secord had conspired to divert millions from the sale of U.S. arms to "Enterprise." Enterprise, a secret organization, conducted an arms-for-hostages deal with Iran and diverted nearly $4 million in profits to the Contras. Both of these activities represented policy disputes between the executive branch and Congress with Oliver North, having lied to Congress and shredded evidence, the designated scapegoat or "fall guy." Was a lieutenant colonel in the U.S. Marines to be held solely responsible for criminal acts, or were higher up individuals, including former CIA chief William Casey (head of Enterprise), who died during the hearings, and President Reagan, to be allowed to conduct foreign policy in defiance of Congress?

North was willing to "hold the bag" (take the rap; accept responsibility) until it became clear that he faced criminal charges without

A well-known recent case of political crime: Lt. Col. Oliver North, shown here on the left, was convicted in 1989 of altering and shredding documents, accepting an illegal gratuity and of aiding and abetting in the obstruction of Congress.

protection from higher-ups. North's boss, General Secord, described how it was possible for the President to truthfully deny knowledge of these activities. Reagan would give general policy guidelines and would let others (North, Secord) carry out the specific details without his specific knowledge. Thus, when asked, he could employ "plausible deniability."

In contrast to our previous discussion of Watergate, the Iran-Contra affair and North's involvement is much more clearly an example of political crime. On May 4, 1989, North was convicted of altering and shredding documents, accepting an illegal gratuity (a $13,800 home security system), and one count of aiding and abetting in obstructing Congress. He was acquitted on nine other counts. North's defense was that he was just following orders: the President's (Rosenthal, 1989).

The Search for the Manchurian Candidate

"Whom the gods destroy, they first make mad"

—Euripedes

In 1958 Richard Condon published a novel (later made into a movie) entitled *The Manchurian Candidate*. In Condon's very clever plot, which takes place during the Korean War, a character named Raymond Shaw and a U.S. Army squad return after having been missing behind enemy lines. The other members of the squad relate Shaw's heroism in saving them from the enemy; he receives the Congressional Medal of Honor for this. In fact, Shaw and his squad were "brainwashed" or "hypnotized-programmed" by the communist Chinese. Asking Shaw to play solitaire until the queen of diamonds appeared would trigger Shaw into zombi-like obedience. His own mother (a Chinese communist "mole" or spy) was his operator, and he was able to function as an assassin of the presidential nominee, thus propelling his father, the vice-presidential nominee, into the Oval Office.

Condon's theme enthralled the Western intelligence establishment, as had the "Moscow show trials" of the period in which dissidents were paraded before cameras and trance-like in appearance admitted treasonable activities against the state (Scheflin and Opton, 1978, p. 437). How could admissions have been obtained from figures such as Hungary's Cardinal Mindszenty? Cold War propagandist Edward Hunter (1951) coined the term "brainwashing," which became a household word; however, it is very likely that Hunter popularized the concept as part of his job with the CIA (Scheflin and Opton, 1978, p. 226).

The Strange Case of Dr. Frank Olson.

> *You've got to trust us. We are honorable men.*
> —*Richard Helms, former director of the Central Intelligence Agency*

In the early morning of November 28, 1953, Frank Olson, a civilian employee of the U.S. Army, inexplicably jumped to his death from the tenth floor window of his New York City hotel room. His distraught widow and family could not understand why he had killed himself, although the CIA had stated publicly that Olson had become mentally unbalanced. Over twenty years later during the Rockefeller Commission (1975) hearings on CIA activities, government documents revealed the actual facts of the incident, facts which had been hidden from Olson's own guilt-ridden widow and family for over two decades. As part of the secret CIA *Project Bluebird* which involved mind-control research, the agency secretly drugged unsuspecting citizens and employees. Olson unknowingly had been slipped a very heavy dosage of LSD and literally "freaked out" (a psychotomimetic or reaction which mimics psychosis). When this occurred, the CIA sent him to an agency allergist rather than a psychiatrist. When Olson killed himself, the agency lied, smearing Olson's reputation in the process (Marks, 1979). When the facts were revealed, the White House issued an apology to the Olson family along with $750,000. The Olson episode was just one in a series of bizarre and frightening mind-control field experiments conducted by the CIA, using as subjects unsuspecting private citizens.

The Brainwashing Myth.   Scheflin and Opton (1978, p. 225) maintain that the brainwashing concept was a myth and that the Communist methods differed little from police interrogation practices:

> That the CIA was able to take an old form of torture, dress it up with a lurid name and convince the public that a new technique for mind subversion was being practiced by the Communist nations, is a propaganda coup of stunning proportion. . . . We do not deny that POWs were subjected to deprivation, torture, interrogation and indoctrination. But we do deny that any mysterious, sinister or unique form of mind control was involved. The Soviet, Chinese and Korean "brainwashing" techniques were fully known to the U.S. intelligence services. There was absolutely no basis in fact to allege that the "communists" had started "brain warfare." It is not entirely impossible that the "brainwashing" scare was created by the CIA because it wanted to do mind-control research and considered that the safest way to get authorization was to allege that the Soviets had done it first.

With various code names—*Bluebird, Artichoke,* and *MKULTRA*— the CIA, FBI and military in the fifties experimented with various behavioral control devices and interrogation techniques including ESP (extrasensory perception), drugs, polygraphs, hypnosis, shock therapy, surgery, and radiation. These projects involved secret testing on private citizens without their permission and, when death or injury took place, a cover-up. In a related example of government agencies using unknowing citizens as guinea pigs, the U.S. Army in the fifties and sixties conducted outdoor tests of poisonous bacteria (serratia) which can cause pneumonia. Due to these bacteriological warfare tests, one hospital reported twelve cases of serratia pneumonia and one death (Cousins, 1979; and Simon and Eitzen, 1982, p. 218).

The Terminal Man.   The Orwellian potential of such uncontrolled invasion of the human mind is illustrated in the case of Thomas R. Michael Crichton (1972) in his best-selling novel (and later movie) *Terminal Man* apparently used as his model a real-life terminal man. The fictional Leonard Kille was one Thomas R., a patient (or more accurately a victim) of the Boston violence project (Scheflin and Opton, 1978, pp. 298–300). In Mark and Ervin's (1970) *Violence and the Brain* it was proposed that brain dysfunction is a major cause of violence; operations to control cerebral functioning were undertaken in the Boston violence project, which had government funding. Thomas R. was paraded as an exhibit of the success of such surgery. His previous violence was described (Ibid.) as primarily associated with "paranoid" charges of unfaithfulness on the part of his wife. Thomas R. had as many as eighty electrodes implanted in order to control his brain dysfunction and, although he was hailed as a success after the removal of the electrodes, he has spent his life in violence and mental hospitalization, and was declared totally disabled by the Veteran's Administration. Mark and Ervin (1970) also fail to mention in their study that, while Thomas R. was being "wired-up," his wife sued for divorce and married a man who had been the subject of Thomas R.'s "paranoia."

Through various fronts during this period, the CIA, apparently unknown to the recipients, also funded social psychological research by such famous names as the Sherifs, Orne, Rogers, Osgood, and Goffman (Marks, 1979, p. 121) and financed the publication of over one thousand books, pretending that they were the products of independent scholarship (Cook, 1984, p. 287).

Requiem for the Manchurian Candidate.   A Canadian teenager seeking medical treatment for an arthritic leg was subjected to LSD, electroshock therapy, and forced to listen to hours of taped messages including one repeating, "You killed your mother." Such bizarre experiments were financed by the CIA and conducted by an American doctor who had been the president of the American Psychiatric Association. Over one hundred Canadians from 1957 to 1961 were unwitting brainwashing guinea pigs, causing them much psychiatric harm. In 1988 the CIA agreed to pay damages to victims of the experiment—$750,000 to be shared by eight of the victims (Witt, 1988, p. 2A).

American Nuclear Guinea Pigs

In 1986 the House Energy and Commerce Subcommittee uncovered the fact that federal agencies had conducted exposure experiments on American citizens including injecting them with plutonium, radium, and uranium over a thirty-year period beginning in the mid 1940s. The experiments included elderly adults being fed radium or thorium at MIT, inmates receiving X-rays to their testes, open-air fallout tests, and people being fed real fallout from a Nevada test site (Lawrence, 1988).

Crimes against Government

Protest and Dissent

As previously indicated, crimes against the government may vary from illegal protests, demonstrations, and strikes to treason, sabotage, assassination, and terrorism. At various times in history, social movements which petition for change are viewed as threatening or subversive to the existing society. The American Revolution, the labor movement, anti-Vietnam War movement, and the struggle for civil rights serve as examples. Demonstrators for civil rights and other causes may purposely violate laws and be arrested for disorderly conduct, breach of peace, parading without a permit, trespassing, loitering, and the like. They may also be arrested for refusing to pay income taxes which may be used for military purposes, for picketing military bases, for student protests, or for refusal to register for military draft. Many student activists of the sixties viewed their universities as involved in the military, industrial, and racial status quo (Skolnick, 1969 p. xxi).

While repression and violation of human rights occur in Western democracies which preach such values, they are systematically violated in totalitarian and authoritarian regimes of both the right and left. Protests against such official control simply are not tolerated in such systems. Lech Walesa's Solidarity labor movement in Poland was finally defined as illegal in that such a union did not fit into Marxist ideology of a proletariat state: Why would a union be necessary in a worker's state? Only later, as part of *glasnost* (openness), was Solidarity recognized.

While dissent and protest activities against the government are usually perceived as "radical" (leftist) in attempting to bring about change in the existing order, they may also represent "reactionary" (rightist) activities which are aimed at preserving the old order, institutions, or organizational schemes that are no longer acceptable. Extremism on the right has been represented in American history by groups such as the Know-Nothing party, a secret political organization formed in 1852 which was opposed to Catholics and foreigners; and the Ku Klux Klan (KKK), begun in 1866, which supported racism and white supremacy through terrorism and violence. Other right-wing groups have included the German-American Bund, the John Birch Society, the Minutemen, the Christian Crusade, and the Black Muslims. In El Salvador in the eighties right-wing "death squads" were responsible for a reign of terror in opposition to government programs of land and labor reform. In China in 1965–75, the "cultural revolution" represented a reactionary youth movement designed to return the society to more orthodox Marxist-Leninist practices.

Groups express dissent and civil disobedience by employing sit-ins, boycotts, and freedom rides (in order to desegregate facilities) to challenge unjust laws. They consciously decide to violate certain laws to call public attention to their cause and to bring about change in the law. Civil rights leader and director of the Southern Christian Leadership Conference, Dr. Martin Luther King, Jr., a Protestant minister, came under heavy criticism from other clergy for neglecting God's work and becoming too involved in disruptive social activities.

Letter from Birmingham Jail

The Nuremberg principle or precedent supports the view that, when one is faced with the imperative of either obeying unjust laws or following a higher moral conscience, the latter holds precedence; to blindly follow orders when they violate basic human rights and dignity is unacceptable. Martin Luther King's (1963) "Letter from Birmingham Jail" very movingly describes his view that immoral laws must be disobeyed:

> My Dear Fellow Clergymen:
>
> While confined here in the Birmingham city jail I came across your recent statement calling my present activities "unwise and untimely". . . . I want to try to answer your statement in what I hope will be patient and reasonable terms. . . . I am in Birmingham because injustice exists here. . . . I cannot sit idly by in Atlanta and not be concerned about what happens in Birmingham . . . Anyone who lives inside the United States can never be

considered an outsider anywhere within its bounds. You deplore the demon-strations. . . . But your statement, I am sorry to say, fails to express a simi-lar concern for the conditions that brought about the demonstrations. . . . Birmingham is probably the most thoroughly segregated city in the United States. Its ugly record of police brutality is widely known. Its unjust treat-ment of Negroes in the courts is a notorious reality. There have been more unsolved bombings of Negro homes and churches in Birmingham than in any other city in the nation. . . . We had no alternative except to prepare for direct action, whereby we would present our very bodies as a means of laying our case before the conscience of the local and national commu-nity. . . . The purpose of our direct action program is to create a situation so crisis-packed that it will inevitably open the door to negotiation. . . . We know through painful experience that freedom is never voluntarily given by the oppressor; it must be demanded by the oppressed. One may well ask, "How can you advocate breaking some laws and obeying others?" The answer lies in the fact that there are two types of laws: just and unjust. I agree with St. Augustine that "an unjust law is no law at all". . . I can urge men to dis-obey segregation ordinances, for such ordinances are morally wrong. . . . I submit that an individual who breaks a law that conscience tells him is unjust and who willingly accepts the penalty of imprisonment in order to arouse the conscience of the community over its injustice is in reality expressing the highest respect for the law. . . . We should never forget that everything Adolf Hitler did in Germany was "legal" and everything the Hun-garian freedom fighters did in Hungary was "illegal."

Martin Luther King, Jr., and his organization, the Southern Christian Leadership Conference, advocated nonviolent, passive resistance, civil disobedience of the form which was employed so successfully by Mahatma Gandhi in overcoming British rule in India. Gandhi taught that violence on the part of those enforcing unjust laws must be met with nonviolence in order to appeal to the public's sense of justice. Incar-cerated members of the Irish Republican Army in Northern Ireland have also borrowed a tactic from Gandhi, the "hunger strike." Members of "H block" starved themselves to death in order to demonstrate their dedi-cation to their cause.

Social Movements

Illegal protests, demonstrations, and strikes are often associated with social movements which advocate change in the existing order. Mem-bers and supporters of such movements are usually deeply committed to altering the status quo. The civil rights battle against racism, the feminist struggle against sexism, the labor and agrarian movements for fair wages, the anti-war movement against the escalation of the Vietnam conflict, the antinuclear, environmental, and the anti- or proabortion movements are all examples. While most such groups are intent upon altering the status quo and may at times resort to violence, sabotage, and other destructive behavior, most do not resort to treason, assassination, or terrorism. Kittrie and Wedlock (1986, p. xxxviii) indicate:

> . . . [P]olitical criminality is an integral part of an ongoing historical process of challenge and response which accounts for many of the liberties and for much of the societal diversity for which America is most admired . . . Dissent, protest, disobedience, violence and rebellion—in pursuit of political change or in opposition to it—have been major forces in the recent history of the nations of the world.

Frequently, political criminals have done nothing more than exist and suffer attack due to race, gender, ethnicity, or nationality. Expulsion, exile, curfews, confiscations, confinement, restrictions on travel, and controls over associations may all be used to subordinate, enslave, or subject to second-class citizenship subjugated groups.

In analyzing black militancy, student riots, and antiwar demonstrations of the sixties, the Skolnick Report to the National Commission on the Causes and Prevention of Violence (Skolnick, 1969, pp. xix–xx) concludes:

> . . . serious analysis of the connections between protest and violence cannot focus solely on the character or culture of those who protest the current state of the American political social order. Rather, our research finds that mass protest is an essentially political phenomenon engaged in by normal people; that demonstrations are increasingly being employed by a variety of groups, ranging from students and blacks to middle-class professionals, public employees, and policemen; that violence, when it occurs, is usually not planned, but arises out of an interaction between protesters and responding authorities; that violence has frequently accompanied the efforts of deprived groups to achieve status in American society; and that recommendations concerning the prevention of violence which do not address the issue of fundamental social and political change are fated to be largely irrelevant and frequently self-defeating.

In the eighties and nineties groups such as "the Sanctuary Movement," "Pro-Life" and "Pro-Choice" groups on the abortion issue, and "Anti-Nuclear" movements participated in various forms of civil disobedience and protest activities. "The Sanctuary Movement" consisted of church and lay workers who ran an "underground railroad" to assist political refugees (often illegal immigrants) from being deported to their Central American homelands where they often faced political repression. The U.S. government claimed that such groups were in violation of the immigration laws and were not political, but economic refugees, and that the government had a right and responsibility to control the nation's borders (Crittenden, 1988; and Tomsho, 1987).

"Pro-Life" (right-to-life) forces are opposed to legalized abortion, viewing it as murder, and seek a reversal of the 1973 *Roe v. Wade* Supreme Court decision which permits abortion on demand. Besides protests and civil disobedience, more extreme elements have bombed abortion clinics. Opponents ("Pro-Choice") argue that such a decision is not the government's decision, but one between a woman and her physician; that one group's morality should not become public policy in opposition to the will of the majority (Paige, 1985).

"Anti-nuclear" forces are convinced that the nuclear industry is unsafe and is sapping funds from more ecologically sane energy policies such as solar energy. Such groups have violated the law in attempts to prevent start-ups of new reactors. Another group that became more visible beginning in the late eighties was "antivivisectionists," those who oppose the use of animals in which maiming, torture, death, or other harm is an essential treatment. Such groups have protested as well as raided laboratories "liberating" animals (Regan, 1982), or photographing and releasing to the press some of the more grisly examples. Scientific researchers who use such animals claim that such experiments are necessary for discovering medical cures and treatments.

Animal-rights activists began committing terrorist acts in the 1980s. This woman was accused of attempting to bomb a company that used animals in research.

Espionage

> Traditionally, roses have been the symbolic emblem of the spying profession. Greek mythology describes an incident in which the god of love offers a rose to the god of silence as an inducement to gain the latter's silence regarding the weaknesses of the other gods. In Medieval Europe a rose was hung from the ceiling of council chambers and those in attendance pledged their silence since the gathering was *sub rosa*, under the rose (Morrell, 1984, p. 83).

Espionage, the secretive theft of information, has been a practice since early recorded history. In the Bible, God commanded Moses to send spies to Canaan and Joshua sent spies to Jericho. In 1987 archeologists discovered a large collection of 3,700-year-old Mesopotamian clay tablets that described, among other things, the capture and ransom of spies (Ancient Records, 1987). Fifth century B.C. Chinese sage Sun-Tzu, in his classic book *Art of War* (1963), provided a chapter on secret agents and types of spies. While the name Benedict Arnold, who betrayed the American colonists to the British during the Revolutionary War, lives in infamy in the U.S., a statue of Nathan Hale, an American spy executed by the British, stands outside Central Intelligence Agency headquarters in Virginia (Hagan, 1987b).

Despite images of "cloaks and daggers," Mata Hari and James Bond, of "black espionage" or "covert agents" ferreting secrets, classical forms of spying have for many years ranked below "white espionage" which uses space satellites, code-breaking, and technical collection (Marchetti and Marks, 1974, p. 186; and Ranelagh, 1986). The technological revolution in espionage has replaced the "seductive, sable-coated countess traveling first class on the Orient Express" (Maclean, 1978, p. 336). "Sub Rosa Criminals" are spies who steal secrets. One form of spying, treason, is one of the earliest crimes punished by society and the only crime discussed in the U.S. Constitution. Despite inattention in the criminological literature, "sub rosa crime" (espionage) is more costly than traditional crime and has altered post World War II economic and political history. Soviet theft of Western technology alone is estimated to cost billions in future defense expenditures to counter Soviet improvements.

Defector and former KGB Major Stanislav Levchenko was apparently the first to reveal the acronym *MICE* for describing the motives of spies (Kneece, 1986): motivation, ideology, compromise, and ego. Others have expanded this acronym to SMICE adding sex as a separate motivation. Vantage Point 11.2 outlines a more detailed typology of spies. There has been a major shift in the motivations of spies East and West from the ideological, Cold War fifties to the materialistic/hedonistic eighties and nineties. The ideological motivation has been replaced for the most part by mercenary considerations.

Many previous discussions of types of spies have concentrated upon specific role performance or tasks (Anderson, 1977; Sun-Tzu, 1963; Copeland, 1974; and Turner, 1985). This writer proposes a *typology of spies* which includes the following (Hagan, 1987b and 1986):

Mercenary	Compromised
Ideological	Deceived
Alienated/Egocentric	Quasi-Agent
Buccaneer	Escapee
Professional	Miscellaneous

Mercenary spies trade secrets for personal monetary reward. Andrew Daulton Lee, "The Snowman" described in Robert Lindsey's book, *The Falcon and the Snowman* (1979), could serve as an example. Lee was a highly successful drug dealer (hence, "the Snowman" title) and began acting as a courier for his friend, Christopher Boyce ("The Falcon"), by transporting American military secrets to the Soviets for financial reward. The majority of spy cases since 1980 have been of the mercenary variety.

The *ideological spy* is motivated by strong ideological beliefs. Such spies are political criminals in that they are often condemned as traitors in one country while heralded as heroes in the recipient nation. Julius and Ethel Rosenberg became the first and only native Americans to be executed for treason in March 1951 for having given the Russians America's atomic secrets (Hyde, 1980). They did so out of devotion to Communism, as did the British "establishment spies," Burgess, Maclean, Philby, and Blunt. Recruited as Cambridge University students in the thirties, they rose to the highest levels as "moles" (deep cover agents) in British intelligence (Pincher, 1984; and West, 1982).

The *alienated/egocentric spy* is one who betrays for personal reasons unrelated to monetary or ideological considerations. In 1985 ex-CIA employee Edward Howard Lee, having been fired by the agency, defected to the Soviets and took with him classified secrets.

The *buccaneer or sport spy* is one who obtains psychological fulfillment through spying. Turner (1985) describes them as "swashbuckling adventurers who spy for kicks." Christopher "The Falcon" Boyce or John Walker serve as examples, although there are many others. Boyce, the partner of Lee in *The Falcon and the Snowman* (Lindsey, 1979 and 1981), was a bored twenty-one-year-old college dropout who gave the Soviets top secret satellite information in an act of defiance against the CIA. Boyce told a federal marshal, "I guess I'm a pirate at heart. I guess I'm an adventurer" (Lindsey, 1983). John Walker, head of a spy ring which included his son, his brother, and his son's friend,

Political "Whistleblowers"

Information usually is classified as secret to protect national security, but also in some instances to misinform the public and shroud questionable activities. It was to protest the latter that Daniel Ellsberg, an employee of the Rand Corporation (a private think-tank and research organization), violated his oath of secrecy and turned over secret government documents, *The Pentagon Papers*, to the U.S. press (Gravel, 1971).

---

was a former naval officer who passed American cryptographic codes to the Soviets from the 1960s through mid-1980s. Walker reflected a Walter Mitty-James Bond image of spying which included props such as umbrella weapons and crossbows. His ring's peddling of American codes to the Soviets cost American pilots' lives in Vietnam and compromised American naval strategy (Kneece, 1986).

Professional spies are agents, careerists, occupational employees of intelligence bureaucracies. Covert professional agents such as Richard Sorge and Rudolf Abel are legends in the history of espionage. Such agents usually operate under diplomatic cover and, when caught, enjoy diplomatic immunity and are dispatched out of the country. Those who lack such cover are usually swapped for other spies at a later date.

Compromised spies are at first reluctant traitors who trade secrets for either romantic purposes or due to blackmail and coercion. Many are victims of the SMICE strategy. The most celebrated case was that of U.S. Moscow Embassy Marine guards, particularly Clayton Lonetree and Arnold Bracey. The guards were allegedly victims of LeCarre's spy fiction gambit, "the honey trap." In spy tradecraft jargon the KGB employs many "swallows" or seductive female assistants to trade sex for secrets (Kessler, 1989; and Schlachter, 1986). Kessler (1989) claims that, although the U.S. government issued denials, the KGB had the run of the embassy and its secrets.

The *deceived spy* ("false flag recruit") is one who is led to believe he or she is working for one organization when, in fact, the work is for another. Edwin Wilson, the subject of Peter Maas' book *Manhunt* (1986), was an ex-CIA employee who recruited assassins, smugglers, technicians, and spies including high-level moonlighters from the CIA to work for Libya. He led them to believe it was a "company" (CIA) operation (Epstein, 1983; and Goulden, 1984). Industrial spies who believe they are working for a rival company may very well be working for the intelligence agency of a rival power.

The remaining types are the *quasi-agents*, dissenters, such as ex-CIA agent Philip Agee, who released classified information to the public. They resemble whistleblowers. *Escapee spies* are individuals who defect in order to avoid personal problems, while the *miscellaneous category* is for those spies who defy classification.

Ellsberg felt that revealing the government's deceit of the public regarding U.S. involvement in the Vietnam War outweighed his duty to keep government secrets. In an even more controversial case, former CIA agent Philip Agee (1975) wrote personal memoirs of his CIA activities in South America in which he named and, according to some, endangered CIA operatives in those countries. He ideologically disagreed with many covert policies the CIA had been carrying out in that region.

Terrorism

We are all too familiar with the obscene tragedy and continuing gothic drama of international terrorism, an all-too-real horror show that enjoys far too many reruns on television. Viewed outside of its political context, international terrorism represents some of the worst examples of mass murder in history.

One can examine the ubiquity of terrorist campaigns by merely reading recent newspaper headlines:

- In January, 1989 a bomb aboard Pan Am Flight 103 exploded over Lockerbie, Scotland, killing all 259 aboard the plane and 11 townspeople. Three Middle East groups claimed responsibility for the attack.
- In Tokyo in May, 1986, during a seven-nation summit to discuss policy related to international terrorism, five homemade missiles fired from two miles away by terrorists fortunately missed the meeting of world leaders.

Definitions and Types of Terrorism

Any definition of terrorism is sure to arouse dispute. Definitions by the U.S. Department of Defense, FBI, State Department, Department of Justice, and Vice President's Task Force on Combatting Terrorism (1986) include:

- the unlawful use of force or violence by revolutionary organizations.
- the intention of coercion or intimidation of governments for political or ideological purposes.
- premeditated political violence perpetrated against noncombatant targets by subnational groups or clandestine state agents.
- use of assassination or kidnapping.

Terrorism may be distinguished from tragic acts of war in the willful and calculated targetting of innocents (Netanyahu, 1986, p. 8). Even during the Nazi occupation of Europe the partisans avoided indiscriminate

Libya, headed by
Moammar Khadafy,
sponsors and encourages
terrorist activities.

killing of the families of German soldiers. No such limitations on non-combatants figure into the plans of many current terrorist groups. The Federal Bureau of Investigation (Pomerantz, 1987, p. 15) defines "terrorism" as ". . . the unlawful use of force or violence against persons or property to intimidate or coerce a government, the civilian population, or any segment thereof, in furtherance of political or social objectives."

The *Report of the Task Force on Disorders and Terrorism* (National Advisory Committee, 1976c, pp. 3–6) provides the following *typology of terrorism*: political terrorism, nonpolitical terrorism, quasi-terrorism, limited political terrorism, and official or state terrorism. The Report defines *political terrorism* as "violent criminal behavior designed primarily to generate fear in the community, or a substantial segment of it for political purposes." *Nonpolitical terrorism* also attempts to elicit fear by means of violence, but is undertaken for either private purposes or gain; examples of this type would include activities of organized crime, the Manson family, or Charles Whitman, "the Texas tower" sniper. *Quasi-terrorism* describes "those activities incidental to the commission of crimes of violence that are similar in form and method to true terrorism but which nevertheless lack its essential ingredient." Rather than being ideologically motivated, many skyjackers and hostage takers, although employing a similar method, are interested in ransom. *Limited political terrorism* refers to "acts of terrorism which are committed for ideological or political motives, but which are not part of a concerted campaign to capture control of the state." Vendetta-type executions and acts of lone terrorists for essentially private motives serve as examples. *Official or state terrorism* occurs in "nations whose rule is based upon fear and oppression that reach terroristic proportions" (Simpson and Bennett, 1985). Wolf (1981) differentiates "enforcement terrorism" from "agitational terrorism," the former being used by governments to control populations.

Brief History

The Assassins of the Middle East were the best known early terrorist groups, although their attacks were confined to officials and authorities. The Jacobin period of the French Revolution and its "reign of terror" provided the name, while the Russian nihilists and "bomb throwers" of the late nineteenth century provided the classic vision of the terrorist. Laqueur (1987, p. 3) notes:

> . . . [T]he popular image of terrorists some 80 years ago was that of a bomb-throwing alien anarchist, disheveled with a black beard and a satanic (or idiotic) smile, fanatic, immoral, sinister and ridiculous at the same time.

Prior to World War II, most terrorism consisted of political assassination of government officials. A second new form of terrorism was inaugurated in Algeria in the late fifties by the FLN (National Liberation Front), who popularized the random attack upon enemy civilians. This is depicted well in the classic film, "The Battle of Algiers." A new third stage of terrorism became popular since the sixties—"media terrorism"—random attacks upon anyone.

Indiscriminate terror has become widespread only in recent times with the invention of more effective explosives and modern mass media. Terroristic action is easier to commit than attacks against hardened targets or well-guarded leaders, and since such actions are unlikely to gain political support, they are more likely to be committed against foreigners. Most of this terrorism has been directed against the democracies with little against the more totalitarian states. Much of it in the eighties had been "war by proxy" or *state-sponsored terrorism* by countries such as Libya, Syria, and Iran. Terrorism became an inexpensive means of waging war or "war on the cheap."

In the late nineteenth century the fate of captured terrorists spelled condemnation and execution, but few since the sixties have suffered such a fate. More likely capture sets off a self-perpetuating cycle with new operations to effect the release of "political prisoners." Fearing retaliation, after World War II, the punishment of terrorists became permissive. Terrorism has become almost respectable with a majority of the members of the United Nations opposing any action against it. The rules of international diplomacy were established by the European colonial powers and are not entirely shared by Third World countries. *State terrorism*, in which nation states and their officials terrorize their own populations, may be the most common form (Herman, 1982).

Terrorism: A Growing Threat?

Laqueur (1977, pp. 213, 218), in discussing terrorism of the seventies, indicates:

> There has been a tendency to exaggerate out of all proportion the cost in manpower and resources needed to combat terrorism. . . . It fascinated millions of people, but it directly affected the life of only a handful. . . . Only a few years ago, newspaper readers in the Western world were led to believe that the German Baader-Meinhof group, the Japanese United Red Army, the Symbionese Liberation Army or the British "Angry Brigade" were substantial movements that ought to be taken seriously. Their "communiques" were published in the mass media; there were earnest sociological and psychological studies on the background of their members and their motivations; their ideology was analyzed in tedious detail. But these were groups of between 5 and 50 members; and their only victories were in the area of publicity. Even more substantial groups, such as the Tupamaros and the Brazilian ALN, the Black Panthers and the Weathermen, were very small indeed and had no significant public support—hence their sudden collapse and disappearance. Elsewhere, terrorists had been more successful, either because their nationalist-separatist appeal guaranteed them wider popular support, or because they receive massive assistance from a foreign power (or powers) or . . . the government . . . was in an advanced state of decay. . . .

Laqueur's account of primarily European terrorist groups may be an accurate description of such activities in the seventies; for instance, as late as 1971, terrorism throughout the world claimed less than two dozen lives per year. Beginning in the eighties, however, these figures escalated dramatically.

Russian anarchist Peter Kropotkin (1842–1921) viewed terrorism as "propaganda by deed" (Nettler, 1982, vol. 2, p. 232). Carlos Marighella, the Latin American author of a handbook on urban guerilla warfare, felt that one purpose of terrorism was as a means of provoking repressive responses by the state and, subsequently, public opposition to the state. While such tactics have in fact destroyed democracies and created more repressive regimes in Argentina, Uruguay, and Turkey, recent brands of terrorism have to date failed to topple any government. Terrorists often assume for themselves a higher morality in which they reject moral limitations in which "righteous homicide justifies killing innocents" (Ibid., p. 231). While members or defenders of a status quo under siege are apt to define any revolutionary or guerilla activities as terrorism, this writer prefers to restrict the term to indiscriminate attacks upon civilians and innocents. While this type of terrorism may never have toppled governments as Nettler suggests, more conventional terrorism aimed at governmental targets certainly has.

Frederick Hacker (1976, p. 69) in *Crusaders, Criminals and Crazies* points out:

> Contrary to widespread belief, terroristic violence is not always futile and ineffective in transforming reality. If it had not been for IRA terrorist activities, the Republic of Ireland never would have come into being. This is also true of independent Cyprus, Algeria, Tunisia, and possibly Israel. . . . Terrorism often is not confined to outlaws and the dregs of society (riffraff theory); it is supported by responsible citizens and organizations, either openly or in secret. . . . Terrorists are *not* all part of a Leninist-Marxist conspiracy. The IRA, particularly its activist Provisional branch, is actually conservative, patriotic, nationalistic, and rightist, and is denounced by opponents as a bunch of fascists and "crazy drunkards."

Myths Regarding Terrorism

Laqueur (1977, pp. 219–222) *discusses what he claims are various myths regarding terrorism*: (1) "Contrary to popular belief, terrorism is not a new or entirely unprecedented phenomenon." It is at least as old as the Russian Narodnaya Volya, nihilistic bomb-throwers of the last century. (2) Since one man's terrorist is another's liberator, the term is "politically loaded" and should be discarded. Most terrorism has been directed at democracies or ineffective authoritarian regimes and ignores totalitarian systems such as Nazi Germany, Fascist Italy, or the Communist regimes. (3) Although terrorism is always assumed to be "left-wing" or revolutionary, intellectual fashions change and slogans should neither be ignored nor taken too seriously. Certainly right-wing death squads in Latin America or the Ku Klux Klan illustrate terror from the right. (4) Terrorism is assumed to take place whenever there are legitimate grievances and amending these conditions will bring about its cessation. The most repressive, unjust societies have been the freest of terrorism. (5) Although terrorism is viewed as highly effective, this is only the case if it is part of a larger strategy. (6) Even though terrorists are viewed as idealists, humane behavior is often sacrificed for revolutionary goals. (7) Terrorism is described as a weapon of the poor, but most terrorists come from affluent backgrounds and are often supported by outside powers such as Russia, Cuba, Libya, and Algeria (see Sederberg, 1989). Terrorism is often an act of desperate revolutionaries, those who lack effective weapons or means of obtaining redress of their grievances through other channels. During the British control of Palestine, Menachim Begin was leader of a group of terrorists, the Irgun, which blew up the King David Hotel, killing innocent victims. Later as President of the new nation of Israel, Begin refused ever to sit across the negotiation table with PLO leader Yassir Arafat because he was a terrorist.

International Terrorism

International terrorism is not simply a sporadic phenomenon born of social misery and frustration, but often represents the ambitious designs of expansionist states and allies. "If a tree falls in the forest and no one hears it, does it make a sound?" In the case of terrorism—no. Terrorism is often aimed at the viewing public, not the actual victims; and modern satellite communication has enabled the "political theatre" or "propaganda by deed" of terrorism to become a subject of "film at eleven."

Some terrorists become, to use Sterling's words, "retail terrorists"; a traveling circus of performers such as "Carlos the Jackal," Abu Nidal's group, or Rengo Sekigun (The Japanese Red Army). Vantage Point 11.3 describes some of the international and national "liberation groups" current in 1990.

Domestic Terrorism, U.S.A.

While incidents of international terrorism, particularly with Americans as targets, grew during the decade of the eighties, domestic terrorism in the U.S. remained at a relatively low level. Most terrorist groups in the U.S. are either international or strongly identified with separatist or leftist movements. Puerto Rican independence, Armenian nationalism, Croatian separatism, anti-Castro groups, the Jewish Defense League, and similar groups were active. An explosion of right-wing KKK/Neo-Nazi hate groups became more prominent in the eighties such as the Order, Posse Comitatus, American Nazi Party, the Aryan Nations, and the Covenant, the Sword and the Arm of the Lord (CSA). Vantage Point 11.4 discusses some of these groups in detail.

Puerto Rican independence groups have historically been the most active. In 1950 one such group attempted to assassinate President

VANTAGE POINT

Some terrorist groups which were active internationally in the late eighties include Abu Nidal's group, Basque ETA, Islamic Jihad, M-19, Palestine Liberation Front, Provisional IRA, Red Army Faction, Red Brigades, Sikh separatists, and Tamil extremists.

Abu Nidal's group (headed by Sabri-al-Banna) is a splinter Palestinian group that has been involved in numerous terrorist attacks often as a proxy for Iraq, and later Syria and Libya. The *Basque ETA* attack Spanish targets in their quest for a separate Basque homeland in northern Spain. *Islamic Jihad* (Islamic Holy War) are Shiite fundamentalist extremists. They are responsible for bombings of the U.S. embassy, of the Marines' barracks in Lebanon, and the holding of U.S. hostages. They are backed by Iran. *M-19* (April 19 Movement) are leftist guerrilla groups in Colombia. In November 1985 they seized the Justice Palace in Bogota in which one hundred died. They are believed to be aligned with Cuba as well as "narco-terrorists." The *Palestine Liberation Front* is a Palestinian faction headed by Abu el-Abbas, who was blamed for the 1986 Achille Lauro hijacking. The PLF is a subgroup of another breakaway group in the Palestinian movement and is aligned with Palestinian Liberation Organization (PLO) leader Yasser Arafat.

The *Provisional IRA* ("Provos" of the Irish Republican Army) are fighting to unite Northern Ireland (which is part of the United Kingdom) with the Republic of Ireland. They wish to drive the British from Northern Ireland and have ambushed British personnel and bombed British facilities. The *Red Army Faction* or RAF (West Germany) is a radical leftist group that attacks NATO targets and West German industrialists. This group is a remnant of the infamous Baader-Meinhof Gang of the early seventies.

The *Red Brigade* (Italy) has killed thousands since 1968 in an attempt to foment a Communist revolution. Having previously murdered former Italian Premier Moro, they suffered a major setback subsequent to their kidnapping of U.S. General Dozier. His rescue and release led to the capture of over five hundred members.

Sikh Extremists seek independence for India's Sikh population in the Punjab. They have been responsible for the assassination of Indian President Indira Gandhi, the bombing of civilian airlines, and booby-trap bombings throughout India. *Tamil separatists* seek independence for the northern part of the island of Sri Lanka, which is currently dominated by the Sinhalese. Both sides in this controversy have massacred civilians.

Vantage Point 11.4—The Turner Diaries, ZOG and
the Silent Brotherhood—The Order

In the 1930s in beer halls in Munich, Germany, a political criminal and racist misfit, Adolf Hitler, advocated a bizarre future: a world of Wagnerian mysticism, a new order, a Third Reich.

> But we are doing something else which is really more important than our campaign against the System. In the long run, it will be infinitely more important. We are forging the nucleus of a new society, a whole new civilization, which will rise from the ashes of the old. And it is because our new civilization will be based on an entirely different world view than the present one that it can only replace the others in a revolutionary manner. There is no way a society based on Aryan values and an Aryan outlook can evolve peacefully from a society which has succumbed to Jewish spiritual corruption (MacDonald, 1980, p. 111).

The above statement is not an excerpt from Hitler's *Mein Kampf*, but rather a book entitled *The Turner Diaries* by Andrew MacDonald (1980), the Nazi penname of William Pierce, a leader of a Neo-Nazi right-wing extremist group (Wiggins, 1986a and 1986b; Holden, 1986; and Sapp, 1986). Groups such as the Order, Aryan Nations, Bruder Schweigen (The Silent Brotherhood), and the Covenant, Sword and Arm of the Lord, and other right-wing extremist groups are linked together by "identity theology." This is an anti-Semitic ideology which views Aryans as God's chosen people and Jews as the children of Satan. Some of these groups also practice "survivalism," a belief that they must stock supplies in order to be self-sufficient as the last hold-outs in some final Armageddon.

The Turner Diaries is a thinly-disguised blueprint for the Order's battle with ZOG, "Zionist Occupational Government" or "Zombies of Government." The book describes a "white revolution" launched by a terrorist group, "The Organization," to topple the U.S. government (ZOG). They support themselves through bank and armored car robbery and counterfeiting. They assassinate key leaders as well as sabotage transportation and power systems. Once in power they intend to kill Jews, blacks, liberals, and other minorities (Klanwatch, 1985, p. 6). In the eighties members of these and related groups murdered Jewish talk-show host Alan Berg in Denver (1984), robbed armored cars and banks, killed and had gun battles with police and federal agents, as well as bombing synagogues and minority-owned businesses—the very things outlined in the Turner diaries.

By the late eighties federal authorities had concluded that the Order had been virtually wiped out due to FBI and local efforts, although others speculate the Ku Klux Klan and other neo-Nazi hate groups simply regroup and reappear in new forms under new names.

Truman and in 1954 shot up the U.S. House of Representatives while it was in session. Such groups want a separate and independent Puerto Rico (which has been a commonwealth affiliated with the U.S.). The two most active groups are the *FALN* and the *Macheteros* (Puerto Rican People's Party). The FALN (Fuerzas Armadas de Liberacion Nacional — Armed Forces for National Liberation) has been responsible for over two hundred bombings in the U.S. and Puerto Rico. The Macheteros (Machete Swingers) have attacked U.S. military personnel and bases in Puerto Rico (Harris, 1987). They were also responsible for a Wells Fargo robbery in West Hartford, Connecticut, of $7.3 million.

Armenian nationalist groups such as ASALA (Armenian Secret Army for the Liberation of Armenia) wish to avenge the Turkish genocide of over 1.5 million Armenians during World War I as well as regain an Armenian homeland. They primarily attack Turkish diplomatic and economic targets. *Croatian separatist* groups with various names are nationalist and anti-Communist with fascist tendencies. They attack Yugoslavian targets. Croatia is part of Yugoslavia (Poland, 1988, p. 84).

While anti-Castro Cuban groups such as *Omega 7* and *Alpha 66* still exist, their activism fades as their leadership (former Cold Warriors and veterans of the Bay of Pigs invasion) ages. Their main targets have been Soviet and Cuban diplomats. The *Jewish Defense League* is an anti-Arab, anti-Soviet group of religious zealots who support a militant Zionism. Through bombing campaigns and harassment they attack targets that they feel are anti-Jewish (Poland, 1988, p. 89).

Radical left terrorist groups declined in the eighties. Groups such as the SLA (Symbionese Liberation Army), the SDS (Students for a Democratic Society), Weathermen, and Black Panthers were quite visible in the sixties and seventies. Spin-offs of the Weather Underground (formerly Weathermen) such as Prairie Fire and the May 19th Communist Organization were involved in some bombings and robberies, but have been superseded by the other groups we have discussed. Although black groups such as El Rukns in Chicago (formerly Blackstone Nation) have been caught planning attacks for Libya in return for money, they have been relatively inactive. Finally, a right-wing faction of interest to law enforcement is the Sheriff's Posse Comitatus, which advocates tax moratorium and disregard for federal and state authority. The FBI has been quite effective in surveillance and deterrence of terrorist acts of such groups by means of "neutralization through preventive interviews"; that is, interviewing members and letting them know that authorities are well aware of their plans (Pomerantz, 1987).

While the Ku Klux Klan has gone mostly underground, their nocturnal activities of cross-burning, arson, vandalism, intimidation and shooting continue.

456

Finally, in a class by itself as the most prevalent terrorist-hate group is the Ku Klux Klan, whose crossburnings, arson and bombing, vandalism, intimidation, shootings and assaults continue, although their movement may have also gone more underground (Klanwatch, 1985).

Criminal Careers of Political Criminals

For political criminals, crime is instrumental; it is a means of achieving what they perceive as being higher moral goals. As Schafer (1976, p. 139) explains:

> The convictional criminal, with his altruistic moral ideology, places less emphasis upon secrecy and even seeks publicity for his cause. Dramatic publicity, moreover, is almost a necessity for the convictional criminal in order to make the public understand his actions; his crime may serve as an example to would-be followers and generate further convictional crimes. His punishment is not a deterrent and may serve to interest others in the given ideal and to recruit other convictional violators of law.

The only exception to this publicity-seeking behavior would be government criminals who in most instances prefer secrecy. Political criminals from the left or right tend to be convinced of the rectitude of their cause and their actions. Rather than viewing their behavior as criminal, political criminals either deny the legitimacy of existing laws or view their violation as an essential step in either preserving the existing social order (crime by government) or in bringing about change in the existing system (crime against government).

A large proportion of revolutionaries are drawn from educated and middle class backgrounds rather than from the ranks of the proletariat, as Marx had predicted. A similar pattern presents itself with terrorists. Laqueur (Ibid., p. 207) points out that in West Germany in the late sixties and early seventies there were more female than male terrorists, and the females were more fanatical than the males. Clutterbuck (1975, p. 65) indicates that "terrorist movements seldom have more than very small minority support from the people . . . [and consist of] earnest young intellectuals increasingly frustrated by their lack of response from the ordinary people."

Political criminals operate within subcultures that define their activities as appropriate or necessary. Whether it be theories of racist supremacy (the Ku Klux Klan), preservation of law and order (illegal police violence), terrorist bombing of innocent victims, the shooting down of civilian airliners (state violence), or nonviolent passive resistance, political criminals feel that they have support of immediate peers. Being convinced of the rightness of their actions, political criminals also assume that others will be impressed with their resolve and also "see the light" and eventually agree with their actions. If proper subcultural support for politically deviant action is not strong, such violators may come to view their actions as illegitimate.

Although some view governmental political criminals as not ideologically committed (Allen, et al. 1981, p. 201–202), they are in fact ideologically committed to preservation of the status quo, and this convictional devotion may be distinct from the quest to preserve personal power (occupational crime). While governmental political criminals tend to be from more privileged backgrounds, many of their agents (servants of power), such as the police, are not. As previously mentioned, political criminals against the government vary considerably in background, although many leaders of the "new left" in the late sixties and early seventies in the U.S. and Western Europe were university educated and drawn from the upper middle class. Even though males dominated numerically, the significant proportion of leaders of radical and terrorist groups during this period were females.

For many terrorists "the end justifies the means;" the rightness of the cause and actions are viewed as reactions to repression, injustice, or hostile acts of the enemy. It is the latter who must bear the burden of guilt for aggression.

The Doctrine of Raison d'État

For political crimes, government officials or their agents historically have sought justification in "the doctrine of raison d'état" (reason of state), usually attributed to Italian political philosopher Niccolò Machiavelli (1469–1527). This doctrine holds that some violations of the common law are necessary for the end of public utility (Friedrich, 1972, pp. 21–22). This Machiavellian "end justifies the means" is a consistent rationalization of political criminals of all stripes: governmental, religious, or political. Friedrich (Ibid., pp. 106–107) indicates:

> The martyrs of Christianity became the saints of a triumphant Christian church; their betrayal of the Roman Empire as seen by its officers was what made them the "functionaries" of a future order. The same may be said of the "saints" of Communism and of national liberation; in the political perspective the sainthood is measured by the rightness of the cause they served, as seen by the beneficiaries of that cause.

In cases of crime committed in the act of political policing, labels of "official" secrets, "national security," and "reasons of state" shroud many incidents and evidence (Turk, 1981). Political crimes by intelligence agencies often have a "keeping up with the Joneses quality" wherein one must match the extreme measures of one's competitor in order to be successful. "To protect ourselves from the tyrannous, we have slowly built up our own tyranny" (Halperin, et al., 1976, p. 236). William Sullivan, former assistant director of the FBI for intelligence, in testifying before the Senate Subcommittee Hearings on Intelligence Activities (U.S. Senate, 1976, p. 141) indicated that the question as to whether Cointelpro was illegal never was discussed. In ten years of membership on the U.S. Intelligence Board, he claimed that legal issues concerning operations were never raised: "As far as legality is concerned, morals or ethics [it] was never raised by myself or anybody else" (Ibid.). In the Iran-Contra case discussed earlier, the conspirators invented a new word for lying—"plausible deniability" or being able to say believably that you did not know about something.

While much of the literature on terrorists plays up their intractability and uncompromising nature, one must also consider the social structural context in which their activities occur. To take but one example, terrorism by the Provisional wing (Provos) of the Irish Republican Army is in part aimed at a united Ireland. How much terrorism or support would the Provos have, however, if a truly successful civil rights movement were to obtain equal jobs, housing, and political influence for Catholics in the North? Similarly, a Palestinian homeland of some form would remove some of the thunder and support for Palestinian terrorists. Certainly legitimate revolutionary and guerilla warfare barring innocents as targets may be a necessary outcome of apartheid, the system of racial separation in South Africa.

Terrorism and Social Policy

Terrorist threats of the future promise to be more nuclear, more urban, and to involve wealthier, more skilled terrorists often as proxy armies for sponsor countries. Terrorism represents a problem to be managed rather than solved. The development of "narco-terrorism," an alliance of terrorists with drug traffickers poses yet another challenge. This will be discussed more fully in the "organized crime" chapter. Attempts at international cooperation are hindered by the very ideological disputes which often give rise to terrorism. A precedent does exist with respect to international cooperation. Piracy, a historically common practice, has been fairly eliminated through international agreement. At one time countries hired pirates in a form of "war by proxy;" but for centuries they have been declared "hostis humani generis" (common enemies of mankind), outlaws with universal jurisdiction given to all states. Perhaps a similar uniform international policy will evolve regarding cross-national terrorism.

Some other possible policies for dealing with terrorism include urging dialogue between terrorist groups and responsible governments, including media coverage of grievances so that such groups cannot claim that they desperately resort to terrorism to call attention to their cause. Media self-regulation (not censorship) is needed similar to media refusal to give camera coverage to exhibitionists who run on the field at athletic events. Terrorism by "lunatic minorities" in democratic countries which provide legal recourse (for example, the ballot box) must be condemned as "crime." Sanctions must be imposed on offending regimes (state terrorism and state-sponsored terrorism). This could include withdrawal of financial aid and diplomatic recognition and invocation of strict liability (holding them legally responsible) rather than conducting business as usual (Martin and Walcott, 1988).

Societal Reaction

The *sociological nature of the concept* political crime is illustrated by its relativity with respect to time and place. Ideologically-committed spies such as the Rosenbergs, who supplied their country's atomic secrets to a foreign enemy, were traitors in the U.S. but heralded as heroes in the recipient country, the Soviet Union. Defecting Polish pilot Frank Jarecki, who delivered the first new Russian MIG to the West, was viewed as a traitor behind the "Iron Curtain" and a freedom fighter in the West. Even the most dastardly terroristic acts, such as the slaughter of almost the entire Israeli Olympic team in Munich, was applauded in many areas of the Arab world.

This very divergence in international ideology explains the relative ineptness of world bodies such as the United Nations to act in unison in condemning global terrorism and atrocities. Often a double standard exists in which deviations of relatively democratic countries are roundly condemned while gross misbehavior of Soviet bloc countries and their surrogates are accepted. In totalitarian regimes such as the latter, dissent is not permitted and human rights groups such as the "Helsinki watch group" or Solidarity are handled as political offenders. While such dissent is permitted in the West, government agencies often employ illegal methods to undermine dissident groups.

Since crimes against the government threaten the status quo of society, societal reaction has been quite strong. However, until recently, public reaction to crimes by the government has been quite mild. This is partly due to the belief that, since the government makes and enforces the law, it is hard to imagine it also violating the law. In the U.S., public innocence in this regard appears to have matured since revelations of CIA and FBI wrongdoing and the events of Watergate.

Turk (1981, p. 236) indicates: "Any conception of legal deviance in political policing inevitably clashes with the fact that such organizations are invented to prevent radical political changes . . . national security . . . political and military considerations override any legal or ethical ones." While some secrecy on the part of intelligence agencies is in the public interest, the level of lying and deceit beyond the public interest is difficult to weigh, indeed the data required for such a judgment is not available until after the fact. The danger lies, of course, in the government, the servant of the people, becoming the master— Big Brother knows best.

The more complex, urban, industrial and interrelated the world community becomes, the easier it is for a small, fanatical minority of the left or right to disrupt, destroy, or endanger not just their political targets, but all of us. At the level of collective behavior and social change, dynamic societies can continue to be expected to generate new social movements and new demands for change and, depending upon the response, new political criminals either in the form of "bell-ringers" of change or overzealous guardians of the gates.

Summary

Ideology refers to distinctive belief systems, abstract ideals which possess a complete design for living. *Political crime* is defined as criminal activity which is committed for ideological purposes. There are *two types of political crime:* crime by government and crimes against the government. *Crimes by government* exclude political corruption, which is an example of occupational crime, and refer instead to violations by secret police, abuses of human rights and constitutional privileges, genocide as well as crimes committed by government officials in the act of enforcing the law. *Crimes against government* range from protests, illegal demonstrations, and strikes to espionage, political whistleblowing, political assassination, and terrorism. The actual definition of political crime is relative to time, place, and ideological views of those making the definition.

All governments have criminal laws forbidding activities which threaten the state. In Anglo-American jurisprudence, political criminals are not recognized as such and are dealt with under more traditional, nonpolitical laws. *The Nuremberg principle,* established by the victorious Allies at the end of World War II, established the precedent that individuals faced with the dilemma of obeying orders which involve war crimes and crimes against humanity or following their moral consciences, should disobey unjust dictates. Similar documents in the Western political tradition as well as the U.N.'s *Universal Declaration of Human Rights* (1948) provide customs or standards for international conduct with regard to respecting integrity of persons, basic human needs, and civil liberties. However, *international law* is handicapped by the lack of a consensual world community as well as by the lack of power of enforcement.

Crime by government is more a sociological than a political entity. Secret police (political policing) are units of the internal security police of the state that have a mandate to suppress all serious or threatening political opposition and to control political activity. Their activities often include illegal surveillance, searches, detention, and violations of human rights. *Political prisoners* may include those who have seriously opposed the existing government, but also prisoners of conscience who are tortured, sent into exile, or murdered. Amnesty International finds totalitarian regimes to be the greatest offenders in this area. Examples were given of Iraq's use of poison gas and those of Klaus Barbie and Kurt Waldheim. *Genocide*, the mass destruction or annihilation of human populations, is the ultimate violent crime by government; in the modern era, political ideologies have replaced religious justifications for genocide. In 1948 the U.N. *Convention on Genocide* defined it as a crime, although this same international body has been less than consistent in condemning such practices. *Political crimes by police* often involve violation of due process, freedom of speech, and invasion of privacy. These and other offenses are committed in the name of "law and order" and preservation of the existing political system.

Other abuses by government agents include illegal surveillance, disruption of democratic processes, including character assassination, and secret experiments upon unsuspecting subjects. One such example was *Operation CHAOS*, which among related activities involved illegal surveillance and harassment of domestic dissidents. *Cointelpro* was the FBI's counterintelligence program to disrupt legitimate political activity such as of the Socialist Worker's Party and black nationalist groups. Harassment of Martin Luther King, Jr., as well as pressure resulting in the suicide of actress Jean Seberg, have been linked to misuse of intelligence agencies such as the FBI by J. Edgar Hoover. The case of Oliver North was also detailed. Further questionable experiments include "the search for the Manchurian Candidate," mind-control experiments conducted in search of a secret *brainwashing technique*. The latter term was coined by Edward Hunter (1951) and, according to Sheflin and Opton, represented a *myth* in order to justify such experiments upon an unsuspecting public. Further examples include the Dr. Frank

Olson case and Thomas R., "*the Terminal Man*." Nuclear exposure experiments were also discussed.

Crimes against the government may involve activities of dissent and protest in opposition to the status quo but may also involve reactionary opposition to changes which have taken place in the existing social or political order. Dissent activities are represented by civil rights, labor, and antiwar groups of the past; reactionary opposition can be found in right-wing "death squads," the Ku Klux Klan, or the American Nazi Party. Excerpts from Martin Luther King, Jr.'s "Letter from Birmingham Jail" provide a very moving defense of civil disobedience and the strategy of the civil rights movement. *Social movements* advocate change in the existing order and often conflict with responding authorities. Some newer examples include the sanctuary, anti/pro abortion, anti-nuclear and anti-vivisectionist (animal rights) groups.

Political espionage involves stealing state secrets and is a standard international practice of intelligence agencies. "Sub rosa criminals" are spies who steal secrets. The motivation of spies often reveals a SMICE strategy (sex, motivation, ideology, compromise, and ego). A typology of spies included: mercenary, ideological, alienated/egocentric, buccaneer, professional, compromised, deceived, quasi-agent, escapee, and miscellaneous. *Treason* involves the betrayal of one's country either out of commitment to a political ideology or foreign power. Political "whistleblowers" such as Daniel Ellsberg violate state secrecy feeling that the public has a right to know the truth.

Terrorism is the use of cruelty and violence in order to spread fear within a population as an instrument of gaining political power. *Types of terrorism* include: political terrorism, nonpolitical terrorism, quasi-terrorism, limited political terrorism, and official or state terrorism. The last type illustrates the fact that not all terrorism involves crime against the government. While observers such as Laqueur feel the threat of terrorism in the seventies was a media event and an exaggeration, statistics from the early eighties suggest a climbing toll of victims. Examples of both international and domestic terrorist groups were detailed. *Some possible myths regarding terrorism* include beliefs that it is: a new phenomenon; an inappropriate, politically loaded term; always leftist in nature; due to legitimate grievances; highly effective; idealistic; and a weapon of the poor.

Examination of the *criminal careers* of political criminals indicates that they view crime as instrumental, a means to ideological ends. Most do not view their activity as criminal and tend to operate within supporting subcultures which reinforce their definitions. For government political criminals "*raison d'état*" (reason of state), national security, and their preservation serves as justification for violations. Some government policies for dealing with terrorism were detailed. *Societal reaction* to political crime varies, with generally strong and disapproving action toward offenders against the government and mild reaction in the past toward governmental offenders. Divergence in ideology prevents any consistent international reaction to political crime.

KEY CONCEPTS

Ideology
Political Crime
Crimes by Government
Crime against Government
Nuremberg Principle
Universal Declaration of
   Human Rights
Secret Police
Human Rights

Genocide
Operation CHAOS
Espionage
Sanctuary Movement
Enterprise
Types of Spies
Cointelpro
Brainwashing
Project Bluebird

The Brainwashing Myth
Terrorism
Types of Terrorism
Myths regarding Terrorism
Raison d'État
Sub Rosa Crime
SMICE

12

Organized Crime

Introduction

Organized crime has been characterized as "the enemy within" (Kennedy, 1960), "the second government" (Valachi, 1969), the "crime confederation" (Salerno and Tompkins, 1969), or "the fifth estate" (Bequai, 1979), which illegally wrings exorbitant profits out of our economy while flaunting authority and corrupting established legal institutions.

In 1986 the President's Commission on Organized Crime (1986a, 1986b, 1985, and 1984b) completed the examination of such activities in the United States. Critics of this commission and earlier ones such as the Kefauver and McClellan commissions view much of the federal attack on organized crime and the Mafia as an example of moral entrepreneurship. These critics view the Mafia as a creation of federal agencies, and as an engineered "alien conspiracy," similar to McCarthyism in the fifties, which "discovered" Communist infiltration in order to raise public fears and justify extraordinary federal legal efforts which invade civil liberties (Smith, 1980, p. 331). Whether menace or myth, cancer or chimera, organized crime remains a topic of heated, albeit at times confusing, debate.

Organized Crime: A Problematic Definition

Organized crime has been variously defined or described by the general public, legislatures, law enforcement agencies, social scientists, and syndicate members themselves. As part of a content analysis of selected criminologists' works, to be discussed shortly, this writer was surprised to discover the large number of works, including textbooks, which failed to offer a definition. That is, organized crime was described, discussed, but often undefined. The Organized Crime Control Act of 1970 failed to provide a definition. In an analysis of the federal law enforcement effort on organized crime, the General Accounting Office (1977) noted a lack of an acceptable definition of organized crime.

Federal agencies such as the FBI and the Department of Justice use the Federal Task Force on Organized Crime's general operational definition, one which best fits the generic type, to be described shortly:

Organized crime includes any group of individuals whose primary activity involves violating criminal laws to seek illegal profits and

power by engaging in racketeering activities and, when appropriate, engaging
in intricate financial manipulations. . . .

Accordingly, the *perpetrators of organized crime may include corrupt business executives, members of the professions, public officials, or any occupational group* [italics mine], in addition to the conventional racketeer element.
(National Advisory Committee, 1976a, p. 213.)

For the purposes of general prosecution and enforcement, most federal and state laws end up including under the definition of organized
crime any group crime of a conspiratorial nature which includes types
of criminal activity that we would more appropriately label as occupational, corporate, political, or even conventional crime (National Advisory Committee, 1976a, pp. 213–215).

These definitions are problematic because in many instances the distinction between organized crime and other types of crime is that the
former involves two or more people; a useful definition must relate to
the nature of the criminal activity and not just the number of people
involved. Like the terms "social class," "culture," "professionalism," and
"personality," "organized crime" already has a popular public definition, which may interfere with its being precisely defined as a legal
or sociological category of criminal activity.

Sources of Information on Organized Crime

While there is no paucity of literature—fiction, nonfiction, journalistic,
law enforcement, and social scientific—on organized crime, much of
this area has been the subject matter of journalists and freelance writers.
In few other subject areas is the literature so confused, undocumented,
and less than scholarly (Albini, 1971, p. 8). Galliher and Cain (1974,
p. 73) point to journalists' need for interesting stories. Block (1978, p. 470)
also points to overreliance upon unsubstantiated informants, while
Abadinsky (1981, p. ix) concludes, on the basis of a variety of sources,
that "none is completely satisfying." Government agencies themselves have
been involved in leaking false information in order to raise havoc within
the ranks of organized crime (Villano, 1978, p. 246–247).

I remember when Joe was testifying before that Senate committee [McClel-
lan] back in 1963. I was sitting in Raymond Patriarca's office [New England
mob boss] . . . and we were watching Joe on television. I remember Raymond
saying: "This bastard's crazy. Who the hell is he?" . . . "What the hell's the
Cosa Nostra?," Henry asked [Tameleo, the underboss]. "Is he a soldier or a
button man?" . . . "I'm a zipper." "I'm a flipper." . . . It was all a big joke to
them. In New England we never used names like "soldiers" or "caporegimes"
(Teresa, 1973a, pp. 24–25, 28).

Joe Valachi broke the underworld blood oath to put the finger on his former bosses in the Cosa Nostra crime empire.

The above account was by Vincent Teresa, author with Thomas Renner of *My Life in the Mafia* (1973b), of the reaction of a mob boss to the testimony of ex-Mafia member Joe Valachi before a Congressional committee. In *The Valachi Papers* (Maas, 1968) Valachi described the inner workings of something he called Cosa Nostra (literally, "this thing of ours"). Other such biographies and autobiographies, although of varying validity, provide rare inside glimpses of organized criminal operations. Pileggi's *Wiseguy* (1985), Pistone and Woodley's *Donnie Brasco: My Undercover Life in the Mafia* (1987), Bonanno's *A Man of Honor* (1983), or Mustain and Capeci's *Mob Star: The Story of John Gotti* (1988) serve as illustrations. Pileggi's *Wiseguy* (1985), for example, details the life of Henry Hill, a career criminal who literally grew up in the mob. Hill gives an inside account of the Paul Vario organized crime family, the 1983 Lufthansa robbery at Kennedy Airport which scored $5 million in cash, the Sindona scandal which nearly collapsed the Vatican bank, and the Boston College basketball point-shaving scandal.

Lupsha (1982) indicates the following *sources of information on organized crime:* informers, hearings and investigations, court trial transcripts and grand jury depositions, news stories, investigative reporting, wire surveillance transcripts, memoirs/biographies, government reports and releases, law enforcement assisted research, archives and historical documents, observation and in-depth interviews. While any source may exhibit varying degrees of validity, far more triangulation (use of multiple methodologies in the same study) is required than has been apparent in past criminological research on organized crime (see also Bynum, 1987; and Morash, 1984).

Types of Organized Crime (Generic Definition)———

Acknowledging the need for a broader (or more generic) definition of organized crime, like operational policy definitions employed by organizations such as the Federal Bureau of Investigation, Joseph Albini (1971), author of *The American Mafia: Genesis of a Legend*, offers the following:

> . . . any criminal activity involving two or more individuals, specialized or nonspecialized, encompassing some form of social structure, with some form of leadership, utilizing certain modes of operation, in which the ultimate purpose of the organization is found in the enterprises of the particular group (Ibid., p. 37).

Albini then identifies *four basic types of organized crime*: political-social organized crime, mercenary (predatory) organized crime, in-group oriented organized crime, and syndicate crime (Ibid., pp. 38–48).

1. *Political-Social Organized Crime.* This category best fits into the "political criminal" activity discussed earlier. These are simply guerrilla and terrorist groups and various militant social movements that use violence, such as the Ku Klux Klan, the Molly Maguires, or the Palestinian Liberation Organization.
2. *Mercenary (Predatory) Organized Crime.* This category refers to crimes committed by groups for direct personal profit, but which prey upon unwilling victims, such as juvenile and adult criminal gangs involved in larceny, burglary, and robbery. The Mano Nera (Black Hand) might serve as an example of the latter. These extortionist gangs (there was no one Black Hand) sent threatening notes to fellow Italian immigrants requesting money. The notes usually contained a sinister mark or sign of a black hand. Often erroneously identified as a forerunner to the "Mafia," the "Black Hand" was more a method of crime than an organization. They provided no other illicit services and could not assure immunity of their own operations through political corruption.
3. *In-Group Oriented Organized Crime.* These groups such as motorcycle gangs and some adolescent gangs whose major goals are

psychological gratification, "kicks," "rep," "highs," "bopping," and "trashing" rather than financial profit. Motorcycle gangs—the post-World War II prototype being Hell's Angels—have branched out since Hollywood portrayals such as Marlon Brando's in *The Wild One*. These gangs are sometimes used as "muscle" (enforcers) and for low-level jobs by larger syndicate groups (see Abadinsky, 1985, pp. 25–40). The Pagans, begun in Prince Georges County in Maryland, in 1959, now has local chapters throughout the East Coast from Connecticut to Florida with the heaviest membership in the Middle Atlantic States (Pennsylvania Crime Commission, 1980, p. 27). Such groups are involved in narcotics distribution, prostitution, extortion, bribery, contract murders, pornography distribution, and other activities. The Hell's Angels have also moved extensively into drug trafficking, allegedly controlling as much as 90 percent of the "speed" market in northern California ("Hell's Angels," 1979, p. 34). Perhaps an apt concept to refer to such gangs would be that they are an example of "semi-organized" crime, ones which lack at least one of the key features of our definition of organized (syndicate) crime, to be discussed next.

4. *Syndicate Crime.* This is the category of organized crime that is the subject of this chapter and to which most writers refer when speaking of organized crime. Syndicate crime (henceforth a synonym for organized crime) may be defined as suggested by Albini (1971, pp. 47–48) as:

   a. a continuing group or *organization* that participates in illicit activity in any society by the *use of force, intimidation or threats*;
   b. the structuring of a group or organization whose purpose is that of providing *illicit services* that are in strong public demand through the use of secrecy on the part of associates;
   c. the assurance of *protection and immunity* necessary for its operation through political corruption or avoidance of prosecution.

In a content analysis of definitions of organized crime provided by various writers and government reports, this author (Hagan, 1983) discovered that many failed to provide any definition. The following characteristics were identified with some consensus: organized (continuing) hierarchy, rational profit through crime, use of force or threat of force, and corruption to obtain immunity. This content analysis supports a core criminological definition of organized crime that is basically consistent with Albini's (1971, p. 126) definition of syndicate crime. The *generic definition* of "organized crime" is not a definition of organized crime, but rather a definition of "group crime," that is, "crime committed by two or more people. . . ." Figure 12.1 summarizes the concept of "organized crime" from both a general (generic) definitional view and a more specialized (sociological/criminological) definitional view.

Figure 12.1: Generic and Specific Definitions of the Concept of "Organized Crime"

Organized Crime	
General Usage (Generic)	Group Crime
Specific Definition (Core Elements)	Violence + Illicit Demanded Services + Immunity ――――― Organized (Syndicate) Crime

The Hells Angels are an example of "semi-organized" crime, lacking at least one key component of organized crime.

"Organized crime" is used in the most generic sense to refer to group crimes and includes many criminal behavior systems as well as "illicit enterprises" that might more appropriately be labeled professional, occupational, corporate, or even conventional criminal behavior. A more specific *criminological definition* would refer to groups which utilize violence or threats of violence, which provide illicit goods which are in public demand, and which assure immunity of operation through corruption and enforcement.

Using these key dimensions, a chief difficulty is that they have been viewed or utilized at a nominal level of measurement and the question asked, "Is this group an example of organized crime?" Attempts to answer this question are in most instances almost futile. We might agree that, if the concept is useful at all, what has been described as the "Cosa Nostra" is an example of organized crime and amateur shoplifters are not. But where does one place the Hell's Angels, the Pagans, drug smuggling organizations, or street gangs?

The Organized Crime Continuum

A continuum or ordinal model of organized crime has been suggested by others (Albini, 1971, pp. 37–38; Cressey, 1972; McIntosh, 1975; and Smith, 1975, 1978, and 1980). In a highly cited "spectrum based theory of enterprises," Dwight Smith (1980) proposes that enterprises take place across a spectrum (or continuum) of possible behavior ranging from the legal to illegal, the saintly to the sinful, and the separation of legitimate business from crime, distinguishing paragons from pariahs from pirates, is an arbitrary point on that range (Ibid., p. 371). This stress upon the term "illegal enterprises" rather than organized crime was proposed by historian Mark Haller (1972) in order to avoid the association of such activities with alien conspiracies such as "the Mafia myth" to be discussed shortly. For a further elaboration of these and related views, the reader is referred to Martin (1981), Albanese (1989), and Abadinsky (1983 and 1985).

What all of these models share is a stress upon the fact that organized criminal activity is not a simple category. Rather than viewing the concept as a matter of *kind*—i.e., is it or is it not?—it is far more useful to conceive of it as a matter of *degree*. That is, the concept "organized crime" is an "ideal type," an abstract generalization which perhaps does not exist in pure form but nevertheless represents a useful, heuristic device for analysis purposes.

The question now becomes: "To what extent does this group and/or its operations resemble organized crime?" Thus the "Cosa Nostra,"

"Mafia," or "Italian-American Syndicate (IAS)" is viewed as a prototype (ideal type) of organized crime, with other criminal groups falling at various points along the continuum, some being designated as "semi-organized crime."

Figure 12.2 outlines a neoteric, continuum model of organized (syndicate) crime. Just as medicine may represent the prototype profession, the "Cosa Nostra" as an "ideal type" could similarly represent a model with which to compare all other groups, but the status of which few groups can hope to attain or, in the case of IAS, may never have attained (Hagan, 1983).

It is important to clarify that the use of the term "Cosa Nostra" (literally, "this thing of ours") is not to suggest an acceptance of the popular and official interpretation of Valachi's testimony, where the term was first introduced, as accurately naming and describing the IAS. The term is used as an "ideal type" with the assumption that the IAS probably never reached the degree of hierarchical structure assumed and, if it had, has most likely experienced an erosion of the traditions described by Valachi (Bonanno, 1983, p. 164).

Many profit-oriented and/or violent criminal groups contain many features which may lead us to describe them as being examples of semi-organized crime. For example, organizations such as the Hell's Angels or the Pagans contain a fairly highly developed hierarchical structure

Figure 12.2: The Organized Crime Continuum

Non-Organized Crime	Semi-Organized Crime	Organized Crime
e.g., Intrafamily assault	e.g., Some Motorcycle Gangs Narcotics Smuggling Rings	e.g., Syndicates "Cosa Nostra"
No	1. Highly Organized	Yes
Not Relevant	A. Hierarchy	Relevant
Absent	B. Restricted Membership	Present
Absent	C. Secrecy (Codes)	Present
No	2. Violence or Threats of	Yes
No	3. Provision of Illicit Goods in Public Demand	Yes
No	A. Profit-Oriented	Yes
	4. Immunity Through:	
Unconnected	A. Corruption	Connected
No	B. Enforcement	Yes

SOURCE: An earlier version of this model appeared in: Frank E. Hagan, 1983, "The Organized Crime Continuum: A Further Specification of a New Conceptual Model," *Criminal Justice Review*, 8: 52–57.

which uses violence, supplies goods (particularly illicit narcotics) which are in high demand by select segments of the public, and has obtained immunity in outlying geographical areas not through corruption so much as through intimidation of local law enforcement. Thus Japanese Yakuza, Chinese Triad Societies, and other international criminal organizations to be discussed shortly can be theoretically if not empirically placed upon the continuum, although application of the model may be limited in a non-Western context.

Types of Organized Crime (Criminological Definition)

While a specific definition of organized crime stresses the three key dimensions of violence, provision of illicit services, and immunity, a variety of types of organized criminal groups or expressions are possible, including:

1. *Traditional Crime Syndicates.* These are comprehensive criminal organizations which place to a high degree on the organized crime continuum shown in Fig. 12.2. They are highly organized and characterized by hierarchy, restricted membership, secrecy, violence, provision of illicit goods, profit orientation, and the obtaining of immunity through corruption and enforcement. Yakuza, Triads, IAS (Mafia or Cosa Nostra), Camorra, Unione Corse, and other such groups serve as examples.

2. *Nontraditional Syndicates.* These are less comprehensive criminal groups which exhibit less development on the dimensions of the organized crime continuum. Large-scale narcotics smuggling organizations, white collar fraud groups, and the so-called "Dixie Mafia" are examples (Hunter, 1983); another is independent crime czars who control local vice operations.

3. *Semiorganized Crime.* These groups are generally smaller and less sophisticated and exhibit a shorter range of criminal goals. Examples are some motorcycle gangs such as the Pagans and Hell's Angels as well as organized burglary and robbery rings.

4. *Local, Politically Controlled Organized Crime.* These are locally controlled organized criminal groups in which the local political and power structure is not simply corrupted or allies, but actual partners in running criminal operations; this type has been suggested by Chambliss in his study of Seattle. As previously mentioned, Block and Chambliss (1981, pp. 112–113) claim that in virtually every American city, those running criminal organizations are members of business, political, or law enforcement communities and not simply "on the pad."

5. *National, Politically Controlled Organized Crime.* In this type, organized crime operates in partnership with elements of the national power structure; national authorities actually participate in the planning and execution of criminal activities. Block and Chambliss (Ibid., pp. 21–25) indicate that the nineteenth-century Asian opium trade controlled and managed by European capitalist countries formed the capital for industrial development. The French and later U.S. in Indochina encouraged tribes to grow narcotics and traffic in them in return for resisting communism (McCoy, 1972). Block and Chambliss (1981, pp. 153–157) claim that Swedish millionaires are the principal financers and organizers of illegal businesses in Sweden, with a crime cartel consisting of political figures, law enforcement officials, and drug traffickers. Reports in the early eighties of the Bulgarian secret service and of the Cuban Castro government's involvement in drug trafficking may also serve as illustrations.

Street Gangs

Street gangs could be viewed as being somewhat near the middle of the continuum, although perhaps not as highly developed as some motorcycle gangs. Juvenile gangs were previously discussed in Chapter 7, where it was indicated that such groups tend to be relatively persistent although only periodically rediscovered by the media. In the 1980s many of the tough American street gangs were rapidly converting themselves to ghetto-based drug trafficking organizations due primarily to the flood of low-cost cocaine (and crack or rock cocaine) from Colombia. At the onset of the nineties many of these groups were about at the same place as Italian-American groups were in the early 1920s during Prohibition (Morganthau, et al., 1988, p. 22). Bloods, Crips (Los Angeles); Montego Bay, Shower, Spangler (Jamaican); Untouchables, 34th Street Players (Miami); or Cobras, Disciples, El Rukns; Latin Kings, and Vice Lords (Chicago) are often big, violent, and increasingly wealthy. In Southern California the majority of street gangs are black or Latino with Anglos normally joining motorcycle gangs. One such group, the POBOBs ("Pissed Off Bastards of Bloomington"), emerged to become the Hell's Angels, perhaps the largest and most notorious outlaw biker gang (Davis, 1982, p. 42).

"Big Hawk 1987 BSVG c 187"

The above illustration of gang graffiti is not a marking of gang turf for bragging rights, but for sales territory and a threat to rivals. The translation is Big Hawk (a member's street name), 1987 (the year), a member of Blood Stone Villain's Gang (BSVG) which is a Bloods set (subgroup of the Bloods' gang). The lower case c, which is usually X'd out, means that Big Hawk kills Crips, and the number 187 is the section of the California criminal code for murder (Morganthau, et al., 1988, p. 23).

For many gang members self-employment in the underground drug economy provides short-term upward mobility, autonomy, a measure of self-dignity, and an opportunity to avoid low-level employment under the direction of what is perceived as hostile, outside ethnic or racial groups (Bourgois, 1988, p. 12). Street gangs, despite their penchant for what might appear to be senseless violence, sometimes represent the minor leagues or incubators; industrial parks for future organized criminals and syndicates. In the early part of the twentieth century a group of teenage hoods who hung around together in New York City were good at their craft and moved into and founded larger syndicates. They were Meyer Lansky, "Bugsy" Siegel, "Lucky" Luciano, and Vito Genovese. Although short of many of the characteristics for full development as organized criminal groups, some gangs are more developed in this regard than others.

International Organized Crime

Internationally, organized crime is not confined to any single political area and thrives especially in political climates such as liberal democracies and corrupt dictatorships. Because laws of liberal democracies such as the United States, Canada, post-World War II Japan, and other Western European and former British Commonwealth countries place a priority upon individual civil liberties, crime control can suffer; such laws make it difficult to crack down on organized criminals and their political allies. Such nations also emphasize private enterprise, which is not restricted to the legal end of the continuum.

Robert Kelly in *Organized Crime: A Global Perspective* (1986) provides examples of organized criminal underworlds in Canada, Great Britain, the Caribbean, Italy, Poland, Israel, Africa, Japan, and Australia. Lupscha (1987, pp. 7–8) describes a number of variables which predict organized crime in an area. These include topographical features which create natural ports or harbors and an important transportation exchange. Cities which are border points of a political jurisdiction or function as international exchange points where a variety of people and trade mix are conditions. New York, Hong Kong, Marseilles, and Naples serve as examples. These geographical factors interact with political, economic, and socio-cultural conditions in such international, cosmopolitan environments. Finally, " . . . the use of street gangs by political machines in the U.S., the use of Triads by Chiang Kai Shek and the Kuomintang, the use of Corsican organized crime groups by the French government in Marseilles, and the use of Yakuza in Japan" (Ibid., p. 8) illustrate the hidden support of organized crime by governmental groups (McCoy, 1985).

Yakuza

The following excerpt from an Associated Press dispatch (Associated Press, 1976) accounts a police roundup of Yakuza (the Japanese term for gangsters or, literally, "good-for-nothings") and of Japan's largest crime family, the Yamaguchigumi:

Japanese Cops Nab 1,554 in Raids

TOKYO (AP) Police arrested 1,554 persons and seized guns, drugs, and other evidence today in their third nationwide crackdown on criminal gangs in seven months. Raids at 1,324 places throughout Japan brought to 26,883 the number of persons arrested since last September in the official drive against organizations dealing in drugs, prostitution, extortion, gambling and other unlawful activities. . . . Police have estimated there are 2,650 criminal gangs with 110,000 members in Japan. They operate restaurants, finance, real estate and other businesses as a front. . . . An arrest warrant was issued for Kazuo Taoka, boss of Japan's largest crime organization, the Yamaguchigumi, with an estimated 11,000 members. . . .

Organized crime figures in Japan in the late seventies affected a curious appearance: crew cuts, elaborate tattoos, and missing little fingers; they often worked as "bouncers" or security guards at corporate conventions, a strategic role which enabled them to gather information with which to blackmail corporate officials ("Japan," 1977, p. 40; and Rome 1975).

Representing a traditional part of Japanese society, the Yakuza originally were recruited by right-wing business leaders after World War II to intimidate left-wing opponents. In the eighties growing concern was expressed regarding Yakuza expansion into the United States (ABC, 1982). Such groups reportedly owned $100 million in Honolulu real estate, where their restaurants, clubs, and pornography shops catered to Japanese tourists. Active also in California, the groups were involved in smuggling drugs to the U.S. and guns to Japan as well as recruiting U.S. female "entertainers" as prostitutes in Japan.

Membership in Yakuza groups is claimed to be twenty times larger than membership in the American "Mafia." There is considerable acceptance and toleration of such groups by both the public and political powers (Kaplan and Dubro, 1986). They serve a useful function for the right wing in intimidating dissent, the free press, and free speech (CBS, 1989a). Yakuza are widely involved in sexual slavery. Thousands of mainly poor Third World women and children are forced into prostitution near military bases, pornography, and mail-order marriages (Kaplan and Dubro, 1986, p. 201). Another major business is debt collection. One-third of the members are Korean and most are from lower class backgrounds (CBS, 1988).

Corrupt dictatorships, particularly in Caribbean vacation areas, were locations for convenient gambling resort areas particularly when organized crime figures such as Meyer Lansky simply "cut in" the authorities, such as Batista in Cuba or Bahamian officials, in return for unencumbered operations.

While organized criminal groups other than black market gangs were not publicized in the past in Communist countries, more has been described by Soviet media since Gorbachev's policies of *glasnost* (openness) and *perestroika* (restructuring). One Soviet police colonel claimed over two hundred "Mafia gangs" in the U.S.S.R. in 1988, whose primary operations include drugs, prostitution, extortion, and the extensive bribery of police officials (Coleman, 1988).

In his *Criminal Brotherhoods*, Chandler (1976) claims that Western organized criminal groups had their beginnings with the Garduna in fifteenth-century Spain. Others, such as the Italian Camorra, the Mafia, the French or Corsican Unione Corse, and the American Cosa Nostra at least initially were secretive, ritualistic, and feudal in structure. The Unione Corse, now headquartered in Marseilles, has been rumored to have existed for years, but was not accepted as reality by the French government until the mid-sixties. It is primarily involved in narcotics, with contacts with French populations in Europe, the Middle East, Africa, Indochina, and Quebec. Organized crime in Africa is described by Opolot (1979) as involving either business persons or well-placed public officials involved in criminal enterprises, "shady" business persons connected to criminal operations, and organizations of criminal operators involved in highway robbery, illegal immigration, smuggling, drug traffic, and poaching. There is, however, little evidence of tribal successions or ringleaders in African organized crime. Perhaps the most secretive and ritualistic of organized crime groups are the Chinese Triads.

Chinese Triad Societies

The operation of Chinese Triad societies was vividly presented to Western audiences in Robert Daley's best-selling novel, *The Year of the*

Dragon (1981). *Triads* are secret Chinese organizations. Referred to as "black societies" by the Chinese, the British called them Triads because of their highly ritualistic use of numerology, a belief in the magical significance of numbers. The number three and multiples of three were accorded major importance by these groups. The symbol of Triad societies is depicted by an equilateral triangle with the three equal sides representing the three basic Chinese concepts of heaven, earth, and man.

Although they are of much more ancient origin and are even more cabalistic, the legends, rituals such as initiation rites, and early history of Triads bear an uncanny resemblance to descriptions of the Mafia legend in Sicily (Bresler, 1980; and Morgan, 1960). The earliest Triads secret societies were founded in China two thousand years ago to oppose warlords (Robertson, 1977; and Daraul, 1969). The modern Triad societies are traced to the latter part of the seventeenth century where members appear as resistance fighters against the Manchu dynasty, "barbarian" invaders who had defeated the Ming dynasty. Legend dates the founding of the first modern Triad to 128 Buddhist monks at a monastery near Foochow, Fukien province, in 1674. They were well trained in Oriental martial arts, including a type they had perfected themselves—kung fu (Bresler, 1980, p. 28; and Chin, 1988, p. 7). A triad called the Fists of Harmony and Justice led the Boxer Rebellion against the European powers.

Although originating as brotherhoods for freedom (Lyman, 1974), Triads also had elements of banditry and were heavily involved in the control of vice activities. All of the Triad groups shared in common highly ritualized initiation ceremonies, blood oaths, passwords, secret signals, and hierarchical positions. Some positions in a Triad society were described by Bresler (1980, p. 28) in his *The Chinese Mafia*:

> The 489, "Shan Chu" (hill chief or head)
> The 438, "Heung Chu" (incense master in charge of ceremonies)

Each cell (branch) would have three lower-level offices:

> 415, the "white paper fan" (financial advisor)
> 426, the "red pole" (kung fu expert)
> 432, the "straw sandal" (messenger/liaison with other groups)
> 49, the ordinary member

The number four in all of the titles reflects the ancient Chinese belief that the world was surrounded by four seas.

> 489 and 438 are said to have been selected because the Chinese characters for 21 (the sum of 4 + 8 + 9) and for 3 and 8, when written together, form

the Chinese characters for Hung, the early Ming Emperor in whose name the whole Triad organization began in the first place. 426 is constructed as 4 × 15 + 4, which equals 64. This refers to the 64 diagrams of Chinese script invented by a legendary Emperor named Fu Teh . . . 432 becomes 4 × 32 + 4, giving us 132, which is the actual number of persons (128 monks and 4 others) supposed to have been living in the original Triad monastery near Foochow. Finally, 49 derives from 4 × 9, which equals 36. This refers to the number of oaths sworn by all new Triad members (Ibid.).

Triads utilize a traditional initiation ceremony called the Hung Mun ritual which includes the taking of thirty-six oaths, one of which says, "If I should change my mind and deny my membership of the Hung family, I will be killed by a myriad of swords" (Hong Kong, 1986, p. 5). Triads are sometimes referred to as the Hung, named after the Ming emperor's grandson, Chiu Hung-chu (Chin, 1988, p. 8). Chin (1988, p. 11) tells us:

> Criminal groups in Taiwan . . . have no structural or spiritual resemblance to the Hung societies. Although the Hung societies and the Ching societies, another major group of secret societies, are [sic] exist in Taiwan, the two societies have not been involved in the local crime scene. Since Taiwan was the colony of Japan . . . crime groups there follow the pattern of Japanese Yakuza.

Chin (1988) claims that many myths, similar to early ones of an omnipotent Italian Mafia, have been created regarding Triads, and that Chinese small-business owners, not Triads, are responsible for most of the drug trafficking, money laundering, and other criminal activities in American Chinatowns. Care must be taken not to label all Chinese groups as being Triads, including a Taiwan-based crime group—the United Bamboo—which clearly is not a Triad organization. Others have warned that we must avoid succumbing to what we will later call another "Mafia myth" (Matheron, 1987).

With the fall of mainland China to the Communists in 1949, many Triads migrated to Hong Kong. With Hong Kong scheduled to be returned to China in 1997, many are believed to be fleeing to the U.S. (Posner, 1988). The largest of such groups were the Green Pang (Green Gang), the Chui Chaos (Chiu Chau), and the 14K. Although the Green Pang originally controlled heroin distribution in the colony, they rely upon the Chui Chaos for supplies of Thai morphine and opium (McCoy, 1972, p. 229). The Chui Chaos had important connections and even members within the Hong Kong police and controlled much of the drug traffic from the "Golden Triangle" (Northern Burma, Laos, and Thailand) and throughout Southeast Asia.

Tongs were Chinese-American fraternal and benevolent organizations, the term meaning "town hall" or "large hall." Some of the important tongs in the U.S. in the nineteenth century were Bing Kung, Hip Sing, Ying On Ton Su, and Hop Sing. New Tong organizations, formed in the post-World War II period, were more ferocious criminal bands made up of many felons who had fled Hong Kong and the Far East. The Flying Dragons, Ghost Shadows, Gray Shadows, and Black Ghost Shadows are some of the names of these groups. While some observers claim that Tongs, like chop suey, were strictly an American invention, organized in the gold fields of California about 1860 (Nash, 1981, p. 337), others see them as branches of Triad societies, mainly the Chee Kung Tong, which generated many feuding rival branches (Bresler, 1980, p. 30). Since the late sixties members of Triad gangs have emigrated and set up operations in the U.S., Canada, and Europe, most notably in the Netherlands and within older established Chinatowns of San Francisco, Vancouver, and Amsterdam (Wilson, 1978). McCoy (1976) reports:

> Seattle was the only American city where the Chiu Chow [Chui Chaos] syndicates had been able to dominate the narcotics supply. After the abolition of Turkish cultivation in 1971 deprived the dominant Montreal Corsican syndicates of their sources, Vancouver's Chinese dealers increased their imports from Hong Kong and were soon supplying Canada's 9000 to 16,000 addicts with 80% of their heroin needs. Vancouver's Chinese began distributing to neighboring Seattle, and Southeast Asian heroin jumped from 12% of the city's identifiable seizures in 1972 to 40% in 1973.

While many modern Triad societies are respected community organizations, many have developed criminal subgroups. Robertson (1977) claims that particularly in Western Europe nearly all Triads are engaged in prostitution, illegal gambling, extortion, and heroin trafficking. They are the major wholesale distributors and processors of opium from the Golden Triangle.

"The China White Trail" is a term used by the DEA to describe the transportation of heroin from Thailand through the secret societies of Hong Kong and finally the Chinese neighborhoods of New York City (Kerr, 1987). In 1989 the FBI seized 828 pounds of heroin valued at $1 billion (the 1971 French Connection was about 220 pounds). This New York City bust was attributed to the China White Trail.

Much more official attention has been paid by government officials in the U.S. than in the past to the issue of Asian organized crime. The President's Commission on Organized Crime (1984a) issued a report on Asian organized crime, as did the Department of Justice in 1988 (Baridon, 1988), as did the Hong Kong Security Forces (Fight Crime Committee, 1986; see also FBI, 1985).

The Nature of Organized Crime

Given our general definition of organized crime, such groups have existed in varying degrees since, or even before, the advent of modern nation states. Large, diversified syndicate crime, with control on an extraregional basis over more than a few illegal activities, is primarily a phenomenon of the post-World War I period. While the focus in discussing organized crime is generally on the prototype, what has been called the "Cosa Nostra," the nature and structure of organized criminal groups is determined by the type of criminal activity they are engaged in as well as by ethnic, subcultural, and cultural values. Criminal gangs, mobs, racketeers, and organized (predatory) criminals share to a lesser degree many of the characteristics of larger syndicates.

Ethnicity and Organized Crime

Some believe that organized crime began in the United States as an import, along with mass immigration of Sicilians and Italians in the late nineteenth and early twentieth centuries. Figure 12.3 contains a random list of names of organized crime figures, none of whom are

Figure 12.3: Ethnicity and Organized Crime

Irish
Dion O'Banion
Owen Madden
George "Bugs" Moran
Legs Diamond (Nolan)
Danny Greene

Jewish
Mo Dalitz
Arnold Rothstein
"Bugsy" Siegel
Meyer Lansky
Arthur "Dutch Schultz" Flegenheimer

WASPs
William Skidmore
Bill Thompson
Joe Hall
Henry Cotton
Sherlock Hillman

Mike McDonald (Scotch)
Murray Humphreys (Welsh)
George Jean De Mange (French)

Afro-American
Leroy "Nickey" Barnes
Roland Bartlett
Jeff Fort
Willie Rispers
Frank Matthews

Hispanic
Favelas
Maciases
Herrera
Valenzuelas
Romero

Italian or Sicilian. Organized crime is not simply a "Mafia transplant" or "alien conspiracy" in the U.S.; it obviously existed before significant Italian immigration and it probably will exist long after Italian-Americans move out of major involvement in organized crime.

Ianni (1973) proposes an *ethnic succession theory* of organized crime in which organized crime acts as a "queer ladder of mobility" (Bell, 1964, p. 115), an alternate means of upward mobility for ethnic minorities who, due to discrimination or lack of skills, are temporarily lodged at the bottom of the system of reward distribution in a society. Thus, while the last fifty years in the U.S. has witnessed the period of Sicilian-Italian domination of syndicate crime, this was preceded by Jewish (sometimes facetiously referred to as the "Kosher Nostra") and Irish domination. Prior to their domination, WASPs (White Anglo Saxon Protestants) controlled organized crime. During these periods, many other ethnic groups—for example, Germans, Lebanese, Greeks, blacks—also participated in organized crime. At the present time with its ethnic base largely middle class, the Italian-American "Mafia" might be described as being in its eleventh hour, as black and Hispanic gangs move into positions of power in organized criminal activity with their base of operations in low-income ethnic ghettoes, long the wellspring of illegitimate careers.

Organized crime in the 1990s is in rapid transition, and much of our image of a dominant Mafia underworld is beginning to resemble an old black-and-white gangster movie starring Edward G. Robinson or James Cagney. Former Attorney General William French Smith in remarks before the President's Commission on Organized Crime (1983, pp. 124–125) indicated:

> Even as federal law enforcement agencies have worked hard to catch up on the traditional crime families found in our major cities, new forms of organized crime have emerged throughout the nation. In just the past few years, new groups have organized in pursuit of the lucrative profits that can be made in drug trafficking. Although traditional organized crime is heavily involved in the drug trade also, these new groups do not have places on that family tree. They are distinguishable. They include motorcycle gangs, prison gangs, and foreign-based organizations. Some of the names of these groups will be familiar, but most are not. They are: Hell's Angels, Outlaws, Pagans, Bandidos, La Nuestra Familia, Mexican Mafia, Aryan Brotherhood, Black Guerilla Family, Japanese Yakuza, Chinese Triad Societies, Israeli Mafia, and many, many more. Of the 425 cases under investigation by the Organized Crime Drug Enforcement Task Force, which this administration established this past year, only a small number involve traditional organized crime. Most involve the new cartels.

This diversity of groups involved in organized crime is certainly well illustrated in the burgeoning international illegal drug business.

Drug Trafficking

While the Italian-American Syndicate has been involved in drug trafficking, the business is so large that no one group can hope to control it. Although there are many international sources of illegal drugs, the three primary centers of supply are: the Golden Triangle, the Golden Crescent, and Latin America. Figure 12.4 depicts the primary drug smuggling routes into the United States.

"The Golden Triangle" refers to the northern border areas of Thailand, Burma, and Laos, which are major heroin-growing areas. Part of this area is called "the Shan States" and is controlled by an Opium Army made up of the descendants of former Chinese Nationalist troops. "The Golden Crescent" includes areas of Iran, Afghanistan, Pakistan, and Turkey which made up the old "French Connection." The latter, which was the basis of a classic movie, involved the smuggling of raw opium to Marseilles, France, for processing into heroin and finally to the U.S. for sale. The third source is Latin America and involves primarily cocaine and marijuana, mainly from Colombia (Abadinsky, 1988; and Inciardi, 1986).

Illegal smuggling and trafficking in drugs of every description is the modern road to riches in the criminal world. The public demand is so vast and the profits to be made so enormous that no one criminal organization can dominate. Occasional successful efforts to close down one major conduit of supply such as the "French Connection" in the early seventies find other sources meeting the demand. Trebach (1984, p. 132) has coined the notion of the "Iron Law of Opium Trade" to describe a situation in which, if one source of supply is closed, another replaces it in order to meet demand. In a six-year observational study of drug smugglers and dealers Adler and Adler (1983) found that, due to the danger and legal penalties, there were "shifts and oscillations" in drug trafficking careers. Involvement was temporary; but due to the large rewards involved, many successful retirees oscillate in and out of smuggling organizations. Lupscha (1988, p. 2) describes state involvement in drug trafficking:

> Finally, there is the model in which drug trafficking is used by nation-states, or their agencies, to gain hard currency. The Bulgarians have, in the past, used KINTEX, the state trading organization to this end and the governments of Cuba and Nicaragua have been accused of this. In addition, we have a number of variants. Syrian Intelligence in the Bekaa valley of Lebanon controlling hashish and heroin production while various factions traffic drugs for guns; pilots of "Air America" in Vietnam, or its

modern reincarnation in Central America, allegedly moonlighting as drug couriers. . . .

The Medellin Cartel

Probably the most powerful international drug trafficking organization in the world is the Medellin Cartel of Colombia, an organization which uses M-19 (the April 19 Movement) revolutionary group as protection for their operation (Gugliotta and Leen, 1989). It was the latter terrorist group which gave birth to the cartel. In 1981 M-19 kidnapped the daughter of Fabio Ochoa, the most powerful cocaine boss. In response the Ochoas formed a cartel of two hundred other narcotics trafficking organizations in the city of Medellin and prepared to wage war with M-19. The latter group wisely released Ochoa's daughter and began a hands-off-the-cartel policy in return for a cut of the profits. The cartel used M-19 to storm the country's Palace of Justice in 1985 killing twelve of the twenty-four supreme court justices (Anderson and Van Atta, 1988b; and Eddy, Sabogal, and Walden, 1988). Narco-terrorist groups also traffic in weapons, launder money, offer mutual assistance, smuggle contraband, as well as share intelligence.

The Underground Empire

In an investigation of "narcotraficantes" (narcotics traffickers), James Mills in *The Underground Empire: Where Crime and Governments Embrace* (1986) makes some serious charges. ". . . [T]he largest narcotics conspirator in the world is the government of the United States whose intelligence agencies conspire with or ignore the complicity of officials at the highest levels in at least 33 countries" (Ibid., p. 1160). As soon as the Drug Enforcement Agency (DEA) closed in on drug domos (bosses), the State Department or CIA sabotaged their investigations in the name of foreign policy (Hagan, 1987a). "The underground empire" is a "fourth world" of nations of institutionalized, state-supported crime. Mills (1986, pp. 1140–1141) indicates:

> The international narcotics industry could not exist without the cooperation of corrupt governments. Our own government leans over backward to conceal this from the public—To recognize it would cripple foreign relations . . . The highly connected, tuxedo-clad criminal is left in place to provide intelligence to the U.S.—and drugs to its citizens . . . To assuage the public, politicians will continue to wage a civil war, one above-ground sector of the government attacking the drug traffic on front pages and the seven o'clock news, another underground sector secretly permitting the traffic, at times, promoting it.

Figure 12.4: Drug Trafficking: Major Routes, Source Countries, and Money Laundering Centers

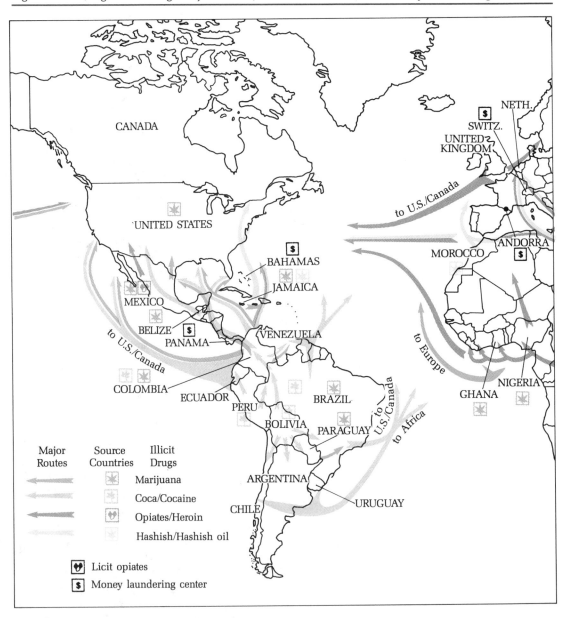

SOURCE: Adapted from U.S. Department of Justice, Drug Enforcement Administration, Office of Intelligence, 1987, *DEA Map 1-1987.*

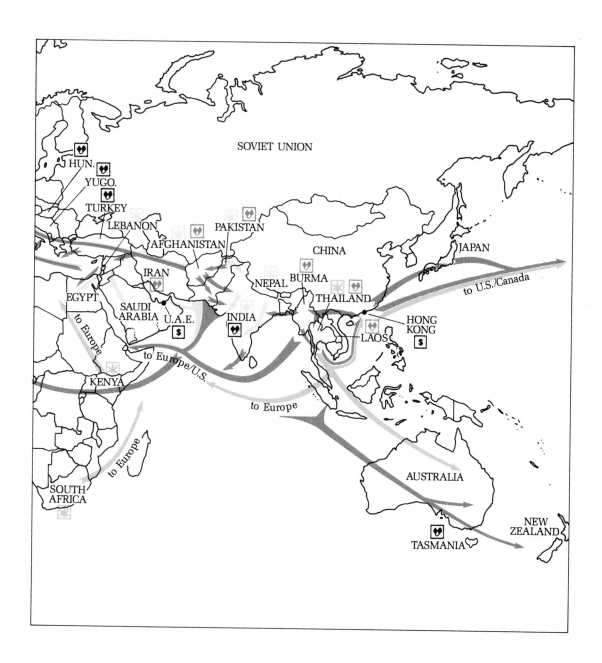

Narco-Terrorism

Until the 1980s the drug traffickers had little contact with terrorist groups, but with the huge expansion of the illegal drug market and shared geographical locales it was inevitable that an alliance of sorts would be forged. The Colombian FARC and M-19, Peruvian Sendero Luminoso ("Shining Path"), Palestinian and Middle Eastern groups, Turks, Armenians, and Tamils all derive portions of their operating capital from drug trafficking or traffickers (Laqueur, 1987, pp. 291–294; and Satchell, et al., 1987). Lupscha (1988) indicates the first time he heard of "narcoterrorismo" was Peru's President Fernando Belaunde Terry speaking of links between Sendero Luminoso (Shining Path revolutionaries) and drug traffickers in the jungle around Tingo Maria. In some areas such as parts of Colombia, guerrilla groups place a "revolutionary tax" on drug activity. Lupscha (Ibid.) views the relationships between drug traffickers and terrorist groups and insurgents as including activities ranging from cooperative interaction between traffickers and terrorists, exploitation of traffickers by insurgents, traffickers using terrorism as a weapon to intimidate the government, states cooperating with traffickers, the use of drug trafficking to promote state policy, and use of connections between drug traffickers and state officials to cover up criminality (see Ward, 1988).

The Nature of "The Mafia"

In an opening quotation for this chapter, informer and former mobster Joseph Valachi, during his testimony before the McClellan Commission, denies that "Mafia" is the name of the organization to which he belonged. As early as 1890 a grand jury investigating the murder of New Orleans Police Chief David Hennessey concluded that a secret criminal group, the Mafia, was responsible (Albini, 1971, p. 167); the existence of an organization by that name was assumed rather than proven.

Origin of Mafia

The origin of the term "Mafia" is often assumed but undocumented, (that is, without sources referenced). Joseph Albini in his *The American Mafia: Genesis of a Legend* (Ibid., pp. 83–106) notes some of the more commonly cited origins:

Maffia (Tuscan word for misery)
Mauvais (French word for bad)

> Ma-afir (Arab tribe which settled in Sicily)
>
> MAFIA (*Mazzini Autorizza Furti Incendi Auvelenamenti*—Mazzini Authorizes Thefts, Arson and Poisons)
>
> Mu'afy (Arabic for protect from death in the night)
>
> MAFIA (Battle cry during the Legend of Sicilian Vespers—a revolt against the French in 1282—*Morte Alla Francia Italia Anela*—"Death to all French is Italy's cry.")
>
> Mafia (The name of a stone quarry in Sicily)
>
> *I Mafiusi Di La Vicaria* (A popular play by Guiseppe Rizzotto in 1860, *The Heroes of the Penitentiary*

Of interest, but not mentioned by Albini, is Ma Fia (my daughter) (cited in Talese, 1971, p. 184). On the basis of extensive research on the subject, Albini concludes that the 1860 Rizzotto play is the most likely explanation. The play, which dealt with life among Cammorristi (organized and professional criminals) in a Palermo prison, was very popular; it was later released simply with the title, *I Mafiusi*, by then a very well known term. This might explain the fact that the term was not popularly known before 1860, while after this period it became almost a synonym for organized crime. Thus rather than being the name of an organization, Mafia refers to a method—syndicate-type organized crime. It is a type of crime, not an organization as such, for example, the Elks or Moose.

Theories of the Nature of Syndicate Crime in the U.S.

Three principal theories regarding the nature of syndicate crime will be discussed in this section. They are:

1. The Cosa Nostra Theory
2. The Confederation Theory
3. The Patron Theory

The Cosa Nostra Theory

The Cosa Nostra theory refers to a theory of organizational structure of syndicate crime that has as its main proponents:

1. Interpretations of the testimony of informant Joseph Valachi before the McClellan Commission in the sixties, in which the term "La Cosa Nostra" (literally, "this thing of ours") was first officially introduced.

2. The organized crime section of the President's Crime Commission Report of 1967 (President's Commission, 1967; pp. 437–486) and theoretical interpretations of its principal consultant, sociologist Donald Cressey (see Albini, 1988).

3. Official although belated policy of federal agencies such as the Federal Bureau of Investigation.

The major elements of "Cosa Nostra theory," as described by Cressey and the Organized Crime Task Force, included:

1. A nationwide alliance of at least twenty-four tightly knit "families" in the United States. (See Figure 12.5 for a map of families.)

2. Membership is exclusively of Sicilian or Italian descent and the organization is referred to as Cosa Nostra particularly by East Coast members. A title of a book by Nicholas Gage (1971) reflects the ethnic exclusivity: *The Mafia Is Not An Equal Opportunity Employer.*

Figure 12.5: Location of Organized Crime Families

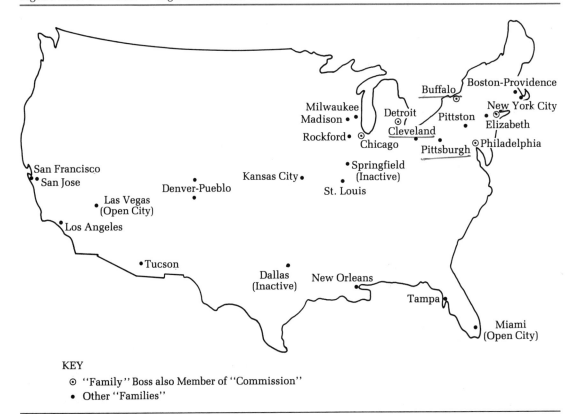

KEY

⊙ "Family" Boss also Member of "Commission"

• Other "Families"

SOURCE: Permanent Subcommittee on Investigations, Committee on Governmental Affairs, 1980, *Hearings on Organized Crime and Use of Violence,* 96th Cong., 2d Sess., April, p. 116.

3. The names and criminal activities of approximately five thousand participants have been assembled and the formal structure (see Figure 12.6) has been pieced together based upon Valachi's testimony.

4. Overseeing the Cosa Nostra is a National Commission made up of the dons (heads) of the most powerful families in the U.S. (Originally consisting of ten to twelve members, according to Fratianno [DeMaris, 1981, p. 294], the commission in 1981 consisted of the heads of the five New York families plus the Chicago boss.) The existence of the Commission was corroborated by means of an electronic bug placed in the dashboard of Anthony "Tony Ducks" Corallo's chauffeur's Jaguar (Powell, et al., 1986, p. 25).

5. LCN controls all but a small portion of illegal gambling in the U.S. and contains the principal loan sharks and importers and wholesalers of narcotics.

6. Much of this information is the result of detailed reports of a variety of police observers, informants, wiretaps, and electronic bugs (President's Crime Commission, 1967, pp. 6–8; Cressey, 1969, pp. 99–107, 241–242).

The description of the internal structure of the LCN in the President's Crime Commission Report was based primarily upon Valachi's testimony. Each of the twenty-four families was described as varying in size from as many as seven hundred to one thousand men to as few as twenty. Only New York City had more than one family, namely five. Family organization was described as being rationally designed with sets of positions similar to any large corporation. Figure 12.6 presents a LCN chain of command headed by a boss (*don*), with an advisor (*consigliere*) and underboss (sort of vice-president). Answering to the underboss are *caporegimas* (literally, heads of regiments or lieutenants or captains). They are chiefs of operating units or soldiers (*soldati*, "buttons"). "From a business standpoint, the *caporegima* is analogous to plant supervisor or sales manager" (President's Crime Commission, 1967, p. 451). Soldiers may run various illicit operations on a commission basis or "own" their own operations within which a portion goes to the boss. All of these individuals are "made members" of the organization.

Below and allied with these families are various nonmember associates and employees, individuals who cooperate, aid, and assist organizational operations. Insulation of the boss and other LCN activity is preserved supposedly according to the "oath of omerta"—a pledge of loyalty, honor, respect, absolute obedience, manliness, and silence. In the old days, accompanying the initiation was an elaborate ritual in which the novitiate was inducted into the LCN.

Figure 12.6: Internal Structure of La Cosa Nostra Families

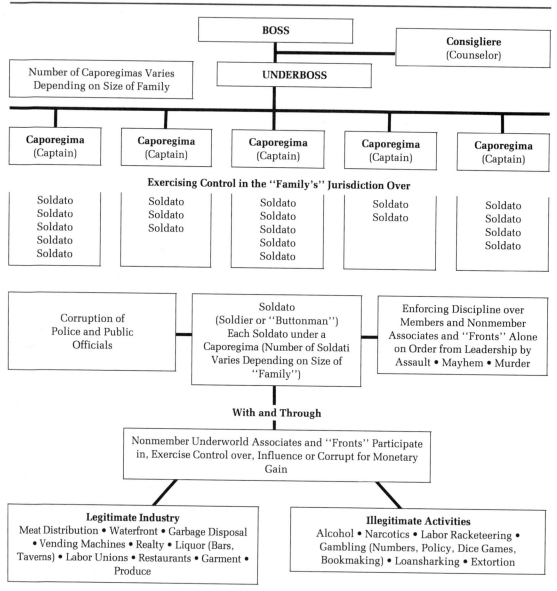

SOURCE: U.S. Senate Permanent Subcommittee on Investigations, Committee on Governmental Affairs, *Hearings on Organized Crime and Use of Violence*, 96th Cong., 2d Sess., April 1980, p. 117.

Confederation Theory

The leading proponent of confederation theory is journalist Hank Messick in books such as *Lansky* (1973) and with Burt Goldblatt, *The Mobs and the Mafia* (1972). In this theory syndicate crime in the U.S. is viewed as having been controlled by a "crime confederation" or "combination," consisting of primarily Jewish and Italian gangsters, with the LCN only a part of the operation. Messick describes Meyer Lansky as having acted basically as the chairman of the board of organized crime. According to Gus Tyler (1962), another advocate of this theory, the basic framework was laid for this National Crime Syndicate with meetings in the late twenties and early thirties. One Atlantic City summit had the following in attendance: Johnny Torrio and Meyer Lansky (master of ceremonies), Moe Dalitz (Cleveland), Isadore Blumenfeld (Twin Cities), Phil Kastel (New Orleans), Hyman Abrams (Boston), Harry Stromberg (Philadelphia), "Longie" Zwillman (New Jersey), and Paul Rica (Chicago). The Italian Syndicate was also represented by Luciano, Adonis, Costello, and Genovese. Supposedly at this meeting the crime leaders divided the U.S. into territories (Messick and Goldblatt, 1972, pp. 105–106). While proponents of the confederation theory point out the continuing power of the old Jewish organization, critics would indicate that the LCN was really in the driver's seat, while others would argue that no one confederation or organization monopolized organized crime. Even if such a theory were historically accurate, it describes an organization long since buried.

Patron Theory

"Patron theory" views organized crime as consisting of a series of patron-client relationships as advocated by Albini (1971). According to this approach, organized crime groups and their leaders resemble a medieval system of shifting warlords in which whoever has the most power and is able to render the greatest services controls support. The occupation of specific positions within a structure is less important than a development-association system of peer relations, ones which are informal, flexible, and constantly immersed in conflict. Feudalism rather than the corporate bureaucracy is a more appropriate analogy for describing organized crime families, a series of shifting alliances (see Albanese, 1989, for other models of organized crime).

The Mafia Myth?

The "Mafia myth" refers to the belief that U.S. organized crime is the result of an imported alien conspiracy which controls all organized crime in America. The "Mafia myth" really has two groups of adherents: the *conspiracy model* and the *moderate model*; while critics tend to lump these models together, separating them will assist in clarifying exactly what is in dispute. The *conspiracy model* suggests that the Mafia is an international organization which controls organized crime, particularly in the United States. Adherents of this view are Harry Anslinger, the former crusading Director of the Federal Bureau of Narcotics, as well as by Edward Allen (1962), Ed Reid (1970), and Frederic Sondern (1959). The moderate model—represented by Donald Cressey (1967), Robert Anderson (1965), and Ralph Salerno and John Tompkins (1969), and reflected in the President's Crime Commission Report—views the Italian American Syndicate (IAS), which the Commission calls Cosa Nostra, as the most powerful of organized crime groups, but not an "alien conspiracy."

The Italian American Syndicate (IAS)

Much of what has been written about organized crime has restricted itself to an analysis of the Italian American Syndicate (IAS), variously referred to as the "Mafia" or "Cosa Nostra." Critics of this approach (Bell, 1967; Ianni, 1972, 1974; Morris and Hawkins, 1970; and Smith, 1975) have largely made their points, among others, that organized crime in the U.S. is home grown and is not the product of an imported, alien conspiracy; that no one ethnic group has a monopoly on organized crime; and that the picture drawn by the Organized Crime Task Force Report (1967) as presented by Donald Cressey (1969) and based largely upon Joseph Valachi's testimony is overdrawn; and that it is doubtful that organized crime, or the IAS, which was the most powerful of such syndicates, ever exhibited the extreme bureaucratic, monolithic structure depicted. These critics do not, however, dispute the existence of organized crime and criminal syndicates as distinct phenomena, nor dispute that an IAS ("Mafia," "Cosa Nostra") is more than a creation of moral entrepreneurs or Hollywood.

However, Lupsha (1981) indicates that testimony of informants such as Valachi and Teresa, which is rejected by these critics, has strong support of wiretaps in New Jersey, Rhode Island, Missouri, and Chicago (Volz and Bridge, 1969; and Zeiger, 1975). While many of the descriptions of organization and structure of the IAS are dated, the vision is "skewed, not false" (Lupsha, 1981, p. 5); the initial description of the Mafia was overdone, but the reaction is perhaps equally overdone. Perhaps there has been a tendency "to throw out the baby of organized crime with the bath water of 'alien conspiracy' theory" (Ibid., p. 4). Some critics of the "alien conspiracy" seem to suggest at times that, since the Mafia does not exist, organized crime does not exist. To say there is no Mafia is quite different than to say there is no organized crime, and some critics seem to border dangerously on this assumption despite disclaimers that, of course, they do not mean to say there is no organized crime. One writer (Gibbons, 1982, p. 340) indicates, apparently not in jest, that the Apalachin meetings (a mob convention to be discussed shortly) were perhaps, as claimed by the participants, a simple barbecue and not a criminal convention. The acceptance of the existence of criminal syndicates does not imply the acceptance of "alien conspiracies," Mafia, or an enemy-oriented model of crime.

While the current version of the IAS has apparently lost much of the power and ritualism associated with its early Prohibition years and probably never resembled a monolithic national or international conspiracy, it has played and continues to play an important role in American organized crime. A recognition of regional syndicates as a component of organized crime or the IAS as a dominant force in no way indicates that federal law enforcement efforts are justified in ignoring corporate crime or other types of non-IAS organized criminal groups.

Testimony during trials of organized crime figures in 1986 has ended this debate—yes, *there is a Mafia*. Albanese (1989, p. 66) explains:

> . . . the debate over the existence of a "Mafia" was finally rendered moot in a 1986 trial when the defendants in the "Commission" trial (i.e., the alleged "bosses' of the New York City crime "families") conceded that the "*Mafia exists* [italics mine] and has members." Furthermore, the defense claimed "there is a commission" which is mentioned in wiretapped conversations of the defendants. Testimony from Sicilian informer Tommaso Buscetta corroborated this claim. He stated that he was told by Joseph Bonanno in 1957 that "it was very advisable" to set up a commission in Sicily "to resolve disputes among criminal groups' (Lubash, 1985). If this testimony is true, it appears that any organization of criminal groups in Sicily was modeled after that in America rather than the common belief . . . that a Mafia organization was imported to America from Sicily.

The Classic Pattern of Organized Crime

In their book, *The Crime Confederation* (1969), Ralph Salerno and John S. Tompkins present a very useful schema for describing and examining both the activities of organized crime and its evolution along the continuum from gangs to powerful syndicates. They describe the "classic pattern of organized crime" as a gradual movement from "strategic and tactical crimes" such as assault, bribery, and extortion to "illegal businesses and activities" to "legitimate businesses" to "big business." Due to their willingness to commit and employ *strategic and tactical crimes*, organized gangs are able to then acquire both the funds and power to be fairly successful at *illegal businesses and activities*. They are, of course, not the only types of criminals engaged in these activities but are more organized, more continuous in their efforts, and simply better at it. The types of crimes committed under strategic and tactical crimes are for the most part disapproved of by the general public, while the illegal businesses and operations often serve demands by segments of the public for vices and other illicit activities. Unwittingly the government, by branding much of this activity, such as narcotics and gambling, as illegal, creates at times a monopoly for criminal groups that are organized well enough to supply these demanded goods and services.

A major problem of some "unconnected" or nonorganized criminals is "laundering" (making "dirty" money appear "clean") of funds obtained in illegal operations. In the earlier history of U.S. organized crime, even "connected" figures such as Al Capone were convicted of income tax violations, and this lesson was not lost on other organized criminals as many began trading in their black shirts and white ties for Brooks Brothers suits. With funds obtained in illegal operations, organized criminals can *infiltrate legitimate businesses*, an even more fertile field for their activities. Finally, experience in such operations enables movement into even *bigger businesses*. Figure 12.7 details businesses which have been cited by appropriate sources as either presently or having at one time had mob influence. (Caution must be used in interpreting this list because the original cited sources of the allegation may be dated.)

Some Activities of Organized Criminals

A detailed account of organized crime activities is beyond the scope of this intended treatment. Readers interested in such detail can consult the latest newspaper or media accounts, though the reading of some of the references cited in this chapter will provide a more systematic starting point.

Strategic and Tactical Crimes

The strength of organized criminal groups is based upon their willingness and ability to use force or threats of force to assure discipline within and outside the organization. Although activities such as assault, coercion, extortion, and murder are not the exclusive property of organized criminals, the protracted nature of their involvement in these exceeds that of most other types of criminals.

Some strategic and tactical crimes committed by organized criminals include: arson, assault, coercion, extortion, murder, blackmail, bribery, and corruption. *Arson,* the deliberate setting of fires, is an activity that organized criminals have either directly or indirectly involved themselves in. Vincent Teresa describes an arson-related "bust out" scam in which, through intermediaries who lack criminal records, he would open a bank account under a corporate name and lease a building, order goods with half the bill paid to build a credit line, place large orders prior to Christmas, remove unsold items from the building and sell them to a fence, then burn the place down, collect the insurance, and declare bankruptcy (Teresa, 1973b, pp. 108–109). Organized criminals also may control the insurance firm that holds the policy on the torched property.

In 1969, due to an error by a defense attorney, 2,300 pages of tape "logs" were made public by the U.S. Department of Justice. These now famous "DeCavalcante Tapes" recorded four years of information gained in a "bugged" plumbing and heating company office of "Sam the Plumber" DeCavalcante, a New Jersey organized crime leader. The transcripts contain a case of Easton, Pennsylvania, racketeer Joseph Migliazzi, who owed DeCavalcante $1,300 which he could not pay back. Sam told him to burn down his Stagecoach Restaurant and give him $5,000 of the

Figure 12.7: Organized Crime is Bullish on America: Businesses and Activities Alleged to Have or that Currently Have Some Organized Crime Influence

Tucson Printing Company[a]	Blue Coal Corporation[b]
Chrysler Office Building[a]	Pocono Downs Racetrack[b]
Moravian Acres Subdivision[a]	Old Forge Bank (Pa.)[b]
Erie Coin and Vending Company[b]	Caesars World, Inc.[b]
Keystone Music Co.[b]	Caesar's Palace[b]
Scotto Pizza[b]	Teamsters Union Pension Fund[c]
Italian Delight[b]	Many Las Vegas Casinos[c]
City Bank of Philadelphia[b]	La Costa Country Club[c]
Forte Oil Company[b]	Miami Beach Hotels[c]
Bonnie Stewart Dresses[b]	Bally Pinball Machines[c]
Medico Industries[b]	International Longshoreman's
Northeastern Pa. TV Cable Co.[b]	Association[d]

[a]Ed Reid, *The Grim Reapers* (1970).

[b]Pennsylvania Crime Commission (1980).

[c]Ovid Demaris, *The Last Mafioso* (1981).

[d]NBC News, 1979, "NBC Follow-Up: A Follow-Up on the 1977 Documentary on 'Racketeering and the International Longshoreman's Association,'" broadcast April 21.

$90,000 insurance. On July 4, 1965, the restaurant was torched (Volz and Bridge, 1969).

Assault, coercion, extortion, and *murder* are bottom-line tools employed by organized crime, weapons of last resort to assure the "rational" pursuit of profit. "Make him an offer he can't refuse" is a black humor saying, but it is an all-too-apt phrase to describe methods used by organized criminals to accomplish their will. Violence and threats of violence, demands for protection money (extortion), and, when necessary as a last resort, murder ("making your bones") is part of the repertoire. Truck driver Joe Smith (pseudonym) told reporter Paul Carpenter how he beat the Commonwealth of Pennsylvania out of $86,400 in one of many trips from North Carolina with a truckload of 48,000 cartons of cigarettes. Characterizing it as a racket that uses brutality, extortion, terrorism, and murder, he claimed that he had the protection of a high Philadelphia city official as well as a state legislator, both of whom were associates of LCN figures running the operation. His truck was sometimes escorted by state police in order to avoid hijacking. Smith expressed fear for his life if he was caught talking to a reporter since the previous year one Rocco Frumento, a state cigarette tax agent and convicted smuggler, was executed gangland style in order to assure his silence (Carpenter, 1977). Decades of internal wars and assassinations within the ranks of organized crime attest to the fact that not only outsiders are the victims of mob discipline.

Blackmail, bribery, and corruption are essential strategic tools of organized crime. The American Bar Association (1952) in their *Report on Organized Crime* (p. 16) concluded: "The largest single factor in the breakdown of law enforcement dealing with organized crime is the corruption and connivance of many public officials." Blackmail is more easily achieved by organized crime figures due to their involvement in gambling casinos, pornography, and servicing of vice-related activities. Bribery and corruption of public officials is the largest operating cost of organized criminal groups, a sort of "underground" tax or license to steal. The history of organized crime's success in corrupting public officials ranges from cities to counties to entire states being "in the bag." Success in strategic and tactical crimes provides the money, "muscle," and "respect" for success at principal illegal businesses and activities. The strategic and tactical crimes are for the most part "rackets," services which are unwanted by or do not require public demand. Organized criminal involvement in illicit enterprises or illegal businesses satisfies public demand for services or vice activities which either cannot be or are not met by legal businesses. Thus the loan shark is a banker of last resort or the fence a less expensive shopping center.

Illegal Businesses and Activities

Since the end of the Prohibition era and until recently, gambling has been viewed as the number one moneymaker for organized crime. Although often described as a Depression and/or ghetto invention, lotteries flourished in the United States as far back as colonial times, used during that period to pay for public works (National Institute of Law Enforcement, 1977). In addition to lotteries, syndicates are involved in other gambling activities, such as bookmaking (taking bets on sporting events), illegal gambling devices (slot machines, punchboards, sports polls), and the running of illegal gambling establishments. The *numbers game* is by far the most popular of these activities. Sometimes called policy or "bolita" in the southern U.S., the basic strategy is similar to legalized state lotteries in that the bettor tries to choose a winning three-digit number. The odds of winning on a straight bet are one thousand to one (digits 000 to 999), while the payoff varies, usually from five hundred to seven hundred to one. A boxed bet increases the odds of winning, for example, 369 would pay if any of the following numbers hit for the day: 369, 396, 936, 963, 639, or 693. The payoffs, of course, would be less. Traditionally numbers differed from lotteries in that the former were chosen on the basis of events such as the numbers of win-place-show horses at a track or Dow Jones averages. Lotteries were spun on a wheel or by some other "honest" gambling device.

Space prohibits detailing of the structure of illegal numbers operations. Very basically, however, the "numbers runner" or "bookie" collects bets and turns over the betting slips to a "controller," who then turns these over to the numbers bank. The local numbers bank, in order to control its losses, may "lay off" bets with larger banks, that is, replace bets on numbers that are heavily bet.

The advent of legal state lotteries may not have made the dent in the illegal numbers business that many had hoped. Many numbers writers simply use the legal daily number as their own, increasing the non-taxed odds and sometimes even laying off bets with the state. Betting on sporting events is widespread, as can be noted by newspaper publication of point spreads, and by a television network featuring "Jimmy the Greek" Snyder and his National Football games picks. Casino gambling still exists in many American communities. Dice or "crap" games, wheels, and "high stake" card games can often be found by simply asking local cabbies, "Where's the action?" In now-famous Wincanton (Gardiner, 1970), a pseudonym for Reading, Pennsylvania, the FBI in 1962 raided what was described as "the largest crap game in the East." It was run nine times per week, with each game involving pots from $50–$100,000. The FBI netted over 150 operators and patrons in the raid, and the game had a weekly payroll for thirty-five employees of $7,800. Links were discovered between local crime czars and Joseph Profaci of New York (Pennsylvania Crime Commission, 1970, pp. 32–33). Reuter, in his book *Disorganized Crime* (1984), is quick to point out that "the Mafia" control of illegal markets is exaggerated and that the numbers, loansharking, and bookmaking are very disorganized businesses.

Related to gambling operations is the loan shark or shylock (the latter name is derived from Shakespeare's money lender character, Shylock, who demands his "pound of flesh.") Loan sharks provide quick loans on the spot to borrowers who are either high risk or in a spot. These loans are given at usurious (illegal and exorbitant rates). Although rates vary, a typical loan might be a "six for five" arrangement. That is, for every five dollars borrowed, six dollars must be repaid (20 percent interest) per week. Sharks are more interested in collecting periodic interest payments (called "juice," "vigorish," or "vig") than having the loan paid off. Often borrowers give their bodies as collateral since, if they were good risks or could share their problem, they could have gone elsewhere. Gambling is the usual manner in which the successful business-person but poor gambler is introduced to loan sharks and, if his or her luck does not improve, his or her likely future business partners.

Other successful illegitimate activities of organized criminals involve labor racketeering; narcotics trafficking; prostitution; pornography (although now much of this is legal); stolen property (such as cars, stocks, and bonds); videotape, film, and record piracy; and even illegal alcohol. Organized criminals will involve themselves in any scam (illegal activity) so long as it is relatively safe and profitable (Kwitny, 1979).

Labor racketeering involves infiltration of unions to use this influence for personal profit. Such operations—which may take the form of bribes, kickbacks, and extortionary threats—permit mobsters to use pension funds and to offer "no strike insurance" (the guarantee that workers will not strike) and sweetheart contracts (collusion between employer and union officials at the expense of workers), as well as other operations.

In one federal sting operation, "Operation Unirac" (Union Racketeering), the FBI reported upon collusion between shipping companies, the International Longshoreman's Association, and organized criminals (NBC News, 1979). According to NBC News (Ibid.) accounts, the operation found that the Genovese, Gambino, and Marcello organized crime families controlled the International Longshoreman's Association (ILA). Hijackings were set up by ILA officials; kickbacks and pay to "phantom workers" were common. In addition, in "Operation Brilab," which disclosed official corruption in Louisiana and Texas among high state officials, the FBI concentrated on Carlos Marcello (reputed boss of New Orleans organized crime), who told two undercover agents, "We own the Teamsters," and bragged of accessibility to the union's pension fund ("Abscam," 1980).

Four unions with substantial organized crime control and influence are the International Longshoremen's Association, the Hotel and Restaurant Employees Union, the Laborers International Union of North America, and the International Brotherhood of Teamsters. Construction costs in New York City are estimated to be 25 percent higher due to the need for organized crime payoffs, and garbage collection $50 million per year more due to mob control (Powell, et al., 1986, p. 28). Mob-controlled Teamster locals 295 and 851 enabled Anthony "Tony Ducks" Corallo to shake down air transport service companies for $1.1 million between 1978 and 1985 (Rowan, 1986, p. 34). "The Outfit" in Chicago charges a "street tax" on all illegal activities. Gamblers, vice operators, even owners of parking lots and legitimate businesses must pay 10 percent to 50 percent of their gross revenues to the Chicago mob.

The largest illegal business of organized criminals is now drugs. In 1986 the President's Commission on Organized Crime (1986a) estimated that organized crime took in as much as $106.2 billion, and by far the biggest money maker was illegal drug trafficking. Success and money from illegal operations, although welcome, present organized criminals with potential tax problems, further encouraging them to move into *legitimate businesses*. Such businesses *provide many opportunities for organized crime*. They provide a source of legal income which can help explain their high life-styles. Due to their methods, the criminal can monopolize markets and make more money than competitors. Such businesses also yield a "cover," or respectable occupation, as well as provide a base of operation and a meeting place, particularly for dealing with public officials. They enable the "washing" or "laundering" of funds, and provide a diversification of operations.

Favorite businesses of organized criminals include: auto sales, bakeries, clothing manufacturing, construction and demolition, import/export, garages, hotels, vending machines, produce, trucking, bars and restaurants, and the like. Businesses such as vending or bars are fertile for "skimming" (hiding or not counting money earned for tax purposes). One hundred dollars skimmed every day from a busy bar would amount to over $30,000 a year, tax free, from just one business. Extortion and monopolization in vending businesses enable organized criminals to force out competitors.

Although estimates of illegal income are hazardous, U.S. Representative Sam Nunn (Georgia) estimates that $121 to $161 billion in unreported, untaxed income is taken out of the economy every year by organized crime (Yema, 1980, p. 7). More conservative estimates place the gross at $48 billion and net revenues at $25 billion in untaxed profits. By comparison, Exxon, the largest U.S. industrial corporation, had gross sales of $97.1 billion in 1982 ("Mafia," 1977a, p. 33; and "Fortune Directory of the Largest U.S. Corporations," 1983).

Claimed levels of profit may be inaccurate, if we are to believe Fratianno, a less successful gangster. Others such as Ianni in *A Family Business* (1972) suggest that the seeds of many American fortunes began with "dirty business" and progressed in a couple of generations to "respectable" business, a natural ethnic succession and progression. In discussing federal enforcement, Ianni is concerned that this progression not be entirely blunted. In the main, however, organized criminals in such enterprises often carry over all the same illegal techniques. Our earlier discussion of extensive corporate criminality already indicates that many legitimate organizations operate with disdain for the law.

Although the veracity of legitimate owners such as Metropolitan Edison and their handling of the Three-Mile Island nuclear accident is questionable as well as scary, imagine if organized crime controlled your friendly local utility. In April 1980, sixty thousand 55-gallon drums of lethal waste stockpiled in the Chemical Control Corporation's Elizabeth, New Jersey, warehouse exploded. Fortunately, prevailing winds prevented the toxic fumes from blowing into New York City (see Szasz, 1986). The mob has owned garbage disposal firms for years and has realized there is big money in illegal disposal of toxic wastes. An alleged member of the Tieri crime family, after threatening the previous owner with a gun, effectively took over the company prior to the incident ("The New Mafia," 1981, p. 39; and Kelly, 1988).

Big Business and Government

It is disquieting to realize that in the course of a normal day the average American is supporting organized crime through patronizing legitimate businesses. Success at small business permits mob infiltration into *big business*, the heartline of our nation's economy. We have already suggested the impact of mob influence in big labor unions such as the Teamsters and the Longshoremen. Banking, construction, entertainment, insurance, real estate, and even Wall Street are not immune. Although mobsters may clean up their violent act in their move from the waterfront to the executive suite, their orientation toward lawbreaking on a more sophisticated level may continue. Mob control of distribution points, kickbacks for labor peace, and actual control of businesses can imperil an economy.

The final stage of the classic pattern of organized crime asks the question, "What remains?"—"Only government." Can or does organized crime have the capability of compromising the government itself? In "Operation Mongoose" (Ashman, 1975), the Central Intelligence Agency used syndicate criminals to put a "hit" on Cuban Premier Fidel Castro in 1963. Although apparently a scam on the part of the mob in that no serious attempts took place (DeMaris, 1981, p. 267), the deal apparently called for cooperation by the CIA in smuggling prostitutes from Marseilles in order to staff mob brothels in Las Vegas (Gangland Enforcer, 1977). One principal figure, John Roselli, who hinted at tie-ins with the Kennedy assassination before the House Assassination Committee, was killed by the "Mafia" before he could testify further (Anderson and Whitten, 1977). The U.S. House of Representatives Select Committee on Assassinations (1979) concluded that there was a conspiracy in the assassination of John Kennedy as well as possible conspiracies in the assassinations of Robert Kennedy and Martin Luther King, Jr. Chief counsel to the committee G. Robert Blakey and Richard Billing (1981) more specifically point the finger, as the title of the book indicates, *The Plot to Kill the President: Organized Crime Assassinated JFK* (see also Scheim, 1988).

The most famous FBI sting operation, ABSCAM (Arab scam), was only one of many such programs, some of which concentrated upon organized crime operations, for example, Brilab, Unirac, or Operation Miporn (Miami pornography). The ABSCAM probe was believed to have been shut down prematurely just as it was about to reach more higher ranking members of Congress than the original eight already accused ("Abscam," 1980). An interesting example at the state level took place in 1954. The U.S. Justice Department had begun deportation hearings against John LaRocca (alleged boss of the Pittsburgh mob). The Pennsylvania Governor, John Fine, sabotaged the federal government's case by first issuing a pardon to LaRocca for previous lottery and larceny convictions. Even though the pardon was issued at the close of the hearings, it was dated to fall before the close of the hearings. Having the grounds for deportation eliminated, the federal government had no choice but to drop the proceedings (Pennsylvania Crime Commission, 1970, p. 19).

The infiltration of organized crime groups into large business enterprises is also assisted by activities of legitimate organizations themselves, some operations of which resemble those of organized crime. Bribery and corruption of national and international public officials, violence either indirectly through the sale of unsafe products or directly in deposing foreign leaders such as Allende in Chile, and pushing of drugs far in excess of the medicinal needs of consumers, are just a few of such examples. A detailing of criminal activities of organized crime syndicates and particularly the IAS is not intended to ignore their corporate counterparts, but to recognized the former as having distinct characteristics of their own. Similarly, while the IAS did not invent, is not the only, and does not control all of organized criminal operations, it has been the most powerful of such groups in the U.S. since the 1930s.

A Brief History of Organized Crime in the U.S. ———

A detailed account of the evolution, development, and continuance of U.S. organized criminal activity is beyond the intended scope of this text. Readers are advised to consult sources cited in the reference list, particularly Abadinsky (1985), Talese (1971), Hammer (1975), MacLean (1974), and Gage (1972). However, a brief account will familiarize the reader with some key events in the history of organized crime. Figure 12.8 contains a brief chronological list.

Figure 12.8: Chronology of Selected Events in the History of Organized Crime in the United States

1700s	Colonial pirates
1800s	WASP, Irish, Jewish gangs
1890	The New Orleans Incident
1920	The Volstead Act (Prohibition)
1930–31	Castellammarese Wars in New York City
1931	Would-be "Capo Di Tutti Capi" Maranzano Murdered
by 1934	Cosa Nostra and/or Confederation Established
1940	Informant Reles Describes Murder Inc.
Post-WWII	Mob Moves into Las Vegas
1950	Kefauver Committee Hearings
1957	The Apalachin "Gangland" Convention
1963	McClellan Commission Hearing Featuring Star Witness Joseph Valachi
1970	Organized Crime Control Act of 1970
1971	Mob Boss Joe Colombo Shot at Columbus Day Rally
1976	Carlo Gambino Dies
1979–80	Mob Wars Continue (Galante, Bruno, Testa)
1980–81	FBI Roundup of Top "Cosa Nostra" Bosses Begins
1983–86	President's Commission on Organized Crime
1983–87	"The Commission Trials"
1985	Paul Castellano Assassinated
1985–86	"The Pizza Connection"
1985–86	"The Great Mafia Trial" in Sicily

Before 1930

Organized crime had its beginnings in the New World with colonial pirates, former naval mercenaries of England in her war with Spain. By the end of the seventeenth century they became an institutionalized component of international trade, intimately tied up with the business and governmental systems of the time. "The pirates, it is clear, were racketeers of their day, bribing officials, corrupting entire governments and looting to maintain a vast underworld market in forbidden goods" (Browning and Gerassi, 1980, pp. 71–72). Organized crime appeared to be an intimate component of American cities from their beginnings, with "robber barons" or "industrial pirates" looting the

In the twenties, public opinion about organized crime was influenced by such acts as the St. Valentine's Day massacre.

landscape in early capitalism (Myers, 1910) and criminals, police, and politicians cooperatively running illicit enterprises in order to satisfy public demand for vice activity. The Irish and Anglo-Saxon street gangs in nineteenth century New York formed organized criminal groups, just as a later generation of mostly American-born street hoodlums of Italian descent would form the most successful prototype of American syndicates, the IAS.

The view has already been espoused in this chapter that organized crime in the United States existed long before major Italian immigration, being dominated in its early history by small local mobs of WASP origin. Also described was the 1890 "New Orleans Incident" in which one of rival Italian-American criminal brotherhoods killed the city's police chief. The aftermath of that incident was a grand jury report naming a secret criminal group, "Mafia," as being responsible. Due to a believed fix in the case, angered citizens stormed the parish prison, executing a number of the gang leaders and almost precipitating a war between the U.S. and Italy (Albini, 1971, p. 167).

Up until 1920, most organized crime was confined to relatively small, local mobs whose operations were not particularly sophisticated. Most were controlled by Irish and Jewish gangsters, although a number began to include as "muscle" a growing number of hoodlums of Italian and Sicilian descent. Prohibition was an absolute bonanza for organized crime, the one factor which made it possible for fledgling gangs to become financially successful syndicates. Frank Costello was one of the first Italo-American gangsters to make it big.

George Wolf (1975, pp. 27–29), Costello's lawyer and advisor, described the Prohibition period before 1924 as one in which bootleggers such as Costello organized a virtual naval flotilla with which to smuggle liquor into the U.S. The few Coast Guard boats were unable to compete with the much faster skiffs, which raced their contraband from freighters anchored beyond the three-mile U.S. territorial limit. When the Coast Guard interdicted supplies, newspapers and the public berated them as "pirates." An $8 case of Scotch from the British Isles was sold for $65 on the freighters, $120 at dockside, and, once doctored with three times as much grain alcohol and water, brought around $400. Since many ships carried twenty thousand cases, Costello's wealth eclipsed that of his former mentor, Arnold Rothstein. "And along with his ships and yachts Frank introduced a new element into bootlegging, one that was to bring gasps of surprise in the courtroom in 1926: seaplanes for air coverage . . . the air wing of Frank's defense department" (Ibid., p. 29).

Costello, who lived in the Waldorf Astoria in Manhattan, would dine daily with city bigwigs and had so compromised and corrupted city officials that he claimed to possess an authentic, handwritten resignation letter penned by then Mayor Paul O'Dwyer, a document which could be turned in any time the later-discredited mayor did not keep his end of the bargain. Naval and air operations by organized crime in the twenties bears an uncanny resemblance to the Colombia runs in Florida beginning in the late seventies by drug smugglers in what has been called "The Colombian Connection," "the Cocaine Cowboys" (1980), and "Air Ganja" (Plate, 1975, p. 119).

It was in Chicago in the twenties and the personage of Al "Scarface" Capone and operations like the St. Valentine's Day Massacre that caused an almost stereotyped picture of the mob to be drawn in the public media. Meanwhile in New York, two old "moustache petes" or "greasers" (names given to old-time, Italian-born mafiosi) were involved in a power struggle. The lineup of contending factions reads like a Who's Who of figures who would dominate the La Cosa Nostra for decades to come. Initially aligned with Joe "The Boss" Masseria faction were *Luciano, Genovese, Adonis, Anastasia, Costello, Gambino, and, through financial assistance, Capone. The rival faction, Castellammarese (named after the home town of most of the members, Castellammare del Golfo, Sicily), was headed by Salvatore Maranzano and included *Bonanno, *Profaci, Lucchese, Magliocco, *Gagliano, and Magaddino. Although the Castellammarese Wars were far from the bloodbath erroneously described by chroniclers (Block, 1978), they were important in that the aftermath gave birth to the modern syndicate. Basically Luciano and Genovese and others doublecrossed Masseria and had him killed.

The victor, Maranzano, often described as the "father of the modern LCN syndicate," was a big fan of Julius Caesar and supposedly modeled the organizational structure after the Roman legions. Unfortunately, Maranzano himself was a victim of overweening ambition, picturing himself as "capo di tutti capi" (boss of all bosses). Six months after taking power he also was killed by Meyer Lansky and "Bugsy" Siegel, who had been hired by Luciano, Genovese, and company.

The Luciano Period

Charles "Lucky" Luciano took power over the new organization, one which would have continual alliance (sometimes called the confederation) with other ethnic gangs but which itself would remain exclusively Italian. Avoiding the top boss role, Luciano supported the autonomy of bosses with a commission for settlement of disputes. This alliance was

---

*Together with Vincent Mangano, those indicated by an asterisk would become the "Charter Dons" of the five New York City families.

apparently further consolidated in the thirties and even a special "hit squad"—Murder Inc.—was set up by Louis "Lepke" Buchalter; this group's existence would be later revealed by informant Abe "Kid Twist" Reles. Murder Incorporated's first victim in 1935 was "Dutch" Schultz, who unwisely had himself been advertising his plan to kill District Attorney Thomas Dewey. In 1934 Genovese fled the country in order to escape a murder charge, and in 1937 Luciano himself was sentenced to a thirty to fifty year term for his prostitution business (so much for insulation from prosecution). It was during this period that Frank Costello acted as boss for the imprisoned Luciano. With the repeal of Prohibition, bookmaking and the numbers racket were now the chief operations.

In 1940 informant Abe Reles, despite police guards, mysteriously plunged to his death from a hotel room prior to further testifying in court. It later came to light that the police had been paid off and mobsters had assisted Reles's plunge. This also was a precursor to the mysterious ".22 Caliber Killings" in the seventies in which key federal witnesses and informants were being killed (Gage, 1977b). Questions such as has the Mafia penetrated the FBI were answered when it was discovered that clerks in certain FBI offices had been selling the information to the syndicate.

In 1946, in part for cooperation in *Operation Underworld*, a program where the U.S. Navy enlisted the cooperation of mobsters to prevent sabotage on the docks during the war (Gosch and Hammer, 1974; Gage, 1974), Luciano was paroled into permanent exile and, although Costello was still acting boss, the Genovese era was about to begin.

The Genovese Period

In a curious series of events, Vito Genovese, who had voluntarily exiled himself in 1934 in order to escape a murder indictment, was not only decorated with Italy's highest citizen award by Mussolini during World War II but had been involved in other intrigue. In 1943 he hired Carmine Galante to murder the U.S. editor of an Italian language newspaper that was critical of Mussolini. Picked up for blackmarketing stolen Allied supplies and extradited to the U.S. for the 1934 murder charge, he was "miraculously" a free man when the chief corroborative witness against him was poisoned in a Brooklyn jail.

The postwar period found the mob moving into casino-building in Las Vegas and also the subject of live televised *Kefauver Commission Hearings*. Only the later Watergate hearings would so captivate the public imagination. After testifying before the Kefauver Committee, Costello was a marked man and, barely escaping an assassination attempt, decided to retire. Behind this attempt and other murders, for example, the well-publicized murder by Joey Gallo of Albert Anastasia in the Park Sheraton barber shop in Manhattan, was Genovese, who was now consolidating his power—power which would elude him in what was to have been the "coronation," a mob convention planned for Chicago three weeks later.

The Apalachin Meetings

Although a major mob meeting was planned for Chicago, Steve Magaddino (the Buffalo boss), for his own health reasons which prevented long travel, offered the Apalachin, New York estate of one of his members. Besides the recognition of Genovese as top boss and assurances of peace to Costello, the meeting agenda included confirmation of the mob's antidrug policy and the need for new memberships (Talese, 1971, p. 213; Bonanno, 1983). The last was a sore point because, due to the lack of new blood, the vitality of the syndicate was of concern. Suspicions regarding informers and of the lack of discipline among American-born recruits led some families to recruit "greenies" from Sicily's *latifondi* or farming areas (Reid, 1970, p. 72).

Before the session ended, a police raid temporarily detaining a large number of those in attendance and obtaining their names was disastrous to the anonymity the syndicate desired. Even more catastrophic than the Kefauver hearings, this evidence of the existence of some type of coordinated, national syndicate was now hard to deny (Bonanno, 1983). In 1958 an informant, Nelson Cantellops, assisted in convicting twenty-four people, including Genovese, Galante, and Joseph Valachi. Having received "the kiss of death" from Genovese in prison, and feeling that he was marked for execution, Valachi murdered by mistake a fellow prisoner and became the first public "made member" informant from the ranks of organized crime and star witness at the McClellan Commission Hearings on Organized Crime.

The Gambino Period

From the mid-sixties until late eighties the IAS, rather than operating as an IBM-type corporation described in Cosa Nostra theory, seemed to more resemble the "patron model." "The Gallo-Profaci Wars," the attempted Colombo assassination, "The Banana Split," and the "Gallo-Colombo Wars" (Diapoulos and Linakis, 1976; Talese, 1971) suggested continuing internal strife. Perhaps a coup-plagued, unstable, small Latin American country would be a better model than a large corporation in describing the IAS. While Carlo Gambino was consolidating his power during this period, a commentary regarding the 1969 truce in the Banana Wars (a rift in the Joseph Bonanno family) may have best described the dilemma faced by the IAS: "What the Mafia needed in New York in 1969 was a health clinic, not a gang war" (MacLean, 1974, pp. 341–342). Most of the leaders were dying or sick. Many of the leaders were in their seventies and their middle-level executives, due to membership moratoriums, were not much younger. Gambino controlled four of the five New York mobs with only the Bonanno family not in the fold. Although forced into involuntary exile in Arizona by the commission, Bonanno still controlled his New York organization through various loyalists. In 1974 his long-time underboss Carmine "The Cigar" Galante was released from a twelve-year stretch in federal penitentiaries. Galante announced his return by blasting off the bronze doors on Frank Costello's mausoleum, warring against blacks and Hispanics for the control of narcotics in the South Bronx and Harlem, and finally, according to unnamed mob sources, arranging for the death of Gambino himself by persuading the elderly, coronary-prone man to get a swine flu shot* ("After the Don," 1976, p. 32).

With the death of Gambino in 1976, many speculations took place as to who was likely to emerge as the most influential boss. Three chief contenders under discussion at a motel near Kennedy Airport in late 1976 were Joseph Bonanno, Anielo "O'Neill" Dellacroce, and Carmine Galante (Ibid., 1976). Bonanno was indicted and Dellacroce died, while Galante was killed gangland style in July 1979 in a New York restaurant with a cigar still in his mouth. Another pretender to the crown, Frank "Funzi" Tieri, head of the old Genovese mob, was convicted as a result of Fratianno's testimony and is since deceased. Continuing assassinations in the early eighties of Philadelphia boss Angelo Bruno and his successor Phil Testa suggest ongoing rivalry and upheaval in the LCN, particularly over organized crime control of Atlantic City gambling, which Gambino, Genovese, and Bruno crime families all have their eye upon.

In 1984 Boss Paul Castellano of the Gambino family and two of his top lieutenants were indicted for extortion, pattern of racketeering, and conspiracies to commit murder. Castellano had emerged as the most powerful of the dons and appeared to be in a position to claim the "national crown" when he was gunned down in Manhattan outside a restaurant December 16, 1985. Upon being indicted he had posted bail of $2 million and his "friends" may have feared that, at age seventy,

---

*During an expected swine flu epidemic in 1976, the U.S. government ran a free inoculation campaign but warned it was unwise for the elderly or those with heart problems to receive the shot.

he might turn informant rather than die in jail. The FBI believes that the person responsible for this assassination was an ambitious younger man, John Gotti, who then seized control of the Gambino family. Maas (1986a, p. 8) claims that, as a result of all of the indictments: "Cosa Nostra is rapidly becoming just another gang of hoodlums, which is all it really ever was."

The Commission Trials

Undoubtedly, the biggest blow ever dealt to the Italian-American Syndicate was a series of prosecutions of organized crime figures by the federal government from 1983–1987. Indictments in 1985 alone reached almost five thousand, and alleged leaders of sixteen of the twenty-four "Mafia" families were indicted. Albanese (1989, p. 3) in accounting the

John Gotti was the only major survivor of the "Commission Trials" and emerged as the most powerful leader of the weakened Italian-American Syndicate.

impact of the trials indicated that both a Mafia and commission were admitted to exist.

The outcome of the trials crippled the aging upper structure of the "Mafia" families. Figures such as the bosses of the Colombo, Genovese, and Lucchese organized crime families were convicted of being members of "the Commission," the same one established by Luciano in 1931, which settled underworld disputes and authorized gangland killings (Doyle, 1987). The only major survivor of the "Commission Trials" was John Gotti, who has emerged as the most powerful of bosses of an organization that now had been weakened by criminal justice and media attention, creating a vacuum to be filled by rival ethnic gangs (Mustain and Capeci, 1988). In referring to Gotti's emergence to head a decimated "Mafia," one magazine article was entitled, "*The Last Godfather?*" (McKillop, 1989).

Some of the competition includes the six thousand-member Herrera family from Mexico, triple the size of the "Mafia" and developing ties with Colombian groups, particularly in Chicago. Outlaw motorcycle gangs, Colombian cocaine crime families, black criminal gangs, and Asian gangs are among the many new mobs contending for this vacated territory.

Other Developments

Jamaican organized crime groups, "posses," operate not only in Jamaica, but increasingly in the U.S. and Canada and are involved in narcotics trafficking, firearms smuggling, money laundering, fraud, kidnapping, robbery and murder. A bizarre relationship exists between rival political parties in Jamaica which are aligned with rival posses. Many of the latter send some of the proceeds from U.S. drug operations back home to finance political campaigns (Pincomb, 1989).

Black organized crime groups are not an example of an emerging group, but have existed for decades (Messick, 1979; Abadinsky, 1985; and Pennsylvania Crime Commission, 1986). While some of the better known organizations were those run by Frank Matthews, Charles Lucas, Leroy Barnes, and Jeff Fort (El Rukns), a variety of groups have been and are involved in such things as drug trafficking, the numbers racket, extortion, and murder. In Philadelphia in the eighties a tightly knit criminal organization calling itself "The Family" specialized in drug distribution and murder.

Organized crime remains a "queer ladder of mobility" (Bell, 1964) for black mobs in Philadelphia and New York, Colombian and Cuban mobs in Florida, and Chinese and Chicano mobs on the West Coast. Although many of these mobs are not fully developed and structured syndicates as in the polar extreme of the organized crime model, they certainly represent an evolving force to be reckoned with. In a dissenting view, Lupsha (1981) argues that Italian organized crime groups still retain predominant power in many key areas of underworld crime, while Reuter (1984a) sees them as paper tigers living off the laurels of their past reputation.

"The Pizza Connection"

In late 1985 to early 1986, a trial of twenty-two defendants took place in New York City, alleging they ran a $1.7 billion drug trafficking organization in the United States, using pizza restaurants as fronts. This group was a "Sicilian Mafia," supposedly separate from and with few links with the existing "American Mafia" according to Tommaso Buscetta, who revealed to U.S. authorities their operations (Ibid.) Federal authorities did, however, find some links with "American Mafia" groups as well as cooperation in money laundering by Swiss and Italian banks and by U.S. brokerage firms, E.F. Hutton and Merrill Lynch. Sicilian immigrants, called "zips" due to their rapid speech patterns, staffed these pizza parlors (Potter, 1989; Blumenthal, 1988; and Alexander, 1988).

The Great Mafia Trial in Sicily

With the closing of the Corsican "French Connection" in the seventies, organized crime figures in Sicily began to supply large amounts of heroin to the U.S. and in the early eighties began a "civil war" over control of this lucrative trade. Their violence spilled over, involving the murder of the head of the Italian anti-mob squad, General Carlo Chiesa, and his pregnant wife, as well as the murder of Judge Caesar Terranova. This enraged the Sicilian public, the church, and public officials, and spelled the doom of Sicilian mafia groups. In February 1986 over 456 members and associates of organized crime groups were put on trial, including Michele "Pope" Greco, according to some to be the "boss of bosses." The trial took place in a specially-constructed courtroom guarded by two hundred crack troops and ended in December 1987 with 338, including Greco, convicted. The key witness in the trial was a former boss, Tommaso Buscetta, who also testified in the "Pizza Connection" trials in the United States (Gage, 1988, pp. 36–37).

Criminal Careers of Organized Criminals

Similar to professional crime, but unlike most other types of crime, organized criminal activity is an example of career crime, in which crime is pursued as a livelihood. Organized criminals exhibit varying degrees of the following characteristics, with those who are members of established syndicates expressing these qualities to a greater degree: they identify with crime and criminal activity, possess strong organizational identity, and tend to belong to structured groups that maintain continuance of operation.

Based upon our previous description of organized crime, such criminals tend to be bred in low income, high crime areas of large central cities, where illegitimate opportunity structures appear more available than legitimate ones. Most begin careers as conventional criminals, but, rather than retiring, as most do in their early twenties, they continue to progress in criminality and in association with organized criminals (Clinard and Quinney, 1973, p. 229). The quick, "high" life-style epitomized by successful local crime figures provides an "attractive" role model for large-city slum dwellers. Neighborhood criminal gangs represent the sandlots or "minor leagues" of organized crime, from which the best players may be selected.

To varying degrees, organized criminal groups subscribe to a code of secrecy, whether it be the "cosa de hombre" (code of manliness) of the "Nuestra Cosa" (Mexican Mafia), rules of conduct of gangs such as Hell's Angels or the Pagans, or the prototype code of "omerta" described by people like Valachi. "Omerta" is a "Cosa Nostra" code of intense loyalty, honor, secrecy, obedience, and "manly" silence—a code which renders loyalty to the organization above that to one's country, God, or family and whose violation means death. Much of the ritual appears tied to more older-generation mafiosi and Albini suggests that rather than being a unique criminal code, omerta was a general condition of Sicilian society (Albini, 1971).

Organized criminals are highly committed to pursuing criminal careers and are also committed to the rational pursuit of crime as an economic livelihood. Modern syndicates attempt to "avoid heat" (violence which causes public and media uproar and subsequent police activity) and "amateurish bravado" and emotional, unplanned elements of criminal activity.

Secrecy, discipline, corruption, planned violence, and public demand for illicit goods in either compromised or inept political climates provide a continuing good occupational outlook for the next generation of Valachis, whatever their ethnicity. The continuing public demand for illicit goods and services and corrupt relationship with government officials may be more important factors in the persistence of organized groups than the imperviousness of their organizations.

Public and Legal Reaction

Later in Chapter 13 we will explore the issue of drug abuse from the standpoint of users, but our concern in this chapter has been drug trafficking in which international drug "kingpins" such as Jorge Ochoa, Pablo Escobar, and Gonzalo Rodriguez are the new Al Capones and Meyer Lanskys. In the late eighties the United States began to go after major drug "kingpins." In May 1988 Carlos Lehder-Rivas, who had been extradited from Colombia, was convicted of being responsible for up to 80 percent of the cocaine smuggled into the U.S. In 1989 leaders of Colombia's Medellin Cartel were indicted on charges of cocaine trafficking, and the slayings of the Colombian justice minister as well as of a U.S. drug informant (U.S. Indicts, 1989). Attempts to put pressure on the "Underground Empire" of drug launderers and officials were illustrated by efforts to depose Panamanian strongman Manuel Noriega.

Drug Control Strategies

Some drug control strategies or options include: "legalization," "use of diplomacy," "interdiction," "targeting traffickers," "coordination of rival departments," and "prevention" (Adler, et al., 1988; and Moore, 1988). *"Legalization"* is viewed as a last resort gamble, an unnecessary risk, and a questionable moral decision. It would appear unwise in overreacting to a crack epidemic to legalize and create more demand for drugs at a time in which overall drug use is declining. *"The use of diplomacy"* or economic and political pressure to halt the drug war being waged against the U.S. by Colombia, Bolivia, Peru, and Mexico in particular is a supply-side strategy which is not without risk. "Anti-Yanqui" feelings may be fueled, and many countries are dependent upon drug money. *"Interdiction"* involves stopping the transport and smuggling of drugs into the U.S. With many ports of entry and endless borders, some deterrence is possible; but complete interdiction is impossible.

"Targetting major traffickers" such as the Medellin Cartel while enhancing street-level enforcement to totally disrupt street traffic in drugs (Hayeslip, 1989) contains possibilities. *"Departmental coordination"* and elimination of rivalry is claimed to be aided by the creation of a federal "drug czar" in 1989 (William Bennett) to oversee and coordinate agencies involved in the drug war. Finally, a "demand-side" strategy of *"prevention"* holds the ultimate hope. Education and rehabilitation programs as well as policy experiments to discover programs which work are in great need.

In *The War on Drugs* Inciardi (1986, p. 211) indicates, " . . . it would appear that contemporary American drug-control policies, with some very needed additions and changes, would be the most appropriate approach." The problem is that the current approach lacks a true commitment and requires more funds and personnel for interdiction, for education and rehabilitation programs. These improvements, plus full use of RICO and new statutes which permit asset seizures (to be discussed shortly), may be the solution.

Organized crime has owed its existence to the vast amounts of money to be earned from a cooperating public that demands the illicit services it regularly offered: illegal alcohol, gambling, drugs, or sex. Such large amounts were and are made and organized on such a national scale that the power of syndicates to compromise and corrupt particularly local officials virtually went unchallenged until the sixties. In the sixties and seventies, rivalry between agencies such as the FBI, IRS, and Drug Enforcement Agency broke down the somewhat successful special federal strike forces organized to fight organized crime. The Strike Force concept, operating at one time in twenty-six cities, combined the efforts of Justice Department lawyers; federal bureaus such as the FBI, DEA, Alcohol, Tobacco and Firearms, Labor, IRS; and local law enforcement. In 1989 Attorney General Dick Thornburgh was considering modifying all such strike forces to resemble a model similar to that for the Southern District of New York, where strike force attorneys were merged into local offices and no longer reported directly to Washington.

Investigative Procedures

Law enforcement in the eighties finally became as organized as organized criminals and began to effectively apply a *variety of investigative procedures including*: financial analysis, electronic surveillance, use of informants and undercover agents, citizens' commissions (Albanese, 1989, pp. 105–120), and computer assistance. *Financial analysis* involves following paper trails (records of transaction) in order to see if expenditures match up with earnings. Classic Internal Revenue Service procedures in enforcing tax codes such as analyzing net worth, expenditures, and bank deposits are utilized.

Electronic surveillance (the use of "bugs" and wiretapping in covert eavesdropping) is viewed by many authorities as one of, if not the, most effective weapon against organized crime. The use of 150 audio and videotapes at the "Commission Trials" was very successful. The *use of informants* (insiders who provide information) as well as *undercover agents* has also been indispensable. Informants such as Jackie Presser (former Teamster President), Angelo Lonardo (former Cleveland don), or Tommaso Buscetta (Sicilian "Mafia" don) have been devastating to syndicate silence. *Citizens commissions* such as the Chicago Crime Commission are essential in providing an independent watchdog function in examining organized criminal activity (Albanese, 1989, p. 116).

Finally, *computer assisted investigation* has great potential for unravelling complicated transactions and network interrelationships. The FBI uses a sophisticated computer data base, the Organized Crime Information System, and is experimenting with artificial intelligence using a super computer called Big Floyd.

Laws and Organized Crime

Some specific laws which have been used against organized crime include: special laws such as the Hobbs Act; features of the Organized Crime Control Act of 1970, especially RICO (Racketeer Influence in Corrupt Organizations), the Bank Secrecy Act (1970), as well as asset seizure (forfeiture).

Hobbs Act

One effective piece of legislation on the books since the mid-forties is the *Hobbs Act,* an anti-racketeering act which basically can be interpreted to mean that any interference with interstate commerce to any degree whatsoever is in violation of the act. This statute has been applied, for example, against politicians in Newark, New Jersey, in accepting kickbacks from contractors who had obtained supplies from out of state.

Organized Crime Control Act

The single most effective piece of federal legislation ever passed in the U.S. to fight organized crime activity is the controversial Organized Crime Control Act of 1970 (1970), a principal feature of which is the RICO statute. RICO (Racketeer Influence in Corrupt Organizations) prohibits proceeds from a pattern of racketeering activity from being used in acquiring legitimate businesses which are involved in interstate commerce. Generally, a "pattern of racketeering" involves participation in any two of specified crimes, such as murder or extortion, within a ten-year period.

Some of the principal features of the act were: the creation of special grand juries to investigate organized criminal activity, and the provision of general immunity for witnesses appearing before the grand jury, in which the privilege against self-incrimination is abrogated in return for protection against the use of such compelled information in a criminal proceeding. It provides for the incarceration of witnesses who refuse to testify (recalcitrant witnesses), authorizes a conviction based on irreconcilably inconsistent declarations under oath (perjury), as well as providing for protected facilities for housing government witnesses and their families. It also authorizes the government to preserve testimony by the use of a deposition ("deposit of papers") in a criminal proceeding, a right which previously existed only for the defendant, and prohibits any challenge to the admissibility of evidence based on its being the fruit of an unlawful government act, if such act occurred five years or more before the event sought to be proved. The act makes it unlawful to engage in the operation of the "illegal gambling business" itself and contains the RICO (Racketeer Influence in Corrupt Organizations) statute, which prohibits the use of the proceeds from a pattern of racketeering activity from being used in acquiring legitimate enterprises which are involved in interstate commerce. It also authorizes increased sentences for dangerous special offenders, provides for regulation of explosives, and calls for a review by a National Commission on Individual Rights of the above and any other federal laws or executive action which may have bearing on individual rights.

The Bank Secrecy Act (1970) is directed at controlling money laundering. It includes features which require that banks must report transactions over ten thousand dollars or file a report if ten thousand dollars or more leaves or enters the country, and requires that citizens must report foreign bank accounts on tax returns (Abadinsky, 1985, pp. 240–243). Assets seizure (forfeiture) has emerged as one of the most powerful tools to break the back of criminal enterprises—"kick them in the assets," so to speak. "Forfeiture, the ancient legal practice of government seizure of property used in criminal activity, may prove a particularly useful weapon against illicit narcotics trafficking" (Stellwagen, 1985, p. 1). Imprisonment and fines have been found inadequate in deterring capital organizations, while seizure of assets curtails the financial ability of such groups to continue criminal operations (Bureau of Justice Statistics, 1988, p. 93). Assets may include money, property, businesses, cars, boats, or any item which may have been involved in or the product of a criminal enterprise. Particularly attractive has been some modifications in federal laws which permit local law enforcement agencies to share in the forfeited assets and then use these to finance police operations. Some controversies have developed regarding overzealous seizures as well as limitations on defense attorney fees by freezing assets in pretrial proceedings (Witkin, 1988, pp. 20–22).

The RICO Statute

The *RICO Statute* authorizes the federal government to seize legitimate operations if they have been purchased with illegally gained funds (laundering) or if they are used for criminal purposes. In addition, defendants can be subject to up to twenty years imprisonment. The law permits prosecutors greater latitude in presenting a broader picture to a jury of patterns of racketeering; this enables them to trace back to formerly insulated bosses. In the trial of John Christopher in Tampa, Florida, prosecutors were permitted to call fifty witnesses to describe Christopher's activity over a thirteen-year period as head of a "white slavery" prostitution ring (Press, Shannon, and Simons, 1979).

While the witness immunity and protection features have been quite useful in obtaining the cooperation of and indispensable services of informants like Jimmy Fratianno, problems have surfaced with regard to adequacy of protection and compensation of protected witnesses. Also due to the broad sweep of the law, lawyers and others are fearful of the pattern of application of the law to nonsyndicate crime, such as crimes by legitimate business.

At the time of the passage of the law many criticized RICO as an exceptional measure (moral entrepreneurship, if you wish) which was passed/engineered in order to grant unusual powers to the government as a result of capitalizing upon public fear of crime, a ploy for the "erosion of justice and equality in America" (Smith, 1980, p. 331). However, it had broadened the classification of "organized lawbreaking" to include political corruption and white collar crime. In 1979 in U.S. District Court, a case was dismissed against five men accused of a Texas oil swindle. The presiding judge was quoted as saying, "RICO was designed to take racketeers out of business, not to make racketeers out of businessmen" (Mitchell, 1981, 41). RICO held that criminal associations need not be *wholly* corrupt; that is, they could be partly legitimate, thus permitting application to private business, labor unions, law enforcement, judicial, and government offices. If the illegal income is derived from, or is used to acquire interest in or in order to conduct an enterprise, then it is eligible for RICO. The following individuals or organizations have been RICO-ed: a hospital equipment business, the Macon County Sheriff's Department, a Florida state judge (his judicial district was named as the enterprise), a pornography operation, bailbondsmen, an oil platform construction company, a Michigan mayor (for shaking down real estate developers), and crooked pharmacists and nursing home operators (Press, Shannon, and Simons, 1979, pp. 82–83).

G. Robert Blakey, the original author of the RICO statute, sees RICO as a radical new way of thinking about criminal prosecution:

Under common law, a crime was committed and only that evidence which was related to that specific crime was admissable in court. RICO changed this and recognized that crime does not occur in a vacuum; that other events precede and follow criminal conduct. It is this concept of continuing criminal activity that RICO brings to modern day law. . . . "RICO" will change the practice of law, as we once knew it (cited in Martens, 1988, p. 11).

RICO charges offer a unique advantage in targeting an entire enterprise and civil RICO laws can be used to seize cash and assets. Application of RICO charges to white collar violations, such as inside trading by brokerage firm Drexel, Burnham, Lambert, raises controversy. Civil RICO permits victims of fraud to bring private civil suits whether or not the Justice Department files charges (RICO, 1989, p. 18). Threatened companies, it is claimed, are forced to settle, rather than be branded racketeers. While some critics see it as a "statute run amok" (Boucher, 1989), others see it as a powerful tool to control white collar crime in addition to organized crime (Waldman and Gilbert, 1989; see also Safire, 1989; and Mansnerus, 1989).

This federal acceptance of the generic definitions of organized crime—which would include corrupt business executives, professionals, and public officials—in the application of the Organized Crime Control Act presents an apparent anomaly for those who would hold that the act represents a strategy of powerful interests to focus upon alien or ethnic conspiracies, such as Italian syndicates, while ignoring the crimes of the powerful. Granted it has not been utilized to attack antitrust activity, which may be beyond its legal mandate; but it has been used in cases involving political corruption, business fraud, and other professional crimes.

In discussing law enforcement efforts and the future of traditional racketeering, Robert Rhodes (1984, pp. 265–269) identifies four policy options: decriminalization, civil/administrative action (regulation through zoning and licensing), reduction of profitability, and suppression by means of criminal sanction. Decriminalization involves the lessening of criminal penalties attached to traditional vice-related crime, organized crime's "bread and butter." Regulation involves licensing and zoning of vice-related activities. Such a policy is aimed at controlling rather than eliminating such activities. Reduction of profitability can be illustrated by better insurance regulations with respect to arson payments (Ibid., p. 268), while suppression can occur through electronic surveillance, special grand juries, and other controversial provisions of the Organized Crime Control Act.

Until 1981 many features of RICO had lain dormant. In a case against IAS boss Frank Tieri the government alleged that Mafia families themselves constituted illegal enterprises. Los Angeles mobsters were also convicted of racketeering and conspiracy charges (Mitchell, 1981, p. 43). As an exercise in what this author would call "creative law enforcement" prior to his assassination, gangster Carmine Galante's parole was revoked on the basis of his knowingly associating with criminal elements. Mention should be once against made of yet another area of "creative law enforcement," which was made most famous with the ABSCAM operation, the undercover sting where police agents pretended to be involved in criminal operations themselves. "Operation Miporn," "Unirac," or "Brilab" are all likely to express the types of aggressive operations necessary to root out aggressive and insulated syndicates.

Summary

The subject of much public interest, organized crime has been defined in a variety of ways. In the United States most federal agency and state statutes use definitions of the generic type, which indicate that organized crime is any criminal activity involving two or more individuals. Utilizing a similar *generic (broad or general) definition*, Albini identifies four types of organized crime: political-social organized crime, mercenary (predatory) organized crime, in-group oriented organized crime, and syndicate crime. With the exception of the last type, syndicate crime, all of the former refer to other types of criminal activity, such as political, conventional, or professional criminal behavior.

A *criminological definition* of organized crime (henceforth synonymous with syndicate crime) as a continuing group or *organization*:

1. that participates in illicit activity in any society by the *use of force, intimidation, or threats*;
2. that *provides illicit services that are in strong public demand*; and
3. that assures protection and *immunity* through corruption.

An *organized crime model* is proposed as a useful device for avoiding confusion in the process of deciding whether a group's activities represent an example of organized crime. Organized crime as a concept is *not a matter of kind*, but is rather *a matter of degree*; that is, to what extent does this type of crime possess the characteristics identified in our criminological definition of organized crime? Types of crime may be viewed as distributed along a *continuum* ranging from nonorganized to organized (syndicate) crime, depending upon the degree to which they exhibit organization, the use or threat of violence, the provision of illicit goods in public demand, and the ability to obtain immunity through corruption and enforcement. *Types of organized (syndicate) crime include:* traditional crime syndicates, nontraditional syndicates, semiorganized crime, local politically controlled organized crime, and national politically controlled organized crime.

In addition to definitional problems, another problematic concern in the study of organized crime is the poor scientific nature of much of the literature which forces the social scientist to rely upon many journalistic and autobiographical accounts. A variety of street gangs were described, and some were noted to be undergoing transition into ghetto-based drug trafficking organizations.

Internationally, organized crime thrives in two types of political environments: liberal democracies and corrupt dictatorships. *Chinese Triad societies,* highly ritualized Chinese secret organizations which are often involved in organized crime, were described. Organized crime, although dominated since the thirties by the Italian-American syndicate, has had and has involvement from a variety of ethnic groups, according to the "theory of ethnic succession," mobs have represented a "queer ladder of mobility" for a variety of minorities.

Primary drug smuggling routes—the Golden Triangle, Crescent, and Latin America—were discussed as were the Medellin Cartel, Underground Empire, and Narco-Terrorism.

Various theories regarding the origin of the term *Mafia* were traced, with the author agreeing with Albini that the most likely explanation was the appearance of Rizzotto's play, *I Mafiusi de la Vicaria* ("The Heroes of the Penitentiary") in 1860. Three *theories of* the nature of syndicate crime in the U.S. were discussed: (1) Cosa Nostra theory, (2) confederation theory, and (3) patron theory. While the first theory, which has been accepted by federal commissions and agencies, views organized crime as centrally controlled by a formally structured Italian-American syndicate, confederation theory views it as controlled by a "combination" of ethnic groups, principally Jewish and Italian. The patron theory views organized crime as a set of shifting alliances, a "client-patron" relationship.

The "Mafia myth" is the belief that organized crime is the product of an alien conspiracy. More moderate expressions of this theme view the IAS (Italian American Syndicate) as the most powerful of organized crime groups, but not the product of an alien conspiracy. Critics of the Mafia or Cosa Nostra (LCN, "La Cosa Nostra") model argue that the terms and descriptions of these organizations are fictitious, the creations of federal law enforcement agencies. A more moderate view admits many of their criticisms, but still argues that the IAS exists, the vision being "skewed, not false."

The *classic pattern of organized crime* involves a gradual evolutionary development from strategic and tactical crimes, to illegal businesses and activities, to legitimate businesses, to an infiltration of big business and government itself. Some typical operations of organized criminal groups are arson, assault, coercion, extortion, murder, blackmail, bribery, and corruption. Typical illegal businesses include gambling operations, loan sharking, labor racketeering, record and tape piracy, and any number of other activities detailed in the chapter. Infiltration of legitimate businesses such as trucking, construction, and the hotel and restaurant industry provides cover for organized crime operations. Although hazardous to guess, estimated gross revenues and untaxed net profits appear to make organized crime wealthier than the nation's largest industrial corporation.

Organized crime infiltration of legitimate businesses may be viewed on one hand as a natural "ethnic succession" out of organized crime, and on the other hand as yet another setting for illegitimate operations. Involvement of organized crime at the highest levels of government is revealed by a "CIA-Mafia link," an attempt to assassinate Fidel Castro.

A *brief history* of organized crime traces its origins back to colonial times. The New Orleans Grand Jury report of 1890 was the first official recognition of the existence of the Mafia in this country. Other important events in the history of organized crime were traced, such as the Prohibition period, the Castellammarese Wars, the Luciano era, the Genovese era, the Kefauver and McClellan commission hearings, the Apalachin meetings, the Gambino era, and other, more recent developments in organized crime such as the Commission Trials, Pizza Connection, and "Great Mafia Trial" in Sicily.

Criminal careers of organized criminals are briefly examined. Highlighted was their strong identification with criminal careers, their recruitment, and relationship with the public. Finally public and legal reaction to organized crime is discussed. While public reaction to organized crime in the past was characterized as a fascinated apathy and sporadic and unorganized legal reaction, recent events suggest major inroads in the war on organized crime. Application of laws such as the Hobbs Act and the Organized Crime Control Act (1970) represent potent tools. The *RICO* (Racketeer Influence in Corrupt Organizations) feature of the latter and "sting" operations by federal agencies represent creative law enforcement efforts in this regard. However, these more aggressive law enforcement efforts have been criticized as threatening civil liberties and operating as a smokescreen for ignoring corporate criminality.

KEY CONCEPTS

Four Basic Types of Organized Crime (Generic Definition)

Three Elements of the Definition of Organized (Syndicate) Crime

Continuum Model of Organized Crime

International Political Climates and Organized Crime

Yakuza

Triads

Classic Pattern of Organized Crime

Activities of Organized Criminals

"Bust Out"

The Numbers Game

Loan sharking

Racketeering

CIA-Mafia Link

Assets Forfeiture

Medellin Cartel

Narco-Terrorism

Ethnic Succession Theory

Theories Regarding Origin of Mafia

Theories of the Nature of U.S. Syndicate Crime

Major Elements of La Cosa Nostra (LCN) Theory

Internal Structure of LCN Families

"Moustache Petes"

"Castellammarese Wars"

Kefauver Commission

Apalachin Meetings

Strike Forces

Hobbs Act

Organized Crime Control Act

RICO

Iron Law of Opium Trade

Pizza Connection

Commission Trials

13 Public Order Crime

Introduction

Public order criminal behavior, sometimes referred to as "crimes without victims" (Schur, 1965) or "legislated morality," refers to a number of activities that are illegal due to the fact that they offend public morality. Such nonpredatory crime generally includes activities such as prostitution, acts related to homosexuality, alcohol and narcotics abuse, gambling offenses, disorderly conduct, vagrancy, and minor forms of "sexual deviance." These crimes outnumber other recorded crimes and have traditionally represented the bulk of police work.

A number of other concepts have been used with which to refer to certain categories of public order criminal activity. Laurence Ross (1961) coined the term "folk crime" with which to refer to relatively common violations which occur in part due to the complexity of modern society. Traffic offenses, fish and game law violations, tax offenses, gambling and sexual deviations all can serve as illustrations. Many, but not all, of the activities to be discussed in this section are examples of crimes which are *mala prohibita*, bad because they have been prohibited by law. They violate various conceptions in society as to appropriate moral conduct, but lack the quality of acts *mala in se*, such as murder or rape, in which there is clear and abhorrent victimization of others. Offenses related to prostitution, homosexuality, gambling, and the like serve as examples of "consensual crimes" (Sanders, 1983, p. 200) in that there is free consent on the part of participants. In many "victimless" crimes, the offenders have customers rather than victims (Silberman, 1978, p. 265).

Nuts, Sluts, Guts, and "Preverts"

Alexander Liazos (1972) published what has now become a classic sociological title, an article entitled "The Poverty of the Sociology of Deviance: Nuts, Sluts and 'Preverts.'" Liazos makes the point that sociologists have concentrated too much on the "dramatic" nature of deviance, such as prostitution, homosexuality, and the like, at the expense of neglecting more serious or harmful forms of deviance such as racism, inequitable taxation, and sexism. He states (Ibid., p. 26):

> As a result of the fascination with "nuts, sluts and preverts [sic]," and their identities and subcultures, little attention has been paid

to the unethical, illegal, and destructive actions of powerful individuals, groups, and institutions in our society. Because these actions are carried out quietly in the normal course of events, the sociology of deviance does not consider them as part of its subject matter.

This chapter will concentrate upon behavior that has been labeled criminal or deviant because it is viewed either as different or as immoral or harmful to the individual. Societal attempts to regulate deviance (nuts), sex (sluts), drug and alcohol consumption (guts), and perversion (other activity) will be explored. The reader may find this "walk on the wild side" vicariously romantic or exciting; in perspective, such behavior is less costly and harmful to the society as a whole than other types which have been examined, such as occupational, organizational, and violent crime. Public order violations often offend the moral sensibilities of some groups and are viewed as undermining the moral fabric of society.

Broken Windows

In their classic article "Broken Windows," Wilson and Kelling (1982) give a different view of the need to regulate such conduct.

> Just as unrepaired broken windows can signal to people that nobody cares about a building and lead to more serious vandalism, untended disorderly behavior can also signal that nobody cares about the community and lead to more serious disorder and crime. Such signals—untended property, disorderly persons, drunks, obstreperous youth, etc.—both create fear in citizens and attract predators (Kelling, 1988a, p. 2).

Neighborhood disorder, drunks, panhandlers, youth gangs, and other incivilities unsettle a community and produce fear and disrupt social, commercial, and political life. Citizens desire the regulation of many activities we would describe as public order crime.

Legal Aspects

In this section we will briefly introduce the legal aspects of each activity and then later in this chapter return to each of these activities and describe them in detail. We will begin with the legal aspects of prostitution.

Prostitution

Prostitution can be defined as the practice of having sexual relations with emotional indifference on a promiscuous and mercenary basis.

In some countries and most U.S. states, prostitution itself is not a criminal offense; it is the act of soliciting, selling, or seeking paying customers which is prohibited. Although sometimes referred to in jest as the "world's oldest profession," prostitution certainly has been widespread in societies, both ancient and modern.

Until the Protestant Reformation in Western society, prostitution was pervasive and tolerated as a "necessary evil." It was often taxed by the church and a major source of community revenue in the Middle Ages. Public health concerns that arose with the introduction of syphilis from the New World and the emergence of the Protestant ethic with its strong emphasis upon individual morality were instrumental in its prohibition. Essentially, concepts of sin were translated into legal notions of crime. Despite its prohibition, prostitution exists internationally, with the exception of some preliterate societies where it would be in little demand. While prostitution is generally regarded as a low-status occupation in societies in which it is approved, in different cultures in the past certain prostitutes have enjoyed high status, such as the *hetaerae* of early Greece, the *lupanaria* in the Roman Empire, the *devadasis* in India, and *geishas* of Japan (Davis, 1961). Such courtesans often were well educated and trained entertainers or religious performers.

In most U.S. states, prostitution is considered a misdemeanor, and laws prohibiting the practice are generally enforced only when the public insists upon it. Typically prostitutes are rounded up, booked, made to pay a small bail or fine, and then are put back on the streets. In order to control the undesirable activities often associated with prostitution and to avoid public complaint, many cities create vice zones or "combat zones," adult entertainment areas.

Homosexual Behavior

Homosexuality refers to sexual relationship with members of one's own sex. While homosexuality itself is not a crime, certain homosexual activities may be considered criminal, depending upon various state or national laws. In certain states, homosexual activity, like some heterosexual activity, may be included under various laws prohibiting adultery, fornication, sodomy, crimes against nature, or lewd and lascivious conduct. Adultery prohibits sexual relations between individuals if at least one of the parties is married to someone else. Fornication refers to sexual intercourse between unmarried persons. Sodomy or "crimes against nature" may cover anal intercourse, mouth-genital contact, and even mutual masturbation. The term *sodomy* is derived from the biblical city of Sodom, which (together with Gomorrah) was destroyed by God's wrath due to its rampant eroticism.

Following Judeo-Christian precepts, homosexuality was strongly forbidden and punished in European countries until the advent of the French Revolution, after which the laws became more tolerant. Although puritanical America was slower in liberalizing its laws, sodomy statutes generally are not enforced or are selectively enforced for extortion or blackmail purposes.

From the standpoint of law enforcement, there is some criminal activity associated with the homosexual community, primarily on the part of those preying upon homosexuals; entrapment, swindling, robbery, blackmail, and sometimes murder may take place. Of primary concern to the criminal justice system are cases in which the behavior is nonconsensual or involves underage minors. Also warranting attention are activities which take place in association with pickups or solicitations in public places, often involving male prostitutes who serve an almost exclusively homosexual clientele.

In 1973 the American Psychiatric Association voted at their national convention that homosexuality was no longer to be considered a mental illness, although a later survey of members found that a majority still regarded homosexuality as immature and abnormal behavior (Rathus, 1983, p. 395). Up to the sixties, all states forbade such conduct.

In 1986 the U.S. Supreme Court upheld a Georgia law which prohibits sodomy (oral or anal sexual relations) between consenting adults. The law carried a punishment of twenty years in prison. That year twenty-six states, mostly in the South and West, prohibited acts defined as sodomy; and in only five states did this refer solely to homosexual activity (Press, et al., 1986).

Sexual Offenses

Albert Ellis (1979, p. 406) lists the following sex-related acts as commonly prohibited and penalized:

1. Forcible sexual assault
2. Forcible rape
3. Statutory rape
4. Incest
5. Noncoital sexual relations with a minor
6. Exhibitory sex acts
7. Obscenity
8. Homosexuality
9. Transvestism
10. Voyeurism or peeping
11. Sex murder

12. Sodomy
13. Adultery
14. Fornication
15. Prostitution
16. Pimping or pandering
17. Brothel-keeping

While sexual assault, rape, and adult sexual relations with minors are taken very seriously by the criminal justice system, most of the other acts have been subject to less attention by authorities in the past two decades and attract response only when they involve other criminal activity (see Lowman, 1986; and Sullivan, 1988).

In addition to prostitution and homosexual offenses, some other sexual offenses which have criminal implications include exhibitionism, voyeurism, fetishism, incest, and pedophilia. Related "deviant" sexual activity that may attract criminal predators includes sadism and masochism. *Exhibitionism* usually involves the purposive and unsolicited indecent exposure of sexual parts, usually of the male penis, to an unsuspecting female. *Voyeurism* involves a person invading the privacy of another by viewing him or her when in either an unclad state or in a sexual situation. *Fetishism* involves the obtaining of erotic excitement through the perception and often collection of objects associated with the opposite sex.

Nonvictimless Sexual Offenses

Of more serious concern are incest and pedophilia. *Incest* involves sexual intercourse between individuals who are legally defined as too closely related to marry. *Pedophilia,* or child molesting, refers to sexual relations between an adult and a child, the latter usually defined as one under the age of twelve or one who has not yet reached the age of puberty. These two types of offenses clearly are not "victimless" and, as will be described in greater detail shortly, are the most widely condemned and seriously punished of sexual depravations. *Sadism* involves the attainment of sexual gratification by means of inflicting cruelty upon others, while *masochism* represents a mirror image in which sexual gratification is obtained through suffering physical pain. Unless both parties consent, sadomasochistic activity, sometimes called "S and M," may entail harm or violent victimization.

While many states still have laws prohibiting certain sexual acts between consenting adults, regulations against homosexuality, cohabitation, fornication, adultery, and the like are usually ignored. Societal attempts to regulate obscenity and pornography continue to stir debate in the 1980s. Vantage Point 13.1 provides a brief sketch of the pornography controversy.

Drug Abuse

Drugs, chemical substances which alter psychological and/or physiological functioning, have been used for centuries in various cultures

Pornography is widely available in America. There is still sharp debate over whether or not it contributes to sexual violence.

as stimulants or depressants for medical, social, and often religious reasons. Even today in many Middle Eastern countries, alcohol is strictly forbidden for religious reasons, while the use of other highly addictive substances is tolerated. The fact that drug abuse has moved into mainstream U.S.A. can be illustrated by reports of widespread abuse particularly by professional athletes, entertainers, and prominent figures. In the 1980s David Kennedy (son of Robert Kennedy), who had a long history of drug abuse, died in a Palm Beach, Florida, motel under circumstances which were believed to be drug related. The near death of comedian Richard Pryor, who caught fire when free-basing cocaine, and the overdose deaths of actor John Belushi and University of Maryland All-American basketball star Len Bias illustrate the mainstream nature of drug abuse.

Vantage Point

Vantage Point 13.1—Pornography

Shortly before his execution in Florida in 1989, serial murderer Ted Bundy blamed pornography for his violent compulsion and, though many questioned Bundy's sincerity, his statements provided further fuel to the pornography debate. *Pornography* refers to erotic or sexually stimulating literature or materials; the term is derived from the Greek, meaning to write about prostitutes. Proponents of liberalized rules regulating pornography point to First Amendment freedom of speech guarantees and argue that in a democracy the state has no right to morally judge what is or is not suitable for reading or viewing. Opponents of pornography argue that such material is grossly repugnant to public morals, is degrading, may inspire sexual attacks against women, and often portrays activities, such as in child pornography, which are clearly beyond freedom of speech guarantees.

The National Commission on Obscenity and Pornography (1970) in a review of previous as well a commissioned studies on the subject concluded that no necessarily harmful behavior resulted from individuals' viewing pornographic material. They found the predominant customers of adult bookstores to be white, middle class, married businessmen. Goldstein et al. (1973) found that rapists, homosexuals, child molesters, and transsexuals had actually experienced less than normal exposure to pornographic materials during adolescence.

Despite these findings, many women's groups and others oppose the content of pornographic material as encouraging the mythical belief among some males that females secretly desire to be raped (McCarthy, 1982), a frequent theme in pornographic literature. McCarthy (Ibid., p. 219) indicates that the findings of the 1970 pornography commission are no longer valid in describing the types of more violent pornography that has emerged since 1970. In "snuff" films, for instance, females are depicted as being tortured and murdered, and sometimes

Figure 13.1 details the *types of common drugs of abuse,* which include:

Cannabis — marijuana, THC, hashish
Depressants — barbiturates, methaqualone, tranquilizers
Stimulants — amphetamines, nicotine, caffeine
Hallucinogens — LSD, mescaline, peyote, PCP, psilocybin
Inhalants — nitrous oxide, butyl nitrite, amyl nitrite, and aerosols
Narcotics — opium, morphine, codeine, heroin, and methadone

In the examination of the legal status of drugs and their known harmful effects the surprising fact is that there is often little relationship between the known harmful effects of a particular drug and its legal status in many societies. Substances such as alcohol or nicotine, while

---

the murder is the real thing. The commission has been criticized for failing to distinguish between erotic, sexually explicit material and pornographic material which exploits women.

The Attorney General's Commission on Pornography (1986) concluded that some forms of sexually explicit material bear a causal relationship to sexual violence and urged that police give a much higher priority to pornography cases. Most critics of the report feel that the commission had decided its conclusions before even conducting investigations and that the literature it cites fails to conclusively prove harmful effects of pornography (Lynn, 1986; Nobile and Nadler, 1986; and Scott, 1988). By way of example, Japan has an extensive amount of pornography, but a comparatively low incidence of rape (Impoco, 1987).

A study by Seymour Fishbach and Neal Malamuth (1978) found that exposure to erotic materials had little association with violent crime, but that a link did exist between viewing violent sexual materials and a greater propensity to view such actions in a favorable light. These findings were supported by others (Goode, 1984, p. 162; Malamuth and Donnerstein, 1982). While the pornography debate continues to rage, a compromise of sorts has been struck in the direction of regulation rather than either banning or further liberalization. The Supreme Court in various rulings has recognized the right of local communities to use zoning, to ban child pornography, and in other ways control some of the more distasteful aspects of pornography. The current state of affairs is perhaps best summed up by McConahay (1988, p. 67), who indicates:

> The new wider audience for X-rated videos means that there are too many pornography consumers, even if they do not think of it as pornography, with too much economic clout to achieve complete suppression and there is too much antipornography sentiment to tolerate complete freedom (read license). Thus, we will have to find a way to muddle through. (See Donnerstein, Linz, and Penrod, 1987).

Figure 13.1: Common Drugs of Abuse

Category	Drugs	Sample trade or other names	Medical Uses	Dependence Physical	Dependence Psychological
Cannabis	Marijuana	Pot, grass, reefer, sinsemilla	Under Investigation	Unknown	Moderate
	Tetrahydrocannabinol	THC	Under Investigation		
	Hashish	Hash	None		
	Hash oil	Hash oil	None		
Depressants	Alcohol	Liquor, beer, wine	None	High	High
	Barbiturates	Secobarbital, Amobarbital Bulisol, Tuinal	Anesthetic, anti-convulsant sedative, hypnotic	High-moderate	High-moderate
	Methaqualone	Quaalude, Sopor, Parest	Sedative, hypnotic	High	High
	Tranquilizers	Valium, Librium, Equanil, Miltown	Anti-anxiety, anti-convulsant, sedative	Moderate to low	Moderate
Stimulants	Cocaine	Coke, flake, snow	Local anesthetic	Possible	High
	Amphetamines	Biphetamine, Dexedrine	Hyperactivity narcolepsy	Possible	High
	Nicotine	Tobacco, cigars, cigarettes	None	High	High
	Caffeine	Coffee, tea, cola drinks, No-Doz	None	Low	Low
Hallucinogens	LSD	Acid	None	None	Degree unknown
	Mescaline and peyote	Button, Cactus	None	None	Degree unknown
	Phencyclidine	PCP, angel dust	Veterinary anesthetic	Unknown	High
	Psilocybin–psilocin	Mushrooms	None	None	Degree unknown
Inhalants	Nitrous oxide	Whippets, laughing gas	Anesthetic	Possible	Moderate
	Butyl nitrite	Locker room, rush	None		
	Amyl nitrite	Poppers, snappers	Heart stimulant		
	Chlorohydrocarbons	Aerosol paint, cleaning fluid	None		
	Hydrocarbons	Aerosol propellants gasoline, glue, paint thinner	None		
Narcotics	Opium	Paregoric	Antidiarrheal, pain relief	High	High
	Morphine	Morphine, Pectoral Syrup		Moderate	Moderate
	Codeine	Codeine, Empirin Compound with Codeine, Robitussin A-C	Pain relief, cough medicine	Moderate	Moderate
	Heroin	Horse, smack	Under Investigation	High	High
	Methadone	Dolophine, Methadone	Heroin substitute, pain relief	High	High

SOURCE: Department of Health and Human Services, 1981, *For Parents Only: What You Need to Know about Marijuana*, Washington, D.C.: Government Printing Office, pp. 26–27.

Effects in hours	Possible effects	Effects of overdose	Withdrawal symptoms
2–4	Euphoria, relaxed inhibitions, increase in heart and pulse rate, reddening of the eyes, increased appetite, disoriented behavior	Anxiety, paranoia, loss of concentration, slower movements, time distortion	Insomnia, hyperactivity, and decreased appetite occasionally reported
1–12 1–16 4–8	Slurred speech, disorientation, drunken behavior	Shallow respiration, cold and clammy skin, dilated pupils, weak and rapid pulse, coma, possible death	Anxiety, insomnia, tremors, delirium, convulsions, possible death
$\frac{1}{2}$–2 2–4	Increased alertness, excitation, euphoria, increase in pulse rate and blood pressure, insomnia, loss of appetite	Agitation, increase in body temperature, hallucinations, convulsions, possible death, tremors Agitation, increase in pulse rate and blood pressure, loss of appetite, insomnia	Apathy, long periods of sleep, irritability, depression
8–12 Variable 6	Illusions and hallucinations, poor perception of time and distance	Drug effects becoming longer and more intense, psychosis	Withdrawal symptoms not reported
Up to $\frac{1}{2}$ hr.	Excitement, euphoria, giddiness, loss of inhibitions, aggressiveness, delusions, depression, drowsiness, headache, nausea	Loss of memory, confusion, unsteady gait, erratic heart beat and pulse, possible death	Insomnia, decreased appetite, depression, irritability, headache
3–6 12–24	Euphoria, drowsiness, respiratory depression, constructed pupils, nausea	Slow and shallow breathing, clammy skin, convulsions, coma, possible death	Watery eyes, runny nose, yawning, loss of appetite, irritability, tremors, panic, chills and sweating, cramps, nausea

possessing mild, short-term, harmful impact, have lethal, long-term effects and enjoy a legal, sometimes subsidized status. Drugs such as heroin, which may be lethal in the short run due to overdoses, are not known to be lethal in the long term, but nevertheless are strongly forbidden. The changing legal status of drugs will be discussed in detail shortly as part of drugs and history.

Drunkenness

Under English common law, drunkenness itself was not a crime; only when a disturbance of peace or disorderly conduct occurred was it punished. In 1982, UCR data indicate that 1,778,400 individuals were arrested for driving under the influence; 1,262,100 for public drunkenness; and 501,200 for liquor law violations (FBI, 1983, p. 167). *Public drunkenness* is covered by a variety of laws in different jurisdictions such as drunk in a public place, breach of peace, disorderly conduct, and inability to care for one's own personal safety. Problem drinking was identified in Chapter 6 as a primary ingredient in other criminal activity, particularly interpersonal violence. The majority of homicides, aggravated assaults, a large proportion of rapes, and about half of all vehicular deaths are believed to be alcohol-related (U.S. Department of Justice, 1980). Alcoholism or problem drinking remains the number one drug abuse problem in the United States, despite official concern with more esoteric drugs.

The Prohibition Experiment

In a period of missionary zeal, the temperance movement, spearheaded by the WCTU (the Women's Christian Temperance Union), pressured by the U.S. Congress to pass a Prohibition amendment. This was ratified in 1919 and would, until 1933, constitute what some called "the noble experiment" and others "the great illusion." Asbury (1969 p. 58) describes this period:

> They [the temperance forces] had expected to be greeted . . . by a covey of angels bearing gifts of peace, happiness, prosperity, and salvation, which they had been assured would be theirs when the rum demon had been scotched. Instead they were met by a horde of bootleggers, moonshiners, rumrunners, hijackers, gangsters, racketeers, trigger men, venal judges, corrupt police . . . And almost total intemperance.

Prohibition did not eliminate the alcohol problem. Bootlegging became a national pastime and one of America's largest industries;

circumvention of the Volstead Act, the enforcement law of Prohibition, spawned corruption, organized crime, and public cynicism. As a result of its own failure as a social control policy as well as due to counter-pressure from rival urban forces, Prohibition was repealed in 1933. Although alcohol use is decriminalized, it is still regulated by state laws.

Other Public Order Crime

Space does not permit detailed discussion of other continuing controversial areas of public order regulation — gambling and abortion. On both of these issues, there is considerable division in public mores; both have also experienced decriminalization. Opponents of the legalization of gambling view such a status as constituting state approval of a depraved sickness in which individuals are encouraged to squander their own and often their family's funds in an almost sure loss situation. Proponents view such activity as a matter of personal choice and not the business of the state. In a similar light, opponents of abortion usually have the personal moral view that it constitutes murder of the unborn, while proponents view its prohibition as state intrusion into personal areas where the government attempts to control a female's body and her personal decisions regarding reproduction. While both the gambling and abortion debates are more complex than has been described, in pluralistic societies such as that of the United States — characterized by a plethora of ethnic, racial, and religious groups — the emergent long-term trend has been for the law to take a morally neutral or secular stance lest it institutionalize the mores of one group to the disadvantage of others. Such decriminalization as will be discussed in the final section of this chapter does not force individuals to gamble or abort, but rather takes the state out of the business of enforcing many areas of individual choice and morality. Though one may personally object to particular activities, utilizing the machinery of the state to try to enforce one's morality upon others is an ineffective and inappropriate use of formal criminal sanctions.

Criminal Careers of Public Order Criminals ————

Most public order offenders do not regard their behavior as criminal, perhaps in part because of general societal ambivalence toward much of it (Clinard and Quinney, 1973, p. 84). Some of the behavior may reflect personal psychological disability, but much of it either reflects adult consensual relations which are agreeable to both parties and harmful to neither or personal choice to participate in activity which the individual desires even though it may be illegal or societally disapproved.

Prostitution

This discussion will concentrate primarily upon female prostitution, which appears to persist despite wide variations in economic, political, and social systems. One explanation is that prostitution serves a function in society: it services otherwise unmet sexual needs. There is a strong demand in many societies for no-strings-attached sexual release, particularly in relatively isolated male environments. City leaders—particularly in seaport cities such as Hamburg, Marseilles, or Baltimore—would argue that toleration of prostitution enabled the servicing of armies, the rejected, strangers, and the perverted, thus protecting "decent" females of the community. In addition to the strong demand for such services, prostitution can offer relatively lucrative rewards for females, depending, of course, upon the status of customers.

Eleanor Miller in *Street Woman* (1986) interviewed sixty-four prostitutes and, similar to Sullivan (1988), found that economic and social problems propelled young women into "hustling" as an alternative to boring, dead-end jobs. For others, it was an escape from abusive or disorganized families. Money and survival became key motivations for street hookers (Ritter, 1988).

Types of Prostitution

Prostitution involves a number of types and settings including: brothel prostitutes, bar girls, streetwalkers, massage parlor prostitutes, call girls, and other variations. As any other occupation, prostitution is stratified, the lowest status and remuneration assigned to brothel or house prostitutes and streetwalkers and the highest prestige and reward attached to expensive call girls, who are able to command higher prices from more exclusive clientele (MacNamara and Sagarin, 1977, p. 99; and Perkins and Bennett, 1985). The many varieties of women selling sexual favors can be illustrated by an early and very general classification offered by Reitman (1931, p. 247) which included: juveniles, potential, amateur, semiprofessionals, professionals, streetwalkers, bats or "over the hill bums," gold diggers, kept women or private mistresses, loose married women, and call girls.

Brothels—sometimes called whorehouses, cathouses or bordellos— were widespread in the U.S. until the post-World War II period. Often clustered together in "red light districts," brothels were managed by madams with whom prostitutes shared the proceeds from their tricks (sexual transactions). The term "red light district" supposedly had its origin when railroad construction workers in the American West hung their red signal lanterns outside whorehouses they were frequenting in order to keep in contact with their dispatchers (Winick and Kinsie, 1971, p. 132). While some illegal brothels still exist, most have disappeared, although legal brothels exist in some counties in Nevada.

The following account of a red-light district in Erie, Pennsylvania, in 1907 is illustrative:

> In the three blocks of French Street mentioned, there are roughly sixteen immoral houses. Within these resorts a conservative total of 75 girls have been leading a life of shame. None of these resorts hold a liquor license, but at all of them, drinks of any description can be obtained at any hour of the day . . . by a visitor of almost any age.
>
> Seventy-five percent of the girls of the tenderloin are under 21 years of age. Ninety percent of the visitors are young men under 20. Fully thirty percent are boys of 16 and 17 (Erie Red Light, 1907).

Streetwalkers or "hookers" parade and negotiate the sale of their wares on the public streets. The term *hooker* was apparently derived from camp or circuit traveling prostitutes who followed and serviced the Confederate troops of General Joseph Hooker during the Civil War (Ibid., p. 58). Such "working girls" earn the least amount of all prostitutes and are most vulnerable to police interference. Streetwalkers also are most likely to have arrangements with pimps who play the combined roles of managers, protectors, and pseudofathers. In the U.S. since the sixties, the majority of street pimps are black; recent research suggests that pimping is held in less regard than in the past and may be of less importance in the world of prostitution than it was at one time (Ibid., p. 120). While relationships between pimps and their stables of prostitutes vary, many hookers are required by their pimp to earn a certain amount per day or suffer physical harm (Milner and Milner, 1972; Slim, 1969; and Sheehy, 1973).

Bar girls, or B-girls, are common in seaport cities or areas serving military populations, such as in combat zones, or adult entertainment sections of some large cities. Such hookers entice customers to buy them drinks, usually nonalcoholic ones, for ridiculous prices, while also arranging for tricks which may occur on the premises or at nearby "hot sheet" hotels.

Call girls represent the top of the prostitution profession. Such "hookers" generally are very selective in their clientele and are highly rewarded. Most are from more educated and middle class backgrounds than streetwalkers or house girls and usually operate on referrals. "Escort services" generally are fronts for prostitution in which clients pay per hour for the company and "services" of usually attractive young women.

According to Rosen (1983), the early twentieth century campaign against prostitution and the banning of "red light districts" have made it the lucrative profession it is today. Previously prostitutes, although exploited, had a certain amount of control over their earnings and working conditions. Their profiteers, madams, landlords, saloon keepers, and other middlemen were more benign than modern pimps, and the brothel was a rational economic alternative to a sweatshop job at starvation wages.

Massage Parlors

"Breslau Executive Health Spa!
15 Lovely Girls Upstairs and
15 Lovely Girls Downstairs
To Serve You"
                    —Advertisement

Sydney Biddle Barrows, nicknamed the "Mayflower Madam," is perhaps the most famous person to run a call-girl operation.

Advertisements such as that quoted above appeared on Canadian commercial television (CKCO-TV, Kitchener, Ontario, September 1, 1983, 12:45 A.M. EST). The massage parlor, in which forms of commercial sex are sold under the guise of a health spa or massage service, became quite common in North America in the seventies. Journalist Gay Talese (1979), who performed extensive participant observation studies of such operations in *Thy Neighbor's Wife*, concluded that for all practical purposes under existing laws such operations constitute legalized prostitution. Since "extras" (prohibited sexual services) must be negotiated and requested by the customer, parlor girls can avoid actual solicitation, and law enforcement agencies must be careful of entrapment or causing illegal activities to occur which would not otherwise have taken place.

A very clever means of rationalizing prostitution surfaced in Los Angeles (Couple Call, 1989) in which a couple offered sexual intercourse to members of their Church of the Most High Goddess. The woman and her husband were arrested on soliciting charges, but insisted the state was violating their freedom of religion. The priestesses absolved the sins of the male followers through sex acts, which they claim was the revival of ancient Egyptian religious rites. She said, "Anything God wants from me, I will give HIM . . . If he wants me to be monogamous, I'll be monogamous. If he says go have sex with 20,000 men, I'll do it" (Ibid.).

Johns

While an extensive literature exists on prostitution, there has been a paucity of information regarding "johns" or customers, except from interviews with prostitutes. Holzman and Pines (1979) note that much of the literature on johns portrays them as socially, psychologically, or physically inadequate, having to pay for that which others can obtain free as a matter of course (Morris and Hawkins, 1970; Laner, 1974; Benjamin and Masters, 1964; Gibbens and Silberman, 1960; and Ellis, 1959). The term "trick" is derisively used to refer to the fact that the hooker tricks the john into paying for what he should be able to obtain free (Milner and Milner, 1972, p. 38). Holzman and Pines (1979) indicate that much of this negative evaluation of johns has come from prostitutes and mental health practitioners and that field studies of such customers by social service researchers present a different picture (Winick, 1962; Armstrong, 1978; Simpson and Schill, 1977; and Stein, 1974).

Stein, employing one-way mirrors in order to observe and record hundreds of sessions between prostitutes and clients, was struck by the normal or "straight" quality of the customers. Employing in-depth interviews of a snowball sample of thirty primarily white, middle class johns, Holzman and Pines (1979) were also unable to support the "pathology-ridden depictions of the clients of prostitutes." All of the subjects indicated current involvements in relationships which involved sex and that they experienced little problem in obtaining sex from non-prostitutes. Some prevailing motivations for visiting prostitutes mentioned by their sample included: expectations of mystery and excitement; special "professional" services; and guaranteed, easy, non-entangled sex, which avoided possible rejection. A controversial, although apparently relatively effective, means of cracking down on open solicitation by prostitutes in given urban areas is the practice of the prosecution and embarrassment of johns by publishing their names and addresses in the local newspaper.

Despite the increased visibility of prostitution beginning in the seventies in the United States, most studies suggest that prostitution has experienced a decline since the pre-World War II period. There appears to be an inverse or negative relationship between sexual permissiveness in a society and the strength of organized prostitution. Prostitution is strongest in countries with traditional concepts of marriage and the double standard. Countries such as France and Italy, for example, discourage divorce and tolerate different expectations of sexual conduct for males and females. Since female sexual expression is discouraged outside of marriage, a small proportion of females serve the illicit, erotic desires of the male population. The decline in prostitution can be noted by comparing Kinsey's 1948 and 1952 surveys with more recent ones (Hunt, 1974, p. 144); they show that, while prior to World War II roughly 50 percent of white males had visited prostitutes, in the seventies only 25 percent of college-educated men had visited prostitutes. The erosion of the double standard and greater female sexual permissiveness has eliminated some of the demand for prostitutes' services.

Underaged Prostitutes

Since the seventies concern has been expressed regarding what appears to be growing participation in prostitution by youths, both male and female, under the age of eighteen. While accurate statistics are difficult to come by, journalistic reports suggest a large recent increase in the sexual exploitation of children, due in part to the youth orientation of society, to growing sexual permissiveness, and to eroding family structures (Booth, 1978, p. 23–A). New York City police authorities claim as many as ten thousand "chicken hawks," male prostitutes under eighteen; another estimate indicates that half of Portland's hookers are girls under eighteen. The so-called "Boy Scout sex ring" in New Orleans involved eighteen Boy Scouts aged eight to fifteen where, in some cases, the youngsters' mothers were aware of their activities.

A large proportion of teenage prostitutes come from "damaged families" and often represent "throw-away children." Many had been raped or sexually abused by surrogate fathers. A Boston ring of homosexual boys was run by the school bus driver, who peddled the bodies of eight and nine year olds and advertised their photographs throughout the East Coast. When the ring was broken, police arrested a child psychiatrist, a clinical psychologist, a former assistant headmaster, and a teacher at a boys' prep school.

The subject of sexual exploitation of children will remain a matter of serious concern, particularly with respect to the long-term psychological impact of such victimizations upon the young people involved (Sullivan, 1988; Ritter, 1988; Burgess, 1984; and Weisberg, 1985).

Homosexuality

Despite decriminalization, homosexual activity is still regulated in most states under sodomy statutes. Attempts to estimate the extent of homosexuality have produced varying figures. An Alfred Kinsey and associates (1948 and 1952) survey indicated that ten percent of their male sample had been exclusively homosexual for at least a three-year period and 4 percent for their lifetimes. Between 2 and 6 percent of unmarried females were exclusively lesbian. A later survey by Morton Hunt (1974) placed the figures at 3 percent for males and 1 to 3 percent for females. Both of these studies have been limited by inadequate sampling procedures, however.

Although many variations could be distinguished, those participating in homosexual activity may be simply divided into two types: situational homosexuals and preferential homosexuals. *Situational homosexuals* are those who may prefer heterosexual activity but participate in homosexual activity as a temporary or substitute means of erotic gratification or a means of monetary reward. *Preferential homosexuals* seek sexual gratification predominantly and continually with members of the same sex. Such individuals tend to develop a homosexual self-concept and to join a gay or homosexual subculture. In actuality, a variety of homosexual roles can be distinguished, including overt or secret, adjusted or maladjusted, true homosexual or situational turnout, as well as primary or secondary (Clinard and Quinney, 1973, p. 87). "This self-conception as a homosexual is derived largely from the reactions of others which results in the homosexual's seeking more and more associations within the homosexual subculture" (Ibid., p. 88).

Many individuals participate in homosexual activity but do not identify themselves as homosexuals. Much situational homosexuality occurs in isolated sexual environments such as prisons, unisexual boarding schools, and military environments. In prisons, for instance, "wolves" exert their masculinity by having fellatio (oral stimulation) performed on them or sodomizing "queens," avowed homosexuals, or "punks," weak males who are forced into performing sexual services (Sykes, 1958, pp. 95–97). Sexual behavior may reflect opportunity and circumstance in addition to preference. In many traditional Islamic countries a high premium is placed upon virgin brides and strong prohibitions against wifely infidelity and even premarital dating. In such a system heterosexual males use other males for sexual outlets. Sexual assaults upon boys are more prevalent than attacks upon women in such countries (West, 1988, p. 183).

Male prostitutes primarily serve the needs of a clientele interested in homosexual activity. In San Francisco these consist of "face-to-face" public prostitutes and "call men." Waldorf, et al. (1988, p. 6) identify the subtypes of face-to-face prostitutes as: trade hustlers (bisexual or homosexual men who exchange sex for money, hence, the term "trade"), drag hookers (transvestites and transsexuals), and young hustlers (very young, gay or bisexual men who openly solicit customers). Call men are less open in obtaining customers and advertise in newspapers and operate by telephone. These include: erotic masseurs, call book men (who have books with names of regular clients), models/escorts, and "stars" of erotic magazines (Ibid., p. 7). Vantage Point 13.2 provides an illustration of impersonal homosexual activity in public places.

Sexual Offenders

In addition to relatively institutionalized forms of "sexual deviance," such as prostitution and homosexuality and seriously regarded activities such as child molesting and incest, there are a variety of activities which might generally be regarded as either nuisance forms of deviation or relatively rare preferences for sexual activities which may on occasion be harmful to one or the other or both parties.

Nuisance Sexual Offenses

Exhibitionism generally involves the purposive public exposure, usually by males, of private sexual parts, in order to elicit shock in unsuspecting female victims. While laws prohibiting indecent exposure are equally applicable to both sexes and are usually brought into force by public complaint, most "flashers" are male (Forgac and Michaels, 1982).

Illustrated by the "dirty old man in a raincoat" who exposes his genitals, exhibitionism may also be demonstrated by adolescent pranksterism by "mooning," displaying one's bare buttocks to an unsuspecting audience, and "streaking," running naked through a public gathering. While "mooning" and "streaking" are performed for kicks, there appears to be little erotic motivation on the part of participants. "Flashers," on the other hand, participate in such activity as a means of sexual arousal and gratification. *Most* are described as the least harmful of sexual offenders; such exhibitionists are generally immature in their sexual development, wish to evoke fear or shock, and actually would be fearful if the victim acted interested or wanted further contact (Gebhard et al., 1965).

Voyeurs attain sexual gratification by viewing others in an unclad state. While legal voyeurism can be practiced in establishments catering to such trade—for example, "topless bars" or adult entertainment districts—illegal voyeurism involves uninvited "peeping" into private homes, parked cars in "lovers' lanes," or other areas. Voyeurs are often called "Peeping Toms," a name derived from the fable of the man who stole a peep at Lady Godiva on her naked romp through Coventry. While some patterns of burglary may be associated with voyeurism, in most instances is appears to be pursued as an end in itself. Primarily practiced by juveniles as a means of achieving erotic excitement, *most* persistent voyeurs are also at a relatively immature level of psychosexual development and, contrary to the fears of many female victims, do not employ voyeurism as a prelude to sexual attack. In this sense, voyeurs are much like obscene phone callers in that they often fear contact with the opposite sex; otherwise they would avail themselves of readily obtainable erotic outlets in the adult sexual marketplace.

Fetishism involves sexual arousal from the perception of inanimate objects or clothing articles usually associated with the opposite sex. While some level of fetishism is normal, it becomes abnormal when an individual acquires such items, often through theft, and venerates such articles as a displaced sexual object. There are, for instance, some episodes of shoplifting associated with fetishistic behavior in which the objects are sought because they have significant value due to the erotic feelings they arouse.

Of possible concern to law enforcement are sexual practices involving sadism and/or masochism. *Sadism* involves the attainment of sexual gratification by means of inflicting pain upon others. Often unable to achieve sexual arousal and/or orgasm through any other means, such individuals may harm unconsenting partners. *Masochism* refers to the attainment of erotic satisfaction through suffering of pain. The masochistic individual must be physically punished in order to gain sexual fulfillment. The leather, whips, and chains school of kinky sex is often serviced by prostitutes who specialize in catering to the even more bizarre needs of their clients.

Not every sexual deviation yields a predictable mode of behavior. While only a very small minority are potentially dangerous, any type may be associated with more serious criminality in the individual case. The vast majority of persistent offenders exhibit immature psychosexual development and, if their behavior elicits police response, such offenders are usually treated under civil commitment proceedings. Since most research on sexual offenders relies upon official statistics and the majority never come to official attention, far more reliable research is required in this area (Toch, 1979, p. 413).

VANTAGE POINT

Vantage Point 13.2 — Laud Humphreys' *Tearoom Trade*

The following is a brief account of Laud Humphreys' (1970) controversial and important study of "tearooms," public restrooms where homosexual activity is common. Such solicitations and activities produce most law enforcement attention and arrests for homosexual activity. Despite public fears of child molesters lurking in wait in such places, surprisingly little information existed prior to Humphreys' (1970) study of such localities. Using the controversial method of disguised observation, Humphreys posed as a "watch queen," a voyeur who obtains erotic excitement by observing such activities, but also serves the crucial role of lookout for police and other unfriendly strangers who may wander upon the scene and interrupt the homosexual trysts. Humphreys traced the automobile license numbers of participants and showed up at their homes sometime later under the guise of performing a mental health survey.

According to Humphreys, tearooms are popular because they provide instant, "no-strings-attached" sex, inexpensive erotic kicks without commitment. They are not gathering places for preferential homosexuals. Such individuals have "come out of the closet," have admitted their sexual preference, and would far more likely be found in gay bars. Tearooms attract a variety of men, only a few of whom are members of the homosexual subculture. The majority have no homosexual self-concept. In fact, over half were married and currently living with their wives.

Humphreys' typology of tearoom participants included: trade, ambisexuals, gay guys, and closet queens. The predominant activity in tearooms is fellatio. Individuals classified as *trade* made up 38 percent of the subjects and were described by Humphreys as "insertors," "fellators," or those who have fellatio performed on them. Most were married, but there was little sex within their

Child Molesting

Child battering, which can be defined as child abuse primarily involving physical assault upon children, was previously discussed in the chapter on violent crime. While it is difficult to draw clear distinctions between abuse and molestation, this discussion will focus upon child molesting, which primarily involves the sexual abuse of children or minors past puberty. A child is defined in most states as one who has not yet reached puberty or age twelve or fourteen.

Pedophiliacs or child molesters are those who have sexual relations with children. For every rape in the United States in a given year it is estimated that twenty children are molested—roughly 500,000, according to official estimates in 1982 (ABC, 1983a). Many myths exist

---

marriages. Other sexual outlets, such as affairs, were viewed as too complicated and expensive. Such individuals at the turn of the century would most likely have visited inexpensive red light districts.

Ambi-sexuals are more likely to be "insertees"; that is, they perform the oral function. Representing 24 percent of Humphreys's sample, most of these men also were married and indicated that their home sex life was satisfactory. Many enjoyed the adventure, excitement, and risk of such illicit activity. *Gay guys* constituted 14 percent of the participants. Such individuals openly associate in the gay subculture. Humphreys claims that most prefer more permanent, "married" homosexual relationships which are not to be found in the transitory atmosphere of the tearoom. *Closet queens,* hidden or unavowed homosexuals, made up the remaining 24 percent. Such persons were usually unmarried and fearful of involvement in other areas of the sexual marketplace. Many were particularly interested in young boys, although few of these are to be found in tearooms. Humphreys feels that the unwillingness of "closet queens" to come to terms with their sexual preference and participate in the homosexual subculture makes such individuals potentially dangerous. For most homosexuals the civil consequences of revelation of their activities are a greater personal concern than the threat of criminal penalties.

While most police departments do not make an active business of pursuing those involved in homosexual activity, an account from Olympia, Washington (More Arrests, 1980), illustrates a tearoom bust. Police investigated and arrested a brewery president, a state legislator, a state official, and others at a lakefront park restroom. Police observed twenty to thirty regular visitors during a two-week period as well as their participation in homosexual activity. An undercover officer was solicited and also observed acts being performed in his presence.

with respect to child molesters. Some common myths are: molesters are usually strangers, molesters will be caught and jailed, and children quickly get over the emotional harm of having been molested. Most molesters, 85 percent, are known to the child and his or her family. Most are not caught and, when apprehended, are more likely to be treated leniently. Less than 10 percent of convicted felon child molesters go to prison. One offender claims that psychiatrists will generally release them as long as they do not appear to be "mad dogs" (Ibid.). Since such offenders are assumed to be mentally ill, they are permitted to plead to lesser offenses, even though victims of child molesters report long-term psychological damage or scars as a result of such incidents. Pressure groups such as SLAM, Society for Laws Against Molesters, are lobbying for stricter laws, insisting that repeat offenders receive mandatory prison sentences consisting of a minimum of four to eight years.

The typical act of child molesting involves an adult male with a female victim usually eleven to fourteen years of age. McCaghy (1967a, p. 87) identified six types of child molesters:

- High interaction molesters, who have known the children for some time and usually perform or have performed genital fondling.
- Incestuous molesters, who take advantage of a child living in their household.
- Asocial molesters, who are involved in illegal careers.
- Senile molesters, who are older, poorly educated offenders.
- Career molesters, who have persistent offense patterns involving child molestation.
- Spontaneous-aggressive molesters, who have had little previous contact with their victims and tend to commit their offense on a very physical and unplanned basis.

While high interaction offenders represented only 10 percent of McCaghy's sample, it is likely that they represent the majority of molesters. Since most are well known to the family and do not employ physical force, they are less likely to be charged with the offense. Given the very sensitive nature of the subject matter, research has been scarce regarding this subject (Mohr, Turner, and Jerry, 1964; Ellis and Brancale, 1965; and Gebhard et al., 1965). Although statistics are unreliable, in many cases of sexual child abuse the offenders are family members.

There have been other attempts to classify child molesters. Groth et al. (1978) describe two types: the "regressed" abuser and the "fixated" abuser. The regressed abuser is one who, having led a fairly normal sexual life, regresses to a sexual interest in children. A previously normal father who suddenly develops such sexual interest in children would serve as an example. Fixated abusers have had an early and strong focused interest in children as sexual objects, often to the exclusion of any other type of sexual activity, such as with adults (Crewdson, 1988). While there has been an increase in literature on the topics of sexual molestation, incest, and pedophilia, more such research is needed (Finkelhor, 1986; Holmes, 1983; O'Brien, 1986; and Vander and Neff, 1986).

Incest

Related to child molestation is the crime of incest which, although varyingly defined by state or national laws, refers to the universal taboo prohibiting sexual relations or marriage between those who are defined as being too closely related either by blood or marriage. At issue in this discussion is not adult relations, but forms of incest that represent a type of child molesting or sexual victimization in which an adult who is closely related to a child has sexual relations with the child.

The incidence of child sexual abuse by a natural parent is difficult to document, even though the American Humane Association has shown a sharp escalation in such statistics since the mid-seventies. "The more 'personal' the relationship between the victim and the offender, the less likely a case of sexual abuse will be reported" (Cardarelli, 1988, p. 9). While a considerable literature has accumulated on this subject, there is still a need for more empirical research (Russell, 1986; and Ekpenyong, 1988).

Since mother-son incest is rare and brother-sister incest is unlikely to involve as gross an age disparity, father-daughter and father-son incestual relationships are the primary subject of this brief presentation. One study found the average age of female victims as 10.2 years of age (Finkelhor, 1979, p. 60). Incestual victimizations may be heterosexual or homosexual. Finkelhor (Ibid., p. 87) found that, although brother-sister incest was by far the most common, father-daughter incest was most likely to come to the attention of authorities, perhaps due to its more traumatic impact upon the family and the child (Janeway, 1981; and Goodwin et al., 1982). Some factors associated with incest include high proportions of stepparent, foster or adoptive parent, family disorganization (Herman, 1981), low mentality, alcoholism, and other personality disorganization. While official reports of child battering tend to be more prevalent among low-income families, the American Humane Association Children's Division (1984) reported sexual abuse and incest are more evenly distributed among social classes. Gordon and O'Keefe (1984), in an analysis of historical records of family violence in the Boston area from 1880 to 1960, did not find that incest offenders were poorer, more alcoholic, or sicker than other assailants. In addition, they questioned the assumption that such violators exhibited pathology or were under external socioeconomic status.

Characteristics of Sex Offenders

Hans Toch (1979, p. 414) summarizes much of the research that has been conducted on characteristics of sex offenders:

- Most, rather than being "sex fiends," are rather harmless, minor offenders.
- Only about 20 percent use force on their victims.
- Untreated, convicted offenders tend to be recidivists in both sexual and nonsexual offenses, but in no greater proportions than nonsexual offenders.
- While few offenders are psychopaths, many are suffering severe neurosis, borderline psychosis, or brain impairment, but most do not fit legal definitions of mental illness.
- Most are emotionally immature and sexually constricted and inhibited, although those involved in rape and incest are more likely to be overimpulsive and oversexed.
- Convicted statutory rapists and those involved in bestiality and incest are more likely to exhibit subnormal intelligence.
- The majority of offenders are young, unmarried, and from poor educational and social class backgrounds (see also Holmes, 1983).

Drug Abuse

Drugs and History

Opium was believed to have been discovered as early as the Neolithic Age and was used by early physicians such as Hippocrates and Galen (McCoy, 1972, p. 3). Opium, the raw base of other derivatives such as morphine and heroin, was first introduced on a wide scale to the rest of the world by Turkish traders around the eighth or ninth century (Block and Chambliss, 1981, p. 20) and was a trade commodity of European mercantilists as early as the sixteenth century, providing at one point almost half of the revenue of colonial governments. Opium dens controlled by European governments could be found in most Asian cities. When one Chinese emperor objected to such trade, the Opium Wars (1839–42) were fought, in which the Europeans (the pushers) were the victors. American "China clipper" ships, known in the trade as "opium" clippers, had a major piece of this trade (Nash, 1981, p. 166).

In 1805 morphine was derived from opium, but widespread medicinal use of morphine and other derivatives such as codeine brought the onset of serious addiction problems. By 1874 heroin, another opium derivative, was developed and was at first believed to be a nonaddicting miracle drug. Cocaine, which was isolated from coca in 1858, was first thought to be a cure for morphinism and was a popular ingredient of tonics such as Coca-Cola when the first soda fountains were introduced in the 1890s. Its inclusion was outlawed by the Pure Food and Drug Laws of 1906. Backwater patent-medicine peddlers of the late nineteenth century American frontier provided highly addictive remedies such as Dover's Powders, Sydenham's Syrup, and Godfrey's Cordial, which were so widely used that by 1900 an estimated one million Americans, mostly women, were opiate users (Brecher, 1972). Brecher (Ibid., p. 4) described turn-of-the-century America as a "dope fiend's paradise."

This relatively unregulated distribution of narcotics by physicians and pharmaceutical companies was creating a tremendous drug abuse problem. By 1924 federal authorities in the U.S. estimated that there were 200,000 addicts (McCoy, 1972, p. 5). International concern over growing drug trafficking led to the Hague Convention of 1912, which called for participating nations to crack down upon drug distribution. The U.S. response was the *Harrison Act of 1914*, which required a doctor's prescription for narcotics and cocaine. The act required the registration of all legitimate drug handlers, but was not intended to interfere with the legitimate medical treatment of addicts. A vague clause in the law to the effect that physicians could dispense such drugs "only for legitimate medical reasons" led some overzealous federal agents to crack down on offending physicians. By the mid-twenties an estimated 25,000 physicians had been arrested, with 3,000 serving jail or prison sentences (Goode, 1984, p. 109). The net result of the Harrison Act was that physicians abandoned the treatment of addicts and the addict as "patient" was replaced by the addict as "criminal," "dope fiend," or outside menace (Lindesmith, 1965; Duster, 1970; and Goode, 1972).

Howard Becker (1963) coined the term *moral entrepreneurs* to refer to individuals who personally benefit from convincing the public to label the behavior of others as deviant or criminal. Vantage Point 13.3 describes two classic moral entrepreneurs, Richard Hobson, "the hero of Santiago Bay," and Harry Anslinger, "the Carrie Nation of marijuana." Thomas Szasz in *Ceremonial Chemistry* (1974), perhaps with some exaggeration, compares the drug war with the war on witches and heretics in Europe from 1430–1730. The latter cost 300,000 lives and was a reflection of ignorance and superstition. In the late eighties an explosion of drug problems was predicted for the twelve-nation European Economic Community with an estimated 1.5 million heroin addicts in 1988 and the Colombian cocaine cartels eyeing it as a new market (Europeans Favor, 1988, p. 4–A). Successive federal legislation from the time of the Harrison Act until the 1970s such as the Marijuana Tax Act (1937), the Boggs Act (1951), and Narcotics Control Act (1956) were all aimed at controlling drug abuse by means of criminalization and harsher penalties.

Vantage Point

Vantage Point 13.3—The Strange Career of Captain Richmond Hobson—Moral Entrepreneur

On June 3, 1898, Captain Richmond Hobson, a recent Annapolis graduate and skipper of the U.S.S. *Merrimac,* piloted his vessel into the mouth of Santiago Bay, Cuba. His mission was to sink his ship in the channel, thus blocking the Spanish fleet. Premature charges sank the ship before the mission could be accomplished and Hobson not only failed in his mission but was captured by the Spanish (Epstein, 1977, p. 24).

Ironically, Hobson became the first hero of that short war when the Navy chose to decorate rather than court-martial him, and upon his release sent him on a cross-country lecture tour. Elected to Congress in 1906, Hobson campaigned first against the "Yellow Peril" and later was an organizer of the Women's Christian Temperance Union. A campaigner against the evils of alcohol, he was the highest-paid speaker on the U.S. lecture circuit in 1915. With the demise of the antialcohol campaign in the thirties, the undaunted Hobson shifted his crusade to an antiheroin Jihad, describing heroin as a vampiric, demonic drug which created the "living dead" and desperadoes. Heroin was viewed as an "enslavement substance" which caused addicts to become criminals. Much of Hobson's theories were expounded in his widely read 1933 book, *Drug Addiction: A Malignant Racial Cancer.*

Hobson's propaganda campaign usefully served the moral entrepreneurship of Harry Anslinger and his efforts to expand the Federal Bureau of Narcotics, which he headed. Anslinger influenced public opinion against marijuana by means of his writing and speeches. One of his articles was entitled, "Marijuana: Assassin of Youth," in which he portrays a marijuana "addict" who axe-murders his family (Anslinger and Cooper, 1937). Another propaganda feat of the period was a film entitled *Reefer Madness,* which similarly displayed marijuana users as rampaging, raving maniacs. Primarily as the result of Anslinger's efforts, U.S. Congress passed the Marijuana Tax Act of 1937, making marijuana use a criminal matter.

The Phantom Army of Addicts

In 1969 the Bureau of Narcotics and Dangerous Drugs (BNDD), using data from police and medical authorities, estimated the number of heroin addicts at 68,088. By 1970 an apparent heroin epidemic took place with the number of addicts set at 315,000 and for 1971, 559,000, a rough eightfold increase in just two years. Edward Epstein (1977, p. 174) in *Agency of Fear* states: "A tenfold increase in the number of heroin addicts would certainly be a cause for national concern; the magnitude of the 1971 epidemic was, however, more a product of government statisticians than of heroin traffickers."

As Epstein explains it, until 1970 the official estimates of heroin addicts were registered by BNDD on the basis of police and medical reports. The 68,088 (1969) figure was based upon the official register, while the increases in 1970 and 1971 were brought about largely due to a new estimating formula, a statistical artifact which in effect created a "phantom army of addicts." This new estimating procedure, "the mark-recapture technique," was one which is widely used in the field of ecology such as the tagged-fish-in-a-pool procedure (see for instance Burnham, 1980; Demaree, 1980; Kenadjian, 1980; and Wanat and Burke, 1980). To guess the number of fish in a pond, a sample of fish is caught, marked or tagged, and released. Then a second sample is caught. If, for instance, one in ten of the second sample have tags, then the entire fish population of the pond would be assumed to be ten times the number of the originally tagged sample. Suppose fifty fish were tagged in the first sample and released, then fifty more caught, of which five bore tags. The estimate of fish population would be ten times fifty or five hundred. Following this same procedure the BNDD compared the number of names on the 1970 addicts' register which had previously appeared (been tagged) on the 1969 register. Finding one in five to be rereports (tagged addicts), the 1969 estimate of 68,088 was multiplied by the calculated ratio of 4,626, providing the 315,000 figure for 1970. This is a classic example of instrumentation—changes in the instrument of measurement being responsible for changes in that which is being measured. While the "mark-recapture" procedure may be useful for estimating fish, it is doubtful that drug addicts follow similar random patterns (Epstein, 1977, p. 175). While the estimates prior to 1970 most likely underestimated the number of addicts, the figures in 1970–71 probably overestimated it. As a validity check, U.S. Army draftees' records at the time indicated no change, treatment centers at the time actually showed a decrease in new addicts for several years (Ibid., p. 177). The politics of these statistics is fascinating as well as frightening, particularly when they became the basis of an extraordinary war upon an "indomitable enemy" which may not exist.

Agency of Fear

Suppose that on an ordinary night you were in bed with your spouse when armed men attired as "hippies" broke into your home and held loaded guns to your heads. Looking at the wife, they say, "Who is the bitch lying there?" and although you are both naked you are not permitted to dress. Saying things such as, "You're going to die unless you tell us where the stuff is," these apparent maniacs, without identifying themselves, unexpectedly apologize, saying they must have made a mistake and leave. These same raiders in what is now called the famous "Collinsville drug raids" repeated this mistake at yet another residence the same evening. They were not a terrorist group, but a new federal law enforcement agency, the Office of Drug Abuse and Law Enforcement (ODALE), a group which Epstein (Ibid.) refers to as the "agency of fear." Using drug statistics such as those which we have just discussed, Epstein maintains that the Nixon administration and G. Gordon Liddy, in a classic example of "moral entrepreneurship," used public fear of addiction and crime in order to create ODALE. In January 1972, by executive order of President Nixon and without congressional approval, the agency was created as an extraordinary investigative agency that was run by the White House and that bypassed usual federal agencies such as the FBI or CIA. Epstein (Ibid., p. 189) claims that—under the cloak of a crusade against an epidemic drug menace—the Nixon administration created this agency to conduct carte blanche investigations of political opponents, dissenters, the media, and the like.

The Nixon statistical strategy almost backfired. After having encouraged a statistical epidemic, they realized that an election year (1972) estimate of 559,000 would reflect badly upon the incumbent Nixon administration. So the figure was arbitrarily reduced to 150,000. Actually, estimates of the number of heroin users and heroin addicts in the U.S. are difficult to make and, depending upon the measuring instrument employed, can supply different figures. Estimating all who have ever tried heroin can supply figures as high as 2 to 3 million (Fishburne, Abelson, and Cisin, 1980).

Drug Use in the U.S.: The Coming Drug Dip?

Patterns of usage of various drugs can be illustrated by examining some of the data presented in Tables 13.1 and 13.2. Alcohol and cigarettes are the most widely used substances by all age groups. The young adult group, ages eighteen to twenty-five, was the most likely to use illicit drugs.

Table 13.1: Estimated Prevalence and Most Recent Use of Alcohol, Marihuana, and Cocaine. By Sex, Race, Age, and Region, United States, 1985.

	Alcohol		Most Recent Use			Marihuana		Most Recent Use			Cocaine		Most Recent Use		
	Never Used	Ever Used	Within Last 30 Days	Within Last 12 Months, but Not Last 30 Days	Not Within Last 12 Months	Never Used	Ever Used	Within Last 30 Days	Within Last 12 Months, but Not Last 30 Days	Not Within Last 12 Months	Never Used	Ever Used	Within Last 30 Days	Within Last 12 Months, but Not Last 30 Days	Not Within Last 12 Months
Total (N = 8,038)	13.9%	86.1%	59.2%	14.3%	12.6%	67.5%	32.5%	9.4%	5.9%	17.2%	88.3%	11.7%	2.9%	3.4%	5.4%
Sex															
Male	9.2	90.8	67.9	10.7	12.2	61.6	38.4	12.3	7.2	18.9	84.6	15.4	3.9	4.5	7.0
Female	18.1	81.9	51.2	17.6	13.1	73.0	27.0	6.8	4.7	15.5	91.7	8.3	2.0	2.4	3.9
Race															
White	11.1	88.9	61.8	14.5	12.6	66.5	33.5	9.1	6.3	18.1	87.6	12.4	3.0	3.4	6.0
Black	25.1	74.9	47.6	11.5	15.8	66.9	33.1	13.1	4.9	15.1	90.1	9.9	3.2	3.0	3.7
Hispanic	26.8	73.2	50.5	13.6	9.1	76.5	23.5	7.4	4.1	12.0	92.7	7.3	2.4	2.7	2.2
Age															
12 to 17 years	44.1	55.9	31.4	20.6	3.9	76.3	23.7	12.2	7.7	3.8	9.48	5.2	1.7	2.5	1.0
18 to 25 years	7.2	92.8	71.5	15.9	5.4	39.5	60.5	21.7	15.2	23.6	74.8	25.2	7.6	8.7	8.9
26 to 34 years	6.8	93.2	70.0	14.0	9.2	41.5	58.5	16.8	8.3	33.4	75.9	24.1	6.1	6.5	11.5
35 and over	12.0	88.0	57.3	12.6	18.1	84.1	15.9	2.2	1.6	12.1	95.8	4.2	(a)	NA	3.0
Region															
Northeast	9.9	90.1	66.1	15.2	8.8	64.4	35.6	10.2	6.3	19.1	86.9	13.1	3.5	4.2	5.4
North Central	11.3	88.7	64.8	13.4	10.5	66.4	33.6	9.5	6.0	18.1	89.8	10.2	2.6	2.3	5.3
South	19.0	81.0	47.2	15.4	18.4	73.4	26.6	8.0	5.1	13.5	90.6	9.4	1.4	2.8	5.2
West	12.9	87.1	65.0	12.4	9.7	62.7	37.3	10.9	6.6	19.8	84.7	15.3	5.2	4.2	5.9

NOTE: These data are from the 1985 National Household Survey on Drug Abuse sponsored by the National Institute on Drug Abuse and the National Institute on Alcohol Abuse and Alcoholism. Households were randomly sampled from all households in the contiguous United States from June to December 1985. The 1985 Survey is the eighth in a series of surveys measuring the prevalence of drug use among the American household population aged 12 and older.

^aLess than 0.5 percent

SOURCE: Timothy J. Flanagan and Katherine M. Jamieson, editors, 1988, Sourcebook of Criminal Justice Statistics, 1987, Albany, N.Y.: SUNY, Albany, Hindelang Criminal Justice Research Center, p. 287.

Table 13.2: Estimated Prevalence and Most Recent Use of Inhalants, Hallucinogens, and Stimulants. By Sex, Race, Age, and Region, United States, 1985.

	Inhalants					Hallucinogens					Stimulants				
			Most Recent Use					Most Recent Use					Most Recent Use		
	Never Used	Ever Used	Within Last 30 Days	Within Last 12 Months, but Not Last 30 Days	Not Within Last 12 Months	Never Used	Ever Used	Within Last 30 Days	Within Last 12 Months, but Not Last 30 Days	Not Within Last 12 Months	Never Used	Ever Used	Within Last 30 Days	Within Last 12 Months, but Not Last 30 Days	Not Within Last 12 Months
Total (N = 8,038)	93.2%	6.8%	0.9%	0.6%	5.3%	93.3%	6.7%	(a)	NA	5.3%	90.8%	9.2%	1.3%	2.8%	5.1%
Sex															
Male	90.9	9.1	1.3	0.9	6.9	91.0	9.0	0.8%	1.4%	6.8	88.9	11.1	1.9	3.6	5.6
Female	95.3	4.7	0.5	(a)	3.9	95.4	4.6	(a)	NA	4.0	92.5	7.5	0.8	1.9	4.8
Race															
White	92.8	7.2	1.0	0.6	5.6	92.4	7.6	0.6	0.9	6.1	89.7	10.	1.5	3.0	5.8
Black	95.1	4.9	(a)	NA	4.0	97.6	2.4	(a)	NA	NA	95.3	4.7	(a)	NA	2.6
Hispanic	95.5	4.5	(a)	NA	3.6	96.8	3.2	(a)	NA	2.5	95.4	4.6	0.6	1.3	2.7
Age															
12 to 17 years	90.9	9.1	3.4	1.6	4.1	96.8	3.2	1.1	1.5	0.6	94.5	5.5	1.6	2.6	1.3
18 to 25 years	87.2	12.8	0.9	1.3	10.6	88.5	11.5	1.6	2.0	7.9	82.7	17.3	3.8	6.3	7.2
26 to 34 years	90.1	9.9	1.0	0.5	8.4	83.2	16.8	(a)	NA	14.5	81.8	18.2	2.2	5.0	11.0
35 and over	96.8	3.2	(a)	NA	NA	97.7	2.3	(a)	NA	NA	95.8	4.2	(a)	NA	3.2
Region															
Northeast	92.4	7.6	1.1	0.6	5.9	93.2	6.8	(a)	NA	5.4	92.1	7.9	1.0	2.5	4.4
North Central	92.8	7.2	0.5	0.6	6.1	92.9	7.1	0.6	0.7	5.8	90.6	9.4	1.8	2.9	4.7
South	94.5	5.5	1.0	(a)	4.2	95.1	4.9	(a)	NA	3.9	93.2	6.8	0.9	2.1	3.8
West	92.6	7.4	1.0	0.9	5.5	90.5	9.5	0.7	1.3	7.5	85.1	14.9	2.0	3.8	9.1

[a]Less than 0.5 percent

SOURCE: Timothy J. Flanagan and Katherine M. Jamieson, editors, 1988, Sourcebook of Criminal Justice Statistics, 1987, Albany, N.Y.: SUNY, Albany, Hindelang Criminal Justice Research Center, p. 287.

Table 13.3 provides some promising findings with respect to future drug use trends. Surveys of student drug use are beginning to show declines in interest in drugs and usage since the late seventies. A recent national survey by Johnston, O'Malley, and Bachman (1987) attributed declining drug use not only to the same demographic shifts that have resulted in an aging population, but to an emergent anti-drug attitude among younger Americans. College surveys have demonstrated similar declines.

Despite the positive sign of a recent decline in teen drug use, the increase in overall U.S. drug use in the last two decades has been enormous and has spread to all social classes. In 1962 roughly 4 percent

Former First Lady Nancy Reagan spearheaded an anti-drug campaign in the 80s geared at getting young children to "just say no" to drug use. Unfortunately, the use of drugs by low-income youth in ghetto areas remained unaffected.

of adults aged eighteen to twenty-five had smoked marijuana, but by 1983 64 percent had. While only a small fraction had tried cocaine in 1962, by 1983 22 million people had done so (McBee and Peterson, 1983, p. 55). In the wake of explosive growth in U.S. drug use, it would be premature to forecast a coming drug dip because very recent data show an emergent antidrug attitude in the nation's youth; however, the aging

Table 13.3: Reported Drug Use within Last 12 Months among High School Seniors. By Type of Drug, United States, 1975–86.

Question: "On how many occasions, if any, have you used . . . during the last 12 months?"

(Percent who used in last 12 months)

Type of Drug	Class of 1975 (N = 9,400)	Class of 1976 (N = 15,400)	Class of 1977 (N = 17,100)	Class of 1978 (N = 17,800)
Marihuana/Hashish	40.0%	44.9%	47.6%	50.2%
Inhalants[a]	NA	3.0	3.7	4.1
Adjusted	NA	NA	NA	NA
Amyl and Butyl Nitrites[b]	NA	NA	NA	NA
Hallucinogens	11.2	9.4	8.8	9.6
Adjusted	NA	NA	NA	NA
LSD	7.2	6.4	5.5	6.3
PCP[b]	NA	NA	NA	NA
Cocaine	5.6	6.0	7.2	9.0
"Crack"[b,c]	NA	NA	NA	NA
Heroin	1.0	0.8	0.8	0.8
Other Opiates[d]	5.7	5.7	6.4	6.0
Stimulants[d]	16.2	15.8	16.3	17.1
Adjusted[d]	NA	NA	NA	NA
Sedatives[d]	11.7	10.7	10.8	9.9
Barbiturates[d]	10.7	9.6	9.3	8.1
Methaqualone[d]	5.1	4.7	5.2	4.9
Tranquilizers[d]	10.6	10.3	10.8	9.9
Alcohol	84.8	85.7	87.0	87.7
Cigarettes	NA	NA	NA	NA

[a]Data based on four questionnaire forms. N is four-fifths of N indicated.

[b]Data based on a single questionnaire form. N is one-fifth of N indicated.

[c]"Crack" is a highly potent and addictive form of cocaine.

[d]Only drug use which was not under a doctor's orders is included here.

Source: Timothy J. Flanagan and Katherine M. Jamieson, editors, 1988, *Sourcebook of Criminal Justice Statistics, 1987*, Albany, N.Y.: SUNY, Albany, Hindelang Criminal Justice Research Center, p. 281.

of the U.S. population and the apparent relative success of antismoking campaigns hold some promise that such a prognosis may have some merit. Unfortunately, this antidrug movement does not appear to be taking place in ghetto areas among low income minority youth, where the recent popularity of crack (a hardened, inexpensive, smokable form of cocaine) has been a scourge.

Class of 1979 (N = 15,500)	Class of 1980 (N = 15,900)	Class of 1981 (N = 17,500)	Class of 1982 (N = 17,700)	Class of 1983 (N = 16,300)	Class of 1984 (N = 15,900)	Class of 1985 (N = 16,000)	Class of 1986 (N = 15,200)
50.8%	48.8%	46.1%	44.3%	42.3%	40.0%	40.6%	38.8%
5.4	4.6	4.1	4.5	4.3	5.1	5.7	6.1
9.2	7.8	6.0	6.6	6.7	7.9	7.2	8.9
6.5	5.7	3.7	3.6	3.6	4.0	4.0	4.7
9.9	9.3	9.0	8.1	7.3	6.5	6.3	6.0
12.8	10.6	10.1	9.3	9.3	7.9	7.7	7.6
6.6	6.5	6.5	6.1	5.4	4.7	4.4	4.5
7.0	4.4	3.2	2.2	2.6	2.3	2.9	2.4
12.0	12.3	12.4	11.5	11.4	11.6	13.1	12.7
NA	NA	NA	NA	NA	NA	NA	4.1
0.5	0.5	0.5	0.6	0.6	0.5	0.6	0.5
6.2	6.3	5.9	5.3	5.1	5.2	5.9	5.2
18.3	20.8	26.0	26.1	24.6	NA	NA	NA
NA	NA	NA	20.3	17.9	17.7	15.8	13.4
9.9	10.3	10.5	9.1	7.9	6.6	5.8	5.2
7.5	6.8	6.6	5.5	5.2	4.9	4.6	4.2
5.9	7.2	7.6	6.8	5.4	3.8	2.8	2.1
9.6	8.7	8.0	7.0	6.9	6.1	6.1	5.8
88.1	87.9	87.0	86.8	87.3	86.0	85.6	84.5
NA	NA	NA	NA	NA	NA	NA	NA

Crack Cocaine

Coke—snow, blow, nose candy, Bolivian marching powder—the drug of Hollywood, of Wall Street, of "sex, drugs and rock 'n roll." Cocaine has become the "hip" drug of the last decade of the twentieth century. While at first believed to be nonaddictive, it has emerged as very dangerous; and what was at first thought to be a scare film, *Cocaine Fiends,* actually bears a close resemblance to reality (Maranto, 1985). A variation of cocaine, "crack" has considerably raised the violence levels associated with drug trafficking in inner city ghettos. Images of twelve- and thirteen-year-olds carrying Uzi submachine guns and earning more than their parents and teachers are no exaggeration (Drug Rings, 1988).

Another emergent drug is related in part to the fitness craze. "Steroid abuse" came to international attention during the 1988 Olympics when Canadian gold medalist Ben Johnson was asked to give up his medals due to such a drug violation. Bodybuilders and athletes utilize steroids to promote tissue growth and to gain weight and muscles. While outlawed in most athletic organizations, it is used despite increasing research which shows tremendous potential harm. This may include injury to organs, early death, and possible increases in aggressive and psychotic behavior (Weaver, 1988).

Drug Abuse and Crime

The term *addicts* is often used to describe a category of drug abusers who have developed severe dependencies. The definition and estimates of number of addicts, however, has been problematic. As part of the war on the "phantom army of addicts," some government figures estimating the amount of street crime due to addicts also practiced statistical overkill. Estimates in the early seventies, such as $18 billion, were several times greater than the total sum of property stolen but unrecovered throughout the entire country using UCR data for the same year (Epstein, 1977, p. 177; and Singer, 1971). Despite the attention called to the danger of these "mythical numbers" (Ibid.), Reuter (1984b, p. 136) indicates that in the thirteen years since Singer's article, "there is a strong interest in keeping the number high and none in keeping it correct." Estimates both of crime by addicts (Chaiken and Chaiken, 1982; and Ball et al., 1982) and of the estimated size of the illegal drug market remain problematic.

The concept of *addiction* is used primarily to describe those who have become dependent upon opium and opium derivatives such as morphine, heroin, and various medicines which contain opiates. Addiction involves a *physiological dependence* commonly referred to as *tolerance,* in which the body requires larger and larger dosages of the substance in order to experience the desired effect. Once this dependence is developed, absence of the required dosage produces the *withdrawal or abstinence syndrome*, physical discomfort experienced by an addict when deprived of the drug upon which he or she has become dependent. Finally, *psychological dependence* involves mentally connecting the withdrawal syndrome with one's physiological dependence and the addict's decision thereafter to continue to use the substance. The fact that addiction is less a permanent condition than believed could be illustrated by the fact that there are few heroin addicts over the age of thirty-five. In addition, a survey of Vietnam veterans found that while about one-third used opiates in Vietnam and one-fifth were addicted, only one percent continued using the drugs upon returning stateside (Robins, 1974).

Much of the crime associated with drug addiction is due to the high cost addicts must pay for illegal sources of supply in order to support their need for a "fix." While costs of heroin vary, assuming a hypothetical $50 per day habit, addicts would have to come up with over $18,000 a year for heroin alone. Unless addicts have occupations which provide either high income or easy access to drugs (such as medicine), most must steal to support their habit; the major means of support for many is dealing in drugs themselves (Inciardi, 1979, 1981; and Stephens and Ellis, 1975). For others, crime is the source of funds. Research in the past has suggested that the majority of crimes committed by heroin addicts are crimes against property, such as burglary and shoplifting or prostitution for females, although 47 percent of the males had committed robbery. Gropper (1985) indicates that, contrary to what has been said in past research, heroin-using criminals are as likely as non-using criminals to kill and rape and are more likely to commit robbery and weapons offenses. In addition there are a wide variety of different types of drug-involved offenders requiring different types of responses by the criminal justice system (Chaiken and Johnson, 1988).

In an ethnographic study of "Hustletown," a neighborhood in northern Manhattan, Strug et al. (1984) describe individuals who are equally addicted to both drugs and alcohol and who "hustle" in order to support these habits. "Hustling" includes a wide variety of illegal and quasi-legal moneymaking schemes including burglary, shoplifting, prostitution, "con" games, and service roles within drug dealing. Such low-level crime becomes "the career" of street hustlers, who despair of finding adequate employment opportunities. Most of their crimes are low-level and nonviolent in nature.

In *Taking Care of Business* Johnson et al. (1985) did a related in-depth study of 201 New York City heroin abusers. They found most of their subjects were polysubstance abusers. None used only heroin and almost all also used cocaine, alcohol, and other drugs. While most were involved in criminal activity such as shoplifting and burglary, they also supported their habits through being "user-dealers." Nurco et al.'s (1988) study of criminal activity by drug addicts found that, for those previously involved in crime, addiction simply increases an already established criminal lifestyle while ". . . for those not involved in preaddiction crime, addiction status is associated with a much sharper exacerbation in criminal behavior" (Ibid., p. 418). In 1988 two-thirds of those arrested in New York City, Washington, Chicago, and Los Angeles tested positive for drugs (Kurtz, 1989, p. A–14; and Anglin and Speckart, 1988). Inciardi (1979) in a study of 356 Miami addicts found that they had committed 118,134 crimes during a one-year period.

In examining the relationship between addiction and crime, it is also important to recognize that many addicts were involved in criminal activity prior to their addictions and that many support their habits through funds earned in legitimate occupations. The relationship between addiction and crime is not a necessary one, as is illustrated by the British program of prescribing legal maintenance doses to heroin addicts; in that case, there is little incidental crime associated with addiction. Recent growth in addiction problems in the United Kingdom has led to some changes (Bennett, 1988; and British Clinics, 1985). Much of the crime related to addiction is due to the high price of drugs due to their prohibition. Erich Goode (1981, pp. 255–256) indicates that there was little crime associated with addiction in the nineteenth century.

Drunkenness

Just as Brecher (1972, p. 39) had described turn-of-the-century U.S. as a "dope fiend's paradise," Rorabaugh (1979) indicates that U.S. consumption of alcohol was much higher during the eighteenth and nineteenth centuries than it is presently. Even today, examination of the problem of drug abuse in America finds alcohol abuse as still constituting the nation's number one drug problem. "Problem drinking," the current preferred term for what is called alcoholism, has already been described as a major lethal ingredient in crimes of violence as well as in vehicular homicide (Collins, 1981). The other major alcohol-related problematic area in criminal justice relates to the chronic inebriates, who make up over half of U.S. misdemeanor arrests and county jail inmates.

Problem drinkers consume alcohol beverages in excess of dietary or social custom to an extent that it affects their health and social relationships. Immersed in a drinking culture, some cross the line into problem drinking or alcoholism. In our previous discussion of "driving under the influence" we touched upon the violent repercussions of driving while experiencing the distorting effects of alcohol or drugs. In the late eighties two incidents occurred which underlined the actual danger. The first was illustrated by a case on the East Coast where a railroad engineer, high on marijuana, ignored stoplights on a railroad siding and directed his train directly into the path of a high-speed passenger train, with obvious results in death and injury. The second occurred in Prince William Sound, Alaska, when an Exxon oil supertanker ran aground when its allegedly drunken pilot turned over the wheel to an untrained third mate. The subsequent huge spill threatened major ecological damage to a fragile subarctic environment.

In May of 1985 Soviet Premier Gorbachev declared alcoholism the Soviet Union's number one domestic enemy and began an antialcohol drive. Fully one-third of the crime in the U.S.S.R. was estimated to be linked to drunkenness in a nation with one of the highest alcoholism rates in the world and one in which the average life expectancy has been declining rather than rising. Strict limits on hard-liquor purchases created an enormous illegal moonshining industry with lethal consequences in poisonings. In the Ukraine alone over thirty-six thousand illegal home stills were destroyed by police in 1987–1988 (Trimble, 1988).

While there is no universally accepted medical or psychological model of alcoholism, many accept a "medical model," which describes it as a disease. A useful descriptive model which illustrates this approach is Jellinek's (1960) profile of the stages of alcohol addiction. These are: the prealcoholic phase, the intermediate stage, the crucial phase, and the final or bottom phase. The prealcoholic phase involves occasional relief drinking as a means of alleviating tension in which, after a time, greater amounts of alcohol are needed in order to generate the desired effect. The intermediate stage occurs when drinking becomes no longer simply a source of relief, but is sought as a drug. Secretive drinking, occasional blackouts or amnesia, alibis, and a compulsion to drink are accompanied by a loss of control. In the crucial phase, the loss of control becomes more complete; the drinker is no longer able to maintain a resolution not to drink. Isolation from others, including family, increases as life becomes alcohol-centered. The final or bottom phase is characterized by the drinker's extensive emotional disorganization. Ethical deterioration, impaired thinking, and obsessive drinking characterize the bottomed-out, chronic alcoholic.

Such chronic inebriates are often handled under what is called the "golden rule disposition" in which, for their own protection, they are picked up by police without formal arrest, jailed overnight, then released in the morning (see Bittner, 1967). Despite frequent arrests or processing, most such individuals do not view themselves as criminals. Arrests for such drunkenness have in fact decreased in many jurisdictions since the early seventies; more police forces have begun to employ strategies of cooperation with local social service agencies which are designed to treat such problem drinkers. Typically local police, when they come across a consistent public inebriate, call such a center. The center's personnel transport the subject to a treatment center where he or she is bathed, dried out, fed, counseled, and provided the opportunity to break the alcohol-obsessive cycle. In addition to providing more meaningful treatment, such programs relieve the police and jails of an improper burden, freeing up law enforcement resources for more appropriate tasks.

Special Populations

A conservative political climate in America in the eighties has led to cuts in social programs and a burgeoning homeless population, as well as a deinstitutionalized mentally ill population. The police, although also cut in manpower, became by default social workers of last resort. "They do so because peace officers are unique in providing free, around-the-clock service, mobility, a legal obligation to respond, and legal authority to detain" (Finn and Sullivan, 1988, p. 2).

Societal Reaction

Popular social philosopher Marshall McLuhan was once quoted as having stated something to the effect that "the past went that-a-way." The rapid pace of social change and subsequent cultural lag which it creates has been endemic in the United States in the post-World War II period. We tend to forget that early in this century cigarette smoking was considered deviant. Similarly, the consumption of alcohol was so dimly viewed that it resulted in a constitutional amendment to forbid its usage.

In democratic societies in the name of civil liberties there is a constant testing of the boundaries of toleration of, as well as decriminalization of, many victimless crimes. Such is less the case under more authoritarian regimes. Nettler (1982, vol. 1, p. 126) indicates:

> Totalitarian regimes are strengthened by an ideology that includes moral conceptions of how people should behave. Modern tyrants therefore have no hesitation about punishing activities they define as immoral, activities ranging from homosexuality and prostitution to drunkenness, absenteeism from work, the use of narcotics, and expression of "wrong" ideas. There is no freedom in Cuba, the People's Republic of China, or the Soviet Union to

be a "drag queen," a whore, an addict, or a dissident. Moreover, there is no public debate in these countries about whether people should be free to choose some of these practices or to criticize their social orders.

As previously indicated, Edwin Schur's (1965) concept of "crimes without victims" refers specifically to consensual, adult activities usually conducted in private in which there is no apparent harm to others. The criminalization of such activities, as illustrated by the Prohibition experiment, often involves ineffective *overcriminalization*, an inappropriate overextension of the criminal law into areas of personal conduct and morality. Most public order crime constitutes violations of legislated morality. Prohibition of such crimes represents an effort to control or regulate moral and personal behavior through formal laws, often without attempts to mold public opinion, which is necessary in order to support the legislative and police activity. Since much of the activity is consensual and private, law enforcement efforts often involve invasion of privacy and the use of extraordinary efforts which threaten civil liberties, leading some observers to describe such efforts as not only expensive and ineffective, but also criminogenic (Morris and Hawkins, 1970, p. 2). In Chapter 1, Sumner's notion that, if laws fail to obtain the support of the mores, they will tend to be ineffective, suggests that criminalization of these offenses has not markedly decreased their activity. Only a small proportion of offenders are reached by the criminal justice system or deterred by the criminal status of the offense.

In harmful, nonconsensual areas the criminal justice system can have an impact in reducing prohibited activity. In 1988 a U.S. Customs Bureau sting, "Operation Borderline," set up a phony child pornography mail-order house in Toronto and then rounded up many pedophiles who ordered such materials. They were charged under a 1984 Child Protection Act, which outlawed the distribution of all sexually explicit material involving children. Such programs are believed to have reduced considerably the child pornography trade (Cohn, 1988; and Anderson and Van Atta, 1986). In consensual vice activities, however, Cook (1988, p. 1) points out: "The criminal law is a cumbersome, costly tool to wield against the harms associated with vice."

The history of the regulation of vice has been one of constant symbolic political posturing with one oftentimes finding little relationship between what is said and what is done. In 1987 President Ronald Reagan not only declared war on drugs but also declared victory, claiming his administration's drug jihad was "an untold American success story." Two years later national news magazines were sensationally declaring that sections of large cities were so overrun by drug gangs they were "dead zones" or "Beirut, U.S.A.," and that "the drug problem and its accompanying violence has clearly outstripped the resources and capability of local governments, police departments, courts, and prisons to cope with them" (Moore et al., 1989, p. 28). While phony wars on drugs were declared, the criminal justice and social service resources to fight the war were cut. For example, in 1973 Washington, D.C., had 5,100 police, but only 3,950 in 1989 (Kurtz, 1989). The DEA had 2,400 agents in 1986, the same number as in 1976 (Ex-Agents Say, 1986). By 1986 the number of public facilities for treating drug abusers had been cut by one-third from their levels in the seventies (Gest, 1986). In a sense it became not a question of more criminal justice efforts or decriminalization, but *do anything* besides talk.

Overcriminalization

Overcriminalization or extension of the criminal law into inappropriate areas of moral conduct results in a number of outcomes:

- Many such laws are virtually unenforceable.
- They often lead to corruption of criminal justice personnel and politicians.
- They undermine public respect for the law.
- They create illicit monopolies for organized crime groups.
- They criminalize activities and stigmatize their participants.
- They reflect no consistent, defensible theory of harm (Richards, 1982, p. 194).
- They isolate and embitter offenders.
- Penalties are often ineffective and/or inappropriate. In the past, for instance, tough drug laws netted many marijuana users and few big drug pushers.
- Such laws tie up law enforcement agencies in thankless tasks which could more appropriately be performed by other social agencies.

Decriminalization

Decriminalization refers to the process of lessening the penalties attached to particular offenses. Some arguments in support of decriminalizing many public order crimes include:

- Such activities should not be the concern of the state and formal agents of social control, but are more appropriately handled by informal modes of control such as the family, community, church, and the like.
- State interference with much of this behavior often makes matters worse. The criminalization of drug users and view of them as crimi-

nals rather than people with medical problems has cut off the legal supply of drugs, created illegal monopolies, and forced many into criminal activity in order to support their habits.

■ Such laws tend to accomplish little with those already favorably disposed to such activity. Homosexuality, prostitution, gambling, and the like have been and will continue to be persistent activities in modern society.

■ A concentration of law enforcement officers upon such public-order crimes overburdens the criminal justice system with inappropriate tasks, preventing the deployment of resources in combatting more serious crimes.

The issue of decriminalization is a matter of degrees of regulation-deregulation rather than of categorical legalization-illegalization. Proposals for decriminalization entail lessening of penalties, but not total abandonment of public or official concern with maintaining some degree of control over the expression of such activities. Fears have been raised that decriminalization of such activities constitutes societal approval.

In 1957 the English Wolfenden Report in examining laws related to homosexuality and prostitution concluded that private, consensual, adult sexual relations were not the law's business. With respect to homosexuality one could ask whether individuals really have much choice in or power to change their sexual orientation. Those who oppose decriminalization of homosexual activities fear proselytizing and seduction of the young. Such a "floodgate theory" (the assumption that decriminalization of homosexuality will increase such behavior) has not been borne out in England (West, 1988, pp. 181, 186). While the menace of AIDS has curtailed some more promiscuous homosexual activity, for example, as in bath houses, it is probably impossible to suppress all homosexuality.

The degree of decriminalization, of course, varies with the type of offense. Few propose decriminalization of predatory or harmful practices such as child molesting or incest, as few would urge that acts which violate privacy, such as exhibitionism or voyeurism, simply be ignored. Civil commitment proceedings by which psychological treatment is prescribed is an important tool for the protection of society. In public inebriate programs, the police remain involved but maximize the use of community social service agencies. Combined with decriminalization public media programs can be used to play a role in discouraging undesirable activity. There has been some recent rethinking of the wisdom of decriminalizing public drunkenness. As our earlier discussion of "broken windows" (Wilson and Kelling, 1982) suggested:

"The presence on the streets of boisterous, obstreperous, and sometimes belligerent drunks contributes to a sense of social disorder" (Jacobs, 1987, p. 2). A field experiment in Lynn, Massachusetts, demonstrated the efficacy of street level enforcement (making it difficult for drug dealers to make a sale and for buyers to "score" or purchase) in improving the quality of life in a community (Kleiman et al., 1988).

The decline in proportion of Americans who smoke tobacco from 42 percent of adults in 1956 to 33 percent in 1980 is illustrative of a more moderate approach to discouraging the use of harmful substances. Arnold Trebach (1984, pp. 136–137) in "Peace without Surrender in the Perpetual Drug War" indicates:

> We did not declare a war on tobacco. We did not make it illegal. We did not say that tobacco addicts . . . were evil. We did not seek to disrupt foreign or domestic tobacco supplies. Indeed, we will subsidize the production of the most dangerous psychoactive drug known to our people.
>
> We did seek to convince our citizens not to smoke through persuasion, objective information and education. . . . Laws do not prohibit smoking entirely, only where and when an addict can take a "fix." In other words, the law did not confront the user head on by absolutely prohibiting this deadly practice. But the law did have a role: it discouraged, it controlled, it curbed, it coaxed.

Evidence related to the criminalization-decriminalization debate is uncertain, as can be illustrated by attempts to control heroin or opium abuse. The pre-1972 British program that medically administered legal doses of heroin to addicts may have meant both a smaller addict population and little crime associated with such addiction (Trebach, 1982). On the other hand, the British Crown Colony of Hong Kong with the same program but a different culture has an addiction problem much greater than that in the United States. Arguments for more zealous law enforcement efforts can point to the People's Republic of China, which through totalitarian policing appears to have nearly eliminated the problem. Such police powers would be culturally unacceptable in Western democracies and have not been particularly successful in brutal authoritarian regimes such as contemporary Iran, where Trebach (1984, p. 137) claims heroin addiction has exploded to include the improbable estimate of one of every twelve Iranians, despite public executions of users and traffickers (see also Trebach, 1987).

Many of the issues that we have examined in this chapter are complex and laden with heavy moral implications. We have, of course, only scratched the surface of some heavy debates which exist on these subjects.

Summary

Public order crime refers to a number of activities that are illegal because they offend public morality. Being primarily nonpredatory, *mala prohibita* acts such as behavior related to prostitution, homosexuality, drug and alcohol abuse, and sexual deviance, they are sometimes called "crimes without victims," consensual crimes, or folk crimes. Liazos's title, "nuts, sluts and preverts," is an attempt to call attention to the fact that studies of deviance have overconcentrated upon the bizarre and kinky at the expense of more serious predatory and elite criminality. The concept of "broken windows" suggests that neglect of public peacekeeping functions encourages disorder.

Prostitution involves sexual relations with emotional indifference on a promiscuous and mercenary basis; the act of soliciting or seeking paying customers is prohibited, not prostitution itself. With the exception of some preliterate societies, prostitution exists internationally and was in fact tolerated throughout most of Western history. *Homosexuality,* sexual relations with members of one's own sex, may be prosecuted under sodomy statutes which prohibit "crimes against nature," often defined as including mouth-genital, anal intercourse, and the like. These same laws, which are generally not enforced, also apply to heterosexual activity. The wide variety of *sexual offenses* includes *exhibitionism* (indecent exposure), *voyeurism* (peeping), and *fetishism* (unusual veneration of sexual attire or objects). *Nonvictimless sexual offenses* include *incest* (intrafamilial sexual intercourse) and *pedophilia* (child molesting); these two are the most seriously regarded deviations. *Sadism* (inflicting pain for sexual gratification) and *masochism* (experiencing pain for sexual gratification) also may entail nonconsensual harm. The legal status of pornography (sexually stimulating media) continues to raise controversy, as does that of gambling and abortion. *Drunkenness-related offenses* are covered under a variety of state laws such as drunk in a public place, breach of peace, disorderly conduct, and the like. The Prohibition experiment, complete criminalization of alcohol usage, was abandoned as a failure. *Drug abuse,* the misuse of chemical substances, has followed much the same pattern as alcohol; that is, primary control has been attempted until recently through criminal laws and penalties. There is an inconsistent relationship between drugs' known harmful effects and their illegality.

Examination of the *criminal careers of most public order offenders* finds that most do not view themselves as criminals. Most are participating in either consensual adult relations or—in the case of activities such as exhibitionism—are suffering from some psychological disorder. *Prostitution* exhibits a variety of types, including brothels, bar girls, streetwalkers, massage parlors, and call girls. *Johns*, prostitutes' customers, do not necessarily fit a pathology-ridden characterization. Underaged prostitution, the sexual exploitation of children, is believed to be becoming more prevalent in part due to the erosion of family structure. *Homosexuality* may be learned as part of the process of socialization; it consists of many types, including preferential and situational patterns. Humphreys' *tearoom* study of homosexual relations in public restrooms identified several types: ambi-sexuals, gay guys, closet queens, and trade. Sexual offenders include the more serious *child molesters* or *pedophiliacs*. The latter type is illustrated by cases in which young children have been molested by teachers or other caretakers, showing that many offenders are known and trusted by the victim and his or her family. Incest is another intimate type of victimization. General characteristics of sex offenders were presented.

The history of drugs and drug abuse portrays increased criminalization of drug usage beginning with the Harrison Act of 1914, which resulted in the concept of addiction as a sickness being replaced with that of addiction as criminal. Much of this legal approach to drug policy was viewed as being brought about in part by *moral entrepreneurs* such as Anslinger and Hobson. Other information was given of the "phantom army of addicts" (statistical shenanigans) and the agency of fear (Nixon's ODALE). Patterns in drug use demonstrate a virtual explosion since the sixties; however, some recent data *may* signal the first signs of a coming drug dip.

Drug trafficking is highly lucrative and practiced by a large number of groups. While statistics regarding the association between drug abuse and crime have been subject to exaggeration, a tremendous amount of primarily nonviolent property crime is committed by addicts because of the high cost of illegal drugs. Addiction—which includes physiological dependence (tolerance), psychological dependence, and the abstinence syndrome—is less a permanent condition than is often suggested. Little crime is associated with addiction, however, if legal supplies are available. *Problem drinking*, alcoholism, is associated with violent crime as well as with the chronic inebriate problem. The law enforcement burden imposed by the latter has been alleviated, in part by means of greater utilization of social service agencies.

Societal reaction to public-order criminality varies between the extremes of overcriminalization and decriminalization. Totalitarian societies simply forbid such activities, while democratic societies must constantly balance the tensions between civil liberties and social morality. Various problems raised by overcriminalization were described, while arguments for decriminalization were also discussed.

KEY CONCEPTS

Public Order Crime
Crimes without Victims
Folk Crime
Exhibitionism
Voyeurism
Fetishism
Pedophilia
Types of Prostitution

Johns
Harrison Act
Moral Entrepreneurs
Broken Windows
Sodomy
Tearoom
Closet Queens
Incest

Mark-Recapture Technique
Addiction
Withdrawal Syndrome
Problem Drinking
Overcriminalization
Decriminalization
Floodgate Theory

14 The Future of Crime

Criminological Theory and Social Policy

Preceding chapters have examined the research methods employed in criminology, some findings with respect to types of criminal behavior which application of these methods has produced, and general theories which attempt to provide explanations for this behavior. Some observers feel, however, that such a search for general causes is "a lost cause in criminology" (Inciardi, 1978, pp. 90–115) or even an illustration of what James Q. Wilson (1975, p. 51) calls the *causal fallacy*, which is "to assume that no problem is adequately addressed unless its causes are eliminated." While these views will be critiqued shortly, they illustrate and perhaps reinforce the state of despair experienced by students who, after reviewing criminological theories, find each of these explanations soundly criticized. They ask which theory is correct and, if none of them is correct, then why study them?

Theory is not truth, fact, or law, but merely a plausible explanation of reality. All social policy is guided either implicitly or explicitly by theoretical assumptions. According to the ancient Hindu fable called the Jain legend, some blind men, upon first encountering an elephant, attempted to explain or theorize as to what it was; each blind man theorized on the basis of touch and smell within his own range of experience—and one indicated "it is a snake," another "it is a wall," and yet another "it is a tree." Various limited theories may yet be linked into an acceptable general theory (Cullen, 1984b) and, while each theory in the two preceding chapters was found to contain certain shortcomings, much criticism related to the failure of each to limit its explanation to the type/s of criminality to which the theory was addressed.

In what he describes as "The Demise of the Criminological Imagination," Frank Williams (1984) laments the lack of any new, imaginative theoretical contributions to the field beginning in the seventies. He explains this hiatus in theory as due to three factors: a recent lack of criminological imagination, the critical environment that made the sixties such a dynamic decade, and the emergence of criminal justice as a discipline. Criminological imagination, "the creative generation of new theory," has been stymied by an overemphasis upon "empirical scientism," which is an overconcentration upon methodological precision at the expense of theory development. The critical intellectual environment nurtured by the sixties emphasized analysis of differences between theories of the expense of the integration of theoretical concepts. Finally, the rise of criminal justice as a discipline in part due to increased federal funds to fight rising crime in the sixties attracted intellectual energy to the issue of the crime control system and programmatic efforts to improve its efficiency. Thus a quantitative, critical, and applied criminology discouraged the type of theoretical developments characteristic of the field prior to 1970. If Williams is correct, this spells intellectual rigor mortis for a field which is satisfied to serve as technician for existing crime control policies and ideology.

Throughout this text, descriptions of the operation of the criminal justice system have been only incidental to accounts of criminals and crime. Much of the future of crime and criminal activity will be influenced by various social policies that are shaped to direct the police, the courts, and corrections. A succinct overview of the criminal justice system as prepared by the Bureau of Justice Statistics (1983) is presented in the Appendix.

The Ill-Fated War on Crime

The "war on crime" in the United States was launched as a social policy with much fanfare in 1967 and, after the expenditure of approximately $8 billion, was all but abandoned in 1981. Begun as a result of rising crime rates in the sixties, it represented the first time in American history that the federal government took it upon itself to fight crime. The rise and fall of the national war on crime is described by Thomas and Tania Cronin and Michael Milakovich in *U.S. v. Crime in the Streets* (1981, p. 11) as originating at a time in which "America . . . did not yet doubt its pragmatic genius. Everything was possible if you just spent enough money!" Despite the fact that the federal executive office could exercise little impact in crime control—primarily a state and local responsibility as well as that of the judicial branch—political candidates for national office seized the issue. This national involvement commenced with the Safe Streets Act and the election of a law-and-order President, Richard Nixon, in 1968. Presidential counselor John Dean (1977, pp. 389–90) explains: "I was cranking out that bullshit on Nixon's crime policy before he was elected. And it was bullshit too. We knew it. The Nixon campaign didn't call for anything about crime problems that Ramsey Clark [Johnson's Attorney General] wasn't already doing under LBJ. We just made more noise."

The Cronins and Milakovich (1981, p. 78) explain that crime was largely viewed as street crime and particularly a problem of unemployed urban black male juveniles. Under the Law Enforcement

Assistance Administration, large amounts of money were expended into many existing criminal justice programs that were simply relabeled in order to meet funding guidelines. By 1972 "LEAA became the unwanted child of the national government. It had become apparent even to politicians that no president could make a promise to end crime and keep that promise. . . . As lowered expectations became policy, LEAA's funding was sharply reduced until the agency was killed off" (Ibid., p. 106). It was perhaps a fitting irony that the national administration leaders who most exploited the law-and-order campaign issue were forced to prematurely resign in disgrace due to their own criminal activity.

The short-lived "war on crime" was primarily an attack upon street crimes and lower class criminals, the "dangerous classes." Hardly mentioned were the most expensive areas of criminality, occupational and organizational crimes—suite crimes. While the issue of crime remained, other items, particularly environmental and economic, became preeminent on the social agenda in the seventies and eighties.

Dirty Secrets

The relatively conservative view that the crime problem can be solved by increasing the technical efficiency of the existing criminal justice system ignores what was described as "the dirty secrets" of crime (Gross, 1980, p. 110). The "dirty little secret" is that most violent street crime is prevalent in structural criminogenic conditions associated with poverty, unemployment, inadequate education, substance abuse, and other economic ills about which the criminal justice system can do little. The "dirty big secret" (Ibid., p. 113) is that the criminal justice system is soft on corporate crime. The war on crime had been a war on some crime, reflecting a distinctive world view or ideology regarding the nature of the crime problem.

Ideology and Social Policy ———————————

Causal vs. Policy Analysis

Ideology was defined previously as a distinctive belief system about what *should* occur, consisting of an aggregate of doctrines, ideas, assumptions, attitudes, and beliefs. Theory and research provide explanations and facts regarding crime and criminal behavior; ideological viewpoints provide the political direction for guiding social policy. Historian Arthur Schlesinger, Jr., in his *The Cycles of American History* (1986) argues that American history and public policy have been punctuated by pendular shifts in which a dominant liberal era runs its course, to be succeeded by a conservative era whose time has come until it also runs its course, to be followed once again by a liberal era. Both Wilson and Herrnstein (1985) and Hirschi (1983) expressed the point of view that the field of the family severed its connections with criminological theory in the fifties and sixties for ideological reasons which favored the examination of larger institutions. Currie (1985, pp. 183–184) also feels that directions in crime and delinquency theory often reflect broader ideological trends in society rather than the fruits of any new research breakthroughs. Conservative political scientist James Q. Wilson (1983a; and 1975, pp. 50–53) draws a distinction between *causal analysis* and *policy analysis* that parallels distinctions made earlier in this text between pure research/theory and applied research/theory. He calls the assumption that "no problem is adequately addressed unless its causes are eliminated" (Ibid., p. 51) the causal fallacy, claiming that ultimate causes cannot be the subject of social policy since they are not subject to change. Advocates of this view tend to consider much causal analysis as an impractical, ivory tower exercise in futility.

Policy Analysis

Policy analysis is practical, applied research and:

> begins with a very different perspective. It asks not what is the "cause" of a problem, but what is the condition one wants to bring into being . . . what policy tools does a government (in our case, a democratic and libertarian government) possess that might when applied, produce at reasonable cost a desired alteration in the present condition or progress toward the required condition? (Ibid., p. 53)

Wilson's causal vs. policy analysis distinction is simply the resurrection of the pure vs. applied research issue discussed in the first chapter. While he is correct in his insistence that something practical must be done about street crime and that policy prescriptions cannot wait until final cause is established, he is incorrect in assuming that his policy approach is atheoretical and not concerned with ultimate cause.

The Social Policy Fallacy

Any policy approach contains inherent theoretical assumptions, acknowledged or not, as can be demonstrated in an analysis of approaches to social policy. In fact, to coin a term, Wilson and others have been guilty of the *social policy fallacy*, the erroneous belief that in a democratic society applied social policy can be effective even though it ignores causal roots. Such solutions, in nonauthoritarian societies, represent only limited, temporary solutions so long as social policy fails to address the critical structural factors which generate the problems it is attempting to resolve.

Ideological Approaches to Criminal Justice Policy

A variety of ideological approaches could be identified, ranging from conservative to radical approaches (Miller, 1973), and is suggested in Herbert Packer's (1968) often-cited *models of the criminal justice process:* the crime control and the due process models. The *crime control model* emphasizes law and order, bureaucratic efficiency in law enforcement, and the prosecution of criminals. Packer compares this model to assembly-line justice in which the criminal justice system is judged on the basis of maximization of apprehensions and convictions. The *due process model* is viewed analogously as an obstacle course in which justice and rights of the accused are held paramount. This emphasis slows down bureaucratic efficiency but is appropriate to a democratic society where the ideal is law, order, and justice, with justice interpreted as protection of legal guarantees of the accused.

Conservative, Liberal, and Radical Approaches

Many ideological stances exist, but this presentation will examine *three ideological approaches to criminal justice policy:* the conservative, liberal, and radical. Each of these is viewed as an "ideal type" in that distinctions between the types are exaggerated and are unlikely to exist in as pure of a form as discussed.

The *conservative approach* to crime control policy is represented by writers such as James Q. Wilson (1975 and 1983a) and Ernest Van den Haag (1975). Though they deny a commitment to any causal theory, most advocates of this approach reflect the classical school of criminological theory. Crime is viewed as the product of free will of the individual actors, who can be deterred by means of more sure, swift, and certain punishment and better application of the crime control model. Such writers tend to concentrate upon crime in the streets as committed by the "dangerous classes," and are oriented toward incapacitation (deterrence through incarceration) and the just-deserts doctrine (retribution).

The *liberal approach*, represented by such writers as Currie (1985) and Reiman (1984), as well as many others, insists that society, in addition to developing crime control measures to contain crime in the streets, must address root causes of crime such as inequality, racism, unemployment, urban blight, and the like. Most liberals also insist that inquiry be directed not only at street crimes, but also at occupational, organizational, political, and other more elite criminal activity. They also tend to be supportive of the due process model, which views crime control as subordinate to upholding the rights of individuals, and have been leading advocates of rehabilitation as a correctional measure.

The *radical approach* usually calls for dramatic alteration in the social structure and its institutions as a means of controlling criminality. Such an approach, discussed in the previous chapter as radical Marxist theory, views crime as an outgrowth of inequalities created in capitalistic economic systems. Represented by the later work of such writers as Richard Quinney (1977) and William Chambliss (1976), radicals tend to overlook political and organizational crimes in noncapitalistic systems.

The Future of Crime

Criminologists lack a crystal ball or some other tool of legerdemain with which to peer into the future and forecast its likely direction. Along with other social scientists and futurists, they can demarcate some likely decisions; however, even these are affected by a myriad of variables whose trends may not be fully anticipated. For example, in examining Canadian crime rates, Daniel Koenig et al. (1983, p. 98) claim:

> Very simply, Canadian crime rates whether of violence, property crime, or other offenses—do not appear to bear any consistent relationship to economic inequality, rates of unemployment or inflation, or changes in per capita income expressed either in current or constant dollars. Nor, for that matter, is there any consistent relationship between Canadian crime rates and either urbanization or the age structure of the population.

The big U.S. crime wave that began in the midsixties apparently stabilized in the decade of the seventies, official statistics to the contrary. "Moreover, forecasts of crime rates based upon projected changes in demographic composition of the population, drug use patterns and other factors lead one to believe that crime will decrease slightly in the future" (Chaiken and Chaiken, 1983, p. 11). Utilizing broad demographic and cultural trends criminologists were accurate in predicting the crime dip which began in the eighties. Crime, being a behavior which is socially defined, can increase or decrease with legislative activity which broadens or lessens the categories included and is responsive to Ferri's "saturation law of criminology" in that it expands to fit the amount of social control activity. Donald Black (1976) has also observed that crime increases with growth in the criminal law.

The orientation of this text is one in which one responds to the question "What causes crime?" with the retort "What type of crime?" In the same light, predictions of the future of crime will vary with the type of criminal activity that is the subject of prognosis.

Public opinion surveys suggest that the public and the media consider upper level occupational crime as very serious. Whether this will be reflected in treating of prominent offenders in the same manner as lower class offenders depends upon ideological directions in politics. The Reagan administration tended to regard federal enforcement in corporate criminal areas and regulatory agency activity as "unnecessary red tape or government interference." The cost, quantity, and international scope of such criminality are likely to increase with the growth of multinational business enterprises.

Gresham Sykes (1972 and 1980) predicts that urban poverty associated with criminality is likely to continue and will continue to play a major role in future street crimes. The future of violent crime in America is uncertain; however, the U.S. is likely to continue to lead developed nations in criminal homicide for the balance of this century, since it will continue to have the largest civilian armed population in the world. Urban robbery rates are likely to remain high, depending upon a number of factors, including employment opportunities for young minority males. Plate (1977, p. 181) suggests that younger criminals have displaced professionals on the streets, and this is unlikely to change as long as national policies use central cities as the dumping ground for national problems such as racism and inequality. Official statistics on violence in the family, spouse and child abuse, and rape are likely to continue to demonstrate increases in response to better reporting and more supportive social programs for such victims.

Most areas of public order criminality are likely to continue to experience decriminalization combined with better regulation and social, psychiatric, and medical support systems. Common property crimes are likely to decrease, being most responsive to the aging demographic profile. Also continuing to decline in importance are many areas of professional criminal behavior, although frauds related to securities, credit, and computer records as well as "knock-offs" or counterfeit products will remain problematic.

In July 1987 United Parcel Service workers in Louisville, Kentucky, opened a leaking package and, to their surprise, discovered five human heads being shipped to a medical laboratory. The heads had been stolen by Philadelphia morgue employees, who had shipped a variety of

These homeless men in Los Angeles are an example of the growing problem of urban poverty in America. Poverty is seen as a leading cause of crime.

body parts to physicians and researchers. Perhaps the illegal marketing of human body parts will emerge as a major crime of the future as an updated version of ghouls and graverobbers (Charges Dropped, 1987).

Organized criminal activity will persist, although dominance by Italian-American syndicates will continue to wane while a multitude of groups capitalize on the new Prohibition Era's criminal seed money— catering to supplying illicit drugs. Political criminality will continue, particularly in the international arena, with terrorism employed as a tool of cheap "diplomatic leverage" and as authoritarian and democratic regimes resort to ideological justifications in their power maintenance activities. Even these very general predictions are hazardous, however; criminologists and others do not agree in their forecasts.

Georgette Bennett in *Crimewarps* (1987) makes a number of interesting predictions for the future of crime, among which were included:

- The computer will be the single greatest crime generator in the future.

Medical quackery and insurance fraud will increase due to the growth in the elderly population; however, industries with older workers will experience less corporate theft.

- The concentration of crime in the U.S. will continue to shift to the Sunbelt and West.
- Low birth rates and high work rates will leave a plethora of unguarded homes ripe for daytime burglary.
- The growing service economy will create many part-time jobs which, combined with fewer student drop outs, will mean less crime.
- More abusive families will emerge as the number of single, poor, young, and undereducated mothers grows.
- Industries with workers of older ages will experience less theft.
- The growth in elderly population will increase medical quackery and insurance fraud.
- Fear of AIDS will reduce the demand for streetwalkers.

Felson (1987, p. 911) argues that:

> Routine activities deliver easy crime opportunities to the offender. Astute planners and managers can interfere with this delivery, diverting flows of likely offenders (such as adolescents) . . . They can engineer traffic to provide "natural surveillance." Past trends encouraged the crime rate increases, but the developing metropolitan facility could reverse this, privatizing substantial portions of the metropolitan turf.

Gendreau and Ross (1987) indicate that the "nothing works doctrine" regarding rehabilitation simply does not match up with the available evidence, perhaps presaging a revivification of rehabilitation programs. Other likely directions include greater use of community policing and problem-solving strategies aimed at mobilizing communities and citizens in crime prevention (Moore, Trojanowicz, and Kelling, 1988) and greater attention to "broken windows" (Wilson and Kelling, 1982) in which the police express concern with enforcing daily civilities without which disorder reigns (Kelling, 1988a).

Policy Experiments

A very promising development in the field of criminology and criminal justice has been the use of "policy experiments," applied field experiments which address themselves to immediate, practical policy questions. In March of 1987 the National Research Council's Committee on Research on Law Enforcement and the Administration of Justice summarized the following steps in designing policy experiments (Garner and Visher, 1988, pp. 7–8):

1. Choose an interesting problem—a policy question that people really care about or an existing procedure that clearly needs improvement.
2. Do some creative thinking to solve legal and ethical issues that may arise.
3. Rigorously maintain the random assignment of persons, cases, or other units into treatment and control groups throughout the experiment.
4. Choose a design and methods of investigation that are appropriate both to the questions to be answered and to the available data.
5. Adopt a team approach between researchers and practitioners and keep working in close cooperation.
6. Put as much into your experiment as you want to get out of it.
7. Use an experiment to inform policy, not to make policy.
8. Understand and confront the political risks an experiment may involve.
9. Insofar as possible, see that the experiment is replicated in a variety of settings before encouraging widespread adoption of experimentally successful treatments.

Policy Options

The Riot Commission

The year 1968 in the United States may be described by future historians as resembling the year of "a national nervous breakdown," a year in which frustration and anger over the Vietnam War, racism, and inequality spilled into the nation's streets. In April 1968, in the wake of the assassination of civil rights leader Martin Luther King, cities across the country exploded into mob fury and, for the first time since the Civil War, the U.S. military set up machine gun batteries on Capitol Hill in order to protect the center of government from its own citizens.

In the late sixties,
the U.S. experienced
what may be described
as "a national
nervous breakdown."

A month prior to this, President Johnson's riot commission, the Kerner Commission (1968) called *The National Advisory Commission on Civil Disorders*, issued their report. They indicated that prejudice and discrimination reflected in white racism had plagued this nation's history, and it now threatened its very survival as a democracy, and that racial divisions or polarization between blacks and whites, expressed in black

concentration in central cities and white flight to suburbia, menaced the very future of American society. More to the point, the commission indicated that unless major commitments to change were undertaken immediately, in twenty years—by 1988—this chasm would most likely become permanent—a divided society refuting the very essence of American democracy.

The Kerner Commission proposed three policy options: the present policies option, a garrison-state option, and a commitment to change option. The *present policies option* proposed that nothing be done. The commission indicated that such a policy would produce a divided society characterized by increasing levels of intergroup violence, fear, and disorder. The *garrison-state option* resembles the conservative approach toward crime control. Without addressing root conditions of discrimination in housing, jobs, education, and the like, better policing would merely represent a temporary or stopgap approach that flirted with creating a "garrison or police state" that would resemble an American version of the South African apartheid system. The third and most advised option was that of a *commitment to change,* a federal policy of encouraging open housing, affirmative action, and desegregation combined with attempts to erase income, educational, and other social deficits experienced by black Americans due to previous institutionalized racism. In short, although many specific recommendations were made by the commission, it was the belief of the members that nothing major could be accomplished without significant structural changes in the economic, social, and political systems.

Criminal Justice Policy Options

Policy options for criminal justice cannot be separated from policies for other social problems. (This statement, of course, places the author in the liberal social policy school of thought and reflects his own views.) *At least three policy options exist for future criminal justice policy:* the present policy option, the conservative option, and the liberal option. The radical-Marxist option, another version of the conservative option, is rejected because a level of minimal social justice is achieved at the expense of democratic freedoms and provides an unacceptable authoritarian political structure. In the *present policy option* the issue of criminal justice is approached from the individualistic, nineteenth-century philosophical viewpoint of the legal profession. Pendular shifts from the crime control to the due process model may or may not assure "legal justice," but do little to address "social justice." Even if the legal rights of the accused are assured under the due process model, this accomplishes little if inequitable conditions continue the criminogenic environments which guarantee future clients. The debate over non-discriminatory provision of legal justice in our local and state courts is an important but moot point: under the crime control model, injustice presents itself in nonenforcement or in weak enforcement of crime in the suites; in the due process model, injustice presents itself in the continued toleration of structural conditions that breed street crime. What good are individual rights—due process—without individual choices—equality? A narrow interpretation of due process can produce the ultimate injustice—the toleration of crimes against the poor in the name of individual rights.

The *conservative option* has been described as an approach to social policy that emphasizes policy analysis, incapacitation, just desserts, and the crime control model; and as one that eschews causal analysis as ultimately impractical, viewing policies directed at resolving causal roots of crime as intractable. At an extreme level, crime control in an authoritarian state can be accomplished through sheer repression and state terrorism. Nazi Germany had law and order, but little social justice. Even in a democratic state, the policies of incapacitating career criminals may be a wise, essential policy in order to address some street crime in the short term. Such policies, if they work, are an elementary expectation in order to protect potential victims particularly against stranger-precipitated violent predations. However, addressing street crimes while ignoring suite crimes institutionalizes a dual system of justice, robbing a democratic society of the legitimizing and fairness elements necessary for political authority. While radical criminologists may be incorrect in charging discrimination in the specific legal processing of conventional offenders, they are absolutely correct in charging discrimination when the pious preeminence of legal sanctions falls upon the dangerous classes while ignoring the glamorous classes.

The *liberal option*, while calling for control of street crime, seeks also to ameliorate root causes of criminality. In addition to a commitment to the due process model of crime control, the liberal option tends also to be committed to the ideals of social justice, insisting that cries for law and order will be ineffective without a concomitant commitment to an eradication of inequality, injustice, and underlying structural criminogenic conditions. Crime is intimately tied to the social structure of society. The relative blindness to upper level crimes furthers inequalities and exacerbates criminogenic environments which foster street crime.

In the late eighties in the United States the top richest 20 percent of families controlled about 44 percent of national income and 79 percent of national wealth (stocks, bonds, real estate, etc.). Indeed the top 5 percent owned over half the nation's wealth. The poorest 20 percent of families had less than 5 percent of national income and less than

1 percent of national wealth (U.S. Bureau of Census, 1989). Perhaps the most foreboding sign for the future is the state of children presently. This theme was examined earlier (see Currie, 1985; and Moynihan, 1986). *Fortune* magazine ("How We can Win, 1989) indicates:

> There is some national embarrassment — if not shame — involved here, beginning with the state of American childhood. Consider a few more statistics remembering that this is no depression, these are "good times": Almost 40,000 of the 3.8 million American children born in 1986 died before their first birthday. Today, we rank 20th in the world, behind Spain and Singapore, in infant mortality; our black infant mortality rate would place us 28th, behind Cuba and Bulgaria . . . Roughly half of the black children live in poverty.

While a commitment to protecting the rights of individuals in the courtroom assures legal justice, only a concomitant commitment to jobs, housing, equal opportunity, and a fair share of society will assure social justice in the streets and suites.

The future of crime will very much depend upon which social policy options are chosen to deal with the issue. The present policies option promises only to condemn American society to continuing unacceptable levels of street crime while tolerating a dual system of justice which is soft on elite crime. The conservative option, while providing minimum expected protection of innocent victims from street predators, serves only as temporary first aid and offers few long-range solutions to ameliorating social forces which assure high crime rates; it also ignores much corporate and occupational criminality. The liberal option, in this writer's opinion, offers the best hope for a long-range amelioration of criminogenic forces. Repression alone is intolerable in a nation which espouses democratic doctrines.

Summary

Some writers such as James Q. Wilson disparage theoretical analysis in criminology as an example of "*the causal fallacy,*" the assumption that no problem can be addressed until the causes are eliminated. Criticisms of major theories do not cancel each theory's usefulness as an explanation of some element of crime or criminality. Even advocates of applied social policy are guided by some theoretical assumptions regarding crime causation. Frank Williams views the *demise of criminological imagination* as due to the rise of empirical scientism, the critical intellectual environment of the sixties, and the emergence of criminal justice as a discipline.

Ideology guides social policy. Wilson's distinctions of *causal analysis vs. policy analysis* in fact parallel the discussion in Chapters 1, 4, and

5 regarding pure research/theory versus applied research/theory. The *social policy fallacy* refers to the erroneous belief that in a democratic society applied social policy can be effective even though it ignores causal roots. The *ill-fated war on crime* describes the period from 1967 to 1981 when the federal government for the first time in American history launched a major battle against street crime. With new laws—the Safe Streets Act—and agencies—LEAA—and increased funds, the federal government made a commitment to fight crimes which were largely a state and local matter. Much of this effort concentrated exclusively upon conventional and violent predatory offenses, ignoring upper level crimes such as those by the Nixon administration, many members of which resigned in disgrace. The *dirty secrets* of crime represent Bertram Gross's notions that violent crimes are due to protracted structural conditions and that the criminal justice system is too lenient with elite economic criminals. Herbert Packer's *crime control model*, which emphasizes law and order and bureaucratic efficiency, wsa contrasted with his *due process model*, which emphasizes justice or the protection of individual rights.

Three *ideological approaches to criminal justice policy* were discussed: the conservative, liberal, and radical approaches. The *conservative approach* is based upon classical theory and advocates incapacitation, just deserts, and the crime control model, whereas the *liberal approach* emphasizes reformation of social structural conditions, more equitable operation of the criminal justice system, and rehabilitation. The *radical approach* calls for revolution against capitalism which it sees as the cause of crime.

Various *trends in future criminality* are cautiously presented since criminologists disagree regarding such forecasts and predictions are highly dependent upon the ideological direction of social policy choices. Policy options proposed by the 1968 Kerner (Riot) Commission were discussed; these included the present policies option, the garrison state choice, and the commitment to change alternative. Similarly *criminal justice policy options* were described as consisting of the present policy, conservative, and liberal options. The author expresses an ideological preference for the last direction.

KEY CONCEPTS

Causal Fallacy	Social Policy Fallacy	Kerner Commission Policy
Demise of Criminological	Policy Experiments	Options
Imagination	Crime Control Model	Criminal Justice Policy
Dirty Secrets	Due Process Model	Options
Policy Analysis	Conservative, Liberal, Radical	
	Approaches	

APPENDIX

An Overview of the Criminal Justice System

The response to crime in the United States is provided primarily by government through the criminal justice system, a loose confederation of more than fifty thousand agencies at all levels of government with varying responsibilities, which together provide the means by which Americans apprehend, try, and punish offenders. The American system of justice has evolved from an adaptation of the English common law into a complex series of procedures and decisions. There is no single criminal justice system in this country; rather there are many systems, which, while similar, are individually unique.

Criminal cases may be handled differently in different jurisdictions, but court decisions based on the due-process guarantees of the U.S. Constitution require that specific steps always be taken in the administration of criminal justice.

The following description of the criminal and juvenile justice systems portrays the most common sequence of events in the response to serious criminal behavior.

Entry into the System

Most crime is not responded to by the justice system because it has not been discovered or reported to the police. Law enforcement agencies usually learn about crime from citizens, from a discovery by a police officer in the field, or from investigative and intelligence work.

Once a law enforcement agency has established that a crime has been committed, a suspect must be identified and apprehended for the case to proceed through the system. Sometimes, a suspect is apprehended at the scene; however, identification of a suspect often requires extensive investigation. Quite often, no one is identified or apprehended.

Prosecution and Pretrial Services

After an arrest, law enforcement agencies present information about the case and about the accused to the prosecutor, who will decide if

Source: U.S. Department of Justice, "An Overview of the Criminal Justice System: The American Response to Crime," *Bureau of Justice Statistics Bulletin*, December 1983, pp. 1–9.

formal charges are to be filed with the court. If no charges are filed, the accused must be released. The prosecutor can also drop charges after making efforts to prosecute (nolle prosequi).

A suspect who is charged with a crime must be taken before a judge or magistrate without unnecessary delay. At the initial appearance, the judge or magistrate informs the accused of the charges and decides whether there is probable cause to detain the accused persons. In some jurisdictions, a pretrial-release decision is made and the defense counsel is assigned at the initial appearance. If the offense is minor, the determination of guilt and the assessment of a penalty may also occur at this stage.

In many jurisdictions, the initial appearance may be followed by a preliminary hearing. The main function of this hearing is to discover whether there is probable cause to believe that the accused committed a known crime within the jurisdiction of the court. If the judge does not find probable cause, the case is dismissed; however, if the judge or magistrate finds probable cause for such a belief, or the accused waives his right to a preliminary hearing, the case may be bound over to a grand jury.

A grand jury hears evidence against the accused presented by the prosecutor and decides if there is sufficient evidence to cause the accused to be brought to trial. If the grand jury finds sufficient evidence, it submits to the court an indictment (a written statement of the essential facts of the offense charged against the accused). Where the grand jury system is used, the grand jury may also investigate criminal activity generally and issue indictments called grand jury originals that initiate criminal cases.

Some felony cases and misdemeanor cases proceed by the issuance of an *information* (a formal, written accusation submitted to the court by a prosecutor). Indictments are usually required in felony cases. However, the accused may choose to waive a grand jury indictment and, instead, accept service of an information for the crime.

Adjudication

Once an indictment or information has been filed with the trial court, the accused is scheduled for arraignment. At the arraignment, the accused is informed of the charges, advised of the rights of criminal defendants, and asked to enter a plea to the charges.

In the great majority of cases, the accused pleads guilty under an arrangement known as plea bargaining. In plea bargaining the attorney for the defense and the prosecuting attorney argue that the accused will plead guilty to an offense less serious than that originally charged or that he will plead guilty to one of several original charges in return for the prosecution's dropping of the other offenses. For pleading guilty the accused receives a less severe sentence than he would have if he had been convicted in court. The prosecution gains the certainty that the accused will not be acquitted and will serve the agreed-upon sentence, and the time and expense of a court trial has been avoided.

Guilty pleas can also be a straightforward admission of guilt by a defendant. This may result from a hope or impression that such a plea will be rewarded by a lighter sentence or from concern that a trial will reveal damaging evidence.

If the accused pleads guilty or pleads nolo contendere (accepts penalty without admitting guilt), the judge may accept or reject the plea. If the plea is accepted, no trial is held and the offender is sentenced at this proceeding or at a later date. The plea may be rejected if, for example, the judge believes that the accused may have been coerced. If this occurs, the case may proceed to trial.

If the accused pleads not guilty or guilty by reason of insanity, a date is set for the trial. A person accused of a serious crime is guaranteed a trial by jury. However, the accused has the right to ask for a bench trial where the judge, rather than a jury, serves as the finder of fact. In both instances, the prosecutor and defense present evidence by questioning witnesses, while the judge decides on issues of law. The trial results in acquittal or conviction on the original charges or on lesser included offenses.

After the trial, a defendant may request appellate review of the conviction or sentence. In many criminal cases appeals are a matter of right; all states with the death penalty provide for automatic appeal of a death sentence. However, under some circumstances and in some jurisdictions, appeals may be subject to the discretion of the appellate court and may be granted only upon acceptance of a defendant's petition for a writ of certiorari.

Sentencing and Corrections

After a guilty verdict or guilty plea, sentence is imposed. In most cases, the judge decides on the sentence, but in some States, the sentence for capital offenses such as murder is decided by the jury.

In arriving at an appropriate sentence, a sentencing hearing may be held at which evidence of aggravating or mitigating circumstances will be considered. In assessing the circumstances surrounding a convicted person's criminal behavior, courts often rely on presentence investigations performed by probation agencies or other designated authorities.

Figure A.1: What Is the Sequence of Events in the Criminal Justice System?

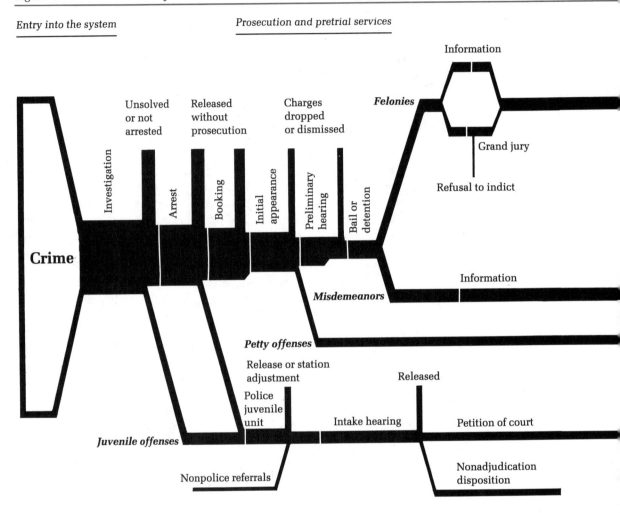

NOTE: This chart gives a simplified view of caseflow through the criminal justice system. Procedures vary among jurisdictions. The weights of the lines are not intended to show the actual size of caseloads.

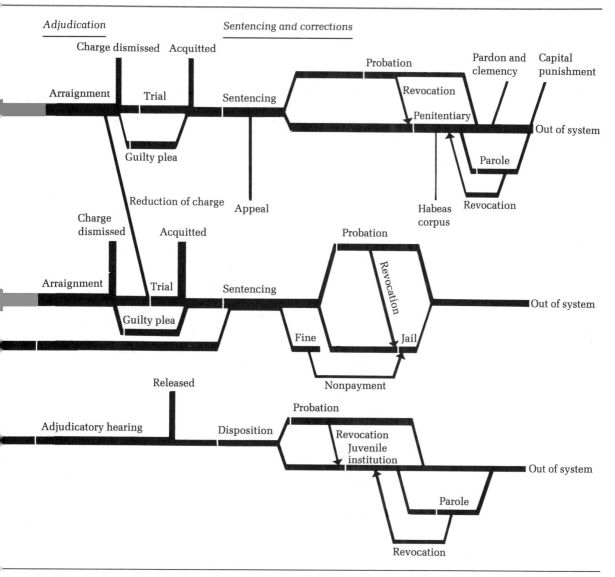

Adjudication

Sentencing and corrections

Charge dismissed   Acquitted

Pardon and clemency   Capital punishment

Probation

Arraignment   Trial   Sentencing   Revocation   Penitentiary   Out of system

Guilty plea   Parole

Reduction of charge   Appeal   Habeas corpus   Revocation

Charge dismissed   Acquitted

Probation

Arraignment   Trial   Sentencing   Revocation   Out of system

Guilty plea   Fine   Jail

Nonpayment

Released

Probation

Adjudicatory hearing   Disposition   Revocation Juvenile institution   Out of system

Parole

Revocation

SOURCE: President's Commission on Law Enforcement and the Administration of Justice, 1967a, *The Challenge of Crime in a Free Society*, Washington, D.C.: Government Printing Office.

The sentencing choices available to judges and juries vary widely among jurisdictions and may include —

- Death penalty
- Incarceration in a prison, jail, or other detention facility
- Probation — allowing the convicted person to remain at liberty but subject to certain conditions and restrictions
- Fines — primarily applied as penalties in minor offenses
- Restitution — requiring the offender to provide financial compensation to the victim.

If sentenced to prison, the convicted person may be eligible for parole after serving a specific portion of his or her sentence. Parole is the conditional release of a prisoner before the prisoner's full sentence has been served. The decision to grant parole is made by paroling authority such as a parole board, which has power to grant or revoke parole or to discharge a parolee altogether. The manner in which parole decisions are made varies widely among jurisdictions.

The Juvenile Justice System

The processing of juvenile offenders is not entirely dissimilar to adult criminal processing, but there are crucial differences in the procedures. Many juveniles are referred to juvenile courts by law enforcement officers, but many others are referred by school officials, social service agencies, neighbors, and even parents, for behavior or conditions that are determined to require intervention by the formal system for social control.

When juveniles are referred to the juvenile courts, their intake departments, or prosecuting attorneys, determine whether sufficient grounds exist to warrant the filing of a petition requesting an adjudicatory hearing or a request to transfer jurisdiction to criminal court. In a few States and at the Federal level, prosecutors under certain circumstances may file criminal charges against youths directly in adult courts.

The court with jurisdiction over juvenile matters may reject the petition or the juveniles may be diverted to other agencies or programs in lieu of other court processing. Examples of diversion programs include alcohol or drug counseling, driver education, or psychiatric therapy.

If a petition for an adjudicatory hearing is accepted, the juvenile may be brought before a court quite unlike the court with jurisdiction over adult offenders. In disposing of cases, juvenile courts usually have far more discretion than adult courts. In addition to such options as probation, commitment to correctional institutions, restitution, or fines, State laws grant juvenile courts the power to order removal of children from their homes to foster homes or treatment facilities. Juvenile courts may also order participation in special schools aimed at shoplifting prevention, drug counseling, or driver education. They may also order referral to criminal court for trial as adults.

Despite the considerable discretion associated with juvenile court proceedings, juveniles are afforded most of the due-process safeguards associated with adult criminal trials. Sixteen States permit the use of juries in juvenile courts; however, in light of the U.S. Supreme Court's holding that juries are not essential to juvenile hearings, most States do not provide for juries in juvenile courts.

Discretion is Exercised Throughout the Criminal Justice System

Discretion is "an authority conferred by law to act in certain conditions or situations in accordance with an official's or an official's agency's own considered judgment and conscience."[1] Traditionally, criminal and juvenile justice officials, in particular the police, prosecutors, judges, and paroling authorities, have been given a wide range of discretion.

Legislative bodies have recognized that they cannot foresee every possibility, anticipate local mores, and enact laws that clearly encompass all conduct that is criminal and all that is not.[2] Therefore, those charged with the day-to-day response to crime are expected to exercise their own judgment within guidelines set by law.

Discretion is also necessary to permit the criminal and juvenile justice systems to function within available resources.[3] The enforcement and prosecution of all laws against all violators is beyond the financial resources available. Therefore, criminal and juvenile justice officials must have the authority to allocate resources in a way that meets the most compelling needs of their own communities.

The limits of discretion vary from State to State and locality to locality. For example, the range of options available to judges when they sentence offenders varies greatly. In recent years, some States have sought

---

1. Roscoe Pound, "Discretion, Dispensation and Mitigation: The Problem of the Individual Special Case," *New York University Law Review* (1960), 35:925, 926.
2. Wayne R. Lafave, *Arrest: The Decision to Take a Suspect into Custody* (Boston: Little, Brown & Co., 1964), pp. 63–184.
3. Ibid.

to limit judges' discretion in sentencing by passing mandatory and determinate sentencing laws.

Who Exercises Discretion?

These criminal justice officials . . .	must often decide whether or not or how to—
Police	Enforce specific laws Investigate specific crimes Search people, vicinities, buildings Arrest or detain people
Prosecutors	File charges or petitions for adjudication Seek indictments Drop cases Reduce charges
Judges or magistrates	Set bail or conditions for release Accept pleas Determine delinquency Dismiss charges Impose sentence Revoke probation
Correctional officials	Assign to type of correctional facility Award privileges Punish for disciplinary infractions
Paroling authority	Determine date and conditions of parole Revoke parole

The Response to Crime Is Founded in the Intergovernmental Structure of the United States

Under our form of government, each State and the Federal Government has its own criminal justice system. All systems must respect the rights of individuals set forth in the U.S. Constitution and defined in case law.

State constitutions and laws define the criminal justice system within each State and delegate the authority and responsibility for criminal justice to various jurisdictions, officials, and institutions. State laws also define criminal and delinquent behavior.

Municipalities and counties further define their criminal justice systems through local ordinances that proscribe additional illegal behavior and identify those local agencies responsible for criminal justice processing that were not established by the State.

Congress has also established a criminal justice system at the Federal level to respond to Federal crimes such as bank robbery, kidnaping, and transporting stolen goods across State lines.

The Response to Crime Is Mainly a State and Local Function

Very few crimes are under exclusive Federal jurisdiction (see table A.1). The responsibility to respond to most crimes rests with the State and local governments. Police protection is primarily a function of cities and towns, while corrections is primarily a function of State governments. More than three-fifths of all justice personnel are employed at the local level.

More Than One Agency Has Jurisdiction Over Some Criminal Events.

The response to most criminal actions is usually begun by local police who react to violation of State law. If a suspect is apprehended, he or she is prosecuted locally and may be confined in a local jail or State prison. In such cases, only one agency has jurisdiction at each stage of the process.

However, some criminal events because of their characteristics and location may come under the jurisdiction of more than one agency. For

Table A.1: Percent of Criminal Justice Employment by Level of Government

	Local	*State*	*Federal*
Police	75%	14%	11%
Judicial	66	29	5
Legal Services and Prosecution	63	27	10
Public Defense	56	41	3
Corrections	38	57	4
Other	38	45	17
Total	64%	27%	9%

example, such overlapping occurs within States when local police, county sheriffs, and State police are all employed to enforce State laws on State highways.

Congress has provided for Federal jurisdiction over crimes that—

- Occur on Federal land
- Involve large and probably interstate criminal organizations or conspiracies
- Are offenses of national importance, such as the assassination of the President.[4]

Bank robbery and many drug offenses are examples of crimes for which the States and the Federal Government both have jurisdiction. In cases of dual jurisdiction, an investigation and a prosecution may be undertaken by all authorized agencies, but only one level of government usually pursues a case.

Within States, the Response to Crime Also Varies from One Locality to Another

This is because of statutory and structural differences and differences in how discretion is exercised. Local criminal justice policies and programs change in response to local attitudes and needs. For example, the prosecutor in one locality may concentrate on particular types of offenses that plague the local community while the prosecutor in another locality may concentrate on career criminals.

The Response to Crime Also Varies on a Case-by-Case Basis

No two cases are exactly alike. At each stage of the criminal justice process, officials must make decisions that take into account the varying factors of each case. Two similar cases may have very different results because of various factors, including differences in witness cooperation and physical evidence, the availability of resources to investigate and prosecute the case, the quality of lawyers involved, and the age and prior criminal history of the suspects.

---

4. *Attorney General's Task Force on Violent Crime—Final Report.* August 17, 1981 (Washington: U.S. Department of Justice, 1981), p. 2.

Table A.2: Percent of Arrests for Serious Crimes That Result in . . .

	Prosecution	Conviction	Incarceration
New York	97%	56%	25%
California	76	57	39
Pennsylvania	76	39	15
Oregon	73	49	22
Arkansas	61	40	18

SOURCE: U.S. Department of Justice, "An Overview of the Criminal Justice System: The American Response to Crime," *Bureau of Justice Statistics Bulletin*, December, 1983, pp. 1–9.

Differences in Local Laws, Agencies, Resources, Standards, and Procedures Result in Varying Responses in Each Jurisdiction

The variation in the outcome of arrests for serious cases among five States illustrates this (see table A.2).[5] At the State level, some of this variation can be explained by differences among States, for example—

- Arrestees released by magistrates during pretrial appearances are considered prosecuted in New York; this raises the proportion prosecuted.
- Pennsylvania uses a pretrial diversion program in which successful participants are not considered convicted; this lowers the conviction rate.

5. The data provided in the table were derived from offender-based transaction statistics (OBTS) from five States. Each of these States has its own system for collecting the statistics. With the exception of Arkansas, which conducted a survey of all 1974 felony arrest records, the data systems rely on reporting of information from criminal justice agencies. Because of nonreporting, some arrests are not included. For example, California estimates that its OBTS data are underreported by about 35 percent. Because each system is unique to its own State, some other differences exist between data sets, such as year of collection and types of crimes.

REFERENCES

Abadinsky, Howard. 1981. *Organized Crime*. Boston: Allyn and Bacon.

———. 1983a. *The Criminal Elite: Professional and Organized Crime*. Westport, Ct: Greenwood.

———. 1983b. "Professional and Organized Crime: A Symbiosis." Paper presented at the Academy of Criminal Justice Sciences Meetings, San Antonio, Tex. March.

———. 1985. *Organized Crime*. 2nd edition. Chicago: Nelson-Hall.

———. 1988. *Drug Abuse: An Introduction*. Chicago: Nelson-Hall.

ABC (American Broadcasting Company). 1982. "Yakuza." *20/20*. Broadcast May 27.

———. 1983a. "Child Molesters." *20/20*. Broadcast February 3.

———. 1983b. *20/20*. Broadcast February 24.

———. 1983c. "The Media and Violence." Broadcast February 24.

———. 1987. "Nightly News." Broadcast August 17.

Abrahamsen, David. 1960. *The Psychology of Crime*. New York: Columbia University Press.

"Abscam (Cont'd): Mafiosi Call off a Summit." 1980. *Time*, February 25, p. 18.

Adams, Virginia. 1976. *Crime*. New York: Time-Life.

Adler, Frieda. 1975. *Sisters in Crime*. New York: McGraw-Hill.

———. 1983. *Nations Not Obsessed by Crime*. Littleton, Col.: Fred. B. Rothman.

——— and Simon, Rita James, eds. 1979. *The Criminology of Deviant Women*. Boston: Houghton Mifflin.

Adler, Jerry, et al. 1988. "Getting Tough on Cocaine." *Newsweek*, November 28, pp. 76–79.

Adler, Patricia A., and Adler, Peter, 1983. "Shifts and Oscillations in Deviant Careers: The Case of Upper-Level Drug Dealers and Smugglers." *Social Problems*, 31: 195–207.

"After the Don: A Donnybrook." 1976. *Newsweek*, November 1, p. 32.

Agee, Philip. 1975. *Inside the Company: CIA Diary*. New York: Stonehill.

Agnew, Robert. 1985. "Social Control Theory and Delinquency: A Longitudinal Test." *Criminology* 23: 47–61.

Agran, Larry, 1982. "Getting Cancer on the Job." In *Crisis in American Institutions*, edited by Jerome H. Skolnick and Elliott Currie, 5th ed. pp. 408–419. Boston: Little, Brown.

Akers, Ronald L. 1967. "Problems in the Sociology of Deviance: Social Definitions and Behavior." *Social Forces* 46:455–465.

———. 1980. "Further Critical Thoughts on Marxist Criminology: Comments on Turk, Toby and Klockars." In *Radical Criminology: The Coming Crisis*, edited by James A. Inciardi, pp. 133–138. Beverly Hills: Sage.

Albanese, Jay S. 1985. *Organized Crime in America*. Cincinnati: Anderson.

———. 1988. "The Impact of the Mob Trials on Organized Crime: Some Observations." *Criminal Organizations* 4:3–4.

———. 1989. *Organized Crime in America*. 2nd edition. Cincinnati: Anderson.

Albini, Joseph. 1971. *The American Mafia: Genesis of a Legend*. New York: Appleton-Century-Crofts.

———. 1986. "The Guardian Angels: Vigilantes or Protectors of the Community?" Paper presented at the Academy of Criminal Justice Sciences Meeting, Orlando, Fla., March.

———. 1988. "Donald Cressey's Contribution to the Study of Organized Crime: An Evaluation." *Crime and Delinquency* 34:338–354.

Alexander, Shana. 1988. *The Pizza Connection*. New York: Weidenfeld and Nicholson.

Allen, Edward J. 1962. *Merchants of Menace: The Mafia*. Springfield, Ill.: Charles C. Thomas.

Allen, Harry E. et al. 1981. *Crime and Punishment: An Introduction to Criminology*. New York: The Free Press.

Allen, John, 1977. *Assault with a Deadly Weapon: The Autobiography of a Street Criminal*. Edited by Diane Hall Kelly and Philip Heymann. New York: McGraw-Hill.

Allison, Dean, and Henderson, Bruce B. 1985. *Empire of Deceit: Inside the Biggest Sports and Bank Scandal in U.S. History*. Garden City, N.Y.: Doubleday.

American Bar Association. 1952. *Report on Organized Crime*. New York: American Bar Association.

———. 1976. *Final Report of the Committee on Economic Offenses*. Washington, D.C.: American Bar Association.

"America Next Target for Terrorism?" 1984. *U.S. News and World Report*, January 9, pp. 24–30.

American Humane Association Children's Division. 1984. *Trends in Officially Reported Child Neglect and Abuse in the United States*. Denver: American Humane Association.

Amir, Menachem, 1971. *Patterns in Forcible Rape*. Chicago: University of Chicago Press.

"An Option to Run." 1978. *Newsweek*, January 30, pp. 64–66.

"Ancient Records Discovered." 1987. *Erie Morning News*, December 29, p. 4–A.

Anderson, Edward J. 1977. "A Study of Industrial Espionage, Parts I and II." *Security Management*, January and March.

Anderson, Jack. 1983. "What's Wrong with Bribes?" *Erie Times News*, July 3, p. 7–A.

Anderson, Jack, and Van Atta, Dale. 1986. "The Amount of Child Pornography Declines." *Erie Times News*, July 13, p. 5–B.

_____ 1987. "Danger Lurks in Counterfeit Bolts." *Erie Times News*, July 19, p. 3–B.

_____ 1988a. "Medical Waste Poses Health Threat." *Erie Times News*, October 16, p. 3–B.

_____ 1988b. "Terrorists Act as Hired Guns for Drug Cartel." *Erie Times News*, August 28, p. 3–B.

Anderson, Jack, and Whitten, Les. 1977. "Mafia Chieftain." *Erie Times News*, March 24, p. 3–B.

Anderson, Robert T. 1965. "From Mafia to Cosa Nostra." *American Journal of Sociology* 71: 302–310.

Anglin, M. Douglas, and Speckart, George. 1988. "Narcotics Use and Crime: A Multisample Multimethod Analysis." *Criminology* 16: 197–233.

Anslinger, Harry, and Cooper, C. R. 1937. "Marijuana: Assassin of Youth." *American Magazine* 74: 19, 50.

Apear, Leonard. 1982. "Amway Distributors' Big Tax Breaks Stir Investigation by Congress and IRS." *Wall Street Journal*, April 16, p. 23.

Archer, Dane, and Gartner, Rosemary. 1980. "Homicide in 110 Nations: The Development of the Comparative Crime Data File." In *Criminology Review Yearbook*, edited by Egon Bittner and Sheldon Messinger, volume 2, pp. 433–463. Beverly Hills: Sage.

_____ 1984. *Violence and Crime in Cross-National Perspective*. New Haven: Yale University Press.

Ardrey, Robert. 1963. *African Genesis*. New York: Atheneum.

"Arson for Hate and Profit." 1977. *Time*, October 31, pp. 22–25.

Armstrong, E. 1978. "Massage Parlors and Their Customers." *Archives of Sexual Behavior* 7: 117.

Asbury, Herbert. 1969. *The Great Illusion*. New York: Greenwood Press.

Ashman, Charles. 1975. *The CIA-Mafia Link*. New York: Manor Books.

Associated Press. 1976. "Japanese Cops Nab 1,554 in Raid." March 10.

_____ 1989. "Ethics Called Key to Computer Security." *The Washington Post*, April 4, p. A–5.

Atkinson, A. B. 1975. *The Economics of Inequality*. Oxford: Claredon.

Attorney General's Office. 1986. *Attorney General's Commission Report on Pornography*. Washington, D.C.: Attorney General's Office.

Attorney General's Task Force on Violent Crime. 1981. *Phase I Recommendations, June 17; Phase II Recommendations, August*. Washington, D.C.: U.S. Department of Justice.

Austin, Roy L. 1987. "Progress Toward Racial Equality and Reduction of Black Criminal Violence." *Journal of Criminal Justice* 15: 437–459.

Austin, Tim. 1986. "Book Review of James Q. Wilson and Richard J. Herrnstein Crime and Human Nature." *Criminal Justice Policy Review* 1: 241–242.

Babbie, Earl R. 1975. *The Practice of Social Research*. Belmont, Ca.: Wadsworth.

Badillo, Herman, and Haynes, Milton. 1972. *A Bill of No Rights: Attica and the American Prison System*. New York: Outerbridge and Lazard.

Bailey, F. Lee, and Rothblatt, Henry B. 1969. *Defending Business and White Collar Crimes: Federal and State*. Rochester: Lawyer's Co-operative Publishing Company.

Bailey, Kenneth. 1978. *Methods of Social Research*. New York: Free Press.

Bailey, William C. 1971. "Correctional Outcome: An Evaluation of 100 Reports." In *Crime and Justice*, edited by Leon Radzinowicz and Marvin E. Wolfgang, vol. 3. New York: Basic Books.

Bakan, David. 1975. *The Slaughter of the Innocents*. San Francisco: Jossey-Bass.

Balkan, S.; Berger R.J.; and Schmidt, J. 1980. *Crime and Deviance in America*. Belmont, Ca.: Wadsworth.

Ball, John C. et al. 1982. "Lifetime Criminality of Heroin Addicts in the United States." *Journal of Drug Issues* 1: 1–2.

Ball, Robert. 1980. "An Empirical Evaluation of Neutralization Theory." *Criminologica*, 4; 22–32.

Banas, Dennis W., and Trojanowicz, Robert C. 1985. *Uniform Crime Reporting and Community Policing: An Historical Perspective*. East Lansing: National Neighborhood Foot Patrol Center, School of Criminal Justice, Michigan State University.

Bandura, Albert. 1973. *Aggression: A Social Learning Approach*. Englewood Cliffs, N.J.: Prentice-Hall.

Baridon, Phil. 1988. *Report on Asian Organized Crime*. Department of Justice, Criminal Division, Washington, D.C.: Government Printing Office.

Baris, Jay G. 1988. "What's New in Bank Theft?" *New York Times*, December, p. 11

Barker, Thomas, and Carter, David L. 1986. *Police Deviance*. Cincinnati: Anderson.

Barlay, Stephen. 1973. *The Secrets Business*. New York: Thomas Y. Crowell.

Barlow, Hugh D. 1984. *Introduction to Criminology*. 3rd ed. Boston: Little, Brown.

Barnett, Arnold, and Kleitman, Daniel J. 1973. "Urban Violence and Risk to the Individual." *Journal of Research in Crime and Delinquency* 10: 111–116.

Barry, Vincent. 1983. *Philosophy: A Text with Readings*. Belmont, Ca.: Wadsworth.

Bartlett, Sarah. 1989. "Saving Fraud Losses Seen as Lost for Good." *New York Times*, April 3, p. 29.

Bartol, Curt H.; and Bartol, Anne M. 1986. *Criminal Behavior: A Psychosocial Approach*. 2nd edition. Englewood Cliffs, N.J.: Prentice Hall.

Battersby, John D. 1989. "Hunger Strikes Grow in South Africa Prisons." *New York Times*, February 10, p. 4.

Baumrind, Diana. 1978. "Parental Disciplinary Patterns and Social Competence in Children." *Youth and Society* 9: 239–276.

Bayer, Ronald. 1981. "Crime, Punishment and the Decline of Liberal Optimism." *Crime and Delinquency* 27: 169–190.

Bayley, David H. 1978. "Comment: Perspectives on Criminal Justice Research." Speech delivered to the Academy of Criminal Justice Sciences, March, New Orleans, La. Reprinted in *Journal of Criminal Justice* 6: 287–289.

Beattie, R. H. 1955. "Problems of Criminal Statistics in the United States," *Journal of Criminal Law, Criminology and Police Science* 46: 178–186.

Beauchamp, Thomas L., ed. 1983. *Case Studies in Business, Society and Ethics.* Englewood Cliffs, N.J.: Prentice-Hall.

Beauchamp, Thomas L., and Bowie, Norman E. 1983. *Ethical Theory and Business.* 2nd ed. Englewood Cliffs, N.J.: Prentice-Hall.

Beccaria, Cesare. 1963. *On Crimes and Punishments.* Translated by Henry Paolucci. Indianapolis: Bobbs-Merrill.

Becker, Gary. 1968. "Crime and Punishment: An Economic Approach." *Journal of Political Economy* 76: 169–217.

Becker, Howard S. 1950. *Through Values to Social Interpretations.* Durham: Duke University Press.

_____ 1954. "Anthropology and Sociology." In *For a Science of Man,* edited by John Gillin. New York: Macmillan.

_____ 1963. *Outsiders: Studies in the Sociology of Deviance.* New York: The Free Press.

_____ ed., 1964. *The Other Side: Perspectives on Deviance.* New York: The Free Press.

Beirne, Piers. 1987. "Adolphe Quetelet and the Origins of Positivist Criminology." *American Journal of Sociology* 92: 1140–1169.

Bell, Daniel. 1953. "Crime as an American Way of Life." *Antioch Review* 13: 131–154.

_____ 1967. *The End of Ideology.* Glencoe, Ill.: The Free Press.

Belson, W. A. 1978. *Television Violence and the Adolescent Boy.* Farnborough, Eng.: Saxon House.

Benekos, Peter J. 1983. "Sentencing the White-Collar Offender: Evaluating the Use of Sanctions." Paper presented at the Academy of Criminal Justice Sciences Meetings, San Antonio, Tex., March.

Benjamin, Harry, and Masters, R. E. L. 1964. *Prostitution and Morality.* New York: Julian Press.

Bennett, Georgette. 1987. *Crimewarps: The Future of Crime in America.* Garden City, N.Y.: Anchor Books, Doubleday.

Bennett, James. 1981. *Oral History and Delinquency: The Rhetoric of Criminology.* Chicago: University of Chicago Press.

Bennett, Trevor. 1988. "The British Experience with Heroin Regulation." *Law and Contemporary Problems* 51: 299–314.

Bennett, Vivo, and Clagett, Cricket. 1977. *1001 Ways to Avoid Getting Mugged, Murdered, Robbed, Raped or Ripped Off.* New York: Mason-Charter Publishers.

Bensinger, Gad. 1987. "Operation Greylord and Its Aftermath." Paper presented at the American Society of Criminology Meetings, Montreal, November 14.

Bentham, Jeremy. 1823. *Introduction to the Principles of Morals and Legislation.* Oxford: Oxford University Press, originally published in 1789.

Bequai, August. 1979. *Organized Crime: The Fifth Estate.* Lexington, Mass.: D. C. Heath.

Berg, Eric N. 1989. "FBI Commodities 'Sting': Fast Money, Secret Lives." *New York Times,* January 30, p. A–1.

Bergamini, David. 1971. *Japan's Imperial Conspiracy.* New York: William Morrow and Company.

Berger, Vivian. 1988. "Review Essay: Not So Simple Rape." *Criminal Justice Ethics* 7: 69–81.

Bergier, Jacques. 1975. *Secret Armies: The Growth of Corporate and Industrial Espionage.* Translated by Harold J. Salemson. Indianapolis: Bobbs-Merrill.

Berk, Richard A., and Newton, Phyllis J. 1985. "Does Arrest Really Deter Wife Battery? An Effort to Replicate the Findings of the Minneapolis Spouse Abuse Experiment." *American Sociological Review* 50: 253–262.

Bernard, Thomas J. 1987. "Structure and Control: Reconsidering Hirschi's Concept of Commitment." *Justice Quarterly* 4: 409–424.

Bertaux, Daniel, ed. 1981. *Biography and Society: The Life History Approach in the Social Sciences.* Beverly Hills: Sage.

Biderman, Albert D., et al., 1967. Report on a Pilot Study in the District of Columbia on Victimization and Attitudes Toward Law Enforcement, Field Surveys I, Commission on Law Enforcement and Administration of Justice. Washington, D.C.: Government Printing Office.

Binder, Arnold, and Meeker, James W. 1988. "Experiments as Reforms." *Journal of Criminal Justice* 16: 347–358.

Bittner, Egon. 1967. "The Police on Skid Row: A Study of Peace Keeping." *American Sociological Review* 32: 699–715.

Black, Donald J. 1970. "Production of Crime Rates." *American Sociological Review* 35: 733–748.

_____ 1976. *The Behavior of Law.* New York: Academic Press.

Blackstock, Nelson. 1976. *Cointelpro: The FBI's Secret War on Political Freedom.* New York: Random House.

Blakey, G. Robert, and Billing, Richard. 1981. *The Plot to Kill the President: Organized Crime Assassinated JFK.* New York: New York Times Books.

Blakey, G. Robert, and Goldsmith, Michael. 1976. "Criminal Redistribution of Stolen Property: The Need for Law Reform." *Michigan Law Review* 74: 1518–1545.

Bloch, Herbert A., and Geis, Gilbert. 1970. *Man, Crime and Society.* 2nd ed. New York: Random House.

Block, Alan A. 1978. "The History and Study of Organized Crime." *Urban Life* 6: 455–474.

Block, Alan A., and Chambliss, William J. 1981. *Organizing Crime.* New York: Elsevier.

Bloom, Murray T. 1957. *Money of Their Own: The Great Counterfeiters.* New York: Charles Scribner's.

Blumberg, Abraham S. 1967. "The Practice of Law as a Confidence Game: Organizational Cooptation of a Profession." *Law and Society Review* 1: 15–39.

Blume, Marshall E., et al. 1974. "Stock Ownership in the United States: Characteristics and Trends." *Survey of Current Business* (U.S. Department of Commerce) 54: 16–40.

Blumenthal, Daniel, ed. 1988. *The Last Days of the Sicilians*. New York: Times Books.

Blumstein, Alfred, and Cohen, Jacqueline. 1987. "Characterizing Criminal Careers." *Science* 237, August 28: 985–991.

———; Cohen, Jacqueline; and Farrington, David P. 1988a. "Criminal Career Research: Its Value for Criminology." *Criminology* 26: 1–35.

——— 1988b. "Longitudinal and Criminal Career Research: Further Clarifications." *Criminology* 26: 57–74.

Blundell, William E. 1978. "I Did It for Jollies." In *Crime at the Top*, edited by John M. Johnson and Jack Douglas, pp. 153–185. Philadelphia: Lippincott.

Bock, Gordon, and McWhirter, William. 1988. " 'The Chairman' and His Board." *Time*, May 30, p. 45.

Bohm, Robert M. 1982. "Radical Criminology: An Explication." *Criminology* 19: 565–589.

——— 1987. "Myths about Criminology and Criminal Justice: A Review Essay." *Justice Quarterly* 4: 631–642.

Bonanno, Joseph. 1983. *A Man of Honor: The Autobiography of Joseph Bonanno*. New York: Simon and Schuster.

Bonger, Willem A. 1969. *Criminality and Economic Conditions*. Bloomington, Ind.: Indiana University Press.

Bonn, Robert L. 1987. "Review of: James D. Wright and Peter H. Rossi *Armed and Considered Dangerous*." *Justice Quarterly* 4: 133–136.

Bookin-Weiner, Hedy, and Horowitz, Ruth. 1983. "The End of the Youth Gang: Fad or Fact? *Criminology* 21: 585–602.

Booth, Cathy. 1978. "Prostitutes in America: Teens, Chicken Hawks, Networks Abound." *Erie Times-News*, March 12, p. 23–A.

Bordua, David J. 1961. "Delinquent Subcultures: Sociological Interpretations of Gang Delinquency." *Annals of the American Academy of Political and Social Science* 338: 119–136.

——— 1962. "Delinquency and Opportunity: Analysis of a Theory." *Sociology and Social Research* 46: 167–175.

Bottomley, A. Keith. 1979. *Criminology in Focus: Past Trends and Future Prospects*. New York: Barnes and Noble.

Boucher, Rick. 1989. "Trying to Fix a Statute Run Amok." *New York Times*, March 12, p. 4–E.

Boudreau, John F., et al. 1977. *Arson and Arson Investigations: Survey and Assessment*. Washington, D.C.: U.S. Department of Justice.

Bourgois, Philippe. 1988. "Fear and Loathing in El Barrio: Ideology and Upward Mobility in the Underground Economy of the Inner City." Paper presented at the American Anthropological Meetings, Phoenix, Arizona, November.

Bowers, William B. 1974. *Executions in America*. Lexington, Mass.: Lexington Books.

Bowers, William B., and Pierce, Glenn. 1975. "The Illusion of Deterrence in Isaac Ehrlich's Research on Capital Punishment." *Yale Law Journal* 85: 164–227.

Bowker, Lee. 1981. "Crime and the Use of Prisons in the United States: A Time Series Analysis." *Crime and Delinquency* 27: 206–212.

Braithwaite, John. 1981. "Paradoxes of Class Bias in Criminal Justice." Unpublished paper, Australian Institute of Criminology. Cited in Francis T. Cullen, *et al.*, 1982, "Dissecting White-Collar Crime: Offense Type and Punitiveness." Paper presented at the Academy of Criminal Justice Sciences Meetings, Louisville, Ky.

Brantingham, Paul, and Brantingham, Patricia. 1984. *Patterns in Crime*. New York: Macmillan.

Brecher, Edward. 1972. *Licit and Illicit Drugs*. Boston: Little, Brown.

Bremer, R. 1980. "Implementing a Three-Part Inventory Shrinkage Control Program." *Retail Control*, June, pp. 36–41.

Brenner, M. Harvey. 1978. "Economic Crises and Crime." In *Crime and Society*, edited by Leonard Savitz and Norman Johnston, pp. 555–572. 2nd ed. New York: Wiley.

Bresler, Fenton. 1980. *The Chinese Mafia*. New York: Stein and Day.

Briar, Scott, and Piliavin, Irving. 1965. "Delinquency, Situational Inducements and Commitment to Conformity." *Social Problems* 13: 35–45.

"British Clinics are Struggling as Heroin Addiction Climbs." 1985. *New York Times*, April 11, p. 15–A.

Brodeur, Paul. 1974. *Expendable Americans*. New York: Viking.

——— 1985. *Outrageous Misconduct: The Asbestos Industry on Trial*. New York: Pantheon Books.

Brown, Bertram S., et al. 1973. *Psychosurgery: Perspectives on a Current Problem*. Washington, D.C.: Government Printing Office.

Brown, Claude. 1964. *Manchild in the Promised Land*. New York: Macmillan.

Brown, Michael H. 1982. "Love Canal and the Poisoning of America." In *Crisis in American Institutions*, edited by Jerome H. Skolnick and Elliott Currie, pp. 297–316. 5th ed. Boston: Little, Brown.

Brown, Richard M. 1969. "Historical Patterns of Violence in America." In *Violence in America*, A Staff Report to the National Commission on the Causes and Prevention of Violence, edited by Hugh D. Graham and Ted R. Gurr, pp. 43–80. New York: New American Library.

Browning, Frank, and Gerassi, John. 1980. *The American Way of Crime*. New York: G. P. Putnams.

Brownmiller, Susan. 1975. *Against Our Will: Men, Women and Rape*. New York: Simon and Schuster.

Bureau of Justice Statistics. 1979. *Computer Crime: Criminal Justice Resource Manual*. Washington, D.C.: U.S. Department of Justice.

——— 1981a. "Measuring Crime." *Bureau of Justice Statistics Bulletin*. February.

—— 1981b. "The Prevalence of Crime." *Bureau of Justice Statistics Bulletin,* March.

—— 1982. "Households Touched by Crime, 1981." *Bureau of Justice Statistics Bulletin,* September.

—— 1983a. "Criminal Victimization in the U.S.: 1980–81 Changes Based on New Estimates." *Bureau of Justice Statistics Technical Report,* March.

—— 1983b. *Report to the Nation on Crime and Justice: The Data.* Washington, D.C.: Government Printing Office, October.

—— 1984a. "Criminal Victimization 1983." *Bureau of Justice Statistics Technical Bulletin,* June.

—— 1984. "Households Touched by Crime, 1983." *Bureau of Justice Statistics Bulletin,* May.

—— 1988a. "Criminal Victimization 1987." *Bureau of Justice Statistics Bulletin,* October.

—— 1988b. *Report to the Nation on Crime and Justice.* 2nd edition. Washington, D.C.: Government Printing Office, March.

Burgess, Ann W. 1984. *Child Pornography and Sex Rings.* Lexington, Mass.: D. C. Heath.

Burgess, Ann W., and Holmstrom, Lynda Lytle. 1974. *Rape: Victims of Crisis.* Bowie, Md.: Robert J. Brady.

Burgess, Ann W., et al. 1987. "Serial Rapists and Their Victims: Reenactment and Repetition." In *Practical Aspects of Rape Investigation,* edited by Robert R. Hazlewood and Ann W. Burgess. New York: Elsevier.

Burgess, Ernest W. 1925. "The Growth of the City." In *The City,* edited by Robert E. Park, Ernest W. Burgess, and Robert D. McKenzie, pp. 47–62. Chicago: University of Chicago Press.

Burgess, Robert L., and Akers, Ronald L. 1966. "A Differential Association-Reinforcement Theory of Criminal Behavior," *Social Problems* 14: 128–147.

Burnett, Cathleen. 1986. "Review Essay." *Criminology* 24: 203–211.

Burnham, Kenneth P. 1980. "Mark-Recapture Techniques for Estimating Animal Populations: What Has Been Done in Ecology." Paper presented at the National Workshop on Research Methodology and Criminal Justice Program Evaluation, Baltimore, Md., March.

Bursik, Robert J., Jr. 1988. "Social Disorganization and Theories of Crime and Delinquency: Problems and Prospects." *Criminology* 26: 519–551.

Bynum, Timothy S., ed. 1987. *Organized Crime in America: Concepts and Controversies.* Monsey, N.Y.: Criminal Justice Press.

Byrne, James, and Sampson, Robert. 1986. "Cities and Crime: The Ecological/Non-ecological Debate Reconsidered." In *The Social Ecology of Crime,* edited by James Byrne and Robert Sampson. New York: Springer-Verlag.

"Cambodia: Pol Pot's Lifeless Zombies." 1979. *Time,* December 3, pp. 55–56.

Cameron, Mary Owen. 1964. *The Booster and the Snitch: Department Store Shoplifting.* New York: The Free Press.

Campbell, Donald T., and Stanley, Julian C. 1963. *Experimental and Quasi-Experimental Designs for Research.* Chicago: Rand McNally.

Cantor, David, and Land, Kenneth C. 1985. "Unemployment and Crime Rate in the Post-World War II United States: A Theoretical and Empirical Analysis." *American Sociological Review* 50: 317–332.

Cardarelli, Albert P. 1988. "Child Sexual Abuse: Factors in Family Reporting." *NIJ Reports* 209, May/June: 9–12.

Carey, Alex. 1967. "The Hawthorne Studies: A Radical Criticism." *American Sociological Review* 32: 403–417.

Carey, James T. 1972. "Problems of Access and Risk in Observing Drug Scenes." In *Research on Deviance,* edited by Jack D. Douglas, pp. 71–92. New York: Random House.

—— 1975. *Sociology and Public Affairs: The Chicago School.* Beverly Hills: Sage.

—— 1978. *Introduction to Criminology.* Englewood Cliffs, N.J.: Prentice-Hall.

Carey, Joseph. 1988. "From Revival Tent to Mainstream," *U.S. News and World Report,* December 19, pp. 52–61.

Carlin, Jerome E. 1962. *Lawyers on Their Own.* New Brunswick, N.J.: Rutgers University Press.

Carlson, Kenneth W. 1979. Statement before the Congressional Committee on Education and Labor, Subcommittee on Compensation, Health, and Safety, "Hearings on Asbestos-Related Occupational Diseases," 95th Congress, Second Session. Washington, D.C.: Government Printing Office, pp. 25–52.

Carpenter, Paul. 1977. "Underworld Uses Bribery, Brutality, Murder to Smuggle Cigarettes." Associated Press, *Erie Morning News,* December 15.

Carson, Rachel. 1962. *Silent Spring.* New York: Houghton Mifflin.

Cary, Peter. 1987. "Dial-a-dupe on Con Man's Coast." *U.S. News and World Report,* December 21, pp. 62–63.

Cater, Douglass, and Strickland, Stephen. 1975. *TV Violence and the Child: The Evolution and Fate of the Surgeon General's Report.* New York: Russell Sage.

Caudill, William A. 1958. *The Psychiatric Hospital as a Small Society.* Cambridge, Mass.: Harvard University Press.

CBS. 1988. "Godfathers of the Ginza." *60 Minutes.* Telecast November 20.

—— 1989a. "Japan." *48 Hours.* Telecast February 23

—— 1989b. *West 57th.* Telecast March 25.

Ceram, C. W. 1967. *Gods, Graves and Scholars: The Story of Archeology.* 2nd ed. New York: Alfred A. Knopf.

Chaiken, Jan M., and Chaiken, Marcia R. 1982. *Varieties of Criminal Behavior.* Report prepared for the National Institute of Justice, U.S. Department of Justice. Santa Monica: The Rand Corporation.

—— 1983. "Crime Rates and the Active Criminal." In *Crime and Public Policy,* edited by James Q. Wilson, pp. 11–29. San Francisco: Institute for Contemporary Studies.

Chaiken, Marcia R., and Johnson, Bruce D. 1988. *Characteristics of Different Types of Drug-Involved Offenders.* Issue and Practices in Criminal Justice, Washington, D.C.: National Institute of Justice, February.

Chambliss, William J. 1975. *Box Man: A Professional Thief's Journal,* by Harry King, New York: Harper.

–––––– 1975b. "Toward a Political Economy of Crime." *Theory and Society* 2: 152–153.

–––––– 1976. "Functional and Conflict Theories of Crime." In *Whose Law, What Order?* edited by William J. Chambliss and Milton Mankoff. New York: Wiley.

–––––– 1988. *On the Take: From Petty Crooks to Presidents.* 2nd edition. Bloomington, Ind.: Indiana University Press.

Chambliss, William J., and Seidman, Robert B. 1971. *Law and Order and Power.* Reading, Mass.: Addison-Wesley.

Chandler, David L. 1976. *Criminal Brotherhoods.* London: Constable and Company.

Chappell, Duncan, and Fogarty, Faith. 1978. *Forcible Rape: A Literature Review and Annotated Bibliography.* Washington, D.C.: National Institute on Law Enforcement and Criminal Justice, May.

"Charges Dropped Against Man Selling Heads." 1987. *Erie Morning News,* January 19, p. 3–B.

"Cheating Medicare 'Easy,' Doctor Says." 1981. *Erie Morning News,* December 10, p. 4–A.

Cheatwood, Derral. 1988. "Is There a Season for Homicide?" *Criminology* 26: 287–306.

Cherrington, David J., and Cherrington, J. Owen. 1982. "The Climate of Honesty in Retail Stores." *Journal of Security Administration* 5 (2): 37–52.

Chesney-Lind, Meda. 1989. "Girls' Crime and Woman's Place: Toward a Feminist Model of Female Delinquency." *Crime and Delinquency* 35: 5–30.

Chin, Ko-Lin. 1988. "Chinese Organized Crime: Myth and Fact." Paper presented at the American Society of Criminology Meetings, Chicago, Illinois, November.

Christensen, Harold T., and Gregg, Christina F. 1970. "Changing Sex Norms in America and Skandinavia." *Journal of Marriage and the Family* 32: 616–627.

Christiansen, Karl. 1968. "Threshold of Tolerance in Various Population Groups Illustrated by Results from a Danish Criminological Twin Study." In *The Mentally Abnormal Offender,* edited by A. V. S. de Reuck. Boston: Little, Brown.

"City Inspectors Extorted Hundreds of Thousands from N.Y. Restaurants." 1988. *Erie Morning News,* March 25, p. 3–A.

Clark, Alexander, L., and Gibbs, Jack P. 1965. "Social Control: A Reformation." *Social Problems* 13: 399–415.

Clark, John P. and Tifft, Larry L. 1966. "Polygraph and Interview Validation of Self Reported Deviant Behavior." *American Sociological Review* 31: 516–523.

Clark, Thurston, and Tigue, Jr., John J. 1975. *Dirty Money: Swiss Banks, the Mafia, Money Laundering and White Collar Crime.* New York: Simon and Schuster.

Clarke, James W. 1982. *American Assassins: The Darker Side of Politics.* Princeton: Princeton University Press.

Clarke, Stevens H. 1974. "Getting 'Em Out of Circulation: Does Incarceration of Juvenile Offenders Reduce Crime?" *Journal of Criminal Law and Criminology* 65: 528–535.

Clébert, Jean-Paul. 1970. *The Gypsies.* Middlesex, Eng.: Penguin Books.

Cleckley, Hervey. 1976. *The Mask of Insanity.* 5th ed. St. Louis: Mosby.

Clinard, Marshall B. 1946. "Criminological Theories of Violations of Wartime Regulations." *American Sociological Review.* 11 (June): 258–270.

–––––– *The Black Market: A Study of White Collar Crime.* Montclair, N.J.: Patterson Smith. (First edition, 1952, New York: Holt).

–––––– 1978a. *Cities with Little Crime: The Case of Switzerland.* Cambridge, Eng.: Cambridge University Press.

–––––– 1978b. "Comparative Crime Victimization Surveys: Some Problems and Results." *International Journal of Criminology and Penology* 6: 97, Cited in John E. Conklin, 1981. *Criminology.* New York: Macmillan.

Clinard, Marshall B., and Abbott, D. J. 1973. *Crime in Developing Countries: A Comparative Perspective.* New York: John Wiley.

Clinard, Marshall B., and Quinney, Richard. 1973. *Criminal Behavior Systems: A Typology.* 2nd ed. New York: Holt, Rinehart, Winston (reissued by Cincinnati: Anderson, 1986).

Clinard, Marshall B., and Yeager, Peter C. 1978. "Corporate Crime: Issues in Research." *Criminology* 16: 255–272.

–––––– 1979. *Illegal Corporate Behavior.* Washington, D.C.: Law Enforcement Assistance Administration.

–––––– 1980. *Corporate Crime.* New York: Macmillan.

Cloward, Richard, and Ohlin, Lloyd. 1960. *Delinquency and Opportunity: A Theory of Delinquent Gangs.* New York: The Free Press.

Clutterbuck, Richard. 1975. *Living with Terrorism.* New Rochelle, N.Y.: Arlington House.

" 'Cocaine Cowboys' Running Rampant in Florida." 1980. Associated Press, *Erie Morning News,* May 6.

Cohen, Albert K. 1951. *Juvenile Delinquency and the Social Structure.* Doctoral dissertation, Harvard University.

–––––– 1955. *Delinquent Boys.* New York: The Free Press.

Cohen, Daniel. 1979. *Mysteries of the World.* Garden City, N.Y.: Doubleday.

Cohen, Lawrence E., and Felson, Marcus. 1979. "Social Change and Crime Rate Trends: A Routine Activities Approach." *American Sociological Review* 44: 588–608.

Cohen, Lawrence E., and Land, Kenneth. 1987. "Age and Crime: Symmetry vs. Asymmetry and the Projection of Crime Rates Through the 1990s." *American Sociological Review* 52: 170–183.

Cohen, Lawrence E., and Stark, Rodney. 1974. "Discriminatory Labeling and the Five-Finger Discount: An Empirical Analysis of Differential Shoplifting Dispositions." *Journal of Research on Crime and Delinquency* 11: 25–35.

Cohn, Bob. 1988. "A Fresh Assault on an Ugly Crime." *Newsweek,* March 14, pp. 64–65.

Coleman, Fred. 1988. "The Mobsters of Moscow." *Newsweek,* October 31, p. 44.

Coleman, James W. 1985. *The Criminal Elite.* New York: St. Martin's Press.

Collins, James J., Jr., ed., 1981. *Drinking and Crime: Perspectives on the Relationships between Alcohol Consumption and Criminal Behavior.* New York: Guilford Press.

Committee on the Judiciary. 1986. S. Rep., No. 433, 99th Congress, 2nd Session, 2.

Comstock, George A. 1975. "The Effects of Television on Children and Adolescents: The Evidence So Far." *Journal of Communication* 25: 25–34.

Comte, Auguste. 1877. *A System of Positive Polity.* London: Longmans.

Condon, Richard. 1958. *The Manchurian Candidate.* New York: Random House.

"Con Game Nets $3600 From Widow." 1972. *Erie Morning News,* November 7, p. 11–A.

Congressional Research Service. 1978. *Human Rights Conditions in Selected Countries and the U.S. Response.* Reports prepared for the House Committee on International Relations, 95th Congress, 2nd Session. Washington, D.C.: Government Printing Office, July 25.

Conklin, John E. 1972. *Robbery and the Criminal Justice System.* Philadelphia: Lippincott.

———. 1977. *Illegal But Not Criminal: Business Crime in America.* Englewood Cliffs, N.J.: Prentice-Hall.

———. 1981. *Criminology.* New York: Macmillan.

"Conning by Computer." 1973. *Newsweek,* April 23, p. 26.

Cook, Fred J. 1982. *The Great Energy Scam: Private Billions vs. Public Good.* New York: Macmillan.

———. 1984. *Maverick: Fifty Years of Investigative Reporting.* New York: G. P. Putnam's Sons.

Cook, Philip J. 1983. "Robbery." *Research in Brief.* Washington, D.C.: National Institute of Justice, June.

———, ed. 1988. "Vice." *Law and Contemporary Problems* 51 (Entire issue).

Cooley, Charles Horton. 1902. *Human Nature and Social Order.* 1964 ed. New York: Schocken Books.

Copeland, Miles. 1974. *Beyond Cloak and Dagger: Inside the CIA.* New York: Pinnacle Books.

Cortés, Juan, with Gatti, Florence M. 1972. *Delinquency and Crime.* New York: Seminar Press.

Coser, Lewis. 1956. *The Functions of Social Conflict.* New York: Free Press.

"Couple Call Sex Cult Sacred (Police Call It Prostitution)." 1989. *New York Times,* April 18, p. 1–B.

Cousins, Norman. 1979. "How the U.S. Used Its Citizens as Guinea Pigs." *Saturday Review,* November 10, p. 10.

Cox, Edward R.; Fellmuth, Robert C.; and Schulz, John E. 1969. *Nader's Raiders: Report on the Federal Trade Commission.* New York: Grove Press.

Crelinstein, Ronald D.; Laberge-Altmejd, Daniel; and Szabo, Denis. 1978. *Terrorism and Criminal Justice.* Lexington, Mass.: D. C. Heath.

Cressey, Donald. 1953. *Other People's Money.* New York: The Free Press.

———. 1960. "Epidemiology and Individual Conduct: A Case from Criminology."*Pacific Sociological Review* 3: 47–58.

———. 1967. "The Functions and Structure of Criminal Syndicates." In *Organized Crime Task Force Report.* Washington, D.C.: Government Printing Office.

———. 1969. *The Theft of the Nation: The Structure and Operations of Organized Crime in America.* New York: Harper and Row.

———. 1972. *Criminal Organization.* New York: Harper and Row.

Crewdson, John. 1988. *By Silence Betrayed: Sexual Abuse of Children in America.* Boston: Little, Brown.

Crichton, Michael. 1972. *Terminal Man.* New York: Alfred A. Knopf.

Crichton, Robert. 1959. *The Great Imposter.* New York: Permabooks.

Crittenden, Ann. 1988. *Sanctuary: A Story of American Conscience and Law in Collision.* New York: Weidenfeld and Nicolson.

Crittenden, Kathleen S., and Hill, Richard J. 1971. "Coding Reliability and Validity of Interview Data." *American Sociological Review* 36: 1073–1080.

Cronin, Thomas E.; Cronin, Tania Z.; and Milakovich, Michael E. 1981. *U.S. vs. Crime in the Streets.* Bloomington: Indiana University Press.

Crowe, Raymond R. 1974. "An Adoption Study of Antisocial Personality." *Archives of General Psychiatry* 31: 785–791.

Cullen, Francis T. 1983. "Public Support for Punishing White-Collar Crime: Blaming the Victim Revisited?" *Journal of Criminal Justice* 11 (6): 481–493.

———. 1984a. "The Ford Pinto Case and Beyond." In *Corporations as Criminals,* edited by Ellen C. Hochstedler. Beverly Hills: Sage.

———. 1984b. *Rethinking Crime and Deviance Theory.* Totowa, N.J.: Rowman and Allenheld.

Cullen, Francis T.; Makestad, William; and Cavender, G. 1987. *Corporate Crime Under Attack: The Ford Pinto Case and Beyond.* Cincinnati: Anderson.

Cullen, Francis T. et al. 1982a. "Dissecting White-Collar Crime: Offense Type and Punitiveness." Paper delivered at the Academy of Criminal Justice Sciences Meetings, Louisville, Kentucky.

———. 1982b. "The Seriousness of Crimes Revisited: Have Attitudes toward White-Collar Crime Changed?" *Criminology* 20: 83–102.

Currie, Elliott. 1985. *Confronting Crime: Why There is So Much Crime in America and What We Can Do About It.* New York: Pantheon.

Dahrendorf, Ralf. 1959. *Class and Class Conflict in Industrial Society.* Stanford: Stanford University Press.

Dale, Robert. 1974. "Memoirs of a Contemporary Cutpurse." In *Streetwise Criminology,* edited by Duane Denfield, pp. 71–75. Cambridge, Mass.: Schenkman.

Daley, Robert. 1981. *The Year of the Dragon.* New York: Signet.

Dalgard, Odd Steffen, and Kringlen, Einer. 1975. "A Norwegian Twin Study of Criminality." *British Journal of Criminology* 16: 213–232.

Dalton, Katharina. 1961. "Menstruation and Crime." *British Medical Journal* 2: 1752–1753.

Daraul, Arkon. 1969. *A History of Secret Societies*. New York: Pocket Books.

Davis, Hugh, and Gurr, Ted. 1969. *Violence in America: Historical and Comparative Perspectives*. New York: The New American Library.

Davis, James. 1982. *Street Gangs: Youth, Biker and Prison Gangs*. Dubuque, Iowa: Kendall/Hunt Publishing Co.

Davis, Kingsley. 1961. "Prostitution." In *Contemporary Social Problems*, edited by Robert K. Merton and Robert A. Nisbet, pp. 275–276. New York: Harcourt, Brace and World.

Dean, John. 1977. *Blind Ambition*. New York: Pocket Books.

"Declaration of the Rights of Man and of the Citizen," Article VIII, 1789. Revolutionary National Assembly of France. In *Classics of Criminology*, edited by Joseph E. Jacoby, 1979, p. 215. Oak Park, Ill.: Moore Publishing.

DeFleur, Melvin L., and Quinney, Richard. 1966. "A Reformulation of Sutherland's Differential Association Theory and a Strategy for Empirical Verification." *The Journal of Research in Crime and Delinquency* 3 (January): 1–22.

Demaree, Robert G. 1980. "Estimating the Size of Drug User Populations." Paper presented at the National Workshop on Research Methodology and Criminal Justice Program Evaluation. Baltimore, Md., March.

Demaris, Ovid. 1981. *The Last Mafioso: The Treacherous World of Jimmy Fratianno*. New York: Times Books.

Denfield, Duane. 1974. *Streetwise Criminology*. Cambridge, Mass.: Schenkman.

Denno, Deborah. 1985. "Sociological and Human Developmental Explanations of Crime: Conflict and Consensus?" *Criminology* 23: 711–742.

Dentler, Robert A. and Monroe, Lawrence J. 1961. "Social Correlates of Early Adolescent Theft." *American Sociological Review* 26 (October): 733–743.

Department of Health and Human Services. 1981. *For Parents Only: What You Need to Know about Marijuana*. Washington, D.C.: Government Printing Office.

_____ 1982. *Television and Behavior*. Washington, D.C.: Government Printing Office.

Detlinger, Chet, with Jeff Prugh. 1983. *The List*. Atlanta: Philmay Enterprises.

Diapoulous, Peter, and Linakis, Steven. 1976. *The Sixth Family: The True Inside Story of the Execution of a Mafia Chief*. New York: Bantam.

di Gennaro, Giuseppe, and Vetere, Eduardo. 1980. "White-Collar Crime: Problems of Definition and Lines of Research." In *International Summaries*, National Criminal Justice Reference Service, vol. 4, pp. 3–12. Washington, D.C.: Government Printing Office.

Doerner, William. 1988. "The Impact of Medical Resources on Criminally Induced Lethality: A Further Examination." *Criminology* 26: 171–179.

Doerner, William G., and Speir, John C. 1986. "Stitch and Sew: The Impact of Medical Resources Upon Criminally Induced Lethality." *Criminology* 24: 319–330.

Donnerstein, Edward, Linz, Daniel, and Penrod, Steven. 1987. *The Question of Pornography*. New York: The Free Press.

Donovan, Robert. 1952. *The Assassins*. New York: Harper Brothers.

Dowie, Mark. 1977. "Pinto Madness." *Mother Jones* 2 (September): 18–32. Reprinted in *Crisis in American Institutions*, edited by Jerome H. Skolnick and Elliott Currie. 1982. Boston: Little, Brown.

_____ 1987. "The Dumping of Hazardous Products on Foreign Markets." In *Corporate Violence* edited by Stuart L. Hills, Totowa, N.J.: Rowman and Littlefield, pp. 47–58.

Doyle, John M. 1987. "Aging Mafia Bosses Get Century in Jail." *Erie Morning News*, January 14, p. 2–A.

_____ 1989. "Court Reverses Convictions in Beech-Nut Juice Case." *The Washington Post*, March 31, p. 5–A.

"Dozens of Officials Implicated." 1980. *Erie Times-News*, February 10, p. 1.

"Drug Rings Hire Gun-Toting Kids." 1988. *Erie Times News*, June 5, p. 4–A.

Dugdale, Robert. 1877. *The Jukes: A Study in Crime, Pauperism and Heredity*. New York: Putnam.

Dunn, Christopher S. 1976. *Patterns of Robbery Characteristics*. Analytic Report 15. Washington, D.C.: National Criminal Justice Information and Statistics Service.

Durkheim, Emile. 1950. *The Rules of Sociological Method*. Glencoe, Ill.: The Free Press.

_____ 1951. *Suicide*. New York: The Free Press.

_____ 1964. *The Division of Labor in Society*. New York: The Free Press.

Duster, Troy. 1970. *The Legislation of Morality: Laws, Drugs and Moral Judgment*. New York: The Free Press.

Dutton, Denis, ed. 1983. *The Forger's Art: Forgery and the Philosophy of Art*. Berkeley: University of California Press.

"Ecology: The Enforcer." 1971. *Newsweek*, October 18, p. 34.

Eddy, Paul; Sabogal, Hugo; and Walden, Sara. 1988. *The Cocaine Wars*. New York: W. W. Norton.

Edelhertz, Herbert. 1970. *The Nature, Impact and Prosecution of White-Collar Crime*. National Institute of Law Enforcement and Criminal Justice. Washington, D.C.: Government Printing Office.

Edwards, Allen. 1957. *Techniques of Attitudes Scale Construction*. New York: Appelton.

Egger, Steven A. 1984. "A Working Definition of Serial Murder." *Journal of Police Science and Administration* 12: 348–357.

Ehrlich, Paul R., and Feldman, S. Shirley. 1977. *The Race Bomb*. New York: Quadrangle.

Eisenhower, Dwight D. 1972. "Farewell Address." In *The Military-Industrial Complex*, edited by C. W. Pursell, Jr., pp. 206–207. New York: Harper and Row.

Ekpenyong, Rosy A. 1988. "Reviews of O'Brien and Goldstein." *The Journal of Criminal Law and Criminology* 79: 569–572.

Elias, Robert. 1986. *The Politics of Victimization: Victims, Victimology and Human Rights.* New York: Oxford University Press.

Elliott, Delbert S., and Ageton, Suzanne S. 1980. "Reconciling Race and Class Differences in Self-Reported and Official Estimates of Delinquency." *American Sociological Review* 45 (February): 95–110.

Ellis, Albert. 1959. "Why Married Men Visit Prostitutes." *Sexology* 25: 344.

_____ 1979. "The Sex Offender." In *Psychology of Crime and Criminal Justice,* edited by Hans Toch, pp. 405–426. New York: Holt, Rinehart and Winston.

Ellis, Albert, and Brancale, R. 1965. *Psychology of Sex Offenders.* Springfield, Ill.: Charles C. Thomas.

Ellis, Lee. 1982. "Genetics and Criminal Behavior." *Criminology* 20 (May): 43–56.

Empey, LaMar T., and Erickson, Maynard L. 1966. "Hidden Delinquency and Social Status." *Social Forces* 44: 546–554.

Engberg, E. 1967. *The Spy in the Corporate Structure.* Cleveland: World Publishing.

Ennis, P. H. 1967. *Criminal Victimization in the United States: A Report of a National Survey.* Field Surveys II, the President's Commission on Law Enforcement and Administration of Justice. Washington, D.C.: Government Printing Office.

Epstein, Edward J. 1977. *Agency of Fear.* New York: G. P. Putnam.

_____ 1983. "Edwin Wilson and the CIA: How Badly One Man Hurt Our Nation." *Parade,* September 18, pp. 22–24.

Erickson, Erik H. 1950. *Childhood and Society.* New York: Norton.

Erickson, Maynard L., and Empey, LaMar T. 1963. "Court Records, Undetected Delinquency and Decision-Making." *Journal of Criminal Law, Criminology and Police Science* 54: 456–469.

"Erie Red Light Resorts Pay More Than $50,000 Annually in Rentals." 1907. *Erie Morning News.* Highlights of 1907 issue, 1988, January 22, p. 6–A.

Erlanger, Howard S. 1974. "The Empirical Status of the Subculture of Violence Thesis." *Social Problems* 22 (March): 280–292.

Ermann, M. David, and Lundmann, Richard J. 1982. *Corporate Deviance.* New York: Holt, Rinehart, Winston.

Esposito, John C., and Silverman, Larry J. 1970. *Vanishing Air: Ralph Nader's Study Group Report on Air Pollution.* New York: Grossman.

Estill, Jerry. 1988. "Feds Start 'Rapsheet' for Doctors." *Erie Morning News,* December 31, p. 1–A.

Estrich, Susan. 1987. *Real Rape: How the Legal System Victimizes Women Who Say No.* Cambridge, Mass.: Harvard University Press.

Etzioni, Amitai, ed. 1969. *The Semi-Professions and Their Organization.* New York: The Free Press

"Europeans Favor Tough Drug Laws." 1988. *Erie Times News,* June 5, p. 4–A.

"Ex-Agents Say Drug War Never Adequately Funded." 1986. *Erie Times News,* October 5, p. 2–A.

Eysenck, Hans. 1977. *Crime and Personality.* 3rd ed. London: Routledge and Kegan Paul.

Fagan, Jeffrey; Piper, Elizabeth; and Moore, Melinda. 1986. "Violent Delinquents and Urban Youths." *Criminology* 24: 439–471.

Fagan, Jeffrey, and Wexler, Sandra. 1987. "Family Origins of Violent Delinquents." *Criminology* 25: 643–669.

Fancher, Raymond E. 1985. *The Intelligence Men.* New York: W. W. Norton.

Farnworth, Margaret, and Leiber, Michael J. 1989. "Strain Theory Revisited." *American Sociological Review* 54: 263–274.

Farrington, David P. 1973. "Self-Reports of Deviant Behavior: Predictive and Stable?" *Journal of Criminal Law and Criminology* 64: 99–110.

_____ 1975. "Age and Crime." Paper presented at the American Society of Criminology Meetings, Cincinnati, Ohio, November.

_____ 1986. "Age and Crime: in *Crime and Justice,* volume 7, edited by Michael Tonry and David Farrington. Chicago: University of Chicago Press, pp. 189–250.

Farrington, David P.; Ohlin, Lloyd E.; and Wilson, James Q., eds. 1986. *Understanding and Controlling Crime.* New York: Springer-Verlag.

Fay, Stephen, *et al.* 1972. *Hoax: The Inside Story of the Howard Hughes Affair.* New York: Viking Press.

Federal Bureau of Investigation. 1985. *Oriental Organized Crime.* Washington, D.C.: Government Printing Office.

_____ 1988. *Crime in the United States, 1987.* Washington, D.C.: Government Printing Office.

"The FBI vs. Jean Seberg." 1970. *Time,* September 24, p. 25.

"Feds Indict TMI Operator Over Reports." 1983. *Erie Morning News,* November 8, p. 1.

Feeney, Floyd, and Weir, Adrianne. 1975. "The Prevention and Control of Robbery." *Criminology* 13 (May): 102–105.

Feldman, Roy E. 1968. "Response to Compatriot and Foreigner Who Seeks Assistance." *Journal of Personality and Social Psychology* 10: 202–214.

Felson, Marcus. 1983. "Ecology of Crime." In *The Encyclopedia of Crime and Justice.* New York: Macmillan.

_____ 1987. "Routine Activities and Crime Prevention in the Developing Metropolis." *Criminology* 25: 911–931.

Fenwick, Charles R. 1982. "Crime and Justice in Japan: Implications for the United States." *International Journal of Comparative and Applied Criminal Justice* 6: 62–71.

Ferracuti, Franco. 1968. "European Migration and Crime." In *Crime and Culture: Essays in Honor of Thorsten Sellin,* edited by Marvin E. Wolfgang. New York: Wiley.

Ferri, Enrico. 1917. *Criminal Sociology.* Translated by Joseph I. Kelley and John Lisle. Boston: Little, Brown.

Fight Crime Committee. 1986. *A Discussion Document on Options for Changes in the Law and in the Administration of the Law to Counter the Triad Problem.* Hong Kong: Government Security Office, April.

Final Report of the Select Committee to Study Governmental Operations with Respect to Intelligence Activities. 1976. U.S. Senate, *Intelligence Activities and the Rights of Americans*, Book II. Washington, D.C.: Government Printing Office.

Finckenauer, James. 1982. *Scared Straight and the Panacea Phenomenon*. Englewood Cliff, N.J.: Prentice-Hall.

Finestone, Harold. 1976. *Victims of Change*. Westport, Ct.: Greenwood.

Finkelhor, David. 1979. *Sexually Victimized Children*. New York: The Free Press.

―――― 1986. *A Sourcebook on Child Sexual Abuse*. Beverly Hills: Sage.

Finn, Peter E., and Sullivan, Monique. 1988. "Police Respond to Special Populations: Handling the Mentally Ill, Public Inebriate, and the Homeless." *NIJ Reports*, 209: 2–8.

Fishbach, Seymour, and Malamuth, Neal. 1978. "Sex and Aggression: Proving the Link." *Psychology Today* 12: 111–122.

Fishburne, Patricia; Abelson, Herbert; and Cisin, Ira. 1980. *National Survey on Drug Abuse: Main Findings, 1979*. Washington, D.C.: Government Printing Office.

Flanagan, Timothy J., and Jamieson, Katherine M. eds. 1988. *Sourcebook of Criminal Justice Statistics, 1987*. Albany, N.Y.: SUNY, Hindelang Criminal Justice Research Center.

Flowers, Ronald B. 1988. *Minorities and Crime*. Westport, Ct.: Greenwood Press.

Fontana, Vincent J. 1973. *Somewhere a Child Is Crying*. New York: Macmillan.

Forgac, Gregory E., and Michaels, Edward J. 1982. "Personality Characteristics of Two Types of Male Exhibitionists." *Journal of Abnormal Psychology* 91 (4): 287–295.

"Fortune Directory of the Largest U.S. Corporations." 1983. *Fortune*, May 2, p. 226.

"42 People Indicted for Smuggling Cocaine." 1984. *Erie Times-News*, May 3, p. 1–A.

"4 Indicted Over Pacemaker Scam." 1988. *Erie Morning News*, September 1, p. 1–A.

Fox, James A., and Levin, Jack. 1985. *Mass Murder: America's Growing Menace*. New York: Plenum.

Fox, Richard G. 1971. "The XYY Offender: A Modern Myth?" *Journal of Criminal Law, Criminology and Police Science* 62: 59–73.

Fox, Vernon. 1976. *Introduction to Criminology*. Englewood Cliffs, N.J.: Prentice-Hall.

―――― 1985. *Introduction to Criminology*. 2nd edition. Englewood Cliffs, N.J.: Prentice-Hall.

Frank, Nancy. 1985. *Crimes Against Health and Safety*. New York: Harrow and Heston.

―――― 1987. "Murder in the Workplace." In *Corporate Violence*, edited by Stuart L. Hills. Totowa, N.J.: Rowman and Littlefield.

Frank, Nancy, and Lombness, Michael. 1988. *Controlling Corporate Illegality*. Cincinnati: Anderson.

Freedman, Monroe H. 1976. "Advertising and Soliciting: The Case of Ambulance Chasing." In *Verdicts on Lawyers*, edited by Ralph Nader and Mark Green. New York: Thomas Y. Crowell.

Freud, Sigmund. 1930. *Civilization and Its Discontents*. Translated by Joan Riviere. Garden City, N.J.: Doubleday.

Friday, Carolyn and Pauly, Jean. 1989. "Hitting Milken Where It Hurts." *Newsweek*, April 10, p. 49.

Friedlander, Kate. 1947. *The Psychoanalytic Approach to Juvenile Delinquency*. New York: International Universities Press.

Friedman, Albert B. 1968. "The Scatological Rites of Burglars." *Western Folklore* 27 (July): 171–179.

Friedman, Milton. 1962. *Capitalism and Freedom*. Chicago: University of Chicago Press.

Friedrich, Carl J. 1972. *The Pathology of Politics*. New York: Harper and Row.

Friedrichs, David O. 1980a. "Carl Klockars vs. the 'Heavy Hitters': A Preliminary Critique." In *Radical Criminology: The Coming Crisis*, edited by James A. Inciardi, pp. 149–160. Beverly Hills: Sage.

―――― 1980b. "Radical Criminology in the United States: An Interpretive Understanding." In *Radical Criminology: The Coming Crisis*, edited by James A. Inciardi, pp. 35–60. Beverly Hills: Sage.

Friedson, Elliot. 1970. *The Profession of Medicine*. New York: Dodd-Mead.

Fry, Fran, Jr. 1986. "Consumer Bag: Airport Theft." *Erie Times News*, September 21, p. 7–B.

Fuller, John G. 1962. *The Gentleman Conspirators: The Story of the Price-Fixers in the Electrical Industry*. New York: Grove Press.

Gage, Nicholas. 1971. *The Mafia Is Not an Equal Opportunity Employer*. New York: McGraw Hill.

―――― 1972. *Mafia, U.S.A.*, Chicago: Playboy Press.

―――― 1974. "Questions Are Raised on the Lucky Luciano Book." *New York Times*, December 17, pp. 1, 28.

―――― 1977. "Has the Mafia Penetrated the F.B.I.?" *The New York Times Magazine*, October 2, pp. 14–17, 44–46.

―――― 1988. "A Tale of Two Mafias." *U.S. News and World Report*, January 18, pp. 36–37.

Gager, Nancy, and Schurr, Cathleen. 1976. *Sexual Assault: Confronting Rape in America*. New York: Grosset and Dunlap.

Galliher, John F., and Cain, James A. 1974. "Citation Support for the Mafia Myth in Criminology Textbooks." *The American Sociologist* 9 (May): 68–74.

Galliher, John F., and McCartney, James L. 1977. *Criminology: Power, Crime and Criminal Law*. Homewood, Ill.: Dorsey.

"Gangland Enforcer Paid with Life for Rifts with Mob Over C.I.A." 1977. *United Press International*, March 31.

Gardiner, John A. 1970. *The Politics of Corruption: Organized Crime in an American City*. New York: Russell Sage.

Garner, Joel, and Clemmer, Elizabeth. 1986. *Danger to Police in Domestic Disturbances: A New Look*. Washington, D.C.: National Institute of Justice.

Garner, Joel, and Visher, Christy A. 1988. "Policy Experiments Come of Age." *NIJ Reports* 201, September/October: 2–8.

Garofalo, Raffaelo. 1914. *Criminology.* Translated by Robert W. Millar. Boston: Little, Brown.

Garrow, David. 1981. *The F.B.I. and Martin Luther King.* New York: Norton.

Gebhard, Paul, et al., 1965. *Sex Offenders: An Analysis of Types.* New York: Harper and Row.

Geis, Gilbert. 1962. "Toward a Delineation of White-Collar Offenses." *Sociological Inquiry* 32 (Spring): 160–171.

_____ 1974a. "Avocational Crime." In *Handbook of Criminology,* edited by Daniel Glaser, pp. 273–298. Chicago: Rand McNally.

_____ 1974b. "Upperworld Crime." In *Current Perspectives on Criminal Behavior: Original Essays on Criminology,* edited by Abraham S. Blumberg, pp. 114–137. New York: Alfred A. Knopf.

Geis, Gilbert, and Meier, Robert F., eds. 1977. *White Collar Crime: Offenses in Business, Politics and the Professions.* Rev. ed. New York: The Free Press.

_____ 1979. "Looking Backward and Forward: Criminologists on Criminology as as Career." In *Criminology: New Concerns,* edited by Edward Sagarin, pp. 173–188. Beverly Hills: Sage.

Gelles, Richard J. 1977. "Etiology of Violence: Overcoming Fallacious Reasoning in Understanding Family Violence and Child Abuse." Manuscript, available through the National Criminal Justice Reference Service, Rockville, Md.

_____ 1978. "Violence toward Children in the United States." *American Journal of Orthopsychiatry* 48 (October): 580–592.

Gelles, Richard J., and Straus, Murray 1979. "Violence in the American Family." *Journal of Social Issues* 35 (March): 15–39.

Gendreau, Paul, and Ross, Robert R. 1987. "Revivification of Rehabilitation: Evidence from the 1980s." *Justice Quarterly* 4: 349–407.

General Accounting Office. 1977. *War on Organized Crime Faltering.* Washington, D.C.: Government Printing Office.

Georges-Abeyie, Daniel, ed. 1984. *The Criminal Justice System and Blacks.* New York: Clark Boardman.

Gest, Ted. 1986. "The Latest Antidrug War: Better Luck This Time?" *U.S. News and World Report,* August 25, p. 18.

Gibbens, T. C. N., and Silberman, M. 1960. "The Clients of Prostitutes." *British Journal of Veneral Disease* 36: 113.

Gibbons, Don C. 1977. *Society, Crime and Criminal Careers.* 3rd ed. Englewood Cliffs, N.J.: Prentice-Hall.

_____ 1982. *Society, Crime, and Criminal Behavior.* Englewood Cliffs, N.J.: Prentice-Hall (4th ed. of 1977 book).

_____ 1979. *The Criminological Enterprise: Theories and Perspectives.* Englewood Cliffs, N.J.: Prentice-Hall.

Gibbons, Don C., and Garabedian, Peter. 1974. "Conservative, Liberal and Radical Criminology: Some Trends and Observations." In *The Criminologist: Crime and the*

Criminal, edited by Charles E. Reasons, pp. 51–56. Pacific Palisades: Goodyear.

Gibbs, Jack B. 1985. "Review Essay of *Crime and Human Nature* by James Q. Wilson and Richard J. Herrnstein." *Criminology* 23: 381–388.

Gil, David. 1971. *Violence against Children.* Cambridge, Mass.: Harvard University Press.

Glaser, Barney, and Strauss, Anselm. 1967. *The Discovery of Grounded Theory.* Chicago: Aldine.

Glaser, Daniel. 1978. *Crime in Our Changing Society.* New York: Holt, Rinehart, and Winston.

Glasser, William. 1965. *Reality Therapy.* New York: Harper and Row.

Glueck, Sheldon, and Glueck, Eleanor. 1950. *Unraveling Juvenile Delinquency.* Cambridge, Mass.: Harvard University Press.

_____ 1956. *Physique and Delinquency.* New York: Harper and Row.

Goddard, Henry H. 1912. *The Kallikak Family.* New York: Macmillan.

Goff, Colin, and Reasons, Charles. 1986. "Organizational Crimes Against Employees, Consumers, and the Public." In *The Political Economy of Crime,* edited by B. MacLean. Toronto: Prentice-Hall of Canada, pp. 204–231.

Goffman, Erving. 1963. *Stigma.* Indianapolis: Bobbs-Merrill.

Gold, Martin. 1966. "Undetected Delinquent Behavior." *Journal of Research in Crime and Delinquency* 3 (January): 27–46.

Goldstein, Michael J., et al., 1973. *Pornography and Sexual Deviance.* Berkeley: University of California Press.

Goode, Erich. 1972. *Drugs in American Society.* New York: Alfred A. Knopf.

_____ 1984. *Deviant Behavior.* 2nd ed. Englewood Cliffs, N.J.: Prentice-Hall.

_____ 1981. "Drugs and Crime." in *Current Perspectives on Criminal Behavior,* edited by Abraham Blumberg, pp. 227–272. New York: Alfred A. Knopf.

Goodwin, Jean, et al. *Sexual Abuse: Incest Victims and Their Families.* Boston: John Wright.

Gordon, David M. 1973. "Capitalism, Class and Crime in America." *Crime and Delinquency* 19 (April): 163–186.

Gordon, Linda, and O'Keefe, Paul. 1984. "Incest as a Form of Family Violence: Evidence from Historical Case Records." *Journal of Marriage and the Family* 46 (February): 27–34.

Gordon, Robert A. 1987. "SES versus IQ in the Race-IQ-Delinquency Model." *International Journal of Sociology and Social Policy* 7: 30–96.

Goring, Charles. 1913. *The English Convict.* London: His Majesty's Stationery Office.

Gosch, Martin A., and Hammer, Richard. 1974. *The Last Legacy of Lucky Luciano.* New York: Dell.

Gottfredson, Michael R., and Hindelang, Michael J. 1977. "A Consideration of Telescoping and Memory Decay Biases in Victimization Surveys." *Journal of Criminal Justice* 5 (Fall): 205–216.

Gottfredson, Michael, and Hirschi, Travis. 1986. "The True Value of Lambda Would Appear to be Zero: An Essay on Career Criminals, Criminal Careers, Selective Incapacitation, Cohort Studies and Related Topics." *Criminology* 24: 213–234.

—— 1987. "The Methodological Adequacy of Longitudinal Research on Crime." *Criminology* 25: 581–614.

—— 1988. "Science, Public Policy and the Career Paradigm." *Criminology* 26: 37–55.

Gould, Leroy C. 1969. "The Changing Structure of Property Crime in an Affluent Society." *Social Forces* 48 (September): 50–59.

Gould, Stephen J. 1981. *The Mismeasure of Man.* New York: Norton.

Goulden, J. C. 1984. *The Death Merchant: The Rise and Fall of Edwin P. Wilson.* New York: Simon and Schuster.

Gravel, Senator Mike, ed. 1971. *The Pentagon Papers.* 4 vols. Boston: Beacon Press.

Green, Mark J. et al. eds. 1973. *The Monopoly Makers: Ralph Nader's Study Group Report on Regulation and Competition.* New York: Grossman.

Green, Mark J.; Moore, Beverly C.; and Wasserstein, Bruce. 1972. *The Closed Enterprise System: Ralph Nader's Study Group Report on Anti-Trust Enforcement.* New York: Grossman.

Greenberg, David. 1975. "The Incapacitative Effects of Imprisonment: Some Estimates." *Law and Society Review* 9 (Summer): 541–580.

—— 1981. *Crime and Capitalism.* Palo Alto, Ca.: Mayfield.

Greene, Robert W. 1981. *The Sting Man: Inside Abscam.* New York: E. P. Dutton.

Greenfield, Lawrence A. 1988. *Drunk Driving.* Bureau of Justice Statistics Special Report. Washington, D.C.: U.S. Department of Justice, February.

Griffin, Katie. 1989. "Nestle Defends Its Third World Policies." *National Catholic Reporter*, February 24, p. 5.

Gropper, Bernard A. 1985. "Probing the Links Between Drugs and Crime." *Research in Brief.* National Institute of Justice, February.

Gross, Bertram. 1980. *Friendly Fascism: The New Face of Power in America.* New York: M. Evans and Co.

Groth, Nicholas, and Birnbaum, H. Jean. 1979. *Men Who Rape: The Psychology of the Offender.* New York: Plenum Press.

Groth, Nicholas; Burgess, Ann W.; and Holmstrom, Lynda L. 1977. "Rape: Power, Anger and Sexuality." *American Journal of Psychiatry* 134 (November): 1239–1243.

Groth, Nicholas, et al. 1978. "A Study of the Child Molester: Myths and Realities." *LAE (Journal of the American Criminal Justice Association)* 41: 17–22.

Gugliotta, Guy, and Leen, Jeff. 1989. *Kings of Cocaine.* New York: Simon and Schuster.

Haas, Scott. 1985. "Bad Seeds and Social Policy: Two Histories." *Psychology Today*, December, pp. 73–74.

Hacker, Frederick J. 1976. *Crusaders, Criminals and Crazies: Terror and Terrorism in Our Time.* New York: W. W. Norton.

Hagan, Frank E. 1975. *Comparative Professionalism in an Occupational Arena: The Case of Rehabilitation.* Unpublished doctoral dissertation, Case Western Reserve University.

—— 1982. *Research Methods in Criminal Justice and Criminology.* New York: Macmillan.

—— 1983. "The Organized Crime Continuum: A Further Specification of a New Conceptual Model." *Criminal Justice Review* 8 (Fall): 52–57.

—— 1985. "Theoretical Range in Criminological Theory." Paper presented at the Academy of Criminal Justice Sciences Meetings, Las Vegas, Nevada, April.

—— 1986. "Sub Rosa Criminals: Spies as Neglected Criminal Types." *Clandestine Tactics and Technology* (A Technical and Background Data Service, International Chiefs of Police) 11: entire issue.

—— 1987a. "Book Review: James Mills' *The Underground Empire: Where Crime and Government Embrace.*" *American Journal of Criminal Justice* 11: 128–130.

—— 1987b. "Espionage as Political Crime? A Typology of Spies." Paper presented at the American Society of Criminology Meetings, Montreal, November (forthcoming in *Journal of Security Administration*).

—— 1987c. "The Global Fallacy and Theoretical Range in Criminological Theory." *Journal of Justice Issues* 2: 19–31.

—— 1988. "Varieties of Treason: Ideology and Criminality." Paper presented at the Academy of Criminal Justice Sciences Meetings, San Francisco: April.

—— 1989a. *Research Methods in Criminal Justice and Criminology.* 2nd edition. New York: Macmillan.

—— 1989b. "Single Subject Designs: Quantitative Case Studies." Paper presented at the Academy of Criminal Justice Sciences Meetings, Washington, D.C., April.

Hagan, Frank E., and Sussman, Marvin B., eds. 1988a. *Deviance and the Family.* New York: Haworth Press.

—— 1988b. "Deviance and the Family: Where Have We Been and Where are We Going?" In *Deviance and the Family*, edited by Frank E. Hagan and Marvin B. Sussman, pp. 1–22. New York: Haworth Press.

Hagan, John. 1987. "Review Essay: A Great Truth in the Study of Crime." *Criminology* 25: 421–428.

Hagan, John; Gillis, A. R.; and Simpson, John. 1985. "The Class Structure of Gender and Delinquency: Toward a Power-Control Theory of Common Delinquent Behavior." *American Journal of Sociology* 90: 1151–1178.

—— 1987. "Class in the Household: A Power-Control Theory of Gender and Delinquency." *American Journal of Sociology* 92: 788–816.

Hagan, John, and Palloni, Alberto. 1986. " 'Club Fed' and the Sentencing of White-Collar Offenders Before and After Watergate." *Criminology* 4: 603–621.

Hagan, John L., et al. 1980. "The Differential Sentencing of White-Collar Offenders in Ten Federal District Courts." *American Sociological Review* 45 (September): 802–820.

Hall, Jerome. 1952. *Theft, Law and Society.* Rev. ed. Indianapolis: Bobbs-Merrill.

Haller, Mark H. 1972. "Organized Crime in Urban Society: Chicago in the Twentieth Century." *Journal of Social History* 5 (Winter): 210–234.

Halperin, Morton H., et al. 1976. *The Lawless State: The Crimes of the U.S. Intelligence Agencies.* New York: Penguin.

Hamilton, Andrea. 1987. "Gang Leader's Manual Gave Youths Pointers on Shoplifting at Malls." *Erie Morning News*, April 17, p. 4–A.

Hamilton, Peter. 1967. *Espionage and Subversion in An Industrial Society.* London: Hutchinson.

Hamlin, John E. 1988. "The Misplaced Role of Rational Choice in Neutralization Theory." *Criminology* 26: 425–438.

Hammer, Richard, ed. 1975. *Playboy's Illustrated History of Organized Crime.* Chicago: Playboy Press.

Haney, Charles; Banks, Curtis; and Zimbardo, Philip. 1973. "Interpersonal Dynamics in a Simulated Prison." *International Journal of Criminology and Penology* 1: 69–97.

Haran, James F. 1982. *The Loser's Game: A Sociological Profile of 500 Armed Robbers.* Unpublished doctoral dissertation, Fordham University.

Hardt, Robert H., and Hardt, Sandra P. 1977. "On Determining the Quality of the Delinquency Self-Report Method." *Journal of Research in Crime and Delinquency* 14 (July): 247–261.

Harlow, Caroline W. 1988. *Motor Vehicle Theft.* Bureau of Justice Statistics Special Report. Washington, D.C.: Government Printing Office, March.

Harmer, Ruth Mulvey. 1975. *American Medical Avarice.* New York: Abelard-Schuman.

Harrington, Alan. 1972. *Psychopaths.* New York: Simon and Shuster.

Harris, John W., Jr. 1987. "Domestic Terrorism in the 1980s." *FBI Law Enforcement Bulletin*, October: 5–13.

Harris, Robert. 1986. *Selling Hitler: The Story of the Hitler Diaries.* London: Faber and Faber.

Hartjen, Clayton A. 1974. *Crime and Criminalization.* 2nd ed. New York: Holt/Praeger.

Hartung, Frank E. 1950. "White-Collar Offenses in the Wholesale Meat Industry in Detroit." *American Journal of Sociology* 56 (July): 25–32.

Haskell, Martin R., and Yablonsky, Lewis. 1978. *Criminology: Crime and Criminality.* 2nd ed. Chicago: Rand McNally.

_____ 1983. *Crime and Delinquency.* 3rd ed. Chicago: Rand McNally.

Hastings, Donald W. 1965. "The Psychiatry of Presidential Assassination." *The Journal-Lancet* 85 (March): 93–100; (April): 157–162; (May): 189–192; and (July): 294–301.

"Havens for Car Snatchers." 1989. *U.S. News and World Report*, January 16, p. 70.

Hawkins, Darnell F., ed. 1986a. *Homicide Among Black Americans.* Lanham, Md.: University Press of America.

_____ 1986b. "Race, Crime Type and Imprisonment." *Justice Quarterly* 3: 253–269.

_____ 1987. "Beyond Anomalies: Rethinking the Conflict Perspective on Race and Punishment." *Social Forces* 65: 719–745.

Hawkins, Gordon. 1969. "God and the Mafia." *The Public Interest* 14 (Winter): 24–51.

Hawkins, J. D., and Lishner, D. M. 1987. "Schooling and Delinquency." In *Handbook of Crime and Delinquency Prevention*, edited by Elmer H. Johnson, pp. 179–221. Westport, Ct.: Greenwood.

Hayeslip, David W., Jr. 1989. "Local-level Drug Enforcement: New Strategies." *NIJ Reports* March/April: 2–7.

Haywood, Ian. 1987. *Faking It: Art and the Politics of Forgery.* New York: St. Martin's Press.

Hazelwood, Robert R., and Burgess, Ann W. 1987. "An Introduction to the Serial Rapist: Research by the FBI." *FBI Law Enforcement Bulletin* 58: 16–24.

Hazelwood, Robert R., and Warren, Janet. 1989. "The Serial Rapist: His Characteristics and Victim (Part I)." *FBI Law Enforcement Bulletin* 60: 10–17.

Healy, William. 1915. *The Individual Delinquent: A Textbook and Prognosis for All Concerned in Understanding Offenders.* Boston: Little, Brown.

Heath, James. 1963. *Eighteenth Century Penal Theory.* New York: Oxford University Press.

Heilbroner, Robert L., et al. 1973. *In the Name of Profit: Profiles in Corporate Irresponsibility.* New York: Warner Paperback Library.

Hellman, Peter. 1970. "One in Ten Shoppers Is a Shoplifter." *The New York Magazine*, March 15, p. 34.

"Hell's Angel's: Some Wheelers May Be Dealers." 1979. *Time*, July 2, p. 34.

Hepburn, John R. 1984. "Occasional Property Crime." In *Major Forms of Crime*, edited by Robert F. Meier, pp. 73–94. Beverly Hills: Sage.

Herling, John. 1962. *The Great Price Conspiracy: The Story of the Antitrust Violations in the Electrical Industry.* Washington, D.C.: Luce.

Herman, Edward S. 1982. *The Real Terror Network: Terrorism in Fact and Propaganda.* Boston: South End Press.

Herman, Judith Lewis. 1981. *Father-Daughter Incest.* Cambridge, Mass.: Harvard University Press.

Hermann, Donald H. J. 1983. *The Insanity Defense.* Springfield, Ill.: Charles C. Thomas.

Herrnstein, Richard J. 1983. "Some Criminogenic Traits of Offenders." In *Crime and Public Policy*, edited by James Q. Wilson, pp. 31–49. San Francisco: Institute for Contemporary Studies.

_____ 1985. "Biology and Crime." *Crime File.* National Institute of Justice.

Herskovits, Melville J. 1930. *The Anthropometry of the American Negro.* New York: Columbia University Press.

"Hertz Admits to Driving Over the Line." 1988. *Newsweek*, February 8, p. 48.

Heussenstamm, F. K. 1971. "Bumper Stickers and the Cops." *Trans-Action* 8: 32–33.

Hickey, Eric W. 1986. "The Etiology of Victimization in Serial Crime." Paper presented at the American Society of Criminology, Atlanta, November.

"Hidden Cameras Project, Seattle, Washington," 1978, Exemplary Projects: A Program of the National Institute of Law Enforcement and Criminal Justice. Washington, D.C.: Government Printing Office. August.

Higham, Charles. 1982. *Trading with the Enemy: An Exposé of the Nazi-American Money Plot, 1933–1949.*. New York: Delacorte Press.

"Highway Safety: Kentucky's Textbook Case in Drunk Driving." 1988. *U.S. News and World Report*, May 30, p. 7.

Hills, Stuart L. 1971. *Crime, Power and Morality*. Scranton, Pa.: Chandler.

_____, ed. 1987. *Corporate Violence: Injury and Death for Profit*. Totowa, N.J.: Rowman and Littlefield.

Hindelang, Michael. 1970. "The Commitment of Delinquents to Their Misdeeds: Do Delinquents Drift." *Social Problems* 17 (Spring): 509.

_____ 1971. "Extroversion, Neuroticism and Self-Reported Delinquent Involvement." *Journal of Research in Crime and Delinquency* 8 (January): 23–31.

_____ 1973. "Causes of Delinquency: A Partial Replication and Extension." *Social Problems* 21 (Spring): 471–487.

_____ 1974. "The Uniform Crime Reports Revisited." *Journal of Criminal Justice* 2 (Spring): 1–17.

_____ 1979. "Age, Sex, and the Versatility of Delinquent Involvements." *Social Problems* 18: 522–535.

Hindelang, Michael; Hirschi, Travis; and Weis, Joseph. 1979. "Correlates of Delinquency: The Illusion of Discrepancy between Self-Report and Official Data." *American Sociological Review* 44: 95–110.

Hindelang, Michael; Gottfredson, Michael; and Flanagan, T. 1981. *Sourcebook of Criminal Justice Statistics, 1980*. Washington, D.C.: Government Printing Office.

Hirschi, Travis. 1969. *Causes of Delinquency*. Berkeley: University of California Press.

_____ 1983. "Crime and the Family." In *Crime and Public Policy*, edited by James Q. Wilson, pp. 53–68. San Francisco: Institute for Contemporary Social Studies.

Hirschi, Travis, and Hindelang, Michael J. 1977. "Intelligence and Delinquency: A Revisionist Review." *American Sociological Review* 42 (August): 571–587.

Hochstedler, Ellen, ed. 1984. *Corporations as Criminals*. Beverly Hills: Sage.

Holden, Richard. 1986. "The Road to Fundamentalist and Identity Movements." Paper presented at the Academy of Criminal Justice Sciences meetings, St. Louis, March.

Holmes, Ronald M. 1983. *The Sex Offender and the Criminal Justice System*. Springfield, Ill.: Charles C. Thomas.

Holmes, Ronald M., and DeBurger, James. 1988. *Serial Murder*. Beverly Hills: Sage.

Holzman, Harold R., and Pines, Sharon. 1979. "Buying Sex: The Phenomenology of Being a 'John.'" Paper presented at the American Society of Criminology Meetings, Philadelphia, Pa. November.

"Home Repair Scam Draws Jail Term." 1986. *Erie Morning News*. May 1, p. 22–A.

"Hong Kong: Battling the Triads." 1986. *C. J. International* 2, September/October: 5.

Hood, Roger, and Sparks, Richard. 1971. *Key Issues in Criminology*. New York: McGraw-Hill.

Hooton, Earnest. 1939. *Crime and the Man*. Westport, Ct.: Greenwood.

"How We Can Win the War on Poverty." 1989. *Fortune*, April, p. 10.

Howery, Carla B. 1988. "New Concerns Surface Over Imprisoned South Korean Sociologist." *Footnotes* (American Sociological Association), December: 14.

Howlett, James B.; Hanfland, Kenneth A.; and Rassler, Robert K. 1986. "The Violent Criminal Apprehension Program: VICAP: A Progress Report." *FBI Law Enforcement Bulletin*, December: 14–18.

Hubbard, L. Ron. 1973. *Dianetics*. New York: Paperback Library.

Huff, Darrell. 1966. *How to Lie with Statistics*. New York: Wiley.

Humphreys, Laud. 1970. *Tearoom Trade: Impersonal Sex in Public Places*. Chicago: Aldine.

Hunt, Morton. 1974. *Sexual Behavior in the 1970s*. New York: Dell Books.

Hunter, Edward. 1951. *Brain-washing in Red China*. New York: Vanguard Press.

Hunter, J. Michael. 1983. "All Organized Crime Isn't Mafia: A Case Study of a Non-traditional Criminal Organization." Paper presented at the Academy of Criminal Justice Sciences meetings, San Antonio. March.

Hutchings, Barry, and Mednick, Sarnoff A. 1977. "Criminality in Adoptees and Their Adoptive and Biological Parents: A Pilot Study." In *Biosocial Bases in Criminal Behavior*, edited by Sarnoff A. Mednick and Karl Christiansen, pp. 127–142. New York: Gardner Press.

Hyde, H. Montgomery. 1980. *The Atomb Bomb Spies*. New York: Ballantine.

Ianni, Francis A. J. 1972. *A Family Business: Kinship and Social Control in Organized Crime*. New York: Russell Sage.

_____ 1973. *Ethnic Succession in Organized Crime*. Washington, D.C.: Government Printing Office.

_____ 1974. *Black Mafia: Ethnic Succession in Organized Crime*. New York: Simon and Schuster.

Impoco, Jim. 1987. "Porn Flourishes in Japan." *Erie Daily Times*, March 11, p. 10–B.

Inciardi, James A. 1970. "The Adult Firesetter: A Typology," *Criminology* 8 (August): 145–155.

_____ 1977. "In Search of the Class Cannon: A Field Study of Professional Pickpockets." In *Street Ethnography*, edited by Robert S. Weppner, pp. 55–78. Beverly Hills: Sage.

_____ 1978. *Reflections on Crime*. New York: Holt, Rinehart and Winston.

_____ 1979. "Heroin Use and Street Crime." *Crime and Delinquency* 25: 335–346.

_____ ed. 1980. *Radical Criminology: The Coming Crisis.* Beverly Hills: Sage.

_____ ed. 1981. *The Drugs-Crime Connection.* Beverly Hills: Sage.

_____ 1983. "On Grift at the Superbowl: Professional Pickpockets and the NFL." In *Career Criminals,* edited by Gordon Waldo, pp. 31–41. Beverly Hills: Sage.

_____ 1984. "Professional Theft." In *Major Forms of Crime,* edited by Robert F. Meier, pp. 221–243. Beverly Hills: Sage.

_____ 1986. *The War on Drugs: Heroin, Cocaine, Crime and Public Policy.* Belmont, Calif.: Wadsworth.

Ingraham, Barton L. 1979. *Political Crime in Europe: A Comparative Study of France, Germany and England.* Berkeley: University of California Press.

Isaacson, Walter, and Gorey, Hays. 1981. "Let the Buyers Beware: Consumer Advocates Retrench for Hard Times." *Time,* September 21, pp. 22–23.

"ITT to Plead Guilty in Defense Case." 1988. *Erie Times News,* October 23, p. 1–A.

Irving, Clifford. 1970. *Fake! The Story of Elmyr de Hory.* London: Heinemann.

Jacks, Irving, and Cox, Steven G. eds. 1984. *Psychological Approaches to Crime and Its Correction: Theory, Research, Practice.* Chicago: Nelson-Hall.

Jackson, Bruce. 1972. *In the Life: Versions of the Criminal Experience.* New York: New American Library.

Jacobs, James R. 1987. "Drinking and Crime." *Crime File.* National Institute of Justice.

_____ 1988. "The Law and Criminology of Drunk Driving." In *Crime and Justice: A Review of Research,* vol. 10, edited by Michael Tonry and Norval Morris, pp. 171–230. Chicago: University of Chicago Press.

Jacobs, Patricia A., et al. 1965. "Aggressive Behavior, Mental Subnormality, and the XYY Male." *Nature* 208 (December): 1351–1352.

Jacoby, Joseph E., ed. 1979. *Classics of Criminology.* Oak Park, Ill.: Moore Publishing.

Jacoby, Tamar. 1988. "A Web of Crime Behind Bars." *Newsweek,* October 24, pp. 76–81.

Jacoby, Tamar; Sandza, Richard; and Parry, Robert. 1988. "Going After Dissidents." *Newsweek,* February 8, p. 29.

Janeway, Elizabeth. 1981. "Incest: A Rational Look at the Oldest Taboo." *Ms.,* November, pp. 61–64, 78, 81, 109.

"Japan: Putting the Mafia to Shame." 1977. *Time,* October 17, pp. 40, 46.

Japan Yearbook. 1944. Tokyo: Foreign Affairs Association of Japan. Cited in *Japan's Imperial Conspiracy,* by David Bergamini, 1971. New York: William Morrow and Company.

Jaroff, Leon. 1988. "Fighting Against Flimflam." *Time,* June 13, p. 72.

Jaworski, Leon. 1977. *The Right and the Power.* New York: Pocket Books.

Jeffrey, C. Ray. 1978. "Criminology as an Interdisciplinary Behavioral Science." *Criminology* 16 (August): 153–156.

Jellinek, E. M. 1960. *The Disease Concept of Alcoholism.* New Brunswick, N.J.: College and University Press.

Jenkins, Philip. 1984. *Crime and Justice: Issues and Ideas.* Monterey, Calif.: Brooks/Cole.

_____ 1988. "Myth and Murder: The Serial Killer Panic of 1983-5." *Criminal Justice Research Bulletin* 3: 1–7.

_____ 1989. "Book Review: Update on Organized Crime Down Under." *Criminal Organizations* 1: 12.

Jensen, Gary, and Eve, Raymond. 1976. "Sex Differences in Delinquency: An Examination of Popular Sociological Explanations." *Criminology* 13: 427–448.

Jesilow, Paul D.; Pontell, Herbert N.; and Geis, Gilbert. 1985. "Medical Criminals: Physicians and White-Collar Offenses." *Justice Quarterly* 2: 151–165.

Johnson, Bruce D., et al. 1983. "Economic Behavior of Street Opiate Users." New York, N.Y.: Narcotic and Drug Research, Inc.

_____ 1985. *Taking Care of Business.* Lexington, Mass.: Lexington Books.

Johnson, Elmer H. 1978. *Crime, Correction and Society.* 4th ed. Homewood, Ill.: Dorsey.

Johnson, Richard E. 1979. *Juvenile Delinquency and Its Origins.* Cambridge, Mass.: Cambridge University Press.

_____ 1986. "Family Structure and Delinquency: General Patterns and Gender Differences." *Criminology* 24: 65–84.

Johnson, Terry. 1987. "A Little House of Horrors: Murder in Philadelphia." *Newsweek,* April 6, p. 29.

Johnston, Lloyd; O'Malley, Patrick M.; and Bachman, Jerald G. 1987. *National Trends in Drug Use and Related Factors Among American High School Students and Young Adults, 1975–1986.* Washington, D.C.: Government Printing Office.

"Judge Agrees to TMI Plea Bargain." 1984. *Erie Morning News,* March 1, p. 3–A.

Judge, Arthur V. 1930. *The Elizabethan Underworld.* London: George Routledge.

Kalish, Carol B. 1988. *International Crime Rates.* Bureau of Justice Statistics Special Report. Washington, D.C.: Government Printing Office, May.

Kaplan, David E., and Dubro, Alec. 1986. *Yakuza: The Explosive Account of Japan's Criminal Underworld.* Reading, Mass.: Addison-Wesley.

Karchmer, Clifford. 1977. "The Underworld Turns Fire into Profit." *Firehouse Magazine.* Read into the *Congressional Record,* U.S. Senate, October 4, 1977, p. S 16263

Karmen, Andrew, 1974. "Agents Provocateurs in the Contemporary U.S. Leftist Movement." In *The Criminologist: Crime and the Criminal,* edited by Charles Reasons, pp. 209–225. Pacific Palisades, Ca.: Goodyear Publishing Company.

Katkin, Daniel. 1982. *The Nature of Criminal Law.* Monterey, Ca.: Brooks/Cole.

Katz, Jack. 1988. *Seductions of Crime: Moral and Sensual Attractions in Doing Evil.* New York: Basic Books.

Kelling, George L. 1988a. "Police and Communities: The Quiet Revolution." *Perspectives on Policing* (National Institute of Justice), June.

———. 1988b. "What Works—Research and the Police." *Crime File*. National Institute of Justice.

Kelly, Delos H. 1975. "Status Origins, Track Position and Delinquent Involvement." *The Sociological Quarterly* 16 (Spring): 264–271.

Kelly, Robert J., ed. 1986. *Organized Crime: A Global Perspective*. Totowa, N.J.: Rowman and Littlefield.

———. 1988. "Review Essay/Dirty Dollars: Organized Crime and Its Illicit Partnership in the Waste Industry." *Criminal Justice Ethics* 7: 47–68.

Kelman, Herbert C., and Hamilton, V. Lee. 1988. *Crimes of Obedience: Toward a Social Psychology of Authority and Responsibility*. New Haven: Yale University Press.

Kempe, Ruth S., and Kempe, C. Henry. 1978. *Child Abuse*. Cambridge, Mass.: Harvard University Press.

Kenadjian, Berdj. 1980. "Estimating the Amount of Unreported Income." Paper presented at the National Workshop on Research Methodology and Criminal Justice Program Evaluation, Baltimore, March.

Kennedy, John F. 1957. *Profiles in Courage*. New York: Pocket Books.

Kennedy, Robert F. 1960. *The Enemy Within*. New York: Popular Library.

Kerner, Otto. 1968. *The Report of the National Advisory Commission on Civil Disorders: The Riot Commission Report*. New York: Bantam Books.

Kerr, Peter. 1987. "Chasing the Heroin from Plush Hotel to Mean Streets." *New York Times*, August 11, p. 1–B.

Kessler, Ronald. 1989. *Moscow Station: How the KGB Penetrated the American Embassy*. New York: Charles Scribner's Sons.

Kidder, Robert L. 1983. *Connecting Law and Society*. Englewood Cliffs, N.J.: Prentice-Hall.

King, Harry, and Chambliss, William J. 1984. *Harry King: A Professional Thief's Journal*. New York: Wiley.

King, Martin Luther, Jr. 1963. "Letter from Birmingham Jail." In *Why We Can't Wait*. New York: Harper and Row.

Kingsworth, Rodney, and Jungsten, Michael. 1988. "Driving Under the Influence: The Impact of Legislative Reform on Court Sentencing Practices." *Crime and Delinquency* 34: 3–28.

Kinsey, Alfred, et al. 1948. *Sexual Behavior in the Human Male*. Philadelphia: W. B. Saunders.

———. 1952. *Sexual Behavior in the Human Female*. Philadelphia: W. B. Saunders.

Kirkham, James F. 1969. *Assassination and Political Violence*. Washington, D.C.: Government Printing Office.

Kirkpatrick, Clifford, and Kanin, Eugene J. 1957. "Male Sex Aggression on a University Campus." *American Sociological Review* 22 (February): 52–58.

Kitsuse, J. I., and Cicourel, A. V. 1963. "A Note on the Use of Official Statistics." *Social Problems* 11 (Fall): 131–138.

Kitsuse, John L., and Dietrick, David C. 1970. "Delinquent Boys: A Critique." In *Society, Delinquency, and Delinquent Behavior*, edited by Harwin L. Voss, pp. 238–245. Boston: Little, Brown.

Kittrie, Nicholas N., and Wedlock, Eldon D., Jr., eds. 1986. *The Tree of Liberty: A Documentary History of Rebellion and Political Crime in America*. Baltimore: Johns Hopkins University Press.

Klanwatch. 1985. "Domestic Terrorists: The KKK in the 'Fifth Era.'" *Klanwatch Intelligence Report* (The Southern Poverty Law Center, Montgomery, Alabama), February, pp. 5–10.

Kleiman, Mark A. R., et al. 1988. *Street-Level Drug Enforcement: Examining the Issues*. National Institute of Justice, August.

Klein, John F. 1974. "Professional Theft: The Utility of a Concept." *Canadian Journal of Criminology and Corrections* 16 (April): 133–143.

Klein, John F., and Montague, A. F. 1977. *Check Forgers*. Lexington, Mass.: Lexington Books.

Klein, Stephen P.; Turner, Susan; and Petersilia, Joan. 1988. *Does Race Make a Difference in Sentencing?* Santa Monica: Rand Corporation.

Klockars, Carl. 1974. *The Professional Fence*. New York: The Free Press.

———. 1979. "The Contemporary Crisis of Marxist Criminology." *Criminology* 16 (Fall): 477–515.

Knapp Commission Report on Police Corruption. 1972. New York: Braziller.

Kneece, Jack. 1986. *Family Treason: The Walker Spy Ring Case*. New York: Stein and Day.

Kobrin, Solomon. 1982. "The Use of Life History Documents for the Development of Delinquency Theory." In *The Jack-Roller at Seventy: A Fifty-Year Follow-Up*, edited by Jon D. Snodgrass, pp. 153–165. Lexington, Mass.: D. C. Heath.

Koenig, Daniel J., et al. 1983. "Routine Activities, Impending Social Change, and Policing." *Canadian Police College Journal* 7 (2): 96–136.

Kornhauser, Ruth. 1978. *Social Sources of Delinquency and Its Origins*. Chicago: University of Chicago Press.

Koski, Patricia R. 1988. "Family Violence and Nonfamily Deviance: Taking Stock of the Literature." In *Deviance and the Family*, edited by Frank E. Hagan and Marvin B. Sussman, pp. 23–46. New York: Haworth Press.

Krahn, Harvey; Hartnagel, Timothy; and Gartrell, John. 1986. "Income Inequality, and Homicide Rates: Cross-National Data and Criminological Theories." *Criminology* 24: 269–295.

Kratcoski, Peter C. 1988. "Families Who Kill." In *Deviance and the Family*, edited by Frank E. Hagan and Marvin B. Sussman, pp. 47–70. New York: Haworth.

Kretschmer, Ernst. 1926. *Physique and Character*. Translated by W. J. H. Sprott. New York: Harcourt, Brace.

Krisberg, Barry. 1975. *Crime and Privilege: Toward A New Criminology*. Englewood Cliffs, N.J.: Prentice-Hall.

Kuhl, Anna F. 1985. "Battered Women Who Murder: Victims or Offenders? In *The Changing Roles of Women in the Criminal Justice System*, edited by Imogene L.

Moyer, pp. 197–216. Prospect Heights, Ill.: Waveland Press.

Kuhn, Thomas S. 1962. *The Structure of Scientific Revolutions*. Chicago: University of Chicago Press.

Kuper, Leo. 1981. *Genocide: Its Political Use in the Twentieth Century*. New Haven: Yale University Press.

Kurtz, Howard. 1989. "Across the Nation, Rising Outrage." *Washington Post*, April 4, pp. 1–A, 14–A, 16A.

Kwitny, Jonathan. 1979. *Vicious Circles: The Mafia in the Marketplace*. New York: W. W. Norton.

Lab, Steven P., and Hirschel, J. David. 1988a. "Climatological Conditions and Crime: The Forecast Is . . . ?" *Justice Quarterly* 5: 281–299.

———. 1988b. " 'Clouding' the Issues: The Failure to Recognize Methodological Problems." *Justice Quarterly* 5: 311–317.

Ladinsky, Jack. 1963. "Careers of Lawyers, Law Practice and Legal Institutions." *American Sociological Review* 28 (February): 47–54.

Laner, Mary R. 1974. "Prostitution as an Illegal Vocation: A Sociological Overview." In *Deviant Behavior: Occupational and Organizational Bases*, edited by Clifton Bryant, pp. 406–418. Chicago: Rand McNally.

Langan, Patrick A., and Greenfeld, Lawrence A. 1983. "Career Patterns in Crime." *Bureau of Justice Statistics, Special Report*. Washington, D.C.: Bureau of Justice Statistics, June.

Langan, Patrick A., and Innes, Christopher A. 1985. "The Risk of Violent Crime." *Bureau of Justice Statistics Special Report*. Washington, D.C.: Bureau of Justice Statistics, June.

Lange, Johannes, 1931. *Crime as Destiny: A Study of Criminal Twins*. Translated by Charlotte Haldane. London: George Allen and Unwin.

Langway, Lynn, and Smith, Sunde. 1975. "Warning! Someone May Try to Steal Your Money." *Newsweek*, October 6, p. 67.

Lappé, Frances M., and Collins, Joseph. 1977. *Food First: Beyond the Myth of Scarcity*. New York: Ballantine Books.

Laqueur, Walter. 1977. *Terrorism*. Boston: Little, Brown.

———. 1987. *The Age of Terrorism*. Boston: Little, Brown.

Laub, John H. 1983. *Criminology in the Making: An Oral History*. Boston: Northeastern University Press.

Laub, John H., and Sampson, Robert J. 1988. "Unraveling Families and Delinquency: A Reanalysis of the Gluecks' Data." *Criminology* 26: 355–380.

Launer, Harold M., and Palenski, Joseph E., eds. 1988. *Crime and the New Immigrants*. Springfield, Ill.: Charles C. Thomas.

Lauter, David. 1988. "Children Must Testify Face-to-Face in Abuse Cases." *Erie Morning News*, June 30, p. 6–A.

"Lavelle Indicted on Five Felony Counts." 1983. *Erie Times-News*, August 5, p. 1.

Lawrence, Jill. 1988. "Feds Used Human Subjects in Radiation Exposure Experiments." *Erie Times News*, October 25, pp. 1–A, 12–A.

LeBeau, James L. 1988. "Comment—Weather and Crime: Trying to Make Social Sense of a Physical Process." *Justice Quarterly* 5: 301–309.

LeBeau, James L., and Langworthy, Robert H. 1986. "The Linkages Between Routine Activities, Weather, and Calls for Police Service." *Journal of Police Science and Administration* 14: 137–145.

Ledeen, Michael A. 1988. *Perilous Statecraft: An Insider's Account of the Iran-Contra Affair*. New York: Charles Scribner's Sons.

Leftkowitz, N. M. et al. 1977. *Growing Up to Be Violent: A Longitudinal Study of the Development of Aggression*. New York: Pergamon.

Lejins, Peter P. 1966. "Uniform Crime Reports." *Michigan Law Review* 64: 1011–1030.

Lekachman, Robert. 1982. *Greed Is Not Enough: Reaganomics*. New York: Pantheon Books.

Lemert, Edwin M. 1951. *Social Pathology*. New York: McGraw-Hill.

———. 1953. "An Isolation and Closure Theory of Naive Check Forgery." *Journal of Criminal Law, Criminology and Police Science* 44 (September): 296–307.

———. 1958. "The Behavior of the Systematic Check Forger." *Social Problems* 6 (Fall): 141–149.

———. 1967. *Human Deviance, Social Problems and Social Control*. New York: Prentice-Hall.

Lemkin, Raphael. 1944. *Axis Rule in Occupied Europe*. Washington: Carnegie Endowment for International Peace.

Leonard, William N., and Weber, Marvin G. 1970. "Automakers and Dealers: A Study of Criminogenic Market Forces." *Law and Society Review* 4 (February): 407–424.

Lesieur, Henry R., and Esposito, Carol. 1982. "Court and Regulatory Agency Processing of Trade and Professional Association Law Violators." Paper presented at the Academy of Criminal Justice Sciences Meetings, Louisville, Ky. March.

Letkemann, Peter. 1973. *Crime as Work*. Englewood Cliffs, N.J.: Prentice-Hall.

Levathes, Louise E. 1985. "The Land Where the Murray Flows." *National Geographic*, August, pp. 252–278.

Levi, Werner. 1980. "Law and Politics in the International Society." In *The Sociology of Law: A Social Structural Perspective*, edited by William M. Evan. New York: The Free Press.

Levine, James P. 1976. "The Potential for Overreporting in Criminal Victimization Surveys." *Criminology* 14 (November): 307–330.

Leyton, Elliott. 1986. *Compulsive Killers: The Story of Modern Multiple Murders*. New York: Washington News Book.

Liazos, Alexander. 1972. "The Poverty of the Sociology of Deviance: Nuts, Sluts and 'Preverts.' " *Social Problems* 20 (Summer): 103–120. Reprinted in *Readings in Social Problems 79/80*, pp. 22–31. Guilford, Ct.: Dushkin.

Lieber, Arnold L., and Sherin, Carolyn R. 1972. "Homicides and the Lunar Influence in Human Emotional Disturbance." *American Journal of Psychiatry* 129 (July): 69–74.

Lieberstein, Stanley. 1979. *Who Owns What Is in Your Head? Trade Secrets and the Mobile Employee.* New York: Hawthorne.

Liebert, R. M., and Baron, R. A. 1972. "Some Immediate Effects of Televised Violence on Children's Behavior." *Developmental Psychology* 6: 469–475.

Liebow, Elliott. 1967. *Tally's Corner: A Study of Negro Streetcorner Men.* Boston: Little, Brown.

Light, Ivan, and Bonacich, Robert. 1988. *Immigrant Entrepreneurs: Koreans in Los Angeles, 1965–1982.* Berkeley: University of California Press.

Lindesmith, Alfred R. 1965. *The Addict and the Law.* Bloomington, Ind.: Indiana University Press.

Lindesmith, Alfred R., and Levin, Yale. 1937. "The Lombrosian Myth in Criminology." *American Journal of Sociology* 42 (March): 653–671.

Lindsey, Robert. 1979. *The Falcon and the Snowman.* New York: Simon and Schuster.

———. 1983. *The Flight of the Falcon.* New York: Simon and Schuster.

Lippman, Matthew. 1987. "Iran: A Question of Justice?" *C. J. International* 3: 5–6.

Loeber, Rolf, and Loeber, Magda Stouthamer. 1986. "Models and Meta-Analysis of the Relationship Between Family Variables and Juvenile Conduct Problems and Delinquency." In *Crime and Justice: An Annual Review of Research,* vol. 7, edited by Norval Morris and Michael Tonry, pp. 29–149. Chicago: University of Chicago Press.

Lombroso, Cesare. 1911. "Introduction." In *Criminal Man according to the Classification of Cesare Lombroso,* edited by Gina Lombroso-Ferrero. New York: Putnam.

Lombroso-Ferrero, Gina, ed. 1972. *Criminal Man according to the Classification of Cesare Lombroso.* Montclair, N.J.: Patterson Smith [reissue of 1911 work].

Londer, Randi. 1987. "Can Bad Air Make Bad Things Happen?" *Parade,* August 3, pp. 6–7.

Lorenz, Konrad. 1966. *On Aggression.* New York: Harcourt, Brace, Jovanovich.

Lowenthal, Max. 1950. *The Federal Bureau of Investigation.* New York: William Sloane Associates.

Lowman, J., et al., eds. 1986. *Regulating Sex: An Anthology of Commentaries on the Badgley and Fraser Reports.* Burnaby, B.C.: Simon Fraser University.

Lupsha, Peter A. 1981. "Individual Choice, Material Culture and Organized Crime." *Criminology* 19 (May): 3–24.

———. 1982. "Networks vs. Networking: An Analysis of Organized Criminal Groups." Paper presented at the American Society of Criminology Meetings, Toronto. November.

———. 1987. "Predicting Organized Crime: Some Variables." *Update* (International Organization for the Study of Organized Crime) 3: 7–8.

———. 1988. "Narcoterrorism." *Update* 3: 1–2.

Lyman, Stanford M. 1974. *Chinese Americans.* New York: Random House.

Lynn, Barry W. 1986. *Polluting the Censorship Debate: A Summary and Critique of the Final Report of the Attorney General's Commission on Pornography.* Washington, D.C: ACLU.

Lyons, Richard. 1980. "Reports on U.S. Oil Companies." *Erie Morning News,* June 23, p. 4.

Maas, Peter. 1968. *The Valachi Papers.* New York: Bantam Books.

———. 1973. *Serpico.* New York: Viking Press.

———. 1975. *King of the Gypsies.* New York: Bantam.

———. 1986a. "The Mafia Today." *Parade,* February 16, pp. 6–8.

———. 1986b. *Manhunt: The Incredible Pursuit of a CIA Agent Turned Terrorist.* New York: Random House.

MacDonald, Andrew. 1980. *The Turner Diaries.* Arlington, Va.: National Vanguard Books.

MacDonald, John M. 1971. *Rapists and Their Victims.* Springfield, Ill.: Charles C. Thomas.

Mack, John A. 1972. "The Able Criminal." *British Journal of Criminology.* 12 (January): 44–54.

———. 1974. *The Crime Industry.* Westmead, Eng.: Saxon House.

Mackay, H., and Hagan, John. 1978. "Studying the Victims of Crime: Some Methodological Notes." *Victimology* 3: 135–140.

MacLean, Don. 1974. *Pictorial History of the Mafia.* New York: Pyramid Books.

Maclean, Fitzroy. 1978. *Take Nine Spies.* New York: Atheneum.

MacNamara, Donal, and Sagarin, Edward. 1977. *Sex Crime and the Law.* New York: The Free Press.

Malamuth, Neil M., and Donnerstein, Ed. 1982. "The Effects of Aggressive-Pornographic Mass Media Stimuli." *Advances in Experimental Psychology* 15: 103–136.

Maltz, Michael D. 1976. "On Defining 'Organized Crime.'" *Crime and Delinquency* 22 (July): 338–346.

"The Man behind Abscam." 1980. *Erie Morning News,* February 12, p. 1–A.

Mankoff, Milton. 1980. "A Tower of Babel: Marxist Criminologists and Their Critics." In *Radical Criminology: The Coming Crisis,* edited by James A. Inciardi, pp. 139–148. Beverly Hills: Sage.

Mann, Coramae Richey. 1984. *Female Crime and Delinquency.* University, Ala.: University of Alabama Press.

Mann, Kenneth J., et al. 1980. "Sentencing the White-Collar Offender." *American Criminal Law Review.* 17: 479–500.

Mannheim, Herman, 1965. *Comparative Criminology.* Boston: Houghton Mifflin.

———, ed. 1969. *Pioneers in Criminology.* Chicago: Quadrangle Books.

Manning, Peter K. 1975. "Deviance and Dogma." *British Journal of Sociology* 15 (January): 1–20.

Mansnerus, Laura. 1989. "As Racketeering Law Expands, So Does Pressure to Rein It In." *New York Times,* March 12, p. 4–E.

Maranto, Gina. 1985. "Coke: The Random Killer." *Discover,* March.

Marbach, William D.; Conant, Jennet; and Rogers, Michael. 1983. "New Wave Computer Crime." *Newsweek*, August 29, p. 45.

Marchetti, Victor, and Marks, John D. 1974. *The CIA and the Cult of Intelligence*. New York: Dell.

Mark, Vernon, and Ervin, Frank. 1970. *Violence and the Brain*. New York: Harper and Row.

Markhoff, John. 1988. " 'Virus' in Military Computers Disrupts Systems Nationwide." *New York Times*, September 4, p. 1.

Marks, John. 1979. *The Search for the Manchurian Candidate: The CIA and Mind Control*. New York: Times Books.

Marsh, Frank H., and Katz, Janet, eds. 1985. *Biology, Crime and Ethics: A Study of Biological Explanations for Criminal Behavior*. Cincinnati: Anderson.

Martens, Frederick T. 1988. "Emerging Trends in Organized Crime." *Criminal Organizations* 1: 11–12.

Martin, David W., and Walcott, John. 1988. *Best Laid Plans: The Inside Story of America's War Against Terrorism*. New York: Harper and Row.

Martin, John M.; Haran, James F.; and Romano, Anne T. 1988. "Espionage: A Challenge to Criminology and Criminal Justice." Paper presented at the Academy of Criminal Justice Sciences meetings, San Francisco, California, April.

Martin, W. Allen. 1981. "Toward Specifying a Spectrum-Based Theory of Enterprise." Paper presented at the Academy of Criminal Justice Sciences Meetings, Philadelphia, March.

Martinson, Robert. 1974. "What Works?—Questions and Answers about Prison Reform." *The Public Interest* 35 (Spring): 22–54.

_____ 1979. "New Findings, New Views: A Note of Caution Regarding Sentencing Reform." *Hofstra Law Review* 7: 242–258.

"Martinson Attacks His Own Earlier Work." 1978. *Criminal Justice Newsletters* 9 (December): 4.

Maser, Werner. 1979. *Nuremberg: A Nation on Trial*. Translated by Richard Barry. New York: Scribners.

Matheron, Michele S. 1987. "Chinese Triads: The Oriental Mafia?" Paper presented at the Academy of Criminal Justice Sciences meetings, St. Louis, March.

Matsueda, Rose L. 1988. "The Current State of Differential Association Theory." *Crime and Delinquency* 34: 277–306.

Matza, David. 1964. *Delinquency and Drift*. New York: Wiley.

Maurer, David W. 1940. *The Big Con*. Indianapolis: Bobbs-Merrill.

_____ 1964. *Whiz Mob*. New Haven: College and University Press.

Maxa, Rudy. 1977. *Dare to Be Great*. New York: William Morrow.

Mayhew, Henry. 1862a. *London Labour and the London Poor*. 2 vols. London: Griffin.

_____ 1862b. *London's Underworld*. London: Spring Books.

McAlary, Mike. 1987. *Buddy Boys: When Good Cops Turn Bad*. New York: G. P. Putnam.

McBee, Susanna, and Peterson, Sarah. 1983. "How Drugs Sap the Nation's Strength." *U.S. News and World Report*, May 16, pp. 55–58.

McCaghy, Charles. 1976a. "Child Molesters: A Study of Their Careers as Deviants." In *Criminal Behavior Systems*, edited by Marshall B. Clinard and Richard Quinney, pp. 75–88. New York: Holt, Rinehart and Winston.

_____ 1976b. *Deviant Behavior*. New York: Macmillan.

_____ 1980. *Crime in American Society*. New York: Macmillan.

McCaghy, Charles; Giordano, Peggy; and Henson, Trudy Knicely. 1977. "Auto Theft." *Criminology* 15 (3): 367–381.

McCandless, Boyd R.; Persons, W. Scott; and Roberts, Albert. 1972. "Perceived Opportunity, Delinquency, Race and Body Build among Delinquent Youth." *Journal of Consulting and Clinical Psychology* 38 (April): 281–287.

McCarthy, E. D., et al. 1975. "The Effects of Television on Children and Adolescents: Violence and Behavior Disorders." *Journal of Communication* 25: 71–85.

McCarthy, Sarah J. 1982. "Pornography, Rape, and the Cult of Macho." In *Crisis in American Institutions*, edited by Jerome H. Skolnick and Elliott Currie, pp. 218–232. Boston: Little, Brown and Company.

McClintock, F. H., and Gibson, E. 1961. *Robbery in London*. London: Macmillan.

McConahay, John B. 1988. "Pornography: The Symbolic Politics of Fantasy." *Law and Contemporary Problems* 51: 31–69.

McCord, William, and McCord, Joan. 1958. "The Effects of Parental Role Model on Criminality." *Journal of Social Issues* 14: 66–75.

McCormick, Albert E., Jr. 1977. "Rule Enforcement and Moral Indignation: Some Observations on the Effects of Criminal Antitrust Convictions upon Societal Reaction Process." *Social Problems* 25 (January): 30–39.

McCoy, Alfred W. 1972. *The Politics of Heroin in Southeast Asia*. New York: Harper and Row.

_____ 1976. *Report from the Golden Triangle*. Unpublished paper. Cited in *Organizing Crime*, by Alan A. Block and William J. Chambliss, 1981, p. 36. New York: Elsevier.

_____ 1985. *Drug Traffic, Narcotics, and Organized Crime in Australia*. New South Wales: Harper and Row Australasia.

McDermott, M. Joan. 1979. *Rape Victimization in 26 American Cities*. Washington, D.C.: Government Printing Office.

McGrory, Mary. 1988. "Owning Up to Atomic Injustice." *Washington Post*, March 27, p. 1.

McIntosh, Mary. 1975. *The Organization of Crime*. London: Macmillan.

McKillop, Peter. 1989. "The Last Godfather?: Going After Gotti." *Newsweek*, February 6: 25.

McKinney, John C. 1966. *Constructive Typology and Social Theory*. New York: Appleton-Century-Crofts.

McMullan, John L. 1984. *The Canting Crew: London's Criminal Underworld, 1550–1700.* New Brunswick, N.J.: Rutgers University Press.

"Meatpackers Hit With Record OSHA Fine." 1988. *Erie Morning News,* October 29, p. 2–A.

Medea, Andra, and Thompson, Kathleen. 1974. *Against Rape.* New York: Farrar, Straus and Giroux.

Mednick, Sarnoff, and Volavka, Jan. 1980. "Biology and Crime." In *Crime and Justice: An Annual Review of Research,* edited by Norval Morris and Michael Tonry, vol. 1, pp. 85–159. Chicago: University of Chicago Press.

Menard, Scott. 1987. "Short-Term Trends in Crime and Delinquency: A Comparison of UCR, NCS and Self-Report Data." *Justice Quarterly* 4: 455–474.

Mendelson, Benjamin. 1963. "The Origin and Doctrine of Victimology." *Excerpta Criminologica* 3 (June): 239–44.

Mendelson, Mary A. 1975. *Tender Loving Greed.* New York: Vintage.

Merry, Robert W. 1975. "The Law Is on Trial." *The National Observer,* November 1, pp. 1–3.

Merton, Robert K. 1938. "Social Structure and Anomie." *American Sociological Review* 3 (October): 672–682.

——— 1957, 1968. *Social Theory and Social Structure.* Revised edition. New York: The Free Press.

——— 1961. "Social Problems and Sociological Theory." In *Contemporary Social Problems,* edited by Robert K. Merton and Robert M. Nisbet, pp. 702–723. New York: Harcourt, Brace and World.

Messick, Hank. 1973. *Lansky.* New York: Berkley Publishing Company.

——— 1979. *Of Grass and Snow: The Secret Criminal Elite.* Englewood Cliffs, N.J.: Prentice-Hall.

Messick, Hank, and Goldblatt, Burt. 1972. *The Mobs and the Mafia.* New York: Ballantine.

Messinger, Phyllis. 1988. "Documents Say FBI Probed More Than 100 Groups." *Erie Morning News,* February 3, p. 5–A.

Messner, S. F. 1980. "Income Inequality and Murder Rates: Some Cross-National Findings." *Comparative Social Research* 3 (January): 185–198.

Messner, Steven F., and Tardiff, Kenneth. 1985. "The Social Ecology of Urban Homicide: An Application of the 'Routine Activities' Approach." *Criminology* 23: 241–267.

"Miami Police Scandal Called Worst in U.S. Since Prohibition." 1987. *Erie Times News,* November 8, p. 1–C.

Milgram, Stanley. 1974. *Obedience to Authority: An Experimental View.* New York: Harper.

Miller, Eleanor. 1986. *Street Woman.* Philadelphia: Temple University Press.

Miller, Walter. 1958. "Lower Class Culture as a Generating Milieu of Gang Delinquency." *Journal of Social Issues* 14 (May): 5–19.

——— 1973. "Ideology and Criminal Justice Policy: Some Current Issues." *Journal of Criminal Law and Criminology* 64 (May): 141–173.

——— 1975. *Violence by Youth Gangs and Youth Groups as a Crime Problem in Major American Cities.* Washington, D.C.: Government Printing Office.

——— 1980. "Gangs, Groups and Serious Youth Crime." In *Critical Issues in Juvenile Delinquency,* edited by David Schichor and Delos Kelly. Lexington, Mass.: Lexington Books.

Mills, C. Wright. 1952. "A Diagnosis of Moral Uneasiness." In *Power, Politics and People,* edited by Irving L. Horowitz, pp. 330–339. New York: Ballantine.

——— 1956. *The Power Elite.* New York: Oxford University Press.

Mills, James. 1986. *The Underground Empire: Where Crime and Governments Embrace.* New York: Doubleday.

Milner, Christina, and Milner, Richard. 1972. *Black Players: The Secret World of Black Pimps.* Boston: Little, Brown.

Minor, W. William. 1981. "Techniques of Neutralization: A Reconceptualization and Empirical Examination." *Journal of Research in Crime and Delinquency* 18: 295–318.

——— 1984. "Neutralization as a Hardening Process." *Social Forces* 62: 995–1019.

Mintz, Morton. 1987. "At Any Cost: Corporate Greed, Women, and the Dalkon Shield." In *Corporate Violence,* edited by Stuart L. Hills, pp. 30–40. Totowa, N.J.: Rowman and Littlefield.

Misner, Gordon E. 1987. "Proces Barbie: Lyons, and the Nazi Trial." *C. J. International* 3: 3–4, 28–32.

Mitchell, G. 1981. "The Trouble with RICO." *Police Magazine,* May, pp. 39–44.

Mitford, Jessica. 1963. *The American Way of Death.* New York: Paperback Library.

Mohr, J. W.; Turner, R. E.; and Jerry, M. B. 1964. *Pedophilia and Exhibitionism.* Toronto: University of Toronto Press.

Monahan, John, and Splane, Stephanie. 1980. "Psychological Approaches to Criminal Behavior." In *Criminology Review Yearbook,* edited by Egon Bittner and Sheldon L. Messenger, vol. 2, pp. 17–47. San Francisco: Sage.

Monmaney, Terence, and Robins, Kate. 1988. "The Insanity of Steroid Abuse." *Newsweek,* May 23, p. 75.

Monroe, Russel R. 1978. *Brain Dysfunction in Aggressive Criminals.* Lexington, Mass.: D. C. Heath.

Moore, Mark. 1988. "Drug Trafficking." *Crime File* (National Institute of Justice).

Moore, Mark, and Trojanowicz, Robert C. 1988. "Policing and Fear of Crime." *Perspectives on Policing* 3, June.

Moore, Mark, Trojanowicz, Robert C., and Kelling, George L. 1988. "Crime and Policing." *Perspectives on Policing* 3, June.

Moore, Thomas, et al. 1989. "Dead Zones." *U.S. News and World Report,* April 10, pp. 20–33.

Moran, Richard, ed. 1985. *The Insanity Defense.* Beverly Hills, Calif.: Sage.

Morash, Merry. 1984. "Organized Crime." In *Major Forms of Crime,* edited by Robert F. Meier, pp. 191–220. Beverly Hills: Sage.

"More Arrest Seen for Lewd Conduct." 1980. *Erie Times-News,* February 17, p. 4–A.

Morgan, W. P. 1960. *Triad Societies in Hong Kong.* Hong Kong: Government Press.

Morganthau, Tom. 1988. "The Drug Gangs." *Newsweek,* March 28, pp. 20–29.

Morganthau, Tom, et al. 1988. "Nuclear Danger and Deceit." *Newsweek,* October 31, pp. 26–29.

Morrell, David. 1984. *The Brotherhood of the Rose.* New York: St. Martin's/Marek.

Morris, Norval. 1987. "Insanity Defense." *Crime File.* National Institute of Justice.

Morris, Norval, and Hawkins, Gordon. 1970. *The Honest Politician's Guide to Crime Control.* Chicago: University of Chicago Press.

Moyer, Imogene L., ed. 1985. *The Changing Roles of Women in the Criminal Justice System.* Prospect Heights, Ill.: Waveland Press.

Moyer, Kenneth E. 1976. *The Psychology of Aggression.* New York: Harper and Row.

Moynihan, Daniel P. 1986. *Family and Nation.* New York: Harcourt, Brace, Jovanovich.

Murray, Charles A. 1976. *The Link between Learning Disability and Juvenile Delinquency.* Washington, D.C.: National Institute of Juvenile Justice and Delinquency Prevention.

Mustain, Gene, and Capeci, Jerry. 1988. *Mob Star: The Story of John Gotti.* New York: Dell.

Myers, Gustavus. 1936. *The History of Great American Fortunes.* New York: Modern American Library.

Myers, Martha A., and Talarico, Susette. 1987. *The Social Contexts of Criminal Sentencing.* New York: Springer-Verlag.

Nader, Ralph. 1965. *Unsafe at Any Speed.* New York: Grossman.

―――― 1970. Foreword to *The Vanishing Air,* by John C. Esposito. New York: Grossman.

―――― 1973. *The Consumer and Corporate Accountability.* New York: Harcourt, Brace, Jovanovich.

Nader, Ralph, and Green, Mark J., eds. 1973. *Corporate Power in America.* New York: Grossman.

Nader, Ralph; Green, Mark J.; and Seligman, Joel. 1976. *Taming the Giant Corporation.* New York: Norton.

Nader, Ralph; Petkas, Peter J.; and Blackwell, Kate. eds. 1972. *Whistle Blowing: The Report of the Conference on Professional Responsibility.* New York: Viking Penguin.

Nagel, Ilene H., and Hagan, John. 1983. "Gender and Crime: Offense Patterns and Criminal Court Sanctions." In *Crime and Justice: An Annual Review of Research,* vol. 4, edited by Michael Tonry and Norval Morris, pp. 91–144. Chicago: University of Chicago Press.

Nash, Jay Robert. 1975 *Bloodletters and Badmen.* 3 vols. New York: Warner.

―――― 1976. *Hustlers and Con Men.* New York: M. Evans and Co.

―――― 1981. *Almanac of World Crime.* Garden City, N.Y.: Doubleday.

National Advisory Committee on Criminal Justice Standards and Goals. 1976a. *Organized Crime: Report of the Task Force on Organized Crime.* Washington, D.C.: Law Enforcement Assistance Administration.

―――― 1976b. *Criminal Justice Research and Development.* Report of the Task Force on Criminal Justice Research and Development. Washington, D.C.: National Institute of Law Enforcement and Criminal Justice.

―――― 1976c. *Report of the Task Force on Disorders and Terrorism.* Washington, D.C.: Government Printing Office.

National Association of Elementary School Principals. 1980. *The Most Significant Minority: One-Parent Children in the Schools.* New York: Charles F. Kettering Foundation.

National Commission on the Causes and Prevention of Violence. 1969. *To Establish Justice, to Insure Domestic Tranquility.* New York: Award Books.

National Commission on Obscenity and Pornography, 1970. *Commission on Obscenity and Pornography Report.* New York: Bantam Books.

National Crime Survey, 1977. "Basic Screen Questions." Form NCJ-1. Washington, D.C.: U.S. Bureau of Census, April 19.

National Crime Survey. 1981. *Criminal Victimization in the United States, 1979.* Washington, D.C.: Government Printing Office.

National Criminal Justice Reference Service. 1979. *We Are All Victims of Arson.* Washington, D.C.: Government Printing Office.

National Institute on Drug Abuse. 1982. *National Household Survey on Drug Abuse.* Washington, D.C.: Government Printing Office.

National Institute on Law Enforcement and Criminal Justice. 1977. *The Development of the Law of Gambling 1776–1976.* Washington, D.C.: Law Enforcement Assistance Administration.

NBC. 1983. "Monitor." Broadcast April 30.

NBC News. 1979. "NBC Follow-Up: A Follow-Up on the 1977 Documentary on 'Racketeering and the International Longshoreman's Association'." Broadcast April 12.

NBC Whitepaper. 1983. "Crime and Insanity." Broadcast April 26.

Netanyahu, Benjamin, ed. 1986. *Terrorism: How the West Can Win.* New York: Farrar, Straus and Giroux.

Nettler, Gwynn. 1974. "Embezzlement without Problems." *British Journal of Criminology* 14 (January): 70–77.

―――― 1978. *Explaining Crime.* 2nd ed. New York: McGraw-Hill.

―――― 1982. *Criminal Careers.* 4 vols. Cincinnati: Anderson.

―――― 1989. *Criminology Lessons.* Cincinnati: Anderson.

Newman, Graeme. 1978. *The Punishment Response.* Philadelphia: Lippincott.

―――― 1979. *Understanding Violence.* New York: Lippincott.

"New Style in Public Enemies—The White-Collar Criminal." 1973. *U.S. News and World Report,* March 12, pp. 53–55.

Nobile, Phillip, and Nadler, Eric. 1986. *United States of America vs. Sex: How the Meese Commission Lied About Pornography.* New York: Minotaur Press.

Normandeau, A. 1968. "Trends and Patterns in Crimes of Robbery." Ph.D. dissertation, University of Pennsylvania, Philadelphia.

Nurco, David N., et al. 1988. "Differential Criminal Patterns of Narcotic Addicts Over An Addiction Career." *Criminology* 26: 407–423.

"Nuremberg Principle." 1970. *The Nation*, January 26, p. 78.

Nye, F. Ivan, and Short, Jr., James F. 1956. "Scaling Delinquent Behavior." *American Sociological Review* 22: 326–331.

Nye, F. Ivan; Short, Jr., James F.; and Olson, Virgil J. 1958. "Socioeconomic Status and Delinquent Behavior." *American Journal of Sociology* 63 (January): 381–389.

O'Brien, Robert M. 1987. "The Interracial Nature of Violent Crimes: A Reexamination." *American Journal of Sociology* 92: 817–835.

O'Brien, Shirley. 1986. *Why They Did It: Stories of Eight Convicted Child Molesters*. Springfield, Ill.: Charles C. Thomas.

O'Connor, Tim. 1987. "The Misfortune Tellers." *Woman's World*, February 2, p. 41.

Office of Management and Budget. 1973. *Social Indicators*. Washington, D.C.: Government Printing Office.

Ogata, R. Craig. 1983. "Understanding Corporate Deviance: The Case of Industrial Espionage." Paper presented at the Academy of Criminal Justice Sciences Meetings, San Antonio, Tex. March.

"OJJDP (Office of Juvenile Justice and Delinquency Prevention) Announces Guidelines Aimed at Juvenile Gangs and Repeat Offenders." 1983. *Juvenile Research* (Bureau of Justice Statistics), November/December.

Opolot, J. S. E. 1979. "Organized Crime in Africa." *International Journal of Comparative and Applied Criminal Justice* 3 (Fall): 177–183.

"Options Scam in Boston." 1978. *Time*, January 30, pp. 49–50.

Orcutt, James D. 1987. "Differential Association and Marijuana Use: A Closer Look at Sutherland (With a Little Help From Becker)." *Criminology* 25: 341–358.

Organized Crime Control Act of 1970, Public Law 91-452. 1970. *Criminal Law Reporter*, 8 (5); October 21, 1–32.

Organized Crime Task Force Report. 1967. Washington, D.C.: Government Printing Office.

Orland, Leonard. 1980. "Reflections on Corporate Crime: Law in Search of Theory and Scholarship." *American Criminal Law Review* 17 (Spring): 501–520.

Owen, Mary Cameron. 1964. *The Booster and the Snitch*. New York: The Free Press.

Packer, Herbert L. 1968. *The Limits of Criminal Sanction*. Stanford: Stanford University Press.

Page, Joseph, and O'Brien, Mary Win. 1973. *Bitter Wages: Ralph Nader's Study Group Report on Disease and Injury on the Job*. New York: Grossman.

Paige, C. 1985. *The Right to Lifers: Who They Are, How They Operate, Where They Get Their Money*. New York: Summit Books.

"Panasonic Gets Zapped, Too." 1989. *Newsweek*, January 30, p. 54.

Panel for the Evaluation of Crime Surveys. 1976. *Surveying Crime*. Washington, D.C.: National Academy of Sciences.

Parenti, Michael. 1980. *Democracy for the Few*. 3rd ed. New York: St. Martin's Press.

Park, Robert E. 1952. *Human Communities*. Glencoe, Ill.: The Free Press.

Patrick, Ted. 1976. *Let Our Children Go*. New York: Dutton.

Patterson, Gerald R. 1982. *Coercive Family Process*. Eugene, Oregon: Castalia.

Patterson, Gerald R., and Dishion, Thomas J. 1985. "Contributions of Families and Peers to Delinquency." *Criminology* 23: 63–79.

Pauly, David, et al. 1987. "New Arrests on Wall Street." *Newsweek*, February 23, pp. 47–50.

Pauly, David, Friday, Carolyn, and Foote, Jennifer. 1987. "A Scourge of Video Pirates." *Newsweek*, July 27, pp. 40–41.

Pavalko, Ronald M. 1971. *The Sociology of Occupations and Professions*. Itasca, Ill.: F. E. Peacock.

Pearsons, Geoffrey. 1982. *Hooligans: A History of Respectable Fears*. New York: Schocken.

Pelfrey, William V. 1980. *The Evolution of Criminology*. Cincinnati: Anderson.

Pelton, L. H. 1978. "Child Abuse and Neglect: The Myth of Classlessness." *American Journal of Orthopsychiatry* 48: 608–617.

Pennsylvania Crime Commission. 1970. *Report on Organized Crime*. Harrisburg: Commonwealth of Pennsylvania.

_____ 1974. *Report on Police Corruption and the Quality of Law Enforcement in Philadelphia*. St. Davids, Pa.: Pennsylvania Crime Commission.

_____ 1980. *A Decade of Organized Crime: 1980 Report*, St. Davids, Pa.: Pennsylvania Crime Commission.

_____ 1986. *The Changing Face of Organized Crime: 1986 Report*. Conshohocken, Pa.: Pennsylvania Crime Commission.

Pepinsky, Harold. 1980. *Crime Control Strategies*. New York: Oxford.

Pepinsky, Harold, and Jesilow, Paul. 1984. *Myths That Cause Crime*. Cabin John, Md.: Seven Locks Press.

Perkins, Roberta, and Bennett, Garry. 1985. *Being a Prostitute: Prostitute Women and Prostitute Men*. Sydney, Australia: George Allen and Unwin.

Perls, Frederick. 1970. "Four Lectures." In *Gestalt Therapy Now*, edited by John Fagan and Irma Lee Shepherd. pp. 14–38. New York: Harper and Row.

Permanent Subcommittee on Investigations of the Committee on Governmental Affairs. 1979. *Illegal Narcotics Profits Hearing*. Testimony of Jack Key, Staffperson to the Subcommittee, 96th Congress, 1st Session, December 7, 11, 12, 13, 14.

_____ 1980. *Hearings on Organized Crime and Use of Violence*. 96th Congress, 2nd session, April.

Peter, Laurence J., ed. 1977. *Peter's Quotations*. New York: William Morrow.

Petersilia, Joan. 1983. *Racial Disparities in the Criminal Justice System*. Santa Monica: Rand Corporation.

Petersilia, Joan; Greenwood, Peter W. and Lavin, Marvin. 1977. *Criminal Careers of Habitual Felons*. Santa Monica: Rand Corporation.

Pfohl, Stephen J. 1985. *Images of Deviance and Social Control*. New York: McGraw-Hill.

Pileggi, Nicholas. 1985. *Wiseguy: Life in a Mafia Family*. New York: Simon and Schuster.

Pincher, Chapman. 1984. *Too Secret, Too Long*. New York: St. Martin's Press.

Pincomb, Ronald A. 1989. "Jamaican Gangs: A Summary." *Criminal Organizations* 2: 7–10.

Pinter, Rudolph. 1923. *Intelligence Testing: Methods and Results*. New York: Holt.

Pistone, Joseph, and Woodley, Richard. 1987. *Donnie Brasco: My Undercover Life in the Mafia*. New York: New American Library.

Piven, Frances Fox. 1981. "Deviant Behavior and the Remaking of the World." *Social Problems* 28 (June): 489–508.

Plate, Thomas. 1975. *Crime Pays: An Inside Look at Burglars, Car Thieves, Loan Sharks, Hit Men, Fences and Other Professional Criminals*. New York: Ballantine.

Plate, Thomas, and Darvi, Andrea. 1981. *Secret Police: The Inside Story of a Network of Terror*. Garden City, N.Y.: Doubleday.

Platt, Anthony. 1974. "Prospects for a Radical Criminology in the United States." *Crime and Social Justice* 1 (Spring): 2–10.

Poggio, Eugene C., et al. 1985. *Blueprint for the Future of the Uniform Crime Reporting Program: Final Report of the UCR Study*. Washington, D.C.: Department of Justice.

Pokorny, Alex D. 1964. "Moon Phases, Suicide and Homicide." *American Journal of Psychiatry* 121 (January): 66–67.

Pokorny, Alex D., and Jachimczyk, John. 1974. "The Questionable Relationship between Homicides and Lunar Cycle." *American Journal of Psychiatry* 131 (June): 827–829.

Poland, James M. 1988. *Understanding Terrorism*. Englewood Cliffs, N.J.: Prentice-Hall.

Police Foundation. 1977. *Domestic Violence and the Police: Studies in Detroit and Kansas City*. Washington, D.C.: Police Foundation.

"Police Lobbying Fails to Save 'Brady' Gun Control Amendment." 1988. *Criminal Justice Newsletter* 19: 1.

Polsky, Ned. 1967. *Hustlers, Beats and Others*. Chicago: Aldine.

Pomerantz, Steven L. 1987. "The FBI and Terrorism." *FBI Law Enforcement Bulletin*. October: 14–17.

Pope, Carl. 1980. "Patterns in Burglary: An Empirical Examination of Offense and Offender Characteristics." *Journal of Criminal Justice* 8 (1): 39–51.

Posner, Gerald L. 1988. *Warlords of Crime: Chinese Secret Societies—The New Mafia*. New York: McGraw-Hill.

Potter, Gary W. 1989. "Book Review: Zips, Pizza and Smack." *Criminal Organizations* 4: 17–18.

Powell, Stewart, et al. 1986. "Busting the Mob." *U.S. News and World Report*. February 3, pp. 24–32.

President's Commission on Law Enforcement and the Administration of Justice. 1967a. *The Challenge of Crime in a Free Society*. Washington, D.C.: Government Printing Office.

_____ 1967b. *Task Force Report: Organized Crime*. Washington, D.C.: Government Printing Office.

President's Commission on Organized Crime. 1983. *Organized Crime: Federal Law Enforcement Perspective*. Record of Hearings I. Washington, D.C.: Government Printing Office.

_____ 1984a. *Organized Crime of Asian Origin*. Washington, D.C.: Government Printing Office.

_____ 1984b. *Organized Crime and Money Laundering*. Record of Hearing II. Washington, D.C.: Government Printing Office.

_____ 1985. *Organized Crime and Gambling*. Record of Hearing VII. Washington, D.C.: Government Printing Office.

_____ 1986a. *America's Habit: Drug Abuse, Drug Trafficking and Organized Crime*. Interim Report. Washington, D.C.: Government Printing Office.

_____ 1986b. *The Edge: Organized Crime, Business and Labor Unions*. Interim Report. Washington, D.C.: Government Printing Office.

President's Task Force on Victims of Crime. 1982. *Final Report*. Washington, D.C.: Government Printing Office.

Press, Aric. 1983. "Mapping the Streets of Crime." *Newsweek*, December 19, p. 68.

Press, Aric; Shannon, Elaine; and Simons, Pamela Ellis. 1979. "Rico the Enforcer." *Newsweek*, August 20, pp. 82–83.

Press, Aric, et al. 1986. "A Government in the Bedroom." *Newsweek*, July 14, pp. 36–38.

Proal, Louis. 1973. *Political Crime*. Montclair, N.J.: Patterson Smith. Reprint of an 1898 edition. New York: D. Appleton.

Queen's Bench Foundation. 1976. *Rape: Prevention and Resistance*. San Francisco: Queen's Bench Foundation.

Quetelet, L. A. J. 1869. *Physique Sociale*. Vol. 2. Brussels. Cited in *The Growth of Crime*, edited by Leon Radzinowicz and Joan King, 1977, pp. 64–65. New York: Basic Books.

_____ 1969. *A Treatise on Man and the Development of His Faculties*. Gainesville, Fla.: Scholar's Facsimiles and Reprints.

Quinney, Richard C. 1963. "Occupational Structure and Criminal Behavior: Prescription Violations by Retail Pharmacists." *Social Problems* 11 (Fall): 179–185.

_____ 1964. "The Study of White-Collar Crime: Toward a Re-Orientation in Theory and Research." *Journal of Criminal Law, Criminology, and Police Science*, 55. Reproduced in *White-Collar Crime: Offenses in Business, Politics, and the Professions*, edited by Gilbert Geis and Robert F. Meier, 1977, pp. 283–295. New York: Free Press.

_____ 1970. *The Social Reality of Crime*. Boston: Little, Brown.

_____ 1974a. *Criminal Justice in America: A Critical Understanding*. Boston: Little, Brown.

_____ 1974b. *Critique of Legal Order: Crime Control in Capitalist Society.* Boston: Little, Brown.

_____ 1974c. *Criminology: Analysis and Critique of Crime in the United States.* Boston: Little, Brown.

_____ 1977. *Class, State and Crime: On the Theory and Practice of Criminal Justice.* New York: David McKay.

_____ 1979. *Criminology.* 2nd ed. New York: McGraw-Hill.

Quinney, Richard C., and Wildeman John. 1977. *The Problem of Crime.* 2nd ed. New York: Harper and Row.

Rabow, Jerome. 1964. "Research and Rehabilitation: The Conflict of Scientific and Treatment Roles in Corrections." The *Journal of Research in Crime and Delinquency* 1 (January): 67–79.

Radzinowicz, Leon. 1966. *Ideology and Crime.* New York: Columbia University Press.

Radzinowicz, Leon, and King, Joan. 1977. *The Growth of Crime: The International Experience.* New York: Basic Books.

Raffali, Henri C. 1970. "The Battered Child." *Crime and Delinquency* 16: 139–150.

Rafter, Nicole Hahn, ed. 1988. *White Trash: The Eugenic Family Studies 1877–1919.* Boston, Mass.: Northeastern University Press.

Randi, James. 1988. *The Faith Healers.* New York: Prometheus.

Ranelagh, John. 1986. *The Agency: The Rise and Decline of the CIA: From Wild Bill Donovan to William Casey.* New York: Simon and Schuster.

Ransdell, Eric. 1989. "Heavy Artillery for Horns of Plenty." *U.S. News and World Report,* February 20, pp. 61–64.

Rashke, Richard. 1981. *The Killing of Karen Silkwood.* Boston: Houghton Mifflin.

Rathus, Spencer. 1983. *Human Sexuality.* New York: Holt, Rinehart and Winston.

Reckless, Walter C. 1961. *The Crime Problem.* 3rd ed. New York: Appleton-Century-Crofts.

_____ 1967. *The Crime Problem.* New York: Appleton-Century-Crofts.

Reckless, Walter C., and Dinitz, Simon. 1967. "Pioneering with Self-Concept as a Vulnerability Factor in Delinquency." *Journal of Criminal Law, Criminology and Police Science* 58 (December): 515–523.

Reckless, Walter C.; Dinitz, Simon; and Kay, Barbara. 1957. "The Self-Component in Potential Delinquency and Potential Nondelinquency." *American Sociological Review* 22 (October): 566–570.

Reckless, Walter C.; Dinitz, Simon; and Murray, Ellen. 1956. "Self-Concept as an Insulator against Delinquency." *American Sociological Review* 21 (December): 744–756.

_____ 1957. "The 'Good Boy' in a High Delinquency Area." *Journal of Criminal Law, Criminology and Police Science* 48 (May): 18–25.

Regan, Tom. 1982. *All That Dwell Therein: Animal Rights and Environmental Ethics.* Berkeley: University of California Press.

Regenstein, Lewis. 1982. *America the Poisoned.* Washington, D.C.: Acropolis Books.

Regoli, Robert, and Poole, Eric. 1978. "The Commitment of Delinquents to Their Misdeeds: A Reexamination." *Journal of Criminal Justice* 6: 261–269.

Reibstein, Larry, and Drew, Lisa. 1988. "Clean Credit for Sale." *Newsweek,* September 12, p. 49.

Reichstein, Kenneth J. 1965. "Ambulance Chasing: A Case Study of Deviation and Control within the Legal Profession." *Social Problems* 13 (Summer): 3–17.

Reid, Ed. 1970. *The Grim Reapers: The Anatomy of Organized Crime in America, City by City.* New York: Bantam Books.

Reid, Susan Titus. 1982. *Crime and Criminology.* 3rd ed. New York: Holt, Rinehart, and Winston.

Reidel, Marc, and Zahn, Margaret. 1985. *The Nature and Pattern of American Homicide.* Washington, D.C.: Government Printing Office.

Reiman, Jeffrey H. 1984. *The Rich Get Richer and the Poor Get Prison,* 2nd ed. New York: Macmillan.

Reiss, Albert J., Jr. 1967. *Studies in Crime and Law Enforcement in Major Metropolitan Areas.* Field Surveys III, President's Commission on Law Enforcement and Administration of Justice. Washington, D.C.: Government Printing Office.

Reitman, Ben L. 1931. *The Second Oldest Profession.* New York: Vanguard Press.

Rengert, George, and Wasilchick, John. 1985. *Suburban Burglary: A Time and Place for Everything.* Springfield, Ill.: Thomas.

Repetto, Thomas A. 1974. *Residential Crime.* Cambridge, Mass.: Ballinger Press.

Report of the National Advisory Commission on Health Manpower. 1968. Quoted in *Crisis in American Institutions,* edited by Jerome H. Skolnick and Elliott Currie, 5th ed., 1982, p. 390. Boston: Little, Brown.

Reuter, Peter. 1984a. "The (Continued) Vitality of Mythical Numbers." *The Public Interest* 75 (Spring): 135–147.

_____ 1984b. *Disorganized Crime.* Cambridge, Mass.: MIT Press.

Revell, Oliver B. 1988. *Terrorism: A Law Enforcement Perspective.* Federal Bureau of Investigation, January.

Rhodes, Robert P. 1977. *The Insoluble Problem of Crime.* New York: Wiley.

_____ 1984. *Organized Crime: Crime Control vs. Civil Liberties.* Westminster, Md.: Random House.

Richards, David. 1982. *Sex, Drugs and the Law: An Essay on Human Rights and Overcriminalization.* Totowa, N.J.: Rowman and Littlefield.

"RICO: Assault with a Deadly Weapon." 1989. *New York Times,* January 30, p. 18.

Ritter, Bruce. 1988. *Sometimes God Has a Kid's Face: The Story of America's Exploited Street Kids.* New York: Covenant House.

Robertson, Frank. 1977. *Triangle of Death: The Inside Story of the Triads.* London: Routledge and Kegan Paul.

Robins, Lee N. 1974. *The Vietnam Drug User Returns.* Monograph, Series A, Number 2. Rockville, Md.: National Institute on Drug Abuse.

Robinson, William S. 1950. "Ecological Correlations and the Behavior of Individuals." *American Sociological Review* 15 (June): 351–357.

Rockefeller Commission. 1975. *The Rockefeller Report to the President by the Commission on CIA Activities.* Washington, D.C.: Government Printing Office.

Roebuck, Julian, and Weeber, Stanley G. 1978. *Political Crime in the United States: Analyzing Crime By and Against the Government.* New York: Praeger.

Roebuck, Julian, and Windham, Gerald O. 1983. "Professional Theft." In *Career Criminals,* edited by Gordon B. Waldo, pp. 13–29. Beverly Hills: Sage.

Rome, Florence. 1975. *The Tattooed Men: An American Woman Reports on the Japanese Criminal Underworld.* New York: Delacorte Press.

Rorabaugh, W. J. 1979. *The Alcoholic Republic: An American Tradition.* New York: Oxford University Press.

Rosanoff, A. J.; Handy, L. M.; and Plesset, I. R. 1934. "Criminality and Delinquency in Twins." *Journal of Criminal Law and Criminology* 24 (May): 923–934.

Rosberg, Robert R. 1980. *Game of Thieves.* New York: Everest House.

Rose, Peter I.; Glazer, Myron; and Glazer, Penina Migdal. 1982. *Sociology: Inquiry into Society.* 2nd ed. New York; St. Martin's Press.

Rosen, Lawrence, and Neilson, Kathleen. 1978. "The Broken Home and Delinquency." In *Crime in Society,* edited by Leonard Savitz and Norman Johnston, 2nd ed. pp. 406–415. New York: Wiley.

Rosen, Ruth. 1983. *The Lost Sisterhood: Prostitution in America, 1900–1918.* Baltimore: Johns Hopkins University Press.

Rosenbaum, Jill. 1987. "Social Control, Gender and Delinquency: An Analysis of Drug, Property and Violent Offenders." *Justice Quarterly* 4: 117–132.

———— 1989a. "Family Dysfunction and Female Delinquency." *Crime and Delinquency* January: 31–44.

———— 1989b. "Women and Crime." Special Issue. *Crime and Delinquency* 35 (January): entire issue.

Rosenthal, Harry F. 1989. "North to Battle Conviction." *Erie Morning News,* May 5, pp. 1–A, 3–A.

Rosenthal, Robert. 1966. *Experimenter Effects in Research.* New York: Appleton.

Ross, Edward. 1907. "The Criminaloid." *The Atlantic Monthly* 99 (January): 44–50. Reprinted in *White Collar Crime,* edited by Gilbert Geis and Robert F. Meier, 1977, pp. 29–37. New York: The Free Press.

Ross, H. Laurence. 1961. "Traffic Law Violation: A Folk Crime." *Social Problems* 9 (Winter): 231–241.

Ross, Shelley. 1988. *Fall From Grace: Sex, Scandal, and Corruption in American Politics From 1702 to the Present.* New York: Ballantine.

Rossi, Peter; Waite, E.; Bose, C. E.; and Berk, R. E. 1974. "The Seriousness of Crimes: Normative Structure and Individual Differences." *American Sociological Review* 39 (April): 224–237.

Rovetch, Emily L., Poggio, Eugene C., and Rossman, Henry H. 1984. *A Listing and Classification of Identified Issues Regarding the Uniform Crime Reporting Program of the FBI.* Cambridge, Mass.: Abt Associates.

Rowan, Roy. 1986. "The Biggest Mafia Bosses." *Fortune,* November 10, pp. 24–38.

Rupe, R. A. 1980. "Formula for Loss Prevention." *Retail Control.* March pp. 2–15.

Russell, Diana E. 1975. *The Politics of Rape.* New York: Stein and Day.

———— 1986. *The Secret Times: Incest in the Lives of Girls and Women.* New York: Basic Books.

Ryan, William. 1971. *Blaming the Victim.* New York: Random House.

Safire, William. 1989. "The End of RICO." *New York Times,* January 30, p. 19.

Sagarin, Edward. 1973. Introduction to *Political Crime,* by Louis Proal. Montclair, N.J.: Patterson Smith.

———— ed. 1980. *Taboos in Criminology.* Beverly Hills: Sage.

Salerno, Ralph, and Tompkins, John S. 1969. *The Crime Confederation.* Garden City: Doubleday.

Sampson, Robert J. 1985. "Structural Sources of Variation in Race-Age Specific Rates of Offending Across Major U.S. Cities." *Criminology* 23: 647–673.

Sanders, William B., ed. 1976. *The Sociologist as Detective.* 2nd ed. New York: Praeger.

———— 1983. *Criminology.* Reading, Mass.: Addison Wesley.

Sapp, Allen. 1986. "Organizational Linkages of Right Wing Extremist Groups." Paper presented at the Academy of Criminal Justice Sciences meetings, St. Louis, March.

Sarbin, Theodore R., and Miller, Jeffrey E. 1970. "Demonism Revisited: The XYY Chromosome Anomaly." *Issues in Criminology* 5 (Summer): 195–207.

Satchell, Michael. 1988. "The Just War That Never Ends." *U.S. News and World Report,* December 19, pp. 31–38.

Satchell, Michael, et al. 1987. "Narcotics: Terror's New Ally." *U.S. News and World Report,* May 4, pp. 30–37.

"Satisfied Workers Don't Steal." 1983. *Criminal Justice Newsletter* 14 (July): 6–7.

Savage, George. 1976. *Forgeries, Fakes and Reproductions.* London: White Lion Publishing.

Savitz, D. 1959. "Automobile Theft." *Journal of Criminal Law, Criminology and Police Science* 50 (July): 132–143.

Savitz, Leonard D. 1978. "Official Police Statistics and their Limitations." In *Crime and Society,* edited by Leonard D. Savitz and Norman Johnston, pp. 69–81. New York: Wiley.

"Scandal Traced to Brezhnev Family." 1988. *Erie Times News,* January 24, p. 1–A.

"Scared Straight Found Ineffective Again." 1979. *Criminal Justice Newsletter* 10 (September): 7.

Scarpitti, Frank; Murray, Ellen; Dinitz, Simon; and Reckless, Walter. 1960. "The Good Boy in a High Delinquency Area: Four Years Later." *American Sociological Review* 23 (August): 555–558.

Scarr, Harry A. 1973. *Patterns of Burglary.* Washington, D.C.: Government Printing Office.

Schafer, Stephen, 1969. *Theories in Criminology: Past and Present Philosophies of the Crime Problem.* New York: Random House.

_____ 1971. "The Concept of the Political Criminal." *Journal of Criminal Law, Criminology and Police Science* 62 (Spring): 380–387.

_____ 1974. *The Political Criminal.* New York: The Free Press.

_____ 1976. *Introduction to Criminology.* Reston, Va.: Reston Publishing Company.

Schauss, Alexander. 1980. *Diet, Crime and Delinquency.* Berkeley, Ca.: Parker House.

Schecter, Leonard, and Phillips, William. 1973. *On the Pad.* New York: Berkeley.

Scheflin, Alan W., and Opton, Jr., Edward M. 1978. *The Mind Manipulators.* New York: Paddington Press.

Scheim, David E. 1988. *Contract on America: The Mafia Murders of President John F. Kennedy.* New York: Shapolsky Publishers.

Schichor, David. 1982. "An Analysis of Citations in Introductory Criminology Textbooks." *Journal of Criminal Justice* 10 (March): 231–237.

Schlachter, Barry. 1986. "Women Find Success in Espionage." *The Buffalo News,* June 15, p. A–14.

Schlesinger, Arthur M., Jr. 1986. *The Cycles of American History.* Boston: Houghton Mifflin.

Schloss, B., and Giesbrecht, N. A. 1972. *Murder in Canada: A Report on Capital and Non-Capital Murder Statistics 1961–1970.* Toronto: Centre of Criminology, University of Toronto.

Schrag, Clarence. 1962. "Delinquency and Opportunity: Analysis of a Theory." *Sociology and Social Research* 46 (January): 165–175.

_____ 1971. *Crime and Justice: American Style.* Washington, D.C.: Government Printing Office.

Schrager, Laura Shill, and Short, Jr. James F. 1978. "Toward a Sociology of Organizational Crime." *Social Problems* 25 (April): 407–419.

_____ 1980. "How Serious a Crime? Perceptions of Organizational and Common Crimes." In *White Collar Crime: Theory and Research,* edited by Gilbert Geis and Ezra Stotland, pp. 14–31. Beverly Hills: Sage.

Schuerman, Leo A., and Kobrin, Solomon. 1986. "Community Careers in Crime." In *Communities and Crime,* edited by Albert J. Reiss, Jr., and Michael Tonry. Chicago: University of Chicago Press.

Schuessler, Karl. 1952. "The Deterrent Influence of the Death Penalty." *Annals of the Academy of Political and Social Sciences* 284: 54–62.

_____ 1954. "Review." *American Journal of Sociology* 49: 604.

Schuessler, Karl F., and Cressey, Donald R. 1953. "Personality Characteristics of Criminals." *American Journal of Sociology,* 55: 166–176.

Schulsinger, Fini. 1972. "Psychopathy, Heredity and Environment." *International Journal of Mental Health* 1 (January): 190–206.

Schur, Edwin M. 1965. *Crimes without Victims: Deviant Behavior and Public Policy.* Englewood Cliffs, N.J.: Prentice-Hall.

_____ 1969. "Reactions to Deviance: A Critical Assessment." *American Journal of Sociology* 75 (November): 309–322.

_____ 1971. *Labeling Deviant Behavior.* New York: Harper and Row.

_____ 1980. *The Politics of Deviance.* Englewood Cliffs, N.J.: Prentice-Hall.

Schwartz, Michael, and Tangri, Sandra. 1965. "A Note on Self-Concept as an Insulator against Delinquency." *American Sociological Review* 30: 922–926.

Schweinhart, L. J., and Weikart, D. P. 1980. *Young Children Grow Up: The Effects of the Perry Preschool Program on Youths Through Age 15.* Ypsilanti, Mich.: High/Scope.

"Scientology Fraud." 1983. *20/20.* American Broadcasting Company. Broadcast January 6.

Scott, Joseph E. 1988. "Book Reviews of Attorney General's Commission on Pornography and Related Works." *Journal of Criminal Law and Criminology* 78: 1145–1165.

Sederberg, Peter C. 1989. *Terrorist Myths: Illusion, Rhetoric and Reality.* Englewood Cliffs, N.J.: Prentice-Hall.

Seidman, David, and Couzens, Michael. 1974. "Getting the Crime Rate Down: Political Pressure and Crime Reporting." *Law and Society Review* 8 (Spring): 457–493.

Sellin, Thorsten. 1938. "Culture Conflict and Crime." *Social Science Research Council Bulletin* 41: 1–7.

_____ 1957. "Crime in the United States." *Life Magazine,* September 9, p. 48.

_____ 1959. *The Death Penalty.* Philadelphia: American Law Institute.

Sellin, Thorsten, and Wolfgang, Marvin E. 1964. *The Measurement of Delinquency.* New York: Wiley.

Senate Permanent Subcommittee on Investigations. Committee on Governmental Affairs. 1979. 96th Congress, First Session, December 7, 11, 12, 13, and 14.

_____ 1983. 98th Congress, First Session, August 3.

Shah, Saleem A., and Roth, Loren H. 1974. "Biological and Psychophysiological Factors in Criminality." In *Handbook of Criminology,* edited by Daniel Glaser, pp. 101–173. Chicago: Rand McNally.

Shaw, Clifford R. 1929. *Delinquency Areas: A Study of the Geographic Distribution of School Truants, Juvenile Delinquents and Adult Offenders in Chicago.* Chicago: University of Chicago Press.

_____ 1930. *The Jack Roller.* Chicago: University of Chicago Press.

Shaw, Clifford R., and McKay, Henry D. 1942. *Juvenile Delinquency and Urban Areas.* Chicago: University of Chicago Press.

Shaw, Clifford R.; McKay, Henry D.; and MacDonald, James F. 1938. *Brothers in Crime.* Chicago: University of Chicago Press.

Shaw, George Bernard. 1941. Preface to *The Doctor's Dilemma,* in *The Doctor's Dilemma* edited by George Bernard Shaw. New York: Dodd, Mead and Company.

Sheehy, Gail. 1973. *Hustling: Prostitution in Our Wide Open Society*. New York: Delacorte Press.

Sheldon, William H. 1940. *The Varieties of Human Physique*. New York: Harper and Row.

———— 1949. *Varieties of Delinquent Youth*. New York: Harpers.

Sheley, J. F. 1979. *Understanding Crime: Concepts, Issues, Decisions*. Belmont, Ca.: Wadsworth.

Shelley, Louise I. 1981. *Crimes and Modernization*. Carbondale, Ill.: Southern Illinois University.

Sherif, Muzafer, and Sherif, Carolyn. 1966. *Groups in Harmony and Tension*. New York: Octagon.

Sherman, Larry. 1987. "Domestic Violence." *Crime File*. National Institute of Justice.

Sherman, Larry, and Berk, Richard. 1984. "The Specific Deterrent Effects of Arrest for Domestic Assault." *American Sociological Review* 49: 261–272.

Shoemaker, Donald L., and Williams, J. Sherwood. 1987. "The Subculture of Violence and Ethnicity." *Journal of Criminal Justice* 15: 461–472.

Short, Jr., James F., and Nye, F. Ivan. 1958. "Extent of Unrecorded Delinquency: Tentative Conclusions." *Journal of Criminal Law, Criminology and Police Science* 49 (December): 296–302.

Short, Jr., James F., and Strodtbeck, Fred L. 1965. *Group Process and Gang Delinquency*. Chicago: University of Chicago Press.

Shover, Neal. 1973. "The Social Organization of Burglary." *Social Problems* 20 (Spring): 499–514.

———— 1983. "The Later Stages of Ordinary Property Offender Careers." *Social Problems* 31 (December): 208–218.

Siegel, Larry J. 1983. *Criminology*. St. Paul: West.

Sigler, Robert T., and Haygood, Donna. 1988. "The Criminalization of Forced Marital Intercourse." In *Deviance and the Family*, edited by Frank E. Hagan and Marvin B. Sussman, pp. 71–85. New York: Haworth Press.

Silberman, Charles E. 1978. *Criminal Violence, Criminal Justice*. New York: Random House.

Silk, L. Howard, and Vogel, David. 1976. *Ethics and Profits: The Crisis of Confidence in American Business*. New York: Simon and Schuster.

"Silkwood Vindicated." 1979. *Newsweek*, May 28, p. 40.

Simcha-Fagan, Ora, and Schwartz, Joseph E. 1986. "Neighborhood and Delinquency: An Assessment of Contextual Effects." *Criminology* 24: 667–703.

Simis, Konstantin M. 1982. *U.S.S.R.: The Corrupt Society: The Secret World of Soviet Capitalism*. New York: Simon and Schuster.

Simmel, Georg. 1955. *Conflict and the Web of Group Affiliations*. Translated by Kurt H. Wolff and Reinhard Bendix. New York: Free Press.

Simmons, Jerry L. 1969. *Deviants*. Berkeley: Glendessary Press.

Simon, David R., and Eitzen, D. Stanley. 1982. *Elite Deviance*. Boston: Allyn and Bacon.

Simon, David R., and Swart, Stanley L. 1984. "The Justice Department Focuses on White-Collar Crime: Promises and Pitfalls." *Crime and Delinquency* 30 (January).

Simon, Rita J., and Aaronson, David E. 1988. *The Insanity Defense: A Critical Assessment of Law and Policy in the Post-Hinckley Era*. New York: Praeger.

Simpson, John, and Bennett, Jana. 1985. *The Disappeared and the Mothers of the Plaza*. New York: St. Martin's Press.

Simpson, M., and Schill, T. 1977. "Patrons of Massage Parlors: Some Facts and Figures." *Archives of Sexual Behaviors* 6: 521.

Sinclair, Upton. 1906. *The Jungle*. New York: Doubleday and Page.

Sinden, P. G. 1980. "Perceptions of Crime in Capitalist America: The Question of Consciousness Manipulation." *Sociological Focus* 13: 75–85.

Singer, Max. 1971. "The Vitality of Mythical Numbers." *The Public Interest* 23 (Spring): 3–9.

Singer, Max, and Levine, Murray. 1988. "Power-Control Theory, Gender, and Delinquency: A Partial Replication with Additional Evidence on the Effects of Peers." *Criminology* 26: 627–647.

Singer, Simon I. 1978. "Comments on Alleged Overreporting." *Criminology* 16 (May): 99–103.

Skinner, B. F. 1953. *Science and Human Behavior*. New York: Macmillan.

———— 1971. *Beyond Freedom and Dignity*. New York: Knopf.

Skogan, Wesley G. 1974. "The Validity of Official Crime Statistics: An Empirical Investigation." *Social Science Quarterly* 55 (June): 25–38.

———— 1987. *Victimization Surveys and Criminal Justice Planning*. Monograph. Washington, D.C.: National Institute of Law Enforcement and Criminal Justice, July.

Skolnick, Jerome H. 1969. *The Politics of Protest: The Skolnick Report to the National Commission on the Causes and Prevention of Violence*. New York: Ballantine Books.

Skolnick, Jerome H., and Currie, Elliott, eds. 1988. *Crisis in American Institutions*. Boston: Little, Brown.

Slim, Iceberg, 1969. *Pimp: The Story of My Life*. Los Angeles: Holloway House.

Smigel, Erwin O. 1970. "Public Attitudes toward Stealing as Related to the Size of the Victim Organization." In *Crimes Against Bureaucracy*, edited by Erwin O. Smigel and H. Laurence Ross, pp. 15–28. New York: Van Nostrand Reinhold.

Smigel, Erwin O., and Ross, H. Laurence, eds. 1970. *Crimes Against Bureaucracy*. New York: Van Nostrand Reinhold.

Smith, Adam. 1953. *The Wealth of Nations*. Cambridge: Harvard University Press.

Smith, Bradley F. 1977. *Reaching Judgment at Nuremberg*. New York: Basic Books.

Smith, Dwight C., Jr. 1975. *The Mafia Mystique*. New York: Basic Books.

_____ 1978. "Organized Crime and Entrepreneurship." *International Journal of Criminology and Penology* 6 (May): 161–177.

_____ 1980. "Paragons, Pariahs and Pirates: A Spectrum-Based Theory of Enterprise." *Crime and Delinquency* 26 (July): 358–386.

Smith, Hedrick. 1989. *The Power Game.* Public Broadcasting System, February 6.

Smith, J. David. 1985. *Minds Made Feeble: The Myth and Legacy of the Kallikaks.* Aspen, Col.: Aspen.

Snider, Donald L. 1978. "Corporate Crime in Canada." *Canadian Journal of Criminology* 20 (April): 142–168.

Snider, L. 1982. "Traditional and Corporate Theft: A Comparison of Sanctions." In *White-Collar and Economic Crime,* edited by Peter Wickman and Timothy Dailey, pp. 235–258. Lexington, Mass.: Lexington.

Snodgrass, Jon D. 1972. *The American Criminological Tradition: Portraits of the Men and Ideology in a Discipline.* Unpublished doctoral dissertation, University of Pennsylvania.

_____ 1982. *The Jack-Roller at Seventy: A Fifty-Year Follow Up.* Lexington, Mass.: D. C. Heath.

Solzhenitsyn, Alexander I. 1975. *The Gulag Archipelago.* New York: Harper and Row.

Sondern, Frederic J. 1959. *Brotherhood of Evil: The Mafia.* New York: Straus and Giroux.

"Soviet Crime Rate Up." 1989. *Los Angeles Times,* February 14, p. 1–A.

Sparks, Richard F. 1980. "A Critique of Marxist Criminology." In *Crime and Justice,* edited by Norval Morris and Michael Tonry, vol. 2, pp. 159–208. Chicago: University of Chicago Press.

Sparks, Richard F.; Genn, Hazel G.; and Dodd, David J. 1977. *Surveying Victims: A Study of the Measurement of Criminal Victimization, Perceptions of Crime and Attitudes to Criminal Justice.* New York: Wiley.

Spencer, C. 1966. "A Typology of Violent Offenders." *Administrative Abstracts* No. 23, California Department of Corrections, September. Cited in *The Nature of Crime,* by Harold J. Vetter and Ira J. Silverman, 1978. Philadelphia: W. B. Saunders.

Spitzer, Stephen. 1975. "Toward a Marxian Theory of Deviance." *Social Problems* 22 (September): 638–651.

Staats, Gregory R. 1977. "Changing Conceptualizations of Professional Criminals: Implications for Criminology Theory." *Criminology* 15 (May): 53–63.

Stafford, Mark. 1984. "Gang Delinquency." In *Major Forms of Crime,* edited by John F. Meier, pp. 167–190. Beverly Hills: Sage.

Stark, Rodney. 1987. "Deviant Places: A Theory of the Ecology of Crime." *Criminology* 25: 893–909.

Steffens, Lincoln. 1904. *The Shame of the Cities.* New York: McClure, Phillips.

Steffensmeier, Darrell. 1978. "Crime and the Contemporary Woman: Analysis of Changing Levels of Female Property Crime, 1960–1975." *Social Forces* 57: 566–584.

_____ 1986. *The Fence: In the Shadow of Two Worlds.* Totowa, N.J.: Rowman and Littlefield.

_____ 1989. "Age and the Distribution of Crime." *American Journal of Sociology* 94: 803–831.

Steffensmeier, Darrell, and Allan, Emilie A. 1988. "Sex Disparities in Arrests by Residence, Race and Age: An Assessment of the Gender Convergence/Crime Hypothesis." *Justice Quarterly* 5: 53–80.

Stein, Martha L. 1974. *Lovers, Friends, Slaves . . . : The Nine Male Sexual Types.* Berkeley, Ca.: Berkeley Publishing Corporation.

Stein, Maurice R. 1964. *The Eclipse of Community: An Interpretation of American Studies.* New York: Harper and Row.

Steinmetz, Suzanne K., and Straus, Murray. 1978. "The Family as a Cradle of Violence." In *Readings in Criminology,* edited by Peter Wickman and Phillip Whitten. pp. 59–65. Lexington, Mass.: D. C. Heath.

"Steinberg Sentenced to Maximum Term." 1989. *Erie Morning News,* March 25, p. 4–B.

Stellwagen, Lindsey D. 1985. "The Use of Forfeiture Sanctions in Drug Cases." *Research in Brief.* National Institute of Justice, July.

Stephens, Richard C., and Ellis, Rosalind D. 1975. "Narcotics Addiction and Crime: An Analysis of Recent Trends." *Criminology* 12: 474–487.

Sterling, Claire. 1981. *The Terror Network: The Secret War of International Terrorism.* New York: Holt, Rinehart and Winston.

Stewart, David W., and Spille, Henry A. 1988. *Diploma Mills: Degrees of Fraud.* New York: Macmillan.

Stewart, James K. 1988. "Foreword." *Research Program Plan, Fiscal Year 1988.* Washington, D.C.: National Institute of Justice.

Stewart, John E., and Cannon, Daniel A. 1977. "Effects of Perpetrator Status and Bystander Commitment on Response to a Simulated Crime." *Journal of Police Science and Administration* 5: 318–323.

"The Sting." 1976. *Newsweek,* March 15, p. 35.

Stirling, Nora. 1974. *Your Money or Your Life.* Indianapolis: Bobbs-Merrill.

"Storm over the Environment." 1983. *Newsweek,* March 7, pp. 16–23.

Straus, Murray A.; Gelles, Richard; and Steinmetz, Susan. 1982. "The Marriage License as a Hitting License." In *Crisis in American Institutions,* edited by Jerome H. Skolnick and Elliott Currie, 5th ed. pp. 273–287. Boston: Little, Brown.

Straus, Murray; Gelles, Richard J.; and Steinmetz, Susan. 1980. *Behind Closed Doors: Violence in the American Family.* New York: Doubleday.

Strug, D., et al. 1984. "Hustling to Survive: The Role of Drugs, Alcohol and Crime in the Life of Street Hustlers." Paper presented at the Academy of Criminal Justice Sciences Meetings, Chicago, March.

Sullivan, Terence. 1988. "Juvenile Prostitution: A Critical Perspective." In *Deviance and the Family,* edited by Frank E. Hagan and Marvin B. Sussman, pp. 113–134. New York: Haworth Press.

Sumner, William G. 1906. *Folkways.* New York: Dover.

Sun-Tzu. 1963. *The Art of War*. Translated by Samuel B. Griffith. New York: Oxford University Press.

Surgeon General's Scientific Advisory Committee on Television and Social Behavior. 1972. *Television and Growing Up: The Impact of Televised Violence*. Washington, D.C.: Government Printing Office.

Survey of Inmates of State Correctional Facilities—Advance Report. 1976. Special Report No. SD-NPS-SR-Z, March. Washington, D.C.: Government Printing Office.

Sussman, Marvin B., and Haug, Marie R. 1967. "Human and Mechanical Error: An Unknown Quantity in Research." *American Behavioral Scientist* 2 (November): 55–56.

Sutherland, Edwin H. 1937. *The Professional Thief*. Chicago: University of Chicago Press. Reissued 1956. Chicago: Phoenix.

_____ 1940. "White Collar Criminality." *American Sociological Review* 5 (February): 1–12.

_____ 1941. "Crime and Business." *Annals of the American Academy of Political and Social Science* 217 (September): 112–118.

_____ 1945. "Is 'White Collar Crime' Crime?" *American Sociological Review* 10 (April): 132–139.

_____ 1947. *Principles of Criminology*. 4th ed. Philadelphia: Lippincott.

_____ 1949. *White Collar Crime*. New York: Holt, Rinehart and Winston.

_____ 1956a. "Crime of Corporations." In *The Sutherland Papers*, edited by Albert Cohen, Alfred Lindesmith, and Karl Schuessler, pp. 78–96. Bloomington: Indiana University Press. Also in *White Collar Crime*, edited by Gilbert Geis and Robert F. Meier, 1977, pp. 71–84. New York: Free Press.

_____ 1956b. "The Development of the Theory." In *The Sutherland Papers*, edited by Albert Cohen, Alfred Lindesmith, and Karl Schuessler, pp. 13–29. Bloomington: Indiana University Press.

Sutherland, Edwin H., and Cressey, Donald C. 1960. *Criminology*. Philadelphia: Lippincott.

_____ 1974. *Criminology*. 9th ed. Philadelphia: Lippincott.

_____ 1978. *Criminology*. 10th ed. Philadelphia: Lippincott.

Swigert, Victoria, and Farrell, Ronald. 1980. "Corporate Homicide: Definitional Processes in the Creation of Deviance." *Law and Society Review* 15 (Autumn): 161–182.

Sykes, Gresham M. 1958. *The Society of Captives: A Study of Maximum Security Prison*. Princeton, N.J.: Princeton University Press.

_____ 1972. "The Future of Criminality." *American Behavioral Scientists* 15 (January): 403–419.

_____ 1978. *Criminology*. New York: Harcourt, Brace, Jovanovich.

_____ 1980. *The Future of Crime*. Rockville, Md.: National Institute of Mental Health.

Sykes, Gresham, and Matza, David. 1957. "Techniques of Neutralization: A Theory of Delinquency." *American Sociological Review* 22 (December): 664–670.

Szasz, Andrew. 1986. "Corporations, Organized Crime, and the Disposal of Hazardous Waste: An Examination of the Making of a Criminogenic Regulatory Structure." *Criminology* 24: 1–28.

Szasz, Thomas. 1974. *Ceremonial Chemistry: The Ritual Persecution of Drugs, Addicts and Pushers*. New York: Anchor Books.

Talese, Gay. 1971. *Honor Thy Father*. Greenwich, Ct.: Fawcett.

_____ 1979. *Thy Neighbor's Wife*. Greenwich, Ct.: Fawcett Crest Books.

Tannenbaum, Frank. 1938. *Crime and the Community*. Boston: Ginn.

Tappan, Paul. 1960. *Crime, Justice and Correction*. New York: McGraw-Hill.

Tarde, Gabriel. 1912. *Penal Philosophy*. Boston: Little, Brown. Reissued 1968. Montclair, N.J.: Patterson Smith.

Taylor, Bruce M. 1989. "New Definitions for the National Crime Survey." Bureau of Justice Statistics Special Report, March.

Taylor, Ian, et al. 1973. *The New Criminology: For a Social Theory of Deviance*. New York: Harper and Row.

_____ ed. 1975. *Critical Criminology*. London: Routledge and Kegan Paul.

Taylor, Laurie. 1984. *In the Underworld*. Oxford, England: Basil Blackwell.

Tennebaum, David. 1977. "Research Studies of Personality and Criminality." *Journal of Criminal Justice* 5 (January): 1–19.

Teresa, Vincent. 1973a. "A Mafioso Cases the Mafia Craze." *Saturday Review*, February, pp. 23–29.

Teresa, Vincent, with Renner, Thomas. 1973b. *My Life in the Mafia*. Greenwich, Ct.: Fawcett Publications.

"13th Victim of Cult Discovered." 1989. *Erie Morning News*, April 14, p. 1–A.

Thomas, Charles W., and Hepburn, John R. 1983. *Crime, Criminal Law and Criminology*. Dubuque, Ia.: William C. Brown.

Thomas, William I., and Swaine, Dorothy. 1928. *The Child in America*. New York: Knopf.

Tiger, Lionel. 1976. "Fearful Symmetry." *New York Times*, February 8.

Tittle, Charles R. 1988. "Two Empirical Regularities (Maybe) In Search of an Explanation: Commentary on the Age/Crime Debate." *Criminology* 26: 75–85.

Tittle, Charles; Villemez, W.; and Smith, D. 1978. "The Myth of Social Class and Criminality: An Empirical Assessment of the Empirical Evidence." *American Sociological Review* 43: 643–656.

Toby, Jackson. 1980. "The New Criminology Is the Old Baloney." In *Radical Criminology: The Coming Crisis*, edited by James A. Inciardi, pp. 124–132. Beverly Hills: Sage.

Toch, Hans. 1979. *Psychology of Crime and Criminal Justice*. New York: Holt, Rinehart and Winston.

Toennies, Ferdinand. 1957. *Community and Society*. Translated by Charles Loomis. East Lansing: Michigan State University.

Tomsho, Robert. 1987. *The American Sanctuary Movement.* Austin: Texas Monthly Press.

Trasler, Gordon. 1962. *The Explanation of Criminality.* London: Routledge and Kegan Paul.

Trebach, Arnold S. 1982. *The Heroin Solution.* New Haven: Yale University Press.

_____ 1984. "Peace without Surrender in the Perpetual Drug War." *Justice Quarterly* 1 (March): 125–144.

_____ 1987. *The Great Drug War.* New York: Macmillan.

Trimble, Jeff. 1988. "Soviets Seek Stills as Spirits Sink." *U.S. News and World Report,* February 22, pp. 59–60.

Truzzi, Marcello. 1976. "Sherlock Holmes: Applied Social Psychologist." In *The Sociologist as Detective,* edited by William B. Sanders, 2nd ed., pp. 50–86. New York: Praeger.

Turk, Austin T. 1969a. *Criminality and the Legal Order.* Chicago: Rand McNally.

_____ 1969b. "Introduction." In *Criminality and Economic Conditions,* edited by William Bonger. Bloomington: Indiana University Press.

_____ 1972. *Legal Sanctioning and Social Control.* Washington, D.C.: Government Printing Office.

_____ 1980. "Analyzing Official Deviance: For Nonpartisan Conflict Analyses in Criminology." In *Radical Criminology: The Coming Crisis,* edited by James A. Inciardi, pp. 78–91. Beverly Hills: Sage.

_____ 1981. "Organization Deviance and Political Policing." *Criminology* 19 (August): 231–250.

_____ 1982. *Political Criminality: The Defiance and Defense of Authority.* Beverly Hills: Sage.

_____ 1984. "Political Crime." In *Major Forms of Crime,* edited by Robert F. Meier, pp. 119–135. Beverly Hills: Sage.

Turner, Frederick Jackson. 1975. *The Frontier in American History.* Huntington, N.Y.: R. B. Krieger.

Turner, James S. 1970. *The Chemical Feast: Nader's Raiders Study Group Report on the Food and Drug Administration.* New York: Grossman.

Turner, Jonathan H. 1974. *The Structure of Sociological Theory.* Homewood, Ill.: Dorsey.

Turner, Stansfield. 1985. *Secrecy and Democracy: The CIA in Transition.* New York: Houghton Mifflin.

Twain, Mark. 1899. *Following the Equator: A Journey around the World.* New York: Harper and Brothers.

Tyler, Gus, ed. 1962. *Organized Crime in America.* Ann Arbor: University of Michigan Press.

United Nations. 1974. *Demographic Yearbook.* New York: United Nations, Publishing Service.

United Press International. 1969. "Text of Terrorist Letter." March 12.

"U.S. Begins Price-Fixing Prosecution." 1975. *Erie Times-News,* September 9, p. 10.

U.S. Bureau of Census. 1970. "Victim Recall Pretest." Washington, D.C., Household Surveys of Victims of Crime. Washington, D.C.: Bureau of Demographic Surveys Division. Mimeograph.

_____ 1983. *Statistical Abstracts of the United States, 1982.* Washington, D.C.: Government Printing Office.

_____ 1989. *Money Income and Poverty Status of Persons in the United States: 1988.* Washington, D.C.: Government Printing Office.

U.S. Congress. 1976. *Hearings before the Subcommittee on Energy and Environment of the Committee on Small Business,* 94th Congress, 2nd Session, April 26, May 20.

_____ 1981. *Hearings before the Subcommittee on Oversight and Investigations of the Committee on Energy and Commerce,* 97th Congress, 1st Session, March 12, April 2, 3.

U.S. Department of Justice. 1974. *Crime in Eight American Cities.* National Criminal Justice Information and Statistics Service. Washington, D.C.: Government Printing Office.

_____ 1975a. *Criminal Victimization Surveys in the Nation's Five Largest Cities.* National Criminal Justice Information and Statistics Service. Washington, D.C.: Government Printing Office.

_____ 1975b. *Criminal Victimization in Thirteen American Cities.* National Criminal Justice Information and Statistics Service. Washington, D.C.: Government Printing Office.

_____ 1976. *Criminal Victimization in the United States.* National Criminal Justice Information and Statistics Service. Washington, D.C.: Government Printing Office.

_____ 1978. *Myths and Realities about Crime.* National Criminal Justice Information and Statistics Service. Washington, D.C.: Government Printing Office.

_____ 1979. *Criminal Victimization in the United States, 1977.* National Criminal Justice Information and Statistics Service. Washington, D.C.: Government Printing Office.

_____ 1980. *Profile of Jail Inmates: Sociodemographic Findings from the 1978 Survey of Inmates of Local Jails.* Washington, D.C.: Government Printing Office.

_____ 1983. "An Overview of the Criminal Justice System: The American Response to Crime." *Bureau of Justice Statistics Bulletin,* December.

_____ 1988. *Bureau of Justice Statistics Annual Report, Fiscal 1987.* Washington, D.C.: Government Printing Office, April.

U.S. House of Representatives. 1979. *Select Committee on Assassinations Hearings.* 95th Congress, 2nd Session.

"U.S. Indicts Colombian Drug Cartel." 1989. *Erie Morning News,* May 23, p. 1–A.

U.S. Select Committee to Study Government Operations. 1979. Cited in *Crime, Criminal Law and Criminology,* edited by Charles W. Thomas and John R. Hepburn, 1983. pp. 279–280. Dubuque, Iowa: William C. Brown.

U.S. Senate. 1976. *Senate Subcommittee Hearings on Intelligence Activities.* Final Report, II. Washington, D.C.: Government Printing Office.

Universal Declaration of Human Rights. 1948. United Nations, General Assembly Official Records, Resolutions, 3, Part 1.

Valachi, Joseph. 1969. Testimony cited in "The Conglomerate of Crime." *Time,* August 22, 17–27.

Van den Berghe, Pierre. 1974. "Bringing Beasts Back In: Toward A Biosocial Theory of Aggression." *American Sociological Review* 39 (December): 777–788.

Van den Haag, Ernest. 1966. "No Excuse for Crime." *Annals of the American Academy of Political and Social Sciences* 423 (January): 133–141.

_____ 1975. *Punishing Criminals.* New York: Basic Books.

Van den Haag, Ernest, and Conrad, John P. 1983. *The Death Penalty: A Debate.* New York: Plenum.

Vander, Brenda J., and Neff, Ronald J. 1986. *Incest as Child Abuse: Research and Applications.* New York: Praeger.

Van Voorhis, Patricia, et al. 1988. "The Impact of Family Structure and Quality on Delinquency: A Comparative Assessment of Structural and Functional Factors." *Criminology* 26: 235–261.

Vetter, Harold J., and Silverman, Ira J. 1978. *The Nature of Crime.* Philadelphia: W. B. Saunders.

Vice President's Task Force. 1986. *Report on the Vice President's Task Force on Combatting Terrorism.* Washington, D.C.: Government Printing Office.

Vigil, James Diego. 1988. *Barrio Gangs: Street Life and Identity in Southern California.* Austin: University of Texas Press.

Vilhelm, Aubert. 1968. "White-Collar Crime and Social Structure." In *White Collar Criminal: The Offender in Business and the Professions,* edited by Gilbert Geis, pp. 173–184. New York: Atherton.

Villano, Anthony. 1978. *Brick Agent.* New York: Ballantine.

"Violence in Canadian Society." 1987. *Juristat.* Ottawa, Statistics Canada, vol. 7, June.

Vold, George B. 1958. *Theoretical Criminology.* New York: Oxford University Press.

_____ 1979. *Theoretical Criminology.* With Thomas J. Bernard, 2nd ed. New York: Oxford University Press.

_____ 1986. *Theoretical Criminology.* With Thomas J. Bernard, 3rd ed. New York: Oxford University Press.

Volk, Klaus. 1977. "Criminological Problems of White Collar Crime." In *International Summaries.* Vol. 4, pp. 13–21. Rockville, Md.: National Criminal Justice Reference Service.

Volz, Joseph, and Bridge, Peter J. ed. 1969. *The Mafia Talks.* Greenwich, Ct.: Fawcett.

Von Hentig, Hans. 1948. *The Criminal and His Victim.* New Haven: Yale University Press.

Voss, Harwin. 1963. "Ethnic Differentials in Delinquency in Honolulu." *Journal of Criminal Law, Criminology and Police Science* 54 (September): 322–327.

Wade, Andrew L. 1967. "Social Processes in the Act of Juvenile Vandalism." In *Criminal Behavior Systems: A Typology,* edited by Marshall B. Clinard and Richard Quinney, pp. 94–109. New York: Holt, Rinehart and Winston.

Wade, Carlson. 1976. *Great Hoaxes and Famous Imposters.* Middle Village, N.Y.: Jonathan David Publishers.

Wade, Wyn Craig. 1987. *The Fiery Cross: The Ku Klux Klan in America.* New York: Simon and Schuster.

Waldman, Michael, and Gilbert, Pamela. 1989. "RICO Goes to Congress." *New York Times,* March 12, p. 4–E.

Waldman, Steven. 1989. "The Revolving Door." *Newsweek,* February 6, pp. 16–19.

Waldo, Gordon, and Dinitz, Simon. 1967. "Personality Attributes of the Criminal: An Analysis of Research Studies, 1950–1965." *Journal of Research in Crime and Delinquency* 4 (July): 185–201.

Waldorf, Dan et al. 1988. *Needle Sharing Among Male Prostitutes: Preliminary Findings of the Prospero Project.* Alameda, Calif.: Institute for Scientific Analysis.

Walker, Samuel. 1989. *Sense and Nonsense About Crime: A Policy Guide.* 2nd ed. Monterey, Calif.: Brooks/Cole.

Wallerstein, James S., and Wyle, Clement J. 1947. "Our Law-Abiding Law Breakers." *Probation,* April, pp. 107–118.

Walsh, Marilyn E. 1977. *The Fence.* Westport, Ct.: Greenwood Press.

Wanat, John, and Burke, Karen. 1980. "Estimating Juvenile Recidivism by Cross-Level Inference." Paper presented at the National Workshop on Research Methodology and Criminal Justice Program Evaluation. Baltimore. Md. March.

"War without Boundaries." 1977. *Time,* October 31, pp. 28–41.

Ward, Richard H. 1988. "Drug Trafficking and Terrorism: A Growing Phenomenon?" Paper presented at the International Conference on Crime, Drugs and Social Control, University of Hong Kong, Hong Kong, December.

Warren Commission. 1964. *Report of the President's Commission on the Assassination of President Kennedy.* Washington, D.C.: Government Printing Office.

"Washington vs. GM: Duel over X-Cars." 1983. *U.S. News and World Report,* August 15, p. 9.

Watson, Russell; Moreau, Ron; and Westerman, Maks. 1983. "On the Trail of the Forger." *Newsweek,* May 23, p. 39.

Weaver, Warren, Jr. 1988. "Justice Department Detects a Gain in Drive on Steroid Abuse." *New York Times,* December 11, p. 2–A.

Webb, Eugene J., et al. 1981. *Nonreactive Measures in the Social Sciences.* New York: Houghton Mifflin.

Weber, Max. 1949. *The Methodology of Social Sciences.* Translated by Edward A. Shils and Henry A. Finch. New York: The Free Press.

Webster, William H. 1984. *Crime in the United States, 1983.* Washington, D.C.: Government Printing Office.

Weinstein, Adam K. 1988. "Prosecuting Attorneys for Money Laundering: A New and Questionable Weapon in the War on Crime." *Crime and Contemporary Problems* 51: 369–386.

Weisberg, D. Kelly. 1985. *Children of the Night: A Study of Adolescent Prostitution.* Lexington, Mass.: Lexington Books.

Wellborn, Stanley N., and Chrysler, K. M. 1983. "The Kyshtym Disaster: Could It Happen Here?" *U.S. News and World Report,* August 15, p. 24.

Wellford, Charles. 1975. "Labelling Theory and Criminology: An Assessment." *Social Problems* 22 (February): 332–345.

Wellford, Harrison. 1972. *Sowing and Wind: A Report from Ralph Nader's Center for Study of Responsive Law.* New York: Grossman.

"Wells Fargo Guard Dopes Boss, Robs Armored Car." 1983. *Erie Morning News*, September 14, p. 5–A.

Wertham, Carl. 1967. "The Function of Social Definitions in the Development of Delinquency Career." The President's Commission on Law Enforcement and Administration of Justice. *Task Force Report: Juvenile Delinquency and Youth Crime*. Washington, D.C.: Government Printing Office.

West, Donald J. 1988. "Homosexuality and Social Policy: The Case For a More Informed Approach." *Law and Contemporary Problems* 51: 181–199.

West, Donald J., and Farrington, David P. 1977. *The Delinquent Way of Life*. London: Heinemann.

West, Nigel. 1982. *The Circus: MI 5 Operations, 1945–1972*. New York: Stein and Day.

Westin, Alan F. 1981. *Whistle-Blowing! Loyalty and Dissent in the Corporation*. New York: McGraw-Hill.

Wheeler, Gerald R., and Hissong, Rodney V. 1988. "Effects of Criminal Sanctions on Drunk Drivers: Beyond Incarceration." *Crime and Delinquency* 34: 29–42.

Whitaker, Mark, et al. 1983. "The Forgotten: The Prisoners of Conscience." *Newsweek*, February 14, pp. 40–55.

"White-Collar Crime: Second Annual Survey of Laws." 1981. *American Criminal Law Review* 19: 173–520.

Whitman, David. 1987. "The Numbers Game: When More Is Less." *U.S. News and World Report*, April 27, pp. 39–40.

"Why So Few Drunk Drivers Go to Jail." 1983. *U.S. News and World Report*. September 12, p. 14.

Whyte, William F. 1955. *Streetcorner Society*. Chicago: University of Chicago Press.

Wickman, Peter, and Whitten, Phillip. 1980. *Criminology: Perspectives on Crime and Criminality*. Lexington, Mass.: D. C. Heath.

Wiggins, Michael E. 1986a. "An Extremist Right-Wing Group and Domestic Terrorism." Paper presented at the Academy of Criminal Justice Sciences meetings, St. Louis, March.

———. 1986b. "The Turner Diaries: Blueprint for Right-Wing Extremist Violence." Paper presented at the Academy of Criminal Justice Sciences meetings, St. Louis, March.

Wilbanks, William. 1985. "Is Violent Crime Intraracial?" *Crime and Delinquency* 31: 117–128.

———. 1987. *The Myth of a Racist Criminal Justice System*. Monterey, Calif.: Brooks/Cole.

Wilbanks, William, and Kim, K. H. 1984. *Elderly Criminals*. Lanham, Md.: University Press of America.

Williams, Frank. 1984. "The Demise of Criminological Imagination: A Critique of Recent Criminology." *Justice Quarterly* 1 (March): 91–106.

Williams, Frank, and McShane, Marilyn. 1988. *Criminological Theory*. Englewood Cliffs, N.J.: Prentice Hall.

Williams, Jay, and Gold, Martin. 1972. "From Delinquent Behavior to Official Delinquency." *Social Problems* 20: 209–229.

Wilson, Edward O. 1975. *Sociobiology*. Cambridge, Mass.: Harvard University Press.

Wilson, James Q. 1975. *Thinking about Crime*. New York: Basic Books.

———. ed. 1983a. *Crime and Public Policy*. San Francisco: Institute for Contemporary Studies.

———. 1983b. *Thinking about Crime*. rev. ed. New York: Basic Books.

Wilson, James Q., and Herrnstein, Richard J. 1985. *Crime and Human Nature*. New York: Simon and Schuster.

Wilson, James Q., and Kelling, George L. 1982. "Broken Windows: The Police and Neighborhood Safety." *The Atlantic*, March, pp. 27–38.

Wilson, James Q., and Lowry, Glenn C., eds. 1987. *From Children to Citizens: Vol. III, Families, Schools and Delinquency Prevention*. New York: Springer-Verlag.

Wilson, Jane. 1975. "Ideological Views of Rape as a State of War." *Los Angeles Times*. December 2.

Wilson, Robert. 1978. "Chinatown: No Longer a Cozy Assignment." *Police Magazine* 1 (July): 19–29.

Winick, Charles. 1962. "Prostitutes' Clients Perceptions of Prostitutes and of Themselves." *International Journal of Psychiatry* 8: 289.

Winick, Charles, and Kinsie, Paul M. 1971. *The Lively Commerce: Prostitution in the United States*. Chicago: Quadrangle Books.

Winslow, Robert. 1970. *Society in Transition: A Social Approach to Deviancy*. New York: Free Press.

Wirth, Louis. 1938. "Urbanism as a Way of Life." *American Journal of Sociology* 44 (July): 8–20.

Wise, David, and Ross, Thomas B. 1967. *The Espionage Establishment*. New York: Bantam Books.

Witkin, Gordon. 1988. "Hitting Kingpins in Their Assets." *U.S. News and World Report*, December 5, pp. 20–22.

Witkin, Herman A., et al. 1976. "XYY and Criminality." *Science* 193 (August 13): 547–555.

Witt, Howard. 1988. "CIA Sued for Attempts at Brainwashing." *Erie Daily Times*, October 3, p. 2–A.

Wolf, George. 1975. *Frank Costello: Prime Minister of the Underworld*. New York: Bantam Books.

Wolf, J. B. 1981. "Enforcement Terrorism." *Police Studies* 3: 45–54.

Wolfgang, Marvin E. 1958. *Patterns in Criminal Homicide*. Philadelphia: University of Pennsylvania Press.

———. 1960. "Cesare Lombroso." In *Pioneers in Criminology*, edited by Hermann Mannheim, pp. 168–227. Chicago: Quadrangle Books.

———. 1963. "Criminology and Criminologists." *Journal of Criminal Law, Criminology and Police Science* 54 (June): 155–162.

———. 1980a. "Crime and Punishment." *New York Times*, March 2, p. E.21.

———. 1980b. "On an Evaluation of Criminology." In *Handbook in Criminal Justice Evaluation*, edited by Malcolm W. Klein and Katherine S. Teilman, pp. 1952. Beverly Hills: Sage.

Wolfgang, Marvin E., and Ferracuti, Franco. 1967. *The Subculture of Violence: Towards an Integrated Theory in Criminology*. London: Tavistock Publications.

Wolfgang, Marvin E.; Figlio, Robert M.; and Sellin, Thorsten. 1972. *Delinquency in a Birth Cohort.* Chicago: University of Chicago Press.

Wolfgang, Marvin E.; Figlio, Robert M.; and Thornberry, Terence B. 1978. *Evaluating Criminology.* New York: Elsevier.

Wood, Arthur L. 1967. *Criminal Lawyer.* New Haven: College and University Press.

Wright, James D., and Rossi, Peter H. 1986. *Armed and Considered Dangerous: A Survey of Felons and Their Firearms.* Hawthorne, N.Y.: Aldine.

Wright, Kevin N. 1985. *The Great American Crime Myth.* Westport, Ct.: Greenwood Press.

Wunderlich, Ray. 1978. "Neuroallergy as a Contributing Factor to Social Misfits." In *Ecologic-Biochemical Approaches to Treatment of Delinquents and Criminals,* edited by Leonard Hippchen, pp. 229–253. New York: Van Nostrand Reinhold.

Yablonsky, Lewis. 1962. *The Violent Gang.* Baltimore: Penguin Press.

———. 1965a. "Experiences with the Criminal Community." In *Applied Criminology,* edited by Alvin Gouldner and S. M. Miller. New York: The Free Press.

———. 1965b. *Synanon: The Tunnel Back.* Baltimore: Penguin.

Yema, John. 1980. "Pictures of the Mob—'Organized,' 'Deadly Serious,' " *Christian Science Monitor,* April 30, pp. 7–8.

Yochelson, Samuel, and Samenow, Stanton E. 1976. *The Criminal Personality.* Vols. 1 and 2. New York: Jason Aronson.

Yoder, Stephen A. 1978. "Criminal Sanctions for Corporate Illegality." *Journal of Criminal Law and Criminology* 69 (January): 40–58.

Zalba, Serapio R. 1971. "Battered Children." *Transaction* 8 (July): 58–61.

Zeiger, Henry A. 1975. *The Jersey Mob.* New York: Signet.

Zeisel, Hans. 1957. *Say It with Figures.* 4th ed. New York: Harper.

Zimring, Franklin E. 1987. "Gun Control." *Crime File* (National Institute of Justice).

Zimring, Franklin, and Hawkins, Gordon. 1973. *Deterrence: The Legal Threat to Crime Control.* Chicago: University of Chicago Press.

NAME INDEX

Aaronsen, David E., 222
Abadinsky, Howard, 327, 467, 470, 472, 484, 504, 512, 518
Abelson, Herbert, 554
Abbott, D.J., 69
ABC, 107, 317, 397, 477, 547
Abrahamsen, David, 113
Adams, Virginia, 319-20
Adler, Freda, 69, 84, 105
Adler, Jerry, 515
Adler, Patricia, 484
Adler, Peter, 484
Agee, Philip, 447
Ageton, Suzanne, 55, 89, 91
Agnew, Robert, 189
Agran, Larry, 399
Akers, Ronald, 181, 193, 201-2
Albanese, Jay, 472, 493, 495, 511, 516-17
Albini, Joseph, 59, 467, 469-72, 488, 490, 493, 506, 514
Alexander, Shana, 513
Allan, Emilie, 84
Allen, Edward, 494
Allen, Harry, 14, 203
Allen, John, 254, 458
Allison, Dean, 358
Amir, Menachem, 236-38
Anderson, Edward J., 445
Anderson, Jack, 326, 380, 392, 485, 503, 565
Anderson, Robert, 494
Anglin, M. Douglas, 562
Anslinger, Harry, 552
Apear, Leonard, 19-20
Archer, Dane, 69, 98, 105
Ardrey, Robert, 210
Armstrong, E., 541
Asbury, Herbert, 536
Ashman, Charles, 503
Atkinson, A.B., 228
Austin, Roy, 96
Austin, Tim, 151

Babbie, Earl, 47
Bachman, Jerald, 557
Badillo, Herman, 261
Bailey, F. Lee, 367
Bailey, William, 61
Bakan, David, 246, 249

Ball, Robert, 186, 560
Banas, Dennis, 32
Bandura, Albert, 107
Baridon, Phil, 481
Baris, Jay G., 361
Barker, Thomas, 353
Barlay, Stephen, 403
Barnett, Arnold, 227
Baron, R. A., 107
Barry, Vincent, 125
Bartlett, Sarah, 383
Bartol, Ann and Curt, 152
Battersby, John D., 429
Baumrind, Diane, 101
Bayer, Ronald, 261
Bayley, David, 42
Beattie, R. H., 36
Beauchamp, Thomas, 394, 409
Becker, Gary, 127
Becker, Howard, 10, 192-93, 343, 551
Beirne, Piers, 129
Bell, Daniel, 483, 494, 512
Belson, W. A., 107
Benekos, Peter, 412-13
Benjamin, Harry, 541
Bennett, Garry, 538
Bennett, Georgette, 581
Bennett, James, 60
Bennett, Jana, 449
Bennett, Trevor, 538, 562
Bennett, Vivo, 309
Bensinger, Gad, 354
Bequai, August, 466
Berg, Eric, 382
Bergamini, David, 419
Berger, Vivian, 233
Bergier, Jacques, 403-4
Berk, Richard, 250
Bernard, Thomas, 125, 128, 130, 153, 157-58, 189, 195, 202
Bertaux, Daniel, 60
Biderman, Albert, 47, 52
Billing, Richard, 503
Binder, Arnold, 250
Birnbaum, H. Jean, 239
Bittner, Egon, 563
Black, Donald, 36, 52, 580
Blackstock, Nelson, 433
Blackwell, Kate, 394

Blakey, G. Robert, 284, 324, 327, 503
Bloch, Herbert, 345-46
Block, Alan, 467, 474-75, 507, 550
Bloom, Murray, 325
Blumberg, Abraham, 367
Blume, Marshall, 587
Blumenthal, Daniel, 513
Blumstein, Alfred, 37, 79
Blundell, William, 382
Bock, Gordon, 360
Bohm, Robert, 200
Bonacich, Robert, 96
Bonanno, Joseph, 468, 473, 509
Bonger, Willem, 134
Bonn, Robert, 231
Bookin-Weiner, Hedy, 288-90
Booth, Kathy, 542
Bordua, David, 172-73
Bottomley, A. Keith, 139
Boucher, Rick, 519
Boudreau, John, 292
Bourgois, Philippe, 476
Bowers, William, 262
Bowie, Norman, 409
Bowker, Lee, 260
Braithwaite, John, 411
Brancale, R., 548
Brantingham, Patricia, 69, 97, 132, 177
Brantingham, Paul, 69, 97, 132, 177
Brecher, Edward, 551, 562
Bremer, R., 271
Brenner, M. Harvey, 106
Bresler, Fenton, 479, 481
Briar, Scott, 189
Bridge, Peter J., 494, 498
Brodeur, Paul, 411
Brown, Bertram, 146
Brown, Claude, 254
Brown, Michael H., 392
Brown, Richard M., 210
Browning, Frank, 343, 388, 398, 505
Brownmiller, Susan, 235, 238
Burgess, Ann, 238, 240, 543
Burgess, Earnest, 174, 181
Burgess, Robert L., 181
Burke, Karen, 553
Burnett, Kathleen, 84
Burnham, Kenneth, 553

635

SUBJECT INDEX